AppleScript

The Comprehensive Guide to
Scripting and Automation on
Mac OS X, Second Edition

Hanaan Rosenthal

apress®

AppleScript: The Comprehensive Guide to Scripting and Automation on Mac OS X, Second Edition

Copyright © 2006 by Hanaan Rosenthal

ISBN 978-1-59059-653-1

ISBN 978-1-4302-0237-0 (eBook)

Trademarked names may appear in this book. Rather than use a trademark symbol with every occurrence of a trademarked name, we use the names only in an editorial fashion and to the benefit of the trademark owner, with no intention of infringement of the trademark.

Lead Editor: Chris Mills
Technical Reviewer: Hamish Sanderson
Editorial Board: Steve Anglin, Ewan Buckingham, Gary Cornell, Jason Gilmore, Jonathan Gennick, Jonathan Hassell, James Huddleston, Chris Mills, Matthew Moodie, Dominic Shakeshaft, Jim Sumser, Keir Thomas, Matt Wade
Project Manager: Beth Christmas
Copy Edit Manager: Nicole LeClerc
Copy Editor: Kim Wimpsett
Assistant Production Director: Kari Brooks-Copony
Production Editor: Ellie Fountain
Compositor: Dina Quan
Proofreader: Lori Bring
Indexer: John Collin
Artist: Kinetic Publishing Services, LLC
Cover Designer: Kurt Krames
Manufacturing Director: Tom Debolski

Distributed to the book trade worldwide by Springer-Verlag New York, Inc., 233 Spring Street, 6th Floor, New York, NY 10013. Phone 1-800-SPRINGER, fax 201-348-4505, e-mail orders-ny@springer-sbm.com, or visit http://www.springeronline.com.

For information on translations e-mail info@apress.com, or visit http://www.apress.com.

The information in this book is distributed on an "as is" basis, without warranty. Although every precaution has been taken in the preparation of this work, neither the author(s) nor Apress shall have any liability to any person or entity with respect to any loss or damage caused or alleged to be caused directly or indirectly by the information contained in this work.

The source code for this book is available to readers at http://www.customflowsolutions.com and at http://www.apress.com in the Source Code/Download section.

Contents at a Glance

PART 1 ▪▪▪ Read Me First

PART 2 ▪▪▪ How to AppleScript

PART 3 ▪▪▪ The Wild World of AppleScript

Contents

PART 3 ▪▪▪ The Wild World of AppleScript

▪CHAPTER 20   Using AppleScript Amenities in Mac OS X 517

▪CHAPTER 21   Extending AppleScript with Scripting Additions 535

About the Author

HANAAN ROSENTHAL: OK, so who are we kidding? This part is not some facts concerning the author's life but rather where I get to write good stuff about myself. So, here I go with some information about myself and how I got to be a scripter.

I started with computer graphics when I was 10 years old. I got a Sinclair 8-bit computer, wrote a couple of graphic programs and a game for it, and published a newsletter that had a one-issue life span.

When I got to Providence, Rhode Island, from Israel at twice that age, I fell in love with Macs after taking a course at the Rhode Island School of Design. I quit my job delivering candy, bought a Mac II with $2,435 of the $2,500 my wife and I had in the bank, and became a computer graphics consultant. In 1996 I started scripting professionally, and my first $100,000+ job came in 1998. This project turned into a disaster when the president of the company I was creating the system for decided to kill the project and blame it on me. Now it's all but a funny memory since over the past eight years I have had the pleasure of creating some pretty cool systems for some pretty neat people from companies such as Fidelity Investments, the *Hartford*, Wellington Management, Showtime Networks, *the Boston Globe*, and others.

During that time I also met with John Thorsen and the rest of the folks from TECsoft Developers Consortium (TDC), which is a national consortium of AppleScripters.

Some of my early clients were financial companies from the Boston area for which I created different graphing and document generation systems (all AppleScript-based!). These jobs led to an AppleScript-based graphing engine I invented that allows me to add custom graphing capabilities to any AppleScript system. The daily stock graphs in *the Boston Globe* and the two-page business graphics extravaganza in the daily *New York Times*, for instance, are created using these systems.

Now I have my own e-publishing company, called TMI, which stands for Too Much Information. I publish ezPrimers, which are short informational pieces about virtually any subject. I mix publishing with other tasks I love such as caring for my two sweet kids, whom Johanne and I home-school; pouring concrete countertops; brewing biodiesel for my old Benz; and rooting for the Boston Red Sox.

About the Technical Reviewer

HAMISH SANDERSON is an experienced United Kingdom–based AppleScripter who first discovered the joys of desktop automation while working as a book illustrator late last century. Since then he has contributed a range of useful libraries and utilities to the AppleScript community and pops up with some regularity on the various AppleScript mailing lists. He is also the author of the highly regarded appscript library, which brings AppleScript-like application scripting support to the popular Python language on OS X.

Acknowledgments

I would like to thank a few people for making this effort possible. The first thanks I owe to my family who were there every step of the way: Johanne, my wife, told me I could write a book and was there for me whenever I was roaming the house aimlessly in search of a sentence, and my kids, Aylam and Olivia, tallied the page count and graciously named the book "That dumb book our dad wrote about AppleScript" (the publisher didn't bite).

I owe thanks to Hamish Sanderson, who kept me honest and didn't hold back. I also drew from the knowledge of people such as Emmanuel Lévy, Shirley Hopkins, Mark Munro, and the folks from TDC who turned every simple question into an election-year debate.

I also owe thanks to the many people at Apress who were on top of everything from guiding the book to crossing the t's and dotting the i's. I'd like to thank Kim and Ellie, and the rest of the folks who worked on this book, for managing to find even the most obscure inaccuracies and Chris and Beth for holding my hand at the last stages of the rewrite as I was, at times, on the edge of insanity.

Introduction

One issue that keeps coming up in the AppleScript world is the place of scripting when it comes to recording macros and programming from scratch. Is scripting more like programming with C++ or more like creating Adobe Photoshop actions or FileMaker Pro scripts? This question doesn't have one answer, but it does raise some interesting issues. Let's establish some facts: AppleScript is an object-oriented programming language that has both depth and beauty in its own right and unlimited potential for expandability by scriptable applications and scripting additions. Although you can use AppleScript for more straightforward tasks such as applying one or two transformations to a mass of files, it shines brightest when taken to a higher level. You really start to tap into the power of AppleScript when you start branching and looping.

Figuring out, however, what AppleScript resembles the most is missing the point. The best aspect of AppleScript is also what makes it like no other programming language. In other programming languages, you write programs, mostly stand-alone packages of code with some supporting files. The program has an interface that the user does something with, and some result is produced. All this happens as part of the package. What makes AppleScript different is that what you create with AppleScript is not so much a program but rather a robot that uses other programs. Imagine being a graphic designer with some modest scripting abilities. Now imagine you have to superimpose a transparent logo at the corner of 1,000 images for an online catalog. Manually, this would take you three days; however, using AppleScript, you fashion yourself a robotic arm, complete with a motor, a trigger, and some controls, that does the job in 12 minutes. Next, you detach the cool gadget from your arm, build it two legs, and set it loose with a remote control. Now, it does the boring repetitive job of three people. You have created an employee that works at phantom speed, is 100 percent accurate, and doesn't need health insurance. In fact, when I meet with clients, I ask them to describe to me the ideal human position they would like the script to function as, instead of a program they need; the scripter's job is to teach the Mac to do the work of that person, using the same applications the human employee would have used. Although other programming languages create programs that need a human operator, in AppleScript you create a superoperator that uses these programs with a speed and precision like no one has ever imagined.

So, what possessed me to take on the task of writing what is undoubtedly the longest book ever written about AppleScript? It started with reading David Blatner's *Real World QuarkXPress 3* book in the early 1990s. That book inspired me because it was written in such a way that any novice could open it and learn from it, but at the same time, the subject matter was advanced enough to keep even the power users happy. Ever since getting involved with AppleScript, I wanted to do the same for this programming language.

What sets this book apart is that it combines a substantial reference with in-depth explanations and real-world examples. This combination of features isn't so much trying to be everything for everyone as creating a complete experience.

I also noticed that other books divided the discussion based on a subject's complexity, not its usefulness. These subjects were organized according to the role they played in the language. That has never made sense to me, and I set out to change it. This book is not about the AppleScript language but rather about the scripter. It is organized from the point of view of a person who needs to perform real tasks with the language. This philosophy shows itself in a few ways. First, the subjects you will find can be described as "things people want to do," things such as work with files, manipulate strings, create interfaces, and so on. In each chapter I cover all aspects related to the issue at hand while giving it the attention it deserves based on how much it is used in the real world, not how many properties and related commands it happens to have. Second, I discuss all information relevant to a specific topic but then take it a step further: I give you the opinion of a professional scripter (that would be me) on what actual uses this feature has, what related tricks there are, what the potential problems are, and more. The chapters also include real-world examples that shed light on every feature from several different directions. My thought was, if I know it, I will write it. There is so much more to a programming language such as AppleScript than meets the eye, and I wanted you to know as much of it as possible.

About the scripts that come with the book: you can download the scripts for the book from www.customflowsolutions.com. Go to that site, and click the AppleScript book link to get to the download area. The scripts are divided into two groups: figure scripts and copy scripts. The figure scripts are the scripts that appear in the screen shots in the book, and they match the number of the screenshot. The copy scripts are the scripts that appear in the copy and have a code caption, such as Script 3-5, which would be script 5 in Chapter 3.

What's Not in This Book, and Why

Shortly after the first edition of this book came out, I started hearing complaints about what's not covered in the book. The complaints revolved around two subjects: Unix shell scripts and AppleScript Studio.

I understand how important both these subjects are to scripters, but I didn't cover either subject in depth because of a practical reason: a 2,500-page book was out of the question. My choice was to either go all the way with subjects or to only briefly introduce them. The fact is, either subject could justify an entire book. This book is mainly about AppleScript. If you want to learn Unix, for any reason, look around—you'll find hundreds of books. About a good AppleScript Studio book: stay tuned!

Another AppleScript-related subject I may disappoint on is Automator. Although you can look at Automator as simplified AppleScript or automation without programming, it isn't a subject that would add much to this book. I do, however, include information about scripting Automator with AppleScript and a bit about the role AppleScript plays inside Automator.

Resources

The following are some resources you can refer to for more information about AppleScript:

- Apple's own AppleScript web pages (www.apple.com/applescript) are full of information, sample scripts, and links to other resources. If you are interested in scripting different Apple applications such as iTunes, iPhoto, Mail, and so on, then refer to the special application pages listed at www.apple.com/applescript/apps/. The resources page lists about 50 links to websites, books, consultants, and more.

- For making some AppleScript friends and getting your questions answered, you can join the AppleScript user mailing list. Join the list by going to www.lists.apple.com/mailman/listinfo/applescript-users.

- Outside the Applesphere, some great websites are dedicated to AppleScript. Chief among them is MacScripter.net. MacScripter.net has a few sections, including the most complete database of scripting additions, AppleScript code shared by other scripters, a BBS, and other features. Another great website is Bill Cheeseman's the AppleScript Sourcebook (www.applescriptsourcebook.com). The AppleScript Sourcebook is known for Bill's detailed explanation of different topics. After Apple releases software updates related to AppleScript, this website is the place to look for explanations of what these updates involve.

- For AppleScript training, the best place to go is www.tecsoft.com. John Thorsen, the founder of TECSoft, has been training people to use AppleScript since the beginning of time and has trained thousands of people on the subject. John also provides online training as well as a training CD for AppleScript.

Many other AppleScript-related websites exist that I haven't included. Please see the resources page on Apple's AppleScript website and the other two websites I mentioned for a complete listing of related sites.

PART 1

...

Read Me First

CHAPTER 1

■ ■ ■

Introducing AppleScript

AppleScript is for Macintosh automation; so, scripts you write can automate tasks you would otherwise have to perform with the mouse and keyboard.

Although you can use AppleScript to automate almost anything you can do with the mouse and keyboard, you probably wouldn't want to do so. So what would you want to automate? The answer to this question falls under two broad categories: small tasks and big tasks.

The main difference between small scripts and big scripts is the amount of thought and planning involved. When writing small scripts, you start out by . . . writing the script. As the script progresses, you add more functions, you add more lines, and you go back to fix and debug until the script works. Big scripts require planning. You have to carefully consider the users, the environment, and the different triggers for tasks the system will perform. You have to deal with where the data for the script comes from, small graphical user interfaces, and return on investment for your script or script project—all the issues that can kill your efforts just as you start to get excited.

Automating Small Tasks

Small scripts are the way one usually starts to become familiar with AppleScript. AppleScript lets you easily create a script, test it, save it as an application, and start using it. This quick turnaround for truly useful utilities is part of the winning recipe that makes AppleScript so great.

A few years ago I was teaching an Adobe Photoshop class, and during my five-minute break, a colleague told me about a problem a client of his, a prepress house, was having. The client couldn't print lines in QuarkXPress documents that were thinner than 0.25 point and was spending hours correcting every document. By the end of my break I had written the following script, saved it as an application, and handed it to him:

```
Tell application "QuarkXPress 4.01"
tell every page of document 1
set width of (every line box whose width < 0.25) to 0.25
end tell
end tell
```

The prepress shop was thrilled for the "utility" we had scrambled to program for them.

Now, since the client got this one for free, you can't measure this return on investment in terms of money. But just for kicks, you *can* figure out the return on investment if you consider it took a person ten minutes to manually fix an average client file and this prepress facility went through ten files a day. Using these numbers, the time investment paid for itself 5,000 times over during the first year. This sounds a bit over the top, but it's not. Little AppleScript efforts can make a big difference.

Automating Big Tasks

Although AppleScript doesn't sweat the small stuff, it can be the base for large-scale custom integrated systems. As far as what to automate, you *could* automate any task that has repeatable logic, and if the cost of automation is less than the amount of money you save—and it usually is—the task is worth automating. *Repeatable logic* is logic that can be applied successfully to similar, but not identical, subjects and that produces a predictable outcome, based on the uniqueness of the subject.

For example, here is a process that is not so suitable for automation:

You take the client's instructions file, and you read the instructions to figure out what corrections the client wants. If the client wants the image to be color-corrected, you open the image in Photoshop and apply curves until it looks better. Otherwise, just correct the typos.

This process is much too arbitrary and relies on the operator's human qualities such as the ability to perform color correction and to correct typos.

Here is a better candidate for automation:

When you get a job from a client, you search for the client in the database to locate the job information. If the job is marked "urgent," you e-mail the imaging room to expect it within ten minutes. You open the Adobe InDesign document and verify that all the fonts were provided. You make sure the document contains the number of pages indicated in the electronic job ticket; if it doesn't, you make a note in the database and e-mail the client. When done, you make a copy of the "job" folder in the "archive" folder on the server, and you send another copy to the "in" folder on the production server. You repeat these steps for all jobs that arrived last night.

Now this is a process for which AppleScript is perfect. Besides having programmatic elements such as a repeat loop for applying the process to all jobs and some branching, the process itself is clear, is logical, and can be applied to any client job that arrives.

If you look more closely at the previous process, you can see that quite a few of the steps happen in software applications. The operator has to know how to use FileMaker Pro for searching and entering data; how to use InDesign for checking fonts, pages, and so on; and how to use the Finder for moving folders. Controlling these and many other applications is one of AppleScript's main strengths. AppleScript can give applications commands and get information from applications, such as retrieving the data in a FileMaker Pro record or the number of pages in an InDesign document.

AppleScript is also ideal for performing repetitive tasks. For instance, how would you like to show up at work one morning and realize that your job for the day is to go through 200 TIFF images in a folder, add a black frame to each one, and export each as a JPEG? Then, you must create a PDF file containing all the images, with four-up (which means having four impressions of similar size on a single printed sheet) and with the image name under each image. Does this sound like hard work? Your reward for a job well done just might be another folder with 200 TIFF images the next day . . . .

Although not sophisticated, this process is repetitive. A script can do it for you while you take a walk to the cafeteria.

Where Is AppleScript?

For more than ten years now, every Mac that shipped with system 7.1.1 (also known as System 7 Pro) and all the following operating systems had everything it needed to use AppleScript—you didn't have to do any special installs, you had hardly any configuration issues from Mac to Mac, and you received a basic array of scriptable applications that grew rapidly (and still does).

What this means is that writing scripts and installing and running them on other Macs requires transporting the script file alone, not a whole array of other resources; everything you need to get started is there. Of course, you have to provide any third-party applications you want to script.

What's truly remarkable about AppleScript is that most of the language's power comes from the applications you automate. For better or worst, the level to which applications can be automated, and the ease in which you can include them in an automated solution, is largely up to the software vendor. It is up to the development team of every application to implement scriptability for any feature they imagine someone would want to automate.

For example, it wasn't until a few years ago that Adobe jumped on the scripting bandwagon and started incorporating AppleScript support into its widely used graphics program. Adobe Illustrator 9 was the first major Adobe application to ship with an AppleScript interface; this was followed by InDesign, which started out boasting a comprehensive scripting vocabulary, and finally Photoshop 7 came out-of-the-box scriptable as well (although you could script Photoshop with the PhotoScripter plug-in from Main Event Software a couple of years before that).

As it stands, the very existence of AppleScript depends on the applications that support it. For commercial-software developers, making an application scriptable doesn't mean simply checking a Make Scriptable check box in a Compile dialog box; rather, they have to spend hours of programming to make it happen and to do it well.

Note When writing applications in the Cocoa environment, you can make some basic scripting dictionaries easily available; however, to allow scripters to automate their applications, developers must put a good amount of thought, planning, and development time into the scriptability of their applications.

To make an application scriptable, the developer has to create special terminology for each feature they want to make scriptable and come up with an object model for the application. That can add up to many hours and can't be done as an afterthought. However difficult, software developers see good return on their investment when companies integrate their applications into automated solutions. This alone ties that application to the client and lowers the chances the client will dump their application for a competing product.

How Do You Write Scripts?

You can't write and run AppleScript scripts from any text editor. To write scripts, you need to use a special script editor, which will allow you to write the script, check the syntax, compile the script, run it, and save it as an applet.

Note Applet who? When you want to save a script in a way that it will run when the user double-clicks it, the option listed in the Apple editor is Application. However, in this book I will refer to it as an *applet*. An applet means the AppleScript code is wrapped with the minimal executable shell that allows it to run in a stand-alone form, just like any other application.

To start, you may want to use Apple's own free tool, Script Editor. Script Editor is a little application that comes preinstalled in the AppleScript folder in the Applications folder and is ready to use with every Mac system. Script Editor has always been a bare-bones AppleScript editor, which makes it rather easy to figure out and leaves few places to get lost. Besides Script Editor, a few other AppleScript editors are available with enhanced editing and debugging features.

Note Other AppleScript editors include Script Debugger from Late Night Software (www.latenightsw.com), which you can pick up for about $199, and Smile from Satimage (www.satimage-software.com), which is a powerful scripting program available as a free download.

As you're writing a script, you can compile and run it right from Script Editor. Even if you save it as a droplet or an applet, you can reopen, change, recompile, and run it right from the script window. This makes your scripts (and other people's scripts, for that matter) easy to look at and try.

Where Do Scripts Reside, and How Do They Run?

Scripts can be saved anywhere! It is up to you where you want to save the scripts you create. This flexibility allows you to create your own super-organized script storage system—and, of course, it allows you to create a holy mess.

Some applications provide special folders, usually called Scripts, to place your scripts in so they will appear in that application's special Script menu.

More and more software vendors realize that providing a special menu for scripts in their applications, or at least placing some scripts in a /Library/Scripts folder (which will appear in the operating system's Scripts menu), is more than just letting users create their own scripts; it also allows them to quickly add "features" to their applications that otherwise would take timely programming resources.

For example, BBEdit from Bare Bones Software has a Script menu with some useful scripts that perform editing functions.

AppleScript File Formats

You can save scripts in several file formats, including as compiled scripts, text files, applets, and variations of these. Scripts are usually saved as compiled scripts, with the .scpt extension. This format can be edited using AppleScript editors only, not just any text editor. Although you write scripts using text and you can usually see the text when you reopen a saved script, the script is actually saved as special tokens that are interpreted by the operating system's AppleScript component when the script runs.

You usually won't notice this "what-you-see-is-not-what-you-saved" situation unless the script has some version issue or an application or scripting addition issue. What you have to remember is that the scripts you write, as discussed earlier, will be composed largely of terminology defined by scriptable applications. An application can define hundreds of keywords that you can include in your scripts. Some of these keywords are the names of commands and classes defined by the application; others are the names of command parameters and object properties, and so on. For a script to compile properly, it needs the applications that are referenced in it to be present, and in some cases it also needs the applications to be open. In fact, if an application referenced in your script isn't present when you try to open the script, you will either have to give up until you install it or trick AppleScript into thinking some other application is the missing one. If you do trick AppleScript, you will have a hard time changing the application-specific terms you used in your script, since they will appear in their raw form inside double angle brackets instead of the easy-to-read English-like AppleScript text you're used to seeing. For instance, a script that used the copy command in InDesign CS2 will show the following code when the application isn't available: <<event misccopy>>.

So how can all that affect you and your script? The main reason why you won't be able to see your code properly is that the application, scripting addition, or application's AppleScript plug-in isn't available.

> **Note** Some applications, mainly from Adobe, don't incorporate their scripting terminology into the actual application but rather have a plug-in manage all the AppleScript-related activity. This will be a noticeable issue only if the application doesn't ship with AppleScript enabled but rather leaves you to activate it. Otherwise, it makes no difference.

Rest assured, however, that the actual script is fine. The next time you open it with the target application available, it will return to its old self and display properly.

As mentioned, when you save a script, you can specify its file format. Three main kinds of script files exist: regular compiled scripts, which are the native AppleScript file format; plain-text files; and applets. On top of that, OS X has a new option for saving compiled scripts and script applets as bundles. *Bundles* are folders that appear and behave as files, which is great when you want your script to appear as a single unit but actually conceal related files as part of it. You can read more about bundles in Chapter 22.

For most purposes, your script will start as text entered in Script Editor but will be most likely saved as a compiled script file. At any point you can save the script as an applet and place it anywhere for use. You can use a script in its AppleScript format state (nonapplet files are saved with the .scpt extension) in one of the following ways: if the script is loaded into another script, you can use it in an application's Script menu where available (InDesign, BBEdit, the Finder, and so on); you can execute it from the Unix command line using the osascript command; or you can simply run it from Script Editor.

Also, two similar application-based formats exist: applet and droplet. A regular *applet* runs the script when you double-click it, and unless it's saved as a "stay-open" applet, it quits after the script is done. A *droplet* can respond to files being dropped on it. This is useful for a script that processes files or folders. Chapter 22 discusses all these variations in detail.

When saving a script as an applet, you can't specify whether you want it to be a droplet or a normal application. Instead, AppleScript determines this based on the contents of your script. Basically, if you tell AppleScript what to do in case some files are dropped on it, it will become a droplet; otherwise, it will be a normal application. I will discuss all that in detail in later chapters.

So, why then would you ever save a script as text? Well, you might do this for a few reasons. First, saving and opening scripts as text doesn't require that the script be compiled. This is useful when something stops you from compiling the script, namely, an error in your AppleScript text. Second, when you send scripts to be used on other Macs, you should try to send them both as compiled scripts and in text format. Getting the script's text allows the other person to open the text version of the script in Script Editor and compile it on the Mac on which the script will eventually run. This helps iron out issues that may stem from using a slightly different version of an application and gives the script a chance to see where all the applications are located on the new Mac.

Another format-related option you have is to save a run-only version of the script. This will allow the script to run, but no one will be able to read it. Distributing a script as a run-only version is useful when you want to protect the rights to your proprietary code.

The Golden Triangle: AppleScript Language, Application Scriptability, and the Scripts You Write

You learned about the role of other applications' scriptability earlier. Now how does that scriptability work with the AppleScript language and with the actual scripts you write?

All this is very much like any other spoken language, say English. The base language has verbs, nouns, adjectives, and some rules. You can use English to talk, but what you say has to have some context in order to be interesting and for you to relate to others. This is where different subjects come in, and I mean big subjects—subjects that have their own lingo. Take, for example, military speak, computer geek speak, or medical language. They all are English, but each has its own special words, some of which no one outside of that business can understand. More than that, the special words add meaning. Take, for example, the following sentence: "Put your masks on, and begin the operation." This means two completely different things whether you're a surgeon or a sergeant, and if you're a computer geek, it means nothing!

It's the same with AppleScript: you can use the make command along with the document class, which is defined by most applications, but simply writing make document has no meaning unless you point it to an application that knows what to do with it. And this application will have its own way of dealing with that command, which is different from the way another application was told to deal with it.

Of all these features, perhaps the most exciting task you can perform (if you're the type of person who can get excited by a programming language) is to define your own commands and objects. You define commands by writing handlers, and you define objects by bundling those handlers along with some properties in script objects.

Let's see whether you can get into the spirit of procreation. What if your script's purpose is to automate the creation of a catalog? Say you have a sequence of commands, and starting at the top and going down, they tell different applications what to do. First you have some database commands for gathering information, and then you use some AppleScript commands to clean and format the text, add some dollar signs to numbers, and so on. Next, you have some repeat loops and conditional statements (if, then) that dump all that text into the page-layout program.

OK, that's not fair. When you start, you just want to get things done, and you don't care really how. Although writing scripts that way is good for shorter scripts and certainly OK when you're just starting, you should have an idea of how you should be writing scripts once you get over the initial euphoria that overcomes you every time your computer does something for you and you have to run to get a cup of coffee just so you can tell everyone that "the script did that by itself while I . . . while I . . . was getting a cup of coffee!"

Teaching the Script New Commands

So how would you make the orderly chain of commands different, and why? The second question has a few answers. For one, short scripts should remain as a collection of statements, without the use of handlers. Once you start working with longer scripts, scripts containing handlers are better organized, are easier to understand and debug, and are more flexible. They're easier to change, and making a change can mean improving the way multiple scripts run. Also, your code becomes more reusable, which is a major part of being a profitable scripter.

And how are better scripts written? Although an entire chapter is dedicated to healthy scriptwriting practices later in the book (Chapter 23), this section touches upon the "better script" model in general terms.

Let's start with redundant code. *Redundant code* is code that performs nearly identical operations in many places in the script. For instance, in the catalog automation script, you may have some code that goes to the database and gets some information from a field, say the price of an item. Then, the script adds a dollar sign to the number and inserts it in a named text frame in the page-layout application. These operations strung together take up, say, thirty lines of code, and they repeat in about five places in your script.

You can make the script much better by defining your own commands to handle each of these tasks! How about a few commands that go by the names get_data_from_database, format_data, and insert_data_into_layout?

This command you write yourself is called a *handler* (or a *subroutine*). It is placed in a special wrapper right inside your script (for the most part), and its functionality is available from anywhere in the script.

Calling handlers is similar to asking someone for a cup of coffee: with a short sentence, you asked them to perform about 20 separate operations.

When you're just starting to script, creating subroutines can be an added complication for which you may not be quite ready. Later, however, writing and calling subroutines can become some of the most important tasks you will do. Organizing your scripts with subroutines makes them easy to read and edit. It also allows you to write special code that can be later reused in other scripts.

You can read about handlers in more detail in Chapter 2 and in Chapter 16, which is dedicated to the subject.

Power Wrap-Up

So, what have you looked at thus far? You saw that although AppleScript provides a rich language to work with, most important for now is that AppleScript allows you to achieve fantastic results by starting out small and simple.

You also saw that in order for AppleScript to be useful, you need to have scriptable applications to which AppleScript can talk; after all, it's the ability to control useful applications that got you started with AppleScript in the first place, right?

PART 2

How to AppleScript

CHAPTER 2

Scripting—From the Ground Up

OK, all you "been-scripting-for-a-year-and-think-you-can-script-the-New-York-City-traffic-light-system" people, listen up. Although this chapter covers fundamental AppleScript concepts, it was written also for you. Nothing is better than rereading the stuff you think is way behind you. Like any other complex subject, AppleScript has a lot of levels, and to get up to the next level, you sometimes have to start fresh and pretend you know nothing.

Script Concentrate: Just Add Water!

In this section, you'll write a script that contains some of the basic AppleScript constructs. Then you'll run the script and try to understand what happened line by line.

This script will be a bit longer than your usual "Hello World" script; however, once you sift through all the lines, you'll be on top of it! Here's what the script will do: It will get a random number and use it to create a name for a folder. Then it will create the folder in the Finder, name it, and finally delete it if the user clicks Yes in a dialog box.

This section will go over many big AppleScript issues. Don't get stressed if it's too much—just go with the flow, read the text, and do the exercises. All of the points covered here will be repeated in great detail throughout the book.

OK, let's start:

1. Open Script Editor. You can find it in the AppleScript folder of your Applications folder (unless the system administrator thought it was a game and deleted it in last night's software raid).

   The main window is divided into two parts: the top is the area where you can write your script, and the bottom is divided into three tabs that display various kinds of useful information. The three tabs are Description, Result, and Event Log. Both the Result tab and the Event Log tab are essential for locating problems and solving them. The toolbar at the top of the window contains buttons for basic AppleScript functions: Record, Stop, Run, and Compile. That's the tour for now; let's start scripting.

2. In the blank, new Script Editor window that should be staring you in the eye right now, type the following two-word command, as shown in Figure 2-1:

   ```
   random number
   ```

The text you typed should be formatted with the font Courier. This is because it has not been compiled yet. To compile your script (which will, amongst other things, check whether your syntax is correct), either press the Enter key or click the Compile button.

Once you compile the script, the font, and possibly the color of the text, changes. Suddenly AppleScript understands what you're saying. Well, it understand what you're saying given you speak to it properly, of course.

Figure 2-1. *The noncompiled script in the Script Editor window*

Take a second to understand what happens when you click the Compile button. Before that, you will save the "random number" script as text to the desktop. Saving the script as text does not require you to compile the script. To save the script as text, choose File ➤ Save As, and choose Text from the File Format pop-up menu. We'll return to the "random number" script later.

To better understand the difference between correct syntax that manages to compile and usable code that compiles and runs correctly, try the following:

1. Start yet another script by choosing File ➤ New, and enter the following:

```
It's time to go
```

When you try to compile this script, you get an error. Ignore the specific error, and just note that what you typed didn't adhere to the AppleScript syntax and also isn't defined in any scripting addition installed on your Mac. In other words, if you were in Greece and couldn't speak Greek but tried to say something you just read in the dictionary, the response of the Greek person you were trying to communicate with would be something along the lines of "Huh?"

2. Back to AppleScript now . . . let's delete the words *to go* to end up with this:

```
It's time
```

Now the script compiles just fine. I bet you're all excited now—let's try to run it. Now what you said was actually a sentence in Greek, but with no real meaning. The Greek person will now smile at the poor foreigner and move on. Even if the script compiles, it still doesn't guarantee that it'll run to completion!

YOU'RE WELCOME TO ENTER, BUT, PLEASE, DO NOT RETURN

The Enter key on the Mac, to all you Windows migrants, is not the same as the Return key. You use the Return key to start a new line, and you use the Enter key for other tasks, such as compiling a script in Script Editor. For the most part, these keys will be marked Return and Enter. On extended keyboards, the Enter key is usually the right-most key on the keypad.

For the script to run successfully, it has to be a correctly written AppleScript code. Being able to compile a script does, however, ensure that you can save it as a compiled script. If you can't compile it (and there may be other reasons for that), you may have to save it as plain text until you figure out what went wrong.

OK, let's return to the "random number" script:

1. If you closed it, open it; if you want to start over, open a new script window, and enter **random number**.

2. Now run the script to see what happens.

As far as folders suddenly synchronizing, catalogs being created, or your iMac suddenly doing the macarena, I can't say that anything really happened. However, the script did run. Take a peek at the result area. If it's hidden, display the pane by dragging the horizontal divider line with the grab bar up until the pane at the bottom fills about a third of the window, and click the Result tab in the center, if not already selected.

The result area shows you the script's result. And since the result area shows the result of the last expression, the result is the result of that first line. What you get is a decimal number somewhere from 0 to 1 (such as 0.582275391438), which is the result of the random number command. In this context, random number is also an expression and therefore responsible for the result of the script line. Much like any other language, expressions and results are the building blocks of AppleScript.

Take, for instance, the following situation: My goal is to play squash, and here is how I go about it—I check what day it is, and the result of that expression is "Thursday." I can play on Thursday! I check the time; it's still early enough. I call my buddy, and he can play. Every single action I took had a result, which in some way led to me taking the next action. In this case, the positive result of each step led to the next step, and a negative result would have caused me to stop.

For that to happen, I need to store the results someplace. This "someplace" is another form of expression called a *variable*. A variable is a word you can invent. This word becomes the name of a container, which holds a value that you can use later in the script. A script without variables is like a bucket with a hole at the bottom. You can put a lot in it, but since nothing is retained, you can't utilize in the script information you were given at an earlier point.

With that said, let's put the random number you picked into a variable so you can refer to it later in the script:

1. Change the single line in the script to the following:

```
set my_number to random number
```

The set statement assigns the result of the expression, and in this case the random number command, into the my_number variable. Later in the script you will retrieve the value that is stored in that variable to name a folder.

2. For now, add the number 100 to the end of the line. This will return a random number from 0 to 100. The new line will now look like this:

```
set my_number to random number 100
```

The number that follows the random number command is a parameter. The random number command has other commands that you'll look at later. The number parameter that follows the command name makes the random number command return a whole number (also called an *integer*) from 0 to that number, instead of a decimal number from 0 to 1 (also referred to as a *real*).

3. To move to the next line, press Return, and then type the following:

```
my_number as text
```

This expression converts the number value stored in my_number to a text value, a process known as *coercion*. Since the result of the random number command is always a number, the new value assigned to the my_number variable is a number. This is all OK, but for this script you won't need that number for its numeric value but rather for including in a name of a folder. For that you need text.

You might be asking yourself why AppleScript should care whether a value is a number or text. Well, AppleScript cares about the type of value far less than most other programming languages, which may make your first few scripts easier to swallow but can create some confusion later when AppleScript's coercion logic doesn't give you the exact conversion you expected. It's better to explicitly specify what you want the *datatype* to be. In fact, since you later attach that random number to the end of a folder name, which is a string, AppleScript will convert the number to text on its own. You will learn much more about that later, so hang on.

4. Now run the script. Before, the result was just a number; now the number appears in double quotes. Double quotes are the distinguishing characteristic of text literals (or, to use a more programming-like term, *strings*).

Note A *text literal* is a text value you enter directly into the script, and such text is always surrounded by double quotes. Notice step 6 in this exercise: there's text stored in the my_number variable, and then there's the text literal "Folder Number ". While the script runs, values in variables can be changed by the script, but literal values can't.

The last line, again, needs to be put in a variable for later use. What you'll do now, however, is just put it back in the same variable, which is OK if you don't need the original value. If you did want to use the value later in the script, you would want to store it in a variable whose name tells you what the value is, such as user_age, current_score, area_code, and so on.

Note Recycling variables is the practice of using a variable for one purpose in the script and then changing the purpose later. Some variable identifiers, such as counter or flag, are natural candidates for recycling. You need them for a short period of time, and then you use them somewhere else for a different assignment.

---

5. Keep the first line of the script, but change the last line you wrote to this:

```
set my_number to my_number as text
```

6. Now you can build the string that will be used to name the folder—type the following new line at the end of the script:

```
set folder_name to "Folder number " & my_number
```

Your script should now look like the one in Figure 2-2.

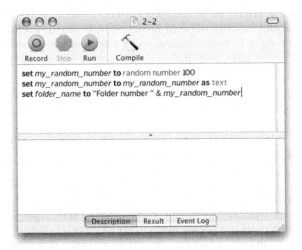

Figure 2-2. *The script so far*

The last statement joined together two values—in this case strings—to produce a new one, a process called *concatenation*. The & symbol, when put between two strings, returns the two strings as a single string. This is an example of an expression, one that includes the concatenation operator.

7. Run the script to see that the result is something like "Folder number 35" (assuming that the random number is 35).

8. Add the following line at the bottom of your script, which will speak directly to the Finder:

```
tell application "Finder" to make new folder at desktop
```

This statement performs two tasks: First, it invokes a command, which is a direct order to make something real happen—to create a folder on the desktop. Second, it also returns an AppleScript result—a pointer to the new folder. This pointer to an item on your disk isn't text or a number, and it is most likely going to be unusable for other applications in its current form. However, it will give you a way to refer to that new folder you just made.

9. Add a fifth line, as follows, to grab that Finder object reference by putting the result of the previous line into a variable:

```
set my_folder to the result
```

Note The `result` variable is a variable used by AppleScript to store the result of the last command that ran. This value of the result, if needed by the scripter, is usually assigned to another variable as well, making the `result` variable itself redundant.

---

10. Run the script, and see what happens—you should get a result along the lines of the following:

```
folder "untitled folder" of folder "Desktop" of folder¬
  "hanaan" of folder "Users" of startup disk
```

This is what's called a *reference*, which is how you can point to a file when scripting the Finder and other applications. Although this will work now, as soon as you run the line that changes the name of the folder, this reference is useless. It's a bit like telling someone whom you've never met before that you are going to be the guy with the beard and then going and shaving it off! You are still you, but the description you gave is no good.

11. To get a more lasting hold on your file, you can use the `alias` data type. Change the last line to this:

```
set my_folder to the result as alias
```

12. Now run the script again, and you should see the following returned:

```
alias "Macintosh HD:Users:hanaan:Desktop:untitled folder:"
```

Any subsequent time you run the script, the resulting folder's name will be `untitled folder 2`, `untitled folder 3`, and so on. This name difference will be reflected in the result of the script as well. This unique way to point to a file works much like aliases in the Finder: it knows what file you're talking about even if it has been moved or renamed! This will come in handy.

13. Let's talk to the Finder again—add the following sixth line:

```
tell application "Finder" to set the name of my_folder to folder_name
```

What you have done here is to use the two variables you collected earlier in the script, `folder_name` and `my_folder`, to rename the folder you created.

14. Now enter the following line—this seventh line will create a dialog box to ask the user whether they want the folder deleted:

```
display dialog ("Delete new folder "& folder_name & "?") buttons {"Yes", "No"}
```

The `display dialog` command has a few optional parameters. You will use the command's direct parameter to denote the dialog box's text and its `buttons` parameter to specify the button labels. By default a dialog box has two buttons: OK and Cancel.

Note You put the `"Delete new folder "& folder_name &"?"` operation in parentheses in this exercise. Although you didn't have to, it keeps your code a little more human readable. In other cases, using parentheses will change the outcome of an operation. Also note that the result of the dialog box is a record. We won't get into records now, but for now you just need to know that you can find out what button the user clicked from that record and then use that information elsewhere in your code.

---

15. The next few lines look inside the dialog box result to determine whether the user clicked Yes or No and act accordingly. Add these lines to the bottom of the script:

```
if button returned of result is "Yes" then
    tell application "Finder" to delete my_folder
end if
```

Notice that the alias value stored in the variable `my_folder` knows what folder you mean even though the folder's name was changed earlier. The script should now look like the one in Figure 2-3.

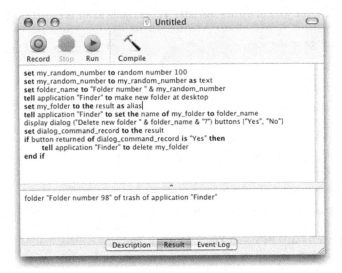

Figure 2-3. *The script so far*

More Results with Less Talk

Let's discuss again the way AppleScript relates to expressions and results. You know that almost every line has a result that can be captured. This is because most lines contain expressions that return results.

A statement can contain a single expression or multiple expressions. For instance, you can write the following:

```
set x to 3 + 4
set y to x * 5
set z to y - 37
set final_number to z / 15
```

or you can make it a more math-like operation and write this:

```
set final_number to (((3 + 4) * 5) - 37) / 15
```

You can perform the same operation by using the result variable instead of creating your own variables:

```
3 + 4
result * 5
result - 37
set final_number to result / 15
```

More on Variables

Variables are, in practical terms, the memory of AppleScript. Anytime you want to figure something out and use it later, you assign your conclusions to a variable. You can later retrieve that value, and use it elsewhere in the script, simply by mentioning the variable.

Naming variables logically can save you a lot of frustration later. The variable name is called an *identifier*.

These are the basic rules for naming variables:

- They must start with an alphabetic character or underscore.

- They can contain alphabetic characters (a–z, A–Z), digits (0–9), and underscores (_).

Note Identifiers are case insensitive; however, once you use a variable in a script, AppleScript will remember how you typed it, and anywhere else that you use it, AppleScript will change the case of the characters in the variable to match the same pattern you used the first time.

Unlike many other programming languages, AppleScript allows you to assign any type of data to any variable. In some languages, when you create a variable, you also tell it what type of data it will hold. In AppleScript, you can create a variable, assign a text value to it, and later replace that value with a number. It makes no difference.

Let's try some variable assignment exercises:

1. Open a new Script Editor window, and type the following:

```
set the_city to "Providence"
```

Since the word Providence is in quotes, AppleScript knows it's literal text or a string, not an identifier. The variable the_city now has the string value Providence assigned to it.

2. Type another line:

```
set the_state to "Rhode Island"
```

3. Now you can do something with these variables. Type a third and fourth line:

```
set my_greeting to "Hello, I live in " & the_city& ", " & the_state
display dialog my_greeting
```

Figure 2-4 shows the script so far.

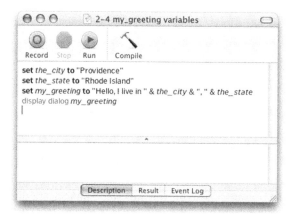

Figure 2-4. *The two variables are assembled into a string that's assigned to a third variable.*

You use the & character to join, or concatenate, the different strings—both the ones that are specified literally and the strings that are stored in the variables. The way in which Apple-Script evaluates the concatenation expression is by retrieving the value each variable contains and then passing these values as operands to the concatenation operator (&), which joins the two values to create a new one; the full expression's final result is assigned to a new variable, my_greeting.

4. When you run the script, the dialog box displays the final greeting, as shown in Figure 2-5.

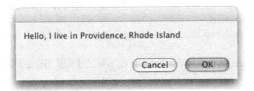

Figure 2-5. *The script's resulting dialog box*

Variables have a scope in which they are visible. If you try to use a variable outside of that scope, what you have is actually two variables that happen to use the same name. Imagine having a co-worker named George; as long as you work at that office, the name George is used to describe your co-worker. If you move to another company and work in another office, the name George may have no meaning at all if no one named George works there. It could also be that there's another George there, so calling George means the wrong person will come. However, if you return to the original office, the name George will again have the old meaning, and the original George still answers to it.

For now, you're not moving to another company, so you have nothing to worry about. But later I will discuss in great detail the implications of using variables in handlers, global and local variables, and properties. As long as a script includes only the run handler, you can be sure that using a certain variable name always refers to the same variable.

Values Come in Many Classes

Value classes in AppleScript define the ways in which information is represented. Information may appear as a number, it may be text, it may be either true or false, or it may be a reference to an object somewhere. The value class is what tells AppleScript how to treat the value when it is used in the script. For instance, the value 12 can be a number you use in the script in a math operation, or you can use it as part of a text string, such as "Expire in 12 days." In either case, the value is 12, but in the first case it's a number, specifically an integer (whole number), and in the second case it's two characters: the character 1 followed by the character 2.

The basic value classes are very logical, as you will see in the following sections.

Text

Also called a *string*, text is just that: a bunch of characters strung together. A *string literal* is the written representation of a piece of data, as used in source code. In other words, a string literal is text you actually type in your script; string literals always have double quotes on either side. Here are some string literals:

```
"A"
"My oh my!"
"IT IS SO ST&@%*"
"75"
```

Your scripts can also obtain string values from other sources. Take, for instance, the following statement:

```
set the_time to time string of (current date)
```

In this line of code, the value of the time string property of the date object returned by the current date command gets stored in the the_time variable. Although the value stored in the the_time variable is a string, its value is assigned while the script is running and therefore isn't shown in the code.

Let's look at the last literal string in the previous examples: "75". Notice that even though you have the number 75, since it is in quotes, it is a string.

To concatenate strings, you use the & symbol. For instance, the result of "to" & "day" is "today".

Other types of strings exist, and chief among them is Unicode text, which I will discuss in Chapter 3.

Number

Numbers come in two flavors: integer and real. An *integer* is always a whole round number, such as 1, 52, or 100,000. A real can be either whole or decimal but always has a decimal point. Here are some real numbers: 0.5, 100.1, 0.003, and 20.0.

When performing math operations, you can mix and match reals and integers; however, with the exception of the div operator, the result will always be a real:

```
8.5 + 70 = 78.5
1.75 + 1.25 = 3.00
```

Boolean

A Boolean is one of the most often used types of values. A Boolean value can be either true or false:

```
3 = 5 --> false
"BIG" is "big" --> true
disk "Macintosh HD" exists --> true
```

Tell Me About It

The tell statement is one of the structures you use to get the attention of the object to which you want to direct commands. Imagine being a fly on the wall in the dean's office at a college. The dean has a helper named AppleScript, who's in charge of making sure the dean's commands get to the right place.

The first command the dean gives is, "Bring me the report by tomorrow." The helper looks at him baffled; something is missing!

Oh, the dean finally gets it, "Tell the student in the second seat in the first row of Ms. Steinberg's class to bring me the report by tomorrow." That's better.

Unless you're using statements that contain only AppleScript commands and objects, you should use the tell statement to direct AppleScript to the right object. Simply throwing the command out there or directing it to the wrong object will most likely generate an error.

For instance, if you happen to be scripting Adobe InDesign and you want to get the font of some text, you use the tell statement to direct AppleScript to the text frame that is found on the page that is found in a specific document. If you tell the page to get the name of the font, you will get an error.

The Many Faces of tell

This section provides a few variations of how you can use the tell statement. They all work the same, but some are better than others in different situations. The main difference between the different ways of using the tell statement is in readability versus the number of lines you use, so the decision is left up to you.

So, what are the different ways to tell?

Let's return to the dean example. The dean used a long sentence that included the target object (the student) and the command in a single line: "Tell the student in the second seat in the first row of Ms. Steinberg's class to bring me the report by tomorrow."

From that statement, you can start to understand the school's object model, which is essential if it is a scriptable application. The model is as follows: the main object is a school, this object contains the classroom objects, and each classroom has a teacher. You can refer to each classroom by the teacher's name! Also, each classroom has seats arranged in rows, and each seat has a student. Each student has a name, age, and other useful school-related properties. In this case, the main school object contains only one object, but it can contain other objects, such as labs, janitors, gyms, and so on.

Now that you understand the object model a bit better, you realize that the dean could have also said to his helper, AppleScript: "Tell Ms. Steinberg's class to tell the first row to tell the student in the second seat that the report is due . . . ."

Notice how things got reversed? Now, instead of starting from the last object, you start at the top and go down: tell the class, followed by the row, followed by the seat. Before it was the seat that is in the row that is in the class.

How about a real example? Open Script Editor, and enter the script shown in Figure 2-6.

Figure 2-6. *Referencing the same object in two ways*

Look at the two ways you provide a reference to the same folder object. In the first example, you wrote a single, complete reference to the object you want: folder "AppleScript" of folder "Applications" of startup disk.

In the second example, you have a series of nested tell blocks, each describing part of the reference. As AppleScript evaluates these tell blocks, it gradually assembles these partial references into a single, complete reference to the object you want, which again is this: folder "AppleScript" of folder "Applications" of startup disk.

To prove that both examples identify the same folder object, run the two examples. The first one opens the AppleScript folder in your Applications folder, and the second one closes it again.

Objects You Can Tell Things To

Let's return to the main topic here, the tell statement. Let's look at some objects that like to be referred to with the tell statement.

The main type of object is application, an object representing a scriptable application. Anytime you want to send commands to an application, you have to direct them to an application object that identifies that application. For convenience, a tell block is normally used to identify that application object as the target for one or more commands within that tell block. Later you will also see how you can load script objects into variables and that the value contained in the variable will become an object that likes to be told things.

Telling in Blocks

The dean scratches his head. He realized that two more students from that same class owe him different reports. Now, when instructing his trusted helper, AppleScript, he may not want to write out the entire reference to a student each time he wants to send that student a command. Instead, he can start with this: "While you're in Ms. Steinberg's class, tell the student in seat 4 of row 2, the student in seat 1 of row 6, and the student in seat 2 of row 3 that they have reports due."

See, when writing scripts, many times you will want to direct more than one command to the same object (or group of objects). What you won't want to do is write the entire object reference (file 1 of folder 4 of folder Applications) each time. Instead, you can use a tell block.

Here is how: in a tell block, you start by identifying the object or objects you want to affect, then you apply one or more commands that will affect these objects, and you finish with the line end tell.

For instance, in the Finder example, you have the folder's position. What if you want to get the modification date of the folder as well? Here is how you can do that:

1. You start with the tell block. Enter the lines shown in Figure 2-7, and click the Compile button. The second line starts with a double hyphen. This turns it into a comment, and AppleScript ignores it.

Figure 2-7. *A* tell *block*

2. Now add the lines shown in Figure 2-8. Notice how each level of the `tell` block starts with the word `tell`, the `tell` block ends with the word `end`, and all the lines in between are indented for readability.

Figure 2-8. *Adding more levels to the* `tell` *block*

3. Now you add statements that collect data from the items inside the folder, as well as from the folder object's own properties. The three lines are as follows:

```
set file_list to name of every item
set time_folder_was_created to creation date
set time_folder_was_modified to modification date
```

Figure 2-9 shows the final script.

Figure 2-9. *The final script with the* `tell` *blocks*

When you run the script, the result shows only the last line's result; however, the rest of the data you collected is safe and sound in the variables file_list, time_folder_was_created, and time_folder_was_changed. Here are typical values:

```
file_list -->
{"AppleScript Utility.app", "Example Scripts"¬
    , "Folder Actions Setup.app", "Script Editor.app"}
time_folder_was_created --> date "Sunday, March 20, 2005 11:24:53 PM"
time_folder_was_changed --> date "Monday, October 31, 2005 7:23:42 PM"
```

More on Script Editor

One of the AppleScript improvements OS X 10.3 provided was a major update of Script Editor; it has many nice new features that are covered throughout the book. It has a customizable Aqua toolbar that gives you access to the main features and easy access to results, the event log, and their respective histories.

Event Log

You can find the event log by selecting the Event Log tab at the bottom of the Script Editor window. The event log records the commands that AppleScript sends to applications and the result returned for each. In Figure 2-10 you can see the previous script and the log it created when running.

Figure 2-10. *The response of the event log*

Result History

The result history feature keeps track of all script results in chronological order.

Choose Window ➤ Result History, and click the clock-shaped History button. Figure 2-11 shows the Result History window.

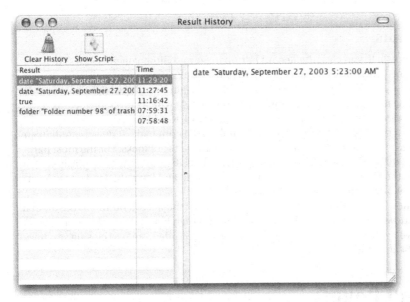

Figure 2-11. *I ran the "random number" script multiple times, and the result history feature captured them all.*

Script Description

Clicking the Description tab at the bottom of the script window in Script Editor reveals a large text field. You can write a description for your script and format it using the Format menu. Change the type size, font, and color as you like.

You can have that formatted text appear in a dialog box every time your script application launches. To display the dialog box at launch, check Startup Screen when you save the script as an application.

Scriptability

Script Editor itself is scriptable. AppleScript can tell Script Editor to create scripts; manipulate text; compile, execute, and save script documents; and more. For example, run the following script; it will create a new script document. Name it My Script, and then compile it and execute it:

```
tell application "Script Editor"
  set my_script to make new document with properties {name:"My Script"}
  set text of my_script to "say date string of (current date)"
  compile my_script
  execute my_script
end tell
```

Contextual Menu

Try Ctrl-clicking the script window to see the contextual menu that will pop up. The bottom of the menu includes folder menus from which you can choose useful scripts that will do everything from inserting `tell` statements, repeat loops, and conditional statements to adding error handlers. You can find the scripts in the menus in this folder: `/Library/Scripts/Script Editor Scripts/`.

Recording Scripts

Here's recording in a nutshell: you click the Record button in Script Editor, you do some stuff in another application, and everything you do is recorded in the AppleScript language.

OK, if that's so easy, why do you need to write a script ever again? Good question.

Although recording is nice, most applications aren't recordable. The recordability feature is rare, since application developers have to put in a lot of extra work to add it.

When you record scripts, you get computer-generated AppleScript code. It doesn't contain any repeat loops, handlers, conditional statements, or easy-to-manage `tell` blocks. For the most part, recording scripts is great if you can't figure out how to script a specific aspect of an application. For instance, in OS X 10.2, the Finder wasn't yet scriptable; in OS X 10.3 and later, the Finder is at least partially scriptable, which can make your life a little easier.

To test it, start a new script window in Script Editor, and click the Record button in the toolbar. Then, create new windows, move them, move files around, and then look at Script Editor to see the recorded actions. As you will see, some basic actions do not get recorded, such as closing windows and moving and duplicating files.

Spaces Don't Count

Extra spaces and tabs will be cleaned up when you check syntax, so don't bother with them. Also, indentation will happen automatically. You can, for readability's sake, leave some blank lines here and there. AppleScript will leave those alone.

To add text that you want the script to ignore, precede it with a double hyphen (--). Any text starting after the double hyphen, all the way to the end of the line, will compile as an inline comment.

Adding comments is essential if you or someone else returns to some code written a couple of months ago and wants to figure out how the code works with the aim of adding functionality or fixing a bug. It is amazing how difficult it can be to decipher even your own scripts after a while, after you can no longer remember what the different parts of the script are supposed to do.

Another reason to comment scripts is that when you're creating scripts that are part of a large system, these comments will be a part of your technical specifications. Clients take well to scripters who comment their scripts.

You can comment out whole blocks of text as well. You do that by starting the block with (* and ending it with *). Here's an example:

```
(* The following statements identify the files
that are a part of the job handled by the script at the time. *)
```

This type of comment is great for longer explanations you want to add to your scripts. Adding a sort of executive summary at the start of the script is a great way to explain what the code does and how it does it.

Note The time you spend writing comments will pay for itself many times over when it comes time for you to change the code, especially if some time has passed since you first wrote it.

The Application Scripting Dictionary

The application dictionary describes all the commands and object classes defined by an application. A dictionary is your first stop when discovering how to script a specific application. You can tell whether an application is scriptable or not just by checking to see whether it has a dictionary.

You can view the dictionary for any scriptable application in Script Editor by choosing File ➤ Open Dictionary and then choosing an application from the application list. The dictionary of the selected application will be displayed in the dictionary window. Figure 2-12 shows the dictionary of the Finder.

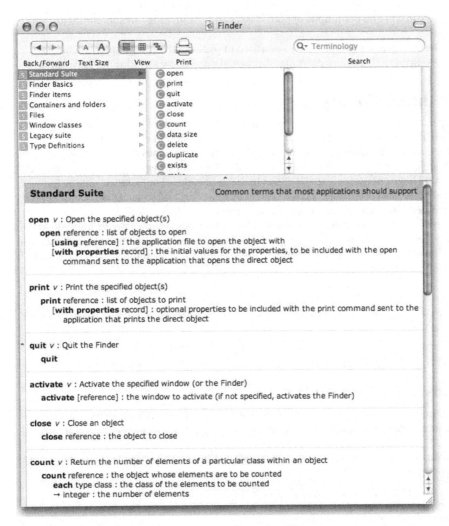

Figure 2-12. *The Finder's dictionary as shown in Script Editor*

Note You can open an application's dictionary in Script Editor in two other ways. You can drag the application's icon and drop it on the Script Editor application's icon. Alternatively, in the Library panel in Script Editor (Window ➤ Library), you can click the plus button in the Library window's toolbar to add the application to the list, then select the application in the list, and finally click the Dictionary button in the toolbar to display that application's dictionary.

As you can see in Figure 2-12, an application's dictionary is segmented into suites. The suites are organized in a logical way in order to help you find the information you need.

In each suite you will find definitions of both classes and commands—or sometimes just one or the other.

Note that the classes and commands are organized in suites so that the scripter will have an easier time browsing them. The suites don't play any actual role in how scripting actually works.

Classes in the Dictionary

Each object type, or class, is listed in the dictionary under the most fitting suite or is sometimes spread over more than one suite. This listing includes specific details about that class.

Besides the class's name and description, you will find two main types of information for every class. *Elements* are the first type of information. Under the "Elements" heading are the potential elements a class could have once it is an actual object in the application. For instance, among the elements of the Folder class are folder, file, alias file, clipping, and so on. Disks do not appear as elements of folders since a folder can never contain a disk.

The other type of information listed for a given class is that class's *properties*. Properties can be read using the get command and can be changed using the set command. Not all properties can be set, however. Properties that are denoted with "r/o" are read-only and therefore can't be changed, only read.

Note There's much to know about classes and commands that is not explained here. Please read on; it will all make sense in time.

Commands in the Dictionary

The commands in the dictionary appear along with a brief description, which is followed by the command's syntax, which also includes the parameters. The optional parameters appear in square brackets.

The following is an example taken from the Finder's dictionary. The example shows the listing of the update command:

```
update: Update the display of the specified object(s)
  to match their on-disk representation
update  reference  -- the item to update
 [necessity  boolean]  -- only update if necessary (i.e. a finder window is open).
    default is false
 [registering applications  boolean]  -- register applications. default is true
```

The description of the update command is great. You read it, and you have no doubt about what the command does. The required parameter for the command is the reference to the object you want to update.

The optional parameters are necessity, which is explained well, and registering applications, which . . . well, I have no idea what it's good for or what it does. The dictionary author either got a bit lazy or simply didn't know the answer either.

At Their Mercy

Although dictionaries are invaluable for any scripter, they are sometimes badly written and incomplete. They don't necessarily lack commands or classes, but many times dictionaries are written as an afterthought; dictionary authors sometimes just do not account for the immense difference a good dictionary can make to the scripter who tries to automate that application. The amount of detail and level of clarity invested in dictionaries are solely up to the dictionary authors, and the range of acceptable detail is high. For instance, when the properties are listed for a specific class, the dictionary usually mentions something in regard to the value that the property accepts. Some properties accept only a list, string, or number; some can accept only specific tokens defined by that application, such as the owner privileges property of the item class in the Finder. The properties can be read only, read write, write only, or none. Although the Finder's dictionary does list these options, some dictionaries lack basic information—something that can make scripting frustrating.

Another fact you can't tell by looking at a dictionary is which classes of objects accept which commands. For instance, the Finder dictionary contains the class window and the command duplicate, but that doesn't mean you can duplicate a window. How commands and classes interact is information you have to find in other places such as books, Internet lists, sample scripts that come with the application, or just good ol', late-night, trial-and-error experimentation.

The Application Object Model

Perhaps the most compelling part of application scriptability is its object model.

The idea of an object model is that one object can contain a number of other objects, which can themselves contain other objects, and so on. An object that contains other objects is known as a *container*, and the objects it contains are described as being *elements* of that container. The number of elements can be anywhere from zero up.

This type of hierarchy is called a *containment hierarchy*, since it describes which objects contain which elements and which objects contain which elements.

Let's look at InDesign's object model as an example: the InDesign application object contains zero or more document elements. (As you know, InDesign allows you to have any number of documents open at the same time.) In turn, each document object contains its own child elements such as spreads, layers, and so on. Spreads can have many pages, and each page has text frames, guides, and so on.

Like in some other applications, in InDesign you can ask for the object model in reverse as well; the parent of a specific text frame may be a specific page, and so on.

Objects and Class Inheritance

Class inheritance is not the same as containment hierarchy. Inheritance tells you how and where some kinds (or classes) of objects share similarities with other kinds of objects. For example, in the Finder a document file and an application file have many features in common: both have a name, a size, and a creation date (amongst other things). They also have a few differences: opening an application file launches that application, whereas opening a document file opens that document in an application. But overall, objects of these two classes are pretty similar. Other kinds of objects may share few, if any, common characteristics; for example, in Apple iPhoto a photo serves a completely different purpose than an album does: one is an image, and the other is a container for holding images. Understanding these sorts of relationships is important if you're going to script applications effectively.

To show you how closely different classes of objects are related and what features and abilities they have in common, each application defines an inheritance hierarchy. For example, to show that the document file class is related to the application file class, the Finder defines an extra class, file, that lists all the features they have in common. The document file and application file classes both then declare file as their parent class. This tells you two facts about document file and application file objects:

- They are all "files" of one kind or another.

- They include (*inherit*) all the attributes declared by the file class, as well as any additional attributes declared by their own classes.

In fact, the Finder's inheritance hierarchy goes even further than this because the file class itself inherits many of its attributes from the item class. The item class is also inherited by the container class, which defines all the attributes shared by its two child classes: disk and folder. Figure 2-13 shows the Finder's item class inheritance hierarchy diagram.

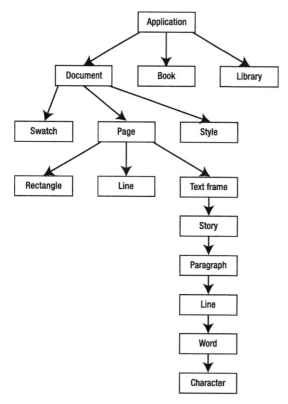

Figure 2-13. *The Finder's* item *class inheritance hierarchy diagram taken from Script Debugger 3*

■**Note** *Superclass* and *subclass* are common synonyms for *parent class* and *child class*, respectively.

Once you've worked out what the Finder's inheritance hierarchy looks like, you can deduce which classes of objects are most similar in nature and will therefore respond to commands in similar, if not identical, ways. You can also determine exactly what properties and elements an object of a particular class possesses when examining the application dictionary. For example, given an object of class document file, you'd work your way up its inheritance chain (document file ➤ document file ➤ item), "adding up" all the attributes you find in each.

For example, you can think of dogs as a class. The dog class has a few subclasses: terrier, herding dog, poodle, and so on. The dog class is also part of another class: mammal; this makes mammal the dog class's superclass. The mammal class by itself is a subclass of the class living-being. That last class, living-being, is the top superclass; any subclass of the living-being class by default inherits all of its properties. For instance, all living beings are born, then they live, and then they die. That is true for mammals, dogs, and terriers. However, every member of the dog class walks on four legs, which is not true for all members of the mammal class, which is is the dog class's superclass.

Classes and Commands

Classes also share commands with their subclasses. For instance, the Finder's item class understands commands such as duplicate and delete. That ability to understand these commands also passes to all of the item class subclasses such as file, folder, and so on.

Classes may be a bit intimidating in the beginning, and you may be asking yourself just how essential is it to get that info down. Well, classes are important, and although you should be grateful they exist and they make life more organized, don't kill yourself trying to understand them right now. You can take care of a dog just fine without dwelling on the evolutionary reasons for the existence of its tail.

What Makes an Object What It Is? A Look at Object Properties

Properties are where the relationship between a class of objects and the objects themselves becomes clear. While a class defines all the properties that all objects of that class have, the objects themselves have something the class doesn't: *values*. For example, in the Finder you have the file class. That class has a property called creator type. The class, however, is not an actual file; it's only the definition of what a file object's structure looks like. On the other hand, a file on the hard disk is a real file, and the creator type property of the object that represents that file actually has a value, which tells you the creator type of that particular file; for example, a value of ttxt would tell you the file was a TextEdit document.

Object properties are much like people properties. We all share the same set of properties in the class human; it's just that the values are different for each of us. For instance, we all have a height property. Each one of us has a weight property that we can give to the nurse at our annual checkup. This number is recorded, and then you are told whether you need to lose some weight! In AppleScript, object properties are used in similar ways. Let's look at the files in the Finder window. In the script, you can pinpoint the file you want to deal with and inspect its properties. You figure out that the size property of the file is 2MB. You write that in your script in a variable and later use it to do something useful.

You can see which object properties AppleScript has access to in two ways. One is the application's AppleScript dictionary, and the other is getting the value of an object's properties property, if it's available.

When you browse the dictionary in OS X 10.4's Script Editor, you start by clicking a suite name at the left column of the top section, which should reveal all the classes and/or commands defined in that suite. From there, you can click any items from the middle column; classes are marked with the letter *C* in a purple square background, and commands are marked with a *C* in a blue circle. After selecting one class (or Shift-clicking to select several), you will then see the elements and properties of the classes you clicked, one after the other in the bottom section of the dictionary viewer. (Remember, *class* is another word for *object type*, so a class defines all the properties and elements of all the objects that belong to that class.)

Figure 2-14 shows the FileMaker Pro 7 dictionary in Script Editor.

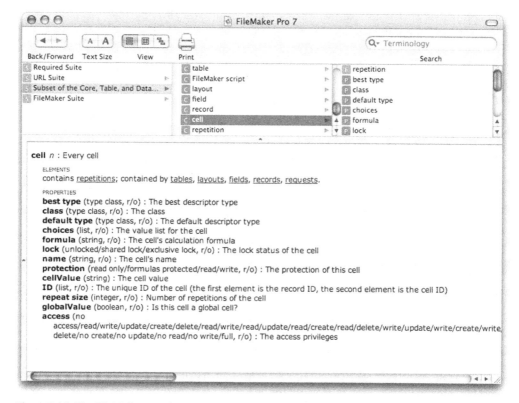

Figure 2-14. *The FileMaker Pro dictionary shown in Script Editor. The* cell *class is selected in the top outline portion, and all the* cell *class properties appear in the lower area.*

The advantage of using the dictionary to examine a class's properties is that the dictionary often comes with helpful hints. As you can see in Figure 2-14, the FileMaker Pro 7 dictionary has a nice explanation after each property. This can be an invaluable source of knowledge, especially because it is not always obvious what type or range of value the property will agree to use. After every property in the dictionary, either the data type or the actual values you can use are specified. For example, the FileMaker Pro 7 dictionary shows you that the lock property of the cell class can have one of three values: unlocked, shared lock, or exclusive lock.

Get Properties

Getting the values of an object's properties using the command get properties is a bit different. Not only do you get the list of property names, but you also get the value of all or most properties for a specific object.

Let's try to get the properties for a single file in the Finder. You will first need to identify the file whose properties you want to get. To do that, you will use the choose folder command, which returns an alias value identifying the folder. After putting that value in a variable, you will ask the Finder to get you the properties of that folder. Create a new script window, and enter the four lines shown in Figure 2-15.

Figure 2-15. *The script and the resulting properties of a chosen folder*

The result of the script is a record that contains about 30 properties associated with the folder class and their values that apply to the actual folder you chose.

Although the get properties of folder the_alias statement seems like its own little command, it is not. The command is actually the verb get, and properties is a reference to the property named properties. Some object properties return a number, such as size, and some return text, such as name. The properties property returns a record that includes most of the other properties. Looking at the folder properties you got (Figure 2-15), you can see that each property label/property value pair is separated by commas and that the value is separated from the label by a colon. Here is part of it:

```
{name:"first book script", index:3, displayed name:"first book script"
name extension:"", extension hidden:false, ...
```

You can easily tell that the value of the property name is "first book script", the index is 3, extension hidden is false, and so on.

The properties property exists in most objects in many applications, so it's almost a sure bet that you will get the results you want if you try it. All you have to do is make sure you have a valid object reference (see the "How to Talk to Objects So They Listen" section later in this chapter).

Read-Only

As you look at a class's properties in the dictionary, some properties will have "r/o" written next to them. These properties are read-only, which means you can ask to see their value, but you can't change it.

Although initially it appears to be a questionable restriction, some properties were simply not meant to be tampered with or are naturally unchangeable. Take the application Address Book, for example. When you create a new person entry, that person automatically gets a creation date value assigned to it. Although being able to use AppleScript to get the creation date of a person is nice, it would not make any sense if you could change that date; it would no longer be the creation date, but just any date.

If you try to change the value of a read-only property, as in the script shown in Figure 2-16, you will get an error, as shown in Figure 2-17.

Figure 2-16. *An unsuccessful attempt at changing a read-only property*

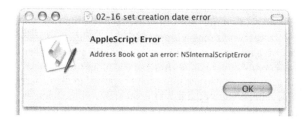

Figure 2-17. *Trying to set the* creation date *property of* person *generates an error*

How to Talk to Objects So They Listen

As you already know, in order to have your commands obeyed, you must address the recipient correctly. In AppleScript, you have many ways to address objects that will make them eligible to receive and obey your script's commands.

These ways of pointing to an object are called *reference forms*. Mastering reference forms is crucial to the success of your script. If you can't point to the right object using the appropriate reference form, your script will not function as expected, if at all. The coming sections will help you understand reference forms and how to use them.

Let's return for a minute to the dean at the made-up school. The dean's job today is to assign the extracurricular duties to students. Before naming the duties that need to be carried out (the commands), he needs to identify the students who will perform the tasks. Based on what you know so far, he can give tasks to each student individually: tell the student in seat 4 of row 8 of Mr. Popokovich's class that his duty is dishwashing at the cafeteria. Or, in other words: the duty of the student of seat 4 of row 8 of Mr. Popokovich's class is dishwashing. Although this is all good, the poor dean will realize soon enough that in order to name all the students and duties for the day, he will need to spend the entire afternoon assigning duties! He needs a better system.

Index Reference Form

The *index* reference form uses an integer to reference objects. To use the index reference form, you type the element's name followed by the position of the specific element you want. For instance, to get the first file of the second folder, you can type file 1 of folder 2. The index reference form uses the order of the elements in the way the application defines that order. In the Finder, for the most part, the files are arranged alphabetically. In page-layout applications, the order of page elements is determined based on their stacking order; the topmost item is always item 1. The order of some objects, such as pages, is easy to determine.

The index reference form is particularly convenient for referring to the frontmost document, since document elements are always ordered from front to back. Thus, to address commands to the front document, just direct them to document 1 (for example, by wrapping them in a tell document 1 block).

The index reference form works from the back as well by specifying negative numbers. The last item is also item –1, one before last is item –2, and so on.

Another way to use the index reference form is with number words such as first, second, and third, like this: third application file of last folder.

Range Reference Forms

The *range* reference form allows you to reference an entire range of elements, instead of one element at a time. You do that by specifying the position of the first element in the range you want, followed by the word thru, and then followed by the position of the last element in the range: pages 3 thru 6, files 1 thru 10, and so on.

Ranges are often used when scripting different aspects of text. The following script extracts a portion of a file's name:

```
tell application "TextEdit"
    set miniaturized of (windows 2 thru -1) to true
end tell
```

This last script will collapse all TextEdit windows other than the front one. Note that the range reference takes place on the second line: (windows 2 thru -1).

Object Names

Many application objects contain a name property. The name property of the object makes it easier to refer to that specific object. Sometimes it is up to you to name it in the first place; in other instances, such as working with filenames or document names, the objects are already named, and all you have to do is refer to the object by name in your script.

The following example creates a new Script Editor document with a name and then refers to the document and to the window by that name:

```
tell application "Script Editor"
  make new document with properties {name:"Great Script"}
  set contents of document "Great Script" to¬
    "tell application \"finder\" to activate"
  compile document "Great Script"
  set bounds of window "Great Script" to {0, 0, 400, 500}
end tell
```

May I See Some ID, Please?

Although names are useful, some applications provide an additional identifier for some or all of their objects: a *unique ID*.

Unlike naming objects, an object's unique ID is assigned by the application and is a read-only property, which means you can't change it; you can only look at it. That aspect of a unique ID is what makes it so useful: although the name of the object can be changed by either a script or in the user interface, an ID is created automatically when the object is created and stays with the object until it is deleted. On top of that, an object's ID is a read-only property and has no way of being seen through the graphical user interface.

Unique IDs are essential reference tools, since unlike the name and index properties, they are truly unique. You have to be aware that the value of the id property for a particular object may change the next time you launch the application. Different applications may use different ID formats; for example, in InDesign object IDs are a three-digit integer, or more. In Address Book, a person's ID may look like this: 03CEBE56-CA2B-11D6-8B0C-003065F93D88:ABPerson.

Applications that assign IDs to objects are InDesign, QuarkXPress, FileMaker Pro, Address Book, iCal, BBEdit, and many more. These applications, for the most part, don't assign IDs to objects: Apple Mail, Adobe Illustrator, Adobe Photoshop, Apple Safari, and Microsoft Excel.

Note Cocoa-based applications will assign an ID to the objects of the window class, since this feature is part of the Cocoa framework.

Here's an example of using the id property of an element. The following script will create a new person in Address Book, extract that person object's id property to a variable, and then use the id property to change the person object:

```
tell application "Address Book"
  set new_guy to make new person with properties {first name:"Pat"}
  set new_guy_id to id of new_guy
  -- new_guy_id value is something like:
  -- 6C244865-51CC-43F5-A563-ECA2861707FE:ABPerson
  tell person id new_guy_id
    set title to "Ms."
  end tell
end tell
```

every . . . whose

The whose clause, also known as the *by-test reference form*, is one of the most powerful programming constructs in the AppleScript language. It gives you the ability to identify elements whose property and/or element values meet certain criteria. Let's break it down. Whenever you examine any group of objects, some of them are similar in different ways. If a folder contains 50 files, 20 of them may be TIFF files, 10 may be aliases, 8 may be larger than 10MB, and some may be older than a month. On an InDesign page, you may have 30 page items: 10 of them may be lines, 22 may have a stroke of 1 point, and 20 may have a blue fill. Notice that I named properties that are unrelated; in the Finder, the same file can be more than 10MB, can be less than a month old, and may or may not be a TIFF file. This way of grouping objects allows you to easily and logically refer to just the objects you want to affect.

The dean, for instance, could have a thought: "I can simply say, 'Every student whose grade average is C or lower has dishwashing duty today.'" Ouch! That is way too mean, but it would have worked.

In some applications, however, you can use an unlimited combination of whose clauses and commands. Let's look at a few examples:

```
tell application "InDesign"
  tell page 1 of document 1
    delete every text frame whose contents is ""
  end tell
end tell
```

The entire set you reference here is the set of text frames on page 1. Using the whose clause, you can single out the text frames that contain no text and delete them as follows:

```
set documents_folder to path to documents folder from user domain
tell application "Finder"
  duplicate (every file of documents_folder whose size is greater than (2¬
    * 1000 * 1000))
end tell
```

Here, the set of objects is all the files in the user's Documents folder. The script wants to duplicate only those files larger then 2MB:

```
tell application "FileMaker Pro"
  tell table  "guests" of database "party"
    set young_kids to cell "name" of every record whose cell "age" is less than 12
  end tell
end tell
```

This script lists the names of all the party guests younger than 12.

When you work with an application that doesn't support the whose clause, you have to settle for slower, clumsier repeat loops, performing each test yourself.

Here's another example:

```
tell application "Address Book"
  get name of every person where (email_address is in (value of every email))
end tell
```

This example searches for a person by giving an e-mail address. Notice that e-mails are stored as elements of the person object, not a property, so you can't simply write every person whose email is email_address. Fortunately, Address Book is pretty clever at interpreting even fairly complex whose clause tests, so you can ask it to look through each email element's value property to see whether the desired address is in any of them. Had this powerful whose clause not been available, you would have had to use a pair of nested AppleScript loops to search through each email element of each person object one at a time—a rather more laborious and far slower solution than getting Address Book to do all the hard work for you.

Relatives

A *relative reference* identifies an element that is positioned before or after another element. For instance, the reference paragraph after paragraph 3 of document 1 of application "TextEdit" requires that paragraph 3 of document 1 of application "TextEdit" will be a valid reference in order for it to be valid itself. If there's no paragraph 3, then you can't use the reference paragraph after paragraph 3 or paragraph before paragraph 3.

The following example selects the photo that follows the currently selected photo:

```
tell application "iPhoto"
    try
        set current_selection to item 1 of (get selection)
        select (photo after current_selection)
    end try
end tell
```

Note The try statement was added to trap the error iPhoto generates in case no photos are selected.

Ordinal Reference Forms

Ordinal reference forms allow you to reference certain elements in a natural way.

All Elements in a Collection

In many situations, you will want a reference to all the elements of a particular object, such as all paragraphs on a TextEdit document, all files of a folder in the Finder, or all pages of an InDesign document.

To indicate a reference to all elements, you can use the optional term every. Here are some examples that use a reference to all elements of an object:

```
tell application "Address Book"
    set people_list to people -- people is the plural of the person object
    --or:
    set people_list to every person
end tell
```

Here are some other examples:

```
tell application "Finder"
    tell startup disk
        set file_names to name of files of startup disk
        --or:
        set file_names to name of every file of startup disk
    end tell
end tell
```

first, last, and middle

As it sounds, these reference forms identify a single element based on its position in the collection of elements. Here are some examples:

```
tell application "Adobe InDesign CS2"
    delete first page of active document
end tell
```

Here are some examples in string manipulation:

```
middle word of "Application automation rocks!" --> "automation"
```

Power Wrap-Up

In this chapter, you discovered Script Editor and used it to write your first AppleScript scripts. You saw how to create values and assign them to variables. You used a few of AppleScript's built-in commands, including the very useful display dialog. You discovered how to send commands to scriptable applications and how to refer to and manipulate objects within those applications. And, finally, you discovered how to define commands of your own.

This was a real whirlwind tour of some of the most interesting and useful areas of AppleScript and application scripting, and it was a lot to master in such a short period of time. But don't worry—you'll slowly work through each of these topics, and a few more besides, in the coming chapters. But right now, just take a deep breath—or ten—and then give yourself a great big pat on the back. Congratulations, you're now officially an AppleScripter!

CHAPTER 3

■ ■ ■

Introducing Values

Values are the bits of information you use when you talk AppleScript: the numbers, text, dates, times, and so on, you use to display, store, and calculate information.

When you speak the AppleScript language, it's important to understand the distinction between merely giving commands and the information you use to make the command mean something. Just like when you speak English, you can have an exchange along the lines of this:

"Hey, what time is it?"

"Hmmm . . . It's quarter of four; I need to get to the bank before it closes and withdraw $60 to pay Dan and Gail for helping me paint."

In AppleScript, this could be represented by the following (although this is not a real script):

```
set list_of_people_to_pay to {person "Dan", person "Gail"}
set time_bank_closes to date "5/22/2003 4:00 PM"
set minutes_to_get_to_bank to 15
set minutes_left_until_bank_closes to time_bank_closes - (current date)
if minutes_left_until_bank_closes > minutes_to_get_to_bank then
    set my_money to withdraw 60 from bank
    give (my_money / 2) to (item 1 of list_of_people_to_pay)
    give (my_money / 2) to (item 2 of list_of_people_to_pay)
end if
```

The preceding example gave a few commands, such as set, withdraw, and give (the withdraw and give commands are found in the application Life, which is yet to be scriptable . . .). The commands themselves, however, don't mean much without the values you attach to them: the bank closing time, amount of money you have to withdraw, and each of the people you have to pay.

These values, or units of information, get their meaning not only from the data itself but also from the *type* of information they represent. For instance, the money you have to pay Dan and Gail is stored in the script as a number. The significance of that is you can perform certain tasks with numbers that you can't perform with text—for instance, math! You could take the amount you withdrew and divide it by 2. The application also does some math with the dates to figure out how much time remains to go to the bank; the result of this is a number. The application then compares this to the length of time it takes to get to the bank to find out whether you'll make it in time; the result of this is a Boolean.

What about the people you have to pay? Each one of them is represented as a person object. The two person objects, however, are clumped together in a *list*, which you will look at in a bit.

The different types of data you use in AppleScript are called *classes*, and the pieces of data are referred to as *values*. In AppleScript, then, the types of information you use are called *value classes*.

AppleScript has the following 14 value classes:

- `class`
- `constant`
- `boolean` (can have one of two values: true or false)
- `integer` (whole number)
- `real` (decimal number)
- `string` (text)
- `Unicode text`
- `date`
- `alias`
- `file`
- `list`
- `record`
- `data`
- `script object`

The value classes I'll cover in this chapter are `integer`, `real`, `string`, `boolean`, and `list`; as I mentioned earlier, a list isn't really a single piece of information but rather a collection of other values. Each value in a list is described as being an *item* of that list, and each item can be a value from any value class. Lists are powerful, flexible values: you can add, replace, and retrieve their items at any time. You will delve more into lists in a bit and explore their many uses throughout the book.

Stringing Characters

One of the tasks you will find yourself doing a lot in AppleScript is working with text in one way or another. The following sections cover the many aspects of text manipulation in AppleScript.

What Can You Do with Text?

Although the official word for text used in this book is *string*, it is basically text. The `string` value class is a sequence of characters. In source code you indicate string literals as zero or more characters between two straight double quotes. For example, `"Hello World!"` is a string literal. Simply having `Hello World` in the script without quotes would cause the script to not compile.

As with any other value, you can assign a string to a variable using the `set` command:

```
set my_greeting to "Hello World!"
```

This line assigns `"Hello World!"` to the variable `my_greeting`.

The length of a string is limited only by your computer's memory. You can assign very long strings to variables—hundreds of thousands of words, really, with no end.

The choice of characters you can use in a string is a different issue, though. AppleScript's original `string` value class can represent a limited range of characters. Your system's language settings determine the exact character set used; for example, for English and most other European languages, AppleScript `string` values will use the MacRoman character set, which contains 256 characters. If your system language is Japanese, then AppleScript `string` values will use the MacJapanese character set, which contains several thousand characters.

■Note To keep things simple, for the rest of the book I'll assume your copy of AppleScript is using the MacRoman character set for its `string` values. But don't worry if it doesn't: most of the differences aren't that important and won't affect how you use AppleScript.

Because older character sets such as MacRoman can display only a small number of characters each, modern operating systems such as Mac OS X have adopted a newer, more powerful character set called Unicode that is large enough to represent every character in common use around the world (with plenty of room to spare). Although some of the details of the Unicode standard are rather complex, fortunately you don't need to know about these details in order to work with Unicode-based text. OS X usually takes care of all the details for you so it "just works," and Apple-Script provides good (though not perfect) Unicode support thanks to its `Unicode text` value class. Older character sets are still supported separately for backward compatibility, though.

Incidentally, the first 128 characters in MacRoman, Unicode, and many other character sets are identical. These 128 characters come from an even older character set called American Standard Code for Information Interchange (ASCII) that was invented back in the days when most computers still filled an entire room and all their users were programmers. The ASCII character set defines letters A–Z in both uppercase and lowercase, numbers 0–9, various common arithmetic and punctuation symbols, spaces, tabs, and returns, which was everything those earlier programmers needed to work their machines. Although the original ASCII character set isn't used much these days, its legacy lives on in its successors, ensuring at least some degree of consistency and compatibility in how computers handle text.

What this means to you, the lone scripter, isn't much, since AppleScript for the most part makes sure to convert between old-style strings and Unicode text when necessary. That conversion in AppleScript is called *coercion*. Coercing a value means converting a value of one class to a similar value of another value class. AppleScript can perform coercions automatically when needed, or you can instruct it to perform specific coercions in your code. You'll learn much more about coercion in Chapter 9. Although AppleScript and OS X in particular are moving toward using Unicode everywhere, they still have many glitches. Some commands don't understand Unicode and are unable to accept Unicode text values as parameters or return them as results. This, however, is becoming better with every release of the operating system and will, I hope, become seamless within a year or two. Almost every update to Mac OS X brings with it updates related to how Unicode text is used in AppleScript. In OS X 10.4, the most important change is that now whenever two strings are concatenated to produce a new string, the text format of the resulting string is the richer of the two. This means a normal string is concatenated to a Unicode text string, and the resulting string is a Unicode text string.

■Note In OS X 10.3.9 and earlier, concatenating old-style strings and Unicode text in AppleScript could produce either a string or a Unicode text result, depending on whether it did "string and Unicode" or "Unicode and string." Unfortunately, squishing `Unicode text` values into `string` values can be problematic: some characters won't translate at all, and the resulting "strings" can behave oddly in some situations because of tricks AppleScript uses to represent other characters. OS X 10.4 changes this behavior so the result will always be Unicode text, which makes life much simpler. If you're scripting for a pre-Tiger Mac, you can deliberately coerce the left value to Unicode text first in order to force the result to be Unicode text: `(value1 as Unicode text) & value2`.

Special Characters in Literal Strings

Although you can include any one of the 256 MacRoman characters in a string, some of them need a slightly different treatment if you want to use them in a literal string in your script. For instance, take double quotes. Since a double quote is the character that specifies the start and end of a string, how can you include quotes in a literal string? If you write the following:

```
set my_string to "Click on the file named "Read me" and open it"
```

then AppleScript will get confused and think the literal string ends at the second double quote, `"Click on the file named "`, and what comes after that won't compile.

The error you get, shown in Figure 3-1, is almost philosophical. I'm glad that AppleScript at least found itself . . . .

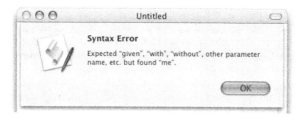

Figure 3-1. *AppleScript expected "without" but found "me."*

The error is meaningless, since the example messed up on the quotes front. The first step to take when an error makes no sense is to check whether you left some quote open somewhere.

To properly include a quote in the string, you escape it with a backslash, also known as the *escape character.* You can find the backslash right under the Delete key on most Mac U.S. keyboards.

To properly assign the string to the variable as the previous example tried to do, you write the following:

```
set my_string to "Click on the file named \" Read me\" and open it"
```

Here's another problem: with the backslash acting as the special escape character in a string literal, what do you do if you want to include the backslash character itself in a string? For instance, if you want to display a dialog box asking users not to use the backslash character, you will need to use it yourself. To do that, you can simply escape it with another backslash character:

```
display dialog "Don't use the \\ character"
```

Figure 3-2 and Figure 3-3 show how to use the backslash character inside double quotes. Fancy stuff!

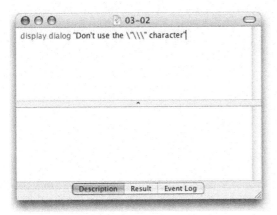

Figure 3-2. *The code*

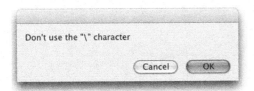

Figure 3-3. *The resulting dialog box*

Another way you can include the double quote character, which is new in Tiger 10.4 or later, is by simply using AppleScript's built-in quote variable, which contains a predefined string value with a single double quote character in it. This might look a little odd at first since the quote variable doesn't go inside the quotes, of course. Using this variable, the previous script line would look like this:

```
set my_string to "Click on the file named " & ¬
    quote & "Read me" & quote & "and open it"
```

Other characters you should know about are the tab and return characters. These two characters won't give you a hard time—just the opposite; you can include them in a string in a few ways. Another way to include these characters is by typing \r for return and \t for tab. Both \r and \t will be replaced with returns and tabs as soon as you compile the script; the similar combination of \n will be replaced with a linefeed character. See Figure 3-4 and Figure 3-5 for an example.

Figure 3-4. *The script before it has been compiled*

Figure 3-5. *The script after it has been compiled*

The other way you can refer to the return and tab characters is by using the corresponding AppleScript built-in variables. AppleScript has four constants: quote, which you looked at already, and space, tab, and return. They're variables that are predefined by AppleScript. Just as with variables, you can't use these three constants in quotes. They're useful when you use the concatenation operator to connect a few strings:

```
set my_own_menu to "coffee" & tab & "$1.15" & return & "donut" & tab & "$0.65"
```

ASCII Is a Sure Thing, Almost . . .

Think about how neat it is to be able to describe characters without typing the character itself. Think about characters that aren't marked on the keyboard or characters that when displayed using certain fonts don't look like anything at all but a square.

Remember, from here on, unless specified otherwise, I will be talking about the MacRoman character set, as listed in Table 3-1. (Some control characters from 0 to 32 were omitted from the table because they don't have a typical visual representation or real use for a scripter.)

Table 3-1. *The MacRoman Character Set*

Number	Character	Number	Character	Number	Character
9	(Tab)	58	:	88	X
10	(Linefeed)	59	;	89	Y
13	(Carriage return)	60	<	90	Z
		61	=	91	[
32	(Space)	62	>	92	\\
33	!	63	?	93	]
34	"	64	@	94	^
35	#	65	A	95	_
36	$	66	B	96	`
37	%	67	C	97	a
38	&	68	D	98	b
39	'	69	E	99	c
40	(	70	F	100	d
41	)	71	G	101	e
42	*	72	H	102	f
43	+	73	I	103	g
44	,	74	J	104	h
45	-	75	K	105	i
46	.	76	L	106	j
47	/	77	M	107	k
48	0	78	N	108	l
49	1	79	O	109	m
50	2	80	P	110	n
51	3	81	Q	111	o
52	4	82	R	112	p
53	5	83	S	113	q
54	6	84	T	114	r
55	7	85	U	115	s
56	8	86	V	116	t
57	9	87	W		

Continued

Table 3-1. *Continued*

Number	Character	Number	Character	Number	Character
117	u	156	ú	196	ƒ
118	v	157	ù	197	≈
119	w	158	û	198	Δ
120	x	159	ü	199	«
121	y	160	†	200	»
122	z	161	°	201	…
123	{	162	¢	202	(Nonbreaking space)
124	|	163	£		
125	}	164	§	203	À
126	~	165	•	204	Ã
127	(Control character)	166	¶	205	Õ
		167	ß	206	Œ
128	Ä	168	®	207	œ
129	Å	169	©	208	–
130	Ç	170	™	209	—
131	É	171	´	210	"
132	Ñ	172	..	211	"
133	Ö	173	≠	212	'
134	Ü	174	Æ	213	'
135	á	175	Ø	214	÷
136	à	176	∞	215	◊
137	â	177	±	216	ÿ
138	ä	178	≤	217	Ÿ
139	ã	179	≥	218	/
140	å	180	¥	219	€
141	ç	181	µ	220	‹
142	é	182	∂	221	›
143	è	183	Σ	222	fi
144	ê	184	∏	223	fl
145	ë	185	π	224	‡
146	í	186	∫	225	·
147	ì	187	ª	226	‚
148	î	188	º	227	„
149	ï	189	Ω	228	‰
150	ñ	190	æ	229	Â
151	ó	191	ø	230	Ê
152	ò	192	¿	231	Á
153	ô	193	¡	232	Ë
154	ö	194	¬	233	È
155	õ	195	√	234	Í

Number	Character	Number	Character	Number	Character
235	Î	242	Ú	249	˘
236	Ï	243	Û	250	˙
237	Ì	244	Ù	251	°
238	Ó	245	ı	252	ˌ
239	Ô	246	ˆ	253	˝
240		247	˜	254	˛
241	Ò	248	¯	255	ˇ

To identify a character, you can ask for its position in the MacRoman character set table (a number from 0 to 255) and then use the number instead of the character. You do that using two (slightly misnamed) commands, ASCII number and ASCII character.

Note The commands ASCII number and ASCII character are actually defined in Standard Additions, a set of scripting additions that comes installed as part of the operating system. You'll learn more about it throughout the book.

The ASCII number command takes a one-character string as its parameter and returns a number from 0 to 255 that indicates its position in the MacRoman character table. For instance, the statement ASCII number space will return 32, which is the ASCII number of the space character.

The opposite command is ASCII character. The ASCII character command accepts a number from 0 to 255 as its parameter and returns the MacRoman character for that number. For instance, the statement ASCII character 36 will return the one-character string $.

Try the following script, and then refer to the resulting dialog box in Figure 3-6:

```
display dialog "I love the big " & ASCII character 240
```

While executing the script, AppleScript evaluates the ASCII character 240 command, which returns a string containing the Apple logo character.

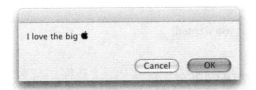

Figure 3-6. *The dialog box with ASCII character 240*

A String Operation

You'd think that performing operations on strings would return different strings as results. In fact, only one string operator returns a string. That operator is the concatenation operator, &.

The rest of the operations you can apply to strings use mainly comparison and containment operators, which return Boolean values. For example, you can check whether *a* comes before *b* or whether the string "Angel food cake" contains the string "food".

The concatenation operator can work on strings, lists, and records, and it's up to you to ensure you know whether the operations you perform with the concatenation operator will return a string, list, or record. On top of that, you have to make sure the result the operation returns is the result you wanted.

What happens here in a sense is that you pay for the AppleScript programming language having relaxed syntax. In many other languages, whenever you declare a new variable, you also have to specify the value class for that variable (whether it will hold a real, an integer, text, and so on). In AppleScript, you can store any kind of value in any variable, so it's up to you to remember which kind it is and how it'll behave when you use it.

You already saw the concatenation operator at work, but now you'll look at a couple of issues with it.

Concatenating strings returns a string result. That makes sense. What else would it return?

Well, try the following in a new script window:

```
set the_price to "$" & 6
```

The result is $6.

The difference here is that you concatenated a string to a number. AppleScript took the liberty to coerce the number into text, so the result is the same as if you had treated the 6 as text in this way:

```
set the_price to "$" & "6"
```

You get the same result.

However, let's see what happens when you switch places:

```
set the_price to 6 & " Dollar"
```

The result this time is different. Since the first operand (the item you operate on) is a number and not a string, AppleScript figures that it is safer to return a list instead of a string. The result then is a list of two items, a number and a string:

```
{6, " Dollar"}
```

To prevent that from happening, you have to include a coercion operator: as.

The operator coerces the resulting value into a different value class. In this case, you should first coerce the number to a string, like this:

```
set the_price to (6 as string) & " Dollar"
```

Now the result is a single string—6 Dollar—just as you wanted.

CONCATENATE WITH CARE

Take care! A common mistake here is to join the two values using the following:

```
6 & " Dollar" as string
```

This may seem to work OK sometimes, but it hides a nasty bug because it works by first creating a two-item list, {6, "Dollar"}, and then coercing that list to a string. If AppleScript's text item delimiters property (which you'll meet shortly) is set to any value except an empty string, you'll find extra characters mysteriously inserted into the result! To avoid such unpleasant surprises, always write it as (6 as string) & " Dollar" instead.

What about the other operators? Well, many operators compare either two strings or pieces of a string to other strings. These operators are =, ≠, >, ≥, <, ≤, starts with, ends with, contains, and is in. Let's start with the simple ones. It's easy to understand how you can see whether strings are equal; consider the following operations. This one:

```
"Ice cream" = "carrot"
```

returns false. And this one:

```
"Me" ≠ "You"
```

returns true.

Incidentally, AppleScript allows each of these operators to be written in any of several ways: as symbols, words, or phrases. This makes no difference to how your script runs, but it does allow you to write your code in whichever style you think reads best. Script 3-1 shows the various alternatives, or *synonyms*, AppleScript provides.

Script 3-1.

```
"Ice cream" is "carrot"
"Ice cream" equals "carrot"
"Ice cream" is equal to "carrot"
"Me" is not "You"
"Me" is not equal to "You"
```

Let's look at some more string comparisons. How about the following statement?

```
"555-1212" = "5551212" --> false
```

or the following one?

```
"ASCII" = "ascii" --> true
```

The result of the first operation is false, and the second one is true. This is because AppleScript makes default assumptions about what characteristics of the text you may want to consider or ignore while comparing text. You should not only be aware of these issues but also always keep in mind that you can overrule AppleScript's assumptions with special clauses that allow you to ignore or consider certain conditions.

Unicode again . . . you know that Unicode is not the same as MacRoman, but in a common-sense effort to make unimportant differences invisible to you, the AppleScripter, comparing strings of different types but with the same content, returns a positive true result.

Take this script, for instance:

```
set string_variable to "it's all text" as string -- this would be string anyway...
set unicode_variable to "it's all text" as unicode text
string_variable is equal to unicode_variable -- the result here is true
class of string_variable is equal to class of unicode_variable -- this is false
```

Considering and Ignoring

AppleScript offers a few consideration attributes that do string comparison. They are (in alphabetical order) case, diacriticals, hyphens, expansion, numeric strings (new in OS X 10.4), punctuation, and white space. By default, when comparing strings, AppleScript ignores case and numeric strings but considers the rest.

These attributes as a group are sometimes overlooked and underrated, but they can play a major role in your scripts, as you're about to see.

Note All the following samples are part of Script 3-2.

Let's start with a simple example of the case clause. To use the case attribute, or any other consideration attribute, you have to wrap your statement in the following way, using either the word ignoring or the word considering, depending on your intention:

```
considering case
    "A" = "a"
end considering
```

The result of the preceding script snippet is false.

The default AppleScript behavior is to ignore the case of characters, so asking AppleScript to consider the case of characters will yield a different result. Simply stating the following:

```
"A" = "a"
```

returns true, and since AppleScript ignores characters' cases by default, the following statement returns true as well:

```
ignoring case
    "A" = "a"
end ignoring]
```

In a recent project, I had to add a feature to a system that would determine whether the content of a Microsoft Excel sheet had changed. The solution was to save every worksheet as a text file and then compare the text files with the older version of that file. Initially, I used the following line:

```
set files_match to (read file_a) = (read file_b)
```

The statement simply compares two strings that are returned from the read command (which you will explore in depth later in this book). The problem with this solution is that if someone simply fixed a capitalization problem in a worksheet, AppleScript would still think the text of the files was identical. The script was retrofitted with the ignoring case clause, like this:

```
ignoring case
    set files_match to (read file_a) = (read file_b)
end ignoring
```

This time, even a simple change of capitalization would show.

The deal with the diacritical, hyphen, and punctuation consideration clauses is a bit different. Each of these refers to a set of special characters that can be ignored when comparing strings. All are true by default, so using them in a considering clause won't normally change the result, but using them in an ignoring clause will.

The ignoring diacriticals clause allows you to ignore any accent marks so that the following statement returns a true result:

```
ignoring diacriticals
    "Résumé" = "Resume"
end ignoring

result: true
```

The ignoring hyphens clause allows you to ignore hyphens in the text:

```
ignoring hyphens
    "stand-alone" = "standalone"
end ignoring
result: true
```

```
ignoring hyphens
    "1-800-555-1212" = "18005551212"
end ignoring
result: true
```

Note, however, that the ignoring hyphens clause ignores only hyphen, or minus, characters, not any typographical dashes such as an en dash or em dash.

The ignoring punctuation clause allows you to ignore any punctuations marks. These marks are as follows:

. , ? : ; ! \ ' " `

In words they are periods, commas, question marks, colons, semicolons, exclamation points, backslashes, single quotes, double quotes, and grave accents (also known as *backticks*). Here's an example:

```
ignoring punctuation
    "That's all, right? Now!" = "Thats all right now."
end ignoring
result: true
```

The ignoring white space clause allows you to ignore spaces, tabs, linefeeds, and return characters when comparing strings:

```
ignoring white space
    "Space craft" = "Spacecraft"
end ignoring
result: true
```

numeric strings is the newest considering/ignoring attribute added to AppleScript (it was added in OS X 10.4).

The considering numeric strings clause is useful for comparing version numbers since it can understand numbers without looking for preceding zeros. Since application version numbers are conveyed as strings and many times contain multiple decimal points (for example, 1.4.2) or multi-digit parts (for example, 1.10.1), it's often not possible, or safe, to convert them into a number. For that reason, version numbers are compared as strings. Take, for instance, these two version numbers (expressed as strings): "version 1.5.89" and "version 1.5.107". If looked at simply as numbers, the digit 8 in the third chunk of the first item is greater than the digit 1 in the third chunk of the second number. Therefore, the following script is false:

```
"version 1.5.89" comes after "version 1.5.107" --> true
```

However, in the version-number world this isn't entirely true, since you know that the version that ends with 107 is a later version than the one ending with 89.

Using the numeric strings clause will correct that, as you can see here:

```
considering numeric strings
    "version 1.5.89" comes after "version 1.5.107" --> false
end considering
```

Comparing numeric strings is also useful when the numbers are part of the string, such as in "Chapter 5.pdf", for example:

```
"Chapter 5.pdf" comes before "Chapter 10.pdf" --> false (not the answer you wanted!)
considering numeric strings
    "Chapter 5.pdf" comes before "Chapter 10.pdf" --> true
end considering
```

The most obscure variation of the ignoring clause, expansion, is probably used more in human languages where ligature characters, such as Æ, æ, Œ, and œ, are used:

```
ignoring expansion
    "Æ" = "AE"
end ignoring
```

```
Result: true
```

Also, since case isn't considered by default, the following is true:

```
ignoring expansion
    "Æ" = "æ"
end ignoring
```

Note As a protest to the elimination of the venerable Key Caps, I've developed my own system that includes opening TextEdit and frantically pressing as many keys as possible while holding different modifier keys. This system isn't so good if you want to trace the key combination for later use.

Using a single considering or ignoring clause may get you what you need, but what if it takes more than one clause? For that you can use multiple parameters and even nest clauses.

Say you want to evaluate words that may or may not include dashes, spaces, or accent marks. Let's assume you want to evaluate a student's response to a test question. Although you need the answer spelled correctly, you want to be lenient when it comes to spaces, dashes, accents, and so on.

Here is how you can evaluate the accuracy of the answer:

```
ignoring white space, hyphens and diacriticals
    set is_answer_correct to student_answer = actual_answer
end ignoring
```

This will ensure that if the answer was El Niño, the responses elnino, El nino, Elñino, and El-Nino would also register as correct.

Another way to state the same intention is by nesting the different consideration clauses like this:

```
ignoring white space
    ignoring hyphens
        ignoring diacriticals
            set is_answer_correct to student_answer = actual_answer
        end ignoring
    end ignoring
end ignoring
```

What if you did want to consider the case of the answer but wanted to give some slack over the accents? Your statement would look like this:

```
considering case but ignoring diacriticals
    a = b
end considering
```

"My Dad" Comes Before "Your Dad"

Much like the = and ≠ operators, the greater than and less than operators always return a result as a Boolean. This means the result of using an operator can be either true or false. To use these operators, you need to understand how a certain character is considered to be greater than another.

In MacRoman text, one character is considered less than or greater than another character depending on whether the first character appears before or after the second one in the MacRoman character table (though don't forget that text comparisons may also be affected by ignoring clauses, of course). Refer to Table 3-1 for the order of characters in the MacRoman table.

To determine in a script whether one string comes before another string, use the less than operator, which can be written in any of several ways:

```
"a" comes before "b"
"a" < "b"
"a" is less than "b"
```

Similarly, the greater than operator checks whether the first parameter is greater than the second or appears later in the sorting chain:

```
"a" comes after "b"
"a" > "b"
"a" is greater than "b"
```

Use the greater than or equal operator to see whether one value is either the same as or greater than another:

```
"a" ≥ "b"
```

You can also write this as follows:

```
"a" is greater than or equal to "b"
```

And you can use the less than or equal operator to see whether one value is the same as or less than the other:

```
"a" ≤ "b"
"a" is less than or equal to "b"
```

Sorting Text

In the spirit of putting characters in order, let's try to analyze a script that sorts a list of strings.

First, Script 3-3 shows the script. Note that this script snippet is a prime candidate for a subroutine. The parameter will be the list you want to sort, and the returned result will be the sorted list. For now, though, you will just concentrate on the code itself and not on how it may fit in a script. (I should also note that I did not write this script. This subroutine is a standard beginner sorting example that has been around for decades.)

Script 3-3.

```
set theList to {"Dell", "Apple", "HP"}

repeat (length of theList) times
    repeat with j from 1 to (length of theList) - 1
        if item j of theList > item (j + 1) of theList then
            set {item j of theList, item (j + 1) of theList} to ¬
                {item (j + 1) of theList, item j of theList}
```

```
        end if
    end repeat
end repeat
theList --> {"Apple", "Dell", "HP"}
```

This script starts with the theList variable that contains a list of the strings to be sorted. At the end of the script, the same list will have the items in sorted order.

The method this script uses to sort the elements is comparing every value with the next value in the list. It loops through the values from the first to the next-to-last one. Each value is paired with the following value in turn, and the two are compared. The script starts by comparing the first item to the second item, then the second item to the third, the third to the fourth, and so on. If the first value in the pair is greater than the second value, then the two switch places and are placed back into the list at the original spots. For example, if the list is {100, 400, 200, 50}, then it'll start by comparing 100 to 400; since 100 is less than 400, nothing will happen. However, when items 2 and 3 (values 400 and 200) are compared, they will be flipped, since 400 is less than 200. The result will be changing {400, 200} with {200, 400}, resulting in {100, 200, 400, 50}. What actually happens is that the two values in every pair of numbers are sorted in relation to each other.

This process, by means of the outer repeat loop, repeats once for each item in the list. When the script is done, because of the constant sorting of the pairs, each value had the chance to move to its appropriate value.

How Long Is a Piece of String?

Since a string is made of characters, the length of the string is also the number of characters it has in it.

Actually, length is a string property. You use it to get a string's character count. Here is how you do that:

```
length of "rope"
```
result: 12

The result is a number, in this case the number 4, since the string "rope" has four characters.

In addition to the length property, you can also use the count command to get the number of characters of a string. Like length, the count command can work on strings, lists, and records:

```
count "Hello world!"
```
result: 12

Breaking Up Strings

A large part of working with text is being able to break apart a string and manipulate different pieces of it. One obvious way to break a string, which is sometimes used, is into a list containing its characters.

Characters

To break a string into characters, you have to use the word characters to refer to all of its character elements along with the get command:

```
get characters of "tic-tac-toe"
```

You can also drop the word get and write the following:

```
characters of "tic-tac-toe"
```

Or you can write every character of ..., which has the same meaning as characters of ...:

```
get every character of "tic-tac-toe"
```

In any case, the result will be the same among all options shown previously, and the class of the result, meaning the type of data returned from the statement, is a list. The list will contain all the characters of the string, with each character taking up one item in the list.

```
{"t", "i", "c", "-", "t", "a", "c", "-", "t", "o", "e"}
```

This can be useful when you want to evaluate each character and perform an action based on specific characters. For instance, having the string broken down into a list of characters can be useful if you wanted to take a string and replace every instance of the character "t" with the string "sl". However, you can perform such a replacement even faster, as you will see in the "The text item delimiters Property" section later in this chapter.

You will start with a variable with a string value and then add another variable that will hold a list containing every character of the string in the first variable:

```
set my_string to "tic-tac-toe"
set my_list to every character of my_string
```

At this point, the value of the variable my_list is as follows:

```
{"t", "i", "c", "-", "t", "a", "c", "-", "t", "o", "e" }
```

Next you will create a simple repeat loop that will loop through the characters and add each one to a new string. If the character is "t", however, the script will add "sl" instead.

You start by defining the empty string variable:

```
set my_new_string to ""
```

In the next few lines of code, you'll add to the variable the_name. The next few lines of code are responsible for building up your new string in this variable. To do this, you get the variable's current value and concatenate it with another string, and then you store the result in the same variable. For instance:

```
set the_name to "Jack"
set the_name to the_name & " B. Back"
get the_name
--> "Jack B. Back"
```

The variable the_name now has the value "Jack B. Back" assigned to it.

Anyway, back to the script.

As you can see in Figure 3-7, you defined the three variables that will be used in the script and created the skeleton of the repeat loop.

Figure 3-7. *The variables are defined, and a* repeat *loop skeleton has been created.*

Note In fact, you don't really need to create a list of characters in this example, because it's also possible (and quicker) to pass the string directly to the repeat loop. But you're looking at breaking up strings in this section, so let's do it this way for now.

Since I will discuss repeat loops in detail later, for now I just want you to understand that when you use a loop like repeat with the_character_ref in ..., the loop variable, in this case the_character_ref, will be assigned a reference to the next list item at every loop revolution. To test the functionality of it, let's add a display dialog command inside the loop:

```
display dialog the_character_ref
```

Now run the script, which should look like the one in Figure 3-8.

When you run the script, a dialog box will be displayed for each character in the string. That should make the function of the repeat statement a bit clearer.

Now that you did that, comment out the display dialog command. This way you can quickly get back to it later if you need to do so.

Next you will explain to the script what to do if the character happens to be a "t" and what to do if it's not.

Add the following lines inside the repeat statement:

```
if contents of the_character_ref is "t" then
    set my_new_string to my_new_string & "sl"
else
    set my_new_string to my_new_string & the_character_ref
end if
```

Your script should look like the one in Figure 3-9.

Figure 3-8. *A temporary* display dialog *command has been added.*

Figure 3-9. *The conditional statement reacts differently if the character is* "t".

The conditional statement checks whether the value stored in the repeat loop variable the_character happens to be a "t". If it is, then the script adds "sl" to the value of the my_new_string variable. If it's any other character, the character itself is added to the my_new_string variable. Since the value of the variable the_character_ref is a reference to an item in a list of strings, you have to use contents of the_character_ref to retrieve the original string value.

As discussed earlier, you build up the new string by getting its existing value, concatenating the new text, and then storing the result in the same variable:

```
set my_new_string to my_new_string & "sl"
```

The last statement of the script, for lack of another use for the new-and-improved string, is as follows:

```
display dialog my_new_string
```

Now the dialog box should look like the one in Figure 3-10.

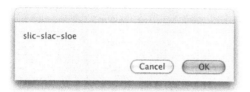

Figure 3-10. *The dialog box showing the resulting variable* my_new_string

Picking the Pieces

So now you know AppleScript can split a string into characters. What you also need to know is how to extract chunks of strings for use in your script. To put it in context, slicing up strings and turning chunks of them into new strings is one task as a scripter you will do all the time: figuring out what date a job is due based on the date embedded in the filename, parsing out text files and using the information there, cleaning out unwanted characters taken from different sources, formatting phone numbers, and so on. The list is endless.

The first and most used tool you have is the ability to extract a number of characters from a string by specifying the starting and ending character. This method is called the *index reference form*, since you refer to a character (in this case) by its position among the other characters.

An easy example is as follows:

```
character 3 of "AppleScript"
```

As you must have guessed already, the result of the preceding statement is a one-character string, p. And since I'm talking AppleScript here, and not some other no-fun programming language, you can also write the following:

```
third character of "AppleScript"
```

The result, as you can imagine, is the same. And if you can refer to the third character, then you surely can refer to the first character, which would've made it cruel and unusual to not allow you to ask for the last character or next-to-last character of AppleScript. Try this:

```
character before last character of "AppleScript"
```

OK, so the only person I know who actually uses these terms in programming is Sal himself (the AppleScript product manager at Apple), but then again, I don't go out much.

Another feature that makes AppleScript a language more suitable for use by humans is that the first character in a string, or the first anything for that matter, is referred to as 1, not 0. This is known as *one-based indexing*.

Note In *zero-based indexing*, the programming language counts from 0, not from 1. "Real" programmer languages use zero-based indexing, which reflects how computers count; languages designed for ordinary users use one-based indexing, because that is how humans usually count.

Let's go back a step and look at the term last character. Of course, using this kind of syntax is useful for that last character, or even the one before it, but what about the one before that? You're in luck, because AppleScript has the perfect solution! The last character is also known to AppleScript as character –1 (that is, minus one). The reason why this is so cool and so useful is that you can use a number to look for a specific character counting from the end of the string, not the beginning. Using that negative-index reference style, you can write the following:

```
character -3 of "AppleScript"
```

which will return the character i.

For your reference, Figure 3-11 shows you different ways you can refer to different characters in a string.

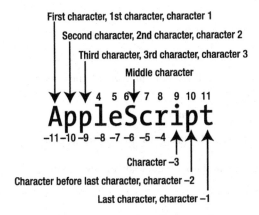

Figure 3-11. *Referring to characters in a string*

Looking at Figure 3-11 you can also see that the word middle is a valid reference, although I've never used that one.

Another way to refer to a character is to use the arbitrary reference form some. The reference some character of a_string returns a random character from a string, which is another reference form I've never used. I prefer to go a different route and first derive a random number and then use that number to refer to a character by index:

```
set my_string to "AppleScript"
set my_random_number to random number from 1 to (length of my_string)
set my_random_character to character my_random_number of my_string
```

OK, so now that I look at it, it does seem neater to just write the following:

```
set my_string to "AppleScript"
set my_random_character to some character of my_string
```

What was I thinking all these years? Oh well, as long as I don't tell anyone . . .

Chunk at a Time

Now that you know all about picking the right character, what about a bunch of characters?

What if you got a filename into a string, and you know that the client's account number is a six-digit number starting from the third character?

OK, so the string is `"JB445091_UTFg12.sit"`. To extract the account number from it, you can write the following statements:

```
set job_file_name to "JB445091_UTFg12.sit"
set account_number to text 3 thru 8 of job_file_name
```

You should notice the word `thru` (which stands for *through*) isn't spelled out. Say "thank you" to the AppleScript team for locking the grammar police in the closet that day. As one who uses the word `thru` in quite a few AppleScript statements, I'm grateful. Using the full spelling `through` is completely legal, however.

In the following code, however, you get the characters of a string as a list. Both statements that follow produce the same result, which is a list with all the characters from the string:

```
get every character of "AppleScript"
get characters of "AppleScript"
```

Here is the result:

```
{"A", "p", "p", "l", "e", "S", "c", "r", "i", "p", "t"}
```

Once you've extracted a string containing only the account number information, the only step that's still left to perform is to convert this string to an integer:

```
set account_number to (text 3 thru 8 of job_file_name) as integer
```

The expression in the first set of parentheses produces a string, and `as integer` at the end coerces that string into an integer.

That same result could have been written in two lines for better readability in this manner:

```
text 3 thru 8 of job_file_name
set account_number to result as integer
```

In the preceding example you didn't store the result of each line in a variable; you didn't even need to reuse the same variable. The `result` variable holds the resulting value of every statement by default, and that saves you the trouble of using `set`.

Another point I will discuss later is that the error-free execution of that script depends on the extracted characters being all digits. You'll learn more about that when I talk about numbers in Chapter 4.

Introducing Words

As would be expected, you can also break down text into individual words. Doing this will also return a list, but unlike breaking text into characters where the integrity of the text remains, breaking text into words cleans out any characters that are considered word delimiters.

Let's start with a little example. Write the script from Figure 3-12, and execute it.

Figure 3-12. *A string being broken into words*

When you run the script, the obvious happens: the result is a list in which each item is a word. What you may not notice right away you're sure to notice in the example shown in Figure 3-13.

Figure 3-13. *Breaking text into words eliminates the delimiters.*

When you ask for the words of a string, you get a list of the words, but the dashes, commas, slashes, and so on, are nowhere to be seen.

WHAT'S A WORD?

Here's the description of a word from the AppleScript Language Guide: "A continuous series of characters that contains only the following types of characters: letters (including letters with diacritical marks), digits, nonbreaking spaces, dollar signs, cent signs, English pound symbols, or yen symbols, percent signs, commas between digits, periods before digits, apostrophes between letters or digits, hyphens (but not minus signs [Option+hyphen] or dashes [Option+Shift+hyphen])."

Here are some examples of words:

```
read-only he's v1.0 $99.99 12c-d
```

This definition of a word applies to English text in the Roman script system. Words in other languages are defined by the script system for each language if the appropriate script system is installed.

The following characters are considered to be words on their own, and even if they're found right next to another valid word, they will be counted as their own items:

$$\& * + > < @ \setminus \setminus \wedge \_ \grave{} \mid \sim \degree £ § \bullet ¶ ß ® © ™ ´ ¨ \neq \infty \pm$$

$$\leq \geq ¥ \mu \partial \Sigma \Pi \pi \int {}^{a} {}^{o} \Omega ¿ ¡ \neg \sqrt{} f \approx \Delta \div \Diamond {-} / \; \langle \rangle \ddagger \cdot {,} {,,} ‰$$

For instance, `words of "you&me"` has no obvious word breaks, and therefore you might expect it to return a list with a single item. However, AppleScript recognizes the ampersand (&) as a word and therefore gives it its own list item. The result is as follows:

```
{" you ", "&", "me"}
```

One more area where AppleScript shows intelligence in the way it breaks apart words is when it deals with U.S. currency marks, periods, and commas. When used in text, the dollar sign ($), cents sign (¢), and percent sign (%) are all considered to be their own words. This means that writing the following:

```
words of "Seven$Flat"
```

returns this:

```
{"Seven", "$", "Flat"}
```

However, if AppleScript recognizes you meant to write a dollar amount, it will bunch $ with the number in one list item:

```
words of "pay me $10"
```

which returns the following:

```
{"pay", "me", "$10"}
```

This works only if the dollar sign is to the left of the number, unlike the percent and cent signs, which are considered part of the same word only if they're to the right of the number. The following:

```
words of "10%"
```

returns this:

```
{"10%"}
```

However, the following:

```
words of "%10"
```

returns this:

```
{"%", "10"}
```

When used between two digits, commas and periods suddenly give up their role as word separators and jump in as part of the word. Take this statement, for example:

```
words of "to get $1,000,000.50, you must give 100%."
```

which returns the following:

```
{"to", "get", "$1,000,000.50", "you", "must", "give", "100%"}
```

Notice that the period and comma that are part of "$1,000,000.50" were left as part of the dollar amount, but the comma that comes right after that amount and the period at the end of the sentence were used as delimiters and are not part of anything in the resulting list.

Paragraphs

Much like breaking strings into words, you can break them into paragraphs. The logic behind a paragraph is much simpler. The first paragraph in the string starts at the beginning of the string and ends at the first instance of one of these characters or character combinations: a carriage return character; a linefeed character, which is the Unix version of a return; or a combination of carriage return and linefeed that ends at the first instance of one of the following:

- A carriage return character (ASCII character 13), which is the standard line break indicator on Mac OS 9 and earlier and which is still used in places on OS X

- A linefeed character (ASCII character 10), which is the standard line break on Unix and often used on OS X

- A carriage return character followed by a linefeed character, which is the standard line break on Windows

If you have only one paragraph (and there's always at least one paragraph, even if the string is empty!), then that one paragraph ends at the end of the string.

The rest of the paragraphs (if you have more than one) start right after the first line break and end right before the next one. The last paragraph ends at the end of the string.

Take, for example, the script in Figure 3-14. You start with a simple string that includes four paragraphs and ask AppleScript to return every paragraph. The result is a list in which every list item contains one paragraph.

Figure 3-14. *AppleScript breaks a string into paragraphs.*

What would happen, though, if you tried to merge the paragraphs back into a string again? See Figure 3-15.

Figure 3-15. *A list of paragraphs coerced into a string become a single paragraph.*

Why did that happen? When you take a string, break it into paragraphs, and then merge them into a string right away, why do you get one long paragraph? This is because when AppleScript breaks down the string into a list, each string in the list contains only the text of a paragraph itself and not the line break character (or characters) itself. I will discuss a quick solution for that in the section "The text item delimiters Property."

Words and Paragraphs in the Real World

That is, for those of us who consider AppleScript to be the real world . . .

From my experience, looking at the words and paragraphs components of strings can be extremely useful. Either breaking down a text file into paragraphs and looping through them or referencing the paragraphs of a string one by one is essential, and asking for every word of some text is great for finding the information you need.

As an exercise, let's create a little script that will parse some text and use the information. The script is a rendition of a script I actually use for scheduling purposes. One of my large clients has scheduling software that sends me e-mails whenever I'm scheduled to be part of a meeting. The e-mails are well formatted, and their content is completely predictable and reliable, since a computer generates them. It contains, in plain-text, information about the location and time of the meeting and some other general information.

Let's say you need to parse that e-mail and create an event in your iCal calendar.

You will start by creating the script as a single flow, from top to bottom. The beginning will gather the text from the message in Apple's Mail application. Then, you will extract the actual meeting information from that text, and you will end by adding a new event to iCal with the information you collected.

After you're done, you will take a minute to better organize the script into subroutines. One subroutine will gather the text, the other will extract the data, and the third will apply it to iCal.

If you grade a script based on code efficiency, the script you're about to write is probably an 8 out of 10. Some slight variations would've worked just as well or better, but for now you'll focus on using words and paragraphs to accomplish the job.

Mail to iCal Script

You will start by extracting the information from Mail. What you will assume is that there's a message selected and that it contains text formatted to your expectations. If this were a script you had to distribute to users in your company, or make public in any way, more than 50% of the code would have been related to idiot-proofing the script: making sure the user selected a message, making sure the user selected the right message, making sure the user knows what the script will do, and so on. You would do everything short of making sure their Mac is plugged in. Idiot proofing your code takes time and makes the script more cumbersome, but it ensures that different errors are filtered to the user as friendly little comments such as "Oh, Great One, please note that in order to select a message, you must have Mail open, and then you must click the message you choose to select. For clicking instructions, please refer to your user manual."

This script, however, will be 100% functional without any error capturing.

Now for the script.

Like many applications, Mail provides a `selection` property that identifies the current graphical user interface (GUI) selection. The `selection` property belongs to the application object and therefore can be accessed from within the initial application `tell` block.

In Mail, like some other applications, the `selection` property contains a list that can include any number of items or no items at all; in this case, it holds only a single item, and you need to retrieve it to get its text.

Before you start writing here, make sure the Mail application is running. Type the content of the message from the following text and send it to your own e-mail address or just assign it to the `message_text` variable without calling Mail at all:

- Meeting Reminder
- Subject: Preapproval of the meeting proposed in the initial proposal draft

- When: Friday, March 2, 2001, 8:30 AM to 9:30 AM (GMT–05:00) Eastern Time

- Where: Break Room in the Marketing Wing

Next, pick up your new mail, and make sure this message is selected in Mail's inbox viewer window. This message will serve as your test data as you write and test this script.

Note If you're unable to use Mail for this exercise, replace all of the previous code with the following:

```
set message_text to "Meeting Reminder
Subject: Preapproval of the meeting proposed in the initial proposal draft
When: Friday, March 2, 2001, 8:30 AM to 9:30 AM (GMT-05:00) Eastern Time
Where: Break Room in the Marketing Wing"
```

I realize you might not be using Mail. If you aren't, you can skip the start and just set the string variable you will see in a minute to the message text. This way you will bypass Mail and get right to cleaning the text.

All this, by the way, isn't just logistics that relate strictly to learning AppleScript from this book; these are different tasks you should perform while writing actual scripts, including creating dummy data, creating objects in an application to use in testing, and so on.

Let's look at the selection property first. Write the following lines, and run the script:

```
tell application "Mail"
    get selection
end tell
```

The result is a list containing one item. Now let's change the script to reference the first item of the list:

```
tell application "Mail"
    get item 1 of (get selection)
end tell
```

Note Notice that you use item 1 of (get selection) here instead of item 1 of selection. That's because you have to get the list from Mail first and then use AppleScript to extract the item you want.

Now the result is the first item of that list. Now let's go all the way and extract the text. In Mail, every message object has a content property that includes the body text of the message. You can see that in Mail's dictionary. What you need is to get the content property of the selected message into a variable. Here is how:

```
tell application "Mail"
    set the_message to item 1 of (get selection)
    set message_text to content of the_message
end tell
```

Notice the message text has four paragraphs and that the meat or nutritional part is concentrated in paragraphs 2, 3, and 4.

Let's add the lines of code that assign the contents of these paragraphs to different variables. You will make the identifiers of these variables as descriptive as you can:

```
set message_subject_line to paragraph 2 of message_text
set message_dates_line to paragraph 3 of message_text
set message_location_line to paragraph 4 of message_text
```

Now you can start to turn the text into the information you need. If you examine iCal's dictionary, you can see there's an event class. That is the class of the object you need to create. An event object has about 12 properties, out of which you care about four: start date, end date, summary, and status.

Of these four properties, two need a value of the class date, one takes a string (summary), and the status property uses a custom class that can be one of four values: none, cancelled, tentative, or confirmed.

You can find all this information in the iCal application AppleScript dictionary. Here's an excerpt from the iCal dictionary that shows these properties of the event class:

```
summary Unicode text   -- The event summary
start date date   -- The event start date
status none/cancelled/tentative/confirmed   -- The event status
end date date   -- The event end date, if defined
```

Notice that the status property uses constants, custom application-defined values that fit this particular property of the event class.

Anyway, your job is to end up with three variables that hold the data that's to go into three of these properties. You'll call these variables start_date, end_date, and the_summary. For the status property, you will just insert the confirmed value directly.

The next portion of the script will mold the plain text you got from the message into data that will fit into these variables. You'll start with the easy one: summary. This is just a text description, and the text in the message_subject_line and message_location_line variables is perfect. Let's concatenate them and assign the result to the the_summary variable:

Add the following line:

```
set the_summary to message_subject_line & return & message_location_line
```

Run the script to make sure it works. The result is as follows:

```
Result: "Subject: Preapproval of the meeting proposed in the initial proposal draft
Where: Break Room in the Marketing Wing"
```

Now you need to attend to the dates. Let's start by breaking down the message_dates_line variable into words. To do that you can type a temporary line that will return the words of the string value of the message_dates_line variable.

At the end of the script, type the following:

```
words of message_dates_line
```

Run the script, copy the result, and paste it in any text editor or into a blank script window. You will use that text as a reference, which will allow you to see what the different words are and their order.

The result should be a list with 15 items:

```
{"When", "Friday", "March", "2", "2001", "8", "30", "AM", "9", ¬
    "30", "AM",  "GMT", "00", "Eastern", "Time"}
```

A quick analysis reveals that items 3, 4, and 5 contain the date; items 6, 7, and 8 make up the start time; and items 9, 10, and 11 make up the end time.

In AppleScript, a date object contains both a date and a time. In fact, if you don't specify a time, AppleScript assigns midnight of that date as the time.

In that case, you can create two strings; one will have the date and the start time, and the other will have the same date and the end time. The AppleScript trick you'll use later is that you'll convert that string into a date value just by adding the word date before the string.

First, though, you need to assemble the strings, as shown in Script 3-4.

Script 3-4.

```
set the_meeting_date to ¬
    word 3 of message_dates_line & space & ¬
    word 4 of message_dates_line & ", " & ¬
    word 5 of message_dates_line
set the_start_time to ¬
    word 6 of message_dates_line & ":" & ¬
    word 7 of message_dates_line & space & ¬
    word 8 of message_dates_line
set the_end_time to ¬
    word 9 of message_dates_line & ":" & ¬
    word 10 of message_dates_line & space & ¬
    word 11 of message_dates_line
```

Let's examine the variables you created. Add the following line:

```
return the_meeting_date
```

What you will get is a string containing the date only, "March 2, 2001". You can do the same with the other variables to examine their values for accuracy.

In the next two lines, you will concatenate the date string and each of the strings containing the start time and end time and convert them into date values:

```
set start_date to date (the_meeting_date & space & the_start_time)
set end_date to date (the_meeting_date & space & the_end_time)
```

Run the script to see how AppleScript has converted each date-time string into a date object. As long as you give AppleScript some sort of a date containing at least the month, day, and year, it'll take it from there and make it into a date it can understand.

Note The way in which AppleScript converts date strings to date objects depends on your system settings. This example assumes you're using U.S.-style dates or similar. If your settings are different and the script reports an error when creating date objects, go to the International pane of the Formats tab in the System Preferences, and temporarily change the region to United States while testing this script. I'll discuss these issues in further detail in Chapter 5.

OK, so it seems like you have all the information you need neatly formatted into dates, text, and so on. Now let's create the event in iCal. iCal's AppleScript object model starts with the application object, which contains calendar elements, each of which can contain event elements. For that reason, you can't create an event element just in iCal's main tell block; instead, you must talk to an existing calendar object. Since a working iCal application must have at least one calendar element, you can safely talk to calendar 1. Here is the tell block you will use to talk to iCal's calendar:

```
tell application "iCal"
    tell calendar 1
        --command here
    end tell
end tell
```

I always complete the `tell` blocks first before inserting the command. This is a way to eliminate nagging little typos that will steal more debugging time than they deserve.

Now, type the following line in the `tell` block:

```
make new event at end with properties ¬
  {start date:start_date, end date:end_date, ¬
  summary:the_summary, status:confirmed}
```

The statement you added starts with the `make` command. The `new` parameter is `event`, which is the class of the object you're creating; you want the `event` element created at the end of the `calendar` object, making it the last event to be entered. The `at` parameter indicates where the new `event` object should appear, in this case at the end of `calendar` 1's existing `even` elements. Notice that you've just written `end` here. When AppleScript evaluates this `make` command, it will use the enclosing `tell calendar 1` block to turn this `end` into the reference `end of calendar 1`. iCal is then smart enough to work out that `end of calendar 1` really means `end of elements of calendar 1`. This saves you some extra typing. Also, as part of the `make` command statement, you can specify initial values for some or all of the new object's properties. This is a fast and efficient way to set the start date, end date, and so on.

If you left any lines in your script that start with the word `return` and are not in a subroutine (you don't have any subroutines here yet . . .), then comment these lines out by adding a double hyphen before them (`--`). They're handy to keep around for testing purposes, but you need to disable them the rest of the time because they'll stop the script's execution. Notice that all four properties you cared about now have the value you supplied; the rest of the properties have default values.

Now run the script to see whether it worked!

As promised, I'll take a minute to show how to streamline the linear script into three subroutines. I will cover subroutines extensively in later chapters; however, it's important to get there with a wee bit of an "I already did it" feeling. So here you go.

The quick-and-dirty idea behind what you're about to do is to segment the linear script into logical stages. Each operation will be determined based on its function and may contain as few or as many lines of AppleScript code as needed.

Note A few reasons exist for changing a script that works and segmenting it into several handlers. One is that it takes the clutter out of the main body of the script: the main body tells the story, and the subroutines contain the gritty details. Another reason is code reuseability.

In this example, you will have three subroutines, each one dealing with one of the following tasks:

1. Get the message text from Mail.

2. Extract and format the information.

3. Create the new event in iCal.

In this example, you'll see that each subroutine has four main components: the subroutine identifier, which is the name of the subroutine; the parameters it takes; the code that makes up the body of the subroutine; and the result it returns.

The first subroutine will have no parameters, but it will return an important result: the text of the currently selected message in Mail. The second subroutine will take that same message text that was the result of the previous subroutine and will return the start and end dates and the summary.

The third subroutine will take the three resulting values (start/end dates and summary) and use them to create the new event in iCal.

Figure 3-16 shows you how the new script will be organized. Notice the three subroutine calls at the top and how the body of each subroutine reflects almost perfectly the chunk of the original script that performed its function.

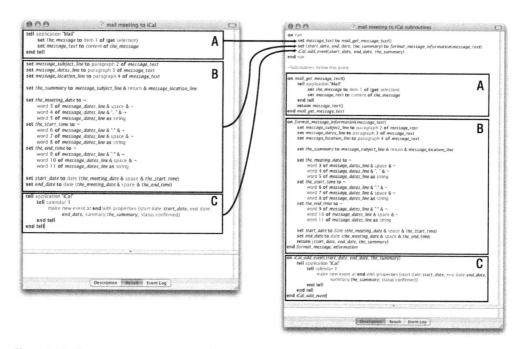

Figure 3-16. *The original script compared with the new subroutine-happy script*

Notice also in the new script that you put all the three subroutine calls inside the run handler. Any lines of code that exist inside the run handler will execute when the script is either launched as an application or set to run from inside Script Editor. The run handler is implied if not supplied, which means if you don't include the run handler, AppleScript will consider any stray line of code that is not in any other handler part of the run handler. (Property declarations must happen outside the run handler; global variable and script object declarations can be outside as well.) The script would run the same whether it includes or doesn't include the run handler. However, since you're in "being organized" mode, it's appropriate to include the run handler too.

Refer to the content of the finished script in Script 3-5, and make the needed changes to your script to bring it to that point.

Script 3-5.

```
1. on run
2.    set message_text to mail_get_message_text()
3.    set {start_date, end_date, the_summary} to ¬
format_message_information(message_text)
4.    iCal_add_event(start_date, end_date, the_summary)
5. end run


6. --Subroutines below this point:

7. on mail_get_message_text()
8.    tell application "Mail"
9.       set the_message to item 1 of (get selection)
10.        set message_text to content of the_message
11.    end tell
12.    return message_text
13. end mail_get_message_text

14. on format_message_information(message_text)
15.    set message_subject_line to paragraph 2 of message_text
16.    set message_dates_line to paragraph 3 of message_text
17.    set message_location_line to paragraph 4 of message_text

18.    set the_summary to message_subject_line & return & message_location_line

19.    set the_meeting_date to ¬
20.    word 3 of message_dates_line & space & ¬
21.    word 4 of message_dates_line & ", " & ¬
22.    word 5 of message_dates_line
23.    set the_start_time to ¬
24.    word 6 of message_dates_line & ":" & ¬
25.    word 7 of message_dates_line & space & ¬
26.    word 8 of message_dates_line
27.    set the_end_time to ¬
28.    word 9 of message_dates_line & ":" & ¬
29.    word 10 of message_dates_line & space & ¬
30.    word 11 of message_dates_line

31.    set start_date to date (the_meeting_date & space & the_start_time)
32.    set end_date to date (the_meeting_date & space & the_end_time)
33.    return {start_date, end_date, the_summary}
34. end format_message_information

35. on iCal_add_event(start_date, end_date, the_summary)
36.    tell application "iCal"
37.       tell calendar 1
38.          make new event at end with properties ¬
39.    {start date:start_date, end date:end_date, ¬
40.    summary:the_summary, status:confirmed}
41.       end tell
42.    end tell
43. end iCal_add_event
```

The text item delimiters Property

Yet another AppleScript pearl, text item delimiters, is a property built into AppleScript, and it's useful for a whole range of text manipulations.

The text item delimiters property is used primarily in two situations: when splitting strings into lists and when coercing lists to strings.

Splitting Strings with text item delimiters

By default, AppleScript's text item delimiters property is set to {""}, which means asking for every text item of a string is the same as asking for every character of a string. See Figure 3-17 for an example. (Actually, it's really a single-item list containing an empty string, but don't worry about this because it makes no practical difference.) The fact that the text item delimiters property is set to an empty string makes AppleScript understand that every single character, including spaces, punctuation marks, and so on, appears as an item in the resulting list.

Figure 3-17. *Every text item here returns a list of characters.*

Where things start to get exciting is when you set AppleScript's text item delimiters property to a different value.

Let's take a phone number, 800-555-1212, that a user entered in a dialog box and see what happens when you change AppleScript's text item delimiters property to -.

Start a new script window, and enter the following script text:

```
set text item delimiters to "-"
get every text item of "800-555-1212"
```

As you can tell from Figure 3-18, the delimiters themselves are discarded, and anything in between them ends up as items in the resulting list.

The once single string with text "chunks" separated by a character called a *delimiter* is now a list where each text chunk is a single list item. In other words, "800-555-1212" changed to {"800", "555", "1212"}.

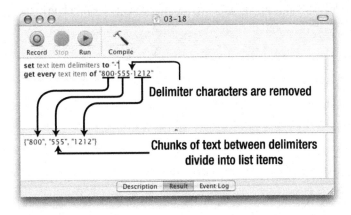

Figure 3-18. *Changing the* text item delimiters *property to a hyphen*

Combining List Items into a Single String

The other function of the text item delimiters property is to provide padding when coercing a list into a string.

Let's take the list you created in the last part:

{"800", "555", "1212"}

Start a new script window, and write a script like the one in Figure 3-19.

Figure 3-19. *When the* text item delimiters *property is set to an empty string, the list items just squish together.*

Now, let's give the text item delimiters property a different value. Change the first line in the script to look like the one in Figure 3-20.

Figure 3-20. *Now that the* text item delimiters *property is set to an asterisk (*), the asterisk string is used as padding between the items when you join the list items into a string.*

What you may be asking yourself, where does the plural in delimiters come from? Can you set the text item delimiters property to multiple delimiters? No, you can't. Although you can currently set AppleScript's text item delimiters property to a list of strings, AppleScript will look only at the first one and ignore the rest. (I guess Apple never quite finished that particular feature . . . .)

You can set the text items delimiters property to a multicharacter string. In Script 3-6, the text item delimiters property is set to the string "mississippi":

Script 3-6.

```
set text item delimiters to "mississippi"
set the_secret_message to ¬
    "memississippiet mississippime mississippiamississippit fimississippive"
set the_items to text items of the_secret_message
set text item delimiters to ""
set the_message to the_items as string
-->"meet me at five"
```

Setting the text item delimiters Property

Until now whenever you wanted to change the value of the text item delimiters property, you just referred to it by name. However, this worked because you weren't talking to any application at the time. In other words, you weren't in any application's tell block.

If you try the script in Figure 3-21, you will get an error. The error, shown in Figure 3-22, lets you know that the Finder doesn't have a text item delimiters property and therefore can't change it.

Trying to use commands and set properties that belong to an object you happen to not be talking to at the time is a common error that can lead to a wild goose chase—or should I say a wild bug chase?

Figure 3-21. *Setting the* text item delimiters *inside the Finder's* tell *block*

Figure 3-22. *The error resulted from running the script from Figure 3-21*

What happened is a bit like saying, "George, your laces are untied." George looks confused, since he's wearing rubber boots. "Oh, I meant Jim's laces!" Now you're being clear.

In this case, you need to specify that the property you want to set belongs to AppleScript rather than to the Finder, which you happen to be addressing at the moment.

Figure 3-23 shows how you can set AppleScript's text item delimiters property inside any application's tell block.

Figure 3-23. *Setting the value of the* text item delimiters *property inside an application* tell *block*

Text Delimiters in the Real World: Search and Replace

One use of the `text item delimiters` property is for the purpose of performing a simple search and replace on strings inside AppleScript.

The way you go about this is by setting the value of the `text item delimiters` property to the text you want to replace and split the text you want to search in into a list. This will remove the search text. Next you set the `text item delimiters` property to the replacement text and combine the list back into a string.

For this example, you will look at a simple way to take template text containing placeholders and personalize it. Imagine having a string that is part of some legal text you need to insert at the end of a document. The text was prepared in advance with the placeholders and looks like this: "Let it be known that [company] is responsible for any damage any employee causes during [company]'s activity while in the conference."

Let's imagine that this text is stored as a string in the variable form_text. You will also have another variable called company_name, which will be set to the string "Disney Inc." for these purposes.

The following is the script that will replace the text "[company]" with the specified company name:

```
set form_text to "Let it be known that [company] is responsible "
set form_text to form_text & "for any damage any employee causes during"
set form_text to form_text & "[company]'s activity while in the conference."

set company_name to "Disney Inc."

set text item delimiters to "[company]"
set temporary_list to text items of form_text
set text item delimiters to company_name
set finished_form to temporary_list as string
set text item delimiters to ""
return finished_form
```

The value of the `finished_form` variable is this text: "Let it be known that Disney Inc. is responsible for any damage any employee causes during Disney Inc.'s activity while in the conference."

The value of the `temporary_list` variable is as follows:

```
{"Let it be known that "}, ¬
{" Inc. is responsible for any damage any employee causes during "}, ¬
{" Inc.'s activity while in the conference."}
```

Note how the "[company]" placeholder is omitted from the temporary list shown previously.

Reading and Using Tab-Delimited Text Files

In the following exercise, you will use AppleScript to read a tab-delimited text file that was exported from a database application. What gives the text meaning is knowing what each column stands for.

The feel-good part of tab-delimited text files is that they're easy to handle. They have no code, no characters to omit, no hidden characters . . . they're just data separated by tabs. The way data is arranged in a tab-delimited text file is just the same as in a database: there are records, fields, and cells. In the text file, each paragraph is a record, each column is a field, and the cells are the text separated by tabs.

For this project's purposes, you will use a text file exported from FileMaker Pro. Granted, you can also use AppleScript to get the data directly from FileMaker Pro, but let's assume you get the data in that form from the company's headquarters.

Figure 3-24 and Figure 3-25 show how the data looks in FileMaker Pro and when opened in a text editor.

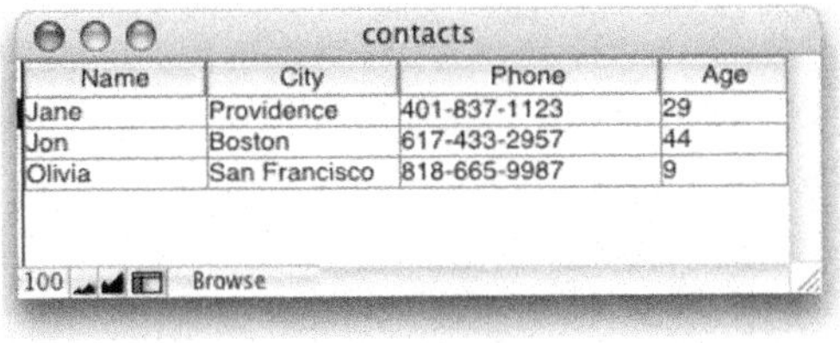

Figure 3-24. *The data in the source FileMaker Pro database*

Figure 3-25. *The data as text in BBEdit; the little gray triangles represent tabs and the line with the 90° angle indicates the return character.*

This script will read the file, loop through the records (paragraphs), and display a little dialog box with a message saying something like "Jane, 29 years old, can be reached at 401-837-1123 at home in Providence."

The first task is to identify the file and read its contents. The result will be a string variable that will contain the entire text contents of the file.

You have a few ways to identify the file you want. It can be in a folder that the script is aware of, or the file can be dropped on a script droplet. What you'll do here is let the user choose the file and process it from there.

The command `choose file` is perfect for that. It's simple to use, and it returns an `alias` value, which is used by AppleScript to identify a file, folder, or hard disk. In this case it'll identify the tab-delimited text file.

A variety of scripting additions and applications use alias values, and although they may look like strings with funny words tacked on their front, they really are values in their own right, just like integers, strings, lists, and so on. Their main characteristic is that, once you create them, they keep track of the same file (or folder) even if you rename that file (or folder) or move it to another location on the same disk. You can also coerce aliases to strings, and vice versa. For example, if you have an alias to a folder, a string containing the name of a file in that folder and an application that wants an alias to that file, you can coerce the folder alias to a string, join the strings, and coerce the result to a new alias value. Other times you might want to keep them as strings: some applications require path strings instead of alias values, and they have other uses too.

Figure 3-26 shows what a path string, a `file` value (another kind of AppleScript value that identifies things in the file system), and an `alias` value look like compared to one another.

Figure 3-26. *A string compared with* file *and* alias *values*

I will spend quite a bit of book real estate on identifying and working with files, so if it's not all clear here, don't beat yourself up (unless, of course, it causes you pleasure).

To thoroughly enjoy this exercise, create yourself a little text file with data similar to the one in Figure 3-25. Save that file as plain text (not RTF) on the desktop.

Let's start with the choose file command. Start a new script window, and type the following:

```
choose file
```

Compile the script, and run it. AppleScript opens the normal Mac open dialog box and allows you to specify any file, just like in Figure 3-27.

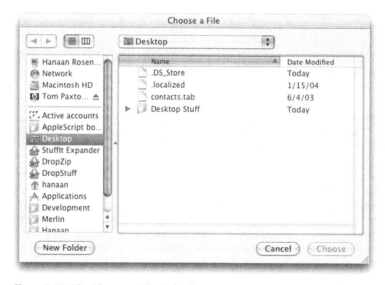

Figure 3-27. *The Choose a File dialog box*

Choose the file you made, and click the Choose button. Now examine the result: the result of that statement containing the `choose file` command is an alias. Speaking of results, you need a home for the resulting alias value. What better place than a variable? Add the variable name with the set command to the beginning of the line like this:

```
set text_file to choose file
```

The next line will read the file and put the text in a variable:

```
set database_text to read file text_file
```

The shorter way to do that is simply have a single line that says this:

```
set database_text to read (choose file)
```

This statement actually performs three commands: it chooses a file, which returns an `alias` value; then it reads the file, which returns a string; and at the end, it assigns that string to a variable.

Although it's a bad scripting practice that makes scripts hard to comprehend, it's great fun trying to see how few lines you can use to perform different actions, although others might not agree. John Thorsen, a longtime AppleScript developer and trainer, tries to stretch each command onto as many lines as he can. He says he does it for readability reasons, but I suspect he does it because he charges his clients by the line :-). In any case, it's the readability of the script you want to worry about, as John does, not condensing it as much as you can.

In any case, you are at the point where you have the text in a variable and you can start playing with it.

What you will do from here, in general terms, is loop through each record, and as you do that, you will split the record and use the information in the cells to build your personalized message.

In AppleScript terms, you have two ways to extract the paragraphs that represent the database records: the obvious choice is to use the `paragraph` element as you loop through the text.

Now you'll loop through the records. Add the following line to your script:

```
repeat with i from 1 to (count paragraphs of database_text)
```

What does i stand for? Well, i is the loop variable. In this type of repeat, its value is a number that changes with each loop. In the first loop, i will have a value of 1; in the next loop, it will have a value of 2; and so on. This can be a useful behavior, and in many cases you make different mathematical operations with it to figure out frame positions, grids, and other graphical aspects.

What will i do for you now? Well, you can use it to get the correct paragraph of database_text. Add the following three lines:

```
    set the_database_record to paragraph i of database_text
    display dialog the_database_record
end repeat
```

Now run the script to see what happens. Every paragraph acting as a database record is a string and displays in a dialog box like in Figure 3-28.

Figure 3-28. *The database record as a string*

Now you need to break each record into a list that will contain the fields. Add a blank line before the display dialog line, and insert the lines shown in Script 3-7.

Script 3-7.

```
set text item delimiters to tab
set field_list to every text item of the_database_record
set the_name to item 1 of field_list
set the_city to item 2 of field_list
set the_telephone to item 3 of field_list
set the_age to item 4 of field_list
set the_message_text to ¬
    the_name & ", " & the_age & ¬
    " years old, can be reached at " & ¬
    the_telephone & " at home in " & ¬
    the_city
```

Now, change the display dialog line to display the message instead of the_database_record:

```
display dialog the_message_text
```

Refer to Figure 3-29 for the finished script. Figure 3-30 shows one of the dialog boxes you get when running the script.

Figure 3-29. *The finished script*

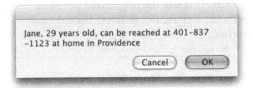

Jane, 29 years old, can be reached at 401–837
–1123 at home in Providence

Cancel   OK

Figure 3-30. *The dialog box resulting from running the script*

Copy and Set

Up until now you've been using AppleScript's trusty set command to assign values to variables.
However, AppleScript provides a second, similar command, copy, which you'll look at now.

First let's compare an example of using set:

```
set the_variable to "Value"
get the_variable
--> "Value"
```

with an example of using copy:

```
copy "Value" to the_variable
get the_variable
--> "Value"
```

As you can see, in both cases the_variable now contains the string "Value". In fact, for simple
values such as numbers, strings, files, and so on, it makes no difference which you use because both
behave the same way.

The situation is different, however, when working with values that can contain other values,
such as lists and records. Consider the following scenario:

```
set my_list to {1, 2, 3}
set my_other_list to my_list
set item 2 of my_list to "a"
get my_other_list --> {1, "a", 3}
```

In the preceding script, you start with a simple list of three items, {1, 2, 3}, which you assign
to variable my_list. Then you set the variable my_other_list to the value of the variable my_list.

The crucial detail here is that the list value now stored in variable my_other_list is the *same
value* that is stored in variable my_list. As you can see, when you change an item in that list via one
of these variables (line 3), you see the same change when you access the other variable (line 4).

The AppleScript Language Guide calls this *data sharing*, which is just a fancy way of saying that
two variables point to the same object in your computer's memory.

Most of the time this "sharing" behavior isn't a problem: it doesn't affect simple values such as
numbers and strings at all, and most of the time isn't a problem with lists and records (for some
tasks it's actually advantage). Sometimes, however, you do want to make an identical copy of a list
or record so that you can then modify the contents of one while leaving the other untouched. To get
around data sharing, all you have to do is use the copy command instead, like this:

```
set my_list to {1, 2, 3}
copy my_list to my_other_list
set item 2 of my_list to "a"
--> my_other_list = {1, 2, 3}
```

This time line 2 uses the copy command to make a perfect copy of the original list stored in my_list and assign this copy to my_other_list. Now you really do have two different list objects so that changing the contents of one has no effect on the other.

Note The copy command makes a perfect duplicate of the value it's copying. For example, if you use copy to duplicate a list of records, then not only is the list itself copied but each of its records is carefully copied too. (And if any of those records contain other lists or records, then those are copied too . . . and so on.) Should you ever want to duplicate the top-level list without duplicating the values in it as well, just use set my_other_list to every item of my_list.

As your scripts become larger and complex, be careful not to let AppleScript's data-sharing behavior confuse you. For example, if you pass an important list value to a handler and that handler quietly modifies the content of that list for its own purposes, other parts of the program that use the same list may get a nasty shock later when they discover its contents have been mysteriously rearranged! In this case, the guilty handler should have made a copy of the original list for its own use; that way, it can tinker with the copy as much as it likes without disturbing anything else.

Anyway, don't worry about this issue for now: most scripters don't run into it until they've been scripting for a while. Just remember that if you someday encounter a bug where a list seems to mysteriously rearrange itself, you heard about it here first!

More on Value Assignment

Remember having fun with shorter scripts that do more with less? Well, here's one for you: in the earlier database-processing script, you used five lines of code to assign the fields' content to the four variables. First you put them all in a list, and then you broke them down to the individual items. However, you can do this in a much better way that will allow you to replace those five lines with just one. If you set a list of variables to a list of values, each variable in the list gets the corresponding value in the value list assigned to it. Observe the following line:

```
set {a,b,c} to {"why","not","today"}
```

The result is that a = "why", b = "not", and c = "today". Pretty cool. You could have used this trick in the script like the one shown in Figure 3-31.

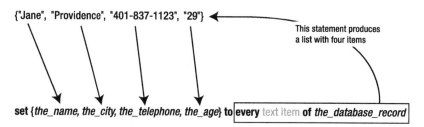

Figure 3-31. *Using a single line to assign each item of a list to a separate variable*

The offset Command

The offset command, which is defined in the String Commands suite of the Standard Additions dictionary, is useful for figuring out where a certain substring starts in another string. This command is a bit limited, but for small operations it can come in handy.

The result of the offset command is an integer that indicates the position of the first instance of the substring in the main string.

Here's a simple example of the offset command:

```
offset of "@" in "info@apple.com"
```

The result is 5.

Figure 3-32 is using the offset command to figure out a domain name in an e-mail address.

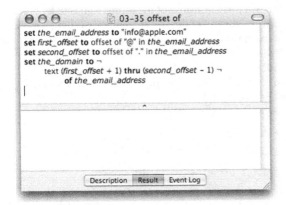

```
○ ○ ○                    📄 03-35 offset of
set the_email_address to "info@apple.com"
set first_offset to offset of "@" in the_email_address
set second_offset to offset of "." in the_email_address
set the_domain to ¬
     text (first_offset + 1) thru (second_offset - 1) ¬
          of the_email_address
|

                    ─────────
           Description  Result  Event Log
```

Figure 3-32. *Using the* offset *command to get the domain from a string*

Of course, if the e-mail address were info@store.apple.com, the script would have still returned apple, while the intent was probably to get store.apple.

A solution to this problem could involve using the text item delimiters property you looked at earlier. The following is the script that returns the correct host name and domain, with or without additional periods:

```
set the_email_address to "info@store.apple.com"
set first_offset to offset of "@" in the_email_address
set text item delimiters to {"."}
set email_address_items to text items of the_email_address
set domain_length to (length of (last item of email_address_items)) + 1
set text item delimiters to {""}
set the_domain to ¬
    text (first_offset + 1) thru -(domain_length + 1) ¬
       of the_email_address
```

The main change in this script is that you use text item delimiters and the text items of the_email_address reference to get the length of the domain. You can figure that if you split the whole e-mail into chunks by using the period as a delimiter, the last chunk will be com or net, and so on.

In line 5 you assign the length of that last chunk to a variable. Line 5 has a pretty complex statement. This statement could've been broken down to two or three lines, which would have made it more legible. It could have read as follows:

```
get last item of address_items
get length of result
set domain_length to result + 1
```

Anyhow, now the variable domain_length holds the length of com plus 1 to account for the period.

The variable domain_length comes back in another statement that needs some analyzing in line 7. Let's look at the complex portion of it:

```
text (first_offset + 1) thru -(domain_length + 1) of the_email_address
```

You start with (first_offset + 1). Remember that first_offset holds the offset of the @ character. In this example, it would have a value of 5. If you start the domain from the fifth character, you will get the @ character as part of the domain, so you must add 1 to it, which is where you get the (first_offset + 1) operation.

The second part is also neat: -(domain_length + 1). The purpose of the minus sign is to let AppleScript know that you want to start counting from the end of the string. Remember that character –1 is the last character, or one character before the end of the string. Now, you know that the domain_length variable has a value of 4 (which is the length of com + 1), which means if you get the characters up to the fourth character from the end, you will *still* get that darn period as part of the result. That's why you need to add 1 yet again to domain_length. You put it in parentheses so it evaluates as a number and only then becomes negative.

Line 7 could also have been broken into three lines in this manner:

```
set start_character_offset to first_offset + 1
set end_character_offset to domain_length + 1
set the_domain to ¬
    text start_character_offset thru -end_character_offset ¬
    of the_email_address
```

Now what else do you have to take into account when joining a list into a string? The text item delimiters property, of course! Not only that, but at the start of the script you changed the text item delimiters property to a period. After line 5 and before line 7 (how about, say, line 6), you need to set text item delimiters back to an empty string in a list: {""}.

Power Wrap-Up

The following sections summarize the chapter in an intensive reference style. Use these sections to look up facts related to the chapter without the chatter.

Value and Variables

Remember the following:

- *Values* are pieces of information you can manipulate in AppleScript.

- *Variables* are named containers you put values into for storage, allowing you to retrieve them later when you need them again.

You assign strings to a variable:

```
set x to "some text"
copy "some text" to x
```

String Values vs. Literal Strings

A string value contains a piece of text as a series, or *string*, of characters.

A string value is represented in AppleScript code as a *literal string*, which is a pair of double quotes with the string's actual text in between:

```
"Hello World!"
"42"
""
```

To include double quotes in your string literals, use the backslash (\) character to *escape* them, like this:

```
set x to "Press the \"OK\" button"
--> x = Press the "OK" button
```

Another way to include double quotes in your string is to use the quote variable, like this:

```
set x to "Press the " & quote & "OK" & quote & " button"
--> x = Press the "OK" button
```

You also have to escape the backslash if you want to include it in a string literal, like this:

```
set x to "This is a backslash: \\"
--> x = This is a backslash: \
```

Including Tabs, Returns, Spaces, and Quotes

To include tabs, returns, and linefeeds in string literals, you can use \t, \r, and \n, respectively:

```
set tab_delimited_text to "Name\tCity\rJoan/tNew York/rJames\tAtlanta"
--Result:
Name  ➤ City
Joan  ➤ New York
James ➤ Atlanta
```

Outside the quotes you can specify the tab, space, double quotes, and return characters using their names, like this:

```
set tab_delimited_text to "Name" & tab & "City" & return & "Joan"
& tab & "New" & space & "York"
--Result:
Name  ➤ City
Joan  ➤ New York
```

To add quotes, do this:

```
set the_string to "Press the" & space & quote & "OK" & quote & space & "button"
```

You can set the constants space, tab, quote, and return to other values; however, this is not recommended.

ASCII Numbers and Characters

Use the ASCII character command to get a character according to its position in the MacRoman character set table:

```
ASCII character 36
--> "$"
```

The ASCII number command works the opposite way: you provide the character, and the result is the character that fits the position in the MacRoman character table:

```
ASCII character "$"
--> 36
```

String Operators

The main operator used with strings is the concatenation operator, which is the ampersand: &.

The two operands are strings, but the right operand can be any value class that can be coerced into a string.

The following line *concatenates* (joins) the string to the left of the operator and the string to the right of it to produce a new string:

```
"Apple" & "Script"
--> "AppleScript"
```

Take care: if the left operand is not a string, the result of the operation is a list, not a string:

```
"$" & 5
--> "$5"
5 & "%"
--> {5, "%"}
```

The correct way to get a string result when the left operand is a real or integer is this:

```
(5 as string) & "%"
--> "5%"
```

Comparing Strings

You can compare strings using the following operators: =, ≠, >, ≥, <, ≤, starts with, ends with, contains, and is in:

```
"Apple" = "Orange" --> false
```

With the >, <, ≥, and ≤ operators, the larger character is the character that appears later in the alphabet:

```
"A" > "B" --> false
```

Considering and Ignoring

You can consider and ignore different attributes of the text to sway the comparison results in different ways:

```
ignoring case and punctuation
    "Hello There!!!" = "hello there"
end ignoring
--> true

considering case and punctuation
    "Hello There!!!" = "hello there"
end ignoring
--> false
```

Length

You can get the length of a string in two ways. You can use the length property of the string:

```
length of "Charles River"
  --> 13
```

or you can use the count command:

```
count "my marbles"
  --> 10
```

Extracting Substrings

The proper form of extracting a substring from a longer string is this:

```
text 1 thru 5 of "AppleScript"
--> "Apple"
```

You can also identify the start and/or end of a substring by word or paragraph:

```
text (word 3) thru (word 6) of "AppleScript is the greatest language in the world"
--> "the greatest language in"
```

String Elements

A string has built-in parts, or *elements*. These parts are characters, words, paragraphs, and text items. Asking for the parts of a string returns a list where each part is an item in that list. For example:

```
characters of "particles"
--> {"p", "a", "r", "t", "i", "c", "l", "e", "s"}

words of "James: 'would you give-up!'"
--> {"James", "would", "you", "give-up"}

paragraphs of "line 1
line 2
line 3"
--> {"line 1", "line 2", "line 3"}
```

Notice that the separators are not part of the result. The words list has no punctuation, and the paragraph list has no line break characters.

Also, when referring to the specific parts in the text, it is better to refer to the direct text element, like this:

```
paragraph 3 of the_text
```

and not like this:

```
item 3 of (paragraphs of the_text)
```

The text item delimiters Property

Text items of a string are the parts of any string, separated by the current text item delimiters property. Although you can set text item delimiters to a list of strings, only the first string will be used.

The default text item delimiters value is {""}, which is an empty string in a list.

You script with text items as you would words and characters:

```
text items of "abc" --> {"a", "b", "c"}
```

Changing the value of AppleScript's built-in text item delimiters property changes how strings are broken up:

```
set text item delimiters to {"b"}
text items of "abc" --> {"a", "c"}
```

```
set text item delimiters to {"@"}
text items of "george@jungle.com" --> {" george", " jungle.com"}
```

```
set text item delimiters to {"i"}
text items of "Mississippi" --> {"M", "ss", "ss", "pp", ""}
```

```
set text item delimiters to {"stop"}
text items of "helpstopmestopJoe" --> {"help", "me", "Joe"}
```

Setting the text item delimiters property inside an application tell block requires that you use the following syntax:

```
set AppleScript's text item delimiters to ...
```

It is also recommended that after setting the text item delimiters property in your script, you return it to the default of {""}.

Offset Command

The offset command returns the index position of a substring in a string or returns 0 if no match is found:

```
offset of "s" in "Music" --> 3
```

```
offset of "Ang" in "Los Angeles" --> 5
```

```
offset of "a" in "1-800-555-1212" --> 0
```

The last statement's result is 0 because the string "1-800-555-1212" does not contain the string "a".

CHAPTER 4

■ ■ ■

Doing the Math: All About Numbers

One of the great challenges in writing complex scripts is dealing with numbers and math. In AppleScript programming, though, your job is not to figure out the solution to a math problem but rather to figure out how to present the problem to AppleScript in a way that it can interpret it and return a useful result to you.

Massaging Numbers

AppleScript supports two classes of numbers: reals and integers. An integer is a whole number without a decimal fraction and with no potential of ever getting one. Integers can, however, be negative numbers. Real numbers, on the other hand, have decimal points, even if the decimal point is ceremonial, like in the case of the real 1.0. It's equal in value to the integer 1, but it is a real nonetheless. Although you, as the scripter, may not ever write a number such as 1.0 (you would use 1 instead), some AppleScript commands always return a real, in which case they would return 1.0 instead of 1, if that were the result.

When coercing numeric strings to reals or integers, AppleScript is specific about which strings it can coerce into numbers and which it can't.

Let's first examine the class of some literal values:

```
class of 2003 --> integer
class of 1.5 --> real
class of "1000" --> string
```

Now, let's take some literal numeric strings and see which ones can be coerced into reals or integers:

```
"1000" as integer --> 1000
"1000" as real --> 1000.0
"1,000,000" as integer -- error: Can't make "1,000,000" into type integer.
"-3.14" as number --> -3.14
```

Funny enough, when coercing strings to numbers, AppleScript respects the `ignoring/considering` attributes. In the following script, the numeric string `"-3.14"` was coerced into the number 314 since both the period (punctuation) and the minus symbol (hyphen) were ignored:

```
ignoring hyphens and punctuation
   "-3.14" as number
end ignoring
--> 314
```

When you do math, some operations return results as reals and some return results as integers. The implications aren't great because you can process both reals and integers pretty much interchangeably without choking AppleScript.

Some areas of AppleScript accept whole numbers only, and using a real with a nonzero fractional part raises an error, but these are obvious enough, such as the following:

```
repeat 1.5 times -- error: Can't make 1.5 into type integer.
    say "Hi"
end repeat
```

Working with "Real" Big Numbers

Real numbers have the tendency to be written using exponential notation, which is the scientific form of a number used to shrink the length of a number while (for the most part) not changing its value. You can write large numbers in AppleScript in their long form (say 120,000,000), but as soon as the script is compiled, these long numbers get converted to their exponential forms, which can prove irritating.

For example, try to write the following in a new script editor window:

```
10000.0
```

When you compile the script, the number will change to this:

```
1.0E+4
```

In scientific terms, the number breaks down into the coefficient, which is always a number from 1.0 up to, but not including, 10.0, and the exponent, which is the number appearing after the E, in this case +4.

The mathematical equivalent of 10,000, or 1.0E+4, is $1.0 * 10^4$.

In other words, AppleScript tells you, "I moved the decimal point four spots to the left." Move the decimal point back, and you have your 10,000 back.

It's simple, really! If you take the number 123,456,789.987654321 and compile it in a script window, it will be displayed as 1.23456789987654E+8. All you have to do is shift the decimal point eight spaces to the right to get the number 123456789.987654.

What? Oh . . . the last three digits after the decimal point . . . . Oh, stop being so picky! Why do you need that precise a number anyway? The same decimal-shifting idea works with negative exponential numbers. That doesn't mean the number itself is negative, just that the direction of the decimal point is.

For example, 1.0E-4 is actually 0.0001. Notice the decimal point moved four spots to the right. Move the decimal, and you get the number.

To become part of that heartless form of displaying numbers, a real number has to be either less than 0.0001 or greater than 10,000; otherwise, it is displayed as is.

Rounding Numbers

Rounding numbers is an important aspect of scripting and programming. Although the round command rounds the number you provide as its direct parameter, you can perform many tasks with the command if you only make some modifications to it.

Let's look at the round command in detail. The parameter you supply it is a real number. This makes sense, since an integer is already rounded!

The result returned by the round command is an integer. Actually, the round command can assist you in converting a real to an integer in several ways. Integers are whole numbers (in other words, they don't have any fractional part), and reals are (usually) not. I write *usually* because I'm not sure if 1.0 is considered round. Hmm.

To test the basic function of the round command, start a new script window, type each of the following lines, and run each line separately to get the result. I included the result on separate lines here:

```
round 1.5
Result: 2
round 2.2
Result: 2
round -6.4
Result: -6
```

You can fine-tune the behavior of the round command by using its optional rounding parameter. The rounding parameter has five possible constant values, if you choose to use any. The constants are up, down, toward zero, to nearest, and as taught in school. If you simply use the round command without specifying the rounding parameter, AppleScript will use the to nearest logic, as described next.

Rounding Up

As it sounds, rounding up will always round to the next higher integer. Here are some examples:

```
round 1.1 rounding up --> 2
round 5.5 rounding up --> 6
round -2.9 rounding up --> -2
```

Rounding Down

The opposite of rounding up, rounding down will always round to the next lower integer. Here are some examples:

```
round 1.7 rounding down --> 1
round 5.5 rounding down --> 5
round -2.1 rounding down --> -3
```

Rounding Toward Zero

rounding toward zero acts the same as rounding down with positive numbers, and with negative numbers it acts like rounding up would. In other words, it simply "chops off" the decimal portion of the number.

Rounding to the Nearest and Rounding As Taught in School

As far as what was taught in school, well, I hate to say that I was probably chasing butterflies the day they taught that . . . but I'll make an effort to understand it anyhow!

rounding to nearest is the default behavior that will be used if none other is specified. rounding to nearest acts as you would expect, other than with rounding in-between numbers: "numbers and a half." When you try to round 0.5, 2.5, 56.5, and so on, the rounding to nearest option will round toward the nearest *even* integer. This is done that way, as explained in the Apple-Script Language Guide, to avoid cumulative errors. Here are some examples:

```
round 5.5 rounding to nearest
--> 6
round 4.5 rounding to nearest
--> 4
```

rounding as taught in school, on the other hand, will round numbers whose decimal part is .5 away from zero. Here are some examples:

```
round 5.5 rounding as taught in school
--> 6
round 4.5 rounding as taught in school
--> 5
round -2.5 rounding as taught in school
--> -3
```

Rounding to Other Increments

When you simply round a real number, you get an integer as a result. That's good for some things, but let's look at two other scenarios that are related to rounding numbers but can't be achieved directly with the round command:

Scenario 1: What if you want to round a real to a certain number of decimal places? Take, for example, currency formatting. If you need to calculate a price, you need only two decimal points. If I'm automating a catalog and I need to use AppleScript to calculate the 7 percent Rhode Island state sales tax on a product that costs $4.99, the total cost with tax will be $5.3393. Rounding that number will give me $5, but what I want to show is $5.34, right?

Scenario 2: You want the script to start with an integer from 10,000 to 99,999 and, using that integer, extract another integer that is the next integer down that can divide evenly by 1,000. For instance, assume that I have the product number 55782. Using the product numbering scheme, I can teach AppleScript that the category number for that product is 55000. Sure, I can coerce it to a string, strip off the last three digits, tack on "000" at the end, and finally coerce the result to an integer again:

```
(text 1 thru 2 of (the_product_number as string) & "000") as integer
```

But you're out of luck: this is the numbers chapter, and the strings chapter of the book is way over, so you're stuck having to find a solution using the round command.

The solution to both of the previous scenarios involves dividing and multiplying the number before and after rounding it.

To be more specific, here is how you would solve each of the needs described in the first scenario: when you analyze the finished script in Figure 4-1, you can see that two mathematical operations involve first multiplying by 100 on line 4 and then dividing by 100 on the last line. This forward-and-back action is the foundation of the script. Figure 4-1 shows the rounding script.

The following is the script, which is followed by a line-by-line breakdown:

```
1. set the_price to 4.99
2. set the_tax_rate to 0.07
3. (the_price * the_tax_rate) + the_price
4. result * 100
5. round result rounding as taught in school
6. set price_with_tax to result / 100
```

Figure 4-1. *The script that rounds currency to only two decimal points*

In lines 1 and 2, you assign values to some variables you will use in the script. This is still a good idea even if the values never change. The tax rate will always be 7 percent, so you should assign it to a variable. This gives it a meaning and makes your script clearer and more flexible, especially if that value is used in multiple places in your script.

From line 3 until line 6, you don't assign any variables. Instead, you rely on the built-in `result` variable that automatically holds the result of the previous expression. You do that since you don't care for the intermediate results. You don't care to store the result of line 4, which happens to be 533.93. You need that resulting value for the following operation, not beyond it. The result of line 3 is used in line 4, the result of line 4 is used in line 5, and the result of line 5 is used in the final operation in line 6.

In line 3, you calculate the actual price with tax. This results in a number with too many digits after the decimal point, a problem you will need to remedy.

In line 4, you multiply the result by 100. You do this because any real number with two decimal points multiplied by 100 should be whole. To figure out the number to use, you can raise 10 to the power of the number of decimal places you want. Get it? You want to end up with two decimal places, so you do 10^2 to get 100.

To make that result whole, you round it in line 5, using the rounding parameter with the value `as taught in school` to ensure that a price ending with half a penny or more rounds up to the next penny.

To give the resulting number its two decimal places back, you divide it by 100 in line 6.

Generally, as you math whizzes already know, if you take a number (n) and first multiply it by another number (say m) and then divide it by that same number (m), you get your original number. You're counting on that fact, but you've added a little twist: you rounded the number in the middle.

This solution is still not complete, though. What if the original price number were 4.5? Using the current program would still return 4.5 and finally end up looking like $4.5.

Scenario 2 is similar; the crucial difference is that you first divide the number and then round it, only then remultiplying it. As you can see in Figure 4-2, I tried to condense the operations from the last script into a single script line.

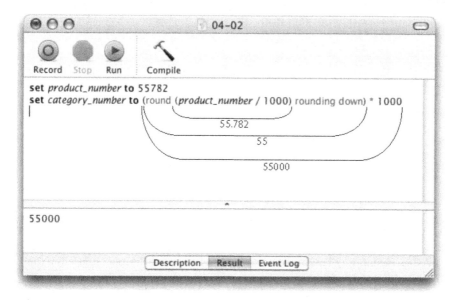

Figure 4-2. *Figuring out the product category from the product number*

Since you don't have script lines to specify the order of operations, you have to rely on either AppleScript's precedence rules or simply on good ol' parentheses. The first operation is in the innermost set of parentheses:

```
product_number / 1000
```

The result is 55.782—this result is then processed by the command in the second set of parentheses:

```
round (product_number / 1000) rounding down
```

You round down since even the product number 55999 still belongs to category 55000. This way, the number 55.782 rounds down to 55.

The final multiplication operation returns the number to its original length:

```
(round (product_number / 1000) rounding down) * 1000
```

which returns 55000.

Rounding Handler

To cap off the rounding discussion, I'll show how to put together a handler that will be in charge of rounding numbers. The handler will accept two parameters:

- The number to round in the real value class.

- The number of decimal places. This will be a small integer that tells the handler what precision you want. For instance, a value of 2 will turn 1.66667 to 1.67.

Here is the complete handler followed by a brief explanation of the steps:

```
1. on round_number(the_number_to_round, the_decimal_precision)
2.     set multiplier to 10 ^ the_decimal_precision
3.     the_number_to_round * multiplier
4.     round result
5.     result / multiplier
6. end round_number
```

I already discussed steps 2 through 4 earlier. You multiply the number you want to round and then you round it and divide it by the same number to return it to its original range.

The neat feature here is how you got to the number you need to multiply and divide by. You use the number of decimal places that you wanted to end up with, and you raise the number 10 by that number. For example, if you want to end up with three decimal places, you would do this calculation: 10 ^ 3. The result will be 1,000, which will be then used in the rounding.

Figure 4-3 shows the handler, a statement calling that handler, and the result.

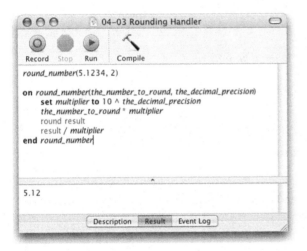

Figure 4-3. *The handler and the handler call*

In the example, the real value, 5.1234, is passed along with 2 as the number of decimal places. The result is 5.12.

Scripting at Random

What's a programming language without the ability to generate random numbers? Incomplete is the answer. Like other languages, AppleScript has a command for generating random numbers and a number of optional parameters to make it work for you in many ways.

Random Number Result

The random number command returns a result that can be either an integer or a real, depending on whether the parameters you provided are reals or integers. In any case, the random number generates a single number result.

Parameters

You can use the random number command as is, without any parameters. The result in that case is a real number from 0 to 1, as shown in Figure 4-4.

Figure 4-4. *The* random number *command used without parameters*

The direct parameter you can use is a number, either a real or an integer, following the command. Try this:

```
random number 5
```

The result is an integer from 0 to 5. Next, try this:

```
random number 5.0
```

Now the result is a real number with up to 12 decimal places, also from 0.0 to 5.0. You can also use the range parameters from and to, like so:

```
random number from 20 to 30
```

or like so:

```
random number from 20.0 to 30.0
```

Note that if you provide a direct parameter as well as to/from parameters, only the direct parameter is used. For instance, the following command will generate an integer from 0 to 3, not a real from 20.0 to 30.0:

```
random number 3 from 20.0 to 30.0
```

The final parameter, with seed, is a bit obscure; it allows you to either get the same random number every time or get a different random number every time.

OK, so these two statements seemed to be contrary to the concept of random numbers. Aren't random numbers supposed to always be random? Well, yes, but you can get the same "random" number every time by using the same seed number, like so:

```
random number with seed 100
```

The result will always be 0.716641089949. Now, try this script:

```
random number from 100000 to 999999 with seed (get current date)
```

Using the current date as the seed ensures that the seed is different every time and therefore that the number you're getting is different every time.

Black Jack!

To cap off the short random number topic, I thought it would be appropriate to invite you to play a little game of black jack.

To keep the script short and simple for the sake of the example, I have simplified a few rules. In the AppleScript black jack, the cards keep their values; for instance, an ace is always 1, a jack is 11, a king is 13, and so on.

If this is too much for your purist self, I suggest you add the necessary lines of code to make the game complete, such as to allow an ace to be 1 or 11.

As for my script, here's how I went about it: the two players are the dealer and you. Each of you has a hand of cards. The information regarding that hand is kept in a record. Each player has their own record that includes two properties labeled total and hand. The total property contains your total score that shows whether either of you reached or passed 21, and the hand property contains a string that's used to show you the cards you have and to show the dealer's hand at the end of the game. In that string, cards may appear like so: [5][K], meaning you have a five and a king.

Note Notice that I'm using a compound value class called a *record*, which is a collection of properties. Each property consists of a unique label (or name), which is an identifier, and a value. To get or set a property's value, you refer to it by its label. You can find more about records in Chapter 6.

This is how the player's record will look:

```
{total:18, hand:" [10] [8]"}
```

Later in the script you'll use the hand property to display the dealer's hand to the player, like this:

```
display dialog (hand of dealer_hand)
```

Note The finished script is Script 4-4 in the Downloaded Scripts folder.

You start the script by setting up some basic variables.

The first is a list of cards, presented in the way they should display. So if the drawn card is 12, for instance, you can ask for item 12 of card_marks and get the string "[Q]". You can use that to build the visual display of the hands:

```
set card_marks to {"[A]", "[2]", "[3]", "[4]", "[5]", "[6]", "[7]", ¬
    "[8]", "[9]", "[10]", "[J]", "[Q]", "[K]"}
```

You also initialize the dealer's hand and the player's hand:

```
set dealer_hand to {total:0, hand:""}
set player_hand to {total:0, hand:""}
```

Then you continue by picking cards for the dealer. You simply repeat in a loop until the dealer's card total reaches 17 points or more. If the dealer gets more than 21, the dealer instantly loses:

```
--setup dealer hand
set total_this_draw to 0
repeat
    set drawn_card to random number from 1 to 13
    set total_this_draw to total_this_draw + drawn_card
    set hand of dealer_hand to ¬
        (hand of dealer_hand) & ¬
        (item drawn_card of card_marks)
```

Get that last statement? drawn_card is an integer from 1 to 13 (random, of course). You associate the card number with the card symbol by using the integer value in drawn_card to get the corresponding string symbol stored in the variable card_marks. card_marks is the string that shows how you want the card to look; for instance, if the number drawn is 1, then item 1 of card_marks will be "[A]".

The following conditional statement first checks whether the card total exceeded 21. If it did, the dealer has lost. If it reached 17 but didn't go beyond 21, then the dealer rests. In both these cases, the script is instructed to leave the repeat loop.

```
    if total_this_draw > 21 then
        set dealer_lost_round to true
        set total of dealer_hand to total_this_draw
        exit repeat
    else if total_this_draw ≥ 17 then
        set dealer_lost_round to false
        exit repeat
    end if
end repeat
```

The next segment of the script adds up the player's hand by drawing the first two cards and then adding them to the player's total:

```
--Draw first two player cards
set total_this_draw to 0
repeat 2 times
    set drawn_card to random number from 1 to 13
    set total_this_draw to total_this_draw + drawn_card
    set hand of player_hand to ¬
        (hand of player_hand) & ¬
        (item drawn_card of card_marks)
end repeat
```

In the next statement, you check whether the dealer lost. If true, the player is notified of the victory:

```
if dealer_lost_round then
    display dialog "You won! "
    return
end if
```

Next, you create a similar loop to the repeat loop that built the dealer's hand, but here you interrupt the loop with a dialog box asking the player to either hit or stay.

If the player stays, the script checks whether he won. If not, the player gets another card, and here you go again:

```
repeat
```

The following statement creates a general string that contains the dealer's hand and the player's hand. This string will be used in dialog boxes that inform the player of either a loss or a win:

```
set final_display to "* * *" & return & ¬
    "Your hand:   " & (hand of player_hand) & return & return & ¬
    "Dealer's hand:   " & (hand of dealer_hand)
if total_this_draw > 21 then
    display dialog ¬
        "You lost! " & return & final_display buttons {"OK"}
```

Figure 4-5 shows the resulting dialog box.

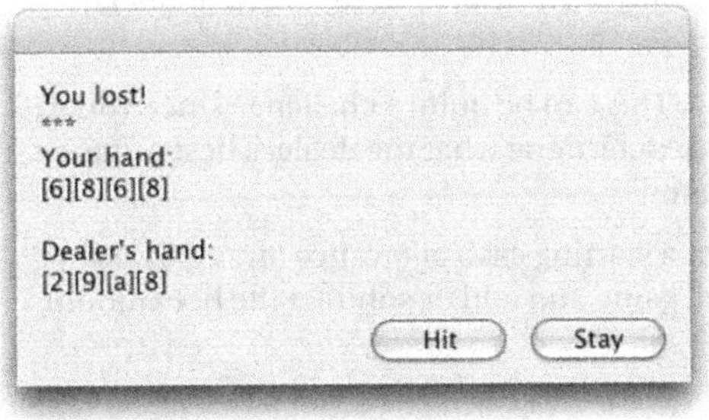

Figure 4-5. *You lost!*

The following lines display the player's hand and request an action from the player:

```
exit repeat
else
    display dialog "Your hand:" & return & ¬
        (hand of player_hand) buttons {"Hit", "Stay"}
```

See the resulting dialog box in Figure 4-6.

Figure 4-6. *The player is prompted for the next move.*

Next, the script acts on the decision made by the user by choosing either to hit and get another card or to stay and compare hands with the dealer:

```
if button returned of result is "Stay" then
        if total of player_hand > total of dealer_hand then
            display dialog ¬
            "You won! " & return & final_display buttons {"OK"}
            return
        else
            display dialog ¬
            "You lost!" & return & final_display buttons {"OK"}
            return
        end if
    else
        set drawn_card to random number from 1 to 13
        set total_this_draw to total_this_draw + drawn_card
```

```
            set hand of player_hand to (hand of player_hand) & ¬
                (item drawn_card of card_marks)
            end if
        end if
    end repeat
end repeat
```

That's it for the example, but I'll give you some exercises to prove your super AppleScript ability. Feel free to e-mail me your solutions:

1. Make the 11, 12, and 13 cards (jack, queen, and king) have a value of 10, not their actual card value as I've programmed them.

2. Make the ace, or 1, have a value of either 1 or 11. This can be quite a challenge since you will need to run an unknown number of scenarios to determine what the dealer's best number is under 21 and when the player exceeds their limit.

3. Put the whole game in a repeat loop, and assign a starting cash allowance of, say, $1,000. Give the player the ability to bet money on each game and add or subtract the bet amount at each round.

You Do the Math

Although you can use numbers in many ways that require no more than some counting skills, when you think numbers, you probably think math. I personally love math and look forward to solving any challenging operations a script may require.

The operators you can use with numbers are the familiar ones such as addition, subtraction, division, and so on, and some less often used ones such as div and mod.

Table 4-1 shows the operators you can use with numbers.

Table 4-1. *Math Operators*

Operator	Description	Example
+	Adds two numbers	5 + 3 --> 8
-	Subtracts the right number from the left number	12 - 9 --> 3
*	Multiplies the two given numbers	3 * 10 --> 30
/	Divides the left number by the right number	7.5 / 2 --> 3.75
^	Exponent; raises the number to its left to the power of the number to its right	2 ^ 3 --> 8.0
div	Divides the number to its left by the number to its right and returns the integral (that is, whole number) part of the answer as its result	7.5 div 2 --> 3
mod	Divides the number to its left by the number to its right a whole number of times and returns the remainder as its result	7.5 mod 2 --> 1.5

You also have the good ol' comparison operators, which return a result in the Boolean value class (that is, true or false). Table 4-2 describes the comparison operations you can use with numbers.

Table 4-2. *Comparison Operators for Numbers*

Operator	Description
=	Returns true if the right operand is equal to the left operand
≠	Returns true if the right operand is *not* equal to the left operand
>	Returns true if the left operand is greater than the right operand
≥	Returns true if the left operand is equal to or greater than the right operand
<	Returns true if the left operand is less than the right operand
≤	Returns true if the left operand is equal to or less than the right operand

Comparing with Logic

Comparison operators can be quite boring when used one at a time. However, when you gang them up, you can create some mighty powerful, and also rather confusing, expressions.

Note My ASP programmer friend Steve says that I use JSL to write my scripts. JSL stands for Job Security Language.

A simple expression may look like this:

```
the_age ≥ 18
```

This evaluates whether the value of the variable the_age is equal to or greater than 18. This expression will return true or false. But, that's not all! What if you needed to write a statement that will approve or reject a credit card application? You'd need to check for a number of true-or-false conditions such as ages, household incomes, bankruptcies, credit ratings, current debts, and so on.

You can use AppleScript's three Boolean, or *logical*, operators—and, or, not—to combine two or more simple comparison expressions into a powerful compound expression.

This expression may look something like the one in Figure 4-7.

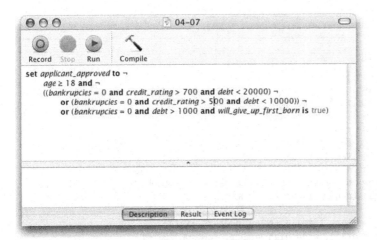

Figure 4-7. *A compound expression that uses multiple comparison operations and no less than nine (!) logical operators to connect everything*

One of the important factors that makes the formula in Figure 4-7 work is the use of parentheses, (and). AppleScript has quite a long list of rules that determine the default order in which the individual operations within a compound expression should be evaluated. Sometimes the default order is the one you want, in which case you don't need to add parentheses. Other times you want AppleScript to follow a different order, in which case using parentheses is essential. I'll discuss all this in Chapter 9. Take care to position the parentheses correctly: poorly placed parentheses may prevent your script from compiling or cause it to error or produce the wrong result when run.

When dealing with complex operations like the previous one, enclosing individual expressions in parentheses can often aid readability, even if AppleScript itself does not require them. It can also be handy to add parentheses when you can't remember (or haven't yet learned!) exactly what order AppleScript will evaluate the various expressions; that way, you don't have to worry about it. You can make the previous script easier for humans to read by changing it from this:

```
(bankruptcies = 0 and credit_ratings > 500 and debt > 10000)
```

to this:

```
((bankruptcies = 0) and (credit_ratings > 500) and (debt > 10000))
```

Alternatively, you can use AppleScript's "nonbreaking line" symbol (¬) to spread the full expression across several lines, like this:

```
bankruptcies = 0 and ¬
  credit_ratings > 500 and ¬
  debt > 10000
```

Doing Basic Math

In the following script, I will show how to create a handler that takes a list of numbers and returns a record with a few mathematical facts regarding the list. The resulting record will include the list average, the highest number, and the lowest number in the list. If you fed the following list to the handler:

```
{10, 3, 5, 4, 13}
```

you'd get the following record as the result:

```
{average:7.0, high:13, low:3}
```

Here is the complete script:

```
1. math_facts({10, 3, 5, 4, 13})
2. on math_facts(numbers_list)
3.     set high_number to item 1 of numbers_list
4.     set low_number to item 1 of numbers_list
5.     set numbers_total to 0
6.     repeat with i from 1 to count numbers_list
7.         set the_number to item i of numbers_list
8.         if the_number > high_number then set high_number to the_number
9.        if the_number < low_number then set low_number to the_number
10.        set  numbers_total to numbers_total + the_number
11.     end repeat
12.     set the_average to (numbers_total / (count numbers_list))
13.     return {average:the_average, high:high_number, low:low_number}
15. end math_facts
```

I started by creating three variables. These variables, for the most part, will hold the values that will return the handler's result. The variables are `high_number`, `low_number`, and `numbers_total`, which will be used to get the list average at the end.

The `repeat` loop between lines 6 and 11 is the main loop that goes through the numbers in the list and analyzes each number to see whether it fits in the high number or low number spots and to add it to the numbers total.

Line 8 determines whether the currently processed number is larger than the value stored in the `high_number` variable. If it is, that number will become the new value of the `high_number` variable. This way, when the `repeat` loop concludes, the `high_number` variable will contain the highest number from the `number_list` variable. Line 9 is responsible for determining the lowest number in a similar fashion.

Line 12 calculates the average of all the numbers by dividing their total, stored in the variable `numbers_total`, by the number of items in the list.

Line 13 puts all this information into a neatly labeled record and returns it.

Using the mod and div Operators

The final math example you'll look at uses the `mod` and `div` operators. Although `mod` and `div` are used less often than other math operators, when you need them, they really shine.

`mod` and `div` deal with how many instances of a number can fit inside a different number without breaking. For instance, `div` can tell you that 2 can fit three times in 6.5, while `mod` will tell you that after you fit 2 in 6.5 three times, the remainder is 0.5.

Why is this so great? Well, I'll discuss a couple of uses of `div` and `mod`. First, what if you want to take a large number of seconds and show it as minutes and seconds? You can do something like this:

```
1. set total_seconds to 735
2. set the_minutes to total_seconds div 60
3. set extra_seconds to total_seconds mod 60
4. set the_time to (the_minutes as string) & ":" & extra_seconds
5. --> "12:15"
```

Second—say you are printing postcards—what if you needed to fit four postcards per page, and the number of postcards changes from job to job? If a job has 27 postcards, how many whole pages will you need? You need the following calculation:

```
set total_postcards to 27
set postcards_per_page to 4
set whole_pages to total_postcards div postcards_per_page
if whole_pages mod postcards_per_page > 0 then
    set whole_pages to whole_pages + 1
end if
return whole_pages
--> 7
```

27 `div` 4 will return 6, since 4 fits 6 times into 27. Then, if the remainder is zero, it means that the division is perfect, like if you had 24 postcards. But if the remainder is more than 0, then you need to add a page.

Reversing Numbers

To convert a number from positive to negative, or visa versa, simply add the minus sign before it, even if the number is in a variable:

```
set my_balance to 500
set my_opposite_balance to -my_balance
--> -500
```

In this situation, the minus operator is the unary *negation* operator, not the binary *subtraction* operator that allows you to subtract one number from the other. (*Unary* means an operator has only one operand; *binary* means an operator has two of them.)

Folder Kitchen Timer

In the next example script, I will show how to convert an ordinary Finder folder into a kitchen timer. The folder's name will change every second to reflect the remaining time. At the end, Apple iTunes will pick a random track and play it to alert you that your food is ready.

Here is the script in its entirety:

```
1. display dialog "How many minutes?" default answer "120"
2. set timer_minutes to text returned of result as integer

3. tell application "Finder" to set folder_alias to ¬
      (make new folder at desktop with properties {name:"Timer"}) as alias
4. repeat with the_minute from (timer_minutes - 1) to 0 by -1
5.    set hrs_left to the_minute div 60
6.    set min_left to the_minute mod 60
7.    set hrs_text to pad_with_zero(hrs_left)
8.    set min_text to pad_with_zero(min_left)
9.    repeat with sec_left from 59 to 0 by -1
10.       set sec_text to pad_with_zero(sec_left)
11.       set displayTime to hrs_text & ";" & min_text & ";" & sec_text
12.       tell application "Finder" to set name of folder_alias to displayTime
13.       delay 1
14.    end repeat
15. end repeat

16. tell application "iTunes"
17.    play some track of library playlist "library" of source 1
18. end tell

19. on pad_with_zero(the_number)
20.    if the_number < 10 then
21.       return ("0" & the_number)
22.    else
23.       return (the_number as string)
24.    end if
25. end pad_with_zero
```

The script utilizes one custom handler, called pad_with_zero, whose purpose is to convert an integer into a string while ensuring that if the integer has only one digit, it will be preceded by a zero. This has to be done as a string since if you ask AppleScript for 01 as an integer or as a real, the preceding zero will be disregarded.

If you have some basic understanding of handlers, you know that they can accept values as parameters and return values as well. This handler accepts a single integer parameter, and it returns a string. If the handler is fed the integer 5, it'll return "05".

The pad_with_zero handler sits at the end of the script (lines 19–25), and you call it to perform three times during the execution of the script.

The script starts by asking the user to set the timer to any number of minutes, and then in line 2, AppleScript takes the text the user typed in the dialog box and converts it to an integer.

This integer will be the starting point of the script. Just like setting a real kitchen timer, the first thing you do is tell the timer how many minutes the timer has to be set to.

Line 3 of the script talks directly to the Finder. The Finder is instructed to make a new folder with a specific name.

You should note a couple of things regarding the syntax of that statement. One is that the Finder's `tell` block is compressed into one line. I was able to do that because I needed the Finder to do one task only.

The second neat feature of this statement is that it obtains an alias value to the new folder (`alias "Macintosh HD:Users:Hanaan:Desktop:Timer:"`), not the usual Finder reference (`folder "Timer2" of folder "Desktop" of folder "Hanaan" of folder "Users" of startup disk of application "Finder"`).

Chapter 14 contains a whole section dedicated to working with files, so for now I'll just add that getting an alias value to the folder you created allows you to change the name of the folder again and again, and the alias value will always remain accurate.

Also notice the use of parentheses. Every expression is surrounded with parentheses to direct AppleScript to the order you would like the expressions executed in and to make the code easier for you to read.

What comes next in the script is the main `repeat` loop starting at line 4 and ending on line 15. This outer `repeat` loop starts from the number of minutes and counts down to 0, stepping –1 step at a time. Actually, just like a real timer, the script starts counting from one second earlier than the requested time. To achieve this, the outer loop actually begins one minute earlier than the inner loop starts at 59 seconds.

Lines 5 and 6 are where you take the current number of minutes and separate that number into hours and minutes. Here's how that's done, assuming for a second that 135 minutes are left:

```
set hrs_left to 135 div 60
```

This statement will return 2, since 60 divides evenly two times in 135:

```
set min_left to 135 mod 60
```

This statement will return 15, since after you fit 60 into 135 twice, you have a remainder of 15.

These two statements repeat for each minute that passes, and they're followed by a handler call that adds a leading zero to the number of hours or minutes, if needed.

The inner `repeat` loop starting on line 9 counts the seconds for each minute. It starts from 59, the number of remaining seconds in that minute, and ends at 0.

Inside that inner loop, the seconds are being formatted with the `pad_with_zero` handler and then concatenated with the hours and minutes to form a single string that contains the time left formatted as you like it. I used a semicolon, but you can also use a period or dash, anything other that a colon, as the separator of choice for your time string; unfortunately, the Finder already reserves the colon character for its own use.

Next, line 12 names the timer folder with the newly formed name, line 13 delays the script by a second, and then the entire process starts again. After the `repeat` loop has ended, the script constructs a reference to identify a random track in iTunes (`some track of library playlist "library" of source 1`) and then passes it to iTunes' `play` command to tell iTunes to start playing a random track. (You can choose a different alert if you want.)

Conclusion

No matter what you do in AppleScript, numbers and math are everywhere—page layout automation, database interaction, and system administration; all require some kind of number
manipulation. Some of my graphic-intensive scripts even forced me to pick up a trigonometry
book and figure out triangles, sines, and cosines!

Throughout the book, you will be attacking number problems and using the concepts covered
in this chapter.

Power Wrap-Up

The following sections give you a quick reference of all the important take-home messages in the
chapter, without the chatter. This will allow you to look up topics quickly.

Dealing with Types of Number

AppleScript supports two types of number values: integers and reals. An integer is a whole number
without a decimal point, while a real number can represent fractions and always has a decimal
point:

```
class of 120 --> integer
class of 3.8 --> real
class of 99999 --> integer
class of 1000.0 --> real
```

Coercing Numbers

You can coerce integers and real numbers to strings:

```
30 as string --> "30"
1.25 as string --> "1.25"
```

Integers can be always coerced into reals:

```
2 as real --> 2.0
```

A real number can be accurately coerced into an integer only if it has no fraction:

```
4.0 as integer --> 4
```

In OS X 10.3, a real number with a fractional part can be coerced to an integer, but the fraction
will be lost:

```
4.0001 as integer --> 4
```

On earlier versions of Mac OS, this will cause an error; however, you can always use the round
command instead.

Dealing with Large Numbers

When working with real numbers of more than a few digits, AppleScript displays the numbers using
exponential notation, instead of their normal form.

The number 10000.0, for instance, will be displayed as 1.0E+4.

See the "Working with 'Real' Big Numbers" section in this chapter for an explanation of how to
decipher the exponential notation code.

Rounding Numbers

The round command takes a real number and rounds it. The round command's optional rounding parameter determines how rounding is decided on by AppleScript. You can use five constants with the round command: up, down, toward zero, to nearest, and as taught in school. The following are examples of using each one.

If no parameter is given, the default behavior is the same as using round to nearest:

```
round 1.5 --> 2
```

Here is rounding up:

```
round 1.1 rounding up --> 2
round -2.9 rounding up --> -2
```

Here is rounding down:

```
round 5.5 rounding down --> 5
round -2.1 rounding down --> -3
```

rounding toward zero rounds positive numbers down and negative numbers up. rounding to nearest and rounding as taught in school round numbers to the nearest whole. The only difference is with numbers that have halves: 1.5, –2.5, and so on. rounding to nearest rounds these to the nearest even integer, and rounding as taught in school rounds them away from zero:

```
round 4.5 rounding to nearest --> 4
round 4.5 rounding as taught in school --> 5
```

Dealing with Random Numbers

The random number command is a part of Standard Additions. In its basic form, the random number command generates a random real number from 0 to 1:

```
random number --> 0.295602678734
```

The random number command has a few optional parameters. The most useful ones are from and to, which specify to the command the number range in which the returned random number has to be in:

```
random number from 1 to 10 --> 5
random number from 1 to 10 --> 3
random number from 1 to 10 --> 1
```

Dealing with Math Operators

AppleScript supports the following math operators: +, –, *, /, ^, div, and mod:

```
set new_number to 5 + 12 --> 17
set new_number to 9 - 3 --> 6
set new_number to 10 * 4 --> 40
set new_number to 12 / 4 --> 3.0
set new_number to 3 ^ 2 --> 9.0 (3 to the power of 2, or three squared)
```

The div operator returns the number of times the right operand completely fits into the left operand. In the following example, without breaking, 5 fits twice into 13:

```
13 div 5 --> 2
```

The mod operator divides the left operand by the right operand a whole number of times and then returns the remainder. After you take 5 from 13 twice, you are left with 3:

```
13 mod 5 --> 3
```

You can use the div and mod operators in scripts in some clever ways. See the "Using the mod and div Operators" section in this chapter.

Using Comparison Operators

AppleScript supports the following comparison operators: =, ≠, >, ≥, <, and ≤. You can also write these operators as is equal to, is not equal to, is greater than, is greater than or equal to, is less than, and is less than or equal to.

These operators always return a Boolean result: either true or false.

CHAPTER 5

■ ■ ■

Picking Up Dates

Dates play an essential part in everyday life—imagine a world without dates! You'd never know if you were on time, and you'd miss out on all kinds of important events, even your birthday! As you might expect, dates are also important in programming—think of how dates come into play in the applications you use every day—your operating system, your e-mail client, a lot of the websites you regularly visit, and so on.

In this chapter, you'll learn how to use dates in AppleScript—as you're about to find out, the date class in AppleScript is versatile and has many hidden aspects worth exploring. I'll cover working with dates, using the date object's properties, and performing simple and complex date operations.

Introducing the date Class and date Object

In AppleScript, objects of a single-value class, date, hold information about a specific second in time. That second includes information about the date, including the time, day, month, and year on which that second falls.

To create a date value, you use a *date specifier*, which is written as the word date followed by a string that describes the date in human-readable form, such as date " Thursday, January 12, 2006 12:00:00 AM". AppleScript is pretty flexible when interpreting that string; for example, you can also write the previous date as date "12 Jan 2006, 12 am" or date "1/12/2006", and AppleScript will figure it out for you, filling in the blanks if needed. You should note, though, that the way it interprets that string can vary from user to user, depending on their system preferences; I'll discuss this shortly.

Note For simplicity, this book assumes your system preferences are set to use the default U.S.-style date and time formats. If they're different, you may need to modify some of the date-processing code in a few of the scripts.

To create a simple date, start a new window in Script Editor, and type the following:

```
date "2/3/06"
```

Now compile the script. As you can see in Figure 5-1, AppleScript takes the liberty of reformatting your date and adding to it the missing time, which is midnight of the date you specified by default. (If your date formatting preferences are set differently, then you may get a different result—more on this in the next section.)

Figure 5-1. date "2/3/06" *after it's compiled on a U.S. Mac system*

You can, of course, also specify your own time, and this is the time AppleScript will use—try this:

```
date "2/3/06 1:54 PM"
```

AppleScript compiles this one as follows:

```
date "Friday, February 3, 2006 1:54:00 PM"
```

Understanding Date and Time Formats

When AppleScript reads or displays a date string, it interprets it according to the settings in the International panel of System Preferences (not the Date and Time panel!).

Figure 5-2 shows the Formats tab in the International panel of the Mac OS X 10.4 (Tiger) System Preferences panels, which you use to modify the format of the date and time for the current user. Although you can change these settings, it may not be a good idea because other applications may rely on them.

Figure 5-1 shows what appears on my own Mac, which uses the U.S.-style "month/day/year" date format when it creates a date object from the string "2/3/06". Other AppleScript users may get different results, however. A U.K.-based Mac will normally use a "day/month/year" format, in which case the same date string is interpreted as 2 March 2006 instead, and a Swedish user who uses "year/month/day" will end up with 6 March 2002. Other times they'll get an error; for example, if the string is "2/15/06", then a U.S. Mac will read it as 15 February 2006, but Swedish and U.K. users are told it's an "invalid date and time" because they don't have a 15th month of the year! Weekday and month names are similarly affected. For example, a French-speaking Mac will understand "12 janvier 2006". An English-speaking one won't but will understand "12 January 2006" instead.

These sorts of inconsistencies are a result of AppleScript's desire to be user-friendly, of course, and are often convenient when writing and running your own scripts. When sharing your scripts with other users, however, you may sometimes need to tweak any date-related code a little to ensure the scripts work smoothly.

Because the user of the computer on which the script runs is able to change the date format, the script is unreliable for many purposes. For instance, if you want to extract the weekday from the date, you should avoid using the string manipulation shown in Figure 5-3.

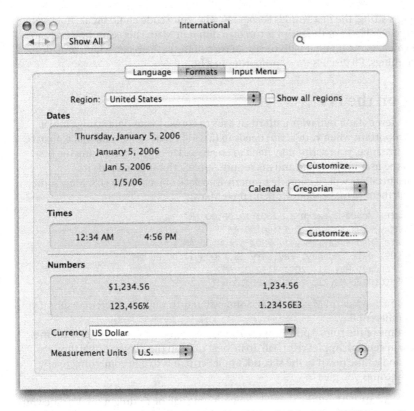

Figure 5-2. *The Formats tab in the International panel of the Mac OS X System Preferences*

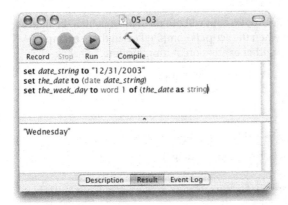

Figure 5-3. *Getting the weekday from a date may work, unless the user has changed the date formats in the International panel of System Preferences.*

In the example shown in Figure 5-3, line 2 will result in the following value:

```
date "Wednesday, December 31, 2003 12:00:00 AM"
```

When converted to a string, the first word is Wednesday. The same code could break, however, if the preferences are changed later or the script is run on a different Mac. This issue, however, becomes moot when you become familiar with the properties of the date object, which provide a much better way to do things. I'll discuss those properties in a bit.

Forming Dates on the Fly

AppleScript does have a few default behavior patterns it uses to convert your date strings into a date object. These are important when your script needs to take different values and make up date objects from them. For instance, your script may need to create a date object containing the first day of the month or let the user input a date and make sure AppleScript understands it.

The following date specifiers will all compile properly into date objects (on a U.S. Mac; some users may need to tweak them to make them work on their Macs):

```
date "03/03/03" --> date "Monday, March 3, 2003 12:00:00 AM"
date "0" --> date "Monday, May 31, 2004  12:00:00 AM"
date "5/1/2002" --> date "Wednesday, May 1, 2002 12:00:00 AM"
date "Feb 28 5:50 AM" --> date "Monday, February 28, 2005 12:00:00 AM"
date "3:30" --> date "Monday, May 31, 2004 3:30:00 AM"
date "May" --> date "Saturday, May 1, 2004 12:00:00 AM"
```

I originally ran these examples on May 31, 2004. Some will return slightly different results if you run them yourself on a different day.

The following are some of the rules AppleScript will use to compile (or parse during runtime) these strings into dates. In general, AppleScript will do its best to fill in the blanks. Since the date object describes a date and a time down to the second, AppleScript has to add something to any partial/incomplete date strings you give it.

- If you specify only a date without the time, the default time will be midnight on the date you specified. If you didn't specify AM or PM, AppleScript will treat your time as if you wrote the time in 24-hour format. That means time strings from 0.00.00 to 11.59.59 are treated as AM, whereas 12.00.00 and greater will translate as PM.

- If you specify only a time without the date, AppleScript will use the date on which the date specifier was evaluated, which could be when the script is compiled (as in these examples) or, if the string is supplied by a variable or other expression, during runtime.

The following are some literal date specifiers, before and after AppleScript compiles them. date "03/03/03" compiles as this:

```
date "Monday, March 3, 2003 12:00:00 AM"
```

AppleScript had to tack on the time, which is, by default, midnight. date "0" compiles as this:

```
date "Wednesday, July 2, 2003 12:00:00 AM"
```

AppleScript uses the date the script was compiled. This book is my only alibi for any crime that happened on that date . . . . date "5/1/2002" compiles as this:

```
date "Wednesday, May 1, 2002 12:00:00 AM"
```

```
date "Feb 28 5:50 AM" compiles as this:
```

```
date "Monday, February 28, 2005 12:00:00 AM"
```

Oops! What happened here is that the year hasn't been specified, so AppleScript took the first digit you intended to use for the time and used it for the year. The minutes you specified appear to have been ignored since AppleScript was looking for an "hours" number by then, and 50 didn't make sense.

```
date "3:30" compiles as this:
```

```
date "Wednesday, July 2, 2003 3:30:00 AM"
```

Here, the time was understood as 3:30 AM, and the date, again, is the date on which the script was compiled.

```
date "May" compiles as this:
```

```
date "Thursday, May 1, 2003 12:00:00 AM"
```

In this case, AppleScript used the first day of May on the current year.

Date "1" compiles as the following, which is the first day of the current month:

```
date "Tuesday, November 1, 2005 12:00:00 AM"
```

You can also experiment with other numbers. As long as a day in the current month corresponds to that number, every number you use will give you a date that corresponds to that day of the current month. Let's look at one more example—date "15" compiles as this:

```
date "Tuesday, November 15, 2005 12:00:00 AM"
```

■**Note** The "day" number has to be in string form, meaning it must be in double quotes, to be recognized. Also, specifying a nonexistent day will result in an error. For instance, date "32" will not compile on U.S. systems. Other examples of date misunderstandings are as follows: date "31 September" is invalid because there's only 30 days in that month; only years in the range 0–9999 are accepted; date "avril 1, 2006" will compile on a French system but break on a U.S. one; and date "April 1, 2006" will compile on a U.S. system but break on a French one.

Specifying a Time Relative to a Date

A nice feature of AppleScript's date values is that they allow you to obtain a particular time relative to a given date. You do this using a simple reference of the following form:

```
date the_time_string of the_date_value
```

For example, the following script creates a date that points to 5 PM of the current date:

```
date "5:00 PM" of (current date)
```

AppleScript allows you to write the of keyword as `relative to` if you'd like; they both mean the same thing. This may make the code more readable, like so:

```
date "6:30 AM" relative to date "September 1, 2003"
```

If you enter this expression and compile it, AppleScript will just change it to a single date literal:

```
date "Monday, September 1, 2003 6:30:00 AM"
```

However, if you use variables, this may be useful, as in the following example:

```
set the_date to (current date)
set the_time to "4:00 PM"
date the_time relative to the_date
--> date "Monday, May 31, 2004 4:00:00 PM"
```

The result shown here, and in many other places in the book, depends on the date you run it.

Specifying a User-Supplied Date

In the following example, you'll create a script snippet that prompts the user to enter a date, and then you will then test to see whether the date is valid. If the date is not valid, you will force the user to reenter it. If it is valid, you will give the user a chance to reenter it.

In the example, you'll use a repeat loop to check whether the user entry is a valid date. In scripts that ask for specific input from the user, it is important to validate the data entered by the user before moving on with the script.

The script shown in Script 5-1 enters a repeat loop with no specified end. The user is allowed out of the loop only if the data provided tests OK. Note that the script starts with a plain repeat and ends with end repeat and that the only way out of the loop is in line 8, which executes only if the user clicks OK in a dialog box.

Script 5-1.

```
1. repeat
2.    display dialog "Enter date" buttons {"OK"} ¬
          default button 1 default answer "MM/DD/YYYY"
3.    set user_date to text returned of result
4.    try
5.       set the_date to date user_date
6.       display dialog ¬
             ("You have chosen:" & return & (date string of the_date)) ¬
                buttons {"Try again", "OK"} default button 1
7.       if (button returned of result) = "OK" then
8.          exit repeat
9.       end if
10.   on error
11.      display dialog ¬
             "Invalid date, please try again using the format \"MM/DD/YYYY\"" ¬
                buttons {"OK"} default button 1 with icon stop
12.   end try
13. end repeat
```

Line 2 of the script asks the user to enter a date and gives a format to follow. Figure 5-4 shows the dialog box.

Figure 5-4. *The input dialog box asks the user to enter a date.*

Line 3 assigns the user's typed text to the user_date variable. The value of user_date is a string that was returned from the display dialog command.

So how do you check whether the date is valid? You try to convert it into a value of class date. You're counting on that if the date is not valid, trying to convert it into a date object will return an error. Therefore, you put the whole statement into a try block.

That try block actually takes over the rest of the script. It starts on line 4 and ends on line 12. If anything goes wrong in lines 5 to 9 that causes an error, the on error part will be executed, telling the user to try again. You start on line 5 by attempting to convert the string the user entered into a date object using a date specifier.

If the date string the user supplied converted properly into a date object, you continue by asking the user whether that was really the date they meant to enter. Maybe they mistyped something, or perhaps AppleScript had a different idea of what date was intended.

So on line 6 you display an interesting dialog box, shown in Figure 5-5. Part of the dialog box's message presents the user's date as a nicely formatted string, which you obtain from the property date string of the date object. I'll discuss this and other properties of the date object in Chapter 5; however, the date string property contains a string that describes the date portion of the date object.

Figure 5-5. *The dialog box confirming the date entered by the user*

Line 7 checks whether the user clicked OK to confirm that the date is fine. If the user approves the date, then line 8 executes and exits the repeat loop and therefore allows the script to continue.

Specifying a Current Date

The current date command is part of Standard Additions, which comes with the Mac OS. The command takes no parameters and returns a date object containing the current date and time, such as date "Sunday, July 2, 2006 10:15:09 PM".

When used as part of a larger operation, the current date command likes to be enclosed in parentheses. Actually, AppleScript is quite aware of that and will many times enclose it, as well as other commands, with parentheses when the script is compiled.

The usefulness of the current date command never ceases to amaze me. Just imagine how many times a day you turn to someone to ask what time or what date it is . . . OK, so its usefulness goes beyond knowing the current date and time. For one, it's a way to get a unique time stamp on which you can perform several operations. You can use the result of the current date command to figure out the time it takes to run a script, as shown in the following example:

```
set start_time to current date
--your script here
--more script
--a few more statements...
set end_time to current date
set time_in_seconds to end_time - start_time
display dialog "The script took " & time_in_seconds & " seconds to run!"
```

Note Although you can time medium to long scripts with the current date command as shown previously, because of its low precision, for short scripts or script portions it's better to use a third-party scripting addition such as GetMilliSec, which is precise to the millisecond. You'll find GetMilliSec and other scripting additions at http://osaxen.com.

Using the time to GMT Command

Another date-related command, time to GMT, returns the time difference between the time zone of the computer that runs the script and Greenwich mean time (GMT). The result is returned in seconds, which means in order to extract any useful information from it, such as the number of hours, you have to divide it by the number of seconds in an hour.

Script 5-2 will return the time difference between your time zone and GMT (provided of course that the time zone is properly set on your computer).

Script 5-2.

```
set time_difference to (time to GMT) / hours
if time_difference mod 1 = 0 then
    set time_difference to time_difference as integer
end if
if time_difference < 0 then
    set time_difference to -time_difference
    set the_message to "You are " & time_difference & " hours behind GMT"
else if time_difference > 0 then
    set the_message to "You are " & time_difference & " hours ahead of GMT"
else
    set the_message to "Your time zone is GMT"
end if
display dialog the_message
```

You start the script by getting the time difference and dividing it by the value of AppleScript's built-in hours constant, 3600, which is the number of seconds in an hour (more about that specific constant in the "Introducing Useful Date-Related Constants" section).

Line 1 returns a real number, but most time zones lie on the hour (0.0, 2.0, –8.0, and so on), and you'd like those numbers to display without the .0 at the end, so you use lines 2–4 to prettify them. Line 2 checks whether the number is a whole number by using the mod operator to divide by 1 and get the remainder. If the remainder is 0, then it's a whole number, and line 3 can safely coerce it to an integer; time zones with an extra 0.25 or 0.5 hours in them remain untouched. The conditional statement that starts on line 5 and ends on line 12 forms a different message whether the time zone of the user is before GMT, after it, or the same.

If the time zone is before GMT, then the value stored in the time_difference value has to be made positive for the dialog box message. That happens on line 4:

```
set time_difference to -time_difference
```

Line 4 uses the unary -, or negation, operator to convert the negative number into a positive number.

Introducing Date Object Properties

So, parsing the date as a string to extract the individual pieces such as the month, weekday, hour, and so on, isn't such a good idea. For these items, you can turn to the properties built into the date object.

class

The first property is class. The value of class is always date. The class property is useful to check whether the value stored in a variable is of class date.

year

The year property contains an integer representing the year of the given date (the value can range from 0 to 9999):

```
year of (current date)
result: 2003
```

month

The month property contains a value representing the month of the given date. The value of the month property isn't a string or a number, rather one of the following 12 constants: January, February, March, April, May, June, July, August, September, October, November, or December.

You can coerce these month constants into strings (which works well for U.S. operating system users), and finally, in AppleScript release 1.9.2 that ships with OS X 10.3 (Panther) and later, you can coerce the month constants into numbers, which is useful if, for example, you want to compare the order of months, like this:

```
December as integer --> 12
```

For example, to get the current month as a number, you'd do this:

```
month of (current date) as integer --> 11
```

weekday

The weekday property can contain one of these constants: Sunday, Monday, Tuesday, Wednesday, Thursday, Friday, or Saturday.

The script shown in Script 5-3 will identify the month containing the first Friday the 13th of a given year.

Script 5-3.

```
set the_year to 2004
repeat with i from 1 to 12
  set date_string to (i as string) & "/13/" & the_year
  set the_date to date date_string
  if weekday of the_date = Friday then
    return month of the_date
  end if
end repeat
```

Notice lines 3 and 4. Line 3 creates a date string with the months changing based on the loop, the day of the month is 13, and the year is specified at the start of the script. In its first trip around the repeat loop, the string will look like this:

```
"1/13/2004"
```

Line 4 converts that string into a date object, and line 5 checks whether the weekday of that date happens to be Friday. If it is Friday, the name of the month is returned.

As an exercise, try modifying the script in Script 5-3 to return a list containing the months of all the Friday the 13ths in a given year. As a hint, you'll need to define a new variable containing an empty list and then add each of the found months to the end of that list. (See Chapter 6 for help on working with lists.)

time

The time property of a date object contains the number of seconds that have passed since midnight of the given date. So for example, the result of this:

```
time of (current date)
```

is 73793. To calculate the time in hours, minutes, and seconds, you have to make some mathematical or comparison operations. You'll do a bunch of them later in the "Doing Math with Dates" section.

NEW FOR OS X 10.4

As of OS X 10.4, you can also coerce the weekday constants into an integer (number), like this:

```
Friday as integer --> 6
```

And you can do it as a part of a script:

```
set todays_weekday to weekday of (current date)
if todays_weekday is in {Saturday, Sunday} then
    display dialog "No work today!"
else if todays_weekday is Friday then
    display dialog "Thank goodness it's Friday!"
else
    set days_left to 6 - (todays_weekday as integer)
    display dialog "Only " & days_left & " more days till the weekend!"
end if
```

date string

The date string property contains a string that represents the date portion of the date object.

The Dates portion of the Formats tab of the International panel of System Preferences, shown in Figure 5-2, determines the exact format of the date string property:

```
date string of (current date)
--result: "Wednesday, July 2, 2003"
```

short date string

This property first came out with AppleScript version 1.9.3, which shipped with Panther.

The short date string property contains a string that represents a short version of the date portion of the date object.

The Dates portion of the Formats tab of the International panel of System Preferences, shown in Figure 5-2, determines the exact format of the short date string property.

time string

The time string property is a string that contains the time portion of the date object.

The Times portion of the Formats tab of the International panel of System Preferences (shown earlier in Figure 5-2) determines the exact format of the time string property. For example, this code:

```
set date_string to "1pm"
time string of date date_string
```

gives the result 1:00:00 PM.

hours

New to OS X 10.4, hours returns the hours of the time of the current date. For example:

```
hours of date "Thursday, November 10, 2005 4:54:04 PM" --> 16
```

The result of this is 16 and not 4 because the value of the hours property is based on the 24-hour clock. You can use hours in a simple if...then loop as follows to give you an alert when it's lunchtime:

```
if (hours of (current date) is 12) then display alert "Lunch!"
```

minutes

This is similar to hours, but this returns the minutes in the time contained in the date object:

```
minutes of date "Thursday, November 10, 2005 4:54:04 PM" --> 54
```

seconds

This is similar to minutes and hours, but this returns the seconds in the time contained in the date object:

```
seconds of date "Thursday, November 10, 2005 4:54:04 PM" --> 4
```

Introducing Useful Date-Related Constants

To assist you in performing date arithmetic, AppleScript was fitted with a few date-related constants. These constants mean you can use them in the script without having to remember their numerical values. Here are the constants and their values:

- minutes = 60
- hours = 3,600
- days = 86,400
- weeks = 604,800

Don't confuse these global variables with the date object properties explained previously. These predefined variables belong to AppleScript itself and can be used anywhere in the script. To get the idea, type the following script, and run it:

```
display dialog weeks
```

This displays the value of the weeks constant, which is 604,800.

So, what exactly do these numbers mean, and what are they good for? They help you perform date-related calculations using specific time spans such as days or weeks.

Let's look at the last two scenarios. If you want to check what the date is going to be three weeks from today, you can use the following script:

```
(current date) + 1814400
```

The number 1814400 is the number of seconds in three weeks. Now, I don't expect you'll want to remember that, let alone figure out the number of seconds in, say, five weeks, three days, and two hours! So since the constant weeks is equal to the number of seconds in one week, you can get the same result like this:

```
(current date) + (weeks * 3)
```

Here are some expressions that return a true value:

```
days * 7 = weeks
24 * hours = days
(date "1/1/2004") - (date "1/1/2003") = 52 * weeks + days
```

So, where are the years and months constants? Well, the number of seconds in a month or in a year isn't fixed; therefore, they can't be defined as constants.

Expect much more fun with these constants in the next section.

Doing Math with Dates

When performing operations on dates, you will be generally performing one of two tasks: subtracting from or adding seconds to a date to get a different date or comparing dates to see whether one is before, after, or equal to another.

Comparing Dates

As with numbers, dates can be compared. You can use the = operator to see whether two dates are equal, for example:

```
set the_date_string to "7/27/2003"
set the_date to date the_date_string
if (current date) = the_date then
  display dialog "happy birthday"
end if
```

You may expect the script, if ran on July 27, 2003, to display a dialog box, right? Wrong—when you run line 2 of the preceding script, the resulting date is `Sunday, July 27, 2003 12:00:00 AM`. This means the script displays the dialog box only if it runs at exactly midnight!

You have a few ways to remedy this problem. One is to compare the day, month, and year separately. You could also take the date portion of the `current date` command and convert that into a date, giving you today's date, at midnight. Script 5-4 shows how that might work.

Script 5-4.

```
set the_date_string to "7/27/2003"
set the_date to date the_date_string
set todays_date_string to date string of (current date)
set todays_date to date todays_date_string
if todays_date = the_date then
  display dialog "happy birthday"
end if
```

Another way to check whether two dates are equal is to get the current date relative to time 0:00:00, like this:

```
set the_date_string to "7/27/2003"
set the_date to date the_date_string
if (date "0:00:00" relative to current date) = the_date then ...
  display dialog "happy birthday"
end if
```

You can also use the `comes after` (same as >) and `comes before` (same as <) operators with dates:

```
set the_date_string to "11/13/2003"
set the_date to date the_date_string
(current date) comes after the_date
```

In this case, you *still* have a chance that you will not get the intended result because any time after midnight on July 27 will be considered after the_date.

As an exercise, modify this code so it also checks that the current date is not more than a day after the_date either and returns true only when both conditions are true. (Hint: you'll need to use an and operator to combine the results of the two comparison tests, and the days constant will be handy too.)

Script 5-5 is an example script that looks at a version of a file both in the server and on the local hard drive. If the hard drive version of the file is newer, the file is copied over to the server version.

Script 5-5.

```
1. set backup_folder_path to "Backup:files:"
2. set file_folder_path to "Macintosh HD:Users:hanaan:Documents:"
3. set file_name to "proposal.pdf"
4. --get modification date of the original file
5. set file_info to info for alias (file_folder_path & file_name)
6. set original_modification_date to modification date of file_info
7. --get modification date of the original file
8. set file_info to info for alias (backup_folder_path & file_name)
```

```
9.  set backup_modification_date to modification date of file_info
10. if original_modification_date comes after ¬
     backup_modification_date then
11.    tell application "Finder"
12.      duplicate file (file_folder_path & file_name) to ¬
13.      folder backup_folder_path with replacing
14.    end tell
15. end if
```

First, as usual, I like to keep paths to files and folders as strings. This allows you to concatenate them and coerce them into alias files or folder references as you want.

In lines 5 and 8 you use the command info for to get file information. In general, this command is great since it's part of Standard Additions, which means you don't have to use it in a Finder tell block.

Calculating Time Differences

When you want to see the time difference between two dates, AppleScript gives you an *integer* result; you can obtain this by using the binary - operator to subtract one date from the other. The resulting integer is the number of seconds between the two dates. At first it looks a bit funny, especially when trying to figure out things such as how long Frank Sinatra lived for:

```
set date_born to date "Sunday, December 12, 1915 12:00:00 AM"
set date_died to date "Thursday, May 14, 1998 12:00:00 AM"
set seconds_lived to date_died - date_born
```

The result (2.6009856E+9) of that script tells you Frank lived for a little more than 2.6 million seconds, but what if you want to make a little more sense out of that number? If you want to know how many minutes, hours, days, or weeks were in that period, you can divide it by the values of AppleScript's built-in minutes, hours, days, and weeks constants. Script 5-6 will ask users for their birthday and tell them how long they have lived.

Script 5-6.

```
1.  set dialog_reply to display dialog "Enter your date of birth" ¬
       default answer "" buttons {"weeks", "days"}
2.  set birthday_string to text returned of dialog_reply
3.  set increment_chosen to button returned of dialog_reply
4.  try
5.    set birthday to date birthday_string
6.  on error
7.    display dialog "Bad date format, birthday boy!"
8.    return
9.  end try
10. set age_in_seconds to (current date) - birthday
11. if increment_chosen = "weeks" then
12.   set age_in_weeks to age_in_seconds div weeks
13.   display dialog "You have been alive " & age_in_weeks & " weeks"
14. else
15.   set age_in_days to age_in_seconds div days
16.   display dialog "You have been alive " & age_in_days & " days"
17. end if
```

This method works well with predictable increments such as weeks or days. However, if you just want to know the age in years, then you are better off comparing the date components: year, month, and day. You have to compare all three, since just comparing years may leave you with the wrong answer. Look at this example:

```
set birthday to date "Wednesday, October 31, 1979 12:00:00 AM"
set today to date "Thursday, July 10, 2003 12:00:00 AM"
set age to (year of today) - (year of birthday)
```

The script returns a result of 24, which is the difference between 1979 and 2003. However, this person won't turn 24 for three more months! You could use the following trick:

```
set birthday to date "Wednesday, October 31, 1979 12:00:00 AM"
set today to date "Thursday, July 10, 2003 12:00:00 AM"
set age_in_days to (today - birthday) / days
--The result is 8653.0
set age_in_years to age_in_days div 365.2425 --23 years
set extra_days to age_in_days mod 365.2425 --252 days
```

Although not perfectly accurate, I used the number 365.2425, which is about the number of days (on average) per year, taking into account leap years.

Another method would be to compare the two dates' year, month, and day values separately. If the month in your birthday comes after the month in today's date, then you have to reduce the year difference by one. However, if the months are the same, then the day has to be compared, and the same rule applies: if the day in your birthday comes after the day in today's date, then you have to reduce the year difference by 1. If the days are the same, then guess what: it's your birthday!

Thanks to the improvements included in OS X 10.3 Panther or higher, you can now compare the month of a date without going to the extreme measures of finding the numerical value of the month using list manipulations, and so on. Script 5-7 shows how you can go about doing that.

Script 5-7.

```
set birthday to date "Wednesday, October 31, 1979 12:00:00 AM"
set today to date "Thursday, July 10, 2003 12:00:00 AM"
set age_in_years to (year of today) - (year of birthday)
if (month of birthday) comes after (month of today) then
    set age_in_years to age_in_years - 1
else if (month of birthday) is equal to (month of today) then
    if (day of birthday) comes after (day of today) then
        set age_in_years to age_in_years - 1
    end if
end if
return age_in_years
```

Another Time-Calculation Example

In the following exercise, you will create a script that allows the user to choose a file and will then tell the user the age of the file in weeks, days, hours, and minutes. You will make handsome use of the four constants you looked at earlier (minutes, hours, days, and weeks) and also look at the mod and div operators.

The script starts by asking the user to pick a file, and then you extract the date from it, as shown in Figure 5-6.

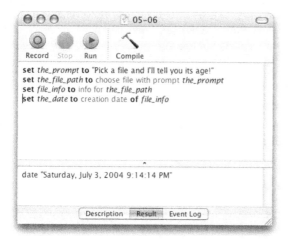

Figure 5-6. *The first four lines of the script have one purpose: to get the creation date of the chosen file.*

Although these four lines will eventually make up the beginning of your script, having to select a new file every time you want to test the rest of the script will slow you down during development. What you want to do is temporarily assign a predefined value to variable the_date as suitable test data. (I've used the value shown in the Result area of the script window in Figure 5-6.) This will allow you to skip the choose file step when you create the script. True, you may want to test your script on more than one date, but having one date for testing can give you consistent results throughout the initial development stage. Don't forget to disable or delete this test code once the script is complete, of course.

In the script shown in Figure 5-7, I have commented the first four lines and inserted a temporary line as described previously.

Figure 5-7. *The script's second stage*

Next, you will get the difference between the creation date and the current date. You do that by simply subtracting the file's creation date, now stored in the the_date variable, from the date returned from the current date command. Figure 5-8 shows this step.

Figure 5-8. *Subtracting a date from another date produces an integer result that is the number of seconds passed between the two dates.*

The result you get is 22031214, which is 22 million and some odd seconds. The rest of the script will convert that number of seconds into a more comfortable format of weeks, days, hours, and minutes.

You start calculating weeks, days, and so on, from the largest down. To figure out how many full weeks fall within that number of seconds, you divide it by the number of seconds in a week using the div operator:

```
22031214 div weeks
 --> 36
```

The result of this statement should be the whole number of weeks. Instead, you could have divided the number of seconds using the normal division operator, /, but then the result wouldn't be a whole number of weeks:

```
22031214 / weeks
--> 36.427271825397
```

You also need to know what the leftover number of seconds is after you extract the number of whole weeks. You get that leftover number by using the mod operator, like this:

```
22031214 mod weeks
--> 258414
```

The result, 258414, is the number of seconds left after you deduct the 36 weeks. Figure 5-9 shows the script with the new statements extracting the number of weeks and the time remaining without the weeks.

Figure 5-9. *The fourth stage of the date script extracts the number of weeks and the leftover seconds.*

Next, you use the same technique to extract the number of days, hours, and minutes from the leftover seconds value. Figure 5-10 shows these lines of code.

Figure 5-10. *Variables have been put in place for the* days, hours, *and* minutes *values.*

The next step is to combine all the variables into a single message you can use to inform the user of the file's age. You do that with simple string concatenation, as shown in Figure 5-11. Also note in Figure 5-11 that I have reinstated the initial script lines that allow the user to choose a file and disabled the temporary line you used for testing.

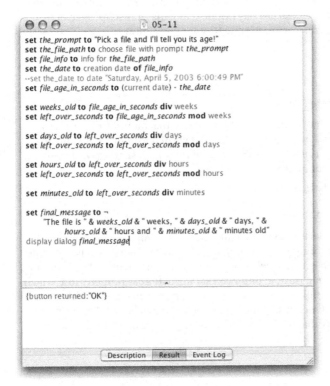

Figure 5-11. *All the values you collected in the script are put into a single string and displayed to the user.*

Using Dates to Get More Dates

As you've just seen, when you test the difference between two dates, you get an integer representing the number of seconds separating the two dates. Similarly, you can add to or subtract any number of seconds from a date and get another date as a result.

This can be useful for several purposes. For instance, you can have a script look in a folder and delete every file that's more than three weeks old. Here is the statement that will test whether to trash the file:

```
if file_modification_date comes before ((current date) - 3 * weeks) then
    --code to delete file...
end if
```

The expression 3 * weeks evaluates as an integer that stands for the number of seconds in three weeks, which you deduct from the current date to obtain the date three weeks ago and compare this against the file's modification date to see whether the file is more than three weeks old. In a script I recently created, I had to figure out the date of the last day of any given month in the current year. Here's how I used date calculations to achieve that: the variable the_month is an integer from 1 to 12, and it stands for the month whose last day I want. (Note that this script specifies months as numbers, not constants, so will work with OS X 10.4 or newer only.)

```
set the_month to 4
set temp_date to current date
set month of temp_date to the_month + 1
set day of temp_date to 1
set last_date_for_month to  temp_date - 1 * days
```

On line 2 you create a new date value for the current year. The actual month and day aren't important because you'll change them. Lines 3 and 4 take advantage of one of the more unusual features of date values: not only can you get the current values of their year, month, day, and so on, properties, you can change them too. For example:

```
set the_date to date "Thursday, July 10, 2003 12:00:00 AM"
set year of the_date to 2008
the_date --> date "Thursday, July 10, 2008 12:00:00 AM"
```

This allows you to perform some clever tricks with date values. First you take the number of the month you want, add 1 to get the month that follows it, and set the date's month property to the result. Don't worry if the current month is 12; AppleScript is smart enough to realize the month 13 really means January of the following year. Next, in line 4 you set the date's day property to 1, which gives you the date of the first day of the following month. You want the day before that, though, so in the final line you deduct the number of seconds in one day. If you want the date to show a specific time, such as midnight, you can specify that too, either by modifying the value of the date's time property:

```
set time of temp_date to 0
```

or by using relative to:

```
date "0:00" relative to last_date_for_month
```

Deleting Old Files

Let's use the same motif as you did earlier with the file's creation date. This time, however, you will look at a file's modification date. You will create a script that looks at a folder's contents and deletes every file that's older than a specified number of weeks. You need to prompt the user to enter the number of weeks and then calculate what the date was that number of weeks ago. You'll call that date expiration_date.

Then, you take the modification date of each file. If it is less than the expiration date, it means the file is more than that number of weeks old and you can delete it. For testing purposes, instead of deleting the file, you can just set its label to red (which requires you to use OS X 10.3 or higher).

Creating the Script

In this script, you will use a property that will hold the path to the folder you want to clean out.

The script will start by checking whether that path is valid, or in other words, whether the folder specified actually exists. If the folder does not exist, the user will be prompted to choose a different one.

Although this is the way the script will start, you will write that portion last. I know that in the previous example you started with the file-choosing portion, commented it out for development purposes, and reinstated it at the end, but don't worry—both ways work. For testing purposes, you should create a folder and put some assorted files in it.

You can create this script in two ways. You can either rely on scripting additions such as info for and list folder or use a scriptable application such as the Finder or System Events, which is very much like scripting the Finder.

Working with files is documented more thoroughly in Chapter 13, but for now you should just note that if you do want to use list folder and info for, you have to get a list of all the items in the folder. You then have to loop through them, testing each one to see whether it's a file and not a folder, and finally you test the date and set the label if needed. This will create a lengthy and slow repeat loop if there are many files to process.

Instead, you can use System Events, which allows you to utilize the whose clause. Using the whose clause, you can condense the entire repeat loop into a single line of code! One problem with System Events, though, is that although it supports deleting files, it does not support labels. For that reason I will write my script using the Finder instead. The final version, which does not use Finder file labels, can be switched back to System Events scripting.

Before you start programming the Finder, you need to have a folder path to work with for testing purposes and an integer indicating the number of weeks old the file has to be in order to be marked. Although specifying the integer isn't a big issue, providing a path may be a bit irritating. It's not that I can't trust myself to spell out the full path, but I really like to make life easy for myself, so I have saved myself some time by creating a little lazy workaround. For the workaround, start a new script, type the command choose folder, and run the script. The choose folder command will force you to choose a folder and return a path to that folder, as shown in Figure 5-12.

Figure 5-12. *The result of the* choose folder *command*

The script in Figure 5-12 is a throwaway script. You can copy the resulting string (without the word alias) to your real script and then close this one without saving.

The script starts with two variables: the_folder_path, which holds the path pointing to the folder you want to clean, and weeks_old, which will be the integer specifying how many weeks old the file has to be to be deleted (or have its label changed in this case). Figure 5-13 shows the initial stage of the script.

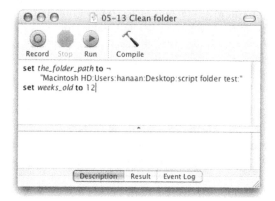

Figure 5-13. *The initial stage of the* clean folder *script*

The next step is to script the part that calculates what the date was *x* weeks ago. I used 12 weeks in my script, which ensures that some of the files in my test folder will be affected and some will not.

The date calculation statement is rather simple, and like many other statements in Apple-Script, you can write it on a single line or spread it out over several lines. The single-line version is as follows:

```
set too_old_date to (current date) - (weeks_old * weeks)
```

The following part of the script will tell the Finder how to treat the old files. Script 5-8 shows how it'll look.

Script 5-8.

```
tell application "Finder"
  tell (every file of folder the_folder_path ¬
    whose creation date comes before too_old_date)
    set label index to 2
  end tell
end tell
```

Notice how you can use a single command to address only the files you want. In the final version of the script, the statement that now says set label index to 2 will simply say delete.

Figure 5-14 shows the script with the added statements.

Adding the User Interaction Portion

The final stage of the script will get the user involved. You need to make sure the user understands what the script will do. You will also allow the user to change the settings stored in script properties, that is, the folder that will be cleaned and the number of weeks.

You start by promoting the first two variables into properties with an initial value. Then, you check the current value of the properties. Remember that even though you assign a value to the properties when you write the script, this value will be changed by user activity, and the new values will stick.

After the properties are declared, the first real part of the script checks whether the folder path is valid and makes sure the number of weeks specified isn't zero or less. If all is well, you show a dialog box reminding the user that the files in a specific folder that are older than a specific date will be deleted. When the OK button is clicked, you will go ahead with the process. Figure 5-15 shows the script with the added properties and conditional statement.

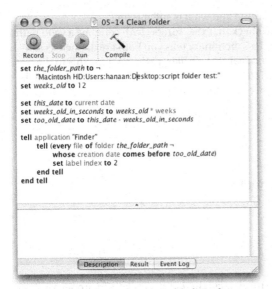

```
set the_folder_path to ¬
    "Macintosh HD:Users:hanaan:Desktop:script folder test:"
set weeks_old to 12

set this_date to current date
set weeks_old_in_seconds to weeks_old * weeks
set too_old_date to this_date - weeks_old_in_seconds

tell application "Finder"
    tell (every file of folder the_folder_path ¬
        whose creation date comes before too_old_date)
        set label index to 2
    end tell
end tell
```

Figure 5-14. *The script with the added Finder statements*

```
property the_folder_path : ""
property weeks_old : 0

--verify folder
tell application "Finder"
    set folder_exists to container the_folder_path exists
end tell
if not folder_exists then
    set the_folder to ¬
        choose folder with prompt "Pick a folder to clean"
    set the_folder_path to the_folder as string
end if
--verify weeks
if weeks_old < 1 then
    set dialog_reply to display dialog ¬
        "Delete files that how how many weeks old?" default answer "5"
    set weeks_old to (text returned of dialog_reply) as integer
end if

set this_date to current date
set weeks_old_in_seconds to weeks_old * weeks
set too_old_date to this_date - weeks_old_in_seconds
set folder_name to name of (info for alias the_folder_path)
set short_date to short date string of too_old_date
set the_message to "Files in folder \"" & folder_name ¬
    & "\" that were created before " & short_date & " will be deleted."
try
    display dialog the_message
on error
    return
end try

tell application "Finder"
    tell (every file of folder the_folder_path ¬
        whose creation date comes before too_old_date)
        set label index to 2
    end tell
end tell
```

Figure 5-15. *The user interaction portion has been added.*

Let's see what was added to the script in this round and what is still missing.

The verify folder section uses the Finder to check that the_folder_path contains a valid path to a folder or a disk (shown in Script 5-9). The Finder's dictionary tells you both are defined as subclasses of container, so you create a reference, container the_folder_path, and pass this to the Finder's exists command, which returns true if a folder or disk exists at that location. If the path is not valid or the Finder finds a file there instead, the command returns false, and the user will be asked to choose a different folder.

Script 5-9.

```
--verify folder
tell application "Finder"
    set folder_exists to container the_folder_path exists
end tell
if not folder_exists then
    set the_folder to ¬
    choose folder with prompt "Pick a folder to clean"
    set the_folder_path to the_folder as string
end if
```

The verify weeks section (shown in Script 5-10) checks whether the weeks_old property is less than 1. What it doesn't do nicely is verify that the user entered a value that can be coerced into an integer. If the user tried to be funny and enter Five, for instance, the script would choke when trying to coerce the result into an integer.

Script 5-10.

```
--verify weeks
if weeks_old < 1 then
    set dialog_reply to display dialog ¬
        "Delete files that are how many weeks old?" default answer "5"
    set weeks_old to (text returned of dialog_reply) as integer
end if
```

The next thing to do is create the message to allow the user to bow out of the deal and cancel. For this you use three new variables: folder_name, short_date, and finally the_message.

The folder's name is obtained using Standard Additions' info for command. This command returns a record containing various labeled values that describe a given file or folder, including its name. The chapter dealing with files thoroughly explains this command.

The short_date variable is assigned the value of the short date string property of the "too old" date, which you figured out earlier in the script.

Finally, the variable the_message collects the last two variables with a bunch of other text into a coherent message used in the display dialog command. Figure 5-16 shows the dialog box.

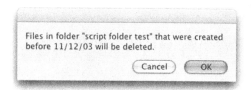

Figure 5-16. *The dialog box informing the user of the action that follows*

You should note a few things about the display dialog statement. First, the entire statement is inside a try block. You do this because if the user clicks Cancel, instead of returning a {button returned:"Cancel"} result, AppleScript raises an error. AppleScript raises a "user cancelled" error, which has an error number of –128 (more about errors in Chapter 15). You can prevent the display dialog command raising this error by using a different button name instead of Cancel, or you can use a try block to trap and handle this error when it occurs. Anyway, if you change the button's name, you have to test which button the user clicked; but in this case, if there's no error, the user must have clicked the OK button.

What follows in Script 5-11 is the part of the script that specifies the variables and displays the dialog box.

Script 5-11.

```
set folder_name to name of (info for alias the_folder_path)
set short_date to short date string of too_old_date
set the_message to "Files in folder \"" & folder_name ¬
    & "\" that were created before " & short_date & " will be deleted."
try
    display dialog the_message
on error
    return
end try
```

▪**Note** Another thing to note is the use of quotes in the dialog box text. If you look at the script, you will notice that in order to include a double quote inside a literal string, you need to escape it; in other words, you need to put a backslash before it, like this: \".

Formatting Time

If you want to display some of your calculated results to the user, which is likely, you'll want to format them a little. The time is returned as seconds, so anything less than about three minutes or so is fairly comprehensible; however, it still looks untidy, and what if the process took 1,519 seconds? You may want to provide the user or system administrator with some more understandable results, such as 0:25:19. Let's look at a handler that will format an integer representing a number of seconds into a nice-looking string.

You'll start by devising a strategy. First you need to break down the total number of seconds into hours, minutes, and seconds and then store these integer values in variables. The variables you'll use are h, m, and s. Although OS X 10.4 adds new hours, minutes, and seconds properties to AppleScript's date class, you'll ensure this script is backward compatible with earlier systems by calculating these numbers yourself. Once you've obtained all three numbers, you'll format them as strings and assemble the finished H:MM:SS-style string.

One more thing you will need to think about: what happens if the number of minutes or seconds is less than ten? You certainly don't want to see 20 seconds formatted as 0:0:20 when you concatenate these single-digit numbers into a string. You will, later, create a little handler that will add a zero before the number if it has only one digit.

Anyway, let's start with calculating the numbers for hours, minutes, and seconds. In building this portion of the script, you will make good use of the mod and div operators. The div operator returns the number of times that the right operand fits into the left operand. In this case, you can use it to extract the minutes from the seconds number. For instance, if the total seconds is 130, you can do this: 130 div 60. The result is 2, which tells you that 60 fits twice into 130. Now what about the rest? If the number 60 fits twice in 130, then the remainder is 10. To get that remainder, you can use the mod operator: 130 mod 60 returns the remainder of 130 div 60. Figure 5-17 shows the start of the script.

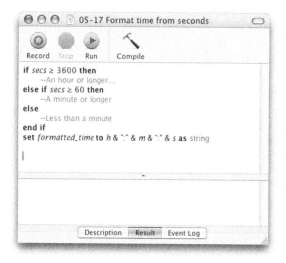

Figure 5-17. *Note the use of* div *and* mod *in figuring out the whole hours and remaining seconds in* secs.

The first step is to define the secs variable that contains the total number of seconds and assign it a value you can use for testing this script:

```
set secs to 10925

set h to secs div 3600
set seconds_left to secs mod 3600
```

Next you calculate the number of whole hours in secs by using the div operator to divide it by 3,600, which is the number of seconds in one hour. You then use the mod operator to calculate the remaining seconds and assign this to the variable seconds_left.

You use the same technique to extract the minutes and seconds values from seconds_left, only this time dividing by 60, which is the number of seconds in one minute. Figure 5-18 shows the script with these lines added:

```
set secs to 10925

set h to secs div 3600
set seconds_left to secs mod 3600
set m to seconds_left div 60
set s to seconds_left mod 60
set formatted_time to (h as string) & ":" & m & ":" & s
```

I've also added a line at the end to format these values as a string. It's not finished yet, but it'll let you check things are working so far. If you run the script now, the result should be 3:2:5, which is the number of hours, minutes, and seconds in 10,295. You should try testing it with a variety of values to see that they all work correctly, such as 0, 4, 60, 130, 3599, and 10925.

Figure 5-18. *The part that calculates minutes and seconds is added.*

Now you get to aesthetics. If you look at the result of the script in Figure 5-19, the string's value indicates three hours, two minutes, and five seconds. Although the result is correct, you would like to display it as 3:02:05. What you need is a little handler that will tack on a 0 before numbers that have one digit, that is, are less than 10.

The handler will take a number, in this case from 0 to 60, and will return a string consisting of two digits. If the number is ten or greater, it will be simply coerced into a string. If it is less than ten, a 0 character will be jammed in front of it. Script 5-12 shows what the handler will look like.

Script 5-12.

```
on make_two_digit(the_number)
    if the_number is less than 10 then
        set the_result to "0" & the_number
    else
        set the_result to the_number as string
    end if
    return the_result
end make_two_digit
```

You could make this handler more sophisticated and allow a number to have any number of digits, but that's up to you. Watch how you call the handler: instead of calling it on a separate line, you just embed the call into the statement that concatenates the hours, minutes, and seconds. Instead of this:

```
set formatted_time to h as string & ":" & m & ":" & s
```

you write the following:

```
set formatted_time to ¬
    (h as string) & ":" & ¬
    make_two_digit(m) & ":" & ¬
    make_two_digit(s)
```

You may also add a 0 to the hours value stored in the variable h, if you want.

The final touch is converting the entire script into a handler. The handler will accept a single integer value and will return a string showing the formatted time. Figure 5-19 shows the final script.

Figure 5-19. *The final script is made out of two handlers. The* format_seconds_to_time *handler takes an integer parameter and returns that number as a string formatted in hours, minutes, and seconds.*

Creating an Alarm Clock Script

The script presented in this section woke me up every morning when I had to be in Boston for a few months. For this script to be useful, it requires two pieces of information: it needs to know what time you want to wake up and which song you want playing when you wake up. You will create a repeat loop for each one for these items, forcing the user to pick a time and then a song. What you'll also do is store these choices in properties so that the user has to pick them only if they need to be changed. Like other scripts you looked at earlier, this one is largely composed of repeat loops. Two large endless repeat loops handle all the user input. Once that's done, the script will wait in a third repeat loop until it's time for the alarm to go off.

If you check the script, you'll see that it has a few other exit repeat statements that lead you out of other endless loops. These are more related to user interaction than to dates. The user interaction trick forces the user to enter a valid value into the dialog box, and this technique is explained in Chapter 12. The basic idea behind it is that you repeat indefinitely, until you manage to convert the user-entered text to the value class you want such as a number or a date, as it is in this case.

Let's go over the script's major parts.

In lines 3–6, you choose the song file and extract the file's name into a variable. Note that you have the user choose a file only if the property `wakeup_tune_file` is set to the default setting of `missing value`. That means these lines will be executed only the first time the script runs. Later in the script, in lines 26, 27, and 28, you give the user a chance to change the song file.

The following part, which starts on line 7 and ends on line 23, allows you to figure out and verify the wakeup time and date. You start this block with line 7, where you simply figure out tomorrow's date:

```
set tomorrow_date to (current date) + (1 * days)
```

You will later apply a new time to the `date` object stored in the `tomorrow_date` variable. This takes place on line 14:

```
set wakeup_date to date requested_time of tomorrow_date
```

Line 8 starts a repeat loop that ends on line 23. The purpose of that loop is to qualify the text the user typed as a valid date. The time the user was asked to provide has to be a time string, such as `"7:00 am"`, that can be converted into a date.

The script first stores the string the user entered in the `requested_time` variable. It then tries to convert this value into a date. This happens in lines 13 through 22. If the conversion is successful, AppleScript will exit the repeat loop (line 15). If the conversion fails, the `try` statement will capture the error, and the `on error` portion of the statement will be executed.

Within this `on error` section, you start a new `try` statement, which is intended to allow the user to cancel. You ask the user to enter a new date, but you give them a way out this time. If the Cancel button is clicked, the `display dialog` command will raise a user-cancelled error. This is caught by the inner `try` block, which executes the `return` statement in its `on error` section, causing the script to stop. This happens on lines 19 and 20.

Line 25 will then collect all the information and will use a self-dismissing dialog box to let the user know when the clock is going to play which song and allow the user to change the tune that'll play, as shown in Figure 5-20.

Figure 5-20. *The script displays a dialog box that allows the user to change the song. The dialog box will give up (close by itself) after 15 seconds.*

Lines 24 through 32 allow the user to change the song file.

Lines 33 through 35 create a loop that makes the script wait until the wakeup time is reached. The `repeat until` loop statement checks to see whether the current date is the same as or later than the wakeup date. If it is, the loop exits automatically; otherwise, it executes the `delay` command to wait ten seconds before trying again.

The final part of the script starts on line 36 and ends on line 43. This tells the QuickTime Player application to open the chosen music file and play it loudly.

Script 5-13 shows the script in its entirety.

Script 5-13.

```
1. property wakeup_tune_file : missing value
2. property requested_time : "7:00"
3. if wakeup_tune_file is missing value then
4.    set wakeup_tune_file to choose file with prompt ¬
         "Pick a wakeup tune" of type {"MPG3"}
5. end if
6. set song_name to name of (info for wakeup_tune_file)
7. set tomorrow_date to (current date) + (1 * days)
8. repeat
9.    set wake_dialog to display dialog ¬
         "Enter time you want to wake up:" default answer ¬
         requested_time buttons {"Stop", "OK"} default button "OK"
10.    if button returned of wake_dialog is "Stop" then return
11.    set requested_time to text returned of wake_dialog
13.    try -- see if time entered is OK
14.       set wakeup_date to date requested_time of tomorrow_date
15.       exit repeat
16.    on error --no good date
17.       try
18.          display dialog "Enter time again"
19.       on error number -128 -- user cancelled error
20.          return
21.       end try
22.    end try
23. end repeat
24. repeat
25.    display dialog "The song \"" & song_name & "\"" & return & ¬
         "should wake you up on: " & return & wakeup_date buttons ¬
         {"Change Song", "OK"} default button "OK" giving up after 15
26.    if button returned of result is "Change song" then
27.       set wakeup_tune_file to choose file with prompt ¬
            "Pick a wakeup tune" of type {"MPG3"}
28.       set song_name to name of (info for wakeup_tune_file)
29.    else
30.       exit repeat
31.    end if
32. end repeat
33. repeat until (current date) ≥ wakeup_date
34.    delay 10
35. end repeat
36. tell application "QuickTime Player"
37.    activate
38.    open wakeup_tune_file
39.    tell movie 1
40.       set sound volume to 300
41.       play
42.    end tell
43. end tell
```

Power Wrap-Up

The following sections summarize the chapter in an intensive reference style. Use these sections to look up facts related to the chapter without the chatter.

Using the date Object

date is a value class intended to store, keep track of, and manipulate dates and times. A value of the date class is an object containing properties that describe the year, month, day, day of week, hour, minute, and second of that date.

The way AppleScript compiles and displays date literals and converts strings into date objects and back depends upon the settings in the International panel of System Preferences.

Specifying Dates

The following statement:

```
date "2/3/06"
```

will compile like this:

```
date "Friday, February 3, 2006 12:00:00 AM"
```

assuming your Mac uses a U.S.-style "month/day/year" date format.

When you use a date string to specify dates, AppleScript is pretty flexible in the values it will accept as a valid date. All the following strings compile properly when converted to dates:

```
date "03/03/03" --> date "Monday, March 3, 2003 12:00:00 AM"
date "0" --> date "Monday, May 31, 2004 12:00:00 AM"

date "5/1/2002" --> date "Wednesday, May 1, 2002 12:00:00 AM"
```

You can also marry a date and a time using the following form:

```
date time_string of date_object
```

For example:

```
date "5:00 PM" of (current date) --> date "Monday, May 31, 2004 5:00:00 PM"
```

AppleScript also allows you to write relative to rather than of if you find it more readable:

```
date "6:30 AM" relative to date "September 1, 2003"
--> date "Monday, September 1, 2003 6:30:00 AM"
```

Using current date

The current date command is a part of Standard Additions. It returns a date object representing the current date and time:

```
current date --> date "Monday, May 31, 2004 12:18:38 PM"
```

When mixing the current date command in a longer statement, AppleScript requires you to place the command in parentheses.

```
set tomorrow_date to (current date) + days
```

Using time to GMT

The time to GMT command returns an integer that stands for the number of seconds between the time zone set on the computer running the script and GMT:

```
time to GMT --> 14400
result / hours --> -4.0
```

Using date object Properties

The date class defines the following properties: year, month, day, weekday, time, hours, minutes, seconds, date string, short date string, and time string.

Examples follow:

```
year of (current date) --> 2004
month of (current date) --> May
```

The following script returns the day of the month:

```
day of (current date) --> 31
```

The following script returns the day of the week as a constant value, not as a string:

```
weekday of (current date) --> Monday
```

The following script returns the number of seconds passed from midnight last night:

```
time of (current date) --> 55956
```

The following script returns the number of minutes in the current time:

```
minutes of (current date) --> 35
```

This number is always from 0 to 59. Using seconds and hours is similar:

```
if (minutes of (current date) > 55) then display alert "Hour is almost over!!"
```

The hours property contains an integer value from 0 to 23 that represents the date object's hour based on a 24-hour clock.

You can alter the date and/or time of a date object by changing the values of its years, months, days, time, hours, minutes, and/or seconds properties:

```
set the_date to date "Monday, September 1, 2003 6:30:00 AM"
set the_date to date "Monday, September 1, 2003 00:00:00 AM"
set year of the_date to 2006
set minutes of the_date to 30
The_date --> date "Friday, September 1, 2006 00:30:00 AM"
```

Using Date Constants

The predefined global variables minutes, hours, days, and weeks help you manipulate dates. Each one has a numerical value, as follows:

- minutes = 60, the number of seconds in a minute
- hours = 3,600, the number of seconds in an hour
- days = 86,400, the number of seconds in a day
- weeks = 604,800, the number of seconds in a week

See earlier sections in this chapter for script samples using these variables.

Comparing Dates

You can use the same operators used to compare numbers to compare dates: =, ≠, >, <, ≥, and ≤. Operations using these operators return a Boolean result. When comparing dates, later dates count as larger. The following is an example:

```
set theDate to "1/1/2000"
(current date) > date theDate --> true
```

You can use the = and ≠ operators to check whether two dates are the same.

Calculating Time Differences

Subtracting one date from another date produces a result that is the number of seconds between the two dates:

```
set theDate to "1/1/2000"
set time_lapse to (current date) - date theDate --> 196961246
set days_passed to round (time_lapse / days) rounding down
```

The result of 196961246 is the number of seconds passed from January 1, 2000, and the time of this writing. The last line returns the number of whole days instead of seconds.

Calculating Earlier and Later Dates

You can add and subtract an integer to/from a date to calculate an earlier or later date. The integer should be the number of seconds between the first date and the second. Doing so is much easier when using the date-related constants minutes, hours, days, and weeks. The result of each of the following script statements is always a new date value.

The following statement returns the date three weeks from today:

```
(current date) + (weeks * 3)
```

The following script returns yesterday's date:

```
(current date) - days
```

CHAPTER 6

■ ■ ■

Working with Lists and Records

Two of AppleScript's most powerful and interesting value classes are `list` and `record`. Unlike simpler values such as numbers and strings, which represent "flat" data, a list or record value is actually a collection of *other* AppleScript values.

Imagine a list as a clothing rack. The rack can be empty, but it can also have a few items hanging from it. The items can be different types, and you can look them over and pick the item you want to wear. A list in AppleScript is a type of rack to which you can add items to, but you can't remove them. When you want to use an item from the rack, you refer to it as "the shirt on the fifth hanger," or you copy it and therefore have a copy of the item in your hand.

Another feature of the clothing rack is that the only way to specify the item you want to work with is by its position on the rack. "Today I will wear the shirt on hanger 3 and the pants on hanger 12, and my socks are on hangers 6 through 7."

It is the same with a list—you can have an empty list that can sit and wait for you to add items to it; you can start with a predefined list, such as a list with the names of the 12 months; and you can obtain a list of values from a scriptable application, such as a list containing the names of all the files in a specific folder, the ID of every text frame on a given page, and so on. Each item in the list can be a value of any class. So, a list is a flexible and expandable storage solution.

AppleScript lists are similar to what are referred to as *arrays* in other programming languages. These arrays, for the most part, allow values only from a single value class. For instance, an array will have only text elements. A list in AppleScript can have text strings, numbers, dates, and, yes, other lists as items.

As you've seen in the scripts in previous chapters, a list literal is written as a pair of curly brackets, with each item separated by a comma. You can see a few examples in Figure 6-1.

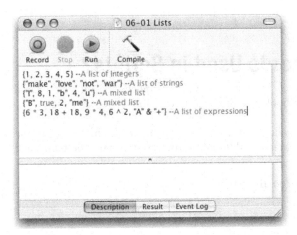

Figure 6-1. *The last list has five items, and each one is an expression.*

So what is a record? Like a list, a record is a collection of values, but in a record every item is labeled. When working with records, you use the label to identify an item. Unlike lists, it's not possible to refer to a record's items by position since their order is not fixed.

If you return to the clothing rack example, in the list scenario I could have grabbed the contents of hanger 3 thinking it was my hat, but if in an earlier script statement I hung my boxer shorts there, things could get pretty interesting. If my hanger rack were a record, I could have just asked the script to hand me my hat, without worrying what position it was in.

A record literal in AppleScript is written as a pair of curly brackets, with each item separated by a comma, but each item now has two parts: the label, which is an identifier, and the value itself. You separate the label and the value with a colon.

One common place you will see records is in the results returned from the `display dialog` command. Figure 6-2 shows a `display dialog` command along with the resulting record.

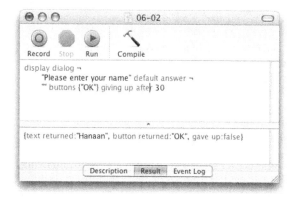

Figure 6-2. *A statement with the* `display dialog` *command, along with the resulting record below*

This record result allows you to extract different bits of information by name—for instance, what text did the user type, and did the dialog box give up?

Note As I'll explain in detail in Chapter 12, the `give up` parameter closes the dialog box if the user hasn't responded in the specified number of seconds.

How Are Lists and Records Used in Scripts?

To understand the difference between the role a list may play in your script versus a record, imagine for a minute your address book. The address book contains information about people: names, numbers, e-mails, and so on.

A list is perfect for storing lots of similar values that you're going to process all in the same way; for example, you might want to create a list of e-mail addresses so you can send a newsletter to each one. Here's an example:

```
{"james12345@cox.net", "jml@myco.com, "etc@mail.com"}
```

Other times you might need to treat all the information for one particular person as a single group, such as when handing it to a script that will generate a selection of letterheads and business cards for that person. Since each value has a different meaning, using a record to group them would make more sense because this allows each value to have a clear, descriptive label:

```
{name: "James Ho", city: "Boston", email: "james12345@cox.net"}
```

More About Lists

One way in which you may want to start with a list is to create an empty one and then add items to it. The syntax you use to create a new list and assign it to a variable is as follows:

```
set my_list to {}
```

The double curly brackets with nothing in between represent the empty list.

You can build up a list of items in two ways, each with advantages and limitations. One is to insert new items at the start or end of an existing list one at a time. The other is to join two lists together using the concatenation operator to produce a new list containing all the items from both. You'll look at each of these techniques next.

Adding Items to a List

You can add new items to an existing list in two ways.

One way is to append an item to the end of a list. To do that, use the following syntax:

```
set end of the_list to the_item
```

For example:

```
set my_list to {1, 2, 3}
set end of my_list to 4
my_list --> {1, 2, 3, 4}
```

Similarly, you can add an item to the beginning of a list, like this:

```
set begining of the_list to the_item
```

For example:

```
set my_list to {1, 2, 3}
set beginning of my_list to 4
my_list --> {4, 1, 2, 3}
```

This approach is the fastest way and the most efficient memory-wise, and since appending an item to the end of a list is one of the more common list-related tasks, you will find yourself using it quite a bit.

Joining Lists

You join lists together with the concatenation operator, &. Whenever you use the concatenation operator to combine two lists, you get a single list as a result, which is made of the items from the list to the left of the operator followed by the items from the list to the right. Script 6-1 shows a few examples of list operations.

Script 6-1.

```
set new_list to {1, 2, 3} & {4 ,5 ,6 }-->  {1, 2, 3, 4 ,5 ,6}
set list_1 to 1 & 2 & 3 & 4 & 5 & 6-->  {1, 2, 3, 4 ,5 ,6}
set list_2 to "a" & "b" & "c" & "d" -->  "abcd"
```

Oops ... what happened here? list_1 ended up as a list, but list_2 ended up as a string.

Remember that the concatenation operator works on strings as well as on lists, and if the left operand in a concatenation is a string, then the result will be a string as well. What you can do is turn the first item into a list, like this:

```
set list_2 to {"a"} & "b" & "c" & "d"
```

This gives you the result {"a", "b", "c", "d"}—that's better.

Replacing Items in a List

Once a list contains one or more items, you can set the value of any item in a list to a different value, like this:

```
set item n of the_list to new_item
```

For example:

```
set my_list to {"A", "B", "C"}
set item 2 of my_list to "Z"
my_list --> {"A", "Z", "C"}
```

Getting Items from a List

Once you have either built a list or returned a list as a result, you need to be able to extract items from it. The example in Script 6-2 creates a list with six items, assigns it to the variable my_list, and then extracts items from it using various references.

Script 6-2.

```
set my_list to {1, 2, 3, 4 ,5 ,6}

item 3 of my_list
--> 3

first item of my_list -- Or "item 1 of my_list"
--> 1

last item of my_list -- Or "item -1 of my_list"
--> 6

middle item of my_list
--> 3
```

You can also use some item to identify a random item in a list, as follows:

```
set winner_name to some item of lottery_entry_list
```

You can also get a range of list items from the same list using the thru keyword:

```
items 2 thru 5 of {1, 2, 3, 4 ,5 ,6}
--result: {2, 3, 4 ,5}
items -2 thru -1 of {"a", "b", "c", "d", "e"}
--result: {"d", "e"}
```

If the script tries to access an item in a list that is out of range, the script will generate a "Can't get reference" error (error –1728), which is a common runtime error:

```
item 4 of {"a", "b", "c}
--error -1728: can't get item 4 of {"a", "b", "c}
```

Getting a range of items from a list is also useful if you want to "delete" an item in a list, because AppleScript doesn't provide a way to delete list items directly. Instead, you have to construct a new list containing all the items except the one you don't want. For example, to "delete" the third item of a five-item list, you get a sublist containing all the items to the left of item 3 and another sublist containing all the items to the right of it and then join these two lists to produce the final four-item list:

```
set the_list to {"a", "b", "c", "d", "e"}
set new_list to (items 1 thru 2 of the_list) ¬
& (items 4 thru 5 of the_list)
new_list --> {"a", "b", "d", "e"}
```

Here's an example of how you'd use this principle in a script:

```
set the_list to {"a", "b", "c", "d", "e"}
set remove_item to 3
set new_list to (items 1 thru (remove_item - 1) of the_list) ¬
& (items (remove_item + 1) thru -1 of the_list)
new_list --> {"a", "b", "d", "e"}
```

This code isn't quite ready for general use, however. Although it works for any item in the middle of the list (2, 3, or 4), it will raise a "Can't get reference" error for the first or last item of the list as it tries to get an item that's out of range:

```
set the_list to {"a", "b", "c", "d", "e"}
set remove_item to 1
set new_list to (items 1 thru (remove_item - 1) of the_list) ¬
    & (items (remove_item + 1) thru -1 of the_list)
--error:
Can't get items 1 thru 0 of {"a", "b", "c", "d", "e"}.
```

So you have to add a conditional statement that checks where the item is in the list and does things differently if it's at the start or end. Check out Figure 6-3 for how you can do that.

Figure 6-3. *Removing an item from a list*

And as usual, I can't leave well enough alone, and I'm compelled to turn this script into a useful little handler that you can use in your own scripts. See Figure 6-4 for the handler version.

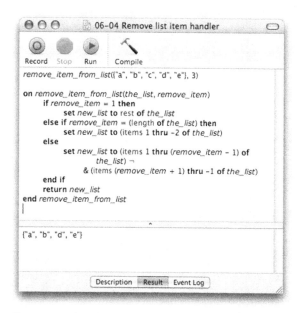

Figure 6-4. *A handler for removing an item from a list*

But even that's not all—there's another way to get the same result, which appears to be much cleaner from a script-writing standpoint. If you look at the solution presented in Figure 6-5, you can see that you can achieve the same result with a couple fewer lines of code.

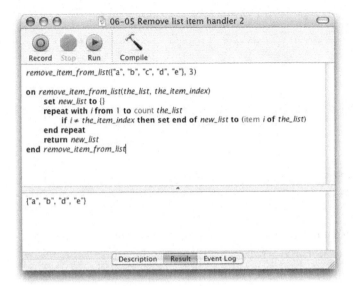

Figure 6-5. *A solution for removing an item from the list appears neater but will take far longer to execute.*

However, don't be fooled—"shorter" doesn't always mean "better." If the handler ends up having to remove an item from a long list, with, say, more than a few dozen items, there will be a significant speed impact. Whenever you can avoid looping, you should. Looping means just that— doing the same thing over and over. And the more loops you do, the longer it takes.

Getting List Items by Class

As you saw earlier, a list can contain items of any value class. But what if you want to extract all the items of a specific class, such as just the strings or integers? AppleScript has an easy way to do this too, which allows you to create a derivative list containing items just of the class you request. All you have to do is ask for the class you want, like so:

```
every string of {"I" ,"Love" ,"You" ,2 , true}
Result: {"I" ,"Love" ,"You"}
```

Setting List Properties

Being a bit more complex than other value classes, the list value class defines a few neat properties that allow you to obtain different kinds of information from lists. The properties are class, length, rest, and reverse. The class property is always the same:

```
class of {1, 2, 3}
```

As you might expect, the result here is always list! That's why I decided to get this one out of the way quickly. The following sections cover the details of the other properties.

length

The length of the list is the number of items it contains. Figure 6-6 shows that the length property of the given four-item list contains the value 4.

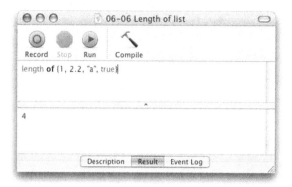

Figure 6-6. *Length of list*

Asking for the `length` property returns the same result as using the `count` command on the list:

```
length of {1 ,2 ,3} = count items of {1 ,2 ,3}
Result: true
```

rest

The value of the `rest` property of a list is a new list containing all the items of the original list except for the first one. So, for example, the result of the following:

```
rest of {"don't", "talk", "while", "you", "eat"}
Result: {"talk", "while", "you", "eat"}
```

is the string `"don't"`, which was the first item in the list and which has been removed.

Also, if a list contains only a single item, the value of its `rest` property is an empty list:

```
rest of {"time"}
Result: {}
```

reverse

As you might guess, the `reverse` property of a list contains a list of the same items, but in reverse order. So the result of the following:

```
reverse of {"start", "middle", "nearly there", "finish"}
```

is as follows:

```
{" finish", "nearly there", "middle", "start"}
```

Treating One List Item at a Time

Often, the purpose of collecting items in a single list is so you can easily go through that list later and do something with each item. Take cooking, for instance: you start by standing in front of the potato bin in the store, going through each potato, and putting only nice ones in your bag—you create a list of potatoes called `nice_potato_list`. Then you go home and peel each potato. You loop through the list, remove defects, if any, and peel each one. You create a list and then loop through it to treat each item—this happens quite a bit in scripting too, so you will explore it in detail in this section.

You can get at every item of a list in succession in two ways, and both ways involve creating a repeat loop. The idea is to repeat an action and have the same variable take on the value of the next item in the list. The example that follows turns the second part of the potato example into a script:

```
set potato_list to {"small potato", "nice potato", "banged potato"}
repeat with the_potato_ref in potato_list
    tell application "kitchen"
        peel the_potato_ref
    end tell
end repeat
```

In the preceding example, you start with a list of potatoes. As you loop through the list, with each repetition the loop variable, the_potato_ref, is assigned a reference to an item of the list, beginning with the first item and ending with the last.

In the next example, the loop variable is a number, not a list item. For that reason, you must add another line that assigns the next list item to your variable:

```
set potato_list to {"small potato", "nice potato", "banged potato"}
repeat with i from 1 to (length of potato_list)
    set the_potato to item i of potato_list
    tell application "kitchen"
        peel the_potato
    end tell
end repeat
```

In this example, the value of the loop variable i is 1, then 2, and then 3; therefore, the variable the_potato is set first to item 1 of potato_list, then to item 2, and then to item 3.

Using List Operations

You already looked at the concatenation operator, &, which can be used to join lists. List objects also support a variety of comparisons and containment operators, which all return a Boolean value.

Comparing Lists

As with any other value class, you can compare two lists to see whether they're equal. You can't, however, check whether a list is greater or smaller than another. For example:

```
{1,2,3} = {1,2,3}
```

The result of this is true, which I know will come as a shock to you!

Using Containment Operators

You can check whether parts of a list match parts of another list. The operators you use to do that are starts with, ends with, contains, and is in. You'll examine these operators in the following sections.

starts with and ends with

The starts with operator can check whether the start of the given list matches another list. The following statements will all return true:

```
{1, 2, 3, 4} starts with {1}
{1, 2, 3, 4} starts with {1, 2}
{1, 2, 3, 4} starts with {1, 2, 3, 4}
```

Now, what if the right operand isn't a list? For example:

```
{1, 2, 3, 4} starts with 1
```

AppleScript's containment operators require that both operands are of the same class, so AppleScript starts by coercing the right operand into a list and then performing the actual containment test as follows:

```
{1, 2, 3, 4} starts with {1}
result: true
```

The next statement, however, returns false:

```
{"abc", "def", "ghi"} starts with "a"
```

This is because in order to see whether a list starts with a specific string or ends with a specific string, you have to use the entire string in the comparison operation. In this case, AppleScript actually checks to see whether the start of the given list matches {"a"}, which it doesn't.

The ends with operator works the same way, but this time compares the end of the given list to see whether it matches another. For example:

```
{1, 2, 3, 4} ends with {3, 4}
--> true
```

contains

You can use the contains operator to see whether a list contains another list:

```
{1, 2, 3, 4, 5} contains {3}
Result: true
{1, 2, 3, 4, 5} contains {3, 4}
Result: true
{1, 2, 3, 4, 5} contains {4, 3}
Result: false
```

The following is an example using the contains operator to check whether the start-up disk contains the essential folders. Of course, you can check that in other ways, but you're currently looking at lists. The script will first create a list using the list folder command and then check to see whether the default folders are part of that list.

```
set folder_list to list folder (path to startup disk)
if folder_list contains "Applications" and ¬
    folder_list contains "Library" and ¬
    folder_list contains "System" and ¬
    folder_list contains "Users" then
    display dialog "Startup disk has all key folders"
else
    display dialog "Startup disk is missing some key folders"
end if
```

The result of line 1 is a list containing the names of every file and folder of the start-up disk. Line 2 then checks to see whether the list contains the four strings "Applications", "Library", "System", and "Users". Since you separated each contains operation with the Boolean operator and, the comparisons operate independently, and the start-up disk gets the OK only if all four values are found.

is contained by

The is contained by operator checks whether the left operand is contained by the list in the right operand. Here's an example:

```
{1, 2} is contained by {1, 2, 3}
Result: true
{"a", "c"} is contained by {"a", "b", "c"}
Result: false
{1, 2} is contained by {1, 2, 3}
Result: true
"treasure" is in (words of "treasure chest")
Result: true --the actual test is: {"treasure"} is in {"treasure", "chest"}
```

As you can see, you can use the term is in instead of is contained by.

More Uses for Containment Operators

Although you will study if statements in much more detail in Chapter 9, I wanted to explain here how using lists can make certain if statements simpler. Sometimes you will want to perform an operation only if a variable has a specific value. This is an easy comparison:

```
if the_variable = "this value" then
  --do something
end if
```

What if, however, the variable can be one of several values? For instance, what if you want to perform an operation only on weekends? The traditional form may look like the following, with a compound if statement separated by the or operator:

```
if the_weekday is Saturday or the_weekday is Sunday then
  --do something
end if
```

Although this is still manageable, imagine if the value could be a choice of 10 to 20 items. This starts to get difficult—lots of or substatements that can be really tricky to manage. The solution is to replace all the is equal operations and their connecting or tests with a single is in test, like this:

```
if the_weekday is in {Saturday, Sunday} then
  --do something
end if
```

Not only is this code simpler to read, but it's also easier to modify later if you need to add and remove items from the list in order to change the conditions.

Here are a few more examples—see whether you can spot which one has the counterintuitive result:

```
{2, 4} is in {1, 5, 2, 4, 3, 0}
--> true
{2, 4} is in {{1, 5}, {2, 4}, {3, 0}}
--> false
{{2, 4}} is in {{1, 5}, {2, 4}, {3, 0}}
--> true
```

The second example is a good reminder that AppleScript's containment operators actually check for a matching range, not a single item. This doesn't matter most of the time, but it can catch you when working with lists of lists unless you're careful.

Using Commands That Produce a List

Asking for multiple elements of an application object or AppleScript value generally returns a list. A simple example of that is as follows:

```
get characters of "abc"
```
Result: {"a", "b", "c"}

Although I will discuss this in much more detail in later chapters that deal with scripting applications, here are a few examples:

```
tell application "Finder"
    set big_file_name_list to name of every file of folder x ¬
        whose size > 10000
end tell
```

The result is a list, each item of which is a string containing a filename. All filenames in the list belong to files larger than 10KB.

Applications can also return lists of references to objects, not only values such as numbers and text. Figure 6-7 shows how InDesign returns a list of references to text frames.

Figure 6-7. *Despite its apparent size, the list contains only six items.*

Another common command that returns a list is the list folder command. This command is a part of Standard Additions, and its purpose is to return a list containing the name of every file and folder in the specified folder.

As shown in Figure 6-8, the list folder command returns a list of filenames only, not the whole path. To do something with the files in the following statements, you have to concatenate the folder path to each of the filenames in the list.

Figure 6-8. *The* list folder *command with its result*

■**Note** The list folder command doesn't distinguish between different types of files, or even between folders, and so on. You can, however, specify whether you want the list to include invisible files.

Figure 6-9 shows a typical set of statements that gets a list of filenames using the list folder command and then repeats in the list and treats each file.

Figure 6-9. *Repeating through filenames in order to process each file*

Understanding Lists of Lists

Let's get fancy now. If list items can belong to any value class, they can also be lists themselves. Not only that, but a list of lists is a useful tool in scripting.

One of the useful features of a list is that it's flexible in length: you can add items to it at will. Imagine a situation, for example, when you work with a list of files in a folder. You don't always know how many files you'll need to handle when the script runs, so instead of putting every filename in its own variable, which wouldn't be practical, you create a single list and make each filename an item in that list.

This is all well and good, but what if you're looking to tackle a more complex problem, such as creating a report that will list all files in a particular folder by file type with a header above each file list displaying the file type? Figure 6-10 and Figure 6-11 show the sample folder and the report the script should generate.

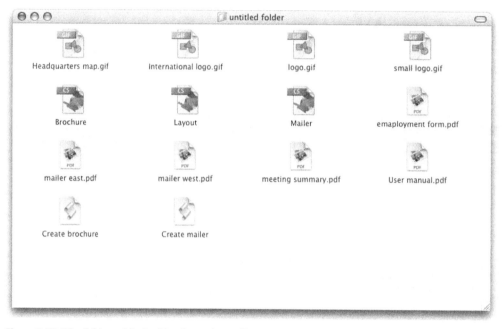

Figure 6-10. *The folder with the files the script will process*

File type: IDd3
***

1. Brochure.indd
2. Layout.indd
3. Mailer.indd

File type: osas
***

1. Create brochure.scpt
2. Create mailer.scpt

File type: PDF
***

1. employment form.pdf
2. mailer east.pdf
3. mailer west.pdf
4. meeting summary.pdf
5. User manual.pdf

File type: GIFf
***

1. Headquarters map.gif
2. International logo.gif
3. logo.gif
4. small logo.gif

Figure 6-11. *The file report the script will create*

To create the folder report, the script will perform several tasks. First it asks the user to select a folder to report on (many scripts that deal with the file system start like that). After the folder has been selected, the script will need to gather the data regarding the files' names and types. After the data has been collected, it has to be formatted and presented.

You can break this process down in more detail:

1. Select the folder to report on, and create a list containing the name of each file in the folder.

2. Create another list containing the file type of each file. This list is in the same order as the filename's list so that when you process the filenames, you can use this file type's list to obtain each file's type. Then create a list of unique file types. This will be used to structure the report.

3. Group filenames that share the same file type together, ready for generating the report. (The result of this operation will be a list of lists.)

4. Assemble the report text, and display the report in TextEdit.

Script 6-3 shows the final script.

Script 6-3.

```
1.  --Select the folder to process and get the names of its files.
2.  set the_folder to (choose folder) as string
3.  set master_file_list to list folder alias the_folder ¬
        without invisibles

4.  --Build the following lists:
5.  --1. a list of unique file types
6.  --2. a list containing the file type of each file
7.  set unique_types_list to {}
8.  set types_of_files_in_master_list to {}
9.  repeat with i from 1 to count master_file_list
10.     set file_name to item i of master_file_list
11.     set file_info to get info for file (the_folder & file_name)
12.     set file_type to file type of file_info
13.     copy file_type to end of types_of_files_in_master_list
14.     if file_type is not in unique_types_list then
15.         copy file_type to end of unique_types_list
16.     end if
17. end repeat

18. --Group file names by type
19. set list_of_file_lists to {}
20. repeat with i from 1 to count unique_types_list
21.     set unique_file_type to item i of unique_types_list
22.     set file_names_with_this_type to {}
23.     repeat with j from 1 to count master_file_list
24.         set the_file_name to item j of master_file_list
25.         set the_file_type to item j of types_of_files_in_master_list
26.         if unique_file_type is equal to the_file_type then
27.             copy the_file_name to end of file_names_with_this_type
28.         end if
29.     end repeat
30.     copy file_names_with_this_type to end of list_of_file_lists
31. end repeat

32. --Format report
33. set report_text to ""
34. repeat with i from 1 to count unique_types_list
35.     set the_type to item i of unique_types_list
36.     set list_of_files_of_that_type to item i of list_of_file_lists
37.     set report_text to report_text & "File type: " & the_type & ¬
            return & "***" & return
38.     repeat with j from 1 to count list_of_files_of_that_type
39.         set the_file_name to item j of list_of_files_of_that_type
40.         set report_text to report_text & j & ". " & ¬
                the_file_name & return
41.     end repeat
42.     set report_text to report_text & return & return
43. end repeat

44. --Show report
45. tell application "TextEdit"
46.     make new document at beginning with properties ¬
            {text:report_text, name:"File Report"}
47. end tell
```

The main challenge in both writing and understanding the script is understanding the different list variables. The script will create and handle four list variables:

```
master_file_list
types_of_files_in_master_list
unique_types_list
list_of_file_lists
```

I'll go over the different lists this script creates and manipulates, explaining each one in turn. The first list is `master_file_list`. This is simply a list where each item is the name of a file in the chosen folder. The number of items then will be the same as the number of files in the folder.

The list `types_of_files_in_master_list` will be a parallel list to `master_file_list`. It'll have the same number of items, but in this list, each item will have a file type. The two lists correspond in that if you take the same item number, one list will contain a file's name, and the other list will contain the file's type. Synchronized lists such as this are a simple way to build database functionality for use at runtime. Figure 6-12 shows the two lists side by side. The windows you're looking at are taken from Late Night Software's Script Debugger, which has some great views of lists, records, and other compound values.

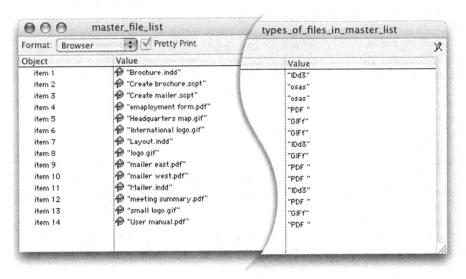

Figure 6-12. *Comparing the lists* `master_file_list` *and* `types_of_files_in_master_list`

In this script you use two separate lists to hold related filename and type data. Another option is to keep related values together by creating a single list of records, where each record holds both the name and type for one file. You'll look at records in the "Working with Records" section of this chapter.

So what is `unique_types_list` responsible for doing? The `unique_types_list` variable holds a list that will have a single item for each unique file type. Since the folder I chose contains files of four different types, the `unique_types_list` list will contain four items by the end.

These three list variables collect their values in the first repeat loop (line 9 to line 17).

Line 19 introduces a new list variable: `list_of_file_lists`. This list will have as many items as `unique_types_list`. Each of the items will be a list in itself, containing the names of the files whose file type is equal to the corresponding item in the `unique_types_list` variable. Figure 6-13 illustrates how the script is designed with corresponding lists.

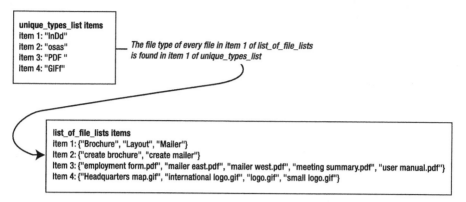

Figure 6-13. *The synchronization between the* unique_types_list *and* list_of_file_lists *variables*

A key to understanding the structure shown previously is that AppleScript isn't aware of any link between the two lists, and it isn't responsible for maintaining their synchronicity. This job is up to you, and it takes planning and confidence; because you are unleashing your script to gather together two separate lists, you are expecting these two lists to match up with each other!

From line 20 to line 31 you actually have a double repeat loop. The outer loop loops through the list of unique file types. The inner loop loops through the entire master_file_list. What happens in the loop is that the type from the type list, which is assigned in line 21 to the variable unique_file_type, is compared with the type of the file, which is assigned in line 25 to the variable the_file_type.

The names of all the files that match the current comparison file type are collected and appended to the list in variable file_names_with_this_type in line 27. Notice the conditional statement between lines 26 and 28.

Line 29 is key. In that line, the list list_of_files_of_that_type is tacked onto the end of the list_of_file_lists variable. Since this happens once in the repeat loop starting on line 20 and since this loop repeats a number of times equal to the number of items in types_list, the result is that the variable list_of_file_lists will have, by the end, as many items as the unique_types_list variable; each item is a list by itself.

In the next portion of the script, a string variable called report_text is created (line 33). This variable slowly gathers the textual data to include in the report. After all, the report isn't a list; it's a string of text.

Following the introduction of the report_text variable, you start another pair of nested repeat loops, this time to extract the data assembled by the loops in the previous section. Here, however, instead of creating the list_of_file_lists variable, you're using the values in it to generate the report.

Now, whenever you look at your script and see that two parts of it are almost identical, you will probably start wondering whether you could have done the job with only one of the parts, slightly rewritten to deal with both jobs. Surely, if you collect the data you need to use in the report in one part of the script and in the other part of the script you use the data you collected, couldn't you have just used the data the first time? Couldn't you just generate the report as you're collecting the information? Wouldn't it be faster and more efficient?

Yes and yes, but this has a catch! Yes, you probably could have just generated the report without creating the elaborate lists. Yes, doing so would have created a faster script. But it's not always better to create faster, smaller, and more efficient scripts.

The same lessons are true for the scripts you write. Sometimes you have to spread them out a little to make it better. The construction of the script clearly distinguishes between data collecting/structuring and the final output of that data, making the code easier to debug and change at a later date if so desired. In addition, now that you have two cool parts to your script, you can actually turn them into handlers and call them something like collect_file_data and create_file_report. Now, they become their own independent self-contained units of code that can be expanded upon and used in other scripts as well—which is much better for code reuse.

See, the construction of that script wasn't an arbitrary attempt to make the script longer and therefore more legible; rather, it was an attempt to separate the input branch (data collecting) from the output branch (report making).

Working with Records

Although lists are wild things with items that only you and God know the meaning of, the values contained in records are meticulously labeled. Figure 6-14 illustrates the differences between a list and a record.

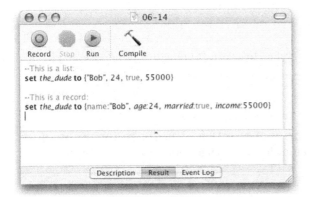

Figure 6-14. *A list and a record, each containing the same four values*

The list contains four items: the values "Bob", 24, true, and 55000. Each value is stored and retrieved according to its index (position) in the list.

The record contains the same four values, only now each one is stored in a property. Each property consists of a label, which is an identifier, and the value. Each value is stored and retrieved using a reference to the property that contains it.

Getting Record Properties

Let's return to the_dude with the following assignment statement:

```
set the_dude to {name: "Bob", age: 24, married: true, income: 55000}
```

To obtain a value from this record, you need to create a reference to the property that holds it. The record's structure—that is, how many properties it has and what their names are—is defined in the script's source code, and the references to access these properties must be defined in the source code too. For example, the_dude's record contains a property with the identifier age, so to obtain the age value from the record, you write a reference to the record's age property—something like age of the_dude, or get age of the_dude if you want to make the get command explicit. If you need to add properties to a record, you can achieve the effect by concatenating two records. Figure 6-15 shows how to get a value from a record.

Figure 6-15. *Getting a value from a record using the property's identifier*

Setting Record Properties

You can use the set command to assign new values to a record's properties. Here's an example:

```
set the_dude to {name: "Bob", age: 24, married: true, income: 55000}
    set income of the_dude to 75000
    return the_dude
result: {name: "Bob", age: 24, married: true, income: 75000}
```

Records are useful when you have a static set of related information that you want to use in a script and you would rather clump that information into a single variable instead of dividing it into multiple single-value variables.

Understanding Records Shortfalls

Although you can count the items in a record, you can't ask to see an item by index. Figure 6-16 shows the error you get when you try to get item 2 of a record.

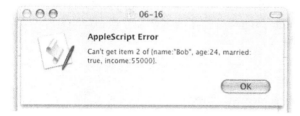

Figure 6-16. *Trying to get an item of a record based on its index (position) generates an error.*

Understanding Where Records Do Make Sense

One area where you'll often meet records lies in application scriptability. Many application objects include a property named properties, which holds a record containing all (or most) of the object's properties. This is convenient when you want to get the values of multiple properties: instead of getting each value one at a time, you just ask the object for the value of its properties property, and it returns them all at once.

Figure 6-17 shows the vast range of information you get when you ask for the properties of a text frame from an InDesign document.

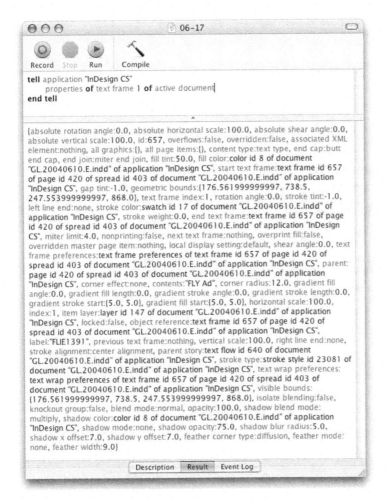

Figure 6-17. *Properties of an InDesign text frame*

Getting the properties of an object as a record is also a useful learning aid while creating the script or familiarizing yourself with the application's object model.

Records make scripts much more legible by allowing complex information to be packaged together in neatly labeled, self-describing structures, and using them will make the job of the poor scripter who'll have to take over your job a wee bit easier (oh, what the heck, let him fry).

Using Commands That Return Records

Being a portable, self-describing set of information, records lend themselves nicely to be used as the result of different commands. The command info for accepts an alias value as a parameter and returns all that file's attributes as a single record. Figure 6-18 shows the attributes of the file Picture 1, which was created by taking a screenshot.

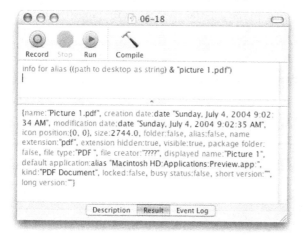

Figure 6-18. *The result of the* info for *command*

Another old favorite is the display dialog command. What's neat about this particular command is that depending on the parameters you give it, the record you get as a result may have different items in it. Figure 6-19 and Figure 6-20 show two different uses of the display dialog command and their respective results.

Figure 6-19. *The* display dialog *command with the* default answer *parameter used*

Figure 6-20. *The* display dialog *command with the* giving up *parameter used*

Notice how the display dialog command returned a different result in Figure 6-19 and Figure 6-20. It is up to you to know what result to expect and how to deal with it when it comes, since you're the one deciding which parameters to include with the command.

Comparing Records

You can test to see whether two records are equal and whether a record contains or is contained by another record.

For instance, the following statement will return true as a result regardless that the properties appear in different order:

```
{model: "Focus", year: "2000"} = {year: "2000", model: "Focus"}
```

Using Records with Containment Operators

You can use containment operators to check whether a record contains another record; see the following examples.

The following two statements return true:

```
{model: "Focus"} is contained by {year: "2000", model: "Focus"}
{year: "2000", model: "Focus"} contains {model: "Focus"}
```

You cannot effectively test whether a record contains a stand-alone value; the value always has to be a part of a record, or the result will always be false:

```
{year: "2000", model: "Focus"} contains "Focus"
```
Result: false

Though the AppleScript Language Guide claims you can use the starts with and ends with containment operators on a record, I've found no evidence of that. It makes sense these operators aren't used, since the order of a record plays no role in comparisons.

Concatenating Records

You concatenate records the same way you concatenate lists: by using the concatenation operator, &. The following is a simple record concatenation operation:

```
{model: "Focus", year: "2000"} & {size: 2}
```

The result of this is {model: "Focus", year: "2000", size: 2}. If the two records contain the same property, the property from the left operand will be used, and the property from the right operand will be discarded:

```
{model: "PB17", RAM: 512} & {RAM: 256, speed: 1000}
```

The result of this is {model: "PB17", RAM: 512, speed: 1000}. Notice how both records contained the property RAM, but the result didn't use that property from the right-side operand.

Coercing Records

Coercing a record into a list creates a list containing the value of each property from the original record. For example:

```
{model: "Focus", year: "2000", size: 2} as list
```

The result of this is {"Focus", "2000", 2}.

Counting Records

Like a list, a record has items that can be counted using either the record's length property or the count command:

```
length of {name: "Bob", age: 24, married: true, income: 55000}
count {name: "Bob", age: 24, married: true, income: 55000}
```

Both of these expressions return 4.

Power Wrap-Up

The following sections summarize the chapter in an intensive reference style. Use these sections to look up facts related to the chapter without the chatter.

Using Lists

The list data type is a container that may contain no items, one item, or multiple items from any other data type. The following list has three items, each one being a string:

```
{"Boston", "Atlanta", "San Francisco"}
```

An empty list looks like this:

```
{}
```

Manipulating Lists

To join two lists, use the concatenation operator, &:

```
set new_list to {"A", "B"} & {1, 2, 3} --> {"A", "B", 1, 2, 3}
```

To add a single item to the end of a list, use this statement:

```
set new_list to {1, 2, 3}
set end of new_list to 4
new_list --> {1, 2, 3, 4}
```

Getting Items from a List

You can get a single item from a list using the item's position in the list, as shown in Script 6-4.

Script 6-4.

```
set city_list to {"Boston", "Atlanta", "San Francisco"}
set the_city to item 2 of city_list --> "Atlanta"
first item of city_list --> "Boston"
last item of city_list --> "San Francisco"
item -1 of city_list --> "San Francisco"
```

You can also get a range of items with the thru term. The result will be a list:

```
set city_list to of ¬
  {"Boston", "Atlanta", "San Francisco", "Providence", "Seattle"}
set the_city to items 2 thru 4 of city_list
--> {"Atlanta", "San Francisco", "Providence"}
```

Using Comparison and Containment Operations with Lists

You can compare two lists or a list with a possible list item:

```
{1, 2, 3} contains 2 --> true
{1, 2, 3} starts with 2 --> false
{1, 2, 3} ends with 3 --> true
```

Using Lists of Lists

A list whose items are also lists is a list of lists:

```
{{1, 2, 3}, {10, 20, 30}, {100, 200, 300}}
```

Setting List Properties

To get the list without the first item, use the rest property:

```
rest of {"Atlanta", "San Francisco", "Providence"}
Result --> {"San Francisco", "Providence"}
```

The reverse property contains the same list in reverse order:

```
reverse of {"Atlanta", "San Francisco", "Providence"}
Result --> {"Providence", "San Francisco", "Atlanta"}
```

Using Records

A record is a list where each item has a descriptive label:

```
{name: "Burt", age: 30, member: true}
```

Record labels can't contain spaces; however, terms defined in an application's dictionary that have a space can be used as a record label in a record created by that application. You can't get a record's item by position, only by label:

```
age of {name: "Burt", age: 30, member: true} --> 30
```

Comparing Records

You can check whether two records are equal:

```
{name: "Burt", age: 30, member: true} = {age: 30, name: "Burt", member: true}
--> true
```

The preceding statement returns true because AppleScript puts no emphasis on the order of the properties in a record.

Using Containment Operators

You can check whether a record contains, or is contained by, another record. The following are a few examples:

```
{name: "Burt", age: 30, member: true} contains {name: "Burt"} --> true
{age: 30, name: "Burt"} is contained by {name: "Burt", age: 30, member: true}
    --> true
```

Concatenating Records

Concatenate records using the concatenation operator.

```
{name: "Burt", age: 30, member: true} & {position: "President"}
--> {name: "Burt", age: 30, member: true, position: "President"}
```

If both operands contain the same property, then the property from the left operand will be used.

Coercing Records

A record can be coerced into a list, in which case the labels will be stripped:

```
{name: "Burt", age: 30, member: true} as list
--> {"Burt", 30, true}
```

CHAPTER 7

■ ■ ■

Giving Commands

If you had to choose a friend from ancient Greece, Socrates may be an interesting choice. You two could sit down for hours reflecting on and discussing the state of things. However, if you needed someone who could get things done—someone in command—you'd probably want to move a few hundred years into the future to ancient Rome and consider someone like Julius Caesar.

AppleScript is more like Caesar than like Socrates; it rules the Mac OS kingdom. When AppleScript talks, most statements it uses contain a command, and after stating most of those, it'll wait there until it gets a result. You use the AppleScript language to get results—to get things done. And since AppleScript has no mouse or keyboard, it gets things done by giving commands.

What Is a Command?

A *command* is an instruction sent to an object, telling it to do something. For example, "Bring me food and wine" is a command; "Invade Gaul" is another.

Mind you, although these sorts of commands may be fine for an emperor's servants and soldiers, I doubt a typical Mac OS X application would understand these particular commands. The kinds of instructions that Mac applications know how to deal with are rather more practical: "Make new document," "Delete every file whose size is 0," "Play the current playlist," and so on. As a Mac user, these are the sorts of tasks that are of particular interest to you, and thanks to the power of AppleScript, you can issue these and many other commands with little effort.

The unit of code that responds to a particular command is called a *command handler*. AppleScript, applications, and scripting additions define their own built-in command handlers, as does AppleScript. Applications, scripting additions, and scripts can define command handlers.

Note The user-defined command handlers you write in your scripts are commonly referred to as *subroutines*, and you can generally talk about "calling a subroutine" rather than "sending a user-defined command to a script." The meanings are essentially the same—it's just less of a mouthful to say.

So far, so good. However, although AppleScript may put all this power at your fingertips, mastering it all can take a bit of time and effort. The commands AppleScript was given at the factory are few—get, set, copy, count, and run—so where does the complexity lie?

Remember that most of the real power of the AppleScript language comes from applications' scriptability. Applications have many more commands built into them. Adobe InDesign, for example, has about 80 of its own commands, FileMaker Pro has about 30, and Adobe Photoshop has more than 65 commands. To control scriptable applications, you have to send them commands—and to do that you first have to learn what commands each application supports and how to use them correctly.

On top of this, scripting additions can define many additional commands that are accessible throughout AppleScript. Mac OS X includes a single general-purpose scripting addition, Standard Additions, as standard. This alone adds several dozen commands for basic tasks such as reading and writing files and displaying simple dialog boxes, and you can add dozens, if not hundreds, more ready-to-use commands by downloading and installing third-party scripting additions available from www.osaxen.com and other AppleScript-related websites.

Finally, as you become more experienced in using AppleScript and as your scripts grow larger and more ambitious, you'll find yourself defining your own commands by adding subroutines to your scripts. Subroutines are great tools for organizing complex code so it's easier to understand and use. They also make it easy to reuse common chunks of code in different parts of your script, or even in other scripts.

The Anatomy of a Command

Commands, even in life, are not just meaningless sentences you throw around. Commands have a purpose: they *make things happen*. One command may create a new document in TextEdit; another may read some data from a file. A third may play a song in Apple iTunes, and a fourth displays a message onscreen. Other commands may create new files or folders, send e-mails, find and replace parts of a string, perform sophisticated mathematical calculations . . . the list of possibilities is almost endless!

So, what makes a successful command?

To start with, even the simplest of commands needs two things: a name and a target (the object to which the command is sent). Commands can also have parameters (values included in the command that will be given to the command's handler to use), and/or return values as their results. Finally, commands may also generate errors when they run into problems they're unable to deal with themselves.

Name

Every command has a name. When an object receives a command, it checks to see whether it contains a command handler of the same name. If it does, it responds to the command by executing the code in that handler. If not . . . well, we'll discuss what happens then later in the chapter (see the "Types of Commands" section).

A command name may be a keyword defined by a scriptable application, scripting addition, or AppleScript itself, or it may be an AppleScript identifier if it's a user-defined command. Here are some examples: run, make, set, display dialog, and find_and_replace.

Target

To have an effect, a command must be sent to an object that knows how to handle it. This is often an application object representing the program you want to script. For example:

```
application "Finder"
```

You can also specify applications by their full path, which is useful if you have several applications with the same name and need to specify one of them in particular:

```
application "Macintosh HD:Applications:AppleScript:Script Editor.app:"
```

You can use AppleScript values such as lists and strings as the target for AppleScript's own count command. For example:

```
count "The quick brown fox jumps over the lazy dog." each word
```

The target can also be a script object, usually your main script. (More advanced scripters may want to target other script objects as well; Chapter 19 explains how and why.)

If you do not specify a particular target for a command, it will be targeted at the current script. Scripting addition commands and user-defined commands are usually sent to the current script, although they can also be sent to other applications if needed. The following example sends a beep command to the current script:

```
beep
```

I'll discuss just what happens to commands when they arrive at the current script a bit later in the chapter (see the "More About Targets" section).

To make targeting commands easier, AppleScript provides the tell block statement, which you already met in Chapter 2. You can use a tell block to specify the default target for all the commands inside the block, which can be especially convenient when you want to direct several commands to the same location.

In the following script, the target for the sleep command is the System Events application:

```
tell application "System Events"
    sleep
end tell
```

Here, the commands activate, enable_logging, and start_next_job are being sent to an application named Job Manager:

```
tell application "Job Manager"
    activate
    enable_logging()
    start_next_job()
end tell
```

Parameters

Many command handlers need additional data in order to do their jobs. The command itself must supply these values—we call these values *parameters*. For example, the following open command has a single parameter, an alias value identifying the file you want to open in TextEdit:

```
tell application "TextEdit"
    open alias "Macintosh HD:Users:hanaan:Notes.txt"
end tell
```

Here's another example, taken from a larger script:

```
set the_list to {"John", "Pete", "Jan", "Mary", "Frank"}
set value_to_find to "Mary"
find_position_in_list(the_list, value_to_find)
```

Here the command find_position_in_list contains two values: a list and a string. As you can see, this command is being targeted at the script itself. In the completed script, a command handler of the same name would take these two values and perform some operations on them—in this case, finding the position of the value Mary in the given list.

You may notice that the find_position_in_list command is written a bit differently than the open command. That's because find_position_in_list is a user-defined command whereas open is defined by an application. Although it may seem a bit odd and inconsistent that one command can have one syntax while another command follows another, this is just one of those quirks that makes AppleScript AppleScript. I'll discuss these differences and how they affect you throughout this chapter.

Result

Many commands return a value as a result. With some commands, usually those that process data, returning a value is their only purpose. For example, the `offset` command (part of the Standard Additions scripting addition) will find the position of one string inside another, returning the index of the first matching substring or 0 if it wasn't found:

```
offset of "cd" in "abcde"
--> 3
```

Other commands may perform an action and then return a useful value related to the outcome of that action. For example, the purpose of the Finder's `make` command is to create a new file or folder on one of your disks, which it does. As an added bonus, it also returns a reference to the object it just created:

```
tell application "Finder"
    make new folder at home
end tell
--> folder "untitled folder" of folder "hanaan" ➥
of folder "Users" of startup disk of application "Finder"
```

This can be useful if you need to refer to that object later in the script: just assign the returned value to a variable, and the next time you need it you can get it from the variable. The following script stores the reference to a newly created folder in a variable named `the_folder` and then uses this value as the parameter to the Finder's `open` command to open the folder on the screen:

```
tell application "Finder"
    set the_folder to make new folder at home
    open the_folder
end tell
```

Errors

Commands that run into unexpected problems while performing a task will usually generate an error to let the script know that something has gone wrong.

For example, unless you happen to have a thousand folders in your home folder, the `open` command in the following script will raise an error when you try to run it:

```
tell application "Finder"
    open folder 1000 of home
end tell
```

The message describing this error is "Finder got an error: Can't get folder 1000 of home." As well as a human-readable description, other information such as error number codes and the value that caused the problem may be provided, allowing scripts to work out what the problem is and try to sort it out themselves, if they want.

I'll discuss errors and error handling in much more detail in Chapter 17.

Types of Commands

One of AppleScript's quirks is that how you write and use commands varies a bit depending on what defines them: applications, scripting additions, scripts, or AppleScript itself. Let's look at the syntax and usage rules for each in turn, noting where the similarities and differences lie.

Application-Defined Commands

Scriptable application commands have a readable, English-like syntax that uses keywords defined by the application's dictionary.

The name of the command is a keyword. For example, iTunes' dictionary defines command names such as open, play, fast forward, quit, and so on. The following script sends the play command to iTunes, telling it to start playing the current track:

```
tell application "iTunes"
    play
end tell
```

Note When you compile a script in Script Editor, AppleScript will highlight each application-defined keyword by coloring it blue (the default setting), making them easier to spot when reading a script. Note that scripting addition–defined keywords and some AppleScript-defined keywords are also styled this way; AppleScript doesn't distinguish between them.

Labeled Parameters

Many application commands also take one or more parameters. Most of these parameters are identified by labels; these are also keywords. For example, the Finder's make command requires you to specify the class of object you want it to create (folder, alias file, window, and so on). To identify this parameter, you give it the label new:

```
tell application "Finder"
    make new folder
end tell
```

An application command can have any number of labeled parameters. Many application commands allow you to omit some or all of its parameters if you want. You can't omit required parameters, though; if you leave one out, the application will report an error when it tries to handle the command.

If you leave out an optional parameter, the command will use a suitable default value instead. For example, you can supply several additional parameters for the Finder's make command if you want; these have the labels at, to, and with properties.

Let's say you want to specify the new folder's name when you create it. You would supply this value via the with properties parameter:

```
tell application "Finder"
    make new folder with properties {name:"Holiday photos"}
end tell
```

The application's dictionary explains what each parameter is for and how and when it should be used. The dictionary definition for the Finder's make command is as follows:

```
make: Make a new element
    make
        new  type class  -- the class of the new element
        at  location reference  -- the location at which to insert the element
        [to  reference]  -- when creating an alias file, the original item to create
                            an alias to or when creating a file viewer window, the
                            target of the window
        [with properties  record]  -- the initial values for the properties of the
                                        element
    Result:    reference  -- to the new object(s)
```

Square brackets indicate optional parameters. (Note that the at parameter in the Finder's make command is actually optional; the Finder's dictionary wrongly lists it as required.)

AppleScript has an extra trick up its sleeve when it comes to a labeled parameter whose value is true or false. When a command parameter is written as a literal true or false directly after the parameter label, AppleScript allows it to be written in a more natural way by using the keywords with and without.

For example, the Finder's duplicate command has an optional replacing Boolean parameter that controls whether it replaces an existing item or raises an error if the destination folder contains an item with the same name as the one it's duplicating. Although you can type the command as follows:

```
tell application "Finder"
    duplicate source_item to destination_folder replacing true
end tell
```

when you compile this script, AppleScript will change it to this:

```
tell application "Finder"
    duplicate source_item to destination_folder with replacing
end tell
```

Similarly, if the replacing parameter is always false, you can write it as this:

```
tell application "Finder"
    duplicate source_item to destination_folder without replacing
end tell
```

You can specify two or more Boolean parameters this way, separating additional parameter labels with commas (the last comma will automatically change to and when you compile):

```
tell application "Finder"
    duplicate source_item to destination_folder ¬
        with replacing, routing suppressed
end tell
```

And you can combine the two forms in the same command when some parameters are true and others are false:

```
tell application "Finder"
    duplicate source_item to destination_folder ¬
        with replacing without routing suppressed
end tell
```

Direct Parameters

Many application commands also take a direct parameter, which immediately follows the command's name and has no label of its own. For example, you've already seen how TextEdit's open command takes an alias value (or list of aliases) as its direct parameter:

```
tell application "TextEdit"
    open alias "Macintosh HD:Users:hanaan:Notes.txt"
end tell
```

Many application commands take a reference as their direct parameter and use this reference to identify the application object (or objects) on which the command should operate. For example:

```
tell application "TextEdit"
    close document 1
end tell
```

```
tell application "Finder"
   move every item of desktop to folder "Old desktop stuff"
end tell
```

AppleScript allows some extra flexibility in how you supply the target reference for these commands. Although you can specify the command's target via its direct parameter, AppleScript also lets you identify the target using a tell block. If the command's direct parameter is omitted, AppleScript will assume that the default target given by the surrounding tell block is the command's intended target:

```
tell application "TextEdit"
   tell document 1
      close --closes document 1
   end tell
end tell

tell application "Finder"
   tell every item of desktop
      move to folder "Old desktop stuff" --moves all the items on the desktop
   end tell
end tell
```

This can be useful for making code easier to read and is particularly convenient when you want to use the same reference as the target for several commands in a row.

Scripting Addition Commands

The syntax rules for scripting addition commands is the same as for application-defined commands: they have keyword-based names, they may have a single direct parameter and any number of labeled parameters, and parameters may be optional or required.

Unlike scriptable applications, scripting additions can't define their own object models: the only objects they can use are AppleScript values: integers, strings, lists, and so on. This means you won't see scripting additions using object references as their parameters like applications do.

You may occasionally meet a scripting addition that uses AppleScript's raw data value class to define its own data types, however. For example, the third-party Satimage scripting addition defines an array of real type that it uses to perform fast mathematical calculations.

Availability

Unlike application commands, scripting additions commands are always available, and you can use them anywhere in your script. AppleScript will automatically recognize all scripting addition–defined keywords whenever you compile a script, as long as you have that scripting addition installed.

For example, the following:

```
display dialog "Hi there!" giving up after 60
```

will compile whether you put it outside or inside an application tell block.

Unlike application commands, where each application is responsible only for handling the commands it defines in its own dictionary (plus a few standard ones such as run, open, quit, get, and set that it may or may not list), *any* application can handle scripting addition commands. How does that work?

Well, anytime you send a command to an application (including the one currently running your script), the application will first check to see whether it defines an application command handler to handle that command. If it doesn't find one, it checks to see whether there is a standard addition that knows how to handle the command, and if there is, then it uses the scripting addition's handler instead.

You can easily see this behavior in action. First create a new document in Script Editor, and then type the following:

```
display dialog "Hi there!"
```

Compile and run this script, and a dialog box will pop up in Script Editor saying "Hi there!" Now wrap the same command in an application tell block as follows:

```
tell application "Finder"
    display dialog "Hi there!"
end tell
```

Now when you run this script, the "Hi there!" dialog box will appear in the Finder instead. This ability to send scripting addition commands to other applications can be useful at times; for example, if your script needs to bring an application to the front in order to work on it, you'll probably prefer that any confirmation, warning, Open and Save File dialog boxes, and so on, appear in front of that application, instead of bouncing the user back and forth between the application you're scripting and the application running your script each time.

Terminology Conflicts

Because scripting addition terminology is available throughout a script, this can sometimes lead to problems when both a scripting addition and a scriptable application use the same keyword to mean different things. If you try to use a scripting addition command inside the tell block of an application with conflicting terminology, this will often result in errors and other strange behaviors.

For example, the Standard Additions scripting addition defines two commands, read and write, that are used to read and write files in AppleScript. Occasionally you will run into a scriptable application that also defines read and write keywords in its dictionary, using them to mean something else. FileMaker Pro is a good example of this: it defines read and write constant values for use in its access properties.

This means the read and write keywords act as Standard Additions commands when used outside a tell application "FileMaker Pro"...end tell block and as FileMaker Pro values when used inside the tell block, where FileMaker Pro's dictionary definitions take precedence. If you try to compile the following script:

```
tell application "FileMaker Pro"
    --some FileMaker Pro code
    write the_text to my_file
    --more FileMaker Pro code
end tell
```

AppleScript refuses to accept the write the_text to my_file line and gives you an error instead: "Expected end of line but found identifier."

The solution in these situations is to move the scripting addition command outside the application tell block where it will compile correctly:

```
tell application "FileMaker Pro"
    --some FileMaker Pro code
end tell
write the_text to my_file
tell application "FileMaker Pro"
    --more FileMaker Pro code
end tell
```

User-Defined Commands

Although AppleScript goes to great trouble to support a really elegant, English-like syntax for application- and scripting addition–defined commands, things are a bit more basic for user-defined commands.

Unlike applications and scripting additions, scripters cannot define new keywords for Apple-Script to use; they can use only those keywords that already exist. Although it is possible to use command name and parameter label keywords for user-defined command handlers (or *subroutines*), the normal approach is to use AppleScript identifiers because these can be defined and used by anyone.

A user-defined command can follow one of two syntaxes. In both cases, the command name is a user-defined identifier, which normally appears in a compiled script as green text (the default Variables and Subroutine Names style in Script Editor's Formatting preferences). However, you can specify the command parameters either by position or by label.

The by-position form is the simpler of the two and consists of a pair of parentheses that immediately follow the command's name, like this:

```
some_command()
```

If the command has parameters, you place them between the parentheses, each one separated by a comment. For example:

```
some_command("Hello", 3, true)
```

The subroutine that receives this command will receive these parameter values in the same order as they were given, so it's up to the command to supply them in the order that the subroutine expects them to be. In the next example, the variable the_phrase in the subroutine shout will contain the string "Hello", number_of_times will contain the number 3, and with_feeling will contain the Boolean value true:

```
shout("Hello", 3, true)

to shout(the_phrase, number_of_times, with_feeling)
    --some statements here
end shout
```

The labeled parameter form is more complex and a bit limited in what you can do with it, so I won't bother going into it here. Chapter 18 goes into much greater detail on user-defined commands and command handlers and on both positional and labeled parameters.

One other significance difference to application and scripting addition commands is that user-defined commands do not support optional parameters. Unfortunately, AppleScript subroutines don't provide a way for you to specify a default value to use when a parameter is missing. That means all parameters are required, and if any are missing, then an error will occur.

AppleScript Commands

The five commands defined by AppleScript all follow the same English-like style used by application-defined commands, with a few minor differences. The run and count commands follow the same pattern as application- and scripting addition–defined commands and are displayed in the application keyword style (blue) when you compile your scripts. The get, set, and copy commands are styled as language keywords (red), however, perhaps to reflect their slightly special nature. They are written as follows (optional portions appear in brackets):

```
[get] some_expression

set some_variable_or_reference to some_expression

copy some_expression to some_variable_or_reference

count some_expression [each some_class]

run [some_expression]
```

You'll look at how these particular commands are used later in the "Standard Commands" section.

More About Targets

Targets are such an important part of using commands that I want to spend a bit more time talking about them—in particular, how to make sure your commands go to the right ones!

Picking the Right Target

For your command to work, the target object needs to know how to handle it. Sending a command to an object that doesn't understand it will (usually) result in an error.

For example, if you send a make command to the Finder, the Finder will recognize it and perform the appropriate action:

```
tell application "Finder"
   make new folder
end tell
--> folder "untitled folder" of folder "Desktop" of folder "hanaan" ➡
of folder "Users" of startup disk of application "Finder"
```

You know that the Finder will recognize this command because make is listed in the Finder's dictionary as one of the commands it understands.

However, if you send the Finder a command such as say_hello, which isn't in its dictionary, you'll get an error instead:

```
tell application "Finder"
   say_hello() --Finder got an error: Can't continue say_hello.
end tell
```

The error message is a bit cryptic but essentially says that the Finder didn't recognize the say_hello command and couldn't pass it to an object that does (hence the "Can't continue" bit).

Likewise, if your script sends say_hello to itself but it doesn't have a say_hello command handler defined, you'll get another error:

```
say_hello() --error: «script» doesn't understand the say_hello message.
```

Again, the error description is a bit cryptic, but as with the previous example, it's just telling you that your command wasn't recognized. «script» is the object the command was sent to—in this case, the current script—and message is just another word for command.

If you add a say_hello subroutine (user-defined command handler) to your script and try again, the say_hello command will now work correctly:

```
say_hello() --this works now, causing the code in the say_hello handler to run

to say_hello()
    display dialog "Hello!"
end say_hello
```

How Script Objects Respond to Commands

Whenever you send a command to a script, the first step it takes is to see whether it contains a handler for handling that command and, if it does, uses that handler to respond to the command. As discussed earlier, when a command cannot be handled, the result is an error. However, script objects don't instantly give up whenever they receive a command that they don't understand themselves; instead, they have one more trick up their sleeve that they always try first.

Run the following script in Script Editor:

```
beep
```

As you can see, you're sending a beep command to the current script, which doesn't contain a beep handler of its own. Yet you hear a beep as intended. How does that work?

The answer is that script objects have the ability to pass commands they don't understand themselves to other objects, in the hope that the next object will know what to do with it. The default parent object to which script objects pass unhandled commands is the AppleScript object, which in turn passes, or *continues*, the command to the current application—in this case, Script Editor—to try answering. After checking its own dictionary for a command named beep (there isn't one), Script Editor checks to see whether there's a scripting addition command by that name (there is; it's in Standard Additions), and at last your command is handled. Whew!

As a scripter, you're hardly aware of all the work that's going on beneath the surface to handle the beep command, but that's the great thing about AppleScript: you don't need to care about these details because it "just works."

Still, it does help to understand a bit about what's really going on in AppleScript's "mind" when you run into problems you weren't expecting, especially when trying to figure out what the heck all those cryptic "Can't continue message" errors are going on about!

Redirecting User-Defined Commands from Inside a tell Application Block

When working with user-defined commands, a common problem that novices run into is trying to use a user-defined command such as find_and_replace inside an application tell block, only to find it doesn't work as intended.

Consider the following example, which is intended to get a list of Finder folder references and then pass each one to a subroutine, process_folder, to be processed:

```
tell application "Finder"
    set folders_list to every folder of home
    repeat with folder_ref in folders_list
        process_folder(folder_ref)
    end repeat
end tell

on process_folder(folder_ref)
    --Do some stuff with the folder here...
end process_folder
```

At first glance this code looks like it ought to work, but as soon as you try to run it, AppleScript reports an error on the fourth line, process_folder(folder_ref), with the cryptic message: "Finder got an error: Can't continue process_folder."

The trouble here is that it's easy to forget that *all* commands within a tell statement will by default be sent to the object the tell block specifies, in this case the Finder application. The user-defined process_folder command may have a different-looking syntax from Finder-defined commands, but it's still a command like any other, so off to the Finder it goes. Unfortunately, applications don't have that special ability to pass ("continue") unhandled commands back to the script, so the Finder has no other choice than to report an error at that point. How then do you make AppleScript send the process_folder command to the current script, not the Finder?

The answer is to use one of AppleScript's special built-in variables, me, as the target for the process_folder command. The value of this variable is the current script. AppleScript provides some flexibility in how you write it (this is nice for making code easier to read), but you'll just look at the most obvious way for now:

```
tell application "Finder"
    set folders_list to every folder of home
    repeat with folder_ref in folders_list
        tell me
            process_folder(folder_ref)
        end tell
    end repeat
end tell
```

As you can see, the tell me block is specifying a new default target for the command inside it. I discuss the me variable in much more detail in Chapter 8.

Standard Commands

The following sections cover the five basic commands defined by AppleScript: get, set, copy, count, and run. All of these commands operate as both AppleScript and application commands. They also have some interesting and unusual characteristics that set them apart from other commands you use, so it's worth spending a little extra time on them.

set

The set command works as both an AppleScript command and an application command.

Using set As an AppleScript Command

In its role as an AppleScript command, set can assign values to variables. (Variables are your script's "memory," allowing you to store values so you can retrieve them for use later.) It can also assign values to the properties of AppleScript records, dates, and scripts and can modify the elements in AppleScript lists.

You'll look at using set as an AppleScript command in much more detail in the next chapter. For now, here is its syntax:

```
set an_AppleScript_variable_or_reference to some_expression
```

And here are a few examples of its use:

```
set first_name to "Jena"

set total_area to the_width * the_height

set end of my_list to new_value
```

The first example assigns a string value, "Jena", to the variable first_name. The second assigns the result of the calculation the_width * the_height to a variable named total_area. The third inserts a value at the end of an AppleScript list.

Using set As an Application Command

In its role as an application command, set is mostly used to assign values to the properties of application objects, although some applications also allow it to modify certain elements (for example, the text elements of a TextEdit document).

Here is its syntax:

```
set an_application_reference to some_expression
```

And here are some examples:

```
tell application "Finder"
    set label index of every folder of desktop to 1
end tell

tell application "TextEdit"
    set word 1 of text of document 1 to "Hello"
end tell

tell application "iTunes"
    set name of the_track to new_name
end tell
```

The first example assigns the value 1 to the label index property of each folder object on the Finder's desktop. The second one will replace the first word element in TextEdit's front document with the string "Hello". The third example will assign a new name to an iTunes track.

How to Tell the Difference

The following is a slightly trickier example containing two set commands. Can you tell which one is an AppleScript command and which one is an application command?

```
tell application "Finder"
    set the_file to file 1 of folder "Jobs"
    set name of the_file to "1.jpg"
end tell
```

Don't let the surrounding tell block fool you: just because a set command is inside or outside an application tell block doesn't tell you whether it's working as an application or AppleScript command. Remember, to figure out whether a set command is an AppleScript or application command, you have to look carefully at the direct parameter (the part after the set keyword and before the to keyword) and work out what it is. If it's a variable or a literal reference identifying a property/element in an AppleScript value, it's behaving as an AppleScript command. If it's a literal reference to a property/element in an application object, it's working as an application command.

In the previous example then, the first set command is actually an AppleScript command, since the part between set and to is an AppleScript variable, the_file, while the second one is working as an application command because it's being used on an application reference, name of file 1 of folder "Jobs" of application "Finder".

Here is another example to try:

```
tell application "Finder"
    set the_list to {}
    set end of the_list to file 1 of folder "Jobs"
end tell
```

Answer: both set commands are working as AppleScript commands.

Here's a third:

```
tell application "Finder"
    set the_file to file 1 of folder "Jobs"
end tell
set name of the_file to "1.jpg"
```

This one is especially tricky, and you'll need to think about what it does when it's run.

Answer: the first set command is an AppleScript command, and the second one is working as an application command—even though it's outside the application tell block!

Remember that AppleScript can often figure out a command's target by examining its parameters. In this case, although the second set command lies outside the Finder tell block, AppleScript realizes its direct parameter is an application reference when executing it, so it sends the set command to the application indicated by this reference: the Finder.

I don't recommend writing code like this yourself, mind you, given how much more awkward it is to read. It does provide a useful reminder that you shouldn't jump to conclusions about what a command will do based solely on whether it's inside or outside a tell block.

copy

The standard copy command is mostly used as an AppleScript command, although it can also operate as various application commands under some conditions.

Using copy As an AppleScript Command

Like the set command, AppleScript's copy command is commonly used to assign values to variables. Here is its syntax:

```
copy some_expression to an_AppleScript_variable_or_reference
```

There is one important difference between using set and copy, however. Although set always puts the original value you give it directly into the variable, when used with certain classes of AppleScript values, the copy command makes an *identical copy* of the original value and puts this in the variable instead.

This duplicating behavior applies only to values that can have editable properties and elements: lists, records, dates, script objects, and AppleScript references created with the a reference to operator. Simpler values such as numbers and strings aren't affected. For example, the following:

```
set variable_1 to "John"
set variable_2 to variable_1
```

and the following:

```
set variable_1 to "John"
copy variable_1 to variable_2
```

do the same thing. The first line assigns a string value, "John", to variable_1. The second line assigns the value of variable_1 to variable_2. Both variables contain the same object.

Similarly, if you use the set command with a list object, like this:

```
set variable_1 to {"John", "Paul", "George", "Pete"}
set variable_2 to variable_1
```

both variables contain the same object.

You can check this by changing one of the items in the list as follows:

```
set variable_1 to {"John", "Paul", "George", "Pete"}
set variable_2 to variable_1
set last item of variable_2 to "Ringo"
```

If you look at the value of variable_2, it's just what you'd expect it to be:

```
variable_2
--> {"John", "Paul", "George", "Ringo"}
```

If you next check the value of variable_1, you'll find it's the same list object:

```
variable_1
--> {"John", "Paul", "George", "Ringo"}
```

This ability to put the same value into multiple variables can be useful in some situations, although it can also easily catch you out if you're not careful! For example, what if you wanted to keep your original list around so you could use it again later in a different part of the script? Obviously, using set is no good for this.

One solution is to make a perfect copy of the original list by using the copy command instead:

```
set variable_1 to {"John", "Paul", "George", "Pete"}
copy variable_1 to variable_2
```

Now each variable contains a different list object. At first, they still look identical:

```
variable_1
--> {"John", "Paul", "George", "Pete"}
```

```
variable_2
--> {"John", "Paul", "George", "Pete"}
```

but you can now safely alter the contents of the second list without affecting the first one:

```
set last item of variable_2 to "Ringo"
```

```
variable_2
--> {"John", "Paul", "George", "Ringo"} --our new list
```

```
variable_1
--> {"John", "Paul", "George", "Pete"} --our original list
```

Lastly, like set, you can use copy to assign an application object or list of objects to an Apple-Script variable. For example, the following:

```
tell application "Finder"
    copy every folder of home to folder_list
end tell
```

is equivalent to the following:

```
tell application "Finder"
    set folder_list to every folder of home
end tell
```

In each case, you're getting a list of folder references from the Finder and assigning this to the variable folder_list.

Using copy As an Application Command

So far you've seen how the standard copy command works when used with AppleScript values and variables. What happens when you start using it as an application command? Here is the syntax:

```
copy some_expression to an_application_reference
```

Once again, the target is a reference to a property or element of an application object (or objects). However, the way this statement actually behaves varies according to how it's used. Most of the time, it behaves the same as an application's set command. For example, when you run the following script:

```
tell application "Finder"
    copy "new name" to name of folder "old name" of desktop
end tell
```

AppleScript will look at the parameters to the copy command and then internally translate it to a standard set command before sending it to the Finder. It's equivalent to writing this:

```
tell application "Finder"
    set name of folder "old name" of desktop to "new name"
end tell
```

How does it know to do this? Well, AppleScript already knows that applications always use set to assign values to their properties. Since the copy command's direct parameter is a string and its to parameter is a property of an application object, it helpfully converts your original instruction to one that the application will understand.

Similarly, the following:

```
tell application "Finder"
    tell desktop
        copy label index of first folder to label index of every folder
    end tell
end tell
```

is equivalent to this:

```
tell application "Finder"
    tell desktop
        set label index of every folder to label index of first folder
    end tell
end tell
```

The one exception is when both parameters are references to the elements of application objects (the to parameter must be a literal reference, though the direct parameter can be either a literal reference or an application reference stored in a variable). In this case, AppleScript will internally translate the copy command into a standard application duplicate command and send that to the application.

Consider the following example:

```
tell application "Finder"
    copy every file of desktop to folder "Archive" of home
end tell
```

The direct parameter is a literal reference to all the desktop object's file elements, and the to parameter is a literal reference to the home folder's Archive folder element. Once again, AppleScript helpfully converts your original instruction into one that the application will understand. Since you're working with an application object's elements here, it figures that what you really want it to do is duplicate those objects to another location. In other words, it's equivalent to writing this:

```
tell application "Finder"
    duplicate every file of desktop to folder "Archive" of home
end tell
```

In both cases, all the files on the Finder's desktop will be copied to a folder named Archive in the user's home folder. Be careful, though; copy acts only as a duplicate command in particular conditions. For example, the following:

```
tell application "Finder"
    set destination_folder to folder "Archive" of home
    duplicate every file of desktop to destination_folder
end tell
```

will duplicate every file of the desktop to the Archive folder the same as before. However, if you now try to substitute copy for duplicate, you will change its behavior:

```
tell application "Finder"
    set destination_folder to folder "Archive" of home
    copy every file of desktop to destination_folder
end tell
```

Now AppleScript will ask the Finder for a list of references to the desktop's files and assign this list to the variable destination_folder instead!

When duplicating application objects, it's probably best if you always use the application's duplicate command and use only copy when you need to make a perfect copy of an AppleScript list, record, or date. That way there's no misunderstandings about what you really meant your script to do.

Other Commands Named "copy"

Note that some applications also define their own copy commands that are completely unrelated to the standard copy command you've looked at here. These application-specific copy commands are used to copy the current selection in that application to the Mac OS's clipboard, similar to choosing Copy from the application's Edit menu. For example:

```
tell application "Adobe Illustrator CS2"
    activate
    copy
end tell
```

This habit of using the same name for different meanings can be a bit confusing at first. Fortunately, you can tell the difference between these application-specific clipboard copying commands and the standard copy...to... command because they don't have a to parameter. Some of these application-specific copy commands take no parameters at all, and others may take a reference to the data to copy as their direct parameter.

In addition, when you compile the script in Script Editor, the clipboard copy command is styled as an application keyword (blue), and the standard copy command is formatted as an AppleScript keyword (red).

You'll explore copying values to the clipboard in Chapter 17.

get

The get command in AppleScript is particularly clever because most of the time when you write and run scripts you're not even aware it's there! It can be written like this:

```
get some_expression
```

where some_expression is a regular AppleScript expression or an application reference. However, the get keyword is almost always optional and is usually left out for simplicity, as you'll see shortly.

The get command can function both as an AppleScript command and as an application command. When used as an AppleScript command, it returns the value of an expression. For example:

```
get 1 + 2
--> 3
```

```
get text 1 thru 3 of "Hi there!"
--> "Hi "
```

When used as an application command, it returns the value of the referenced objects:

```
tell application "TextEdit"
    get front document
end tell
--> document 1 of application "TextEdit"
```

```
tell application "Finder"
    get name of every folder of home
end tell
--> {"Desktop", "Documents", "Library", "Movies", "Music", "Pictures", ...}
```

In both cases, it assigns the resulting value to a special AppleScript variable named result, which is something you'll look at in more detail in the next chapter.

What's unusual about the get command is that you hardly ever have to write it yourself because AppleScript is smart enough to send a get command for you whenever you need one. So, you can just as easily write some of the earlier examples as follows:

```
1 + 2
--> 3
```

```
tell application "TextEdit"
    front document
end tell
--> document 1 of application "TextEdit"
```

and AppleScript will take care of any "getting" for you.

Because get usually works automatically, it's almost always a matter of personal taste whether you write get, although most code looks better if you leave it out. For example, the following:

```
tell application "InDesign CS2"
    set my_doc to document 1
end tell
```

is nicer to read than this:

```
tell application "InDesign CS2"
    set my_doc to get document 1
end tell
```

When Are Explicit gets Necessary?

Although AppleScript is good at working out the right time to send an implicit get command, it doesn't always get it 100% right when dealing with literal references. As a result, sometimes you need to help AppleScript out a bit by adding them yourself.

First you'll look at how AppleScript decides when to send an implicit get when evaluating a literal reference. Consider the following example:

```
tell application "Finder"
    set the_name to name of home
end tell
--> "hanaan"
```

This code actually involves two commands:

- An implicit application command, get, to get the value identified by the literal, reference name of home [of application "Finder"]

- An explicit AppleScript command, set, to assign the result of the right-side expression to the variable the_name

AppleScript looks at the expression on the right side of the set command, sees that it's all a single reference, and sees that the start of the reference identifies an application property, home. So, it bundles the entire reference, sticks it in an implicit get command, and sends it off to the Finder.

The Finder responds by evaluating the reference and returning the value it identifies, in this case a string value containing the name of the current user's Home folder. Lastly, the AppleScript set command assigns this string to the variable the_name. Whew!

So far, so good. As I've said, AppleScript is pretty good at guessing the right thing to do. Now let's look at what happens when it gets it wrong. Let's say that instead of the full folder name, I want only the first three characters of it—"han" instead of "hanaan" in this case. Here's the code I originally wrote to do this:

```
tell application "Finder"
    set abbreviated_name to text 1 thru 3 of name of home
end tell
```

When I try to run this script, however, instead of getting "han," I get an error: "Finder got an error: Can't get text 1 thru 3 of name of home." I know the folder name is at least three characters long, so the problem isn't that I asked for text that was out of range. Something else must have gone wrong, but what?

Well, remember how AppleScript performed its implicit get command in the earlier example? It saw a literal reference that must be intended for the Finder, name of home, so it slurped up the entire reference and sent it off as the direct parameter to a Finder get command. In this example, it's using the same approach, only this time the reference it's sending to the Finder is text 1 thru 3 of name of home.

If you look at the Finder's dictionary, you'll see that the name property defined in the item class (which is where the folder class gets it from) contains a string value (Unicode text, to be precise). Here is the part of the Finder's dictionary you're interested in, the definition for the item class:

```
Class item: An item
Plural form:
    items
Properties:
    name  Unicode text  -- the name of the item
    ...
```

You already know that AppleScript knows how to get text 1 thru 3 of an AppleScript string... and there's the problem: AppleScript may know how to do it, but right now you're not talking to AppleScript; you're talking to the Finder. And the Finder, like all scriptable applications, knows how to manipulate only the contents of *application* objects.

In other words, the Finder knows how to resolve the name of home part OK, since the home property contains a folder object and the folder object contains a name property—all things the Finder understands. However, its dictionary clearly states that the content of the name property is a simple string value, not an application object, and the Finder doesn't know how to manipulate the contents of values such as strings, lists, and records: its object model just doesn't stretch that far.

So, what do you do? You know that the Finder understands a reference such as `name of home`, and you know that AppleScript understands a reference such as `text 1 thru 3 of some_string`. The answer is clear: you need to split the one big reference into two, giving the Finder one and AppleScript the other.

You can write this in a couple of ways. Here's the first way:

```
tell application "Finder"
    set the_name to name of home
    set abbreviated_name to text 1 thru 3 of the_name
end tell
--> "han"
```

Here you put the two references on separate lines. This makes AppleScript send an implicit get command to resolve the reference `name of home` on line 2. Line 3 then takes the resulting string value and asks AppleScript to extract the part you want.

Another way you can do it is insert an explicit get command:

```
tell application "Finder"
    set abbreviated_name to text 1 thru 3 of (get name of home)
end tell
--> "han"
```

Once again, you force AppleScript to send a get command to the application at the exact point you want. You then use AppleScript to deal with the resulting string value. Both approaches are fine, although the second way has the advantage of being a bit more compact.

Another common situation where AppleScript fails to send a get message when you need it to is when using a `repeat with...in...` loop with an application reference. For example:

```
tell application "Finder"
    repeat with folder_ref in every folder of home
        --Do some stuff with folder_ref here
    end repeat
end tell
```

You might expect the previous code to get a list of folder references from the Finder and loop over that. Unfortunately, somebody must have forgotten to tell AppleScript this, because instead it creates a series of references like `item 1 of every folder of home of application "Finder"`, `item 2 of...`, and so on, assigning those to the `folder_ref` variable instead. As you can imagine, these sorts of references can cause all sorts of problems when you try to use them, since instead of identifying a folder in the home folder, each one points to an item (file, folder, and so on) in each of the folders of the home folder—not what you meant at all!

Once again, you need to help AppleScript, persuading it to send the Finder a get command that returns a list of folder references that you can then loop over yourself:

```
tell application "Finder"
    set folders_list to every folder of home
    repeat with folder_ref in folders_list
        --Do some stuff with folder_ref here
    end repeat
end tell
```

Or for example:

```
tell application "Finder"
    repeat with folder_ref in (get every folder of home)
        --Do some stuff with folder_ref here
    end repeat
end tell
```

You'll explore repeat loops and how to use them in much more detail when you get to Chapter 11.

count

The count command returns the number of items in a list, a record, or a string. Here are some simple examples:

```
count "abc"
--> 3

count {"alef", 2, "gimel", "dalet"}
--> 4

count {name: "Jerry", occupation: "singer", outlook: "grateful", status: "dead"}
--> 4
```

If you want the count command to count only those items of a particular class, you can use the optional parameter, each:

```
count {"alef", 2, "gimel", "dalet"} each string
--> 3

count {"alef", 2, "gimel", "dalet"} each number
--> 1
```

Strings, lists, and records also have a length property that allows you to find out the number of items they have:

```
length of {"alef", 2, "gimel", "dalet"}
--> 4
```

Or if you're interested only in a single class of items, you can use a reference like this:

```
length of every number of {"alef", 2, "gimel", "dalet"}
--> 1
```

It's largely a matter of personal preference whether you use AppleScript's count command or an object's length property when dealing with AppleScript values. Just use whichever one you think looks best.

Counting Objects in Applications

AppleScript isn't the only one to define a count command: many scriptable applications also define count commands for counting their own application objects: documents, windows, tracks, folders, and so on. For example, to count the number of pages in the front document in InDesign, use this:

```
tell application "InDesign CS2"
  count document 1 each page
end tell
```

Scriptable applications' count commands almost always use the same syntax and behavior as AppleScript's count command does, so you shouldn't find this confusing. (One rare exception is File-Maker Pro, which for some reason names its labeled parameter class rather than the usual each.)

run

The run command works as both an application command and as an AppleScript command.

Running Applications

You can use the run command with any application. If the application isn't already running, then the run command will cause it to launch. For example:

```
tell application "Script Editor"
    run
end tell
```

You can also write this as follows:

```
run application "Script Editor"
```

If the application is already running, the run command often does nothing, although some applications such as TextEdit may respond by creating a new blank document if they don't already have any documents open.

Note If you want to bring an application to the front, use the activate command instead.

Most of the time, you don't need to include explicit run commands in your scripts because AppleScript is smart enough to launch applications as needed. For example, if you run the following script:

```
tell application "Script Editor"
    make new document
end tell
```

AppleScript will check whether Script Editor is already running before sending it any commands. If it isn't, AppleScript will automatically start the application before sending it the make command.

Running Scripts

When used as an AppleScript command, the run command tells a script to execute its run handler, which may be implicit or explicit. An explicit run handler typically looks like this:

```
on run
    --some statements
end run
```

If there's no explicit run handler, AppleScript will treat all top-level statements (except those declaring global variables, properties, handlers, and named script objects) as the script's implicit run handler.

You'll rarely need to send a script a run command. You might occasionally find it useful if you have a script that needs to load another script from disk and run it. For example, save the following script to your home folder as my script.scpt:

```
property i : 1

say i as string
set i to i + 1
```

Now create a new script as follows (you'll need to alter the file path in the first line to point to your copy of my script.scpt):

```
set my_script to load script (alias "Macintosh HD:Users:hanaan:my script.scpt")
repeat 10 times
    tell my_script to run
end tell
```

When you run this script, it will load a copy of your saved script and run it repeatedly, causing it to count from 1 to 10. (Incidentally, you could also use Standard Additions' run script command to load and run the script in a single step. The only difference with using run script is that it loads a fresh copy of the saved script each time so would say "one" each time.)

Other Common Application Commands

All OS X applications should respond to the following application commands, as well as to the run command discussed in the previous section.

launch

The launch command works similarly to the run command with one difference. When you use the run command to start an application, the application will start normally, and a new blank document will be created. If you use the launch command instead, a new document is not created:

```
tell application "BBEdit 6.5" to launch
```

activate

The activate command brings a running application to the foreground. This is particularly useful when you need to display dialog boxes, attract the user's attention to a particular application, use graphical user interface (GUI) scripting to manipulate its menu bar, and so on. For example:

```
tell application "iTunes" to activate
```

or for example:

```
activate --make sure user can see the following dialog box
display dialog "Enter your name" default answer ""
```

If the application is not already running, AppleScript will start it automatically.

open

All applications that work with files should respond to the open command. The open command takes a single direct parameter: an alias or list of aliases to the files you want opened:

```
tell application "Safari"
    open alias "Macintosh HD:Users:Hanaan:Sites:index.html"
end tell

tell application "Preview"
    open {alias "Macintosh HD:Users:Hanaan:Pictures:birthday_001.jpg", ¬
        alias "Macintosh HD:Users:Hanaan:Pictures:birthday_002.jpg", ¬
        alias "Macintosh HD:Users:Hanaan:Pictures:birthday_004.jpg"}
end tell
```

quit

You can use the `quit` command to tell a running application to quit itself. For example:

```
tell application "Preview" to quit
```

Many applications include an optional `saving` parameter that takes one of three constant values: yes, no, or ask. This allows you to specify how you want documents with unsaved changes to be treated. The following script will tell Tex-Edit Plus to quit, saving any changes to existing files automatically:

```
tell application "Tex-Edit Plus"
    activate
    quit saving yes
end tell
```

Unless you use the no option, if the user has previously unsaved document windows open, Tex-Edit Plus will still display the standard Save Changes Before Closing? dialog box. If you want to make sure the user sees these dialog boxes, you can place an `activate` command before the `quit` command to bring the application to the foreground first. If the user clicks Cancel in the Save dialog box, the application will halt its shutdown procedure, and the `quit` command will generate a "User canceled" error instead.

Application Command Control Statements

Whenever AppleScript sends a command to another application, it usually waits in order to get some communication from the application. This communication may be information your script wanted from the application or an indication that a command has executed properly.

Two issues are related to the exchange between AppleScript and the scriptable application: should AppleScript wait for a response in the first place, and if it does, then just how long should it wait? By default, AppleScript will wait up to two minutes for an application to respond to a command. However, you can use its `considering`, `ignoring`, and `with timeout` control statements to modify this behavior in various ways.

Considering/Ignoring Application Responses

Using the `considering` and `ignoring` control statements with the `application responses` attribute determines whether AppleScript will wait to see what response the application gives after AppleScript sends it a command.

By default, when you use AppleScript to tell an application to do something, AppleScript won't continue the script until it hears from the application. Although this is usually OK, sometimes you want to send a command to an application and move on with the script.

To tell AppleScript not to wait for a response to specific application commands, wrap those commands in an `ignoring application responses` block. Here is its syntax:

```
ignoring application responses
    --one or more application commands go here
end ignoring
```

This will cause AppleScript to ignore any result values or error messages the application may generate in response to the commands within the `ignoring` block. Using this feature means you trust the application to complete the appointed task or you have other ways to verify that the task has been completed.

The following script tells Photoshop to play an action but does not hang around to see how things worked out:

```
tell application "Photoshop CS"
    ignoring application responses
        do script "Convert folder to JPG" from "Conversion action set"
    end ignoring
end tell
```

In the following script, you ask Adobe Acrobat Distiller to distill an Adobe PostScript file. Although you tell AppleScript to ignore any responses from Acrobat, you do check whether the file has been generated before reporting the job completed. In between, the script is free to get on with any other work you may want it to do.

```
set source_posix_path to "/Users/hanaan/Desktop/temp_document.ps"
set destination_hfs_path to "Macintosh HD:Users:hanaan:Desktop:final.pdf"
set destination_posix_path to POSIX path of destination_hfs_path

--Start the distilling process without waiting for it to complete
tell application "Acrobat Distiller 6.0.1"
    ignoring application responses
        Distill sourcePath source_posix_path destinationPath destination_posix_path
    end ignoring
end tell

--While we're waiting for Acrobat to finish distilling the file,
--the script can get on with performing other tasks here...

--Wait here until we know that Acrobat has created the finished PDF file
tell application "Finder"
    repeat until exists file destination_hfs_path
        delay 0.1
    end repeat
end tell

--Perform any remaining operations involving the PDF file here...

display dialog "PDF Done!"
```

Note Yes, Acrobat Distiller 6 now uses the command `Distill` instead of `open`, and if you want it to take you seriously, you better supply it with POSIX paths for source and destination file paths.

One limitation of the previous script is that if Acrobat encounters a serious problem while distilling the file, the script will end up looping forever as it waits for a file that will never appear! (Remember, ignoring application responses ignores application errors too.) You could solve this problem by improving the repeat loop so that as well as checking for the finished PDF file it also looks to see whether an error log file has appeared; if one has, then it can raise an error itself.

considering/ignoring Blocks and Subroutine Calls

When using `considering` and `ignoring` blocks, be aware that they affect *all* the statements that are executed while inside the block. If you call a subroutine from inside a considering/ignoring block, all the statements within that subroutine will be affected too.

In the following script, you call a `delete_file` subroutine that uses the Finder to delete a file, but on this occasion you ask it to delete a nonexisting file. The `delete` command in the subroutine will usually generate an error if the file isn't found, but in this case the `ignoring application responses` block surrounding the subroutine call means AppleScript will ignore this response:

```
ignoring application responses
    delete_file("lala:bimbim")
end ignoring

on delete_file(file_path)
    tell application "Finder"
        delete file file_path
    end tell
end delete_file
```

You may find this ability to change the `considering`/`ignoring` behavior of the subroutine code from outside the subroutine useful in some situations. Be careful, though: it could also cause unexpected problems if the code in your subroutine depends on specific `considering`/`ignoring` settings to do their job correctly. (Incidentally, this is true when using any `considering`/`ignoring` attribute, not just `application responses`.)

If you want to override the current `ignoring application responses` behavior while executing the `delete_file` subroutine, you can wrap the `delete_file` call in a `considering application responses` block as follows:

```
ignoring application responses
    considering application responses
        delete_file("lala:bimbim")
    end considering
end ignoring
```

If you want to guarantee that the code in your subroutine always considers application responses, even if called from inside an `ignoring application responses` block, you may prefer to put the `considering` block inside it instead:

```
on delete_file(file_path)
    considering application responses
        tell application "Finder"
            delete file file_path --this command's response will always be considered
        end tell
    end considering
end delete_file
```

Timeouts

By default, when AppleScript sends a command to an application, it waits 120 seconds for a response. If the application returns no response by then, AppleScript throws a timeout error. You can use the `with timeout` control statement to tell AppleScript to wait for a longer or shorter amount of time when executing certain commands. This is especially useful when you have to send an application a time-consuming command that is likely to take more than two minutes to complete.

For example, the following script is intended to back up the entire start-up disk:

```
tell application "Finder"
    duplicate disk "Macintosh HD" to folder "BU" ¬
        of disk "Backup Volume" replacing yes
end tell
```

With so much data to copy, however, the Finder is bound to take longer than 120 seconds to perform this duplicate command. Figure 7-1 shows the timeout error generated by the application script running the preceding script.

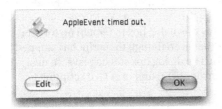

Figure 7-1. *The timeout error generated by a command that took longer than the allowed timeout, 120 seconds by default*

It is important to understand that even though AppleScript gives up on the application and throws a timeout error, the application will continue to perform the task assigned to it. In the case of the preceding script where you duplicate the entire hard drive to the backup folder, the duplication will still continue despite that the script that initiated the command has already errored out and stopped.

Setting a New Timeout Value

You can increase (or decrease) the maximum amount of time AppleScript allows an application to perform a command with the with timeout control statement. Here is its syntax:

```
with timeout of some_integer seconds
   --one or more application commands here...
end timeout
```

For example, to allow up to five minutes for a command to complete, you would use this:

```
with timeout of 300 seconds
   --your application commands here...
end timeout
```

You can include any statements in a with timeout block, but only application commands will be affected by it. As with considering and ignoring blocks, if you call a subroutine from inside a with timeout block, the code in that subroutine will also be affected.

The following script allows up to 20 minutes for a script to resize an image in Photoshop:

```
with timeout of (20 * minutes) seconds
   tell application "Photoshop CS"
      tell document 1
         resize image resolution 120 resample method none
      end tell
   end tell
end timeout
```

If you want, you can tell AppleScript to wait virtually forever for a command response just by specifying a really large number of seconds in the with timeout block. Most times, however, you'll want to set a more reasonable upper limit so your script isn't left waiting forever if some sort of holdup problem occurs.

Trapping Timeout Errors

Even though you can use with timeout to allow extra time for a command to complete, sometimes the command takes longer than you're willing to wait for it. In this case, you may want to provide extra protection by placing the with timeout block inside a try statement that catches and handles any timeout errors that occur.

The following script lets the user choose a file. It will allow the dialog box to remain up for one hour before automatically exiting the script. The problem is that even though the script has stopped because of the choose file command timing out, the Choose File dialog box still displays. To deal with this issue, it uses a try block to trap the timeout error (error –1712) and uses GUI scripting to gracefully dismiss the dialog box.

```
1. try
2.     with timeout of 3600 seconds
3.         tell application "Finder"
4.             choose file
5.         end tell
6.     end timeout
7. on error number -1712
8.     tell application "Finder" to activate
9.     tell application "System Events"
10.         tell application process "Finder"
11.             click button "Cancel" of window "Choose a File"
12.         end tell
13.     end tell
14.     return
15. end try
```

CHAPTER 8

■ ■ ■

Working with Variables

In AppleScript, as in many other programming languages, variables consist of two parts: the identifier and the value. The *identifier* is a name that describes the value, and the *value* is what you actually want to use. Here's an example:

```
set first_name to "Sponge"
```

This example assigns the value "Sponge" to the variable first_name. If you want to either retrieve the value of that variable or assign a different value to it somewhere else in the script, you use the identifier first_name. When the script is run, AppleScript evaluates the identifier and returns the variable's value.

Picture variables as a container on your desk. The container has a label on it that says "today's newspaper." What would you imagine you would find in this container? You would surely expect to find today's newspaper. Will that be the case every day, though? Well, yes and no. As the new newspaper is delivered each day, the size, shape, and layout may be the same, but the information will not. When asked what's in the container on January 10, 2006, you can either say "the newspaper from January 10, 2006" or say "today's newspaper." The former will be accurate only in a certain case and will be liable to change, so it's like a specific variable value. The latter will always be the same, so it's more like the variable itself. But the value contained within the newspaper is what you really care about—the information itself—rather than the description (it's a newspaper). This is also true of variables when programming.

Understanding How Variables Are Created

You can define three kinds of variables in AppleScript: local variables, properties, and global variables. I'll discuss the similarities and differences between these throughout this chapter, but I'll start here with how they're created.

The type of variable you'll use most is a local variable. Local variables are normally defined automatically the first time you assign a value to them using the set and copy commands, although you can declare them separately using the local statement. For example, the following script will implicitly declare i and j as local variables and assign them the values 0 and 1, respectively:

```
set i to 0
copy 1 to j
```

Since variables i and j have not been previously defined, AppleScript automatically makes them local variables by default. Alternatively, you can explicitly declare i and j as local variables first and assign them values later:

```
local i, j
```

Another way to create a variable is by declaring a property or a global variable. The most obvious difference between the two is that you don't assign a value to a global variable when declaring it, but you do assign an initial value to a property.

You define a property like this:

```
property main_folder_path : path to applications folder
```

You define a global variable like this:

```
global main_folder_path
```

It is important to understand that although you can implicitly declare a local variable anywhere in the script by simply assigning a value to it, you have to explicitly declare global variables and script properties. These declarations must appear before the code that uses them in order to work correctly. I recommend always putting them at the top of the script before all your other code, because this also makes them easy to see. Script 8-1 shows the start of a well-structured script.

Script 8-1.

```
property identifier1:"starting value"
property identifier2:"starting value"
global identifier3, identifier4

on run
    local identifier5, identifier6 -- optional declarations
    -- other statements
end run

-- other handlers
```

You'll explore some other differences between locals, properties, and globals throughout this chapter.

Naming Variables

You define variables when you write the script. Variable identifiers, the actual labels you use to assign or get a value from a variable, are words you make up, and you don't have to follow any syntax rules in order for your variables to work. Once you consider all the basic no-nos in variable naming, you are pretty much on your own. What's good is that you don't usually have to wait until you run your script to discover that you can't use a variable name. For the most part, the script will simply not compile since the AppleScript compiler will detect and reject invalid names.

Basic Variable Naming Rules

The basic rules for naming variables are as follows:

- The variable name must start with an alphabetic character (a–z, A–Z) or an underscore (_).
- It may contain alphabetic characters (a–z, A–Z), digits (0–9), and underscores (_).

You'll also want to avoid certain characters when deciding on a name, or identifier, for a variable, specified in the following three rules. The first rule is easy to learn because if you break it, the script will simply not compile.

Rule 1: An identifier can't start with a digit or contain spaces, dashes, or any other nonalphanumeric characters.

Here are some valid identifiers:

```
my_total_solitare_score
x
RatioBetweenTaxibleIncomeAndCharitableContribution
And some bad ones:
2_times_dose
price*tax
first&last
```

The following two rules are a bit more problematic since they will reveal themselves as problems only during runtime. Even then, though, they're easy to detect and fix.

Rule 2: An identifier can't be the same as a reserved word.

AppleScript has quite a few words it reserves for its own use, including if, then, data, log, month, file, and so on. Trying to use a reserved word as a variable will generate an error when the script tries to compile.

In addition to the words reserved by the AppleScript language, every scriptable application or scripting addition can reserve its own words. For example, FileMaker Pro reserves the words database, record, field, cell, and more.

Note AppleScript also defines several preset variables as constants, such as pi, space, hours, and so on. These are different from reserved words. Trying to set the value of a predefined variable has the potential of messing up your script, and trying to use a reserved word as a variable will generate an error when the script tries to compile. Although AppleScript won't actually prevent you from changing the value of these constants, you should avoid doing so because it will make your code more confusing to follow and increase the risk of bugs.

Instead of listing all these words just for the purpose of remembering not to use them, you can simply use AppleScript's built-in syntax coloring. In the Apple Script Editor and third-party script editors, you can use the preferences to set AppleScript's syntax coloring and formatting. These attributes, as shown in Figure 8-1, are per-user preferences, which means if you use more than one AppleScript editor, the changes will affect them all.

Figure 8-1. *Script Editor allows you to set AppleScript's syntax coloring.*

Anyway, notice the categories Language Keywords, Application Keywords, and Variables and Subroutines. Out of the box, the coloring is that language keywords are red, application keywords are blue, and user-defined variable and subroutine names are green.

If you change these settings, you will notice right after compiling your script whether the variables you typed have the color and formatting you assigned to the Variables and Subroutines category.

Rule 3: You can't use a handler's identifier as a separate variable identifier.

In your own scripts, you assign names to both variables and subroutines, so not repeating the same name shouldn't be hard, although AppleScript won't be any help in detecting this issue.

The trouble with using the same identifier for a variable and a handler is that starting from the time you assign a value to the variable, calling the handler will cause an error.

As a rule, I always name my variables with word caps and name my handlers with underscore separators, like this:

```
this_is_my_handler(argumentPassedToIt)
```

Safe Naming Tactics

Try to make your variables and subroutine names stand out. I always use at least two words in my variable identifiers, such as in document_file. This way I can tell them apart from other elements, and I avoid inadvertently using a reserved word (reserved words are rarely compound words). The syntax coloring is a big help, too.

Break All the Rules!

OK, so now that you've recited all the rules and know them perfectly, I'll give you the invisibility cloak that will allow you to bypass all those rules! Use spaces, start with a number, and use reserved words—anything you want!

All you have to do is wrap your identifier in a pair of pipes, like this:

```
|my variable|
```

This shields the variable from any naming rules. Doing this allows you to use spaces, use special characters, start the name with a number (inside the pipes), and so on. Here are some legal names:

```
|#$%@ That!|
|        |
|2b or not 2b|
```

When AppleScript decompiles a previously compiled script to source code, it will automatically apply pipes to an identifier if that identifier would otherwise conflict with an application or scripting addition–defined keyword.

Understanding How Variables Live and Die

So far you know that assigning a value to a variable allows you to retrieve that value later. That is true to some extent, but as your scripts become more sophisticated, you will need to understand where variables are useful, why they're useful, and for how long they're useful.

As stated earlier in the chapter, when you simply assign a value to a variable, you are actually getting AppleScript to perform two actions: declaring the variable and assigning a value to it.

The variable that was created, however, has been declared as a local variable, by default.

Local variables are simple to understand until you start creating your own handlers. Once handlers enter the scene, you must also consider the *scope* of the variables—that is, which parts of the script can see them. Examine Script 8-2 to better understand what I mean:

Script 8-2.

```
set user_name to "Ben"
display dialog ("Hello " & user_name & "!")
```

When you run the script, AppleScript displays the dialog box shown in Figure 8-2.

Figure 8-2. *Hello Ben! dialog box*

Line 1 of the script declared the local variable user_name and then assigned the value "Ben" to it. Line 2 created a dialog box displaying the value stored in the variable—so far, so good.

What you'll do now is put the display dialog statement from line 2 in the preceding script into a subroutine. Script 8-3 shows what it looks like.

Script 8-3.

```
set user_name to "Ben"
say_hello()

on say_hello()
   display dialog ("Hello " & user_name & "!")
end say_hello
```

The subroutine is declared between lines 3 and 5. It is called to action on line 2.

If you try to run the preceding script, you will get the error shown in Figure 8-3.

Figure 8-3. *Apparently, the variable* user_name *has not been declared.*

So, what went wrong? You specifically assigned a value to the user_name variable in line 1, so why did line 4 raise the error it did? This is because the local variable was visible in the body of the script but *not* to the code inside the say_hello handler.

The scope of a local variable—since you didn't specify otherwise, user_name is a local variable—is the current handler only.

What handler is that exactly? It's the run handler. The lines that declare (start and end) the run handler can be left out, but even without the declaration, any code that is not a property or a handler is part of the implied run handler. The script could have explicitly specified the run handler, as shown in Figure 8-4.

Figure 8-4. *The* run *handler, which was implied in Script 8-3, is described explicitly here.*

Now, looking at the script in Figure 8-4, things come into focus a bit. The user_name variable was declared in the run handler and therefore not recognized in the say_hello handler.

You can remedy this problem with a couple of solutions. You can either tell the handler what the value is by passing it as a parameter to the say_hello command or make the variable visible to all handlers in the script by declaring it as a property or global variable.

Up front, the second choice sounds simpler—why pass a value as a parameter to multiple handlers when you can just make it directly visible to all handlers? One good reason is portability. This may not seem like a big deal at the start, but later, when you try to take those brilliant handlers you created and use them in a different script, figuring out which global variables or properties are used by the handler may just drive you out of your mind. You may also start with code that is part of the run handler, then choose to move it to a handler, and finally, when the script gets too long, choose to port some of the handlers to a separate library.

Variables make handlers harder to test and debug individually. If a handler uses only local variables, it should be easy to call it directly, passing it test data as parameters and checking that the value it returns is correct. If a handler uses global variables too, you'll also need to assign test data to those before calling the handler and then check that their values are still correct once the handler is finished.

Perhaps the best reason to avoid gratuitous globals, however, is that they make your scripts harder to read and understand. One of the big advantages of handlers is that they allow you to split up a large, complex script into lots of small, simple units that can be understood and worked on independently while ignoring the rest. Because a global variable is visible to every part of the script, any part of the script is able to use or change it at any time. This means to work safely on a piece of code that uses global variables, you must also pay close attention to all the other parts of the script that share this variable—that's a lot of extra factors to juggle in your head when you want to concentrate on just one.

Although these issues aren't so important in small scripts where the code is simple and easy to understand all at once, in a large script with many handlers and lots of global variables, keeping track of all these extra connections and making sure they all interact correctly can be a lot of extra work.

Despite a handler needing many variables in some cases, it is almost always better to pass them as arguments rather than declare them as global variables, especially if the reason for it is blatant laziness. I'll discuss the justifiable exceptions to this rule later in the "Understanding When Properties Are a Good Idea" section.

Passing Values to Handlers

Although AppleScript handlers are always the same wherever you go, you can specify their parameters in a couple of ways: by position or by label. Chapter 17 covers the two methods extensively, but this section contains a primer for passing values by position, which is the simpler way. To pass a value to a handler, you include it in the parentheses following the handler name. Figure 8-5 shows how you can do that.

Figure 8-5. *Passing the value of the* user_name *variable to the* say_hello *handler*

What's important to understand is that what you're passing isn't the variable but rather the value of the variable. The user_name variable in the run handler is completely separate from the one in the say_hello handler—that is, they're two different variables that just happen to use the same name. The two scripts shown in Script 8-4 and Script 8-5 should help to make this clear.

Script 8-4.

```
on run
    set user_name to "Ben"
    say_hello(user_name)
end run

on say_hello(somebody)
    display dialog ("Hello " & somebody & "!")
end say_hello
```

In the preceding script, the handler call passes the value of the variable user_name. The say_hello handler receives the value and assigns it to the somebody variable, where it is used in the handler.

Script 8-5.

```
on run
    say_hello("Ben")
end run

on say_hello(somebody)
    display dialog ("Hello " & somebody & "!")
end say_hello
```

In this script, you don't pass the value of a variable but rather the value itself.

Passing Multiple Values

To pass multiple values to a handler, provided you use positioned parameters and not labeled parameters (until now you dealt only with positional parameters), you must separate the values you pass in the handler call with commas and do the same with the parameter variables in the handler definition. The handler call must have a single value for each parameter variable in the handler definition.

You must not confuse that with a list, however. The parameters are passed as single values. You could pass a list as a value to the handler, but it would be put into a single variable. You'll learn more about that when I cover handlers in Chapter 18, but for now, here's an example:

```
on run
    say_hello("Ben", "Brown")
end run

on say_hello(first_name, last_name)
    display dialog ("Hello " & first_name & space & last_name & "!")
end say_hello
```

Introducing Properties

Earlier I discussed that global variables are visible to all handlers. Another way to make a value visible to any handler in the script is to assign it to a property. Properties are just what they say they are: pieces of information that describe different aspects of the script. Much like an application object that may have properties such as name and version, a script is an object that can have its own properties. As far as AppleScript is concerned, however, a property is just a variable you predefine in your script, with a wider scope than a local variable.

Here are some examples of setting properties and global variables:

```
property my_name : "Jane Smith" -- value set on same line
property office_zip : "02906"

global quit_now -- global variable declared first
set quit_now to false -- value assigned later
```

For instance, if you're creating a script that is responsible for backing up some files to the server, one of its properties may hold a value that identifies the destination folder for the backed-up files.

Both global variables and properties share another important feature: when the script assigns a different value to a property, the property will retain that value even after the script is done running. This means the script can remember values you give it from run to run.

If you open the script, however, you will not see the new value assigned to the property, because Script Editor displays the original source code, which is not modified. If you open the script and recompile it, the values of the properties will be reset to the original values you gave them. To test it, type the script in Figure 8-6, and save it as an application. Then run the script a few times.

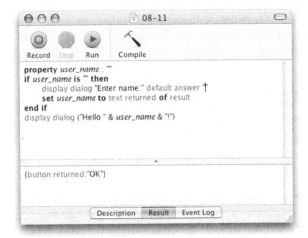

Figure 8-6. *This script has a property that will retain its value from run to run.*

When you run the script for the first time, the value of the user_name property is "", or a blank string. The second line in the script picks up on that and asks the user to enter their name.

The fourth line assigns the text the user typed to the property user_name. From this point on, the script has the value embedded into it, and the way this particular script is structured, the user has no way to reenter their name. The script in Figure 8-6 verifies that the user typed the right name and gives them the chance to enter a new name.

There's always a big question as to whether to use properties or global variables. For the most part, there's no functional difference between them, especially when dealing with relatively simple scripts.

As with global variables, you should think carefully before adding properties. Overusing script properties instead of local variables can make the script difficult to understand and debug.

Understanding When Properties Are a Good Idea

In the following sections, you'll look at three typical situations in which utilizing script properties can be useful.

Development and Testing Settings

Once in a while some pieces of information belong at the top of the script. For instance, I always include a debugMode property, which has a Boolean value. Certain functions I want performed only if I'm debugging, but I would hate to forget to turn them off before I put the script to use, or worse, send it to a client. So, any debugging-related function I just wrap in an if debugMode then block, and all I have to do in order to turn them all off is to set the debugMode property to false.

Script Object Properties

Although I will cover this issue in detail when I talk about script objects in Chapter 19, it's appropriate to discuss in this section the aspect of including properties in script objects that you load into the main script.

A *library* is just a script containing one or more general-purpose handlers that you regularly use in other scripts. Rather than cutting and pasting these handlers into every script that needs them, you place them in a library script and save it somewhere convenient such as your /Library/ Scripts folder. When another script needs to use these handlers, it loads this library into a property. This allows the library's handlers to be called from anywhere in the script, like this:

```
property ListLibrary : load script ¬
(alias "Macintosh HD:Library:Scripts:ListLibrary.scpt")

on some_handler()
   --some statements here that create an unsorted list of names
   tell ListLibrary to set sorted_names_list to sort_list(names_list)
   --some statements here that use the sorted list of names
end some_handler
```

User Preferences

Although requiring users to modify a script themselves in order to use it is often undesirable, some situations just call for it. Take, for example, a droplet script that creates titles in Adobe Illustrator and exports them as TIFF files. The user may indicate they want to change the font the script uses sometime down the road. Well, you could build a way for that user to gracefully change the font, but that would be one more thing to get broken later and . . . you're already out the door . . . so you add the title_font property to the top of the script and tell the user to change it later to a different font.

Although I do that sometimes, it can be sometimes difficult to support scripts you know the user is messing with. Anytime you let the user modify your scripts, you're asking for trouble; besides, it's hardly as nice as facilitating a way for the user to change some script settings.

Your Script's Preferences Pane

Unless you go for an AppleScript Studio application, you can't really create a preference pane with radio buttons and so on; however, you can present a series of dialog boxes intended for collecting different settings from the user.

The way you can let the user set preferences here is by starting the script with a single dialog box at the beginning with three buttons:

- Cancel, in case the user didn't mean to launch the script
- Run, used for normal operation, which should also be the default button
- Settings, which allows the user to change some preferences

If the user clicks the Settings button, they will be presented with a series of dialog boxes whose results will supply values to the script's properties. In the next example, in Script 8-6, pretend you have an Illustrator script that replaces variables with data in a template and applies the font specified in the title_font property. The template file path is specified in the template_path property. The only twist with this script is that if the file specified in the template path property doesn't exist, you will force the user to pick one.

Script 8-6.

```
property template_file : missing value
property title_font : missing value

on run
    if title_font is missing value or template_file is missing value then
        set_preferences()
    end if
    display dialog "Run the script or change settings?" buttons ¬
        {"Quit", "Settings", "Run"} default button "Run"
    set dialog_result to button returned of result
    if dialog_result is "Quit" then
        return
    else if dialog_result is "Settings" then
        set_preferences()
    end if
    --The rest of your code is here...
end run

to set_preferences()
    set template_file to choose file with prompt ¬
        "Pick an Illustrator template" of type {"PDF "}
    tell application "Adobe Illustrator 10"
        set font_list to get name of every text face
    end tell
    set user_selection to choose from list font_list with prompt ¬
        "Pick a font for the title"
    if user_selection is false then error number -128 -- user clicked cancel
    set title_font to item 1 of user_selection
end set_preferences
```

In the preceding script, you have a run handler and another handler, set_preferences, that is in charge of collecting settings from the user.

Two scenarios will cause the script to call the set_preferences handler: the first time the script runs, in which case the value of the properties will be missing value, or when the user clicks the Settings button in the start-up dialog box. Once invoked, the set_preferences handler allows the user to choose a template path in one dialog box and choose a font in another. Once selected, the chosen font and template are assigned to the properties and are used the next time the script runs.

Introducing AppleScript-Defined Variables

AppleScript has a few predefined variables available for use in your scripts. Some of these variables—namely, it, me, and result—are rather dynamic, with AppleScript automatically updating their values as the script runs, and some (see the next sections) have a predefined value that should not be changed.

The variables return, space, tab, quote, weeks, days, hours, minutes, and pi are constant-like global variables with a preset value. The purpose of these variables is to save your work and make your script easier to read by supplying a selection of useful values ready for use. Although it's possible to change the value of these scripts, it is highly discouraged.

The first four variables in the list have string values and are used to make literal strings in your script more legible. For example, the following statement:

```
item_1 & tab & item_2 & space & item_3 & tab
```

is much easier to understand than this one:

```
item_1 & "    " & item_2 & "    " & item_3 & "    "
```

The weeks, days, hours, and minutes constants are useful when working with times and dates. The other variables—it, me, and result—are a bit more sophisticated, and you'll get to those variables shortly. The following sections describe the built-in variables in detail.

return

The return variable's default value is the return character, or ASCII character 13, and it's useful in text concatenations.

Although you can set return to any value you choose, you probably shouldn't, unless you're playing a practical joke on someone. Here's an example of using the return variable:

```
set names_message to "Peter" & return & "Paul" & return & "Mary"
```

The result is as follows:

```
"Peter
Paul
Mary"
```

Script 8-7 shows another, more flexible way to perform the same general function, this time with added line numbers.

Script 8-7.
```
set names_list to {"peter", "paul", "mary"}
set names_message to ""
repeat with i from 1 to (count names_list)
  set the_name to item i of names_list
  set names_message to names_message & i & ". " & the_name & return
end repeat
display dialog names_message
```

In line 5, you concatenate a bunch of text into a single string and add it onto itself in a repeat loop. The last item you add in each loop is return, which adds another line to the string.

In scripts where I use this a lot and want a shorter version of return, I create a global variable called cr for *carriage return*. Then I add the following statement:

```
set cr to return
```

From that point on, I can use cr as I would the return character.

space, tab, and quote

Just like the return variable, the predefined space, tab, and quote variables hold a one-character string.

The value of the space variable is a single word space, or ASCII character 32, and the value of the tab variable is a single character string with one tab character, or ASCII character 9.

The quote constant contains a single double quote (", or ASCII character 34). Usually when you're writing a literal string, such as "Say hello, Bob", and want to include a double quote, you have to remember to escape it with a backslash first, or the script won't compile correctly. In other words, you use `"Say \"hello\", Bob"`, not `"Say "hello", Bob"`. However, you can use the quote constant instead if you find it more convenient:

`"Say " & quote & "hello" & quote & ", Bob".`

Using these variables produces the same result as typing the actual character or using the command ASCII character with a character's respective number. These variables are useful, though, since by looking at a string with a few spaces or tabs, you can't always see right away what characters are used and how many of them are used.

The script handler shown in Script 8-8 uses the tab and space variables to trim them from the start or end of a string. It takes one parameter, which is the string you want trimmed.

Script 8-8.

```
1. on trim_tabs_and_spaces(the_text)
2.    repeat while the_text starts with space or the_text starts with tab
3.       if length of the_text is 1 then
4.          set the_text to ""
5.       else
6.          set the_text to text 2 thru -1 of the_text
7.       end if
8.    end repeat
9.    repeat while the_text ends with space or the_text ends with tab
10.      set the_text to text 1 thru -2 of the_text
11.   end repeat
12.   return the_text
13. end trim_tabs_and_spaces
```

pi

The pi variable has the value 3.14159265359 assigned to it. You can use it anytime you need to figure out a circle circumference from its radius, or vice versa. Script 8-9 calculates the amount of ribbon you would need to tie around a given number of pies.

Script 8-9.

```
on how_much_ribbon(pie_count, pie_radius)
   set pie_circumference to pie_radius * pi
   set ribbon_length to pie_circumference * pie_count
   --add 10% to compensate for bow-tie at end
   set ribbon_length to ribbon_length * 1.1
   return round ribbon_length
end how_much_ribbon
```

it

The it variable contains a reference to the target of the current tell block. This value isn't up to you to set, but rather AppleScript sets this value automatically. The it variable is mostly implied by AppleScript, which means you don't often write it into your code, but it can be used literally for readability: `set first_word to word 1 of it` vs. `set first_word to word 1`. In some cases, the use of the it variable is required.

In another example, Figure 8-7 shows a script using InDesign, in which the variable it has been placed inside the tell application "InDesign CS2" block. In this case, the value of the it variable is therefore a reference to the application.

Figure 8-7. *The value of the* it *variable is a reference to the application InDesign.*

So when is the it variable used, and when is it implied? Consider Script 8-10, which is a variation on the script in Figure 8-7.

Script 8-10.

```
tell application "InDesign CS2"
    tell active document
        get name of it
    end tell
end tell
```

The it variable used in line 3 of Script 8-10 refers to the active document, since that is the target of the inner tell block. In the following script, the it variable is implied, but AppleScript knows that name is a property defined by InDesign so can deduce the of it part of the reference itself:

```
tell application "InDesign CS2"
    tell active document
        get name
    end tell
end tell
```

Although the it variable can be implied instead of written out, in some cases you would want to use it in order to make your script read more easily. Although saying the following:

```
if name of it is "Document 1"
```

is more English-like, you may prefer the more concise version:

```
if name = "Document 1"
```

me

The variable me refers to the current script object. This is usually the script you're running. There aren't many distinct uses for the me variable; however, the few uses it has (see the next sections) are used in real-world scripts quite a bit.

path to me

One of the nice uses of the me variable is using it with the Standard Additions' path to command. path to me is often used to get the path to the script's file. This is useful in helping your scripts find the files they count on for execution.

Note path to me doesn't work in all situations. Prior to OS X 10.4, it was not an official AppleScript feature and was actually interpreted by the path to command as path to current application. As a result, path to me would return the desired result only in script applets and a few attachable applications (for example, Smile) that provided special support for it. Otherwise, it would return the path to the current application instead. In OS X 10.4 and later, path to me is directly supported by AppleScript itself so should now produce the desired result in most applications. Although I'll introduce path to here, I'll explain it in more detail in Chapter 13.

Say you have a script that generates a text file called settings as part of its execution. The script needs a reliable folder to write the file to and find the file in for reading.

One solution is to use one of OS X's many unmovable folders in the user's library folder or other places. This, however, complicates things, because if the script is stopped from being used on a specific Mac, you either have to hunt for these files or just leave a mess.

Another solution is to get the user to always put the script folder in the root directory, on the desktop, or somewhere you can teach your script to find. This is also not so good since, well, you just made a crucial mistake—you counted on the user to listen to your instructions!

Here's a solution that has worked for me with many different projects: I create a folder that I designate as the main folder. This folder can have any name, and the user can also change the name and it won't matter. All scripts, including the main script, are stored in folders nested inside that folder.

Then, I create a folder structure, and, yes, I do have to ask the user not to rename folders in there. In this case, I might have a folder in the main folder called Scripts where I put my scripts. I have a Settings folder and a Utilities folder where I usually put my application script that the user launches. I also make sure to create an alias to the main applet or application that the user launches in a more convenient location such as the main folder or the desktop. I also have a folder I call System where I put files I absolutely don't want the user to touch. Figure 8-8 shows this sample folder structure.

Figure 8-8. *A sample automated system folder structure*

Now let's see how this works. To create a Settings file, all I need is the path to the Settings folder. Since I told the user to put the main folder anywhere, I can't count on a specific location. I have to do an inside job in order to find the location. Script 8-11 creates a few variables whose string values describe the location of different folders in my folder structure.

Script 8-11.

```
set this_applet_path to (path to me) as string
tell application "Finder"
    set utilities_folder_path to (container of file this_applet_path) as string
    set main_folder_path to (container of folder utilities_folder_path) as string
end tell
set scripts_folder_path to main_folder_path & "Scripts:"
set settings_folder_path to main_folder_path & "Settings:"
set system_folder_path to main_folder_path & "System:"
```

In line 1 the main script applet gets the path to itself. Line 3 gets the path to the folder that contains the main applet, which is the Utilities folder, and line 4 gets the path to the Utilities folder's container, which is the main folder. From there, I simply concatenate the names of the other folders to the main folder path to get the paths to the other folders.

Let's assume for a minute that the main folder is located in the root directory of the hard disk. In this case, the following expressions will return the results right below them:

```
this_applet_path
--> "Macintosh HD:Main Folder:utilities:Launch me..."
utilities_folder_path
-- (the path to the containing folder of the "Launch me..." applet)
--> "Macintosh HD:Main Folder:utilities:"
main_folder_path -- (the path to the containing folder of the "utilities" folder)
--> "Macintosh HD:Main Folder:"
```

This main folder can be put anywhere and named anything. Thanks to the path to me command, you can always locate it from within the utility script.

Tell me Something

The me variable also comes in handy when you want to call a handler in your script from within an application tell block.

If you try to run the script shown in Figure 8-9, you will be presented with the error message shown in Figure 8-10. The reason is that when you call a handler from within a tell block, Apple-Script sends that command to the target object specified by that tell block. If the target object contains a handler for that command, it will handle it. If it doesn't, you get an error.

I always get a kick from the message "Can't continue." I guess what I want is more details, something like "Can't continue because my feet hurt" or something. Anyway, the message actually means that the Finder didn't know how to handle the say_hello command and couldn't find a scripting addition that could handle this command either.

What you have to do in this case, or whenever you want to call a local handler from within a tell block that's directed to an application, is to direct the command toward the script, not the application. Figure 8-11 shows how you do that.

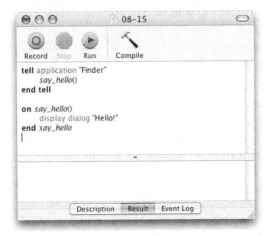

Figure 8-9. *Calling the* say_hello *handler from within the Finder* tell *block generates an error since the Finder doesn't have a* say_hello *command defined in its dictionary.*

Figure 8-10. *The error you get from calling a command within an application* tell *block*

Figure 8-11. *To call a handler that belongs to the main script from within an application's* tell *block, you have to target the script using the* me *variable.*

Another way to get the same result, as explained in the following section, is to just add the word my before the command:

```
tell application "Finder"
    my say_hello()
end tell
```

my

Another problem you may encounter is when you try to retrieve values of properties whose names are used both as a property in your script and as a property in the application. Take, for example, Script 8-12.

Script 8-12.

```
property name : "Olivia"
tell application "Finder"
    tell file 1 of disk "Macintosh HD"
        display dialog (get name)
    end tell
end tell
```

In line 4 you want to get the value of the script's name property and have the Finder display this value in a dialog box. However, the dialog box displays the name of file 1 of disk Macintosh HD instead.

If you want the dialog box to display the property name defined in the script itself, you must specify it using this:

```
get name of me
```

Or you can use its slightly better-looking equivalent:

```
get my name
```

Either way, the name Olivia will be displayed, not the name of the file.

result

The result variable is the most often updated and most used variable in AppleScript.

After evaluating all the expressions within a statement, AppleScript assigns the final result to the result variable. In practical terms, this means the result of any line of code that whose expression produces a result will have that resulting value assigned to the result variable.

Examine the simple statement in the script in Figure 8-12.

Line 1 of the script in Figure 8-12 contains a simple mathematical expression that isn't assigned to any specific variable—it is simply expressed into the air. But, thanks to the result variable, the value it returns is safe. The value 6 that was returned from the expression in line 1 was put in the result variable. Line 2 retrieves the value of the result variable and shows that it is 6.

Figure 8-12. *The* result *variable is assigned the value returned by the expression* 2 + 4 *in the previous statement.*

Destroying Variables

Generally, the AppleScript Language Guide does not recommend or explain any way to completely get rid of variables. The way to do that is by creating a small handler that returns no value, as shown in Script 8-13.

Script 8-13.

```
to destroy_variable()
  return
end destroy_variable
```

To use the handler to actually destroy a variable, you need to set the variable to the result of this subroutine, as follows:

```
set variable_i_no_longer_want to destroy_variable()
```

Figure 8-13 shows the complete variable-killer script, and Figure 8-14 shows the error that follows its execution.

■**Note** Technically, this hack doesn't destroy a variable; it merely assigns "no value" to it. Also, it's rarely useful but possible nonetheless.

Figure 8-13. *The variable-killer script*

Figure 8-14. *The error generated by running the script in Figure 8-13*

Power Wrap-Up

The following sections summarize the chapter in an intensive reference style. Use these sections to look up facts related to the chapter without the chatter.

Declaring Variables

You can declare variables explicitly or implicitly. To implicitly declare a variable, just assign a value to it. The two statements that follow use two different commands to assign a string value to a variable whose identifier is my_variable:

```
set my_variable to "the value"
copy "the value" to my_variable
```

Using Properties

Properties are variables that are normally declared at the top of a script. You have to assign a value to a property right from the start:

```
property identifier_name : "initial value"
```

The value of a property is available throughout the script, including inside all subroutines, and is retained even between script runs.

Using Global Variables

Much like properties, global variables are normally declared at the top of a script. You don't supply them with an initial value, and you can declare multiple global variables with one statement:

```
global identifier_1, identifier_2, identifier_3
```

Once the value of a global variable has been set, it will be available throughout the script, including all subroutines, and will come back even between script runs.

Using Local Variables

Any variables you created and did not declare as either a global variable or a property are local variables by default. The value of a local variable is available only inside the handler in which it was defined. To use the value of a local variable in another handler, you must pass it as a parameter.

Explicitly declaring local variables is not necessary but is good practice:

```
on run
    local identifier_1, identifier_2
    --statements
end run
```

Naming Variables

The basic variable naming rules are as follows:

- An identifier must start with a letter (A–Z, a–z) or an underscore (_) and may contain (after the first character) any alphanumeric character (A–Z, a–z, 0–9) or underscore.

- An identifier can't start with a digit or contain spaces, dashes, or any other nonalphanumeric characters.

- An identifier can't be a reserved word. You will know right away if it is by looking at the compiled script's syntax coloring, if the script compiles at all.

- An identifier can't have the same name as a handler identifier in the same script.

Use straight lines (pipes) at the start and end of a variable identifier, and you can break all the rules:

```
set |123 GO! Yes, this is a legal variable!| to "string value"
```

A good variable name has at least two words to help distinguish it from reserved words or pre-defined variables.

The words can be capitalized in word case or separated by an underscore, for example user-Name and page_count.

Using Not-Good Variables

Variables whose values have not been set will generate an error if you try to use them. For example:

```
local x
x * 2 -- error: The variable x is not defined.
```

Using Predefined Variables

AppleScript has a few predefined variables that are mentioned and used throughout the book. These variables are as follows:

- return, which has the value of a return character
- space, which has the same value as a space character
- tab, which has the same value as a tab character
- quote, which has the same value as a straight double quote
- pi, which has the real value of 3.14159265359
- minutes, which has the value of 60 seconds
- hours, which has the value of 3600 seconds
- days, which has the value of 86400 seconds
- weeks, which has the value of 604800 seconds

Using it and me

The variable it describes the object currently targeted by a tell block. In Script 8-14, the value of it is document 1 of Script Editor:

Script 8-14.

```
tell application "Script Editor"
    tell document 1
        display dialog (text of it)
    end tell
end tell
```

The value of me is always the current script.

You can use me in the Standard Additions' path to command to get the path to the script's file or applet, although this doesn't work in all applications:

```
path to me
```

You can use me within an application's tell block to direct handler calls to the script itself instead of the targeted application. For example, the following script will raise the error "Can't continue do_this_thing" when it attempts to call the do_this_thing handler from within the tell application block:

```
tell application "Script Editor"
    do_this_thing() --Script Editor got an error: Can't continue do_this_thing.
end tell

on do_this_thing()
    display dialog "Just doing my thing!"
end do_this_thing
```

Script 8-15 shows how to direct the do_this_thing command to the script instead.

Script 8-15.

```
tell application "Script Editor"
    do_this_thing() of me
    --or...
    my do_this_thing()
    --or...
    tell me to do_this_thing()
end tell

on do_this_thing()
    display dialog "Just doing my thing!"
end do_this_thing
```

Using result

The result variable contains the result of the last statement that ran, provided that the last statement returned a result. In the following example, the value of the result variable will be 12 after the first line and 36 after the second line:

```
5 + 7
result * 3
```

CHAPTER 9

■ ■ ■

Introducing Operations and Coercion

Look around you, and you will find that the environment in which you script is chock-full of raw material—numbers, text, data, dates, and other values taken from files, documents, web pages, databases, and user input. All these values won't amount to anything without you molding them into something else. In fact, a large portion of scripting is taking values, changing them, and forming new values to your liking.

Since operators and operations are everywhere in AppleScript, they are covered extensively throughout the book. You will mainly find operations covered in the chapters devoted to numbers and math, text and strings, dates and time, and so on.

This chapter aims to tie up the loose ends but not to cover what is extensively covered in other, more targeted chapters.

What Are Operations?

As the *AppleScript Language Guide* describes it, "Operations are expressions that use operators to derive values from other values." In simple terms, *operators* are tools for manipulating data.

Operations turn flower, milk, and sugar into pancakes; a few words into a sentence; some numbers into a meaningful result . . . you get the picture.

In the pancake's case, the ingredients are the *operands*, the mixing is the *operator*, the mixed batter is the *expression*, and the steaming pancake on your plate is the *result*.

Although AppleScript doesn't have operators that can be used for cooking, it does have operators for comparing values, doing math with numbers, performing Boolean operations, calculating dates and times, and doing much, much more.

Understanding Operations and Coercion

Several rules govern operations, and operations fall into certain categories. Let's start with a few basic assumptions. An operation means having an operator act on one or two values (operands) to produce a new, usually different value. Operations in AppleScript are performed with operands from any value class. You can perform operations with integers and reals, with strings, with dates, with lists, and with any other available value class. If there are two operands, each one will sit on one side of the operator.

Most AppleScript operations consist of two operands with a binary operator in the middle (*binary* here means "has two operands"); for example, in the operation 2 + 4, the left operand is the integer 2, the right operand is the integer 4, and the operator is +. When AppleScript evaluates this operation, its result will be the integer 6. As you know from math, in some cases it is important which operand is on the left and which one is on the right, as in division or subtraction.

Some operations use a unary operator and a single operand to its right. (*Unary* here means "has one operand.") For instance, in the following example, the hyphen acts as a unary minus operator and will make any positive number to its right negative and any negative number positive:

```
set x to 12
set y to -x
get y --> -12
```

What about mixing operands? Can you have an operation with operands from two different value classes? What if you wrote "2" + 2? The result will be 4, but not because AppleScript adds a string to an integer. Instead, AppleScript identifies the + operator as one requiring two numbers and therefore automatically tries to coerce any operand that is not a number into a number. In this case, it works. In other cases, the operations may return an error, such as in the following operation: "gazillion" + 3. AppleScript identifies the + operator as one requiring a number value on either side of the operator and therefore tries to coerce the string "gazillion" into a number. This, as you can imagine, causes an error.

What Is Coercion, Anyway?

Coercion is when a value of one class is converted to a comparable value of another class. For instance, the value 5 is an integer, and the value "5" is a string. You can't do math with "5", and you can't concatenate 5 to another string as long as it is an integer.

So, to do math with the string value "5", you must convert it, or *coerce* it, into a number, and to use the number value 5 in a string, you must coerce it into a string.

How Can You Explicitly Coerce Values?

In parts of the script where you explicitly want to coerce values from one value class to another, you use the as operator.

The as operator is the coercion operator. The left operand is a value of a specific value class, and the right operand is the value class into which you want the left operand coerced. Figure 9-1 and Figure 9-2 show a couple of examples.

Figure 9-1. *A string value is coerced into an integer.*

Figure 9-2. *An integer value is coerced into a string.*

A single expression can combine a few levels of coercion, as shown in Figure 9-3.

Figure 9-3. *A single statement with two levels of coercion*

In Figure 9-3 you can see that each of the operands had to be coerced into an integer individually before the multiplication could take place. In this case, you did the coercions yourself; if you didn't, AppleScript would do them for you. However, since you wanted the result to be a string, you had to coerce the result of the multiplication operation into a string.

■**Note** Parentheses can also help improve the readability of complex expressions by making the order in which they're evaluated immediately obvious to the eye.

The script in Figure 9-3 could have been broken down into a few lines, as shown in Figure 9-4.

Figure 9-4. *The script from Figure 9-3 broken down into lines*

Sometimes you *must* explicitly coerce values in order to obtain the results you need, but the rest of the time AppleScript will perform the desired coercions for you if you leave it to do so. In the latter case, you have the option of inserting explicit coercions if you want, and sometimes you'll find it's useful to do so in order to make your intentions obvious to anyone who reads your code.

For example, if you want to concatenate a string and a number to produce a new string, the number value will have to be coerced to a string along the way. In some situations, you must explicitly coerce the number yourself; otherwise, you won't get the correct result. Other times you can safely leave AppleScript to perform an implicit coercion itself—although you can still use an explicit coercion if you prefer. See Script 9-1 for an example. As you can see, the result for the first script returns a string. However, what if you change the composition to the second one?

Script 9-1.

```
set the_age to 35
set the_text to "I am " & the_age
--> "I am 35"

set the_age to 35
set the_text to the_age & " is my age"
--> {35, " is my age"}
```

Oops, now it's a list. If you counted on the result here to be a string, you would have gotten an error. To get the result you're after, you need to provide AppleScript with some extra guidance by coercing the value of the_age to a string yourself:

```
set the_age to 35
set the_text to (the_age as string) & " is my age"
-> "35 is my age"
```

Implicit coercion—the ability of a language to coerce values between classes "on the fly," without you even thinking about it—is one of those AppleScript features intended to make it easier to use. So why doesn't every language do that? There's a very good reason. Once a programming language tries to guess your intention, it moves away from being transparent. AppleScript does take some of the work out of your everyday scriptwriting, but it does that with a heavy set of rules that you eventually have to learn.

I prefer to coerce values myself even when it's not essential. Although it adds a bit more code, it also means anyone reading my script can immediately see where coercions are performed. So, for example, I'd write that first script as follows:

```
set the_age to 35
set the_text to "I am " & (the_age as string)
--> "I am 35"
```

That way, if somebody modifies the code later, they're not likely to break it because they didn't notice an implicit coercion was involved.

When Does AppleScript Perform Coercion on Its Own?

AppleScript attempts to coerce values automatically during some operations. A binary operation has three elements: the left operand, the operator, and the right operand. For most types of binary operations to be successful, the left and right operands must belong to the same class, and the operator must be compatible with that class. For example, the + operator requires two numbers, and both numbers must be integers or reals. Here's how it works:

1. When an operation is encountered, AppleScript determines the value class of the left operand. If the left operand is of a legal class, and the operator can work with that operand, then the right operand is checked to see whether it also matches.

2. If the left operand isn't compatible with the operator, AppleScript attempts to coerce it. If it can't, AppleScript will raise a coercion error (error number –1700), which means AppleScript can't coerce a value into the needed value class.

3. If the left operand is compatible with the operator or AppleScript manages to coerce it, then the right operand is evaluated and, if needed, coerced to match the left operand.

Let's look at some script snippets—in the script that follows, the left operand is compatible with the operator, but AppleScript will have to coerce the right operand to a real (or integer, if no decimal point) to make it compatible with the left operand:

```
5 + "12.3"
```

In the following script, AppleScript will first coerce the left operand into an integer to make it compatible with the + operator. It will then coerce the right operand into a real to make it compatible as well:

```
"5" + "12.3"
```

The result will be a real number, since any operation that happens between a real number and an integer results in a real value.

One side effect of the left-to-right operation evaluation method is that an operation with the same values and same operator can produce a different class of results based on the order of the operands Take, for example, the concatenation operator. If the left operand is a string, then AppleScript will attempt to coerce the right operand into a string as well and return a string result. If the left operand is a record, then AppleScript will attempt to coerce the right operand into a record as well and return a record result. If the left operand is any other value class, AppleScript will attempt to coerce both operands to lists and return a list result. Refer to Figure 9-5.

Figure 9-5. *The* display dialog *command fails since the operation evaluates as a list, not a string.*

The script in Figure 9-5 will result in an error since AppleScript evaluates the operation as a list, not a string, and because the display dialog command requires a string (see Figure 9-6).

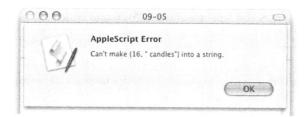

Figure 9-6. *The error shows that the value passed to* display dialog *was indeed a list, not a string.*

The error message in Figure 9-6 shows the list value that AppleScript evaluated from the operation in the script in Figure 9-5. Figure 9-7 shows the corrected script, where a string value is passed to the display dialog command.

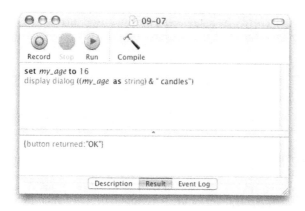

Figure 9-7. *The* display dialog *command has no problem now since its parameter is a string.*

Performing Boolean Logic Operations

boolean is a value class that allows only two possible values: true or false. AppleScript provides three Boolean logic operators for working with Boolean values: and, or, and not. In operations that use these operators, both operands and the result are Booleans. The meaning of the operators and, or, and not is pretty self-explanatory, much like the use of these words in the English language.

Using and, or, and not correctly in AppleScript takes a little more care, however. Although it's OK to say something like "If the score is 9 or 10, then say 'Excellent!'" in English, if you try that in AppleScript, you'll get an error when you run it because 10 is not a Boolean value. You have to phrase the test expression in strictly logical terms: the score is 9 or the score is 10.

You should not confuse Boolean operators with comparison operators, although they're often used in conjunction with one another. Although comparison operators also produce a result in the boolean value class, they serve a different purpose, and their operands are, for the most part, not Boolean values. I'll discuss comparison operators later in the "Introducing Comparison Operators" section.

not

The not operator takes a Boolean value as its sole, right-side operand and returns the opposite Boolean value. If the operand is true, the result is false. If the operand is false, the result is true.

The following script snippets show the not operator in action:

```
not true
```
Result: false

```
not false
```
Result: true

```
not (1 + 2 = 3)
```
Result: false

Since the expression (1 + 2 = 3) results in the Boolean value of true, putting the not operator before it reverses the result to false.

The not operator is useful in a few situations. One is reversing a Boolean value when testing its value in a conditional statement. Here's a practical example that creates a folder named TO DO on your desktop if it doesn't already exist:

```
tell application "Finder"
    if not (folder "TO DO" of desktop exists) then
        make new folder at desktop with properties {name:"TO DO"}
    end if
end tell
```

and

The and operator takes two Boolean operands and returns true only if both operands are true. If either operand is false, it returns false. Here are some examples of the and operator in action:

```
true and true --> true
true and false --> false
false and true --> false
false and false --> false
```

And here are some practical examples of using and:

```
if (email_address contains "@") and (email_address contains ".") then
    --Create and send an email...
else
    --Display an "invalid email address" error dialog...
end if
```

Or, if you just want a variable whose value is true or false, use something like this:

```
set valid_email_address to (email_address contains "@") and ¬
    (email_address contains ".")
```

Notice the use of the parentheses. They are not required in this case, but they visually distinguish the different operations, making the code easier to read.

To perform the command do_something if the variable x is within a range of numbers, say between 10 and 20, you can use the following statement:

```
if (x ≥ 10) and (x ≤ 20) then do_something()
```

or

The or operator takes two Boolean operands and returns true if either operand is true. If both operands are false, it returns false. Here are a few examples:

```
true or true --> true
true or false --> true
false or true --> true
false or false --> false
if (email ends with ".net") or (email ends with ".com") or
(email ends with ".org") then...
```

The script in Figure 9-8 first assigns some color values of lines on an Adobe InDesign page to two variables: swatch_name and line_tint.

If either the value of swatch_name is "None" or the value of line_tint is 0, then the line is deleted.

Figure 9-8. *Notice the Boolean* or *operation in the* if *statement.*

Learning More About the and or Operators

One important feature when using the and operator is if the value of the left operand, which is evaluated first, is false, the right operand will never get evaluated.

This is useful in situations where you have two test expressions joined by an and operator and attempting to evaluate the second test when the first one had already returned false would cause an error. Refer to the following example:

```
tell application "TextEdit"
    if (document 1 exists) and (text of document 1 is not "") then
        -- process the document's text
    end if
end tell
```

Look at the and operator in line 2. The command on its left side checks whether document 1 exists, while the expression on its right checks whether document 1 has any text. If AppleScript saw that the document didn't exist but went on to ask for its text anyway, this would cause TextEdit to raise a "Can't get document 1" error.

Fortunately, AppleScript is smarter than this and knows that if the first operand is false, the and operation's eventual result must always be false as well. This means there's no point in it getting the second operand and therefore no need for it to evaluate the second expression, so it doesn't. If the document does not exist, the entire and operation immediately returns false, and AppleScript moves straight to the next statement without any trouble.

The or operator is "short-circuited" in a similar fashion; however, in its case, the right operand is ignored when the left one is already true.

Mixing Operators

Since the result of a Boolean operation is a Boolean value, you can combine multiple Boolean operations in order to perform more complex multipart tests. Here's one:

```
(email contains "@") and ¬
    ((email ends with ".com") or (email ends with ".net")) and ¬
    ((offset of "@" in email) > 1)
```

The preceding script includes four expressions that result in a Boolean value:

- email contains "@"
- email ends with ".com"
- email ends with ".net"
- (offset of "@" in email) > 1

The final result is true if 1 and 4 are true and either 2 or 3 are true.

Figure 9-9 shows a script that uses this Boolean operation to validate an e-mail address that a user enters. The script is in a closed loop and doesn't allow the user to leave unless a proper e-mail address has been entered. It's a good use of Boolean but is very irritating for the user!

Figure 9-9. *A complex expression that includes several* not, and, *and* or *operations validates a user-supplied e-mail address.*

Notice that the conditional statement starts like this:

```
if not...
```

Everything after the not operator is in parentheses. If the expression in the parentheses ultimately evaluates as true, the not operator will reverse this value to false. This means the if statement's test condition is not met, in which case it evaluates the code after the else keyword that ends the loop. If the e-mail isn't valid, the test condition evaluates as true, and the user is told to try again.

Introducing Comparison Operators

Comparison operators basically ask a simple question: is the left operand the same as the right one? Sometimes the values belong to different—but closely related—value classes but are still considered equal; you'll look at these later in the "What Value Classes Can You Use?" section. The result of a comparison can be either true or false. Let's look at how AppleScript deals with comparing values.

The most commonly used operator is the equals (=) operator. It returns true if the left and right operands are the same:

```
"a" = "b"
-->false
(5 + 5) = 10
-->true
```

The opposite of the equals operator is the unequal operator: ≠. On a U.S. keyboard you can insert it by pressing Option+=. However, this may vary for other keyboard layouts.

The following operation returns a true value because 17 is not the same as 17.5:

```
17 ≠ 17.5
Result: true
```

The less-than (<) and greater-than (>) comparison operators can help you figure out whether the left operand is smaller or larger than the right operand:

```
5 > 3
Result: true
```

```
12.1 < 12
Result: false
```

Cousins of the greater-than (>) and less-than (<) operators are the greater-than-or-equal-to (≥) and less-than-or-equal-to (≤) operators. You insert them by pressing Option+. (period) to get ≥ and Option+, (comma) to get ≤, (again, this works on U.S. keyboards and may vary on other layouts). The ≥ operator checks to see whether the right operand is greater than or equal to the left operand. The ≤ operator checks whether the right operand is smaller than the left operand or equal to it.

When comparing numbers, AppleScript acts as you would expect. However, when comparing text, things can get a little more complicated. We will look at the different possibilities in the "Using Considering/Ignoring Clauses" section later in this chapter.

Using Synonyms

AppleScript allows each comparison operator to be written in several ways. Some of these synonyms are very English-like and have minute differences.

Table 9-1 shows the different comparison operators and their synonyms. Square brackets show optional words. Note that some of these variations will compile differently depending on the way you type them. If you type =>, for instance, AppleScript will compile it into ≥.

Table 9-1. *Operator Names and Synonyms*

Symbol	Synonyms
=	is equal equals [is] equal to
≠	is not isn't isn't equal [to] is not equal [to] doesn't equal does not equal
>	[is] greater than comes after isn't less than or equal [to] is not less than or equal [to]
<	[is] less than comes before isn't greater than or equal [to] is not greater than or equal [to]

Continued

Table 9-1. *Continued*

Symbol	Synonyms
≥ or >=	[is] greater than or equal [to] isn't less than is not less than does not come before doesn't come before
≤ or <=	[is] less than or equal [to] isn't greater than is not greater than does not come after doesn't come after

Here are some examples of these operator synonyms in use:

```
50 ≥ 50
Result: true

51 ≥ 50
Result: true

"Zebra" comes after "Armadillo"
Result: true

"Zebra" > "Armadillo"
Result: true

50 is not greater than 50
Result: true

date "Tuesday, January 1, 2002 12:00:00 AM" comes after (current date)
Result: false
```

What Value Classes Can You Use?

Although the result of the comparison operators is always a Boolean, the operands can be of various classes. The rules for how AppleScript treats different classes on either side of the operator vary from value class to value class and among operators.

You can use the = and ≠ operators with values of any value class on either side. However, if the value classes are incompatible, the result of the comparison will be false. For instance:

```
"2" = 2
Result: false
```

The <, >, ≤, and ≥ operators require both operands to be of the same class or closely related classes such as integer versus real. If they aren't, AppleScript will attempt to coerce the right operand to the same class as the left operand first:

- When the left operand is a number and the right operand isn't, AppleScript will try to coerce the right operand into a number as well. If it can't, an error will be raised:

  ```
  50 > "20"
  Result: true

  50 > "hello"
  Error: Can't make "hello" into type number.
  ```

- Similarly, when the left operand is a string and the right operand isn't, AppleScript will try to coerce the right operand into a string as well. If it can't, an error will be raised:

```
"hello" < 50
Result: false
```

```
"30" < 5
Result: true
```

Notice that the second example returns true because AppleScript is comparing two strings, not two numbers, and the character "3" comes before the character "5".

- When comparing a string value with a Unicode text value, AppleScript will perform the operation as if both were from the same value class:

```
"B" as Unicode text > "A"
Result: true
```

Using Containment Operators

Containment operators check whether one value can be found inside another. AppleScript provides six containment operators and the operand classes they support, as listed in Table 9-2. Like the comparison operators, the result of operations using containment operators is always a Boolean.

Table 9-2. *Containment Operators*

Operator	Class of Operands	Synonyms
starts with	list, string	start with, begin with, begins with
ends with	list, string	end with
contains	record, list, string	contain
does not contain	record, list, string	doesn't contain
is in	record, list, string	is contained by
is not in	record, list, string	isn't in, isn't contained by, is not contained by

Containment operators don't work on numbers of any kind.

The following are some examples of operations taking advantage of containment operators:

```
"Apple Pie" contains "Apples"
--> false
"Apple Pie" starts with "Apple"
--> true
"art" is contained by "start"
--> true
{1, 2, 3} starts with {1}
--> true
```

The following two operations show that you can test whether a list starts with another list:

```
{"abc", "def", "ghi"} starts with {"abc", "def"}
--> true
{"abc", "def", "ghi"} starts with {"abc"}
--> true
```

You can also test to see whether a list starts with a value of any other value class. In this case, however, AppleScript will first coerce the operand to the right into a single-item list and then perform the comparison:

```
{"abc", "def", "ghi"} starts with "abc"
Implicit coercion: {"abc", "def", "ghi"} starts with {"abc"}
Result: true
```

In the following example, even though the first item of the list starts with the right operand, the result is false. The starts with and ends with operators evaluate only whole-list items when comparing them.

```
{"abc", "def", "ghi"} starts with "a"
Result: false
```

```
"the end" ends with "the end"
Result: true
```

The preceding operation shows that when strings are equal, the starts with and ends with operators will return a true result. This is also the case with two list values.

Using Math Operators

Next are the math operators. I will list them briefly in this section, but for comprehensive coverage, you should look at Chapter 4.

All math operators can have operands that are either integers or reals, or a mix of the two. The result of these operators may be either an integer or a real, depending on the type of operation and the class of each operand.

Table 9-3 lists the math operators, their names, their functions, and the key combinations that will work on U.S. keyboard.

Table 9-3. *Math Operators*

Syntax	Name	Key Combination (U.S.)	Function
–	Unary minus	-	Converts the single operand to its right from positive to negative or from negative to positive.
+	Plus	Shift+=	Adds the left and right operands.
–	Binary minus	-	Subtracts the right operand from the left operand.
*	Multiply	Shift+8	Multiplies the left and right operands.
/ or ÷	Division	/ or Option+/	Divides the left operand by the right operand.
div	Integral division		Returns the number of times the right operand fits whole in the left operand.
mod	Modulo, remainder		The right operand is subtracted from the left operand repeatedly until the remainder is smaller than the right operand. That final remainder is the result.
^	Exponent	Shift+6	The result is the left operand raised to the power of the right operand (that is, the left operand is multiplied by itself the number of times indicated by the right operand).

Introducing Concatenation

Probably the most used operator in AppleScript is the concatenation operator, &.

To *concatenate* means to join together. AppleScript's concatenation operator can concatenate two strings into a third string, two lists into a third list, and two records into a third record. Other classes and combinations of operands will result in either a string or a list.

The following sections describe concatenation and give a few examples of the concatenation operator; however, for more complete coverage, see the individual chapters dealing with strings and with lists and records (Chapter 3 and Chapter 6, respectively).

Concatenating Strings

When both operands to the concatenation operator are strings, AppleScript produces a new string made up of the characters of the left string followed by the characters of the right string. If only the left operand is a string, AppleScript tries to coerce the right operand to a string before joining the two values, raising an error if the coercion fails. The most common usage is concatenating two or more strings, where at least one is a variable. Take a look at this example:

```
set user_name to "Olivia"
set user_greeting to "Hello" & space & user_name
--> "Hello Olivia"
```

In the preceding example, I concatenated the literal string "Hello"; the value of the space constant, which is by default a single space; and the value of the variable user_name, which happened to be Olivia.

Building Up a String Stored in a Variable

In many cases you will need to build up a string in multiple steps, such as when you're building a list or a report. To do this, you start by creating a variable containing the initial string. Each time you want to add more text, you use the concatenation operator to join the string that's currently stored in this variable with the string containing the text to add and then assign the new string back to the same variable:

```
set my_var to "Hit"
--The initial value of my_var is "Hit"

set my_var to my_var & space & "the"
--The value of my_var is now "Hit the"

set my_var to my_var & space & "road"
--The value of my_var is now "Hit the road"
```

Concatenating Records

When two records are concatenated, the result is a new record containing the properties from the left record followed by the properties from the right record. Figure 9-10 shows two records concatenating (in their natural habitat . . .).

Figure 9-10. *Simple concatenation of records*

When both records contain properties with the same label, only the property from the left record appears in the resulting record, as shown in Figure 9-11.

Figure 9-11. *If a duplicate label is found in the second record, it is dropped from the resulting record.*

Concatenating Lists

Concatenating two lists results in a single list containing the items of the left operand followed by the items of the right operand, as shown in Figure 9-12.

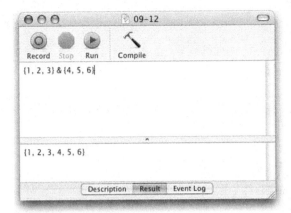

Figure 9-12. *Two lists being concatenated*

If one or more of the lists' items are lists themselves, these lists will remain intact and will not become part of the main list. Figure 9-13 contains two lists. The items of the two lists are themselves lists, but they don't merge with the main list. The left operand is a two-item list, and the right operand is a one-item list; therefore, the result is a three-item list.

Figure 9-13. *Only the two main lists combine into a single list when concatenating. List items that are lists remain intact.*

Inserting into a List Handler

As a little example of list concatenation, Script 9-2 shows a subroutine that adds a given item to a given list at a given position.

The parameters are, as mentioned earlier, the list you want to add to, the item you want to add, and the position. The result is a new list that contains all the items from the original list plus the new item.

Script 9-2.

```
set the_list to {1, 2, 3, 4}
insert_into_list(the_list, "a", 2)

on insert_into_list(the_list, the_item, the_position)
    if the_position ≤ 1 then --add to start
        set new_list to {the_item} & the_list
    else if the_position > (count the_list) then --add to end
        set new_list to the_list & {the_item}
    else --add in middle
        set new_list to ¬
            (items 1 thru (the_position - 1) of the_list) & ¬
            {the_item} & ¬
            (items the_position thru -1 of the_list)
        end if
    return new_list
end insert_into_list
```

You can add a value to the start of the list by wrapping the value as a single-item list and then concatenating this with the original list to produce the new list. Notice that you don't use `set beginning of the_list` to `the_item` here because quietly altering the original list could give unsuspecting users a nasty surprise. You can add a value to the end of the list in a similar fashion, while inserting an item in the middle involves splitting the original list first.

In each case, make sure to wrap the new item as a single-item list. If you don't, you'll get an incorrect result when adding a string to the start of a list (the concatenation operation would return a string, not a list) or inserting a sublist (the concatenation operation would merge the two lists instead). For example, the following:

```
insert_into_list({"Jane", "Mary"}, "Bob", 1)
```

should return the list `{"Bob", "Jane", "Mary"}`, not a string like `"BobJaneMary"`. And the following:

```
 insert_into_list({{1, 3}, {4, 9}}, {5, 8}, 2)
```

should return `{{1, 3}, {5, 8}, {4, 9}}`, not `{{1, 3}, 5, 8, {4, 9}}`.

Concatenating Other Value Classes

Concatenating operands of value classes other than a string, list, or record produces a list with two items: the left operand and the right operand. In the following code, the concatenation operator appears with two date values. The result is a list with the two dates in it.

```
(current date) & (current date)
--> {date "Saturday, October 25, 2003 10:35:30 AM", ¬
  date "Saturday, October 25, 2003 10:35:30 AM"}
```

Understanding the a reference to Operator

The `a reference to` operator allows you to turn a literal reference that identifies a property or element(s) of a particular object into a reference value that can be assigned to variables and passed to and from subroutines just like any other value.

Usually when AppleScript evaluates a literal reference, it immediately retrieves the value from the location:

```
set my_rec to {name: "John", age: 18}
set my_age to age of my_list
--> 18
```

```
tell application "Finder"
    set the_disks to every disk
end tell
--> {startup disk of application "Finder", disk "Backup" of application "Finder"}
```

Most of the time this is what you want, but occasionally it's useful to specify a reference at one point in a script without resolving the reference until later. A common example where this happens automatically is AppleScript's repeat with...in... loop, where the loop variable is assigned a reference to each list item in turn. This allows the code within the loop to not only obtain each item in the list but also to replace that item with a new value if it wants:

```
set the_list to {1, 2, 4, 5}
repeat with number_ref in the_list
    set contents of number_ref to contents of number_ref * 2
end repeat
the_list --> {2, 4, 8, 10}
```

However, you can also create your own reference values by placing the a reference to operator in front of a literal reference:

```
set my_rec to {name: "John", age: 18}
set my_age_ref to a reference to age of my_rec
--> age of {name:"John", age:18}
```

```
tell application "Finder"
    set the_disks_ref to a reference to every disk
end tell
--> every disk of application "Finder"
```

To obtain the current value of the referenced location, just ask the reference for the value of its contents property:

```
set my_age to contents of my_age_ref
--> 18
```

```
set the_disks to contents of the_disks_ref
--> {startup disk of application "Finder", disk "Backup" of application "Finder"}
```

Similarly, to replace the value at the referenced location with a new value, assign a new value to the reference's contents property:

```
set contents of my_age_ref to 19
get my_rec
--> {name: "John", age: 19}
```

Should the original value change at some point, then the new value will be returned the next time you get the reference's contents:

```
tell application "Finder" to eject (every disk whose ejectable is true)
get contents of the_disks_ref
--> {startup disk of application "Finder"}
```

The a `reference` `to` operator can be useful when you want to assign a reference for an application object to a variable for later use. With some applications, it's fine just to use the reference returned by the application:

```
tell application "Finder"
    set source_folder to folder "Movies" of home
end tell
--> folder "Movies" of folder "Hanaan" of folder "Users" of startup disk of ➡
application "Finder"
```

A reference that identifies elements by name or ID should be quite reliable over time. Some applications, however, return references that identify elements by position. For example, in Script 9-3, say you'd like to set variable my_layer to a specific layer in an Adobe Illustrator document.

Script 9-3.

```
tell application "Adobe Illustrator CS2"
    set my_layer to layer "images" of document "brochure.ai"
end tell
--> layer 1 of document 1 of application "Adobe Illustrator CS2"
```

As you can see, AppleScript takes the original "by name" reference on line 2 and immediately sends it to Illustrator, which trades it for a less precise "by index" reference. If you'll be moving documents or layers, then this sort of reference isn't desirable because it could easily end up identifying a completely different object than the one you want.

This script would be much more reliable if you could keep the original, more precise "by name" reference and always use that. Thanks to the a `reference` `to` operator, you can. Script 9-4 shows how.

Script 9-4.

```
tell application "Adobe Illustrator CS2"
    set my_layer to a reference to layer "images" of document "brochure.ai"
end tell
--> layer "images" of document "brochure.ai" of
application "Adobe Illustrator CS2"
```

Now, instead of immediately asking Illustrator to get `layer` `"images"` of document "brochure.ai", line 2 assigns the original reference directly to the my_layer variable. The script can use this reference later just like it would any other reference. The only difference is that it'll be more reliable than the one Illustrator would have given you otherwise.

Using Considering/Ignoring Clauses

Considering and ignoring clauses allow you to alter AppleScript's behavior when comparing text. Using them in the right places can essentially save you a lot of code and allow your scripts to be more useful. All consideration clauses, with the exception of the application `responses` clause, are used in text comparisons.

The most common clause in text comparison is the case clause. You will notice it outside of AppleScript when you try your password for the fifth time and start wondering whether the password is case sensitive. What does *case sensitive* mean exactly? Well, are the words *free* and *FREE* the same? If you ignore that one is uppercase and the other is lowercase, then they are the same. This point is exactly what consideration clauses are all about. In AppleScript, by default, the following statement is true:

```
"FREE" = "free" --> true
```

But what if you want to be a bit stricter and check to also see whether the case is identical? You have to put the statement in a consideration clause, like this:

```
considering case
    "FREE" = "free" --> false
end considering
```

Since the comparison operation in the preceding script happens inside the consideration clause block, AppleScript is forced to also check whether the case of the letters match and therefore returns a false result from the operation.

Ignoring Clauses

Although the letters' case is ignored during text comparison by default, some conditions you could possibly want to ignore are considered. Take, for example, white space and hyphens: by default, the two statements that follow will return a false result:

```
"White-house" = "Whitehouse"
"Apple Script" = "AppleScript"
```

But what if you want to see whether the correct answer was provided to the question "Where does the president live?" and you want to allow some latitude? What you can do is make the comparison while asking AppleScript to return a true result even if there's an extra hyphen or white space. Script 9-5 shows how you would do that.

Script 9-5.

```
set the_quiz_question to "Where does the president live"
display dialog the_quiz_question default answer ""
set user_answer to text returned of result
ignoring white space and hyphens
    set answer_is_correct to (user_answer equals "Whitehouse")
end ignoring
if answer_is_correct then display dialog "You got it!"
```

In the preceding example, even if quiz takers spelled the answer *White house* or *White-house*, they would still come up on top.

Now, what if you want to consider capitalization? For instance, what if the question is "Which is the smallest state?" and you want to accept *Rhode Island* and *Rhode-Island* but not *rhode island*? You need to consider case during comparison but ignore dashes. Script 9-6, which includes two scripts, shows how you do that.

Script 9-6.

```
considering case
    ignoring white space and hyphens
        "Rhode Island" is equal to "Rhode-Island" --> true
        "Rhode Island" is equal to "rhode island" --> false
    end ignoring
end considering

considering case but ignoring white space and hyphens
    "Rhode Island" is equal to "Rhode-Island" --> true
    "Rhode Island" is equal to "rhode island" --> false
end considering
```

The reason that *Rhode Island* was found to be not equal to *rhode island* in the second case is that you asked AppleScript to consider the case of the letters.

Understanding Consideration Attributes

So far you have looked at three attributes that AppleScript can consider when comparing strings: case, white space, and hyphens. The following sections describe all possible consideration attributes.

case

If considered during string comparisons, AppleScript will check to see whether the capitalization is equal in the two strings being compared. By default, case is ignored, and therefore when making string comparisons without case consideration, AppleScript ignores the case of the different strings.

white space

By default, spaces, tab characters, and return characters are considered in string comparisons, which will make *whitehouse* different from *white house*. If white space is included in the ignore clause, the preceding two strings would come out equal. See Script 9-7 for an example.

Script 9-7.

```
"slow motion" is equal to "slowmotion" --> false

ignoring white space
    " slow motion" is equal to " slowmotion " --> true
end ignoring
```

diacriticals

Diacritical marks, or accents, can be either considered or ignored during string comparisons. (These are character accents such as ´, `, ^, ¨, and ~.) Diacriticals are considered by default, so if you want the string "résumé" to be considered equal to "resume", then you have to ask AppleScript to ignore diacriticals. See Script 9-8 for an example.

Script 9-8.

```
"resume" is equal to "résumé" --> false

ignoring diacriticals
    "resume" is equal to "résumé" --> true
end ignoring
```

hyphens

As you saw earlier, by default strings with hyphens will evaluate to be not equal to the same string with hyphens. See Script 9-9 for an example.

Script 9-9.

```
"Wall-Street" is equal to "Wall Street" --> false

ignoring hyphens
    "Wall-Street" is equal to "Wall Street" --> true
end ignoring
```

expansion

Expansion deals with the letter combinations (ligatures) found in some European languages and their two-letter counterparts. For instance, by default AppleScript would consider Æ not equal to AE, Œ not equal to OE, and so on, unless of course you tell AppleScript to ignore expansion. See Script 9-10 for an example.

Script 9-10.

```
"AE" is equal to "Æ" --> false

ignoring expansion
    "AE" is equal to "Æ" --> true
end ignoring
```

punctuation

By default, AppleScript considers punctuation marks (. , ? : ; ! \ ' " `) when comparing strings. If the punctuation attribute is ignored, the strings are compared as if these punctuation marks were not there. See Script 9-11 for an example.

Script 9-11.

```
"it's" equals "its" --> false
"1,000.00" equals "1.000,00" --> false

ignoring punctuation
    "it's" equals "its" --> true
    "1,000.00" equals "1.000,00" --> true
end ignoring
```

numeric strings

Let's say you have two filenames, Image version 5.9.12 and Image version 5.13.3, and you need to figure out which is the most recent one based on the version numbers at the end of each name. If you were to compare them as strings, AppleScript would tell you that the filename ending with 5.9.12 is the latest version, since 5.9 is greater than 5.1. However, by considering the numeric strings attribute, AppleScript realizes that the end of the string consists of three numbers: 5, 9, and 12 on one end and 5, 13, and 3 on the other. Since the 5s are the same, the order is determined by 13 being greater than 9. See Script 9-12 for an example.

Script 9-12.

```
set fileName1 to "Image version 5.9.12"
set fileName2 to "Image version 5.13.3"

considering numeric strings
  fileName1 comes after fileName2
end considering
--> false
```

Which Value Classes Can Be Coerced?

As discussed before, coercing a value creates a similar value of a different value class. AppleScript will often coerce values automatically when necessary, or you can coerce them yourself by using the as operator:

```
13 as string
Result: "13"
```

```
"13" as real
Result: 13.0
```

In these two examples, you coerced an integer value into a string and then coerced a string value into a real. These operations worked for two reasons. The first condition for a successful coercion is that AppleScript knows how to convert values of the given class to values of the desired class. AppleScript supports many kinds of coercions as standard, including integer-to-string and string-to-real coercions as used previously. If you ask it to perform an unsupported coercion, an error will occur, as shown in Figure 9-14 and Figure 9-15.

Figure 9-14. *In this script, you try to coerce a list value into a record.*

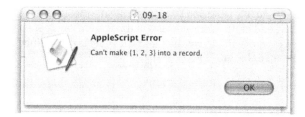

Figure 9-15. *The result of the script shown in Figure 9-14 is an error, telling you that you can't coerce a list into a record.*

This is not to say, though, that the reverse wouldn't work; in this case, it would have done just fine.

The second condition for a successful coercion is that the values themselves fit well with the new value class. For instance, here is what may happen when converting a string into an integer:

```
"3" as integer --> 3
```

This example worked, but what about this next one?

```
"Hello" as integer --> error number -1700
```

This didn't work because, although the string-to-integer coercion is supported, the actual value you tried to coerce can't be represented as a number.

So which classes can be coerced to which? The following sections describe most of the common value classes and the coercions supported between them, with some notes and exceptions.

The class and constant value classes can be each coerced into a single-item list and into a string. Some constants, such as weekdays and months, can be also coerced into an integer. Here are some examples:

```
Class of {1, 2, 3} as string
--> "list"

 weekday of (current date) as string
--> "Monday"

weekday of (current date) as integer
--> 2
```

Boolean Values

Boolean values can be coerced into a string or an integer (but not into a real):

```
true as string
Result: "true"

false as string
Result: "false"

true as integer
Result: 1

false as integer
Result: 0
```

A Boolean value can also be coerced to a single-item list:

```
true as list
Result: {true}
```

Integer

An integer can be coerced into a string without any restrictions. In addition, an integer can also be coerced into a real, which will be the integer with a decimal point and a zero behind it:

```
3 as string
Result: "3"

3 as real
Result: 3.0
```

An integer can also be coerced to a Boolean: 0 coerces to `false`, and any other number coerces to true.

```
1 as boolean
Result: true
```

And as with most other value classes, you can coerce an integer into a single-item list.

Real

A real value can be coerced into a string and a single-item list without any trouble.

If the real value has no fractional part, such as 10.0 or 2.0, then it can be coerced into an integer as well without changing the numerical value. A nonwhole real value gets rounded automatically in OS X 10.3 and later; in pre–OS X 10.3 AppleScript, coercing a nonwhole real into an integer would raise an error.

String

Strings that match the required format can be coerced into integers or real values. Strings can also become a single-item list. Strings can also be coerced to Booleans: "true" and "yes" coerce to true, and all other strings coerce to `false`.

Date

Dates can be coerced into strings and into a single-item list:

```
(current date) as string
Result: "Tuesday, October 28, 2003 5:06:29 PM"
```

The exact format of the resulting date string is determined by the Date and Time tabs in the International panel in System Preferences.

Single-Item List

A single-item list can be coerced to any other class as long as the item in the list can be coerced into that class:

```
{3} as integer
Result: 3
```

```
{3} as string
Result: "3"
```

```
{"lalala"} as real
error -1700
```

Multi-Item List

A list with multiple items can be coerced into a string only as long as all the items themselves are cool with the notion of turning into strings:

```
{1, 2, {"a", "b"}, (current date), "bumbum", 33.33} as string
Result: "12abTuesday, October 28, 2003 5:22:03 PMbumbum33.33"
```

```
{"garage", "band"} as string
Result: "garageband"
```

Note that in the previous example, the strings from the lists appear to have been concatenated without anything between them. What actually happened is that when a list is coerced into a string, the value in AppleScript's text item delimiters variable becomes the separator between the items. See the following example:

```
set text item delimiters to "; "
set display_items to {"London", "France", "Athens"} as string
Result: "London; France; Athens"
```

Record

Records can be coerced only into a list. All that happens is that they shed their labels.

Mixing Expressions and the Mighty Parentheses

One of the fun things about forming expressions is that the same expression with the same result can be spread over multiple lines in the script or be crammed into a single line. In some cases, you would want to create expressions that contain more than one simple operation.

What's important to remember is that an operation has one or two operands and a single operator. Complex operations, then, are really expressions made up of many nuclear operations. Let's look at the following operation as an example:

```
5 + 5 + 3
```

It appears to have three operands and two operators, right? Well, yes and no. The way AppleScript attacks this statement is by first resolving the leftmost operation: 5 + 5. The result of this is then used as the left operand for the following operation: 10 + 3. So as you can see, there are really four operands after all. In a sense, AppleScript does this:

```
5 + 5 = 10
10 + 3 = 13
```

Table 9-4 lists AppleScript's operators in precedence order. When resolving these sorts of complex expressions, AppleScript uses different rules of precedence to determine two things—the order in which operations of different precedence should be resolved (shown in the Order column in the following table, which originally appeared in the AppleScript Language Guide) and the direction in which to resolve operations whose operators have the same precedence level, such as multiplication and division (shown in the Form of Association column).

Table 9-4. *AppleScript's Operators in Precedence Order*

Order	Operators	Form of Association	Type of Operator
1	( )	Innermost to outermost	Grouping
2	+, -	Unary	Plus or minus sign for numbers
3	^	Right to left	Exponentiation
4	*, /, div, mod	Left to right	Multiplication and division
5	+, -	Left to right	Addition and subtraction
6	&	Left to right	Concatenation
7	as	Left to right	Coercion
8	<, ≤, >, ≥	None	Comparison

Continued

Table 9-4. *Continued*

Order	Operators	Form of Association	Type of Operator
9	=, ≠	None	Equality and inequality
10	not	Unary	Logical negation
11	and	Left to right	Logical for Boolean values
12	or	Left to right	Logical for Boolean values

Understanding Precedence Rules

Although the order of precedence resolves some of the confusion, quite a few operators have the same order of precedence, such as plus and minus. The Form of Association column in Table 9-4 explains how AppleScript deals with statements that contain multiple operators with the same precedence level.

Left to Right and Right to Left

Operators marked "left to right" are evaluated in that order when more than one operator from the same precedence exists. For instance, the following operation:

```
12 + 5 + 30 --> 47
```

will be resolved as follows:

```
12 + 5 = 17 -- leftmost
17 + 30 = 47
```

The result of the previous operation (17) is now the left operand.

Unary

A unary operator, as used in AppleScript, is one that takes a single operand to its right; for instance:

```
-7
```

The minus operator in this case turns the positive number operand to its right into a negative number and a negative number into a positive one.

If you type multiple unary operators of equal precedence all in a row, they start evaluating from the one closest to the operator, going further and further away. Look at the following statement:

```
not not not true
```

Here's how AppleScript looks at the preceding statement:

```
not (not (not true))
```

In fact, if you do use the statement without the parentheses, when you compile the script, AppleScript will add parentheses for you!

Understanding When You Should Use Parentheses

You should be using parentheses in three instances:

- You should use parentheses to make the code do what you want by changing the order in which AppleScript evaluates subexpressions within a larger expression. For instance, without parentheses, the following expression will have a different result:

```
(2 + 5) * 7
Result: 49
```

```
2 + 5 * 7
Result: 37
```

- You sometimes need to add parentheses to help the AppleScript compiler understand your code correctly. For example, AppleScript will complain about the get keyword when you try to compile the following:

```
tell application "Finder"
    repeat with the_window_ref in get windows --this line won't compile
        --do stuff here
    end repeat
end tell
```

Wrapping the get windows part in parentheses prevents this confusion:

```
tell application "Finder"
    repeat with the_window_ref in (get windows) --this will compile
        --do stuff here
    end repeat
end tell
```

- Optionally, you should use parentheses at your own discretion to make code easier to understand.

Power Wrap-Up

The following sections summarize the chapter in an intensive reference style. Use these sections to look up facts related to the chapter without the chatter.

Performing Operations

Operations are expressions that use operators to derive values from other values.

Using Coercion

Coercion is when a value is converted to an equivalent value of another value class.

Using Explicit Coercion

To explicitly coerce a value from one class to another, use the as operator:

```
"120" as integer
Result: 120
```

```
set the_string to 75.5 as string
Result: "75.5"
```

```
(not true) as string
Result: "false"
```

Since the coercion operator has a lower precedence than math operators, each coercion that is part of a larger math operation should be enclosed in parentheses. In the following statement, AppleScript will wrap at least the first coercion statement in parentheses if you don't:

```
("120" as integer) + ("120" as integer)
Result: 240
```

Coercion from list to string is common, especially when working with text.

```
set text item delimiters to " - "
set the_string to {"Bob", "Ben", "Bill"} as string
Result: "Bob - Ben - Bill"
```

Here's another example:

```
set the_price to (text 2 thru -1 of "$12.95") as real
Result: 12.95
```

Using Automatic Coercion

AppleScript will try to coerce values on its own when it sees fit.

For example, when concatenating two values of different classes, AppleScript will try to coerce one or both operands to the same class before joining them. When concatenating a string and an integer, if the string comes first, then AppleScript will coerce the integer into a string as well before joining them:

```
"July " & 15
Result: "July 15"
```

In this statement, however, the integer comes first, so AppleScript coerces both values to single-item lists and joins those:

```
15 & " of July"
Result: {15, " of July"}
```

When concatenating a string value to a Unicode text value, the result will always be a Unicode text value (OS X 10.4 or later).

Using Boolean Logic Operators

Boolean operators operate on Boolean values and expressions. Any expression in a Boolean operation must evaluate as a Boolean. These are AppleScript's Boolean operators: not, and, and or. The following are some examples of using Boolean operators.

The not operator is a unary operator. It works by changing the operand to its right from true to false or from false to true:

```
not true --> false
set slept_well to not had_bad_dreams
```

The and operator will return true if both left and right operands are true. (Note that the parentheses are used to highlight the expressions but are not needed in these cases.)

```
true and true --> true
(12 > 6) and (length of "Shaq" is 4) --> true
(5 = 5) and ("Yes" is "no") --> false
```

The or operator will return true if either the left or right operands are true:

```
true or false --> true
false or false --> false
(12 > 6) or (12 < 6) --> true
```

You can create complex logical expressions that contain multiple Boolean logic operations:

```
set is_valid_email to (email contains "@") and ¬
    ((email ends with ".com") or (email ends with ".net")) and ¬
    ((offset of "@" in email) > 1)
```

Using Comparison Operators

Comparison operators can operate on many types of values, but the result of a comparison operation is always either true or false.

AppleScript includes the following comparison operators: =, ≠, >, <, ≥, and ≤.

Check out Table 9-1 in this chapter for other ways to write each operator, such as is greater than.

The way in which a comparison operator compares two values depends on the class (or classes) of those values. For more information, see the corresponding chapters: Chapter 3 for strings, Chapter 4 for numbers, Chapter 5 for dates, and Chapter 6 for lists and records. The following are a few comparison operations:

```
3 > 2 --> true
8 = "8" --> false
(current date) > date "1/1/2000" --> true
```

Using Containment Operators

Containment operators also return either true or false. They check whether a particular value contains, or is contained by, another value.

The containment operator group consists of the following operators: starts with, ends with, contains, doesn't contain, is contained by, and isn't contained by. Each operator listed here has synonyms that you can find in this chapter. The following are a few containment operator examples:

```
"Friendship" contains "Friend"
```
Result: true

```
{12, 14, 16} contains 14
```
Result: true

Both operands must be the same class, so in the second example AppleScript coerces the value 14 to a single-item list and evaluates the expression as {12, 14, 16} contains {14}.

Using Math Operators

AppleScript allows you to use the following math operators: * (multiply), + (plus), - (minus), / (division), div (integral division), mod (modulo, remainder), and ^ (exponent).

Here are a few examples:

```
3 * 5 --> 15
72 / 12 --> 6
3 ^ 2 --> 9
```

For a complete explanation of math operators in AppleScript, see Chapter 4.

Using the Concatenation Operator

AppleScript uses the ampersand (&) as the concatenation operator.

You can concatenate strings, lists, and records, like this:

```
"Micro" & "Soft" --> "MicroSoft"
"Steely" & space & "Dan" --> "Steely Dan"
{1, 2, 3} & 4 & {5, 6} --> {1, 2, 3, 4, 5, 6}
{name:"Jane"} & {age:23} --> {name:"Jane", age:23}
```

Using the a reference to Operator

The a `reference` to operator returns a reference to a property or elements of an object, instead of the value of the property or elements.

Using Considering/Ignoring Clauses

You can use considering or ignoring blocks to alter the way in which two strings are compared. These clauses tell AppleScript to either consider or ignore specific attributes. The attributes that can be considered or ignored are case, white space, diacriticals, hyphens, expansion, punctuation, and numeric strings.

The following are two examples of using the different consideration clauses. For more examples, see earlier in this chapter.

Use this for considering case:

```
"AppleScript" = "applescript" --> true

considering case
    "AppleScript" = "applescript" --> false
end considering
```

Or, use the following for ignoring white space and hyphens:

```
"800 555-1212" is equal to "8005551212" --> false

ignoring white space and hyphens
    "800 555-1212" is equal to "8005551212" --> true
end ignoring
```

CHAPTER 10

■ ■ ■

Teaching Your Script to Make Decisions

The AppleScript language, like other programming languages, revolves around two things: a few simple concepts and a lot of syntax. One of these concepts is the conditional statement, which is a concept so basic that most kids can master it by the time they can put a sentence together. A conditional statement decides whether to execute a specific section of code depending on whether a certain condition is met.

In AppleScript, the ability to make decisions is what gives your script artificial intelligence. The more conditional statements you use, attached to different sensors, the more organic and fluid your script is.

In AppleScript, you can refer to conditional statements as if statements, in honor of their syntax.

Conditions are everywhere! They do not need a conditional statement to exist. The state of every property of every object of every application, the text or buttons that are returned from a dialog box, the value and properties of any variable you use in your script—these are all conditions you can test and use to your advantage. The only thing stopping you is your imagination (and how many hours you can bill for!).

The idea of a condition is that as complex as it may be, the result is primal: it can be either true or false. Even the most complex conditions boil down to true or false.

Understanding the Basic Conditional Statement

The basic syntax, shown in Figure 10-1, is arranged in what we call a *conditional statement*. A conditional statement starts with the word if, is followed by the first conditional test, and ends with the line end if.

Figure 10-1. *The basic conditional statement*

In Figure 10-1, line 1 contains the conditional test. You test whether the value of the variable customer_age is less than 21.

The execution of the second line depends on the condition being true. This means the code in line 2 will execute only if the test in line 1 is true. If the test isn't true (it returns a false value), then AppleScript will skip the rest of the code in the conditional statement block and proceed directly to the next statement that follows it.

In the case of the script in Figure 10-1, the third and last line indicates the end of the conditional statement.

Looking at Conditional Statement Definitions

A bit later in this chapter I will go into the different ways you can use the if statement. This section gives you a dictionary definition–style description of the different flavors of the if statement.

For the purposes of this discussion, the following examples represent their test expressions as boolean_expression. This could be a variable containing the values true or false, or it could be a more complex expression that evaluates to either true or false. We refer to these as *Boolean expressions* because they are expressions that always return a Boolean result.

The following is a one-liner:

```
if boolean_expression then single_statement
```

The following is an if-then statement block:

```
if boolean_expression then
    -- One statement or more
    -- execute only if boolean_expression is true
end if
```

The following is an if-then-else conditional statement:

```
if boolean_expression then
    -- One statement or more
    -- execute only if boolean_expression is true
else
    -- One statement or more
    -- execute only if boolean_expression is false
end if
```

The following is an if-then-else statement block, where there are two or more different conditional tests to follow:

```
if boolean_expression then
    -- One statement or more
    -- execute only if boolean_expression is true
else if another_boolean_expression then
    -- One statement or more
    -- execute only if another_boolean_expression is true
...more else if clauses...
end if
```

The following is an if-then-else statement block. It's the same as the previous one, but with a provision in case none of the conditional tests used is true:

```
if boolean_expression then
    -- One statement or more
    -- execute only if boolean_expression is true
else if another_boolean_expression then
    -- One statement or more
    -- execute only if another_boolean_expression is true
...more else if clauses...
else
    -- One statement or more
    -- execute only if none of the previous expressions is true
end if
```

Let's look at an example that will help explain the difference between the last two conditional statement variations. The following conditional statements will return the shipping cost based on the shipping method:

```
if shipping_method = "Next day" then
    set shipping_rate to 40
if shipping_method = "2nd day" then
    set shipping_rate to 30
if shipping_method = "Ground" then
    set shipping_rate to 10.50
end
```

The previous statement is OK, but what if the script suddenly gets a new value from the database and the value of the shipping_method variable is not "Next day", "2nd day", or "Ground"? In that case, none of the conditions will be met, so the shipping_rate value will not be set.

For this situation, you can add the final else condition, which will include lines that can handle any condition that is not explicitly defined:

```
if shipping_method = "Next day" then
    set shipping_rate to 40
if shipping_method = "2nd day" then
    set shipping_rate to 30
if shipping_method = "Ground" then
    set shipping_rate to 10.50
else
    error "Shipping method not recognized"
end
```

Offering Alternatives

The following script contains a single conditional statement. If the condition is `false`, then line 2 of the script will be skipped, and the statement will end without anything happening.

```
if exists document 1 then
    set text of document 1 to "Hello!"
end if
```

The previous script will execute the statement in line 2 only when the condition, in this case whether `document 1` exists, is `true`. But what will happen if the statement is `false`? What if you want the script to make a new document if none exists? In that case, you use the `else` clause. The `else` clause divides the conditional statement into two parts: what happens when the condition is `true` and what happens when it is `false`. It's that simple!

In this case, the script will look like this:

```
if exists document 1 then
    set text of document 1 to "Hello!"
else
    make new document with properties {text: "Hello!"}
end if
```

The script in Figure 10-2 shows another example of the `else` clause being used.

Figure 10-2. *A conditional statement is used with the* else *clause.*

The example in Figure 10-2 should be clear enough, but just to make sure, Figure 10-3 shows a flowchart that describes the script.

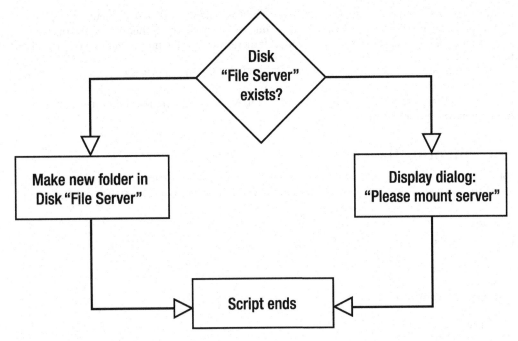

Figure 10-3. *A conditional statement's flowchart*

Learning More About Conditions

Often, a conditional statement will test for multiple conditions. In this case, AppleScript will look for the first test clause whose condition is true and execute its statements, and then the conditional statement will end.

Here's how it might work logically—you're at a party, and you want something to drink. If there's soda, you drink that. If there isn't, you look for beer. If there's no beer, you check for vodka instead. If there's no vodka left, the party has run dry, and you'll probably want to think about heading home.

In AppleScript, the conditional statement for this search for liquid may look like this:

```
if exists "soda" then
    set contents of glass to "soda"
else if exists "beer" then
    set contents of glass to "beer"
else if exists "Vodka" then
    set contents of glass to "Vodka"
else
    set contents of glass to ""

end if
```

The first condition checks for soda. If there is soda, it makes no difference whether there's also beer or vodka—you will fill your glass with soda and skip the beer part. If there's no soda, the beer gets a chance. If there's no beer, it'll try for vodka. If there's no vodka, it means nothing is left, and it's time to head home.

Now, suppose you go hunt for drinks for yourself and a friend. Your friend, for argument's sake, has the same preference as you: he would rather get soda, but if not, then beer is OK, and so on. To write a script that will fetch drinks for both of you, you will need to run the conditional statement twice—you will look at this next.

Implementing the Party

You can do run the conditional statement twice in a couple of ways. If the script will always look for drinks for two people only, you can explicitly run the condition twice, as shown in Script 10-1.

Script 10-1.

```
1. local my_drink, friend_drink

2. property sodas_left : 4
3. property beers_left : 1
4. property vodkas_left : 5

5. -- pour me a drink
6. if sodas_left > 0 then
7.    set my_drink to "soda"
8.    set sodas_left to sodas_left - 1
9. else if beers_left > 0 then
10.    set my_drink to "beer"
11.    set beers_left to beers_left - 1
12. else if vodkas_left > 0 then
13.    set my_drink to "Vodka"
14.    set vodkas_left to vodkas_left - 1
15. else
16.    set my_drink to "nothing"
17. end if

18. -- pour drink for a friend
19. if sodas_left > 0 then
20.   set friend_drink to "soda"
21.    set sodas_left to sodas_left - 1
22. else if beers_left > 0 then
23.    set friend_drink to "beer"
24.    set beers_left to beers_left - 1
25. else if vodkas_left > 0 then
26.    set friend_drink to "Vodka"
27.    set vodkas_left to vodkas_left - 1
28. else
29.    set friend_drink to "nothing"
30. end if

31. display dialog "I'm drinking " & my_drink & return & ¬
        "My friend is drinking " & friend_drink
32. display dialog "Drinks remaining:" & return & ¬
        sodas_left & " soda, " & beers_left & " beer, " & vodkas_left & " vodka"
```

Understanding How This Script Works

Let's examine the preceding script. Lines 2, 3, and 4 set the inventory. Each type of drink is represented by a variable that indicates how many single servings are left in the bottle.

Later, lines 6 through 17 contain the conditional statement block that determines your drink, or what the script calls `my_drink`. By the end of that conditional statement, the inventory has been updated to compensate for the drink you got.

Lines 19 through 30 do the same thing, but this time the result assigns a drink value to the `friend_drink` variable.

Can You Make This Script Better?

What instantly irritates me about the preceding script is that the two main chunks, lines 6–17 and lines 19–30, are nearly identical. This is wasteful coding and will simply not do! When you encounter two parts of your script that are similar, you usually can condense them and make one block take care of both tasks.

The two main forms of doing this are subroutines and repeat loops (or a combination of both).

I know we are getting slightly sidetracked here, but I just can't leave the poor script looking like that. So what I'll do is put the conditional statement into a subroutine and call it twice, as shown in Figure 10-4.

Figure 10-4. *The conditional statement appears only once but can be called multiple times.*

With a bit more thought, you can make the script handle parties of any size by creating a list of people you want to get drinks for and then looping through that list. Each loop will determine the drink for the next person in the list:

```
property sodas_left : 4
property beers_left : 1
property vodkas_left : 5

set partygoers_names to {"Sue", "Jane", "Sarah", "Steve", "Hanaan", "Jon"}
repeat with name_ref in partygoers_names
   display dialog name_ref & " is drinking " & get_drink()
end repeat

on get_drink()
   ...
```

In a real-world situation, I would start by loading the inventory from a database (or user input) and then outputting the final inventory (in other words, after the drinks have been taken) at the end of the script.

Clarifying Your Conditionals

What's important to remember when working with conditional statements is that when the script runs, the expression that lies between the word if and the word then will be evaluated and reduced to one thing: a value that is either true or false.

Although the Boolean result may be simple, the logic used to arrive at it may be complex. Until now you have seen a simple Boolean expression, sodas_left > 0, which simply evaluates one number.

Figure 10-5 shows a complex Boolean expression used in the conditional statement.

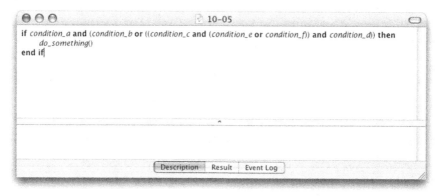

Figure 10-5. *A conditional statement using a complex Boolean expression*

To make this situation a bit easier to swallow, what I usually do is start by assigning the result of the complex Boolean expression to a well-named variable. I can then use that variable in the conditional statement instead of the monstrous expression itself. Figure 10-6 shows an example of this.

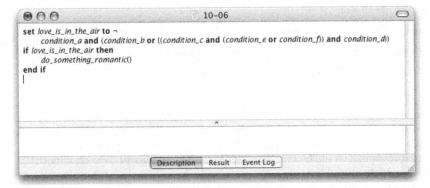

Figure 10-6. *The same complex Boolean expression assigned to a variable before being used in a conditional statement*

Nesting Conditional Statements

Another way to organize complex conditional code is by nesting several simple conditional blocks one inside another. You put forth one condition—if it evaluates to true, the next condition is tested, and so on.

Figure 10-7 shows a simple nested conditional statement.

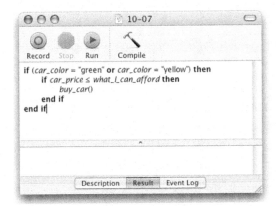

Figure 10-7. *A simple nested conditional statement*

By the nature of their functionality, some scripts will contain more conditional statements than others. Some scripts contain so many that their entire structure is one huge conditional statement.

Another way to form complex conditional statements is to use small conditional statements and nest them in other conditional statements. It does make the script longer, but as the script as a whole becomes larger and more difficult to handle, you may see the benefits of this style of writing.

Let's look at an example—say you're in the market for a car. You travel from dealership to dealership and present your requirements in two different formats. The first format is this single statement:

If you have a car that is yellow or green, gets more than 30 miles per gallon, can fit five, is less than three years old, and costs less than $10,000, I'll take it!

The second format goes like this:

Do you have cars that are yellow and green?

Hmm, OK, of these cars, do any get more than 30 miles per gallon?

OK now, out of these cars, are any three years old or newer?

And so on . . .

The first format is better since it'll get you out of the dealership more quickly. However, since it's in the nature of scripts to change, what if new requirements pop up? Let's say that if the car costs more than $8,000, it also needs to have a CD changer. Although you could build that into your original conditional test expression, it would be much simpler to modify your script if the conditional statement consists of multiple nested statements.

From looking at the two scripts in Figure 10-8 and Figure 10-9, you can see that when you nest conditional statements inside other conditional statements, the script is longer, but it is also easier to read and will be much easier to add to later.

Figure 10-8. *The car search script in one conditional statement with a long conditional test expression*

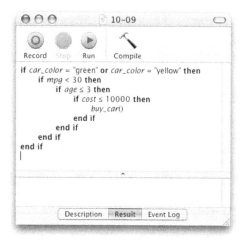

Figure 10-9. *The same car search script with the conditional test broken down into multiple levels in the conditional block*

Another big advantage of spreading your conditions over multiple nested statements is that you can add more statements in the different levels of the conditional statement, something you can't do with one conditional test.

Using Shortcuts

The following are some neat tricks to help you make the most of conditional statements and save you some typing too.

Using a Condition in a Single Line

Conditional statements can start and end on a single line, like in the following script:

```
if time_left = 0 then blow_whistle()
```

This form of conditional statement is useful when the statement is simple because it makes the statement more concise and easier to read.

Avoiding Unneeded Conditional Statements

Sometimes you want to check whether a condition is true or false just in order to set the value of a variable to that true or false value. You may be tempted to write the script shown in Script 10-2.

Script 10-2. *(includes the following scripts)*

```
if stoplight_color is "green" then
  set walk_now to true
else
  set walk_now to false
end if
```

This works, but it is unnecessarily complex. Instead, you should just use the following:

```
set walk_now to stop_light_color is "green"
```

The expression stoplight_color is "green" evaluates to either true or false. That value can be directly assigned to the walk_now variable without a conditional statement.

Is It True?

To check whether a Boolean value assigned to a variable is true or false, it isn't necessary to perform a full-blown equality test like this:

```
if Boolean_variable = true then do_something()
```

Simply use the variable, like this:

```
if Boolean_variable then do_something()
```

If you want to find out whether the variable's value is false, simply add the not operator before the variable, like this:

```
if not tired_yet then write_another_chapter()
```

This last line says that the handler write_another_chapter will be called if the variable tired_yet is false.

One word of caution with this scripting technique is that if the variable you're testing ever contains a value other than `true` or `false`, the conditional statement will raise an error. This is because conditional statements insist on their test expressions returning a Boolean value. Unlike some other parts of AppleScript, if they receive a value of any other class, they won't even try to coerce it to a Boolean; they'll just raise an error immediately.

For example, look at the script in Script 10-3 that utilizes the `choose from list` command. This command returns a list if the user clicks OK, but it returns the Boolean value `false` if the user clicks the Cancel button. In the script, I start by asking the user to choose from a list, and then I test right away if the user clicked Cancel.

Script 10-3. *(includes the following scripts)*

```
set list_of_items to {"New Job", "Save Job", "Close Job"}
set chosen_item to choose from list list_of_items
if not chosen_item then
  display alert "You canceled"
end if
```

This script will work just fine if the user clicks Cancel, but if they choose anything from the list (I chose the first item) and click OK, you will get this error:

```
Can't make "New Job" into type boolean.
```

To solve the problem, use the `equals` operator to check whether the variable's value is `false`, like this:

```
set list_of_items to {"New Job", "Save Job", "Close Job"}
set chosen_item to choose from list list_of_items
if chosen_item is false then
  display alert "You canceled"
end if
```

Using Lists for Manageable Statements

One point I made earlier is worth discussing in more detail here. Let's explore a situation in which you want to check whether the value of a variable is one of several possibilities. For instance, say you want the script to do something if the month of a given date, for example, is between September and November. In this case, you can create a compound test expression, like this:

```
set the_month to month of some_date
if the_month is September or the_month is October or the_month is November then
  -- do something
end if
```

Although this works, you will be better off with the following simpler `if` statement that uses the `is in` containment operator along with a list of months to achieve the same result:

```
if the_month is in {September, October, November} then
  -- do something
end if
```

Writing in Shorthand

Like in other AppleScript statements, you can omit certain words, and AppleScript will fill them in for you. The only problem with this is that when you then switch to programming in another language that doesn't have the same shortcut facilities (such as REALbasic), you have to remember to write everything. One such shortcut AppleScript has is the word then. Simply omit it, and AppleScript will add it for you when it compiles. The other word you can omit in every control statement is the word if that immediately follows the word end.

Let's try an example: start a new script window, and write the script shown in Figure 10-10. Compile the script, and it will end up looking like the code shown in Figure 10-11.

Figure 10-10. *The words* then *in the first line and* if *in the last line have been omitted.*

Figure 10-11. *AppleScript adds these words as the script compiles.*

Power Wrap-Up

The following sections summarize the chapter in an intensive reference style. Use these sections to look up facts related to the chapter without the chatter.

Using a Basic Conditional Statement

When your script has to decide between executing one set of statements or not, you use a conditional statement. You can write conditional statements in a few ways, but they all include the two words if and then. Script 10-4 shows an example of a simple conditional statement.

Script 10-4. *(includes the following scripts)*

```
if some_boolean_expression then
   display dialog "The answer is right"
end if
```

In the preceding example, only if the variable some_boolean_expression is true will the line containing the display dialog command execute. The Boolean expression doesn't have to be a variable; it can be a complex some_boolean_expression representing a Boolean expression, which is an expression that evaluates to either true or false, as in this example:

```
if (the_chip contains "G5") or (the_chip contains "G5") and ➥
the_model contains "Power" and ((the_RAM ≥ 1000) or ➥
(the_MHZ ≥ 1000)) then
   buy_mac()
end if
```

No matter how complex, if the expression between if and then on the first line evaluates as either true or false, it is legal. You could have written the two preceding scripts using one line only, like this:

```
if some_boolean_expression then display dialog ¬
"The answer is right"
```

Using if-then-else

If the script is going to choose from two options, the else part of the statement has to separate those choices, as shown in Script 10-5.

Script 10-5. *(includes the following script)*

```
if some_boolean_expression then
   --perform these statements
else
   --perform these other statements
end if
```

To allow even more options, you can add branching with additional else if lines, like this:

```
if some_boolean then
   --perform these statements
else if some_boolean_2 then
   --perform these other statements
else if some_boolean_3 then
   --perform these other statements
else
   --perform these other statements
end if
```

The final else line is not required. If included, it handles all the cases that did not fall within the previous conditions. For example, Script 10-6 assigns a reference to Adobe InDesign's front document to the variable this_document. It uses a conditional block to check whether the front document already exists, and if not, it creates one for this purpose.

Script 10-6.

```
tell application "InDesign CS"
  if (exists document 1) then
    set this_document to document 1
  else
    set this_document to make new document
  end if
end tell
```

CHAPTER 11

■ ■ ■

The Assembly Line: Creating Repeat Loops

The repeat loop is one of the two programming concepts that separate AppleScript from other automation solutions such as recording macros or running actions in Adobe Photoshop (the other one being conditional statements). This loop allows you to perform a single set of actions multiple times. Figure 11-1 shows an example of a simple repeat loop.

Figure 11-1. *A simple* repeat *loop*

OK, so this didn't do much; it just beeped. Also, the operation was performed identically each time, without any variation. But that's the idea I'm demonstrating here—an assembly line that performs the same operation every time. If you have an assembly line in a soda can factory, for instance, you may want a tool to apply a label to each can. The operation will be identical, but the can will be a different can every time. In other words, you'll have identical cans but different instances—one tool is used to perform as many operations as you want, saving you a lot of time!

This is the most basic form of a repeat loop:

```
repeat
  --Do something...
end repeat
```

Notice that the statement starts with the word repeat and ends with an end repeat line. This is a requirement for all repeat statements. Between these two lines you will put all the statements that will be executed every time the loop repeats. What's sorely missing in the preceding repeat statement is a consideration that the wizard's apprentice didn't take into account: what will make the repeat loop stop?

AppleScript has two basic ways to specify when the repeat loop should end and move on to the statement following the repeat loop:

- Predetermined count, which means the number of repetitions will be known to the script before the loop starts

- Signaled condition, which means the loop will continue repeating until a condition is met

AppleScript provides a few variations on these two themes. Some loops repeat a predetermined number of times, and some loops keep repeating until a specific condition is met. For instance, if you loop through a list of folders and do something to each folder, the number of repetitions will normally depend on the number of folders, which is unknown at the time you write the script but will be determined by the script when it runs.

You can also include one or more statements inside the repeat statement block that set a condition that if true, the repeat loop will stop; otherwise, the loop will just continue. What follows are the variations of the repeat control statement, followed by a detailed explanation of each one.

Understanding the Code Variations of Repeat Loops

Script 11-1 lists the different flavors of repeat loops. These flavors are explained in detail later in the chapter.

Script 11-1. *(includes the six following scripts)*

```
repeat
  --statement/s to repeat
end repeat
```

The previous script repeats forever.

The following one repeats a specific number of times:

```
repeat n times -- n is an integer
  --statement/s to repeat
end repeat
```

This repeats with a loop variable:

```
repeat with i from start_integer to end_integer -- i changes value
with each loop
  --statement/s to repeat
end repeat
```

And the following is an extended version of the previous repeat form; it repeats with a loop variable, jumping by intervals other than 1:

```
repeat with i from start_integer to end_integer by step_interval
-- i changes value with each loop by the step_interval
  --statement/s to repeat
end repeat
```

This repeats until a certain Boolean condition becomes true:

```
repeat until boolean_expression
  --statement/s to repeat
end repeat
```

This repeats while a certain Boolean condition is true:

```
repeat while boolean_expression
  --statement/s to repeat
end repeat
```

Repeating (Forever)

Well, you never would really repeat forever, although I'm sure OS X is capable of running continuously for that long! By forever, I mean that the repeat statement itself doesn't contain any provisions for ending the loop.

Although you can loop forever, you can, and should, include a way for the loop to terminate inside the repeat loop block. You'll learn more about terminating loops a bit later in the "Exiting a Loop Programmatically" section.

Interrupting a Script That's Stuck in a Loop

A script that is in the middle of an endless loop, or a loop that doesn't appear to end, can be interrupted only by pressing Command+. (period) or, if that doesn't work, by force quitting using Command+Option+Escape.

Exiting a Loop Programmatically

One of the ways to terminate the simple repeat statement without specifying an end to it is by using the exit repeat statement.

This statement is contained for the most part in a conditional statement. If it isn't, the loop will end after the first repetition.

The advantage of using the exit repeat statement instead of some other repeat statement type is that the condition can be placed anywhere in the repeat block, not stuck in the first line. The problem with it, however, is that it makes the code harder to understand, since it isn't immediately apparent under which condition the loop is terminated.

Figure 11-2 shows an example of a repeat loop with an exit repeat statement inside a conditional statement.

Figure 11-2. *A plain* repeat *loop that will exit when a certain condition is met*

You may be asking yourself what happens if the condition is never met. Well, then AppleScript will run the script forever. It is your job as a scripter to make sure your loops run their course and come to an end when appropriate. Remember, pressing Command+. (period) will stop a script or quit a script application that's in the foreground. You will need to use that during testing.

Repeating *n* Times

This simple repeat variation is intended to be simple and concise. It is useful when you want to perform the same set of actions a certain number of times with no variation from one loop to the next. Figure 11-3 shows an example of a repeat loop that repeats five times.

Figure 11-3. *A* repeat *loop that repeats five times*

You can also use a variable to specify the number of repetitions, like in Script 11-2.

Script 11-2.

```
Display dialog "How many times should I beep?" default answer "5"
Set beep_count to text returned of result as integer
repeat beep_count times
    beep
    delay 1
end repeat
```

The preceding script asks the user to enter a number and then executes a beep command the number of times dictated by the user.

What happens is that the user's response (which comes as a string) is coerced into an integer. However, there's no verification to make sure the user doesn't cancel or enter a value that cannot be coerced into an integer.

Using Loop Variables

Loop variables are variables whose values change incrementally with every loop repetition. Like kids playing jump rope and counting each jump aloud, AppleScript automatically updates the value of that special variable with every loop. In this section, you'll see an example of using a loop variable. Let's say you have a list of U.S. phone numbers, and you want to add area codes to the ones that have only seven digits. Looking at the loop requirements, you see that each repetition will treat each item of the phone number list in turn. The loop variable i changes its value starting with 1 and incrementing up by 1 with every repetition. Here's the script:

```
repeat with i from 1 to count phone_list
    if length of (item i of phone_list) is 7 then
        set item i of phone_list to area_code & (item i of phone_list)
    end if
end repeat
```

Repeating with Numbers in a Range

When you repeat with numbers in a range, you include a variable that automatically changes in value based on the current loop count. This allows you to specify a numerical range, and while the loop is repeating, the value of that variable increases (or decreases) in value with each repetition. See Figure 11-4.

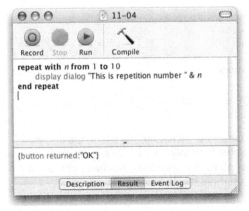

Figure 11-4. *The variable* i *increases in value with each repetition, starting with 1 all the way to 10.*

This repeat flavor also allows you to play with the way the repeat variable increases or decreases. You'll see a few examples in the following sections.

Using an Expression to Define the Range

As you may imagine, you can use any integers stored in variables to specify the start and end of the range, as shown in Script 11-3.

Script 11-3.

```
repeat with n from start_integer to end_integer
--do something with n...
end repeat
```

This is useful when you don't know in advance the range of numbers you want to count over.

This is one of the most widely used variations of repeat loops and is useful when you need to perform a certain operation on a range of application objects—for instance, all the pages of an Adobe InDesign document, the records in a FileMaker Pro found set, or all the files in a particular folder. For that, you use the repeat loop along with the count command. The count command along with the object range returns the number of applicable objects, which in turn becomes your repeat loop's number of repetitions. Figure 11-5 shows an example of this. In the example, the script needs to add the word *folder* to the end of the folder name.

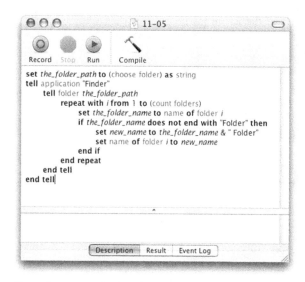

Figure 11-5. *A* repeat *loop with a variable used for the range*

Specifying Increments

The first variation of this repeat loop flavor lets you change the increments by which the loop variable increases. In the previous examples, the loop variable increased by 1 each time, but what happens if you want to increase it by another number? All you have to do is add the by phrase followed by the increment you want to use. Refer to the example shown in Script 11-4.

Script 11-4.

```
set the_list to {}
repeat with i from 1 to 50 by 5
    set end of the_list to i
end repeat
the_list = {5, 10, 15, 20, 25, 30, 35, 40, 45, 50}
```

The following example will change every third word in the front TextEdit document into the word *carrot*:

```
tell application "TextEdit"
  tell document 1
    repeat with i from 3 to (count every word) by 3
      set word i to "carrot"
    end repeat
  end tell
end tell
```

Make sure not to run this script if the front TextEdit document has something important in it, such as a recipe for a carrot cake.

If you take this concept a step further, you can create the entire multiplication table, and what the heck, let's present the result in HTML (see Script 11-5).

Script 11-5.

```
1. set html to ""
2. set html to html & "<html>" & return
3. set html to html & "<head>" & return
4. set html to html & "<title>Multiplication table</title>" & return
5. set html to html & "</head>" & return
6. set html to html & "<body>" & return
7. set html to html & "<table border=1 cellpadding=2>" & return
8. set html to html & "<tr>" & return

9. repeat with i from 1 to 10
10.    repeat with j from (1 * i) to (10 * i) by i
11.        set html to html & "<td>"
12.        set html to html & j
13.        set html to html & "</td>"
14.    end repeat
15.    set html to html & "<tr>" & return
16. end repeat
```

Although this is quite a complicated loop, it demonstrates a specific form of repeat loop; you can also achieve the same result in other ways.

Here are two repeat loops nested one inside the other. The outer repeat loop simply counts from 1 to 10, assigning the loop value to the variable i, which becomes the driving force behind the inner repeat loop.

The inner repeat loop uses the variable j. What gives j the correct integer value for the multiplication table is that every time the loop executes, the start point and end point move up. Here is the inner repeat statement the way it appears in the code:

```
repeat with j from (i * 1) to (i * 10) by i
```

In the first loop, the value of the variable i is 1, and the inner repeat loop looks like this:

```
repeat with j from 1 to 10 by 1
```

In the second loop the value of i is 2, and therefore the repeat statement translates into this:

```
repeat with j from 2 to 20 by 2
```

The third loop is where i is 3 and the values of j are 3, 6, 9, 12 . . . 30:

```
repeat with j from 3 to 30 by 3
```

This continues all the way to the final loop where the value of the variable i is 10:

```
repeat with j from 10 to 100 by 10
```

The values of j here are 10, 20, 30, 40 . . . 100.

Inside the loop, you add the <td> tag, followed by the actual value assigned to the variable j, followed by the closing </td> tag.

Figure 11-6 shows the resulting web page.

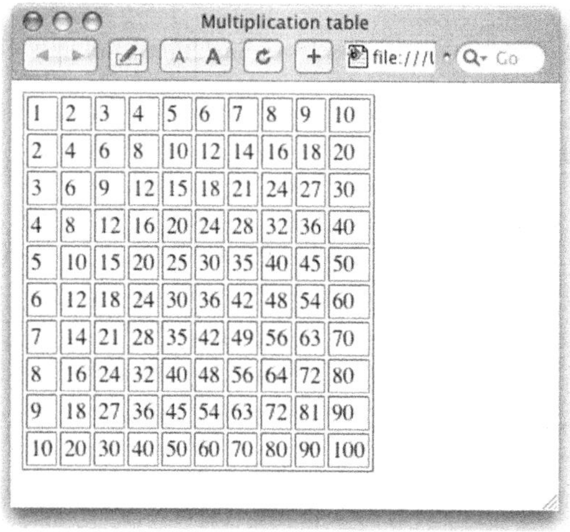

1	2	3	4	5	6	7	8	9	10
2	4	6	8	10	12	14	16	18	20
3	6	9	12	15	18	21	24	27	30
4	8	12	16	20	24	28	32	36	40
5	10	15	20	25	30	35	40	45	50
6	12	18	24	30	36	42	48	54	60
7	14	21	28	35	42	49	56	63	70
8	16	24	32	40	48	56	64	72	80
9	18	27	36	45	54	63	72	81	90
10	20	30	40	50	60	70	80	90	100

Figure 11-6. *The web page resulting from the multiplication table script*

Counting Backward

In a repeat loop, the repeat variable can also count backward. This means the value of the repeat variable is higher at the start than at the end. To do that, you must use a negative integer for the step value (see Script 11-6).

Script 11-6.

```
Repeat with i from 100000 to 1 by -1
Display dialog "Shuttle launch in " & i & " seconds" giving up after 1
End repeat
```

Although the preceding script won't land me a job at NASA, it shows how a repeat loop starts high and counts down. Note that it is not enough to specify from high to low numbers; you must include the by <negative number> at the end.

Counting Forward and Backward in the Same Loop

What if a loop calls for one variable to count both up and down? For that you will need some sort of a rig. You'll need to count up and reverse the value of the repeat variable inside the loop, as shown in Script 11-7.

Script 11-7.

```
repeat with i from 1 to 10
  set negative_i to -i
end repeat
```

The variable negative_i will start from –1 and go all the way to –10.

Repeating Actions on Items in a List

In many cases, you will have a list and want to perform one or more actions using each item in the list in turn. For instance, if you have the following list of names:

```
{"Ben", "Jen", "Stan"}
```

you can assign the value of a different list item in every loop, as shown in Figure 11-7.

Figure 11-7. *A* repeat *loop that allows the script to use one item from a list in each turn*

This script will display a dialog box with the value of the variable the_name_ref in each repetition.

Naming the Loop Variable

You will sometime encounter single-number variables such as i and j as the repeat variables. I did that because the variable's value had no special meaning other than being an integer. In this case, the variable points to an item from a list. So if the list is called names_list, then it's only fitting that the repeat variable will be called the_name_ref. Also notice that instead of using the statement display dialog the_name_ref, I used display dialog (contents of the_name_ref). This made the script get the actual value of the list item rather than the reference to the list item, which is stored in the variable the_name_ref.

Another Example Regarding Treating Items in a List with a Repeat Loop

In this section, you will take the name list you looked at earlier and create a script that will generate a personalized letter for each person in the list. The script will open the template you're about to create, replace the name placeholder text, and save the letter with the person's name in the filename.

To start, you'll create the template. Start a new TextEdit document, and type the following text:

```
"Dear NAME_PLACEHOLDER,
You're invited to join us in the office on Monday for pizza"
```

Next, save the document on the desktop to a file named `report template.rtf`. Script 11-8 shows the script.

Script 11-8.

```
set names_list to {"Ben", "Jen", "Stan"}
set desktop_path to (path to desktop) as string
set report_template to desktop_path & "report template.rtf"

repeat with name_ref in names_list
  set report_file to desktop_path & name_ref & " report.rtf"
  tell application "TextEdit"
    activate
    open alias report_template
    tell document 1
      set (every word where it is "NAME_PLACEHOLDER") ¬
        to contents of name_ref
      save in file report_file
      close saving no
    end tell
  end tell
end repeat
```

Notice that throughout the script you use the repeat loop variable twice: once to set the report file path and again when inserting the person's name into the report template.

Using repeat while and repeat until

In some situations, the termination of a loop will be determined by a condition being met rather than by a predetermined count.

Using repeat while and repeat until, you can attach a condition to the repeat loop that will stop the loop repeating when the result of the condition changes. For instance, if you have a cookie jar you're trying to empty (one cookie at a time), the condition is whether the jar is empty. Here's how you can script it:

```
Repeat until (jar is empty)
  Eat cookie
End repeat
```

In the preceding script, which won't run on any of my Macs, the condition jar is empty comes back false as long as there are still cookies in the jar. As soon as there aren't, the loop stops repeating.

Now in the preceding example, you could've theoretically counted the cookies and repeated a number of times that is equal to the number of cookies; however, in some cases, there's no way to know in advance just how many times a loop is going to repeat. We'll look at a couple of examples later.

Two forms of repeat loop can break on a condition: repeat while and repeat until. Both forms use a condition; when using repeat while, the loop goes on *while* the condition is true, and when using repeat until, the loop repeats *until* the condition is true.

Note that you can use the repeat while and repeat until methods interchangeably by adding the not operator before the condition. You choose one over the other simply by how it sounds and how well it fits what you do.

Script 11-9 shows the syntax for the two examples.

Script 11-9.

```
repeat while condition_is_true
-- do something
end repeat
The opposite of that is
repeat until condition_is_true
-- do something
end repeat
```

Figure 11-8 and Figure 11-9 show simple examples of repeat until and repeat while.

In Figure 11-8 you have a virtual pile of playing cards. You want to see how many cards you flip before the card total exceeds 100. So, you have a variable that adds the card values and a variable that counts the cards. The script will loop until the cards total reaches 100 and will return the number of cards flipped so far.

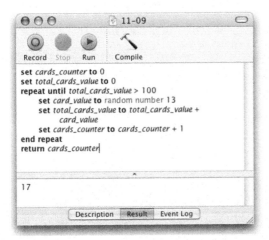

Figure 11-8. *Repeating until the total card value exceeds 100*

In the script shown in Figure 11-9, the loop simply checks whether the file exists. When distilling an Adobe PostScript file into a PDF file using Acrobat Distiller 5, for instance, Acrobat Distiller won't tell you when the PDF is complete. This loop can come in handy for delaying the script until the PDF file has been created.

Figure 11-9. *Repeating while the file doesn't exist*

The script in Figure 11-10 is a modification of the script in Figure 11-8. It repeats while the card total is less than 21. Look at the record that the script returns: it contains the card count, the total card value, and the cards themselves.

The problem? You asked the script to loop while the card value is *less* than 21, but the card value at the end is *greater than* 21. This happens because when the repeat loop condition executes, the card value has already been exceeded 21! At that point, all the repeat loop can do is stop, but the damage has already been done, and the card total has climbed beyond 21.

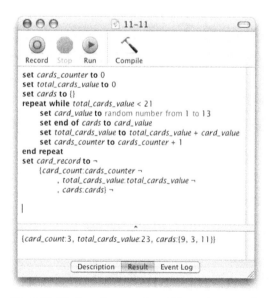

Figure 11-10. *Does the* repeat until *continue one loop too many?*

So how do you fix this problem? You use a simple repeat loop with a slightly more complex conditional statement, as shown in Script 11-10.

Script 11-10.

```
repeat
    set card_value to random number from 1 to 13
    if (total _value + card_value) > 21 then exit repeat
    set end of cards to card_value
    set total_value to total_value + card_value
end repeat
```

In the preceding script, the condition to stop the repeat isn't part of the repeat statement but rather a separate conditional statement. It checks whether the total exceeds 21 before it actually adds the new card to the total.

Script 11-11 shows a neat example of the repeat until command. This example shows a script that arranges files in folders for archiving. The script has to make sure each folder has files whose accumulated file size is almost, but not quite, 600MB (or any other specified size) so that they can fit on a disk. The script contains two loops.

Script 11-11.

```
1.  set max_archive_size to 600 * 1024 * 1024 -- 600 MB
2.  set source_folder to path to pictures folder
3.  tell application "Finder"
4.  set files_to_process to document files of folder source_folder ¬
        whose size < max_archive_size
5.     set archive_number to 0
6.     repeat until files_to_process is {}
7.        set archive_number to archive_number + 1
8.        set archive_folder to make new folder at desktop ¬
            with properties {name:"folder " & archive_number}
9.        set total_size to 0
10.       repeat until files_to_process is {}
11.          set file_size to size of item 1 of files_to_process
12.          if total_size + file_size > max_archive_size then exit repeat
13.          move item 1 of files_to_process to archive_folder
14.          set files_to_process to rest of files_to_process
15.          set total_size to total_size + file_size
16.       end repeat
17.    end repeat
18. end tell
```

The first loop in the preceding script starts at line 6. It will repeat until the folder you're archiving is empty. Notice that there's no mention of how many files there are or should be, only a simple condition: keep looping until there are zero files.

The second repeat loop, starting on line 10, relies on a variable called total_size. This variable is a real value and is being added to incrementally. The size of every file that the script processes is added to the total_size variable. As indicated in the condition set in line 12, the second loop repeats until the value of the total_size variable is less than the specified amount set in the max_archive_size variable.

Using Other Ways of Counting Loops

The looping method of repeat with some_expression from start_integer to end_integer is the only one that has a built-in loop counter. This does not mean you can't create your own loop counter. It is common practice to use a counter variable in some instances with any of the other repeat loop flavors, such as when the increment has to be a fraction.

What you do is start by assigning an initial value to your counter variable and then increase it, decrease it, multiply it, or divide it by any value you want. This method gives you the most flexibility over your counter variable. Here's an example:

```
Set counter_variable to 1
repeat
  set counter_variable to counter_variable * 2 - 3
  do something with counter_variable
end repeat
```

The variable counter_variable will have the following values: –1, –5, –13, –29, –125, –253, –509, and so on. Why would you need such an odd set of numbers? Well, I doubt you'll ever need this one, but it does demonstrate what flexibility you have with your counter variable, should you ever need it.

Avoid Looping When Possible

Although the repeat loop is a staple you can't do without, sometimes the application you're scripting may allow you to use the whose clause to target a collection of elements.

In some cases, you can use the whose clause instead of a repeat loop. If supported by the application's scripting interface, the whose clause can target multiple elements at the same time and allows you to apply an action to all of them together. Since the whose clause is implemented inside the application, it generally runs much faster than if you had a repeat loop target each element individually. Imagine standing in front of 100 people all wearing different color hats and having to ask all the red-hat wearers to take off their hats. With a repeat loop, it would go like this: first person with red hat, take it off; second person with red hat, take it off; third person with red hat, take it off; and so on.

With a whose clause, it would go like this: every person whose hat is red, take your hats off. In the following example, we will delete all files that have the word *temp* in the name. First, this is the repeat version:

```
tell application "Finder"
   repeat with file_ref in (get files of folder theFolder)
      if name of file_ref contains "temp" then
         delete file_ref
      end if
   end repeat
end tell
```

Script 11-12 shows the smart version that uses the whose clause.

Script 11-12. *(includes previous script)*

```
tell application "Finder"
   delete every file of folder theFolder whose name contains "temp"
end tell
```

It's not only that the code is shorter and more to the point, but the execution time will be shorter—much shorter in situations where there are many objects to loop through. When using the whose clause, you're not forcing the scripting application to send commands and reference objects time and time again; instead, the command will be sent once.

Power Wrap-Up

The following sections summarize the chapter in an intensive reference style. Use this part to look up facts related to the chapter without the chatter.

Using a Simple Repeat Loop

The simplest repeat loop will repeat until stopped either by an `exit repeat` statement inside the loop or by the user pressing Command+. (period). With every repetition, the script will be executing the statements between the `repeat` line and the `end repeat` line.

```
repeat
  --Do something...
end repeat
```

Exiting a Repeat Loop

You exit a repeat loop with the `exit repeat` statement. This statement usually sits in a conditional statement that determines when the loop has reached its potential. Here's how you use the `exit repeat` statement:

```
repeat
   --Do something...
   if time_to_stop_loop is true then
      exit repeat
   end if
end repeat
```

Using the Simplest Repeat Loop

Use the following version of the repeat statement to repeat a specific number of times:

```
repeat 12 times
  --statements to execute repeatedly
end repeat
```

Using Loop Variables

Loop variables are variables that automatically change with each repetition. In the following script, the variable i is the loop variable. It will start with the value of 1 and increment by 1 with every repetition. The loop will stop when the value of i has reached the number indicated at the end of the repeat line:

```
repeat with i from 1 to 10
  --The value of the variable i starts with 1
  --and grows by 1 with each loop
end repeat
```

Here's another example:

```
repeat with i from 1 to (count characters of user_name)
  --statement to execute repeatedly
end repeat
```

You can use the by parameter to change the repeat variable to any other number. The loop in the following script will have 20 repetitions:

```
repeat with i from 5 to 100 by 5
  --The value of the variable i starts with 5 and grows by 5 up to 100.
end repeat
```

You can also count backward (see Script 11-13).

Script 11-13.

```
repeat with i from 20 to 0 by -2
  --The value of the variable i starts with 20 and
  --decreases by 2 until it reaches 0.
end repeat
```

Repeating Actions on Items in a List

When you have a list whose items need to be processed in order, you can make the loop variable take on the value of the next item in the list each time. In Script 11-14, the value of the loop variable will be a different value from the employee_names list.

Script 11-14.

```
set employee_names to {"Jena","Jack","Bonnie","Frank"}
repeat with the_name in employee_names
  --The value of the variable the_name
  -- starts with "Jena" in the first loop, then "Jack", etc.
end repeat
```

Using repeat while

You can repeat while a certain condition is true. This allows you to repeat the execution of statements without setting a predefined loop count. Script 11-15 will loop as long as there's an open document in FileMaker Pro. Since the repeating statement closes the front open document, all documents will be eventually closed, the Boolean expression document 1 exists will evaluate as false, and the loop will conclude.

Script 11-15.

```
tell application "FileMaker Pro"
   repeat while (document 1 exists)
      close document 1
   end repeat
end tell
```

Using repeat until

The repeat until flavor of the repeat loop works the opposite way from the repeat while statement. You supply the repeat loop with a Boolean expression, and as soon as that expression evaluates as true, the loop will stop. See Script 11-16.

Script 11-16.

```
tell application "FileMaker Pro"
    repeat until (count documents = 0)
        close document 1
    end repeat
end tell
```

Using Counter Variables

Counter variables are like loop variables, but you decide on their value. The typical counter variable will increase in value by 1 with every loop. You can have multiple counters that serve different purposes, as in Script 11-17.

Script 11-17.

```
set year_counter to 0
set dog_year_counter to 0
repeat
    set year_counter to year_counter + 1
    set dog_year_counter to dog_year_counter + 7
    set the_message to "After " & year_counter & ¬
    " years, your dog is really " & dog_year_counter & " years old."
    try
        display dialog the_message
    on error -128 -- user canceled
        exit repeat
    end try
end repeat
```

CHAPTER 12

■■■

Interacting with the User

In various situations you'll need to get the user involved during the execution of your script, so this chapter details the AppleScript features related to user interaction.

Although AppleScript provides ways for the user to interact with the script and to provide some input during script operation, these interaction facilities are minimal. AppleScript was designed for accessing data and manipulating it and therefore doesn't include robust interface tools. If your solution calls for a more complex interface than the commands provided by AppleScript (and detailed in this chapter), you'll have to look to other tools. These tools include third-party scripting additions such as 24U Appearance OSAX, which allows you to design more robust dialog boxes. To create solutions that include multiple complex windows with controls such as pop-up menus, images, movies, and so on, you should look into using a development tool such as Smile, FaceSpan, or the more complicated AppleScript Studio.

AppleScript's user interaction commands are all part of the Standard Additions suite, and they allow you to interact with the user in three ways: you can display information and gather text input from the user; you can allow the user to specify items such as files, folders, servers, and disks; and you can allow the user to perform other tasks such as picking an item from a list or choosing a color.

Creating Basic Dialog Boxes and Gathering Text Input

The best example for user interaction in AppleScript is, perhaps, the `display dialog` command, which can display a message and request the user to enter text or click a button.

Until OS X 10.4 came along, you had to use the `display dialog` command for most simple user interaction. Now, you can use a new command: `display alert`.

The `display alert` command is a cousin of `display dialog`. It displays a similar-looking dialog box but offers an easier way to display a quick alert on the screen.

The `display dialog` command and other user interaction commands you'll look at in this chapter are all part of the Standard Additions suite that comes installed as part of the Mac OS.

Introducing the display dialog Command

The `display dialog` scripting addition is one of the most useful commands and one of the first you will try in AppleScript.

The Standard Additions dictionary defines two `display dialog`–related items: the `display dialog` command and the `dialog reply` record.

From the Dictionary: display dialog

The following is the Standard Additions dictionary definition for display dialog:

```
display dialog v : Display a dialog box, optionally requesting user input
    display dialog string : the text to display in the dialog box
        [default answer string] : the default editable text
        [hidden answer boolean] : Should editable text be displayed as bullets?
            (default is false)
        [buttons list of string] : a list of up to three button names
        [default button number or string] : the name or number of the default button
        [cancel button number or string] : the name or number of the cancel button
        [with title string] : the dialog window title
        [with icon number or string] : the resource name or ID of the icon to
            display...
        [with icon stop/note/caution] : ...or one of these system icons...
        [with icon file] : ...or an alias or file reference to a '.icns' file
        [giving up after integer] : number of seconds to wait before automatically
            dismissing the dialog
    Result: dialog reply : a record containing the button clicked and text entered
        (if any)
```

From the Dictionary: dialog reply

The following is the specification for the dialog reply record:

```
Class dialog reply: Reply record for the 'display dialog' command
Properties:
    button returned  Unicode text  [r/o]
        -- name of button chosen (empty if 'giving up after'
            was supplied and dialog timed out)
    text returned  Unicode text  [r/o]
        -- text entered (present only if 'default answer' was supplied)
    gave up  boolean  [r/o]
        -- Did the dialog time out? (present only if 'giving up after'
            was supplied)
```

Using the Basic Form of the Command

The basic form of the command allows you to display a simple message in a dialog box along with two buttons, OK and Cancel. Figure 12-1 shows the basic display dialog command and its resulting record, and Figure 12-2 shows the dialog box itself.

If you look at the script result in the Result area in Figure 12-1, you will notice that the result is a record with a single property. The label is button returned, and the value is OK. This record will actually have more items in it when you add more parameters to the display dialog command.

For now, you can see that the button returned (the button the user clicked) was the OK button.

Figure 12-1. *The basic* display dialog *command*

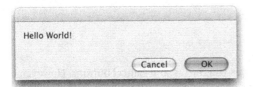

Figure 12-2. *The dialog box resulting from the basic* display dialog *command*

Dealing with the Erroneous Cancel Button

Let's try to run the script and click the Cancel button.

Hmm . . . where's the result? No record this time? What happened is that the display dialog command generates an error when the Cancel button is clicked. You can get more information about it if you trap it using the try...on error control block.

Create a new script, and copy the text from the script in Figure 12-3.

Figure 12-3. *Trapping the Cancel button error using the* try...on error *block*

Now run the script, and click the Cancel button in the first dialog box. This causes the display dialog command on line 2 to generate an error. This error is caught by the enclosing try block, causing the try block to execute its on error portion.

As will be explained in detail in Chapter 17, you can place a variable name, in this case error_text, immediately after the on error portion on line 3. When the try block catches an error, it assigns the error message string to this variable.

The second dialog box will display that error message string. This will be, in effect, your own error message dialog box.

As you can see in the dialog box shown in Figure 12-4, the error AppleScript returned was a "User canceled" error. This error has an error number of –128.

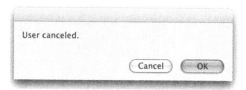

Figure 12-4. *The dialog box showing the error message*

Creating Custom Buttons

By default, AppleScript's display dialog command gives you the OK and Cancel buttons. However, you can easily define one, two, or three buttons of your own. To define buttons, you use the buttons parameter followed by a list of button names as strings. Each string will become a button. A list with more than three items will generate an error, and an empty list will prompt AppleScript to use the default OK and Cancel buttons.

When running the script in Figure 12-5, the dialog box shown in Figure 12-6 will be displayed. When you click a button in that dialog box, the display dialog command returns a record with a buttoned returned property containing the button's name. For example, the Result area in Figure 12-5 shows the result of clicking the No button.

Figure 12-5. *You can create your own dialog box buttons.*

Figure 12-6. *The dialog box with the custom buttons*

If you use longer names for your buttons, AppleScript will produce a dialog box with wider buttons to try to accommodate your text. In OS X versions prior to Tiger (10.4), all buttons in the dialog box were stretched equally, and the widest button you could have was about 20 characters. In Tiger, buttons are made to fit the size of the button text, which means that if the button titles are longer than a few characters, each button will have its own size. If the titles of all buttons force the dialog box to be wider than 600 pixels, the button titles will get truncated from both ends.

You have no way to change the font size or font style of the dialog box. For that kind of control, you need to upgrade your skills to the "everything is possible" land of AppleScript Studio, FaceSpan, or third-party scripting additions.

Specifying a Default Button

What's missing from the dialog box in Figure 12-6 is a button that will execute when the user presses the Return key. This is called the *default* button. You can turn a button into the default button by passing its name as the `default button` parameter. Running the script in Figure 12-7 will produce the dialog box shown in Figure 12-8.

Figure 12-7. *The default button is specified.*

Figure 12-8. *The dialog box with a default button*

The default button parameter can also take an integer from 1 to 3. Specifically, 1 would be the leftmost button in the dialog box. This means to get the same result as shown in Figure 12-8, you could specify the default button as 3 instead of Maybe.

Note Deciding which button is the default one can be important. What you have to assume is that for the most part, people don't read dialog boxes. There's even the saying "It's a Mac, just click OK . . . ." This aspect of human nature means you should make the default button the button with the least harsh consequences. For instance, the default button in a dialog box that reminds users for the last time that the script is about to erase their hard disk should be the Cancel button, not the OK button.

Specifying a Cancel Button

cancel button, a new parameter to the display dialog command in Tiger, allows you to specify which button is executed when the user presses the Esc or Cmd key. This is useful when you want a button that isn't named Cancel to cancel the dialog box.

The script in Figure 12-9 displays a dialog box (shown in Figure 12-10). The dialog box has three buttons, arranged a bit differently this time. Notice that instead of the evenly spaced buttons in the dialog box shown in Figure 12-8, these buttons have been automatically arranged to send a message. The default (Maybe) and cancel (No) buttons are on the right side of the dialog box. For that to happen, you have to specify both the default and cancel buttons, and you have to order them so that the default button is the rightmost button and the cancel button is the second from the right.

Figure 12-9. *This script displays the dialog box shown in Figure 12-10.*

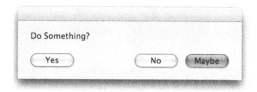

Figure 12-10. *The dialog box with default buttons*

No matter which button you specify as the cancel button, clicking it will generate the benign "User canceled" error number –128.

Adding a Title

As of Tiger, dialog boxes can now have titles. Adding a title to a dialog box is great; many times you want to use the actual dialog box text to ask a simple question, so some title explaining what the dialog box is about can be useful.

You add a title with the `with title` parameter. The following example will display the dialog box shown in Figure 12-11:

```
display dialog "Delete older files?" with title "Now performing backup"
```

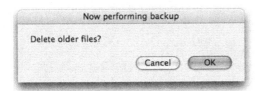

Figure 12-11. *The dialog title tells the user that the script is performing a backup routine.*

Showing Icons in Dialog Boxes

Displaying an appropriate icon in a dialog box is a bit like a score of a movie: it sets the mood.

Four icon choices are built in:

- `stop`
- `note`
- `caution`
- And, the default choice, having no icon at all

Note A dialog box that informs the user that the process has completed should probably have the `note` sign; you can alert the user that something did or might go wrong with the `stop` icon.

You specify an icon by adding the `with icon` parameter to the `display dialog` command, followed by the choice of icon.

For example:

```
try
    -- your main code here
on error error_text
    display dialog error_text buttons {"Quit"} with icon stop
end try
```

Notice that `stop` isn't a string; instead, it's a constant defined in Standard Additions.

You can also specify an icon by number. The number 0 will give you the `stop` icon, the number 1 will display the `note` icon, and number 2 will show the yellow `caution` icon.

Using an Icon File in a Dialog Box

You can go beyond the three built-in icons in a dialog box and display pretty much any icon you want, as long as it is stored in an .icns file.

.icns files are the OS X version of the icon files used by most OS X applications. You can create your own .icns file by using the Icon Composer utility that comes bundled with the free Developer Tools from Apple included on Mac OS X installer disks or available from https://connect.apple.com. Simply drag and drop or even copy and paste any graphics into the squares, shown in Figure 12-12, and save. I prefer to use Adobe Illustrator to compose my icons and then copy the art directly from Illustrator and paste it into Icon Composer.

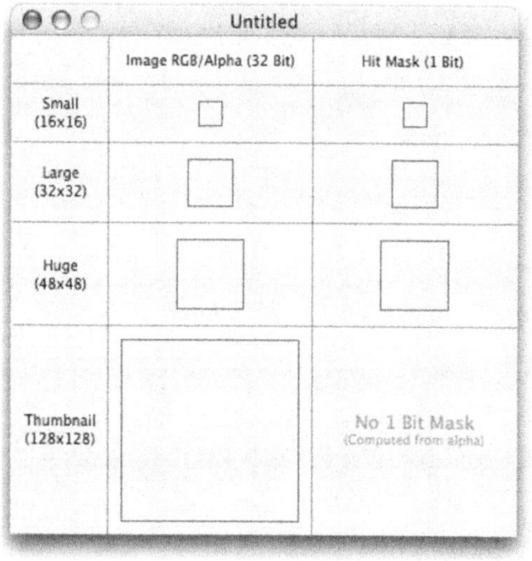

Figure 12-12. *The Icon Composer application window*

In addition, you can use icons from any existing OS X application. To do that, you have to locate the icon files. They usually reside in the Contents/Resources folder in the application bundle and end with the .icns extension.

Figure 12-13 shows a script that uses the icon from Apple GarageBand. If you don't have GarageBand, use the following line instead of line 2, which will use the vCard icon from Address Book:

```
set the_icon_file to alias (applications_folder_path & ¬
    "Address Book.app:Contents:Resources:vCard.icns")
```

Figure 12-14 shows the dialog box with the icon created by the script in Figure 12-13.

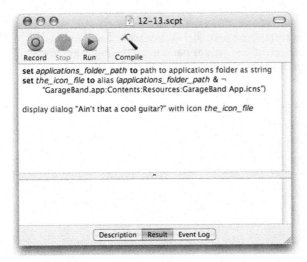

Figure 12-13. *Specify a path to an* `.icns` *file to use that icon in your dialog box.*

Figure 12-14. *The dialog box created by the script in Figure 12-13*

Dealing with Missing Icons

Up to Tiger 10.4, AppleScript didn't generate an error if an icon specified in a `display dialog` command was not found. In OS X 10.4 or later, an error will be generated, and the script will stop.

Getting Text Input from the User

Beginning programmers derive special satisfaction from getting information from users, and AppleScript makes that really easy to do. All you need is to add a `default answer` parameter to your `display dialog` command, followed by a string. For an example, check out Figure 12-9 and Figure 12-10 again.

Specifying the `default answer` parameter in the `display dialog` command will tell AppleScript to add the input field to the dialog box. The string you supplied as part of the `default answer` parameter is the text that appears by default in the field when the dialog box is displayed.

Out of the box, AppleScript allows only a single text field. With some creativity, you can stretch this field a bit, but you get only one.

You can create custom dialog boxes in a few ways, and you may be able to find a third-party scripting addition with some more dialog box support. One such scripting addition is 24U Appearance OSAX from 24U Software (`www.24usoftware.com`).

My favorite way to create custom dialog boxes is to create a stand-alone AppleScript Studio application. The application runs without a menu bar or dock icon and provides a selection of useful windows, such as password entry boxes and progress bars, that can be shown or hidden as needed.

Creating Password Dialog Boxes

In some instances, you may want the user to enter secret text, such as a password, without having the text actually display. For that, use the Boolean hidden answer parameter. The following script asks the user to enter a password, but as you can see in Figure 12-15, the password the user types appears as bullets:

```
display dialog "Enter your database password:" default answer "" with hidden answer
```

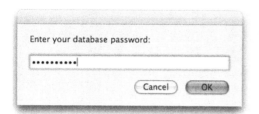

Figure 12-15. *The dialog box with the hidden "bullet" text*

■**Note** Notice in the previous script how the hidden answer parameter of the display dialog command is written. The command looks like this: display dialog ... with hidden answer. The hidden answer parameter is actually a Boolean parameter, but instead of writing it as hidden answer true or hidden answer false, you can use the word with before the names of all the parameters whose values are true and use without before the names of all the parameters whose values are false. AppleScript does this automatically to make the command easier to read.

Using User-Entered Text

Notice the Result area in Figure 12-16. Until now, the result record had a single property labeled button returned. Now, it has another property: text returned.

Figure 12-16. *The* text returned *property of the* dialog reply *record contains a string that is the text the user typed.*

Only dialog box commands that include the `default answer` parameter will have the text returned property in the `dialog reply` record.

Later in the "Validating User-Entered Text" section, you will learn different ways to validate the text that users enter.

How Long Do Dialog Boxes Display?

A `display dialog` dialog box will normally remain on the screen until manually dismissed by the user. You can, however, take control of the length of time the dialog box lingers by using the `giving up after` parameter.

Consider the following `display dialog` command:

```
display dialog "Click this within ten seconds!" giving up after 10
```

If you clicked the OK button within ten seconds, the dialog box would return this result:

```
{button returned:"OK", gave up:false}
```

Otherwise, the dialog box would automatically close itself, and the result would be as follows:

```
{button returned:"", gave up:true}
```

As you can see, using the `giving up after` parameter is responsible for the `gave up` property in the `dialog reply` record.

The value of the gave up property is Boolean, and it is true if the dialog box gave up since no one clicked any button. It's false if the user clicked a button.

Script 12-1 shows an example of how you can use the `giving up after` parameter for speed quizzing.

Script 12-1.

```
set dialog_reply to display dialog "5472 ÷ 57 =" buttons {"56", "76", "96"} ¬
    giving up after 7
if (gave up of dialog_reply) then
    set qResponse to "Not fast enough!"
else
    if button returned of dialog_reply is "96" then
        set qResponse to "You got it!"
    else
        set qResponse to "Wrong answer"
    end if
end if
display dialog qResponse
```

The preceding script places the `dialog reply` record in the variable dialog_reply. The script counts on that the `dialog reply` record will contain a gave up property that will have a Boolean value.

Validating User-Entered Text

The nature of asking the user to enter data involves expecting a certain type of data. When the data you expect is a string, such as the user's name, a city, or a company name, you may want to check that the field isn't empty or is a certain length. This is rather easy to do, since AppleScript returns a string as the text returned item in the `dialog reply` record.

You may, however, run into issues when you expect the user to enter a value that has to be later converted into a valid date or integer or has to be a specially formatted string such as an e-mail address or uniform resource locator (URL).

The method I found most effective is to put the dialog box inside an endless repeat loop that won't relent until the user either enters a conforming string or cancels. As an example, imagine you want the user to enter a meeting date and that the date, besides being a valid date, has to be in the future. What you'll need is a variable that will hold the final date. You can start the script by creating the loop and displaying the dialog box:

```
repeat
    set dialog_reply to display dialog "Enter date" default answer ""
    --more script here...
end repeat
```

Next, you can try to convert the string the user typed into a date. If successful, you will check whether the date is after today's date. If it is, you will release the user from eternal bondage and exit the repeat loop. If anything goes wrong, then the user is requested to reenter the date, and the loop repeats again.

Script 12-2 shows all this in action.

Script 12-2.

```
1. repeat
2.     display dialog "Enter date" default answer ""
3.     set user_date to text returned of result
4.     try
5.         set the_date to date user_date
6.         if the_date comes after (current date) then
7.             exit repeat
8.         end if
9.     end try
10.    display dialog "Reenter date" buttons {"OK"} ¬
           default button 1 with icon caution
11. end repeat
12. the_date
```

The try statement that extends from line 4 to line 9 is responsible for capturing the error generated in the event that the string the user typed doesn't want to be coerced into a date class. There's no on error in this case; the repeat loop simply doesn't end. Also, the if statement that starts on line 6 doesn't have an else clause. If the condition isn't fulfilled, the repeat loop simply makes another revolution.

You can take this script a step further and check once more with the user that the date AppleScript coerced the string into is indeed the date intended.

You do that by inserting yet another layer containing a dialog box and a conditional (if) statement. The conditional statement will simply check to see whether the button returned is Keep, which keeps the date, or Change, which changes it.

Script 12-3 shows the script with the new portion added.

Script 12-3.

```
1.  set dialog_text to "Enter date"
2.  repeat
3.      set date_dialog to display dialog dialog_text default answer ""
4.      set date_string to text returned of date_dialog
5.      try
6.          set the_date to date date_string
```

```
7.        if the_date comes after (current date) then
8.            set msg to "You've entered the following date:" & ¬
                 return & (date string of the_date) & ¬
                 return & "Keep it or change it?"
9.          display dialog msg buttons {"Change", "Keep"} with icon 1
10.         if button returned of result is "Keep" then
11.             exit repeat
12.         end if
13.      end if
14.   end try
15.   set dialog_text to "Reenter date"
16. end repeat
17. the_date
```

The main difference is a dialog box on line 9 asking the user whether the date is correct. If the user clicks Keep, then the conditional statement in line 10 will exit the repeat loop and continue with the script.

The nice part is that you do all that with one dialog box. This is also better since it makes the same impression with one instead of two dialog boxes.

Introducing the display alert Command

display alert, the new kid on the block, is a welcome introduction to Tiger and is a cousin of the display dialog command. In other words, display alert shares some parameters with display dialog but serves a different purpose.

The main idea behind the new display alert command is to allow the scripter to easily display a standard OS X alert box. Figure 12-13 shows the basic dialog box, which is a bit bigger than the dialog box used by display dialog and which displays a single OK button and application icon by default. As you can tell by comparing Figure 12-17 and Figure 12-18, the default dialog box that the two commands display is a bit different. The controls in the alert are smaller, and the dialog box itself is larger. Also, the alert shows the icon of the current application by default, but the dialog box does not. I'll talk more about the differences between the commands in the following sections.

Figure 12-17. *The result of a basic* display alert *command*

Figure 12-18. *The result of a basic* display dialog *command*

From the Dictionary: display alert

The following is the Standard Additions dictionary definition for display alert:

```
display alert v : Display an alert
    display alert string : the alert text (will be displayed in emphasized
        system font)
        [message string] : the explanatory message (will be displayed in small
            system font)
        [as critical/informational/warning] : the type of alert (default is
            informational)
        [buttons list of string] : a list of up to three button names
        [default button number or string] : the name or number of the default button
        [cancel button number or string] : the name or number of the cancel button
        [giving up after integer] : number of seconds to wait before automatically
            dismissing the alert
    Result: alert reply : a record containing the button clicked

alert reply n : Reply record for the 'display alert' command
    properties
        button returned (Unicode text, r/o) : name of button chosen (empty if
            'giving up after' was supplied and alert timed out)
        gave up (boolean, r/o) : Did the alert time out? (present only if
            'giving up after' was supplied)
```

The display alert command has four parameters in common with the display dialog command: buttons, default button, cancel button, and giving up after. The following sections describe its other parameters.

Using the message Parameter

You can use the message parameter to add an explanation or other descriptive text to the alert box. Figure 12-19 shows the alert generated by the following script:

```
set theAlert to "The script has encountered the wrong file type"
set theMessage to "A PDF file should be placed in the 'In' folder." ¬
  & return & "Any other file type would not process." & return ¬
  & "I'm not going to be as nice about it next time :-["
display alert theAlert message theMessage
```

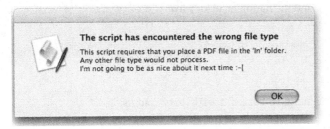

Figure 12-19. *The alert with the main alert message in bold, followed by a more detailed explanation of the problem*

Notice how the text of the alert is now bold and appears a little higher up; also, the text supplied for the message parameter is smaller.

You can manipulate the look of the alert by including an empty message parameter. Doing this will force the alert text to be bold, but this will produce an unexplained space below the alert text.

Using the as Parameter

The display alert command's as parameter allows you to manipulate the mood of the alert by specifying one of three possible constants: informational, warning, or critical.

The difference will show in the icon of the dialog box. informational will show the icon of the current application, warning will show the icon of the current application reduced in the corner of a warning yellow triangle (as shown in Figure 12-20), and critical, although I assume it's supposed to show the stop icon, seems to behave the same as informational.

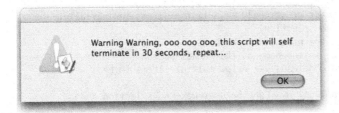

Figure 12-20. *The alert with the* as *parameter set to* warning

Setting the Button Behavior

Unlike in the display dialog command, if you don't specify a default button, the display alert command will designate the rightmost button as the default button.

Using an alert Handler

Not using Tiger yet? Try this alert handler.

It so happens that a dialog box style that repeats quite often is what I call alert. It is a simple dialog box with one OK button and a stop icon. For this dialog box I create a special handler called alert, which has a single parameter: the text to display. I call that parameter msg (short for *message*).

Script 12-4 shows what my handler and the handler call look like.

Script 12-4.

```
alert("Did it again!") --the call

on alert(msg)
    display dialog msg buttons {"OK"} default button 1 with icon caution
end alert
```

Now, I could certainly spice it up a bit and add more parameters, such as one for the icon, and so on. But the idea of my alert handler is that it's simple. I have other dialog box–related handlers that include more options—not this one.

Introducing the choose from list Command

The choose from list command allows you to display a special dialog box that lists a number of strings. The user can then choose one or more items from the list.

You can also determine which items are selected by default.

From the Dictionary: choose from list

The following is the dictionary specification of the choose from list command:

```
choose from list: Choose one or more items from a list
    choose from list  a list of number or string  -- a list of numbers and/or
            strings to display
        [with title  string]  -- the dialog window title
        [with prompt  string]  -- the prompt to be displayed in the dialog box
        [default items  a list of number or string]  -- a list of items to initially
            select (an empty list if no selection)
        [OK button name  string]  -- the name of the OK button
        [cancel button name  string]  -- the name of the Cancel button
        [multiple selections allowed  boolean]  -- Allow multiple items to be
            selected?
        [empty selection allowed  boolean]  -- Can the user make no selection and
            then choose OK?
    Result:   a list of number or string  -- the list of selected items
```

Getting the Results of the Command

The choose from list dialog box has two buttons: OK and Cancel. Although you can customize the titles of these buttons, you can't add buttons or change the functions of these buttons.

Clicking the OK button, which is always the button on the right and the default button, will always return a list. By default, this list is always going to be a one-item list. You can use parameters (shown later) to allow an empty selection or a multiple-item selection.

Clicking the Cancel button, however, will return the value false. The reason for that, I assume, is to spare you from a record result with the list and button in separate items, like with the dialog reply record.

It is, however, a bit frustrating not knowing the value class of the result you're expecting. This situation forces you to first check whether you got false as the answer, as shown in Script 12-5.

Script 12-5.

```
set item_choice to choose from list {1, 2, 3}
if item_choice is false then
    --Cancel button was clicked
else
    --OK button was clicked
end if
```

If you want choose from list to behave like display dialog and generate a "User canceled" error when the Cancel button is clicked, just use the following one-line conditional statement:

```
set item_choice to choose from list {1, 2, 3}
if item_choice is false then error number -128 -- User Canceled
```

Using the Basic Command

In its simplest form, the choose from list command takes a single parameter: the list you want the user to choose items from.

When the user clicks OK, the result is always a list.

The following is an example of the simplest use of the choose from list command. Figure 12-21 shows the dialog box that the following script line produces:

```
choose from list {"a", "b", "c"}
```

Figure 12-21. *The simplest* choose from list *dialog box*

Notice how the list expands to fit the number of items.

Creating a Custom Prompt

The first thing you will want to change about this dialog box is the text that tells the user how to use it. You do that with the with prompt parameter.

For example:

```
choose from list {"a", "b", "c"} with prompt "Pick a letter"
```

Figure 12-22 shows the dialog box resulting from this script.

Figure 12-22. *A* choose from list *dialog box with a custom prompt message*

Adding a Title

As of Tiger, you can add a title to the choose from list dialog box.

The following script displays the choose from list dialog box shown in Figure 12-23:

```
choose from list {"Petrol", "Diesel", "Veg Oil"} ¬
    with title "Energy Helper" with prompt "Choose your fuel"
```

Figure 12-23. *A* choose from list *dialog box with an Energy Helper title*

Setting the Default Selection

If you want one or more items to be initially selected when the dialog box displays, you can specify this with the default items parameter.

In the following example, the user has to pick from a list of five cities. A property called previous_city captures the selection the user made the previous time the script ran.

This time, the list will display but will have the city that was previously chosen selected by default.

Figure 12-24 shows the dialog box resulting from Script 12-6.

Script 12-6.

```
property the_city : ""

set the_selection to choose from list city_list with prompt ¬
    "Pick a city" default items {the_city}
if the_selection is false then error number -128 -- User Canceled
set the_city to item 1 of the_selection
```

Figure 12-24. *The dialog box resulting from the* choose from list *command with the* default items *parameter*

Restricting the Selection

The choose from list command allows you to restrict the selection the user can make. You can choose to allow or disallow the selection of multiple items and to allow or disallow the user to select nothing. By default, the user must choose one item and one item only.

To allow the user to select multiple items, set the multiple selections allowed parameter to true, as shown in Script 12-7.

Script 12-7.

```
set state_list to {"NY", "RI", "GA", "CA", "WA"}
set chosen_states to choose from list state_list ¬
   with multiple selections allowed
--> {"RI", "GA", "WA"}
```

In the preceding script, the user selected three items: RI, GA, and WA. In a similar fashion, you can allow the user to click OK while making no selection at all.

Now, about selecting nothing, the user can always click Cancel, but by default, if the user hasn't picked any item from the list, the OK button will be disabled. You can allow the user to pick no items and still click OK with the empty selection allowed parameter:

```
set chosen_states to choose from list state_list ¬
   with empty selection allowed
```

If the user selected nothing and clicked OK, the result would be an empty list:

```
--> {}
```

Customizing Buttons

The choose from list command has two buttons: OK and Cancel. As discussed earlier, the functions and positions of these buttons are set. The right button will return a list containing the selected items, and the left button will always return the value false.

You can, however, change the title of these buttons. To do that, you can use the OK button name and cancel button name parameters. Each one of these parameters is a string containing the new title for the button.

Script 12-8 displays the choose from list dialog box shown in Figure 12-25.

Script 12-8.

```
set state_list to {"NY", "RI", "GA", "CA", "WA"}
set chosen_states to choose from list state_list ¬
    OK button name "Make a Pick" cancel button name "Na..."
```

Figure 12-25. *The dialog box resulting from Script 12-8*

Choosing Files, Folders, and Disks

The Standard Additions suite gives you a few ways to allow the user to choose files, folders, disks, and servers. Although the procedures are user interaction functions and are discussed in the upcoming text, they will be covered extensively in the file management realm in Chapter 13.

Getting Common Results

All file-related choose commands return an alias or file value (or a list of them) identifying the chosen file, folder, or disk. You can ask to get the result returned as a string simply by adding the as string coercion after the command.

Recognizing Operating System Differences

Note that although the command and result remain the same no matter which Mac OS version you use, the look of the dialog box will change. OS X 10.1 will show the generic file-list dialog box, Jaguar (OS X 10.2) will let you choose a file using the outline style view, and Panther (OS X 10.3) or later adds the sidebar to the left of the dialog boxes.

Introducing the choose file Command

The choose file command has many uses. It allows the user to specify a file using the Open dialog box.

From the Dictionary: choose file

The following text is the dictionary definition of the choose file command:

```
choose file: Choose a file on a disk or server
    choose file
        [with prompt  plain text]
            -- a prompt to be displayed in the file chooser
        [of type  a list of plain text]
            -- restrict the files shown to only these file types
```

```
[default location  alias]  -- the default file location
[invisibles  boolean]
    -- Show invisible files and folders? (default is true)
[multiple selections allowed  boolean]
    -- Allow multiple items to be selected? (default is false)
[showing package contents  boolean]
    -- Allow multiple items to be selected? (default is false)
Result:   alias  -- to the chosen file
```

Getting the Results of the Command

The choose file command will either return an alias or list of aliases or generate an error, depending on the user action and parameters.

The dialog box will generate a "User canceled" error if the user clicks the Cancel button.

If the user clicks OK, then the command will return a single alias by default. However, if the multiple selections allowed parameter is set to true, then the result will be a list of aliases, even if the user chose only one file.

This means you probably have to put your choose file command in a try block to handle any "User canceled" errors and know whether to expect a list of aliases or a single alias based on your use of the multiple selections allowed parameter.

Figuring Out When to Use the Command

The choose file command is the AppleScript version of the Open dialog box—not that the command opens anything, but it presents the user with the Open dialog box and allows them to specify a file. From that point on, what happens to the file is up to you and your script.

You use choose file when you need the user to specify a file that the script has to deal with.

Allowing the user to choose a file has the same sort of effect as a script droplet. The user has the ability to specify a file that the script will then process.

Imagine you create a script that opens an Adobe InDesign file, exports all the images, and then catalogs them.

Sure, if you have a strict filing convention and folder hierarchy, the script may be able to find the files that need processing. However, if the file can be any InDesign file from anywhere on the hard disk or network, you will want to use the choose file command to allow users to specify the file themselves.

One of the most important features of the choose file command is its ability to restrict the user to choosing files of specific types. For example, when you select File ➤ Open in an application, you are restricted to choosing files that the application supports; the same is true for the restrictions you can put on your script's users by specifying which file types they can choose with the choose file command. I'll provide more details about this in the "Restricting to Specific File Types" section.

Using the Basic Command

To invoke the basic choose file command, you don't need to specify any parameters, just the command itself.

This script line will produce the dialog box shown in Figure 12-26:

```
choose file
```

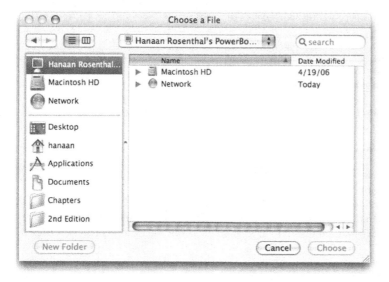

Figure 12-26. *The basic dialog box produced by the* choose file *command*

Creating a Custom Prompt

The first parameter you can change is the prompt. The prompt is the text that appears at the top of the dialog box.

The default choose file dialog box shown in Figure 12-26 has no prompt.

The script that follows produces the dialog box whose top is shown in Figure 12-27:

```
choose file with prompt "Pick a file to use as template"
```

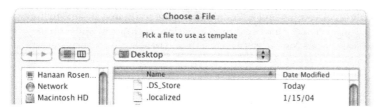

Figure 12-27. *The top of* choose file *dialog box with a custom prompt*

Restricting to Specific File Types

One of the parameters that makes the choose file command so useful and powerful is the of type parameter.

The of type parameter takes a list of strings, each representing a file type. Although in Tiger you can specify any number of types, pre-Tiger releases limit you to four types. When the dialog box is displayed, the user can choose only those files whose file types appear in the list.

The following example limits the user to choosing a text file:

```
choose file of type {"TEXT"}
```

The following script prompts the user to pick a background image (for something) and restricts the user to choosing a JPEG, TIFF, GIF, or PSD (Photoshop) file:

```
choose file with prompt "Choose a background image" ¬
    of type {"JPEG", "TIFF", "GIFF", "8BPS"}
```

In OS X 10.4 and later, you can also use uniform type identifiers (UTIs) with the of type parameter. For example, the following script will allow the user to choose only Microsoft Word documents:

```
choose file of type {"com.microsoft.word.doc"}
```

Using UTIs provides some significant advantages over using file types in that they're a lot more flexible in how they recognize files.

In the days of OS 9, you could pretty much count on files always having a file type code because they probably wouldn't work without one! In OS X, however, it's quite common to encounter files that have filename extensions but no file type code, so if you use file type codes in the choose file command's of type parameter, users won't be allowed to select these files even though they should be able to do so.

For example, let's say you want to limit the user to choosing only JPEG files. If you use a file type for the of type parameter, like so:

```
choose file of type {"JPEG"}
```

then only files with the file type JPEG will be selectable in the resulting choose file dialog box. Unfortunately for the user, any JPEG files that don't have a file type—perhaps because they've been downloaded from the Internet or created by a program that doesn't use creator and file type codes—won't be selectable. However, if you use a UTI, like so:

```
choose file of type {"public.jpeg"}
```

then any file that has a JPEG file type *or* a .jpg or .jpeg filename extension will be selectable.

Another advantage of UTIs is that they allow you to be more general or more specific about the types of files you want to be selectable. For example, if you want to let the user choose *any* kind of image file, just use the following:

```
choose file of type {"public.image"}
```

Mac OS X defines some common UTIs, and individual applications can add their own. You can find more information about UTIs at this location:

```
http://developer.apple.com/documentation/Carbon/Conceptual/understanding_utis/
```

■**Note** If you're not sure what the file type or type identifier for a particular type of file is, don't worry: it's easy to find out using AppleScript. See the "Determining the File's Type or Identifier" section.

Showing Package Contents

By default, when you use the choose file command, applications will behave as files, allowing you to choose the application as a single file. As you know, however, Cocoa applications are actually bundles that are more like folders with files in them. If you set the showing package contents parameter to true, the choose file dialog box will treat application bundles and other types of bundles such as .rtfd and .scptd files like ordinary folders, allowing you to select files from inside the application's bundle.

The following script displays the choose file dialog box in Figure 12-28:

```
choose file default location (path to applications folder) ¬
    with showing package contents
result: alias "Tiger:Applications:Chess.app:Contents:Resources:1.rgb"
```

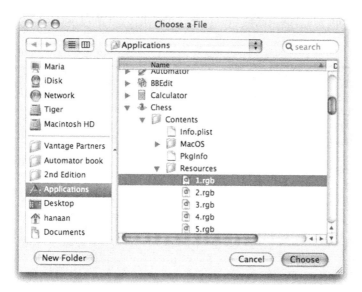

Figure 12-28. *The* choose file *dialog box with access to bundle contents*

Determining the File's Type or Identifier

Looking at the list of four file types I used previously, you might be wondering how I figured them out. Getting TIFF and JPEG is kind of obvious, but how did I know that the Photoshop file type is 8BPS? Is there a list of file types somewhere? A list may exist, but I don't have it. To get the file type, I use, well, a script!

The following script line will return the four-letter string that is the chosen file's file type. It uses, as you can see, the choose file command:

```
file type of (info for (choose file))
```

Or, to get the identifier, you can use this:

```
type identifier of (info for (choose file))
```

The preceding script is a combination of two commands: choose file, which returns an alias, and info for, which returns a file information record describing the file.

As you can see in Figure 12-29, the script's result is the chosen file's four-character code.

Figure 12-29. *The four-character code result*

To use the code, just copy the result from the Result area and paste it in your list.

Here's a fun exercise for you: create a scripter's utility script that builds a list of file types for use with the `choose file` command. The script should be a `repeat` loop that loops four times. On every loop the user should be asked to choose a different file for the file type list. If the user clicks Cancel at any point, exit the loop.

The result of the script should be a list of file types of the files the user picked. To make it even better, make sure the user is notified if they pick a file with the same file type.

Picking Invisibles

By default, the `choose file` command will allow you to pick invisible files. To restrict the user to visible files only, set the `invisibles` parameter to `false`.

The difference between the invisibles and file type restriction is that when you set the `invisibles` parameter to `false`, invisible files won't even show. When you restrict to only specific file types, all files will show, but files with different file types will be disabled.

The following script will show the `choose file` dialog box but will not allow users to pick invisible files:

```
choose file without invisibles
```

Setting the Default Location

The optional `default location` parameter allows you to set a starting point for the `choose file` dialog box. When the dialog box appears, you may want to direct the user to a specific folder.

The following script lets users start the search at the Documents folder in their home directory:

```
choose file default location (path to documents folder from user domain)
```

You can also specify a folder path in the usual way. In Script 12-9, the `jobs_folder_path` variable is set to a path referencing the `jobs` folder. Note that the variable itself contains a string, not a file reference; therefore, you need to add the word `alias` before it when you use it to specify the default location.

Script 12-9.

```
set jobs_folder_path to "Macintosh HD:Clients:Jobs:New Jobs:"
choose file with prompt "Pick a job to process" ¬
    default location alias jobs_folder_path
```

If the folder you specify as the default location doesn't exist, the starting location will revert to the default, but no error will be generated.

Allowing Multiple Selections

You can allow the user to pick multiple files at one time. To do that, set the `multiple selections allowed` parameter to true.

The natural restriction of the `multiple selections allowed` parameter is that all files have to be visible to you in the same `choose file` dialog box. If you want to pick one file from the `Documents` folder in your home domain and one file from some nested folder on the server, you may have a problem. OS X 10.3 does allow you to switch from list view to outline view in the `choose file` dialog box. The list type will allow you to collapse and expand folders and therefore choose files from different locations. Still, it will be most comfortable for the user to choose multiple files from the same folder.

Setting the `multiple selections allowed` parameter to true will alter the command's result from a single alias to a list of aliases. Even if the user ends up choosing one file only, this alias will be returned as the only item in a list.

The following script allows the user to choose multiple files:

```
choose file with multiple selections allowed
```

Two files were chosen:

```
--> {alias "Macintosh HD:image 1.gif", alias "Macintosh HD:image 2.gif"}
```

Introducing the choose file name Command

The `choose file name` command allows you to add a Save As–like dialog box to your scripts. The result is a path to a not-yet-existing file.

From the Dictionary: choose file name

The following is the dictionary specification of the `choose file name` command:

```
choose file name: Get a new file reference from the user, ➥
    without creating the file
  choose file name
    [with prompt  plain text]
       -- the text to display in the file creation dialog box
    [default name  plain text] -- the default name for the new file
    [default location  alias] -- the default file location
  Result:  'file' -- the file the user specified
```

choose file name vs. choose file

The difference between the choose file and choose file name commands is the same as the difference between the Open and Save dialog boxes. When you open, you can choose a file. When you save, you specify a filename and location, but the file may not yet exist. If the file you specified is already there, the usual "Are you sure you want to replace this item?" dialog box will appear.

Figuring Out When to Use the Command

You use the choose file name command whenever you want the user to specify a file that the script has to create in some way—for instance, use it if the script creates a text log and you want to let the user decide where that log is saved and what the log's name is. Or, use it if you're creating an InDesign project from a template and you want the user to specify where the project should be saved.

Getting the Results of the Command

The choose file name command can return one of two types of values based on the button the user clicks. If the user clicks the OK button, the command returns a file reference to the yet-to-exist file. If the user clicks Cancel, then a "User canceled" error will be generated.

The reason why the choose file name command returns a file specifier (file "filepath"), instead of an alias (alias "filepath") as in the choose file command, is that alias values can identify only those files that actually exist, and the file you specify here may not yet exist.

Using the Basic Command

The basic choose file name command used in the following script will display the dialog box shown in Figure 12-30:

```
choose file name
```

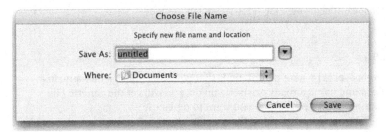

Figure 12-30. *The basic dialog box displayed by the* choose file name *command*

Creating a Custom Prompt

As with other file-related dialog box commands, you can add a custom title to your dialog box. As you can see in Figure 12-30, the default prompt says, "Specify new file name and location." Using the with prompt parameter, as in the following script line, will replace that prompt with a custom message:

```
choose file name with prompt "Save the log file"
```

Setting a Default Name and Location

As with the `choose file` command, the `choose file name` command also contains a parameter, `default location`, that allows you to set the default folder location. This location will be the first folder shown in the dialog box.

The `choose file name` command also allows you to provide a default name for your file via the `default name` parameter.

Script 12-10 lets the user choose a filename while directing the user to the `log files` folder and providing a default filename of `log.txt`. Figure 12-31 shows the resulting `choose file name` dialog box.

Script 12-10.

```
set default_log_folder to (path to documents folder from user domain ¬
    as string) & "log files:"
choose file name with prompt "Save the log file" ¬
    default location alias default_log_folder default name "Log.txt"
```

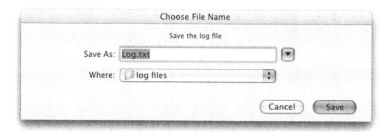

Figure 12-31. *A* `choose file name` *dialog box with a default path and filename*

If the user accepted the defaults and clicked OK, the result would be as follows:

```
file "Macintosh HD:Users:hanaan:Documents:log files:Log.txt"
```

Replacing an Existing File

An interesting feature of the `choose file name` command is that you can choose a filename in a folder in which a file with the same name already exists. If you do, you will get the generic File Already Exists dialog box asking whether you're sure you want to replace it.

Remember that `choose file name` creates only a file specifier. It doesn't create or replace any files itself, so merely clicking Replace won't affect the existing file. It's up to your script to move, delete, or simply overwrite the existing file as appropriate.

Seeing an Example in Action

As a simple example of using the `choose file name` command, I will show how to create a new InDesign document and save it using a name and location the user chooses with the `choose file name` command.

Script 12-11 shows the script, which is followed by the explanation.

Script 12-11.

```
1. set docs_folder to (path to documents folder)
2.    set new_file to choose file name ¬
            default location docs_folder ¬
            default name "job name.indd"
3. set new_file_path to new_file as string
4. tell application "InDesign CS"
5.    set new_doc to make new document
6.    tell new_doc
7.       save it to new_file_path
8.    end tell
9. end tell
```

The script starts with line 1 setting a variable to a string value that refers to the user's Documents folder. In line 2, the script uses the variable docs_folder to specify the default location.

In line 3, the script coerces the file reference into a string. Strings are easier to work with since they can be later converted to aliases, converted to file specifiers, or written to a text file themselves if needed.

Lines 4 through 9 instruct InDesign to create a new file and save it to the file path the user chose in line 2.

Introducing the choose folder Command

The choose folder command allows you to make the user choose a folder using a standard Choose a Folder dialog box.

From the Dictionary: choose folder

The following is the dictionary definition of the choose folder command:

```
choose folder: Choose a folder on a disk or server
    choose folder
        [with prompt  plain text]
            -- a prompt to be displayed in the folder chooser
        [default location  alias]  -- the default folder location
        [invisibles  boolean]
            -- Show invisible files and folders? (default is false)
        [multiple selections allowed  boolean]
            -- Allow multiple items to be selected? (default is false)
        [showing package contents  boolean] -- Show the contents of packages?
            (Packages will be treated as folders. Default is false.)
    Result:  alias  -- chosen folder
```

Using the Command

The choose folder command presents users with the Choose a Folder dialog box and allows them to choose a folder. The result is an alias value identifying that folder.

If the user clicks Cancel, however, the "User canceled" error will be generated.

Figure 12-32 shows the dialog box that the choose folder command generates. The following script shows the basic form of the choose folder command, without any parameters:

```
choose folder
```

Figure 12-32. *The dialog box shown by the* choose folder *command. Notice how certain files are disabled.*

Figuring Out When to Use the Command

You should use the choose folder command when you need to create an alias, path, or Finder reference to a folder and you want the user to choose the folder for you.

For example, you might write a script to batch convert TIFF images to JPEG format. This script would use the choose folder command twice, first to ask the user to choose the source folder containing the original TIFF images and then to choose the destination folder for the newly created JPEG files.

Setting the Parameters

The choose folder command is similar to the choose file command:

- Both allow you to choose file system items.
- Both will produce an error if the user clicks Cancel.
- Both share the following parameters: with prompt, invisibles, default location, multiple selections allowed, and showing package contents.

To read more about these parameters, refer to the "Introducing the choose file Command" section earlier. Here are the descriptions in short: the Boolean invisibles parameter determines whether invisible folders appear in the list. The default location parameter determines the location that the Choose a Folder dialog box starts in.

The Boolean multiple selections allowed parameter allows the user to select multiple folders at once.

If the multiple selections allowed parameter is true, then the choose folder command returns a list of aliases instead of a single alias.

Setting showing package contents to true will allow you to choose a folder located inside an application bundle or other "files" that are actually bundles such as .rtfd, which is used by TextEdit for saving rich-text files containing images, or .scptd, which is a compiled AppleScript file saved as a bundle.

Choosing a Folder Once

Although allowing the user to specify a folder in a Choose a Folder dialog box is often more convenient than having them edit the script directly, this can become tiresome if the folder being chosen is the same every time, such as a permanent drop box or log file folder. It'd be much less annoying if the script needs to ask the user to choose a folder only the first time it's run and then remembers that folder for future use. Script 12-12 shows a folder_path property. The property starts out having the value missing value assigned to it; later it will hold a string containing the path to the chosen folder.

The script starts by figuring out whether the folder path currently stored in variable folder_path is valid. If it isn't, the user is prompted to choose a different folder.

Script 12-12.

```
property folder_path : missing value

tell application "Finder"
    if folder_path is missing value or not (container folder_path exists) then
        tell me to set folder_path to (choose folder) as string
    end if
end tell
folder_path --> "Macintosh HD:Users:hanaan:Pictures:"
```

The preceding example uses the Finder to tell you whether the value of the variable folder_path is a valid folder path. When the folder path isn't good, you make the user choose a different folder. Also notice that I keep the folder path as a string. This helps me keep my options open.

Introducing the choose application Command

The choose application command lets the user pick an application on the machine running the script. The choose application command can return either an alias pointing to the application or an application object, as you will see a bit later.

From the Dictionary: choose application

The following is the dictionary definition of the choose application command:

```
choose application: Choose an application on this machine or the network
    choose application
        [with title  plain text]  -- the dialog window title
        [with prompt  plain text]
            -- the prompt to appear at the top of the application chooser dialog box
        [multiple selections allowed  boolean]
            -- Allow multiple items to be selected? (default is false)
        [as  type class]
            -- the desired type of result. May be application (the default) or alias.
    Result:  app  -- the application chosen
```

Using the Command

The choose application command, if used by itself with no parameters, displays the dialog box shown in Figure 12-33. The default result is an application object, as shown here:

```
application "Finder"
```

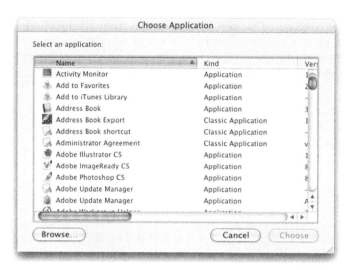

Figure 12-33. *The basic* choose application *dialog box*

Using the as parameter, you can ask for the result to be returned as an alias to the application, as shown here:

```
choose application as alias
--> alias "Macintosh HD:Applications:FileMaker Pro 7:FileMaker Pro.app:"
```

You can also use the with title and with prompt parameters to add a title and a prompt to the dialog box. In Figure 12-33, you can see the default title Choose Application and the default prompt "Select an application."

Choosing Other Types of Items

In the following sections, you will read about the user interaction commands that allow the user to specify a remote application, a URL, or a color.

Introducing the choose remote application Command

The choose remote application command allows you to choose an application on another Mac on the network. This command is more a utility command used by scripters than a command you will incorporate into final scripts.

The result of the command, shown next, is a reference to a specific application on a remote Mac that you choose. You use this reference to control the application on the remote Mac.

```
application "InDesign" of machine "eppc:// ➥
    francd0101.wellmanage.com/?uid=502&pid=1565
```

Figure 12-34 shows the dialog box resulting from the `choose remote application` command.

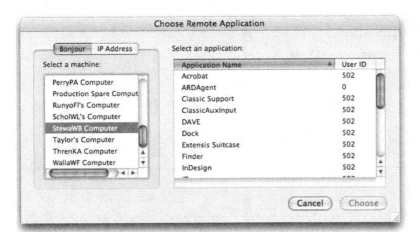

Figure 12-34. *The dialog box resulting from the* `choose remote application` *command*

Introducing the choose URL Command

The `choose URL` command allows the user to specify a URL to a server via FTP servers, file servers, remote applications, and so on.

The result of the command is a URL string that can be used as a parameter with other commands such as `mount volume` (described in Chapter 13).

From the Dictionary: choose URL

The following is the dictionary definition of the `choose URL` command:

```
choose URL: Choose a service on the Internet
    choose URL
        [showing  a list of ¬
            Web servers/FTP Servers/Telnet hosts/File servers/¬
            News servers/Directory services/Media servers/¬
            Remote applications]  -- which network services to show
        [editable URL  boolean]  -- Allow user to type in a URL?
    Result:  URL  -- the URL chosen
```

Using the Command

The `choose URL` command has two parameters. The `showing` parameter allows you to specify a list of protocols that will appear in the protocol pop-up menu at the bottom. By default the list shows seven protocol service types (listed previously in the "From the Dictionary: choose URL" section). The following script restricts the command to three of the seven protocols. It also uses the Boolean parameter `editable URL` with a `false` value. This prevents the user from entering a URL rather than choosing one from the list.

```
choose URL showing {Web servers, FTP Servers, Telnet hosts} without ¬
    editable URL
```

Figure 12-35 shows the dialog box resulting from the previous script.

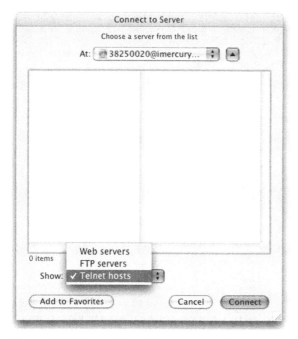

Figure 12-35. *The resulting dialog box from the* choose URL *command*

The following script will ask the user to specify a file server URL, by either choosing it from a list or entering it, and then mount the specified volume:

```
set server_address to choose URL showing {File servers} with ¬
    editable URL
mount volume server_address
```

The choose URL command now supports Common Internet File System (CIFS) file servers, which is new to Tiger 10.4.

Introducing the choose color Command

The choose color command allows you to make the user specify a color.

From the Dictionary: choose color

```
choose color: Choose a color
    choose color
        [default color RGB color] -- the default color
    Result: RGB color  -- chosen color
```

Getting the Results of the Command

The result is a list of three integer values, representing the red, green, and blue values of an RGB color. Each number is from 65,535, which corresponds with the bright, full presence of the color, to 0, which means the color is dimmed all the way. For example, this result was returned after specifying a reddish color: {60790, 5233, 6667}. Notice that the first value, indicating the red value, is almost at the full brightness of 65,535, and the green and blue are relatively close to 0. The value of pure red will be {65535, 0, 0}.

Although the color picker the users are presented with allows them to specify hex colors for web colors and CMYK colors, the result will always be the RGB color equivalent.

Figuring Out When to Use the Command

Use this command whenever you're in a situation that the user has to specify a color. This feature wasn't intended for precise color use in production or design environments, but rather for picking colors in a more general way: pinkish, light blue, and so on.

In Chapter 13, you'll see an example that creates an RTF file. The example uses the choose color command to specify RGB colors that are later used in the RTF file.

Using the Basic Command and Using It with Parameters

The choose color command has one parameter: default color. It allows you to specify the color that is displayed by default when the dialog box appears.

The following script will display the Colors dialog box without a predefined default color:

```
choose color
```

The following script will display the Colors dialog box shown in Figure 12-36:

```
choose color default color {65535, 0, 0} -- default color is red
```

Figure 12-36. *The dialog box resulting from* choose color

Focus Points

I usually prefer to stay away from shorthand and personal acronyms. They cause general confusion, and if you manage to remember what you meant two years ago when you wrote the script, your replacement certainly won't. Unless this is what you're aiming for, which is a language my ASP programmer buddy Steve Adler calls JSL (short for Job Security Language), you should spell things out AMAP (As Much As Possible). Acronyms are perfectly acceptable, however, when they are a part of a well-defined naming convention.

Creating small scripts that give you the results you need to use in your script, as I did in this chapter to get the file's four-character type, is one of the scripter's best tools.

The alias value class requires that the string that follows the word alias is a valid path to a file or folder that actually exists. If the alias isn't pointing at a valid file, the file won't compile. If the string following the alias prefix is stored in a string variable, then a runtime error will occur. You'll learn more about that in Chapter 13.

In Chapter 17, you can read more about dealing with errors, trapping errors, and figuring out which errors have which numbers. Also, look for Chapter 20, which deals with user interface (UI) scripting to see how to isolate the button you need in the jungle of UI elements.

Power Wrap-Up

The following sections summarize the chapter in an intensive reference style. Use these sections to look up facts related to the chapter without the chatter.

User Interaction and AppleScript

Since the AppleScript language was designed for data manipulation, the user interaction portion of it is minimal. This chapter dealt with the few user-interaction commands AppleScript does possess.

All user interaction commands are defined in the Standard Additions dictionary.

display dialog

The display dialog command displays a simple dialog box with buttons and an optional text field. This is the basic display dialog command, which displays a dialog box with some text and two buttons, OK and Cancel:

```
display dialog  "Something interesting"
```

You can see screenshots of the different resulting dialog boxes throughout this chapter.

Canceling a Dialog Box

When clicking the Cancel button, the command will generate a special error. The error is the "User canceled" error, –128. It will stop the script if not captured in a try block, but most applications won't display an error message. Here's how to trap the cancel error:

```
try
   display dialog  "Something interesting"
on error number -128
   display dialog  "You canceled"
   return
end
```

Creating Custom Buttons

The display dialog command allows you to define up to three custom buttons. You do this with the buttons parameter. To specify custom buttons, you supply the buttons parameter with a list of up to three strings, where each string is one button's title. The buttons will be displayed in the dialog box in the same order they appear in the list.

The following script will display a dialog box with the buttons Yes, No, and Maybe:

```
display dialog  "Click a button:" buttons {"Yes", "No", "Maybe"}
```

To specify which button is the default button, use the default button parameter. This parameter accepts either a string that is the name of the button you want to make the default button or an integer that specifies the button by position.

The following script lines both define the Yes button as the default button:

```
display dialog  "Click a button:" buttons {"Yes", "No", "Maybe"} ¬
    default button 1
display dialog  "Click a button:" buttons {"Yes", "No", "Maybe"} ¬
    default button "Yes"
```

You can also specify the button that executes when the user presses Cmd-period or Esc. You do that with the cancel button parameter:

```
display dialog  "Click a button:" buttons {"Yes", "No", "Maybe"} ¬
default button "Yes" cancel button "Maybe"
```

To extract the button the user clicked, get the button returned item of the dialog reply record (see the "Introducing the dialog reply Command" section).

Specifying Dialog Box Icons

AppleScript dialog boxes can have one of three icons, no icon at all, or an icon file or resource you specify. You specify icons with the with icon parameter.

For the stop icon, use the constant value stop or 0; for the note icon (in Tiger it's the current application icon), use either note or 1; and for the caution icon (yellow triangle), use either caution or 2. The following two script lines will display a dialog box with the stop icon:

```
display dialog  "The script will now stop"  with icon  stop
display dialog  "The script will now stop"  with icon  0
```

To use an icon file with a dialog box, specify the file path to the .icns file, like this:

```
set icon_file_path to (path to applications folder as string) & ¬
    "Chess.app:Contents:Resources:chess.icns"
display dialog "Time to play some Chess!" with icon alias icon_file_path
```

Getting User Input

The display dialog command allows you to solicit user input by using the default answer parameter. The default answer parameter takes a string value. Including that parameter will cause the dialog box to include a text field. The string you provide as the parameter's value will be the default text in the text field. To have a blank text field, use a blank string ("") as the parameter's value.

The following script will display a dialog box with a blank text field for user input:

```
display dialog  "Enter your name:"  default answer ""
```

The following script will display a dialog box with default text:

```
display dialog  "Enter your date of birth:" default answer "MM/DD/YYYY"
```

To extract the text the user entered, get the text returned item of the dialog reply record (see the upcoming "dialog reply" section for more information).

Hiding Text User Input

In Tiger (OS X 10.4.3), you can make the font of the user input field bulleted. This will allow the user to enter information that can't be read.

To display a dialog box with the hidden text, use the hidden answer parameter:

```
display dialog  "Enter your server login password" default ➡
answer "" with hidden answer
```

Creating Dialog Boxes That Give Up

The giving up after parameter of the display dialog command allows you to specify a time period in seconds after which the dialog box will "give up" and close itself.

If you include the giving up parameter, the dialog reply record will include the Boolean property gave up. A true value indicates that a button was not clicked and the dialog box gave up after the specified number of seconds.

The following script will give up after 20 seconds:

```
display dialog  "Click a button, quick!" giving up after 20
```

dialog reply

The dialog reply is a record returned by the display dialog command. The dialog reply record is a bit different depending on the parameters you use. The following are pairs of statements using the display dialog command, followed by the resulting dialog reply record.

This is a simple dialog box:

```
display dialog  "Click a button"
--> {button returned:"OK"}
```

This is a dialog box with text input:

```
display dialog  "Enter your name" default answer ""
--> {text returned:"Joe", button returned:"OK"}
```

This is a dialog box with a giving up after parameter:

```
display dialog  "Click a button, quick!" giving up after 20
--> {button returned:"", gave up:true}
```

display alert

As of Tiger, the display alert command works similarly to display dialog, with a few differences. The display alert command displays a dialog box that always has an icon and has only the OK button by default. This is the basic command:

```
display alert "The file couldn't be found"
```

Using Parameters Consistent with the display dialog Command

The four parameters that have the same function as they do when used with the `display dialog` command are as follows: `buttons`, `default button`, `cancel button`, and `giving up after`.

See information about these parameters in the earlier "Introducing the display dialog Command" section.

Using the default message Parameter

The `message` parameter adds a message to the alert that appears in smaller text and underneath the main alert text:

```
display alert "The file couldn't be found" ¬
    message "The settings file should be in the 'Settings' folder"
```

Using the default as Parameter

The `as` parameter changes the icon in the alert dialog box to one of three styles. The value for this parameter can be one of the following constants: `critical`, `informational`, or `warning`.

choose from list

The `choose from list` command is defined in the Standard Additions dictionary. It allows a user to choose an item from a list of strings. The result can be a list of items or simply `false` if the user clicks the cancel button.

The following script allows the user to choose from a list of three cities:

```
choose from list {"Los Angeles", "Boston", "Atlanta"}
```

The `choose from list` command has a few parameters that define the titles of the buttons and the item-selection behavior.

Specifying Prompts and Button Titles

Use the `with prompt` parameter to specify a prompt to the dialog box. To specify alternate titles for the OK and Cancel buttons, use the `OK button name` and `Cancel button name` parameters, as shown in the following script:

```
choose from list {"Los Angeles", "Boston", "Atlanta"} with prompt "Pick a city" ¬
    OK button name "Get there" Cancel button name "Forget it"
```

Specifying Multiple-Item Selection

By default, the user must make a single choice. No empty selection or multiple selections are allowed. To change these defaults, use the Boolean `multiple selections allowed` and `empty selection allowed` parameters.

The following script will allow the user to click OK even if no selection has been made:

```
choose from list {"Los Angeles", "Boston", "Atlanta"} ¬
    with empty selection allowed
```

The following script will allow the user to select multiple items from the list:

```
choose from list {"Los Angeles", "Boston", "Atlanta"} ¬
    with multiple selections allowed
```

You can also specify which items will be selected by default. The following script starts with the U.S. item selected:

```
choose from list {"US", "France", "Mexico"} default items {"US"}
```

choose file

The `choose file` command allows the user to specify an existing file using the Open dialog box. This command returns an alias to the chosen file and generates an error if the cancel button is clicked. The following script will display the basic Open dialog box using the `choose file` command:

```
choose file
```

Using the with prompt Parameter

The `with prompt` parameter allows you to specify a custom prompt. By default, there is no prompt. The following script will display the dialog box with a custom prompt:

```
choose file with prompt "Pick a text file to clean:"
```

Restricting File Types Parameter

The `of type` parameter allows you to specify a list of file types. The `choose file` command will allow the user to choose only files whose type is mentioned in the list of types you provide. The following script will restrict the user to choosing plain-text and Word files:

```
choose file of type {"W8BN", "TEXT"}
```

Starting with Tiger, the `of type` parameter can also be a list of type identifiers. Using file types works only for files that already have a file type code, but type identifiers will recognize all the files that have either a suitable file type or a filename extension. For example, the following script will allow the user to choose any kind of image or movie file:

```
choose file of type {"public.image", "public.movie"}
```

Using the default location Parameter

`default location` is an alias to a folder that the `choose file` dialog box will point to as it opens. The following script will ensure that the Open dialog box starts out by pointing to the desktop:

```
choose file default location (path to desktop)
```

Using the invisibles Parameter

The Boolean parameter `invisibles` determines whether the `choose file` command will allow the user to choose invisible files.

Using the multiple selections Parameter

The Boolean parameter `multiple selections allowed` determines whether the `choose file` command will allow the user to choose multiple files.

Using the showing package contents Parameter

The showing package contents parameter makes bundle-based files such as Cocoa applications appear as regular folders instead of single files. Use this to choose files inside bundles.

choose file name

The choose file name command displays a dialog box similar to the Save dialog box. It allows you to specify a filename and location of a nonexistent file. The command doesn't create any file; it only returns a path to the new file the user specified.

The choose file name command has three parameters: with prompt, default name, and default location.

The with prompt parameter adds a prompt to the top of the dialog box.

The parameters default name and default location allow you to specify the default file name and default folder location to which the Save dialog box will be pointing.

The following script will allow the user to choose a filename and location with a default location of the desktop and a default name:

```
choose file name default name "Image.JPG" default location (path to desktop)
--> file "Macintosh HD:Users:hanaan:Desktop:Image.JPG"
```

choose folder

The choose folder command is nearly identical to the choose file command, but instead of a file, the user will be able to select only a folder.

choose application

The choose application command allows the user to pick an application from the applications on the computer. The parameters with title and with prompt allow you to customize the choose application dialog box. The multiple selections allowed parameter allows the user to pick multiple applications.

The result is an application object, as shown here:

```
application "Finder"
```

Or you can use the as parameter to have the command return the result as an alias to the application file instead, as shown here:

```
choose application as alias
--> alias "Macintosh HD:Applications:FileMaker Pro 7:FileMaker Pro.app:"
```

choose remote application

New in Tiger, this command allows you to choose an application on another Mac on the network. The result of this command is a remote application object, like this:

```
application "InDesign" of machine "eppc://192.168.2.2/?uid=502&pid=1565"
```

choose URL

The choose URL command displays a Connect to Server dialog box and returns a string containing the URL of the chosen server. You can use the showing parameter along with one or more of the following constant values to limit the type of URL the user can choose. The possible values for that parameter are Web servers, FTP servers, Telnet hosts, File servers, News servers, Directory services, Media servers, and Remote applications. For example, the following command will allow you to select a Mac server that has the Remote Apple Events option enabled in the Sharing panel of its System Preferences:

```
choose URL showing {Remote applications}
```

The Boolean parameter editable URL determines whether the user can also specify a URL by entering it in directly. A false value means that the user will not get a text field in which the URL can be edited or entered.

choose color

The choose color command allows the user to specify a color using OS X's Colors dialog box. The color is returned as a list of three integers from 0 to 65,535, which describes the color as three 16-bit red, green, and blue values. The command's one parameter, default color, allows you to specify the color that the dialog box will have when it first appears. The following script will allow the user to pick a color, and the default color in the dialog box will be red:

```
choose color default color {65535, 0, 0}
```

Advanced User Interaction

Although using the tools provided in the User Interaction suite of Standard Additions gives you useful capabilities such as displaying dialog boxes and alerts, allowing the user to choose an item from a list, specifying Finder items and more, it can leave you looking for more. For example, you may want to present a dialog box containing several text fields, pop-up menus, and buttons, or you may just want to make your script look more like a utility with a better-organized window, even if a text field and a couple of buttons are all you need.

Using the right tools, you will be amazed just how quickly you can equip a run-of-the-mill script with a useful interface.

One obvious choice that comes to mind is AppleScript Studio. Because covering AppleScript Studio in detail would require a whole other book, I'll just show you how to use it for creating an interface that can be used with your scripts. After all, the interface of a typical AppleScript Studio application is scriptable and therefore can be controlled by script outside the Studio application as well as by the script (or scripts) inside it.

Another subject this chapter will touch on is FaceSpan for OS X. FaceSpan is a simple-to-learn application that allows you to create AppleScript-based applications with robust interfaces.

Quick Custom Dialog Boxes for Your Script Using AppleScript Studio

Undoubtedly the biggest boost AppleScript has gotten in the past few years is AppleScript Studio. With Studio you can create full-blown Cocoa applications for Mac OS X using Xcode and AppleScript.

AppleScript Studio consists of two parts:

- The AppleScriptKit framework, which provides a collection of "AppleScriptable" classes representing application windows, buttons, text fields, and so on

- The AppleScript application authoring tools provided by Apple's powerful Xcode and Interface Builder (IB) applications

The AppleScriptKit framework is included in Mac OS X, allowing AppleScript Studio applications to run on any Mac OS X computer. To develop AppleScript Studio applications of your own, you have to install Apple's Developer Tools, which are included with your OS X installer disks or can be downloaded from http://developer.apple.com but are not installed by default. Although you can use AppleScript Studio to create fully programmed applications, here I will teach you a neat technique for using an AppleScript Studio application with minimal AppleScript programming to create a series of rich custom dialog boxes that you can use in your scripts.

You'll take advantage of one of the AppleScript Studio environment's coolest features: any application you build with it is automatically "scriptable." OK, so it doesn't have an object model with rich properties relating to the application's subject matter like traditional scriptable applications do, but all the user interface (UI) elements are fully scriptable from external scripts such as the scripts you're writing in Script Editor.

What you will create in this chapter is a simple application with a minimal amount of programming (as little as four lines!) that will act as a repository for dialog boxes and panels.

Later, using this script, you can display those panels, return any buttons that were clicked, and extract any text from the text fields, the status of check boxes, the selections of pop-up menus, and so on.

Note You could also utilize another new AppleScript feature and embed the application inside a bundle-based script applet. This would mean the user doesn't see multiple files, just your script applet. Chapter 24 covers bundle-based applets in more detail.

Now, why go through this trouble instead of just creating an AppleScript Studio application? Although Studio is a powerful and flexible tool, it is overkill for many tasks. Often all you need is a simple, double-clickable applet that launches, asks the user for a few initial values, performs some tasks, and quits again when it's done. It might be a new applet that you've just started writing, or it may be one you wrote earlier and now want to enhance a bit. These sorts of scripts are quick and easy to develop in Script Editor, but what happens when Standard Additions' display dialog and choose from list commands are just a little too limited for the job?

One option is to rework your script from the ground up as a Studio-based application, and for scripts with lots of complex user interaction, this is probably the right thing to do. For less demanding projects, however, it's quicker, easier, and more flexible if you could keep it as is and just use AppleScript Studio to create a sort of turbocharged version of display dialog in the places you need the extra dialog box support.

This more limited approach also allows you to dip your toe into Studio programming without having to jump all the way in. AppleScript Studio is a large and rather complex environment, and it can be quite intimidating to new users attempting to dive in headfirst. Building a few simple standalone dialog boxes first is a great way to "warm up" to Studio programming before finally taking the plunge.

How Will It Work?

The custom "dialog box" will actually be a window in the AppleScript Studio application you'll create. This window will contain text fields and other controls where users will enter their details and will contain some buttons they'll click to accept or cancel the dialog box when they're done. The rough design in Figure 13-1 shows how the planned dialog box will look in use.

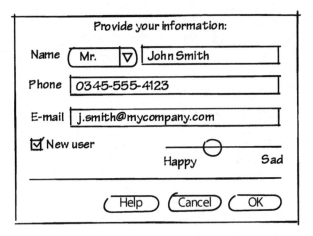

Figure 13-1. *A sketch of how the dialog box will look in use*

All three clickable buttons in the application will perform the same task: they will copy their own title to a hidden text field in the window called chosen button and then make the window invisible again. This will allow the external script to detect when the user has dismissed the dialog box and which button they clicked to do so.

The other controls will just have names that the script can later use to identify them when extracting information from them. The user can enter text and otherwise manipulate these controls as normal, but unlike clicking buttons this won't have any direct effect on your scripts.

From the script, you will invoke the dialog box in three steps:

1. Tell the dialog box's application to show the window you want.

2. Use a repeat loop to wait while the window is still visible.

3. Once the window has become invisible, the script will extract the values from the different text fields and other UI elements. You are able to do this because the text fields and other UI elements retain their values even after the window is invisible.

You will start by creating the application, and then you will create the script tidbits that will display the dialog box and get the dialog box information.

Creating the Application

You will create a new project in AppleScript Studio called dialog. This project will be the application you'll use to edit and later show dialog boxes from.

Launch Xcode, which is an application that is part of the Developer Tools package (/Developer/ Applications/Xcode.app), and start a new AppleScript Application project, as shown in Figure 13-2. Name the project dialogs, as shown in Figure 13-3.

Figure 13-2. *Creating a new AppleScript Application project*

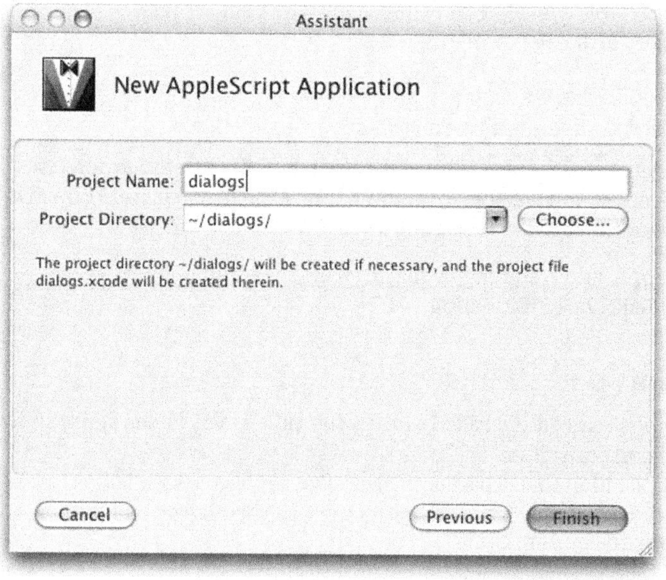

Figure 13-3. *Naming the new project*

After you've created the project, locate the icon for the MainMenu.nib file (highlighted in Figure 13-4), and double-click it.

The MainMenu.nib file is the interface of your application. Double-clicking its icon in Xcode opens this .nib file in Interface Builder, allowing you to edit it.

Figure 13-4. *The* `MainMenu.nib` *interface file icon in your Xcode project*

In the `MainMenu.nib` file window (at the top of Figure 13-5), locate the icon for the default window, click it, and click Delete. You will create a panel to replace it. In the toolbar of the Palettes panel (shown at the bottom of Figure 13-5), click the fourth icon (the one that looks like a miniature window) to show the palette with the window elements. Drag an instance of the panel object to your `MainMenu.nib` file window, as shown in Figure 13-5.

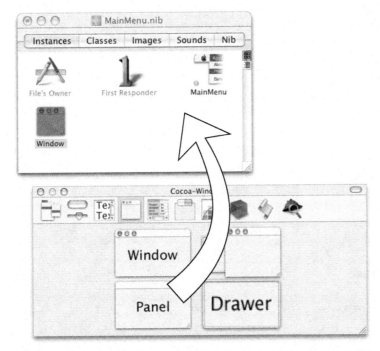

Figure 13-5. *Dragging a new panel to the* `MainMenu.nib` *file window. Make sure you also delete the original window object in the* `MainMenu.nib` *file window.*

Editing Your First Dialog Box

In the `MainMenu.nib` file window of Interface Builder, double-click the newly created panel to open it.

Next, go to the Tools menu, and choose Show Inspector (or Show Info if you're on Panther). This will display the Inspector palette (or Info palette in Panther). If not selected, select Attributes from the pop-up menu at the top of the Inspector palette.

In the Inspector palette, you can give your dialog box a title and apply a brushed steel texture to it if you want. Many people poke fun at the brushed steel windows; call me uncool if you want, but I like them! To give your panel the brushed steel look, select the Has Texture check box. Also, type a title in the Window Title field at the top. I used the title Provide Your Information:.

The check boxes for the window's three controls—Close, Minimize, and Zoom (and resize), or Miniaturize, Close, and Resize in Panther—should be checked. This will help ensure that the window stays open until one of the buttons is clicked.

Note When you start creating your own Studio-based dialog box applications, if you don't create a new panel but instead use the default window supplied by Interface Builder, you'll have to uncheck the window's Visible at Launch Time check box in the Inspector palette. Remember, when the application launches, you don't want any windows to show; you want the windows showing only when your script specifically makes them visible.

Figure 13-6 shows the Inspector palette with the appropriate settings.

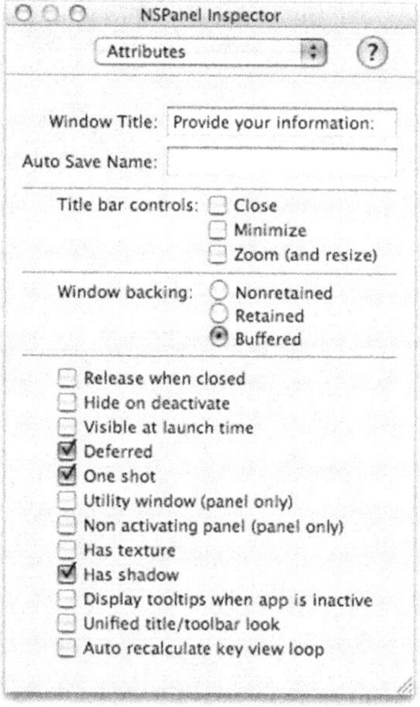

Figure 13-6. *The Inspector palette*

Giving Your Window Its AppleScript Name

As well as giving your window a human-readable title, you must also give it an internal name that AppleScript can see and use. The external script will use this name when referring to the window object it wants to show.

To name the window, choose AppleScript from the top pop-up menu in the Inspector palette.

Note When naming a window object, if the window contains any controls, such as buttons, and so on, make sure that none of these controls are selected. If they are, you will be naming them, not the window.

Now, type the name **user info** in the Name field, as shown in Figure 13-7.

Figure 13-7. *The window's Inspector palette with the new window object's name*

Adding Dialog Box Elements

The dialog box you'll create will be fairly simple, housing three text fields, a check box, a pop-up menu, a slider, and a few buttons. You'll also add some text labels so users know what to put in each text field. These labels are for information only and don't serve any programming-related purpose. The purpose of the dialog box you're creating will be to collect the user's information, but you're welcome to experiment with any other fields, labels, and UI elements.

Set up your panel the way I did, as shown in Figure 13-8. Just drag each of the desired text fields, buttons, and other UI elements from the Palettes panel to your own window. You'll find all the controls you need under the second and third tabs of the Palettes panel. You can resize the text fields by dragging the small dots that appear at their corners while they're selected.

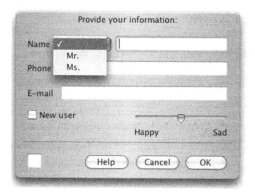

Figure 13-8. *The finished dialog layout. Notice the small extra text field in the bottom-left corner; this will have a special purpose in your finished dialog box application.*

Naming and Editing Dialog Box Elements

The dialog box you created has several types of elements, some of which you need to name so that AppleScript can refer to them when getting their values: the editable text fields, pop-up menu, check box, and slider. You could also name the three buttons at the bottom, but since you're keeping things simple, you'll cheat a little and just use their titles when working with those.

You name the elements in the AppleScript pane of the Inspector palette. Make sure the Inspector palette is visible, and choose AppleScript from the pop-up menu at the top, as shown in Figure 13-9.

To name an element, click it in the window, and type the element's name in the Name text field in the Inspector palette, also shown in Figure 13-9.

Give the top three text fields the following names: name, phone, and email.

Name the pop-up salutation, the check box newuser, and the slider mood.

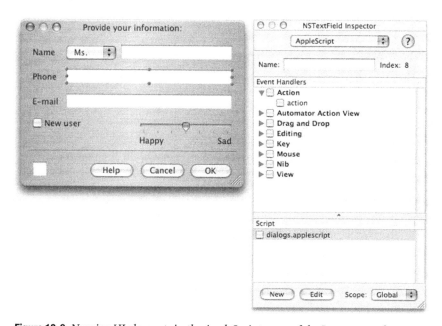

Figure 13-9. *Naming UI elements in the AppleScript pane of the Inspector palette*

Setting Up the Hidden Button Field

Notice the label-free square text field at the bottom left of the window you designed, as shown in Figure 13-9. Name this field chosen button. External scripts will use this field to work out which button the user clicked. When any button is clicked, the Studio application's internal script will take the title of that button and place it in that field, which will be hidden. Later, you can use the script to get the contents of the chosen button text field to know which button was clicked.

To make this text field invisible so the user won't see it when the application is run, check the Hidden check box in the Attributes pane of the Inspector palette.

Testing the Interface

In IB, you can press Cmd+R (or choose File ➤ Test Interface) at any point to see how the interface will look and to try all the controls you put on it.

Connecting the Buttons to the Script

One more thing you have to do to make the buttons perform is set them up so they'll send events to the application's internal script whenever the user clicks them.

To configure a UI element to send events to a script, first select that UI element. Then go to the AppleScript pane of the Inspector palette, and check all the event handlers you want it to trigger, along with the script those handlers are in. In this case, you want each of the three buttons to send a clicked event to the main dialogs script, as shown in Figure 13-10.

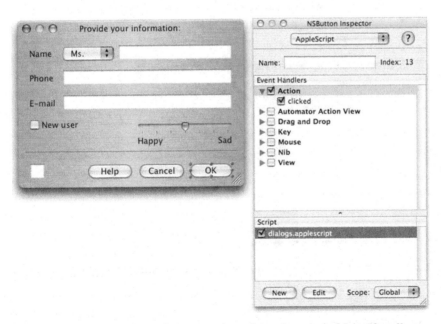

Figure 13-10. *Setting up the OK button to trigger the main script's* clicked *handler*

Follow these steps:

1. Click the first button.

2. Choose AppleScript from the pop-up menu at the top of the Inspector palette.

3. In the Event Handlers outline list, expand the Action triangle, and check Clicked.

4. In the script pane, check dialogs.applescript.

Notice that you didn't give the buttons names. In a full Studio application, you'd normally name them, but since you're keeping it simple here, you'll just rely on their titles, like you do in the `display dialog` command.

Repeat steps 1 through 4 for the other two buttons as well.

In the AppleScript Studio application, all those buttons will invoke the same event handler in the script.

To create that event handler in the script automatically, click one of the buttons to select it (any one), and click the Edit button (or Edit Script on 10.3) at the bottom of the AppleScript pane of the Inspector palette.

Once you do, the script in the Xcode project will open, and a new, empty `clicked` event handler will be added, as shown in Figure 13-11.

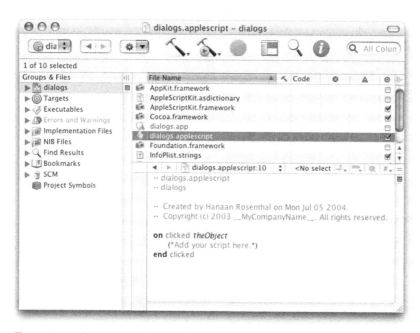

Figure 13-11. *The Xcode project window with the script, and the* `clicked` *event handler that has been added by IB*

Setting Up the clicked Event Handler

The `clicked` event handler will be invoked whenever the user clicks a UI element that is configured in IB to send that event. Since all the buttons in the panel you designed send `clicked` events to the same script, clicking any of them will invoke the same `clicked` event handler.

The way you structure the application will allow you to treat all buttons with one simple script. All you want is to copy the title of the button that has been clicked to the text field named `chosen` button. IB and Xcode should have already added the on clicked theObject and end clicked lines to dialogs.applescript for you, so fill in the rest of the handler's code as shown here:

```
on clicked theObject
    tell (window of theObject)
        set contents of text field "chosen button" to title of theObject
        set visible to false
    end tell
end clicked
```

The handler will start by making the window on which the clicked button sits the target of the current tell block.

Since the variable theObject contains a reference to the button that has been clicked, when you refer to the window of theObject (line 2), you instantly identify the window to which this button belongs.

This window property is defined in Studio's view superclass, so you'll find it in buttons, sliders, pop-up menus, text fields, and all other objects that inherit from view. Looking up the window this way makes your code more flexible than if you hardwired it into the handler as tell (window "user info")...end tell. If you want to add extra dialog boxes to the application later, they can all use the same clicked handler, and it will find the right window automatically.

In line 3 you set the contents of the text field named chosen button to the title of the clicked button.

Line 4 makes the window invisible again.

At this point, the application is done, and this is all the internal code your application will require.

The rest of the work will be up to the external script—it will need to extract the values from the different text fields and other UI elements.

Testing the Application

In Xcode, choose Build ➤ Build and Run, or press Cmd+R. This will build the application and launch it. Click the Save All button if Xcode prompts you to save changes.

The default location for the application is in the Build folder inside the project folder. Later you can move it to any other location. You must beware, however, because if you leave a copy of it in the Build folder, AppleScript may try to launch this version of the application when it is mentioned in the script.

When you see the application in your dock, you can switch to your script editor, where you will complete the exercise.

To test the scriptability of your application, try something like this: create a new script window in Script Editor, or other script editing application, and type the following script lines:

```
tell application "dialogs"
    get name of every window
end tell
```

As a result, you should get a list of one item, the name of your one window:

```
{"user info"}
```

Now, let's test for the text fields. Change the script to look like this one:

```
tell application "dialogs"
    tell window "user info"
        name of every text field
    end tell
end tell
```

And the result will be as follows:

```
{"name", "phone", "email", "chosen button", missing value, ¬
missing value, missing value, missing value, missing value}
```

The reason for all the missing values is that you haven't named all the text labels that are also considered text fields by AppleScript.

Using the Custom Dialog Box in a Script

Now that you have created the application and tested its scriptability, let's see whether you can put it to use. Your strategy will be to start by telling the application to show the window you want to use as a dialog box. Then, you will wait until the window isn't showing anymore, and finally, when that happens, you will extract the values from the different controls.

Show the Dialog Box

The part of the script that shows the dialog box will look like this:

```
tell application "dialogs"
    activate
    tell window "user info"
        repeat with name_ref in {"chosen button", "name", "phone", "email"}
            set contents of text field name_ref to ""
        end repeat
        set visible to true
        --more to come here
    end tell
end tell
```

You start by activating the application. This brings the application to the front so users will be able to enter data into its dialog box window. Then, you clear the text from all the editable text fields. This is important since you don't want the dialog box to retain the values from the last time you used it.

Instead of clearing the text fields, you could use this part to populate them with default values as well.

Then you set the value of the window object's `visible` property to true, which simply makes the window visible onscreen.

Wait for the User to Close the Dialog Box

Next, you will create a `repeat` loop that will go on as long as the window is visible. Since you want to replicate the script's natural behavior, the script has to sit there until the user clicks a button.

The script with the waiting repeat loop looks like this:

```
tell application "dialogs"
    activate
    tell window "user info"
        set contents of every text field to ""
        set visible to true
        --Wait for window to close:
        repeat while visible
            delay 0.1
        end repeat
        --more to come here
    end tell
end tell
```

The script could, if you needed to, track the time the dialog box is open and close it after a while. This would make the dialog box behave like Standard Additions' display dialog command does when you use its giving up after parameter. For example, to make the dialog box automatically dismiss itself after ten seconds, you would use the following waiting loop:

```
set seconds_passed to 0
repeat while visible and seconds_passed < 10
    delay 0.1
    set seconds_passed to seconds_passed + 0.1
end repeat
```

The external script can then check to see whether the chosen button text field contains an empty string; if it does, it means the dialog box must have expired by itself.

Extract User-Entered Values

Next you will go control by control and extract the values the user chose or typed in. To figure out which button the user clicked, just use this line:

```
set buttonReturned to contents of text field "chosen button"
```

Here's the script in its entirety:

```
1. tell application "dialogs"
2.      activate
3.      tell window "user info"
4.          repeat with field_name_ref in {"chosen button", "name", "phone", "email"}
5.              set contents of text field field_name_ref to ""
6.          end repeat
7.          set visible to true

8.          repeat while visible
9.              delay 0.1
10.         end repeat

11.         set buttonReturned to contents of text field "chosen button"
12.         set userName to contents of text field "name"
13.         set userPhone to contents of text field "phone"
14.         set userEmail to contents of text field "email"
15.         set userSalutation to ¬
                title of current menu item of popup button "salutation"
16.         set userMood to integer value of slider "mood" -- 0=happy, 100 = sad
17.         set userIsNew to contents of button "new user"
18.     end tell
19. end tell

20. activate

21. display dialog "Button: " & buttonReturned & "
        Name: " & userName & "
        Phone: " & userPhone & "
        Email: " & userEmail & "
        Salutation: " & userSalutation & "
        Mood: " & userMood & "
        User is new: " & userIsNew
```

Once you've finished retrieving all the user values, you use another activate command to bring the application running the external script back to the front again. The display dialog command in the last line simply displays the user's input for testing purposes.

Using FaceSpan for OS X

In 2005, Late Night Software, creator of Script Debugger, bought the rights to FaceSpan and is working on new updates. You can download a demo or buy a full copy of the latest FaceSpan at Late Night Software's website (www.latenightsw.com). Whether you want to develop a fully functional application or just provide an interface for an AppleScript you have already written, FaceSpan provides the tools you need.

■**Note** These FaceSpan sections were written by Shirley Hopkins of DTI, maker of FaceSpan.

What is FaceSpan? It is an integrated development environment that allows you to create the user interface, add resources (movies, graphics, and so on), define the code, and build a Macintosh application that looks and runs like an "off-the-shelf" application. FaceSpan 4.0 does this for you in an easy-to-use, high-level environment. Everything you need to build an application for OS X is at your fingertips. Its predecessors, versions 1 through 3.5, work with earlier versions of the operating system. This discussion will cover only FaceSpan 4.

FaceSpan 4 is deceptively easy to use, but there is a lot of power "under the hood." By using a full complement of objects from tables and tab views to a secure text field that hides user entries as they are typed, you can create FaceSpan interfaces with simple drag and drop. FaceSpan 4 has much built-in functionality and provides handlers that you can use as is or modify to suit your specific needs. You can even make calls directly to Cocoa if the need arises.

Best of all, FaceSpan takes advantage of AppleScript's object-oriented structure. Events generated at the window item level can be handled in the script for the item, in the script for its parent window, or in the project script. If an event is handled at the window item level, it can be continued to a same-named handler in a window or the project script. Properties assigned at the project script level can be "seen" by the window's scripts and by window item scripts using the my qualifier. It's like having a well-organized team at your command, with each item and each script working in concert. You can even add Script Object scripts (FaceSpan scripts) to your project to extend the object-oriented functionality.

For the more advanced user, FaceSpan interfaces nicely with Script Debugger, which can be set to work as its editor and/or debugger.

Nine Steps to Success

Basically, the process of creating a project in FaceSpan consists of nine easy steps:

1. **Start a new project**: To start a new project, select File ➤ New Project in FaceSpan. In the New Project dialog box (see Figure 13-12), give your project a name. For most applications, you will want to select the Use Project Name As Executable Name check box. Select the application type from the Project Type pop-up menu, and if needed, designate where the project will be saved. You can also start a project by selecting a template from the templates list, if desired. Once you have given FaceSpan this information, click OK.

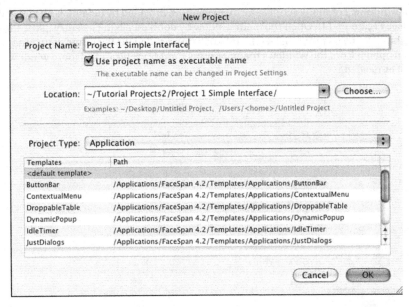

Figure 13-12. *New Project dialog box*

2. **Add resources**: The project has a main window and main menu created by default. A script also exists for the project, the project script. You can add artwork, movies, sounds, and files to your project using the Project dialog box (see Figure 13-13) or by selecting Project ➤ Add Files.

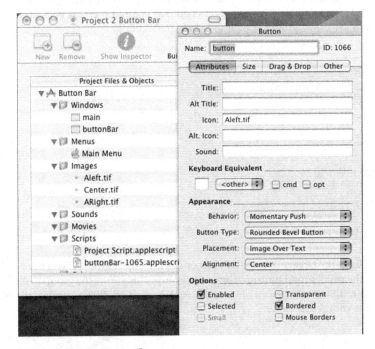

Figure 13-13. *Button attributes*

3. **Set up windows**: For many scripts, the main window, provided by default, is all you will need (see Figure 13-14). Open the main window by double-clicking its entry in the Project dialog box. Define its properties in the Info palette provided. (If the Info palette is not open, you can open it from the Windows menu or press Cmd+I.) You can add more windows (or panels) as needed.

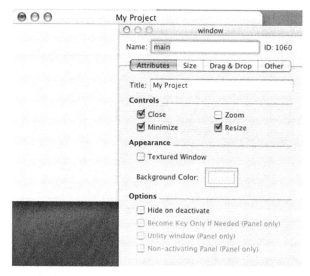

Figure 13-14. *Window attributes*

4. **Design the user interface**: You add objects to windows (and panels) by dragging objects from the Objects Palette and placing them as needed (see Figure 13-15). As you move objects around in a window, guides appear to help in positioning.

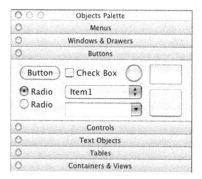

Figure 13-15. *The Objects Palette*

Clicking a title bar in the Objects Palette window opens the object group. If you need only one object, use the small round button to open the group. This allows the group to close automatically once the item is placed on the window. You can Ctrl-click a window to select an object from its contextual menu.

Tip Hold the cursor over an object in the Objects Palette to see its description.

Set the properties for each object in the Info palette. If the Info palette is not open, you can open it by using the Window menu or by pressing Cmd+I.

The Info palette shows information for the interface element currently selected and indicates its class in its title bar (see Figure 13-16). In naming objects, select names that are easy to remember. Names are used to reference objects in scripts and are case sensitive.

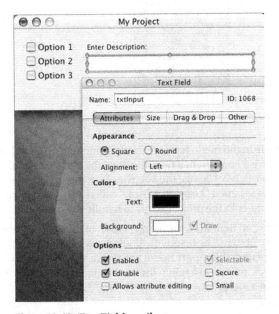

Figure 13-16. *Text Field attributes*

Tip Get in the habit of pressing Tab after typing an entry into one of the Info palette's text fields. This will move your cursor to the next field automatically.

5. **Edit main menu**: Change, add, or remove items from the main menu as needed (see Figure 13-17). To work with the main menu, double-click its entry in the Menus folder of the Project dialog box.

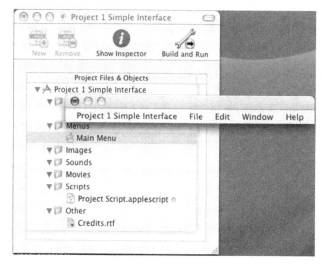

Figure 13-17. *The main menu*

To change an item, click a menu title in the menu bar to disclose its menu items and high-light the one you want to edit. To give a menu item a new title, type the new text into the Title field of the Info palette's Attributes tab. Change the behavior for a menu item in the Actions list of the Info palette. Items assigned "<execute script>" will need to have code written in the choose menu item handler in the project script to handle them being selected.

To add an item to the menu bar, drag an item from the Menus group of the Objects Palette (an insert line will appear where the item will be inserted). A Submenu item added to the menu bar will be initially empty; opening this empty menu will reveal a blank space where you can add new items to it. Ctrl-click an item in a menu list (or the blank space if it's empty) to add, delete, or move items within a menu list.

Close the main menu when complete.

6. **Attach scripts**: A project script is provided by default. You can put all your code here, or you can manage your scripts in an object-oriented manner by attaching scripts to windows or window items.

   To create a script, select the item to which the script will be attached, and press Cmd+E (or select Script ➤ Add Script). To open an existing script, double-click its entry in the Project dialog box.

   To get references to the window and to window objects, you can use the Object Browser in the Scripting Help drawer of the Script Edit window. Double-click an object in the Object Browser, and its full reference appears at the cursor location in the script.

   Create functionality by adding code to scripts. FaceSpan helps you by providing a wealth of handlers that can be used as is or modified to suit your needs. Many are written as templates requiring that you replace placeholder text (designated by ALL CAPS) with references to objects or values.

   Check your code's syntax by clicking the Compile button in the Script Edit window. Correct errors as needed. Most errors will be typographical in nature: you forgot to end a quote with a quotation mark, misspelled a word, forgot to close a parentheses pair, and so on (see Figure 13-18).

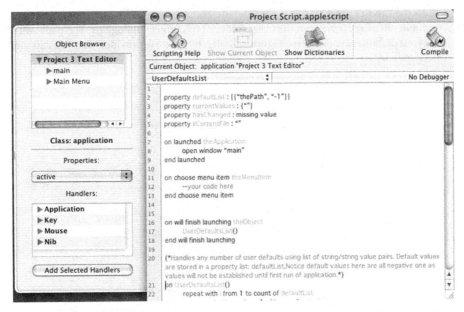

Figure 13-18. *The Script Edit window*

7. **Test and debug:** Click the Build and Run button in the Project dialog box (or press Cmd+R) to build the project and test run the resulting application. Debug as needed. The Message window can be a great aid for simple debugging. To check the values of variables at runtime, place log commands within the code with the following format:

```
log variableValue
```

The value for variableValue in the preceding example would be printed to the corresponding Event Log window in FaceSpan as the application runs (see Figure 13-19).

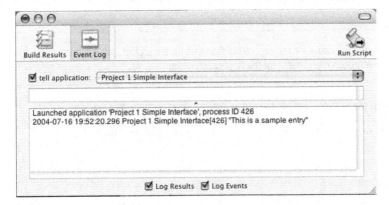

Figure 13-19. *An Event Log window*

The Build and Run button in the Project dialog box changes to a Stop button while a project is running. Click this button to stop a test run.

8. **Edit the Credits page**: To add author details, comments, and so on, to the Credits page, double-click Credits.rtf in the Other folder of the Project dialog box. The page will open in your default text editor (see Figure 13-20). A template is provided that you can modify as needed.

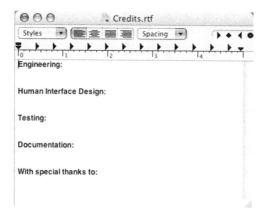

Figure 13-20. Credits.rtf *file*

9. **Save the project**: You may want to select the Save Unsaved Projects option on the Building tab of FaceSpan's Preferences to Ask Before Building. This will make FaceSpan ask you whether you want it to save a project before building it. Once the project is working as desired, save the project.

Establish settings for the executable (application created) if desired. The name of the executable will be the same as that of your project if you checked Use Project Name As Executable Name when you created the project. You can give your executable a different name. You can also assign a custom icon, an identifier, and an information string to be used by the system. You can find these settings in the Executable Settings dialog box (see Figure 13-21), which you can open by selecting Project ➤ Executable Settings.

Note If you do use a different name for the executable than that for the project, you will need to change the name of the project in the various menu items for the Application menu.

Build and run (or build) your project after editing the Credits page.

You can now save and close the project (or throw it away, if you choose).

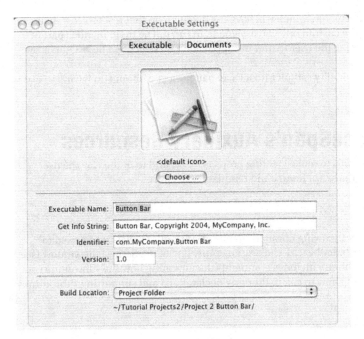

Figure 13-21. *Executable Settings dialog box*

After completing the preceding steps, you should have a folder that looks like Figure 13-22.

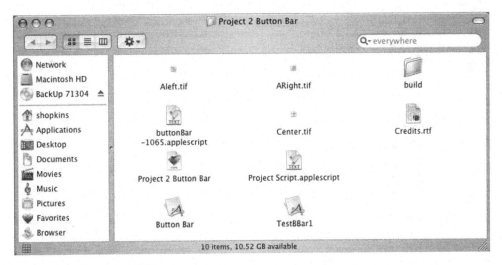

Figure 13-22. *The project folder*

You can double-click the executable, which will have the default icon that resembles a sheet of paper with a letter *A* on it (or the custom one you assigned), to run it. The main menu is part of your application by default, allowing the user to quit the application by selecting File ➤ Quit or by pressing Cmd+Q.

As you can see, a lot of functionality is built into a FaceSpan project without you having to even think about it.

A Word About FaceSpan's Auxiliary Resources

FaceSpan gives users a wealth of aids to make creating projects easier and to fit the way the user wants to work. Among these are the script library and template collection.

Library

One of the features of FaceSpan is a growing library of standard subroutines that can be used to build scripts. You can access the library by Ctrl-clicking an empty line of the Script Edit window (see Figure 13-23). Code found in this library includes comments documenting how the subroutine can be used and example code showing how to call it. Property declarations and supporting subroutines are also supplied as needed.

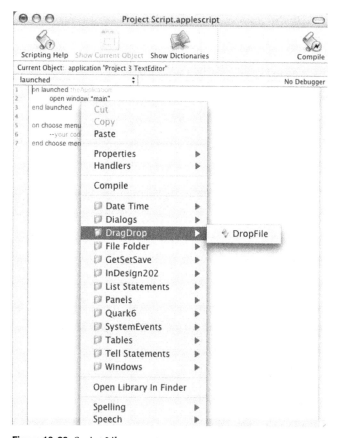

Figure 13-23. *Script Library entry*

If the code includes a property statement, you should cut and paste this at the beginning of the script where the property will be managed (usually the project script). An example call to the subroutine is often included and will need to be cut and pasted at the appropriate location in the script and modified as needed. Some entries act as templates, with placeholder text (indicated with ALL CAPS). These will need to be replaced with actual object references or values.

The Library folder is installed in the same folder as FaceSpan. You can add your own routines to this collection by saving scripts as text with the .applescript extension and placing them in the appropriate folders.

Templates

Another great resource is the Templates folder, which is also installed in the same folder as FaceSpan. Templates are a great way to start a project quickly. You can save a project at any stage as a template. Just save the project to the Templates folder using Save As. Take note that your current project is now the template project, so you will want to close the current project and reopen the original project from which the template was created before continuing.

Keep Up-to-Date

Because new templates and library scripts are being added periodically, you may want to check FaceSpan's downloads web page (www.FaceSpan.com) to make sure you have all the latest treats.

You can also find the completed projects described in the following tutorials on the downloads page.

Writing Code

When writing a script in Script Editor, there is a strong tendency to write statements as one big monolithic piece of code. When you work with an interface, however, each action or event that can take place in the interface can potentially be "handled" in a separate event handler.

Event Handlers

Writing code for FaceSpan depends heavily on the use of event handlers. For example, when an object in a window is clicked, it sends a clicked event. Statements included in the clicked event handler that responds to this event dictate what happens when the button is clicked.

Many event handlers include the variable theObject as part of the on line. This parameter variable contains a reference to the object that sent the event. If you have a clicked handler in a script that's attached to the object itself, the clicked handler will receive only the clicked event sent by this object. However, if you put a clicked handler in the script for a window or in the project script, the code will need to determine which object sent the event, since more than one button may be sending clicked events to the same window script or project script. To do this, you'll need to give each button a different name and then use name of theObject in the clicked handler to work out which button sent the event and execute the appropriate code.

To add an empty template for an event handler that responds to a particular event sent by an interface object, find and select the object in the Object Browser of the Scripting Help drawer. The handler choices for the object then appear in the Handlers browser in the same drawer. Double-clicking an entry in the Handlers browser will place the handler template in the script at the current cursor location. Make sure the cursor is in an open area of the Script Edit window before double-clicking.

Subroutines

You can also include any number of subroutines (user-defined command handlers) in your project's scripts. Although you write event handlers specifically to respond to events sent by the application's graphical user interface (GUI), you use subroutines to organize your general code better. The more you can group related statements into meaningful blocks of code that perform a single, well-defined function, the more reusable and easier to understand your code will become.

For the sake of consistency, the user-defined subroutines in the tutorials all use positional parameters. Positional parameters were briefly introduced in Chapters 2 and 8 and are covered in detail in Chapter 18, if you need to remind yourself of how to use them.

Commands vs. Events: What's the Difference Anyway?

The reason I'm making a distinction between command handlers and event handlers is to indicate their different purposes when discussing them. That is, all these handlers work in the same basic way, but how you use them is different:

When I say *event*, I'm talking about a message sent by an application's GUI to its internal script to let it know the user has just done something interesting (clicked a button, selected a menu item, and so on).

When I say *command* or *subroutine call*, I'm talking about a message sent by a script demanding that a specific operation be performed (make a new document, sort a list, and so on). Similarly, an *event handler* is a handler written to respond to a particular kind of event, whereas a *command handler* or *subroutine* is a handler written to carry out a specific command.

Making this mental distinction between commands and events is an important part of writing GUI applications where so much of an application's behavior relies on being triggered by various events—especially since the timing and order in which events might (or might not) occur can greatly vary depending on how users interact with the application's interface. Whether you're using FaceSpan or AppleScript Studio, this sort of "event-driven" programming is quite a change from writing simple step-by-step processing scripts that run, perform a specific sequence of operations, and quit when done. But once you get used to this new way of thinking, it can be great fun to do and allows you to produce sophisticated applications with rich user interaction and a professional look and feel.

FaceSpan Scripts

If you like the idea of having reusable subroutines in a script library, you will love the concept of using FaceSpan scripts. FaceSpan scripts serve the same purpose as regular AppleScript "library" scripts (discussed in Chapter 19), but they are automatically included in the finished application bundle and are saved and loaded in a slightly different way.

With a FaceSpan script, you put a collection of subroutines together into one script file. For instance, you could put all your subroutines that work with text in your favorite scriptable text editor in one file. Just stack the subroutines in the file, as you collect them, but be sure to keep documentation handy to remind you of the subroutines and what parameters are required. Save the script as a text file with the `.applescript` extension.

When you want to use the subroutines in the collection, add the file to your project. To add a file, select Project ➤ Add Files, or drag the file to the `Scripts` folder in the Project window. The subroutines inside the file are not available to your scripts until you actually load the file. You'll usually do this in the project script so that all parts of the project can have access to the loaded script:

1. Define a global variable to contain the loaded script object in the project script. You might want to call it gTextScripts:

```
global gTextScripts
```

2. Before you need to use the subroutines, load the script into the variable using the name of the file as shown in the Project dialog box but without the .applescript extension. A good place to do this is at the start of the project script's launched handler:

```
on launched theApplication
    set gTextScripts to load facespan script "FSTextScripts"
    --rest of this handler's code goes here
end launched
```

3. When you need to call one of the subroutines in the loaded script object, first make sure the script from where the call is being made has declared the same global variable at the top of the script:

```
global gTextScript
```

4. Now any statement in the script can refer to the script object in this global variable in order to call its subroutines. For instance, if the FaceSpan script contains a getText subroutine, you would call the subroutine using this:

```
set theText to gTextScript's getText()
```

In all other respects, the subroutines found in a FaceSpan script are used like the subroutines found in any other script within a project.

More advanced users will appreciate the simplicity with which you can create FaceSpan script files for an individual project directly in FaceSpan. Ctrl-click the Scripts folder in the Project window, and select New Script from the contextual menu. A new unattached script is created for the project. You can accept the default name or change the name by clicking the Show Inspector button. This script file will be included in the finished application and can be loaded and used within a project in the same manner as described previously.

Tutorials

The best way to examine how an application functions is to work with it. The following are several simple projects to demonstrate some of FaceSpan's features. The tutorials will follow the basic nine-step procedure outlined previously with further explanation as needed. Remember to refer to the nine-step outline as you work through the projects for more information.

Even if you do not currently have access to FaceSpan, the projects are short enough that you can mentally work through them to see how FaceSpan makes it easy to create working applications using AppleScript.

Preliminaries

Before you start putting your first project together, you might want to set up a folder where you want your projects to be saved. You may also want to establish some preferences for how you want to work.

Once you launch FaceSpan, select Application ➤ Preferences. If nothing else, you will want to establish the location for your projects. To target the folder that you set aside for your projects, select Other from the Default project location drop-down list in General Preferences and navigate to the folder you created. Most preferences are pretty self-explanatory.

For general preferences, the following are suggested:

- When adding files, copy files into project folder.
- Sync script names with object names.
- When working with windows and panels, remember document states.
- When FaceSpan launches, show the Objects Palette.
- Show the Info palette.

For editing, the following is suggested:

- All options are checked. You may want to uncheck allow text completion.

For building, the following is suggested:

- As default

Project 1: Put a Face on It

The first project will demonstrate how to turn an existing script into a FaceSpan-based application. You can apply the basic procedure outlined here to any number of scripts you might have that could benefit from a user-friendly interface.

For demonstration, assume that the existing script presents users with a list of options from which they must select one or more options (choose from list). There is also a text string that must be entered by users (display dialog). From there the script performs some functionality depending on the choices made. Putting this all in a FaceSpan project is a no-brainer. The run handler in the current script could read something like the following:

```
on run
    set userChoiceList to {"Choice 1", "Choice 2", "Choice 3"}
    set defaultString to "Input string here"
    --call subroutine that uses choose from list to return user's choices
    set userChoice to getUserChoice(userChoiceList)
    --call subroutine that uses display dialog to get string entry
    set userInput to getUserInput(defaultString)
    --call main processing subroutine using input from user
    doMainProcess(userChoice, userInput)end run
```

This run handler is then followed by the subroutines that perform the various functions: getUserChoice, getUserInput, and doMainProcess.

Here are the steps for re-creating this script as a FaceSpan-based application (refer to the nine-step outline earlier for details):

Step 1: Start a New Project

Select Application for the type. No template will be used, so select <default template> in the Templates list.

Step 2: Add Resources

No resources will be added to the project; skip this step.

Step 3: Set Up Windows

This project will require only one window, main, which is provided by default.

Step 4: Design the Interface

Analyzing the script should help in deciding the design for the project. The script dictates the need for a main window with one text field for text entry (see Figure 13-24). You can use a check box matrix in place of the choose from list command. The window will also require a button for the user to click to "trigger" the functionality.

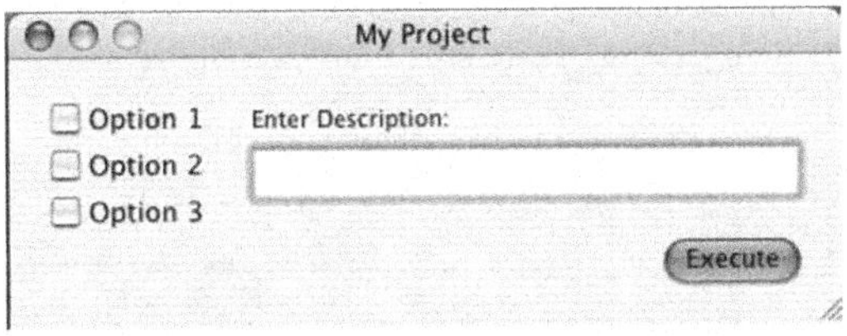

Figure 13-24. *Project 1:* main *window*

Open the main window, and set its properties (use your discretion for settings, but don't change the window's name to anything other than main).

Check Box Matrix

To create the check box matrix, drag a check box from the Buttons group of the Objects Palette. Once you've placed the check box on the window, hold down the Option key. Click and drag one of the sizing handles for the check box to create three check boxes stacked vertically. The Info palette will display the word *Matrix* in its title bar. Use the Info palette to name the matrix matCheck (see Figure 13-25).

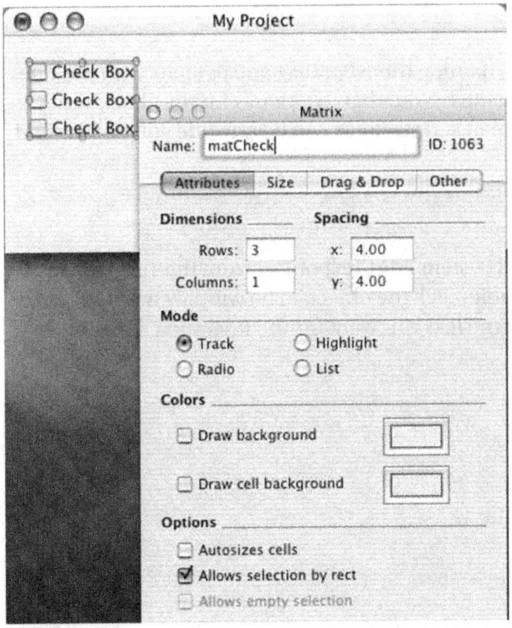

Figure 13-25. *Matrix*

Now double-click the first check box in the matrix. (The window will dim, indicating that a nested object is selected, and the Info palette will display *Button Cell* in its title.) Set the name for the first check box to Option1. Set the title to Option 1 (see Figure 13-26).

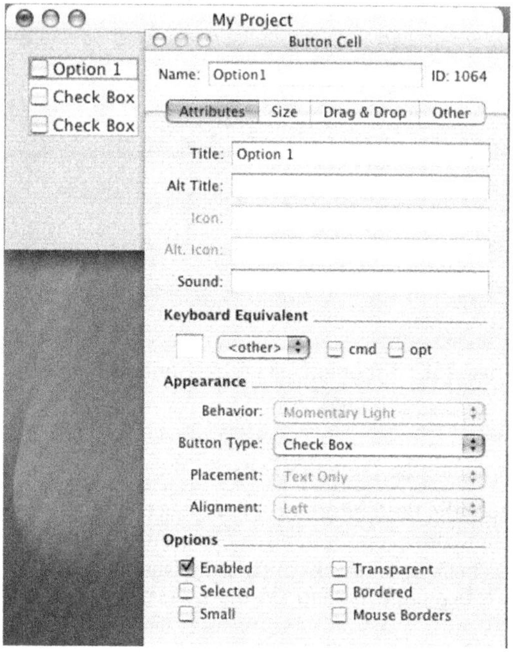

Figure 13-26. *Button Cell's Attributes pane*

Click each of the next check boxes and repeat, naming them Option2 and Option3 with the titles Option 2 and Option 3. Click the window when finished. Note that the names for the check boxes need to correspond to the names used for reference in scripts; titles can be any title you choose and will be read by the user.

Label

To create the label above the text field, drag a Small System Font Text object from the Text Objects group in the Objects Palette. Once it's in place, double-click the object. (The window will dim, indicating that the text field editor is now active.) Type the text you want for the title, such as **Enter Description:** (see Figure 13-27).

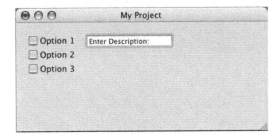

Figure 13-27. *Editing the label text*

Text Field

The text field is the box in the Text Objects group that does not have a scrollbar. Add one to the window, and resize as desired. Name the text field txtInput in the Info palette. You may want to set a text formatter for this field to ensure that only text can be entered. For this, select Add Formatter from the Format menu. The formatter type should be Text by default. You may want to experiment with the various format options (see Figure 13-28).

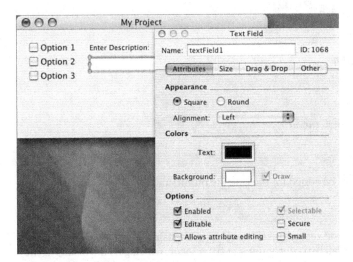

Figure 13-28. *The Text Field Attribute pane*

Push Button

Add a button to the main window. Name the button pshExecute. Label it Execute. You may want to give the button default behavior so it sends a clicked event when the user presses the Return key. For this, set Keyboard Equivalent in its Info palette to the Return option found in the pop-up (see Figure 13-29).

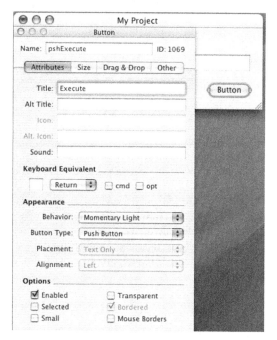

Figure 13-29. *The Button Attribute pane*

Step 5: Edit Main Menu

No alterations will be made to the main menu.

Step 6: Attach Scripts

This project will require that a script be added for the Execute button and the main window.

Execute Button Script

Create a script for the push button pshExecute by selecting it and choosing Script ➤ Add Script. The clicked handler for the button will call two subroutines: getUserInput, which gets the results of the user's input, and doMainProcess, where most of the code from the existing script will be placed.

   If FaceSpan preferences are set to Add Code for Standard Handlers (in Editing Preferences), the script will have a clicked handler as part of the button's script. Complete it as follows:

```
on clicked theObject
    set {userOptions, userEntry} to getUserInput()
    doMainProcess(userOptions, userEntry)
end clicked
```

Main Window Script

Create a script for the main window. A subroutine in this script, getUserInput, will collect the result of the user's interaction with the window items (see the listing that follows). While writing this subroutine, use the Object Browser in the Scripting Help drawer to add references to the user interface's objects. For instance, after typing set userOptions to name of every cell of in the first statement, double-click the entry for the matCheck matrix in the Object Browser (see Figure 13-30).

Figure 13-30. *The Object Browser*

Notice that a complete reference to the matrix object, matrix "matCheck" of window "main", is added to your script. Since you want only the names of the check boxes that are checked, add the filter clause whose state is on state to the end of the full reference. Follow this procedure for adding a reference to the text field in the next statement. The completed subroutine looks like the following:

```
on getUserInput()
    set userOptions to name of every cell of matrix "matCheck" of window "main" ¬
        whose state is on state
    set userEntry to string value of text field "txtInput" of window "main"
    return {userOptions, userEntry}
end getUserInput
```

Main Process Subroutine

Once the previous subroutines have obtained the data from the user interface, the main processing subroutine, doMainProcess, will process this data. Most of the code in the doMainProcess subroutine is taken directly from the existing script. Since this subroutine is called from the button's script, it could be placed in the script for the main window, in the script for the push button, or in the project script. This is one of the nice features of FaceSpan: you can place most subroutines wherever it makes the most sense to you (and perhaps the script). For demonstration, we have created the following "dummy" subroutine to indicate how this subroutine would be written.

Note If you put the procedure in the script for the main window, you can use the Scripting Help drawer to create a reference to the text field.

In the main window's script, include the following:

```
on doMainProcess(userOptions, userEntry)
    if "Option1" is in userOptions then
        --statements to perform if Option1 check box is checked
        say "Option 1 is selected."
    end if
    if "Option2" is in userOptions then
        --statements to perform if Option2 check box is checked
        say "Option 2 is selected."
    end if
    if "Option3" is in userOptions then
        --statements to perform if Option3 check box is checked
        say "Option 3 is selected."
    end if
```

```
    --statements to perform using the entered text
    say "The text entered is " & userEntry
    set string value of text field "txtInput" of window "main" to ¬
        "Script completed successfully"
end doMainProcess
```

Step 7: Test and Debug

If the project runs successfully, the message "Script completed successfully" will appear in the text field. As you test a project, you may see the need to add code or functionality. Often this becomes apparent as you experience how user behavior might cause a project to fail.

In this project, should the user fail to check a check box or fail to add information to the text field, the project could fail. You can prevent this by having the doMainProcess subroutine initially check that the userOptions list and userEntry string aren't empty before going any further. A more sophisticated design might even check the check boxes' and text field's values as soon as the user alters them and immediately reject any changes that would lead to problems later.

For the user's convenience, you might also design the window so that at least one option is initially checked and a default entry is placed in the text field. An opened handler in a script attached to the window object would be an appropriate place for such setup code.

Main Window Script Opened Handler

Open the main window's script. To create the handler, select main in the Object Browser, and disclose the Window entry in the Handlers browser. With the text cursor on an open line in the script, double-click Opened from the Handler list. The handler wrappers are added to the script. Add statements to the handler so it reads as follows. (Use the Object Browser to get the references to the matrix and text field.)

```
on opened theObject
    set state of cell 1 of matrix "matCheck" of window "main" to on state
    set string value of text field "txtInput" of window "main" to "Default value"
end opened
```

Step 8: Edit Credits Page

Refer to the outline in "Nine Steps to Success" for details.

Step 9: Save Project

Although this project has no real functionality, the hope is that this introductory project will give you a quick overview of using FaceSpan to create a simple user interface.

Project 2: Multiple Functionality for a Button Bar

This project demonstrates using a template to start a project. Perhaps you have a number of scripts that work in the same environment such as ones for automating Adobe InDesign or QuarkXPress. Think how handy it would be to have a floating button bar so that all you (or your user) need to do is click a button to get script functionality. The following tutorial demonstrates this. You will want to have some graphics handy that measure 36 pixels by 36 pixels (or however large you want your buttons to be). These can be just about any common format, such as TIFF.

Step 1: Start New Project

In the New Project window, enter **Script Launcher** for the name, and select the ButtonBar template from the template list to start this project quickly (see Figure 13-31).

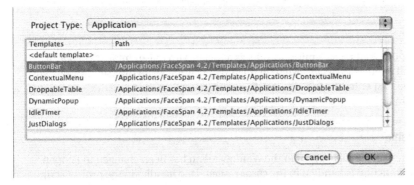

Figure 13-31. *Selecting the ButtonBar template*

Step 2: Add Resources

You can add a number of graphics to your project at one time by Shift-selecting your image files in the Finder and dragging them to the Images folder in the Project window. Just make sure you do not release the graphics until the line below the Images folder appears.

Step 3: Set Up Windows

The template provides all you will need for this project.

Step 4: Design the Interface

The template provides much of what is needed for the interface, but you can modify the project to fit your particular needs.

Bevel Buttons

The template provides a panel buttonBar that is set up to float. It has one bevel button. Duplicate this bevel button to create the number of buttons you want on your button bar. You may need to resize the window. To duplicate the bevel button, select it, and press Cmd+D. Enter values in the fields (the demonstration project uses 39 in the Horizontal Offset field, 0 in the Vertical Offset field, and 8 for Repeat Count). Click OK (see Figure 13-32).

Figure 13-32. *The* buttonBar *panel*

To assign an image to a button, click the button, and enter the name of the graphic in the Icon field for the Info palette. Type the filename as it appears in the Images list in the Project dialog box.

Note In FaceSpan 4.2 and newer, you can drag the entry from the Project dialog box to the button to assign the image.

Alternately, you could set it up so a button works as a toggle with one graphic to display when in the "on" position and another to display when in the "off" position. To do this, set the behavior for the button to Toggle, and enter the "off" image's filename in the Icon field and the "on" image's filename in the Alt. Icon field.

Step 5: Edit Main Menu

The title of the menu item Bring All to Front in the Window menu has been changed to Reopen panel in the template. Its action is handled in the choose menu item handler in the project script.

Note Projects created with a template inherit the name of the template. You will need to open the menu editor and change the title of the application menu and several menu items in the application and Help menus to replace the template's name with your own. (Use the title field in Info palette to change the title.)

Step 6: Attach Scripts

Now it's just a matter of adding scripts and code to the project to respond to the buttons being clicked. One way you can do this is to put a lengthy if-then statement in a clicked handler inside the panel's script. This will test for the button being clicked and then call procedures depending on which button it was. This has been started for you in the template and reads as follows:

```
on clicked theObject
    set theName to name of theObject
    if theName is "button" then
        --call to procedure for bevel button "button"
        processImage()
    else if theName is "button1" then
        --call to next procedure
        --repeat for all buttons
    end if
end clicked
```

The routines called could be in the same script, could be in the project script, or could even be part of an imported FaceSpan script. The template provides a dummy routine:

```
on processImage()
    --statements for called routine
    activate
    display dialog "Button was pushed"
end processImage
```

Code to accommodate the floating panel is part of the project script that is included in the ButtonBar template. This includes code to respond to the Reopen panel menu item in the choose menu item handler:

```
on choose menu item theMenuItem
    if title of theMenuItem is "Reopen panel" then
        display panel thePanel
    end if
end choose menu item
```

Step 7: Test and Debug

Click the Compile button to check that your scripts' syntax is correct. Once it is, click the Build and Run button to build the application and test all its features to make sure they work correctly. A project with this limited scope should run without a hitch.

Step 8: Edit Credits Page

If you decide to save this project, you may want to put your name and any contact information on the Credits page.

Step 9: Save Project

Projects that use a template inherit the name of the template's executable. You will need to open the Executable Settings dialog box (select Executable Settings from the Project menu). Change the name of your project there.

Project 3: Simple Text Editor

This project demonstrates how using scripts from the script library can reduce the amount of actual code writing required in a project to a bare minimum. You will create a simple text editor using scripts provided as part of FaceSpan's Script Library to work with User Defaults, which is used to load and save an application's preferences, and to work with the Open panel (see Figure 13-33).

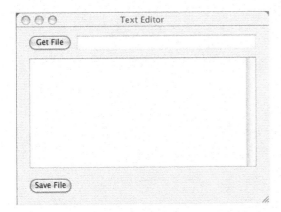

Figure 13-33. *Final project interface*

Step 1: Start New Project

Enter **My Text Editor** for the name, and select Application for Project Type. No template will be used.

Step 2: Add Resources

No resources will be added to the project.

Step 3: Set Up Windows

Open the main window, and set its properties. (Use your discretion in setting its properties, or you may leave the default settings as they are.)

Step 4: Design the Interface

You will set up the main window to allow the user to click or drop a file onto the Get File button to open it. The name of the file opened will display in the text field, and the contents of the file will display in the text view (the large text box with the scrollbar). When the user clicks the Save File button, the text in the text view will be saved over the original file if changes have been made. You will add some buttons, a text view, and a text field to the window.

Buttons

Add a button to the window, and place it at the top left. Name the button pshFiles, and give it the title Get File.

Duplicate the button by pressing Cmd+D with the button still selected. You will want a horizontal offset of 0; the vertical offset is not critical. Try 200 as a value. Rename the duplicated button pshSave, and give it the title Save File.

To handle a drop event (should your user drop a file on the pshiles button), you need to set the pshFiles button up to accept a drop. To do this, click the button and select the Drag & Drop tab in the Info palette. Click the check box next to Filenames in the list. The button is now ready to accept a filename (see Figure 13-34).

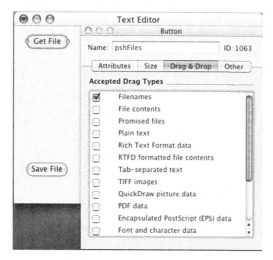

Figure 13-34. *Drag & Drop tab in the Info palette*

Text View

The text view is identified by a scrollbar on the right side. Add a text view to the window, and resize by dragging resize handles as needed.

Several objects in FaceSpan 4 are nested inside other objects. The text view is an example. When you drag the text view onto a window, you will notice that the title for the Info palette is Scroll View. The scroll view is the parent of the text view and gives it scrollbar behavior. Make sure you name the scroll view txtScroll.

To access the text view, double-click the scroll view. Notice that the window dims to indicate you are inside a nested structure. To "back out" of the structure, you can click the little up arrow in the lower-right corner of the text view, use the Cmd-up arrow key combination, or click the window. If you want to set properties for the text view, make sure the Info palette displays the words *Text View* in its title bar (see Figure 13-35).

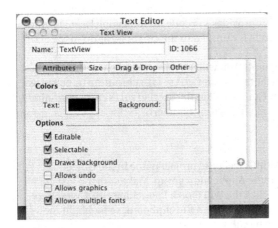

Figure 13-35. *Text view*

Text Field

Add a text field to the window, and resize as needed. Name the text field txtFile. You will also want to uncheck the Editable option in the Attributes pane because this field is for display purposes only.

Step 5: Edit Main Menu

A contextual menu is connected automatically to a text view and a text field to provide access to text formatting and spelling functionality. You may also want to add a text formatting menu to the application's main menu bar.

Double-click Main Menu in the Project window to open the menu editor.

Drag the Format item from the Menus group in the Objects Palette to the main menu bar (a line will appear where the menu will be inserted). The Format menu has a Font item and a Text item that open to display submenus. The functionality for the menu items in the Format menu is built in (see Figure 13-36).

Figure 13-36. *Main menu*

Close the menu editor.

Step 6a: Attach Scripts

Open the project script. If Add Code for Standard Handlers is checked in the Editing tab in Face-Span's preferences, the project script will include two handlers by default: launched and choose menu item. The project script is an ideal place to manage values that need to be available to various objects within the project.

The functionality for managing values that are permanently stored with the application is provided by User Defaults. User Defaults is a system for storing an application's preferences as a collection of key/value pairs, allowing you to look up a value according to its key. The demonstration project will use code found in the Script Library to manage User Defaults.

Ctrl-click an empty line in the script window to open the Script Library. In the GetSetSave collection you will find the entry UserDefaultList. This provides the code for managing User Defaults as a list of values. When the entry is selected, the code is dumped to the cursor location in the Script Edit window.

Notice that the code includes property statements. You will need to cut and paste them at the top of the project script. The comments suggest that the UserDefaultsList subroutine be called as part of the project's will finish launching event. Cut the call to the UserDefaultsList subroutine (it will be pasted in the next step into the will finish launching handler).

The will finish launching Handler

To add a will finish launching handler to the script, select the project name in the Object Browser. From the list of handlers presented, close the Application group. Make sure the text cursor is on an open line in the edit window, and double-click the Will Finish Launching entry. Wrappers for the handler are added to the script. The call should still be on the clipboard, so highlight the single statement inside the will finish launching handler, and paste.

Define the user defaults by editing the defaultList property. For this project, leave the list as defaulted. Notice that there is only one item in the defaultList: thePath with a default value of –1. Each entry in User Defaults is a key/value pair. Each item in your default list is a list of two items: the key and the value.

The currentValues list needs to have a list of empty strings to correspond to each item in the defaultList. This variable will keep track of the values at runtime. User defaults usually are not saved to the application until right before the application quits. Notice that a will quit handler is included as part of the code.

If you use User Defaults, you will need to identify the executable settings for the application.

Click the Compile button for the project script. Once compiled, you can close the script if you want.

pshFiles Button Script

Create a script for the pshFiles button. This will need a handler to take care of a filename drop. In the DragDrop collection of the script library, there is an entry called DropFile. Add it to the GetFiles button's script. Notice that the code includes a property, kCurrentFile. Cut and paste this property declaration at the top of the project script. It also makes a call to a populateWindow subroutine.

Should the user click the button (instead of dropping a file), the script will need a subroutine to let the user select a file from an Open Panel dialog box. In the File Folder collection of the Script Library, find the entry for GetFileOpenPanel. Add this to the button's script. The code includes statements to be provided as part of a call to the subroutine. Cut the call statements, and paste them into the clicked handler for the button. The value for thePath (the default folder path) is item 1 of the currentValues list. The theTitle and thePrompt values can be any string value. Add a call to the populateWindow subroutine, and update the value for the kCurrentFile property. The clicked handler should read similar to the following:

```
on clicked theObject
    set thePath to (item 1 of my currentValues)
    set theTitle to "Place Title Here"
    set thePrompt to "Select file"
    set theFiles to getFiles (thePath, theTitle, thePrompt, false)
    populateWindow (theFiles)
    set my kCurrentFile to theFiles
end clicked
```

Main Window Script

Create a script for the main window. Again, the script code will come from the Script Library. In the Window collection, you should find the entry Initialize Window. Add it to the main window's script. This handler can set up initial values and flag your project when a condition changes. Cut the hasChanged property, and paste it at the top of the project script.

PopulateWindow

The PopulateWindow subroutine will call a readFileText subroutine and place the contents of the file in the text view. The name of the file will be placed in the text field. This routine will be placed in the script for the main window. The PopulateWindow code, found in the Windows collection of the Script Library, is a subroutine template designed just for this purpose. Add it to the main window's script. Words shown in ALL CAPS need to be replaced with actual references and values pertinent to the script. Highlight TEXT FIELD REFERENCE in the first line, and double-click the entry for txtFile in the Object Browser. For VALUE, replace this with the variable fileRef. Notice that the next line calls a subroutine that is included with the template. Highlight TEXT OBJECT REFERENCE, and double-click the entry for TextView in the Object Browser. (You may need to click the twisty triangle next to the txtScroll entry to see the entry for TextView.) Compile the script.

Step 6b: Test and Debug

This may be a good place to test what has been done so far. When the project runs, drag a text file onto the Get File button, or click the button and select a file from the Open panel. Stop the run. If nothing happened when you dragged a file to the button, check to make sure the name of the button is the same as is required by the drop handler.

```
if name of theObject is "pshFiles" then
```

Also, double-check to make sure you have set the button to recognize a file (check Filenames in the Drag & Drop tab of Button's Info palette).

Step 7a: Attach Scripts

Once you've finished testing the code written so far, it's time to add the rest.

Save Button Script

Create a script for the pshSave button. This will call a routine to verify whether there is text in the text view. If the value of the application property hasChanged is found to be true, the routine will need to save the text to the current file. (The reference to the current file is in the kCurrentFile property.)

You can find the routine you will use, GetTextandSave, in the GetSetSave collection of the Script Library. Place this in the script for the pshSave button. The call to the GetTextandSave routine needs to be cut and pasted into the clicked handler for the Save Button script. The properties hasChanged and kCurrentFile are already defined in the project script, so you can delete them.

All that is left is to add a reference to the text view in place of the TEXT VIEW REFERENCE place-holder.

Main Window Script

You need to attend to just one detail. The hasChanged property will have the value false until you add code that will set the value of hasChanged to false when new text is placed in the text view or set the value of hasChanged to true when the text view gets a changed event.

For the first step, the populateWindow subroutine in the script for window main would be a good place to initialize the value for the hasChanged property. Add the following statement as the last line:

```
set my hasChanged to false
```

For the second step, you can add a changed handler to the window's script. This will set the value of hasChanged to true when the window receives a changed event from the text view. You can find the changed handler in the Editing group of handlers for a text object. Select the text view entry in the Object Browser, and close the Editing handlers. Double-click the changed entry to add its wrappers to the window's script.

Add code so the handler reads as follows:

```
--toggles false to true for application property hasChanged
on changed theObject
    if name of theObject is "TextView" and my hasChanged is false then
        set my hasChanged to not my hasChanged
    end if
end changed
```

Step 7b: Test and Debug

Compile the script to check its syntax. Again, test run the project to make sure that both the earlier code and the new additions are all working correctly.

Step 8: Edit Credits Page

Even though adding a Credits page may seem like an unnecessary step, it adds a touch of professionalism to your project.

Step 9: Save Project

When you are satisfied, save the project.

This is just the beginning of what could be a fully functional text editing application. As is, it can read text from a file and save the edited text. You may want to run it just to explore all the text-editing capability that comes with a text view without you having to write one line of code.

Tutorial Wrap-Up

The goal of the tutorials was to introduce you to some of the ways you can use FaceSpan and to give a better understanding of what you can do with it. This is just the tip of the iceberg. There is so much more waiting for your creativity. The possibilities for creating stunning interfaces with custom views and the ability to nest objects within one another are just some of the options.

There is no right and wrong way to put a project together. The tutorial examples use a style that is referred to as a *distributed approach*, because code is "distributed" among the various objects. Nothing is wrong with putting all your code in the project script; it's just that a distributed approach makes a project easier to read and maintain. No hard-and-fast rules exist for how this is done, but the following steps are a good guideline:

1. Put variables whose values need to be used throughout the project in property statements in the project script.

2. If FaceSpan scripts are used, define a global variable to hold each FaceSpan script in the project script and every other script that uses it, and then have the project script load the script into this variable at launch time.

3. Reserve the project script for managing persistent properties, handling menu actions, and for working with subroutines and handlers that need to be available to more than one window.

4. Subroutines that work with "outside" applications are often placed in the project script or are part of a collection that is loaded from a FaceSpan script.

5. All activity that is generated in a window should be handled in the window's script or in individual scripts for its window items.

6. If a window contains a number of similar buttons, you may want to handle their clicked events in a single clicked handler using if-then tests to determine which button sent the message.

7. Use prebuilt scripts from the Script Library when possible. There should be no need to re-create the wheel. Make sure you cut the property statements and paste them to the top of the project script. Copy and paste the sample calls to the subroutines into your code where appropriate.

A Word About my

Watch for the little qualifier my: it can make or break a project:

- Use the my qualifier as part of a call to a subroutine when you are making the call within a tell statement.

- Use the my qualifier to reference a property in a parent object. If a property statement is declared at the application (property script) level, my is needed to reference the property from a script at either the window level or the window item level.

Code in the Script Library assumes that property declarations will be made at the application (property script) level with the code at the window or window item level. Notice that references to properties include my.

The Unsung Heroes

Within FaceSpan are a number of functionalities and windows you can use to facilitate project building. You may find them seldom used or may wonder how you could work without them.

The Dictionary Viewer

Dictionaries are online references of an application's object classes and methods (commands). Besides being able to display its own, FaceSpan's dictionary viewer displays the dictionaries for other scriptable applications. You can even set it to show the information as raw event codes. And, you can save a dictionary so you can view without having to find it each time you want to use it (see Figure 13-37).

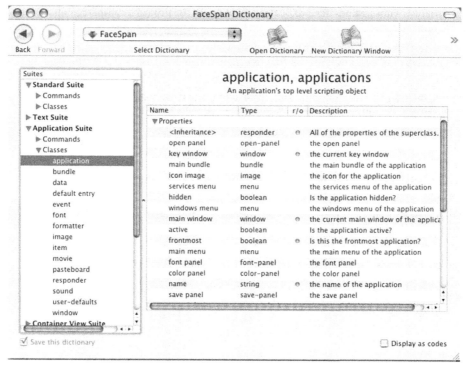

Figure 13-37. *Dictionary viewer*

Contextual Menus

Just about every object in FaceSpan has a contextual menu to give an alternate method for creating and managing objects. Ctrl-click an object to see the options available. It's enough to make you want a three-button mouse (if you don't have one already).

Object Inspector

To get information about a resource in the project, the Object Inspector is the place to go. Click the Show Inspector button in the Project window, and activate one of the three tabs. You can preview graphics and movies on the Preview tab (see Figure 13-38).

Figure 13-38. *Object Inspector's Preview tab*

Formatting Helps

If you find yourself needing to align objects, the Alignment panel is a handy tool. Cmd-click the objects you want to align, and select Format ➤ Align (Cmd+Shift+A). Hold the cursor over an icon in the tool to get its description if you can't discern its functionality (see Figure 13-39).

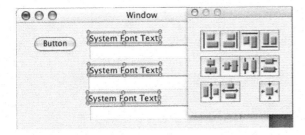

Figure 13-39. *Alignment panel*

The Format menu also has some handy formatting aids that respond to keyboard shortcuts: Shift Right (Cmd+]), Shift Left (Cmd+[), Comment Selection (Cmd+}), and Uncomment Selection (Cmd+{).

Test Interface

Objects have built-in behavior such as changing appearance when selected. You can try these behaviors by putting a project in Test Interface mode, which you do by choosing File ➤ Test Interface. To indicate when a project is in Test Interface mode, FaceSpan's icon changes in the document. To return to Edit mode, press Cmd+Q.

To Explore Further

To see the tutorial projects and other sample projects at work, visit FaceSpan's download page, and download the projects desired. I hope you will soon experience the variety of ways that AppleScript and FaceSpan can make a world-class application, or just a much-used utility, from your Apple-Script scripts.

CHAPTER 14

■■■

Working with Files

In this chapter, you will see how you can use scripts to identify files, folders, and disks and how to read and write files using Standard Additions. In the next chapter, you'll look at how to manipulate files and folders by copying, moving, and deleting them via the scriptable Finder.

Identifying Files, Folders, and Disks

When you work with files, what you need is a way to refer to the files you use. No matter whether your goal is creating a text file, backing up some folders, or deleting the entire contents of a hard disk, the ways you refer to a file are the same.

AppleScript can refer to a file, folder, or disk in three general ways, and your job is to choose the method that works best with your specific situation and with the application you're using:

- An HFS/POSIX path or uniform resource locator (URL) string

- A file specifier (an alias, file, or POSIX file value)

- An application reference to the Finder or System Events

Script 14-1 shows a typical example of each approach.

Script 14-1.

```
--An HFS path string:
"Macintosh HD:Applications:Adobe InDesign CS:Adobe InDesign Technical Info: ➥
Scripting:InDesign CS Scripting Guide.pdf"

--An AppleScript alias value:
alias "Macintosh HD:Applications:Adobe InDesign CS:Adobe InDesign Technical Info: ➥
Scripting:InDesign CS Scripting Guide.pdf"

--A Finder application reference:
document file "InDesign CS Scripting Guide.pdf" of folder "Scripting" ➥
of folder "Adobe InDesign Technical Info" of folder "Adobe InDesign CS" ➥
of folder "Applications" of startup disk of application "Finder"
```

All three values identify the same file, though in different ways. Figure 14-1 shows the hierarchy leading to this file.

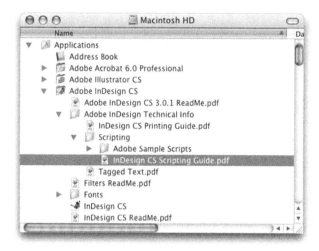

Figure 14-1. *A Finder window showing the file identified by each of the values in Script 14-1*

Path Strings

Path strings provide a basic way to describe the location of files, folders, and disks. Since path strings are just ordinary AppleScript strings, they're useful when you want to assemble, modify, and pull apart paths using AppleScript's string-handling facilities: text item delimiters, the concatenation operator, and so on. They are also helpful for creating file specifier values for use in application and scripting addition commands and for creating application references in the Finder and the System Events application.

AppleScript understands two types of path strings: HFS paths and POSIX paths. HFS-style paths first appeared with the original Mac OS and are still used by various parts of Mac OS X, including the AppleScript language. POSIX-style paths are the standard path name format used on Unix operating systems and are also commonly used on Mac OS X, which is Unix-based. Here are some examples:

```
--Typical HFS path strings:
"Macintosh HD:Applications:TextEdit.app"
"Macintosh HD:Users:hanaan:Documents:Manuscript.doc"
"Backup Disk:Work Files:"

--Typical POSIX path strings:
"/Applications/TextEdit.app"
"/Users/hanaan/Documents/Manuscript.doc"
"/Volumes/Backup Disk/Work Files/"
```

About HFS Paths

Let's start with an example of an HFS path: `Macintosh HD:documents:reference.pdf`.

This path identifies a file called `reference.pdf` in a folder called `documents` on a start-up disk whose name is `Macintosh HD`. The path starts with the name of the volume the file is on, is followed by the name of each folder in the folder hierarchy that leads to the file, and ends with the name of the file. Each name in the path is separated by a colon (:), which is reserved for this purpose.

An HFS path that identifies a disk or folder usually has a colon at the end, although this is not essential:

```
Macintosh HD:
Macintosh HD:documents:
```

Putting a colon delimiter at the end of disk and file paths is clearer, however, and will matter if you later decide to extend this path string by concatenating it with additional folder and filenames:

```
"Macintosh HD:documents:" & "reference.pdf"
--> "Macintosh HD:documents:reference.pdf" --Correct

"Macintosh HD:documents" & "reference.pdf"
--> "Macintosh HD:documentsreference.pdf" --Oops!
```

About POSIX Paths

Because of their Unix nature, POSIX paths work a bit differently than HFS paths and require a little more explanation. Here's an example of a POSIX path that identifies the same reference.pdf file as the HFS path shown earlier:

```
/Volumes/Macintosh HD/documents/reference.pdf
```

The first difference you'll notice is that a POSIX path uses a slash (/), not a colon, to separate each name in the path. The second difference is that POSIX paths view the file system hierarchy in a slightly different way than HFS paths do. Although each HFS path begins with a disk name, a POSIX path treats the entire file system as one big tree-shaped structure. The top of this tree structure is called the *root* and is indicated in a POSIX path by the leading slash character, /. Each mounted disk appears further down in this hierarchy, at /Volumes.

The Unix view of the file system does have one extra trick up its sleeve, however: the top-level folders in the start-up disk—Applications, Library, System, and Users are the four common ones—also appear at the root level. Since the folder documents in the example is located on the start-up disk, this means you can also identify the reference.pdf file using the following path:

```
/documents/reference.pdf
```

As with HFS paths, POSIX paths that identify a folder or disk are usually shown with a trailing slash for clarity, although again this is not required:

```
/Volumes/Macintosh HD/
/Volumes/Macintosh HD/documents/
```

You'll look at ways to convert HFS paths to POSIX paths and back again later in the "Creating POSIX File Values" section.

File Specifiers

AppleScript provides three value classes for describing files, folders, and disks in the OS X file system: alias, file, and POSIX file. File specifier values are commonly used by scriptable applications, particularly in open and save commands and in file system–related scripting addition commands such as choose file, info for, read, and write.

AppleScript can easily convert file specifier values to and from path strings. The Finder also knows how to convert them to and from Finder-specific references.

Here are some examples of literal file specifiers. Each one identifies a file named Report.doc on the start-up drive:

```
alias "Macintosh HD:Report.doc"
file "Macintosh HD:Report.doc"
POSIX file "/Users/Report.doc"
```

As you can see, each file specifier consists of two parts: a keyword—alias, file, or POSIX file—followed by a path string. The first two take HFS path strings, and the third takes a POSIX path string.

One odd thing you'll notice is that when you compile the POSIX file literal, it'll appear in the compiled code as follows:

```
file "Macintosh HD:Report.doc"
```

This transformation can be a bit confusing at times, particularly since the Finder and System Events define their own file keywords that look the same but have different meanings. You'll learn more about this in the "System Event's File System Object Model" section in Chapter 15.

Alias Values

Values of AppleScript's alias value class (not to be confused with the Finder's alias file class, by the way) are written as the word alias followed by an HFS path string. For example:

```
alias "Macintosh HD:AppleScript Reference.pdf"
```

Alias values refer to files, folders, and disks that already exist. Their most interesting feature is that, once created, they can keep track of a file or folder even if it is renamed or moved to another location on the same disk.

Most scriptable applications take an alias (or a list of aliases) as the direct parameter to their open commands:

```
set the_file_alias to alias "Macintosh HD:AppleScript Reference.pdf"
tell application "Preview" to open the_file_alias
```

They are also used by various scripting addition commands; for example, the Standard Additions' choose file command returns an alias value identifying a file selected by the user, and its info for command can accept an alias value (amongst other things) as its direct parameter.

How Aliases Work

One of the first aspects you'll notice about aliases is that when you create them, AppleScript checks whether a file (or folder or disk) corresponds to the supplied path string. For example, if your script includes the following statement:

```
alias "Macintosh HD:AppleScript Reference.pdf"
```

as you compile the script, then AppleScript will check to see whether a file named AppleScript Reference.pdf exists on a mounted volume named Macintosh HD. If there isn't such a file, AppleScript will return a syntax error. For example, the following alias literal identifies a file that doesn't exist on my Mac:

```
alias "Macintosh HD:Windows XP source code.TXT"
```

When I try to compile this statement, AppleScript generates the error shown in Figure 14-2.

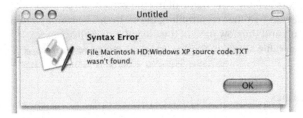

Figure 14-2. *The script won't compile since the file specified by the alias literal doesn't exist.*

Now why would AppleScript go to the trouble of checking the file's existence right away? The answer is that as soon as AppleScript creates an alias value, it finds the specified file and creates an internal reference to it. This internal reference works in a similar way to alias files in the Finder: the file is remembered even if its name or location has changed. Yes! For as long as the alias value exists in the script, AppleScript will keep track of that file. The only way it will lose track of a file is if the file itself is deleted.

All alias values work this way, whether they're created when the script is compiled (as in this example) or while the script is running. This feature makes aliases especially useful in scripts that rename files and folders or move them.

Alias File-Tracking Example

To test and demonstrate that alias capability, you will create a script that tracks a file you pick and reports whether the location or name has changed. For that, you will need two properties: one for the alias itself, which will keep track of the file even if it's moved or renamed, and one that will hold the previous path name as a string.

Script 14-2 shows the script. The script starts by checking whether the the_alias property has been set (line 3). If the script is running for the first time and the the_alias property has not been set, then the script will ask you to choose a file (line 4). The choose file command returns an alias that will be assigned to the the_alias property.

From there, the script compares the string variable containing the previous location to the alias to check whether the file has moved (line 7). If the file has moved, AppleScript shows you the old path and the new path in a dialog box (line 10).

Script 14-2.

```
1. property the_alias : missing value
2. property last_pathname : ""

3. if the_alias is missing value then
4.     set the_alias to choose file
5. else
6.     set this_pathname to the_alias as string
7.     if this_pathname = last_pathname then
8.         display dialog "The file hasn't moved"
9.     else
10.         display dialog "Old file path:" & return & ¬
                last_pathname & return & ¬
                "New location: " & return & ¬
                this_pathname
11.     end if
12. end if
13. set last_pathname to the_alias as string
```

Run the script once to choose the file. Next, change the name of the file you chose, or even move it to a different folder. Run the script again (without recompiling the script!). The script should display a dialog box showing you the old path and the new path of the file you originally chose.

To force AppleScript to let go of the alias value stored in the the_alias property, recompile the script.

Converting Aliases to and from Other Values

You can convert an HFS path string to an alias value in two ways. The first way is by using the alias specifier on a variable containing the path string:

```
set the_path_name to "Macintosh HD:Windows XP source code.TXT"
alias the_path_name
--> alias "Macintosh HD:Windows XP source code.TXT"
```

The other way is by coercing the string to an alias using AppleScript's as operator:

```
set the_path_name to "Macintosh HD:Windows XP source code.TXT"
the_path_name as alias
--> alias "Macintosh HD:Windows XP source code.TXT"
```

These approaches are useful if you don't want to create the alias value until the script is running. For example, if the file doesn't exist when the script is compiled, putting a literal such as alias "Macintosh HD:Windows XP source code.TXT" in your script will prevent it from compiling. Creating the alias at runtime avoids this problem and allows the script to compile normally.

Another time it's useful to create an alias on the fly is when you want to assemble the full path string while the script is running. For example, to get an alias to a folder named Work on the current user's desktop, you can write this:

```
set desktop_path to path to desktop folder as string
set work_folder to alias (desktop_path & "Work:")
--> alias "Macintosh HD:Users:hanaan:Desktop:Work:"
```

Creating an alias at runtime will still work only if the corresponding file or folder exists by then; otherwise, you'll get error number –43, which means "File not found."

To convert an alias to an HFS path string, you just use the as operator again:

```
(alias "Macintosh HD:Applications:TextEdit.app") as string
--> "Macintosh HD:Applications:TextEdit.app"
```

You can also obtain a POSIX path string by asking the alias for the value of its POSIX path property:

```
POSIX path of (alias "Macintosh HD:Applications:TextEdit.app")
--> "/Applications/TextEdit.app"
```

So What About File References?

You can write an AppleScript file reference (not to be confused with a Finder file reference, by the way, which can look similar but is specific to the Finder) as the word file followed by an HFS path string. For example:

```
file "Macintosh HD:AppleScript Reference.pdf"
```

File references are different from aliases in a few ways. The main difference is that an alias points to an existing file or folder, but a file reference can be pointing to a file that doesn't yet exist. Getting them to work on Mac OS X can be a bit fiddly, though, because of some under-the-hood changes since OS 9.

Back in the pre–OS X days, AppleScript traditionally had two value classes for representing file system objects: alias and file specification. You could use aliases for identifying existing files, and you could use file specifications to identify a nonexistent file in an existing folder or disk. An AppleScript object specifier such as file path_string would always produce a value of class file specification, as would the coercion path_string as file specification. Things could get a little confusing if you got AppleScript's file keyword and the Finder's file keyword muddled up, but on the whole it was all pretty straightforward and worked as expected.

In Mac OS X, AppleScript's file keyword gets a bit more complicated to use. The original file specification value class is still around in OS X, but unfortunately it lacks proper support for Unicode-based filenames and names longer than 32 characters, both of which are used in OS X. As a result, this class has become obsolete in OS X, and its use nowadays is discouraged; alias and POSIX file value classes are generally used instead.

However, even though file specification values may be going away, AppleScript's file keyword is still in common use amongst scripters: Apple has just "rejigged" how it works a bit in OS X. Although in a few situations it may still produce a file specification value, in most cases an expression such as file "Macintosh HD:Some file.pdf" actually behaves more like a typical application object reference. Unfortunately, this new behavior doesn't work quite as well as it should.

To demonstrate the problem, create a new document in Script Editor 2, and type a line like the following:

```
file "Macintosh HD:Applications:"
```

This code looks like it ought to work without any problems; and longtime scripters may well remember lines like this working perfectly in earlier Mac OSs. You also know that the equivalent alias "Macintosh HD:Applications:" will compile and run just fine (assuming the path string is valid for the current user's system), returning an alias value for your Applications folder.

Unfortunately, when you run the previous code, you actually end up with a bizarre-sounding error like this: "Can't make file 'Macintosh HD:Applications:' into type reference." This sort of thing is really annoying if you want to, say, create an AppleScript file reference in one part of your script and assign it to a variable so it can be used in another part of the script later. For example:

```
set file_ref to file "Macintosh HD:Some file.pdf"
```

Or, for example:

```
set file_ref to file the_file_path
```

In both cases, when AppleScript tries to execute these statements, it raises an error instead; alas, AppleScript just can't seem to evaluate these file specifiers by itself. I hope this will be fixed in some future version, but for now it's just something you have to accept.

Fortunately, there isn't any problem when the literal file specifier appears as a parameter in an application or scripting addition command. For example, both of the following commands work as you'd expect:

```
tell application "TextEdit"
   open file the_file_path
end tell
```

```
read file "Macintosh HD:Some file.txt"
```

You can also "trick" AppleScript so it won't try to evaluate the file some_path specifier itself. You do this by adding the a reference to operator in front of it. The resulting code is a bit clumsy looking, but it gets the job done. For example, to assign a file reference to this variable:

```
set file_ref to a reference to file "Macintosh HD:Some file.pdf"
```

the value assigned to the variable file_ref will be a reference that looks like this:

```
file "Macintosh HD:Some file.pdf" of «script»
```

Later, you can use this reference value in application and scripting addition commands without any problem:

```
tell application "TextEdit"
   open file_ref
end tell
```

```
read file_ref
```

POSIX File Values

The POSIX file value class is a slightly more recent addition, first appearing in AppleScript on Mac OS 9.2.2 and OS X 10.1.2. Together, the POSIX file value class and the POSIX path property found in all file specifier values enable AppleScripts to work with the Unix-style POSIX paths used in many parts of OS X, as well as the traditional HFS-style paths inherited from the original Mac OS.

Unlike aliases, POSIX file values can refer to *any* location in the file system, even nonexistent files in nonexistent folders on nonexistent disks. For example, the choose file name command in Standard Additions will return a POSIX file value identifying a file that may or may not exist yet.

Creating POSIX File Values

To create a POSIX file value, you write POSIX file followed by a POSIX path string. For example:

```
POSIX file "/Applications/Chess.app"
```

The POSIX path string must provide an absolute path name, that is, one that begins at the file system's root (/) and that describes the full path to the desired file, folder, or disk. (If you're familiar with Unix, you'll know that the Unix command line also understands the concept of *relative* path names; AppleScript isn't this clever unfortunately.)

One strange thing you'll notice when you compile a POSIX file literal such as this:

```
POSIX file "/Applications/Chess.app"
```

is that the AppleScript compiler will "helpfully" rewrite it as this:

```
file "Macintosh HD:Applications:Chess.app"
```

This can be quite annoying if you need to recompile the script again later, because AppleScript will treat the file "..." code differently. (See the previous section for more information.) However, you can always prevent AppleScript from rearranging your code by writing it in a slightly different way:

```
POSIX file (get "/Applications/Chess.app")
```

You can also supply the POSIX path string via a variable or other expression:

```
set path_string to "/Applications/Chess.app"
set posix_file to POSIX file path_string
```

The resulting value will appear in Script Editor's Result area as follows:

```
file "Macintosh HD:Applications:Chess.app"
```

Should you need to, you can find out whether this value is of the POSIX file class by getting the value of its class property:

```
class of posix_file
--> «class furl»
```

I have no idea either why the class name is «class furl» instead of POSIX file as you'd expect, but it works OK, so this isn't a problem.

Converting POSIX Files to Other Values

Most of the time you don't need to worry about the difference between a POSIX file and other file values because modern OS X applications and scripting additions should accept both. If you do have to deal with difficult older applications that won't accept POSIX file values for some reason, you can always coerce them to one of AppleScript's other classes (assuming the new class can represent the same item, of course). For example:

```
POSIX file (get "/Applications/Chess.app") as alias
--> alias "Macintosh HD:Applications:Chess.app:"
```

You can also obtain an HFS path string by coercing the POSIX file value to a string:

```
POSIX file (get "/Applications/Chess.app") as string
--> "Macintosh HD:Applications:Chess.app:"
```

Finally, you can convert a POSIX file value to a POSIX path string by asking it for the value of its POSIX path property:

```
set posix_file to POSIX file (get "/Applications/Chess.app")
POSIX path of posix_file
--> "/Users/hanaan/ReadMe.txt"
```

You can convert paths in the opposite direction, from HFS to POSIX, using the posix path property of a file object, like this:

```
set posix_path to POSIX path of (alias hfs_path)
```

Although this method is the safest, it'll work only when converting references to files that actually exist, which is no good if you need to refer to files that are not yet there. In that case, use this:

```
set posix_path to POSIX path of hfs_path
```

The previous example won't work correctly for paths that start with a volume that isn't mounted. For instance, the POSIX path "Server:Folder:File" will become "/Server/Folder/File" instead of "/Volumes/Server/Folder/File".

The following subroutine will reliably convert HFS paths of existing and nonexisting files into POSIX paths by evaluating each character and converting it if needed:

```
set hfs_path to "Backup CD:3/19/2006:Client Files:Catalog.indd"
set posix_path to convert_hfs_to_posix_path(hfs_path)
--> "/Volumes/Backup CD/3:19:2006/Client Files/Catalog.indd"

on convert_hfs_to_posix_path(hfs_path)
    set posix_path to "/Volumes/"
    repeat with char_ref in hfs_path
        if contents of char_ref = ":" then
            set posix_path to posix_path & "/"
        else if contents of char_ref = "/" then
            set posix_path to posix_path & ":"
        else
```

```
        set posix_path to posix_path & char_ref
      end if
    end repeat
    return posix_path
end convert_hfs_to_posix_path
```

Finder References

So far you've looked at two ways in which most applications, scripting additions, and AppleScript refer to files, folders, and disks: path strings and file specifiers.

The other way you can refer to files, folders, and disks is using the Finder and System Events applications. Both of these applications treat files, folders, and disks as individual objects in a well-structured object model whose structure is defined in the application's dictionary. Each application also provides various commands for performing actions on objects in its object model, allowing AppleScripts to perform a wide range of file system operations: creating, copying, moving, renaming, and deleting files and folders; erasing and ejecting disks; and obtaining lots of useful information about these items as well.

You'll look at System Events in Chapter 15; for now, you'll concentrate on the Finder.

The Finder's Object Model

Like most scriptable applications, the top object in the Finder's object model is the application object. Each mounted disk on your Mac is represented as a disk element of this application object. Each of these disk objects has various file and folder elements representing the files and folders contained by that disk; in turn, each of those folder objects has file and folder elements . . . and so on. Figure 14-3 shows a simplified view of this containment structure. Notice how folder elements can contain their own folder and file elements all the way to infinity (or at least until the Finder decides it has had enough!).

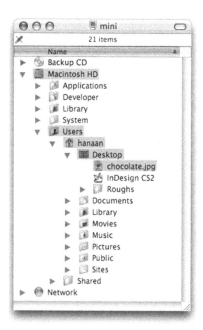

Figure 14-3. *The* chocolate.jpg *file in its Finder window*

Like other scriptable applications, the Finder uses AppleScript's English-like object reference forms to refer to objects within this object model. For example, let's say you have a file named `chocolate.jpg` on your desktop. (Figure 14-4 shows the Finder's file/folder/disk containment structure.)

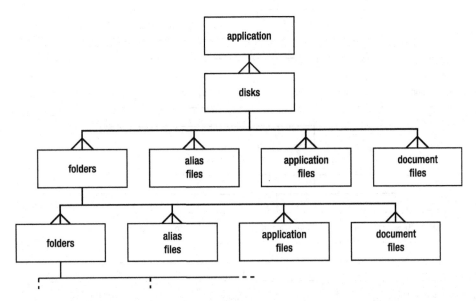

Figure 14-4. *A simplified diagram of the Finder's file/folder/disk containment structure*

The HFS path string for this file is as follows:

`"Macintosh HD:Users:hanaan:Desktop:chocolate.jpg"`

while the alias value identifying this file is as follows:

`alias "Macintosh HD:Users:hanaan:Desktop:chocolate.jpg"`

By comparison, the Finder describes the location of this file using a reference to an object in its object model:

```
document file "chocolate.jpg" of folder "Desktop" of folder "hanaan" ➥
of folder "Users" of startup disk of application "Finder"
```

How does the Finder arrive at this reference? Look at Figure 14-5, which shows a portion of my file system as the Finder sees it: as a series of objects nested one inside another.

Like all AppleScript references, this one begins by identifying the desired object, so it starts by specifying the document file element named `chocolate.jpg` in the folder element named `Desktop`, and it works its way back to the Finder's top-level application object. Figure 14-5 highlights the full route taken by this reference in gray.

One slight difference you might notice between the Finder reference and alias reference is that the reference identifies the disk `Macintosh HD` using a property, `startup disk`, rather than an element reference form, `disk "Macintosh HD"`. The Finder knows this particular volume is my start-up disk, so it automatically uses `startup disk` to make this obvious. You'll learn more about this in Chapter 15.

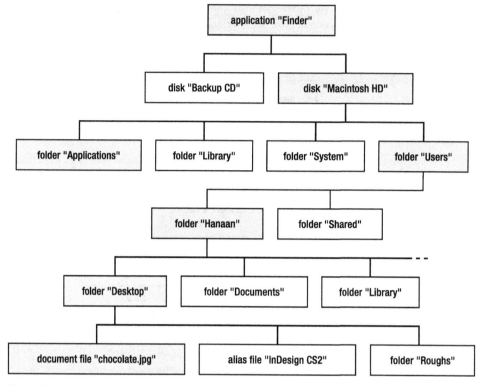

Figure 14-5. *How the Finder sees my file system (or part of it, at least)*

Creating Finder References

You can construct a Finder reference in several ways. The first and most obvious way it to write out the full reference as follows:

```
tell application "Finder"
    document file "chocolate.jpg" of folder "Desktop" of folder "hanaan" ¬
        of folder "Users" of disk "Macintosh HD"
end tell
```

As you'll recall from Chapter 2, you can also write the same reference as follows:

```
tell application "Finder"
    tell disk "Macintosh HD"
        tell folder "Users"
            tell folder "hanaan"
                tell folder "Desktop"
                    document file "chocolate.jpg"
                end tell
            end tell
        end tell
    end tell
end tell
```

Or you can use any combination in between:

```
tell application "Finder"
    tell folder "hanaan" of folder "Users" of disk "Macintosh HD"
        document file "chocolate.jpg" of folder "Desktop" of it
    end tell
end tell
```

(The of it part is optional, but including it here makes this particular piece of code easier to read.)

The Finder's application object also contains several properties that act as shortcuts to important and commonly used locations in the file system:

- startup disk, which contains a reference to the current start-up disk

- home, which contains a reference to the current user's Home folder

- desktop, which contains an object representing the current user's Desktop folder

- trash, which contains an object representing the current user's hidden Trash folder

Using these properties can save quite a bit of typing when constructing Finder references. For example, you can also locate the chocolate.jpg file using any of the three following references:

```
tell application "Finder"
    document file "chocolate.jpg" of folder "Desktop" of folder "hanaan" ¬
        of folder "Users" of startup disk

end tell
tell application "Finder"
    document file "chocolate.jpg" of folder "Desktop" of home
end tell

tell application "Finder"
    document file "chocolate.jpg" of desktop
end tell
```

These shortcuts also help make scripts more portable because they save you from having to include the exact names of the start-up disk or current user in a script's code when referring to items in those locations.

Notice that when the Finder evaluates each of the references shown previously, it will automatically expand each one according to its own set of built-in rules. In each case, the resulting reference is as follows:

```
document file "chocolate.jpg" of folder "Desktop" of folder "hanaan" ➥
of folder "Users" of startup disk of application "Finder"
```

Once you have a Finder reference, you can get, and in some cases set, the values of its properties, or pass it to other Finder commands to manipulate it in different ways. For example, to get some information about the file, use this:

```
tell application "Finder"
    set the_file to document file "chocolate.jpg" of desktop
    get {name, name extension, size, modification date} of the_file
end
--> {"chocolate.jpg", "jpg", 1361.0, date "Sunday, March 12, 2006 21:14:37"}
```

To open the file in its default editor/viewer application (such as Preview), use this:

```
tell application "Finder"
    tell desktop
        tell document file "chocolate.jpg"
            open it -- (the "it" keyword is optional)
        end tell
    end tell
end tell
```

More About Finder References

If you look at the inheritance hierarchy for the document file class in the Finder's dictionary, you can see that document file is a subclass of the file class and file is a subclass of the item class. This means you can also identify the chocolate.jpg document file using the less-specific file and item elements of the desktop object:

```
file "chocolate.jpg" of desktop
item "chocolate.jpg" of desktop
```

The Finder will figure out exactly what class the item named chocolate.jpg is when it resolves the reference.

Using a more general element name is useful when you want to identify an item but aren't sure of its exact class. For example, if there's an item on my desktop called Work but I don't know whether it's a document file, alias file, or folder, I could just say this:

```
item "Work" of desktop
```

and the Finder will understand this. Whereas if I write document file "Work" of desktop and Work turns out to be a folder instead, the Finder will generate an error: "Can't get folder 'Work' of desktop."

Similarly, if I know Work is some sort of file but don't know exactly which kind, I can just write file "Work" of desktop, and the Finder will be happy. In fact, it's often convenient to write file instead of document file, application file, alias file, and so on, just because it's less typing! The Finder will figure out exactly which class of file it is when it resolves the reference.

Converting to and from Finder References

As with any other scriptable application, only the Finder knows how to interpret Finder references. This isn't an issue in scripts where only the Finder interacts with the file system, but often you'll want to combine Finder scripting with other applications and scripting additions. Since other applications and scripting additions can understand only AppleScript values such as strings, aliases, and so on, you'll need a way to convert Finder references to and from those other formats in order to use them there. If you accidentally pass a Finder file reference to an application such as TextEdit or Adobe InDesign, all you'll get is an error.

Fortunately, the Finder makes it easy to convert path strings and file specifier values to Finder references and back again. For instance, look at the following script and at the result:

```
tell application "Finder"
    document file "Macintosh HD:Users:hanaan:Desktop:chocolate.jpg"
end tell
--> document file "chocolate.jpg" of folder "Desktop" of folder "hanaan" ➡
of folder "Users" of startup disk of application "Finder"
```

As you can see, the Finder also allows you to use a regular HFS path string when specifying a file or folder object and will expand this to a full Finder reference when it evaluates it. You can even mix the two approaches if you want:

```
tell application "Finder"
    document file "hanaan:Desktop:chocolate.jpg" of folder "Users" of startup disk
end tell
```

This flexibility makes it easy to take a path string stored in a variable and convert it to a Finder reference ready to use in one or more Finder commands. For example:

```
set the_file_path to "Macintosh HD:Users:hanaan:Desktop:chocolate.jpg"
tell application "Finder"
    open document file the_file_path
end tell
```

You can also supply alias and other file specifier values in the same way:

```
set the_alias to alias "Macintosh HD:Users:hanaan:Desktop:chocolate.jpg"
tell application "Finder"
    open document file the_alias
end tell
```

In most cases, you can omit the document file part if you want. For example:

```
set the_alias to alias "Macintosh HD:Users:hanaan:Desktop:chocolate.jpg"
tell application "Finder"
    get name of the_alias
end tell
--> "chocolate.jpg"
```

Converting Finder references to path strings and alias values is even simpler. In both cases, you use the as operator to coerce the reference to the desired type:

```
tell application "Finder"
    document file "chocolate.jpg" of desktop as string
end tell
--> "hd:Users:has:Desktop:chocolate.jpg"
```

```
tell application "Finder"
    document file "chocolate.jpg" of desktop as alias
end tell
--> alias "hd:Users:has:Desktop:chocolate.jpg"
```

File URL Strings

The file URL string is useful for opening local files using with the browser. You can get a file's URL by tapping into the URL property defined in the Finder and System Events dictionaries. Script 14-3 gets the URL property of the file you choose.

Script 14-3.

```
set the_alias to (choose file)
--alias "Macintosh HD:Developer:Documentation:ADC Reference Library:index.html"
tell application "System Events"
    set the_url to URL of the_alias
end tell
--> "file://localhost/Developer/Documentation/ADC%20Reference%20Library/index.html"
```

Although you can get the URL of any existing file, folder, or disk, it is really useful only with Internet-related files such as HTML, JPG, GIF, and so on.

You can use the URL in Safari, or you can use the open location command.

The following script will display the URL in the variable the_url (from Script 14-3) in the front Safari window:

```
tell application "Safari" to set URL of document 1 to the_url
```

You can also use a URL when creating a new Safari document:

```
tell application "Safari" to make new document with properties {URL:the_url}
```

However, if you're opening a local file, it may be easier to use Safari's open command for this:

```
tell application "Safari"
  open alias "Macintosh HD:Developer:ADC Reference Library:index.html"
end tell
```

You can also use the open location command to open a URL in the default browser:

```
open location the_url
```

The open location command is part of Standard Additions:

```
open location: Opens a URL with the appropriate program
  open location [string]  -- the URL to open
    [error reporting boolean] -- Should error conditions be reported in a dialog?
```

About Filename Extensions

One more present the new Unix-based OS X gave us is the introduction of filename extensions. Yup, just like that, I have to say goodbye to years of taunting my PC programmer buddies about their antiquated dependency on easily changeable filename extensions . . . . OK, enough of that. Filename extensions are great! I love them.

Files either can have an extension or not. Despite the irritation, it is always better to have a name extension. It makes it easier to spot the purpose of the files and makes you a better network citizen.

If the file has a name extension, it might be hidden. In the Finder, you can see the name extension and its status in the Info panel.

Click a file, choose Get Info from the File menu, and expand the Name & Extension pane. Figure 14-6 shows the Finder's Info box with the Name & Extension pane.

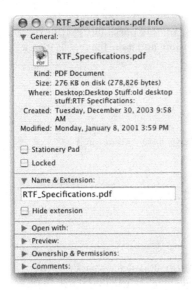

Figure 14-6. *The Finder's Get Info dialog box*

Using AppleScript, you can check the status of the name extension in a few ways. The best way to gain information about the existence, type, and visibility of a specific file's extension is by tapping into the file information record.

As you'll see in the next chapter, you can use Standard Additions' info for command to return records containing useful information about any files you want. Although OS 9 had one name-related property called name, OS X has four name-related properties. Three of them are Unicode strings: name, displayed name, and name extension. The fourth property, extension hidden, contains a Boolean value that is true if the extension is hidden and false if it is visible. The following is part of the Standard Additions dictionary, showing the definitions for the four name-related properties in the record returned by the info for command:

```
Class file information: Reply record for the 'info for' command
Properties:
    name  Unicode text  [r/o]  -- the name of the item
    displayed name  Unicode text  [r/o]  -- the user-visible name of the item
    ...
    name extension  Unicode text  [r/o]  -- the name extension of the item
                                            (such as "txt")

    ...

    extension hidden  boolean  [r/o]  -- Is the item's name extension hidden from
                                         the user?

    ...
```

Another way to obtain information about filenames and extensions is via the Finder, because its file class defines four similar properties. (System Events is yet another possibility.) Script 14-4 is a little script that goes through any file that doesn't have an extension, and if the file type is PDF, it adds a .pdf name extension to its name as well.

Script 14-4.

```
1. set the_folder to choose folder
2. tell application "Finder"
3.    set files_list to every file of folder the_folder whose name extension is ""
4.    repeat with file_ref in files_list
5.       considering case
6.          if file type of file_ref = "PDF " then
7.             set name of file_ref to name of file_ref & ".pdf"
8.          end if
9.       end considering
10.   end repeat
11. end tell
```

In line 3 of the script you obtain the names of any files that don't already have a name extension. In lines 4 to 10 you loop through each name in the list, checking to see whether the file with that name has the file type PDF. If it does, you ask the Finder for its original name and then concatenate this string with the new extension, .pdf, to create the new name. Lastly you set the file's name to this new string. (It would be simpler if you could just say set name extension of file_ref to "pdf", but the Finder's dictionary states that the name extension property is read-only unfortunately.)

Also notice that the script wraps the file type comparison test, file type of file file_name_ref = "PDF ", in a considering case block. File and creator type codes are actually case-sensitive; for example, abcd, ABCD, AbCd, and so on, are all different file types as far as Mac OS is concerned. If you want to be absolutely sure you don't get any false matches, then this is a good precaution to take, although it probably won't matter if you forget because the chances of meeting two codes that differ only in case are probably quite low.

Reading and Writing Files

When I started using AppleScript, one of the tasks that fascinated me the most was writing text files. Man, that was almost as much fun as displaying my first dialog box.

AppleScript has a few commands for reading data from files and for writing the data. For the most part, you will use these commands to read and write text, but you can pretty much read and write any data: graphic formats, PDFs, and so on. The reason why you will mostly work with text files is that you can easily create text in strings, see what you created, and understand it. Any other data is a bit more complex. You can't really look at the data of a PDF file and understand what's going on in there. When working with these sorts of complicated binary files, it's usually best to use a scriptable application that already knows how to process them.

But text doesn't have to be dull. Plenty of text-based file formats allow you to create richly formatted files, such as XML, RTF (see the "Writing RTF Files" section later in this chapter), SVG (an XML-based format used to describe line-based graphics), and so on. Also, both QuarkXPress and InDesign use their own tagged text file format, which you can create.

Commands for Reading and Writing Files

You can read and write files using the file read/write scripting additions, which are part of Standard Additions. The main commands are read and write, but to use them, you use other commands that open and close access to the files you want to read and write to and then get and set the end of file (EOF) of the files you want to use.

The following sections explain the different file-reading and file-writing commands.

Reading

The read command allows you to read the text data or binary data of a file.

From the Dictionary

Here's the definition:

```
read: Read data from a file that has been opened for access
read anything
        -- the reference number, alias, or file reference of the file to read
    [from double integer]
        -- starting from this position;
        -- if omitted, start at last position read from
    [for double integer]
        -- the number of bytes to read from current position;
        -- if omitted, read until the end of the file...
    [to double integer] -- ...or stop at this position...
    [before string] -- ...or read up to but not including this character...
    [until string] -- ...or read up to and including this character
    [using delimiter string] -- the value that separates items to read...
    [using delimiters a list of string]
        -- ...or a list of values that separate items to read
    [as type class] -- the form in which to read and return data
  Result: anything  -- the data read from the file
```

Using the read Command

Reading files is fairly straightforward: you furnish the read command with the required file reference, and the result is the contents of the file.

Try the following: Use TextEdit to create a text file. Make sure to convert the file to plain text (not RTF). Type the phrase **Hello World!**, and then save this document as the file work.txt in your Home folder.

Now, start a new script document, and write a line equivalent to the following:

```
read alias "Macintosh HD:Users:Hanaan:work.txt"
```

(You may need to adjust the previous path name to suit your own file system, of course.) The result of running the script is the text stored in the file: "Hello World!"

Opening and Closing Access to Files

Standard Additions defines two file-access-related commands: open for access and close access. These commands create a longer-lasting connection between AppleScript and the file being worked on, allowing you to perform more complex operations on it.

Although you can read data from files without opening them for access, the read command operates differently when you do or don't open the files. I describe this difference in the "Reading Files and Open for Access" section. When writing to files, you must always open them for access first; otherwise you'll get errors.

From the Dictionary

Here's the dictionary definition of the open for access and close access commands:

```
open for access: Open a disk file for the read and write commands
open for access file
   -- the file or alias to open for access.
   -- If the file does not exist, a new file is created.
     [write permission boolean] -- whether to allow writing to the file.
   Result: small integer
      -- a file reference number; use for 'read', 'write', and 'close access'

close access: Close a file that was opened for access
close access anything
      -- the file reference number, alias, or file reference of the file to close
The open for access result
```

Notice the result section of the open for access command: it's an integer.

When you open access to a file, the result is a unique ID number generated by the open for access command. You can use this ID number to identify this file in Standard Additions' other read/write commands: read, write, get eof, set eof, and close access.

The following script shows how to use the integer resulting from the open for access command:

```
set the_file_path to "Macintosh HD:work.txt"
set file_ID to open for access file the_file_path
-- (The variable file_ID now contains a unique ID number, e.g. 5680.)
set file_data to read file_ID
close accessfile_ID
```

This unique ID number will refer to the file for only as long as the file remains open, however, so you don't need to hold onto this number after you close the file. A new ID number will be assigned every time you open a file for access, even if it's the same file.

You can use the original path string, alias, and so on, in all these commands as well—after all, you had to have a normal file reference to the file for the purpose of opening the file for access.

What If There's No Such File?

The open for access command is used not only for opening connections to existing files but also for creating them!

Try the following script:

```
set new_file_path to (path to desktop as string) & "not there yet.txt"
open for access file new_file_path with write permission
close access file new_file_path
```

After running this script, look at your desktop, and see that a new file named not there yet.txt was created there. It does happen to be empty (has zero bytes), so reading it will generate an EOF error; however, you could write text to it.

Opening a File for Writing

The open for access command also has an optional Boolean parameter, write permission.

When this parameter is false (the default), you can only read from the file. Setting it to true allows you to write to the file as well. Trying to write to a file that has not been opened with write permission will generate an error.

The open for access command in the following example opens a file for access with write permission:

```
set the_file_path to "Macintosh HD:Users:hanaan:work12345222.txt"
open for access the_file_path with write permission
```

Close What You've Opened

Every time you open a file for access, you should use the close access command to close it once you're finished with it. Not closing a file is a bit like leaving the phone off the hook. So, the last command relating to reading or writing to or from a file should be followed by a command closing access to that file.

You shouldn't worry, however, that leaving a file open for access will cause any damage to the file. The file itself isn't actually affected by the open for access or close access command.

Even if you open a file for access with write permission, the file's busy status remains unchanged. In fact, once you open access to a file from one script, you can use another script to write to that file using the same file reference number.

Also, you should know that quitting the script editor will close access to any files you opened.

Read Command Parameters

The read command has a number of optional parameters that make it even more powerful.

Reading Different Kinds of Data

By default, the read command reads a file's data into an AppleScript string. The as parameter allows you to read files that contain data in a number of other formats. The most common use for the as parameter is in reading Unicode text files. Unlike the MacRoman character set where each character is represented by a single byte, the Unicode character set uses multiple bytes to represent each character. The two most common Unicode file formats you'll encounter are UTF-8 and UTF-16. I'll discuss these later in this section.

You can also make the read command read a number of common binary file formats. For example, to read a PICT, TIFF, JPEG, or GIF file, you'd use picture, TIFF picture, JPEG picture, or GIF picture for its as parameter. The resulting value will appear in AppleScript as raw data («data ...») and can—at least in theory—be used in scripting additions and applications that understand it. For example, to read a TIFF file from disk and put it onto the clipboard, you'd use this:

```
read alias "Macintosh HD:Users:hanaan:Desktop:chocolate.tif" as TIFF picture
set the clipboard to result
```

Finally, you can use the as parameter to read other AppleScript values such as lists and records that have been saved as binary files using Standard Additions' write command. You'll look at doing this in the "Writing Files" section.

Using a Delimiter to Read Text into a List

The using delimiter parameter allows you to read a text file directly into a list. You do that by specifying a delimiter character. This character acts as the text delimiter, which separates the text read from the file into list items. For example, if you have multiline text saved in a return-delimited file, you can read that file into a list, where each list item is a paragraph, simply by setting the using delimiter parameter to the return character, like this:

```
set paragraph_list to read alias "Macintosh HD:other work.txt" ¬
    using delimiter return
--> {"First paragraph", "second paragraph", "next line"}
```

Be careful, though: although older Carbon-based Mac applications often use return characters (ASCII 13) to indicate line breaks, Cocoa-based OS X applications use Unix-style linefeed characters (ASCII 10). Fortunately, the using delimiter parameter can also accept a list of characters, allowing you to specify more than one delimiter at a time if you're not sure:

```
set paragraph_list to read alias "Macintosh HD:other work.txt" ¬
    using delimiter {ASCII character 10, return}
```

Reading a Specific Number of Bytes

The for parameter allows you to read a specific number of bytes of data from the current position. This is most useful when your copy of AppleScript and the text file you're reading both use a character set like MacRoman where one byte equals one character. (Chapter 3 discussed character sets in detail.) For instance, the following script will read the first ten characters of a MacRoman text file:

```
read alias "Macintosh HD:somefile.txt" for 10
```

You may also find this parameter occasionally useful if you need to extract specific sections of data from binary files whose structure you already know.

Avoid using the for parameter when reading Unicode text files, though, because it's not really safe for working with them. If you need to extract a section of text from a Unicode file, read in the whole file first, and then use a reference to get the bit you want. For example:

```
text 1 thru 10 of (read alias "Macintosh HD:anotherfile.txt" as Unicode text)
```

The from and to Parameters

The from and to parameters allow you again to specify the starting and ending points for reading data. Although the for parameter reads a certain number of bytes from the file marker (or from the start), the from and to parameters read data from a specific byte counted from the start of the file.

Let's assume you have a MacRoman text file with the contents applescript. The following script uses the from and to parameters to read the text from character 3 to character 6:

```
read alias "Macintosh HD:work.txt" from 3 to 6
--> "ples"
```

As with the for parameter, you should avoid using from and to when dealing with Unicode files.

The before and until Parameters

The before and until parameters are similar: they both allow you to specify a character at which the read command should stop reading. The before parameter tells the read command to read up to before the specified character, and the until parameter includes the indicated character.

Let's assume you have a text file with the contents abcde-abcde. The following scripts illustrate how to use the until and before parameters:

```
read alias "Macintosh HD:work.txt" before "d"
--> "abc"
```

Notice that the character d is omitted from the end of the returned string, unlike in the next script:

```
read alias "Macintosh HD:work.txt" until "d"
--> "abcd"
```

You can also combine the before and until parameters with the from parameter. For example, let's start from the fifth byte and read until d:

```
read alias "Macintosh HD:work.txt" from 5 until "d"
--> "e-abcd"
```

This time, the script started from the fifth character and continued until the following instance of d.

Combining the read and open for Access Commands

Two more commands in Standard Additions' File Read/Write suite are open for access and close access. These commands open read and write access to files.

As you can see in the following read example, for simple tasks the read command does not require that the file is first opened for access:

```
read alias "Macintosh HD:some text file.txt"
--> "Contents of the text file"
```

Opening the file with the open for access command prior to reading it changes the scene a bit.

When a file is opened for access, one of the things Standard Additions does is create an internal marker that determines the position in that file where the next read (or write) operation should start. To understand that better, imagine reading a book. When you start reading the book, you begin at page 1 and you read, say, five pages. When you put the book down, you insert a marker at page 5 so you'll remember where you stopped last time. The next time you pick it up again, you continue reading from the point of the marker, and as you read more, the marker advances. When you get to the end of the book, you close it and put it away.

The same is true with reading a text file that has been opened for access; the only difference is that Standard Additions takes care of moving the bookmark for you. As an example, use TextEdit to create a new document, and type the alphabet: abcde...wxyz. Save the file as work.txt in your Documents folder, and close it.

Now you will learn to write a script that uses the read command with the for parameter. Start a new script, and write what's shown in Script 14-5.

Script 14-5.

```
set the_file to alias ((path to documents folder as string) & "work.txt")
open for access the_file
repeat
    set the_text to read the_file for 4
    display dialog the_text
end repeat
```

Now run the script.

The script will loop, each time reading the next four bytes as a four-character string (assuming AppleScript and TextEdit are using MacRoman or a similar single-byte character set), until it gets to the end of the file. At that point, you will get an EOF error, number –43.

Unless you use the read command's from parameter, you will not be able to read this file again until you use the close access command to close access to that file. Try to run your script again, and you will get the error right away. To fix the problem, do the following: to close the file left open by the previous script, create another script file, then type this line, and finally run the script:

```
close access alias ((path to documents folder as string) & "work.txt")
```

This tells Standard Additions to forget the last-read position in this file so the next time you use the command read the_file, it will start reading from the start of the file again.

As mentioned, running this script will end up causing the script to try and read bytes that don't exist. To prevent that, you can use the following script to catch the EOF error:

```
set the_file to alias ((path to documents folder as string) & "work.txt")
open for access the_file
try
    repeat
        set the_text to read the_file for 4
        display dialog  the_text
    end repeat
on error number -39 --handle the end-of-file error
    close access the_file
    display dialog  "All done!"
end try
```

Working with the End-of-File (EOF) Commands

EOF is a whole number that signifies the number of bytes in a given file. AppleScript allows you to both get a file's EOF and set it using Standard Additions' get eof and set eof commands.

The value returned by the get eof command is the same as the file size as returned by the info for command, as you can see here:

```
set the_file to alias "Macintosh HD:work.txt"
size of (info for the_file) = get eof the_file
--> true
```

From the Dictionary

The following are the dictionary entries of the get eof and set eof commands:

```
get eof: Return the length, in bytes, of a file
get eof anything
        -- a file reference number, alias, or file reference of a file
    Result: double integer  -- the total number of bytes in the file

set eof: Set end of file location for the specified file
set eof anything -- a file reference number, alias, or file reference of a file
        to double integer -- the new length of the file, in bytes. Any data beyond
                        -- this position is lost.
```

Getting a File's EOF

To get the EOF value of a file, you use the get eof command. The get eof command takes a single argument (a valid file specifier value) and returns a whole number.

The following script returns the EOF value of the file work.txt from your hard disk:

```
set the_file to alias "Macintosh HD:work.txt"
set byte_count to get eof the_file
```

The get eof command returns a real value, although the digit after the decimal is always 0. The reason is that get eof represents the EOF number as a 64-bit double-integer value, but AppleScript can't represent double integers itself so it automatically converts them to reals instead. No big deal, though.

Setting a File's EOF

When you set a file's EOF, you in fact determine the new end of the file. Setting the EOF to a smaller number than it already is will permanently delete the data after the new EOF you set. For instance, if the text of a MacRoman file is I Love Christina, the EOF of it is 16 bytes. If you set the EOF to 12, you will find your file saying I Love Chris, which is still perfectly valid but may not be what you intended.

On the other side of the coin, if you set the EOF to a larger number than it is, AppleScript will pad the end of the file with extra bytes, each one equivalent to ASCII number 0. These will appear in a text editor as invisible characters, but if you use the arrow keys, you can actually advance through them.

The following script sets the size of the file Work.txt to 10 bytes:

```
set the_file to alias "Macintosh HD:work.txt"
set eof of the_file to 10
```

The following script takes the same file and discards the second half of it:

```
set the_file to alias "Macintosh HD:work.txt"
set byte_count to get eof of the_file
set eof of the_file to (round (byte_count / 2))
```

Writing Files

AppleScript allows you to write data to files using the write command as defined in Standard Additions. Although you can write any type of data, for the most part, you'll stick to what you understand, which is text. You can see it, read it, and understand it. (For writing JPEGs, I suggest you use Adobe Photoshop!)

From the Dictionary

The following is the dictionary definition of the write command:

```
write: Write data to a file that was opened for access with write permission
write anything  -- the data to write to the file
      to anything -- the file reference number, alias or file reference
                  -- of the file to write to
      [starting at double integer] -- start writing at this position in the file
      [for double integer] -- the number of bytes to write; if not specified,
                           -- write all the data provided
      [as type class] -- how to write the data: as text, data, list, etc.
```

Using the write Command

The write command returns no result. It simply writes text or other data to a file. Before writing to a file, you should use the open for access command to get it ready for use. To grant yourself writing privileges, you must set the open for access command's write permission parameter to true. If you forget this, you'll get a "File not open with write permission" error when you try to write to it.

Using the open for access and close access commands guarantees that always there's a file for the write command to write to. If the file doesn't already exist, open for access will create one automatically. In fact, it is possible to use the write command without opening the file first, but this will work only if the file already exists; otherwise, you'll get a "File not found" error instead.

Next, unless you plan to insert your new data into the file's existing data (for example, adding a message to the end of a permanent log file), you need to clear any existing file data using the command set eof the_file to 0. This is another important step when writing to a file: for example, if a text file contains "Hello World" and you write the string "Goodbye" to it without resetting its EOF first, the result will be a file containing "Goodbyeorld"—not "Goodbye" as you intended!

With the preparations complete, you can now write some data to the file. The write command has two required parameters: the data you want to write and a value identifying the file to write to. This value may be a path string, a file specifier such as an alias or POSIX file value, or a unique ID number returned by the open for access command. Lastly, you should use the close access command to close the file again when you're done.

The following example creates a new text file (if none exists) and writes some text into it:

```
set the_file_path to "Macintosh HD:Users:hanaan:work.txt"
set file_ID to open for access file the_file_path with write permission
set eof file_ID to 0
write "abc" to file_ID
close access file_ID
```

(As with other examples in this chapter, remember to adjust the file path to suit your own file system before trying it yourself.)

The same script could be different, if you choose to forgo the integer result of the open for access command and just use the original file path each time:

```
set the_file_path to "Macintosh HD:Users:hanaan:work.txt"
open for access file the_file_path with write permission
set eof file the_file_path to 0
write "abc" to file the_file_path
close access file the_file_path
```

Notice that, in both cases, you cleaned up after yourself by closing the file.

How Much to Write and Where to Start

Two of the write command's parameters help you specify how much data or text you want to write to the file and at which position in the file you want to start.

The starting at parameter takes an integer argument and is useful for writing text or data to an existing file, when you don't want to start the writing from the beginning of the file.

One of the most common uses of the starting at parameter is appending text to the end of a file. For example, a script that needs to keep a written record of its activities would write each entry to the end of a permanent log file. For that, you will simply tell the write command to write at the end of the file, or starting at EOF. Script 14-6 shows the example script.

Script 14-6.

```
set the_file_path to "Macintosh HD:Users:hanaan:work.txt"
open for access file the_file_path with write permission
set eof file the_file_path to 0
write "this is the beginning" to file the_file_path
close access file the_file_path

open for access file the_file_path with write permission
write " and this is the end!" to file the_file_path starting at eof
close access file the_file_path
```

The resulting text file will have the text this is the beginning and this is the end!

Notice that the first write command started writing at the beginning of the file as usual. However, by setting the second write command's starting at parameter to the eof constant, you tell that command to add its data to the end of the file instead.

If you want to limit the amount of data that gets written, you can do that with the for parameter, which takes an integer as an argument and limits the number of bytes written to that number.

In Script 14-7, only the first five bytes of data will be written.

Script 14-7.

```
set the_file_path to "Macintosh HD:Users:hanaan:work.txt"
open for access file the_file_path  with write permission
write "abcdefghij" to file the_file_path for 5
close access file the_file_path
```

Useful File Writing Subroutines

The following are two subroutines you can use for basic text file saving. The first one saves the given text to a given text file, and the second handler adds the given text to the end of the given text file.

```
--Saves a text file
on write_text_to_file(the_file, the_text)
    set file_ref to open for access the_file with write permission
    set eof file_ref to 0
    write the_text to file_ref as string
    close access file_ref
end write_text_to_file

--Adds text to a text file
on append_text_to_file(the_file, the_text)
    set file_ref to open for access file theTextFilePath with write permission
    set file_length to get eof file_ref
    write the_text to file_ref as string starting at eof
    close access file_ref
end append_text_to_file
```

Using the write Command to Create a Script Log

In this little exercise you will create a handler that I use in all my systems. The purpose is to create a detailed log of script activity. This log will help you determine what went wrong if the script crashes and you're on the other end of the phone with a communicationally challenged individual trying to describe the problem to you.

The idea behind the logging system is that instead of collecting all the messages into a long string and writing the whole thing to a file at the end, the script constantly writes the latest information to the end of the file. This way, if the script gets an error, you can pinpoint the error location in the script. You can make the log as detailed as you want by calling the handler from more areas in your script.

The handler really is pretty simple. It receives a message to add to the log and adds it along with the date and time.

■**Note** You can make the log file folder structure more complex by incorporating a date-based folder structure: a year folder containing a folder for each month, containing all the log files for that month. For now, you will keep it simple. Instead, you will create a log file whose name will include the date and the file extension .log. You will use .log because on OS X, files with this extension are automatically opened by the console application, which adds a level of coolness to the mix. To keep things simple, the handler shown here just saves the log files to the current user's desktop, but you can easily modify it to use a different location if you want.

Script 14-8 shows the finished add_to_log handler. To use it, call it from anywhere in the script with a simple text message that describes your current location in the script.

Script 14-8.

```
1. on add_to_log(the_message)
2.    set YY to year of (current date)
3.    set MM to month of (current date) as integer
4.    if MM < 10 then set MM to "0" & MM
5.    set DD to day of (current date)
6.    if DD < 10 then set DD to "0" & DD
7.    set log_file_name to (YY as string) & "_" & MM & "_" & DD & ".log"
8.    set log_file_path to (path to desktop as string) & log_file_name
9.    set full_message to return & (current date) & return & the_message
10.    set file_ID to open for access file log_file_path with write permission
11.    write full_message to file_ID starting at eof
12.    close access file_ID
13. end add_to_log
```

In lines 2 through 8 you create the file path for the log file. This consists of the path to the user's desktop and a filename containing the date upon which the log entry was added. Getting the desktop folder path automatically allows this script to work on any machine without needing to be altered, and using today's date for the filename means that the add_to_log handler will automatically start a fresh log file for every day it's run.

Line 9 puts the message together.

Line 10 opens the log file for access, which will also create a new log file if one doesn't already exist. Line 11 appends the message to the end of the file, and line 12 closes the file again.

To add an entry to the log, I just call the add_to_log handler like this:

```
add_to_log("1044 Adding client name to job ticket")
```

Another technique I use is to include a property called debug at the top of my scripts. This property contains a Boolean value that is used to enable or disable extra debugging code in a script. I then put add_to_log commands inside conditional blocks so they'll call the add_to_log handler only when debug is true. This makes it really easy to turn debugging messages on during testing and off again during normal use.

Here's an example:

```
if debug then add_to_log("1044 Adding client name to job ticket")
```

Saving and Loading AppleScript Lists and Records

Another fantastic feature of the write command is its ability to save almost any kind of AppleScript value to a file, not just strings and Unicode text.

Besides being able to save binary data, you can write AppleScript lists and records to files and read them right back! This is great for saving script preferences and data that can be shared among scripts or backed up. It's true you can coerce most things into strings and save them as text, but here you can save lists containing real numbers, date values, and more embedded lists; write them all to a file; and later read them back exactly as they were before.

All you have to do is specify the value's original class using the write command's as parameter. For example, if you wanted to save a record value to a file, you'd add as record to the end of the write command.

The following script writes a simple list to a file, and the script following it reads it back:

```
set the_list to {"Anthony", 37, date "Sunday, December 4, 2067 12:00:00 AM"}
set file_path to (path to desktop as string) & "list file"
set f to open for access file file_path with write permission
write the_list to f as list
close access f
```

Now, let's read it back (see Script 14-9).

Script 14-9. *(includes previous script)*

```
set file_path to (path to desktop as string) & ➡
  "list file"set the_new_list to read file_path as list
--> {"Anthony", 37, date "Sunday, December 4, 2067 12:00:00 AM"}
```

Dealing with Text File Encodings

Although reading and writing plain-text files in AppleScript might sound like a simple enough procedure, it's actually a bit more complicated than I've let on up until now. Here's the issue: there's more than one way character data can be represented, or encoded, in a text file. When reading and writing text files in AppleScript, it's essential you use the correct text encoding; otherwise the results will appear as gibberish. This applies both to the text files you read and write using AppleScript alone and to the text files that are created by AppleScript for use by other programs, and vice versa.

If you're lucky, you won't run into these issues straightaway. However, you're almost certainly going to run into them sooner or later. When you do, you'll want to know a bit about how text—especially Unicode text—is actually represented in files and how AppleScript reads and writes those files.

About MacRoman and Unicode Character Sets

AppleScript itself can represent text in two ways: as values of class string and as values of class Unicode text. The string class normally represents characters in your Mac's primary encoding, which in turn is determined by your system's language settings in the International panel of System Preferences. For example, if your first language is English, your primary encoding will be MacRoman. (To keep the rest of this discussion simple, I'll assume that's what it is.)

The MacRoman character set represents 256 different characters, where each character is described by a single byte of memory. When you write a MacRoman string to a file using Standard Additions' write command, the result is a text file where each character is represented as a single byte in that file. To read this file correctly later, you need to know it contains MacRoman-encoded text data. If you try to view its data using a different encoding—for example, Latin-1 or UTF-8—some or all characters will appear incorrectly, or you may even get a "File is unreadable" error.

The Unicode character set is a more recent development that can represent a *much* larger range of characters than MacRoman can. The Unicode character set currently represents roughly 100,000 characters, which includes every character in common use around the world today, with enough space for up to a million or so in total. It does this by using multiple bytes to represent each character in the Unicode character set.

The technical details of the Unicode system are a bit complicated, but fortunately you can almost entirely ignore these in normal use. The only thing you really need to know about is how Unicode data is represented in plain-text files so you can use Standard Additions' read and write commands correctly.

Although it's not quite there yet, this huge "one-size-fits-all" character set is gradually superceding the older, smaller, and much more limited character sets of MacRoman, MacGreek, Latin-1, and so on. This will eliminate a lot of confusion that comes from having dozens of different and mostly incompatible character sets being used in different parts of the world. Although a great improvement on these earlier systems, Unicode is not without a few interesting characters of its own. Most notable is the ability to represent the same Unicode characters in more than one encoding scheme, something I'll get to shortly.

Reading and Writing Text Files in Different Encodings

Text-editing applications such as TextEdit commonly include an option in their Open and Save dialog boxes for specifying which encoding you want them to use when reading and writing a plain-text file. Similarly, Standard Additions' read and write commands give you some control over how you read and write plain-text files in AppleScript by way of their optional as parameters. In both commands, the as parameter takes a class name constant that indicates how the character data is (or should be) encoded in the text file.

You can use three class names for specifying how AppleScript reads and writes text files: string, «class utf8», and Unicode text.

Reading and Writing MacRoman Files

To read and write text files in MacRoman (or whatever your primary encoding is), use string for the as parameter. For example:

```
read the_file as string
```

And for example:

```
write the_text to the_file as string
```

If you don't specify an as parameter for the read command, it will use string as the default. The write command's default behavior is a bit trickier to describe, however. In Panther and earlier, the write command's default as parameter was also string; however, this behavior has significantly changed in Tiger. I'll discuss the details and implications of the new behavior later in the "Changes to the write Command in Tiger" section.

Reading and Writing Unicode Files

To read and write Unicode text files, you need to use either «class utf8» or Unicode text. Which one you should use depends on how the Unicode character data has been (or will be) encoded in the text file. The two main Unicode encoding schemes in common use today are UTF-8 and UTF-16. (In fact, there's actually two kinds of UTF-16 encodings: UTF-16LE and UTF-16BE; I'll discuss the difference in this section.)

The UTF-8 encoding scheme is a cleverly designed encoding that uses a variable number of bytes to represent each character. The first 128 characters in the Unicode character set—this includes commonly used characters such as A–Z, a–z, 0–9, and basic punctuation—are represented by a single byte each, and all other characters are represented using unique combinations of two to six bytes apiece. The first 128 characters in the Unicode character set are also identical to the 128 characters of the 7-bit ASCII character set, an even older system that has been influential over the decades.

Many other character sets, including MacRoman, are also supersets of ASCII. This overlap gives UTF-8 a degree of backward compatibility, since tools that understand ASCII (much of Mac OS X's Unix-based command line, for example) can still make some sense of UTF-8 encoded files. It also means that UTF-8 files containing mostly English text are more compact than UTF-16 files, which can be handy if you need to keep file size to a minimum. These advantages make UTF-8 a popular modern encoding for plain-text files.

To read and write UTF-8 encoded text files, use this:

```
read the_file as «class utf8»
```

and this:

```
write the_text to the_file as «class utf8»
```

Note If you accidentally read a UTF-8 encoded text file as if it was MacRoman, the result will be readable where characters 0–127 are used since both UTF-8 and MacRoman represent those characters in the same way. Other characters will appear as gibberish, however. For example, a UTF-8 encoded text file containing the phrase "37·5°C" would show up as "37¬∑5¬∞C" if interpreted as MacRoman instead of UTF-8. Each of the number and letter characters is represented by the same single byte in both the MacRoman and UTF-8 encoding systems, so would appear correct either way. However, the decimal point and degree sign are both represented in UTF-8 using two bytes apiece, so they show up as nonsense characters when interpreted as MacRoman.

The UTF-16 encoding scheme is a bit more straightforward than UTF-8, although it lacks the backward compatibility and compactness aspects when dealing with English text. In UTF-16, the majority of characters are encoded as two bytes of data each. (Some characters are actually represented using four bytes, but you don't need to worry about this.)

To read and write UTF-16 encoded text files, use this:

```
read the_file as Unicode text
```

and this:

```
write the_text to the_file as Unicode text
```

Note If you accidentally read a UTF-16 file as MacRoman, the resulting value may look at first glance like an ordinary string, especially if it contains English text. You'll quickly discover that something is very wrong when you try to use it, however: a common symptom is that each visible character in your "string" seems to have an invisible character in front of it. For example, reading a UTF-16 encoded text file containing the phrase "Hello World!" as a string would produce a string like "*H*e*l*l*o* *W*o*r*l*d*!", where each "*" is really an invisible ASCII 0 character.

UTF-16's simpler, fairly regular structure means it's also a popular choice for representing Unicode data in plain-text files.

UTF-16 has one significant twist: although a single character is represented using two bytes of data—a "high" byte and a "low" byte—the order in which those two bytes appear can vary. Some processors, such as those in the Power PC family, represent multibyte numbers with the most significant (highest) byte first; what's known as *big endianness*. Others, including Intel-compatible X86 processors, represent multibyte numbers with the least significant (lowest) byte first, or *little endianness*. Since all characters are ultimately represented at the hardware level as numbers, this means—for efficiency—some platforms like to encode characters in UTF-16 files in big-endian form, and others prefer to use the little-endian form. These two UTF-16-based formats are known as UTF-16BE and UTF-16LE—I'm sure you can guess what the BE and LE suffixes mean.

Byte order doesn't matter when working with Unicode text inside AppleScript but is important to get it right when reading and writing Unicode text into and out of AppleScript using Standard Additions.

When you use Standard Additions' write command to write a text file as Unicode text, it will always produce a UTF-16 file in big-endian form; that is, it will produce UTF-16BE. When you ask Standard Additions to read a text file as Unicode text, the read command will automatically assume the file is encoded as UTF-16BE . . . *unless* it finds a special sequence of bytes at the start that explicitly indicates the byte order used. If it finds one of these special byte order marks (BOMs), it will use that to determine whether the file's encoding is UTF-16BE or UTF16-LE and read it accordingly.

Although including a BOM in a Unicode text file is optional, it's a good idea to add one when writing a UTF-16 file in AppleScript. Here is a simple subroutine for writing a UTF-16BE file with the appropriate BOM at the start:

```
to write_UTF16_file(the_file, the_text)
    set file_ID to open for access the_file with write permission
    set eof file_ID to 0
    write ((ASCII character 254) & (ASCII character 255)) to file_ID
    write the_text to file_ID as Unicode text
    close access file_ID
end write_UTF16BE_file
```

A Summary of Common Text File Encodings

Figure 14-7 summarizes how the string "37·5°C" is represented under each of the four encoding systems described earlier: MacRoman, UTF-8, UTF-16BE, and UTF-16LE.

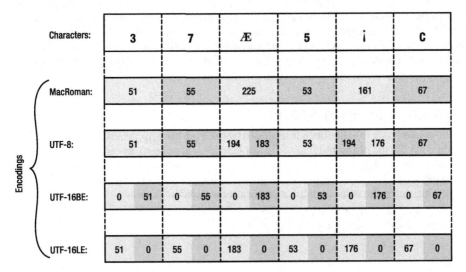

Figure 14-7. *How characters are represented in different text encodings. Each gray box indicates a single byte of data in the text file.*

As you can see, in MacRoman each character is represented as a single byte of data. In UTF-8 some characters are represented by a single byte whose value is 0–127, and others are represented by two or more bytes whose values are in the range 128–255. In the two UTF-16 encodings, each character is represented by two bytes, and the order of those bytes depends on whether the encoding is UTF-16BE (big-endian) or UTF-16LE (small endian).

Further Reading on Text Encoding

Unicode, MacRoman, and the entire text-encoding subject is much greater than I can cover in this chapter or would want to bore you with. For further reading, you can start at the following URLs:

```
http://www.joelonsoftware.com/articles/Unicode.html
http://en.wikipedia.org/wiki/Universal_Character_Set
```

Changes to the write Command in Tiger

On Mac OS X 10.3.9 and older, if you didn't specify an as parameter for the write command, it would use string as the default, and the resulting file would contain text data in your primary encoding. On Mac OS X 10.4 and newer, if you pass the write command a value of class string as its direct parameter, it will write the file using your primary encoding. However, if you pass it a Unicode text value, it will now write the file using a UTF-16 encoding instead.

Since many application and scripting addition commands already return Unicode text and AppleScript treats string and Unicode text values as largely interchangeable, it's easy to end up passing Unicode text to the write command without even realizing it. This means many scripts that may have written MacRoman files on Panther are now writing UTF-16 files on Tiger—often to the great annoyance of their authors and users who can't understand why scripts that worked perfectly under Panther now produce apparently "broken" files on Tiger. The files themselves aren't really broken, of course; they're just in a different encoding from what they were before. But you can guess what happens when the next script or program tries to open these files, believing them still to be in MacRoman format . . . .

Fortunately, the solution is simple enough: when using the write command to write text files, always supply the as parameter yourself as either string, «class utf8», or Unicode text. This way there'll never be any doubt as to which encoding the resulting file will be in. In the case of updating Panther-era scripts that broke when moved to Tiger, you should add as string to the end of all write commands that previously relied on the default behavior.

Writing Sound Files with Speech

Another fun file-related trick that has been introduced by the ever-busy AppleScript team is the ability to create and save spoken sound files using AppleScript. These aren't any sound files but rather text that is read back by one of the Mac's voices.

The following script will allow you to choose a new file (make sure its name ends in .aiff), and it'll save an AIFF file that is the voice of Ralph reciting a verse from the Bible:

```
say "The lord is my Shepherd, I shall not want" ¬
    using "Ralph" saving to (choose file name)
```

Power Wrap-Up

The following sections summarize the chapter in an intensive reference style. Use these sections to look up facts related to the chapter without the chatter.

Recognizing Files, Folders, and Disks

You can identify items on a hard drive or network volume in three ways: path strings, file specifiers, and Finder (or System Events) references.

Path Strings

Two kinds of path strings exist: HFS paths and POSIX paths. HFS path strings start with a volume name, and the names in the path are separated by colon delimiters. For example, you refer to the file Reference.PDF in the folder Documents in the hard disk Macintosh HD like this:

```
"Macintosh HD:documents:reference.pdf"
```

POSIX path strings start with a forward slash that indicates the file system's root, and the names in the path are separated by slash delimiters. For example:

```
"/documents/reference.pdf"
```

Unlike HFS paths, in POSIX paths all mounted volumes appear at /Volumes, such as /Volumes/ Macintosh HD; however, when referring to the start-up disk, you can skip this bit and just use /.

Alias and File Specifiers

Most commands that need a file reference as a parameter or return a file reference as a result use one of three forms. First, alias values identify files, folders, and disks that already exist. An alias value keeps track of the same file even if the file is renamed or moved to another location on the same volume. A typical alias value looks like this:

```
alias "Macintosh HD:documents:reference.pdf"
```

Second, file references identify files and folders that may or may not already exist. They are understood by many applications and scripting additions, although they can be a bit quirky to create. A typical file reference looks like this:

```
file "Macintosh HD:documents:reference.pdf"
```

Finally, many applications and scripting additions also understand POSIX file values. You create a POSIX file value using a POSIX path string, and it can identify files and folders that may or may not already exist. You can create a typical POSIX file value using an object specifier like this:

```
POSIX file "/documents/reference.pdf"
```

However, AppleScript will display the resulting POSIX file value so it looks the same as a file reference.

You can convert alias, file, and POSIX file values to HFS path strings by coercing them to a string or Unicode text. For example:

```
alias "Macintosh HD:documents:reference.pdf" as string
--> "Macintosh HD:documents:reference.pdf"
```

You can also convert them to POSIX path strings by getting the value of their POSIX path properties:

```
POSIX path of alias "Macintosh HD:documents:reference.pdf"
--> "/documents/reference.pdf"
```

Finder References

Finder references are references to Finder items as returned after being evaluated by the Finder in one way or another. The Finder references uses an object-model look to point to files (file "file.txt" of folder "the folder" of disk "Mac HD") rather than the colon ("Mac HD:the folder:file.txt") used in HFS-style file pointers or slash-separated ones ("/folder/file.ext") used in Unix file references.

Here's an example:

```
tell application "Finder"
    return first file of (path to documents folder)
end tell
--> document file "my document.txt" of folder "Documents" of folder "hanaan" ¬
of folder "Users" of startup disk of application "Finder"
```

About Filename Extensions

In OS X, most files have Windows-style filename extensions that indicate their type, although these may often be hidden in the Finder depending on the user's preferences. AppleScript allows you to get information about a file's name, displayed name, and name extension. You can get this information with the info for command. The info for command returns a large record with plenty of information about the given file.

The following four properties are connected to the name and name extension:

```
set file_info to info for ¬
    file "Macintosh HD:Applications:AppleScript:Folder Actions Setup.app:"
name of file_info --> "Folder Actions Setup.app"
displayed name of file_info --> "Folder Actions Setup"
name extension of file_info --> "app"
extension hidden of file_info --> true
```

Reading Files

You can read files into a variable with the read command. The following script will read a chosen text file:

```
set file_text to read (choose file of type {"TEXT"})
```

You can also open the file for access before reading it. Opening a file before reading it has some implications detailed earlier in this chapter.

Reading a File to a List

By default, when you read a file, you get all the text as a string. Using the using delimiter parameter, however, you can break the text into a list of items using one or more characters as delimiters. The following script reads a return-delimited file to a list, where each list item is a paragraph:

```
set text_paragraphs to ¬
   read alias "Macintosh HD:report export.txt"  using delimiter {return}
```

Reading Specific Data

The read command has three parameters—from, for, and to—that allow you to specify exactly the bytes you want to read from the file:

- from: (An integer.) Start to read from this position and on. If omitted, start from byte 1.
- for: (An integer.) The number of bytes you want to read.
- to: (An integer.) Read up to this point. If omitted, read to the end.

Two other parameters, before and until, allow you to specify a particular character it should read up to:

- before: (A string.) Read all characters up to, but not including, the specified character.
- until: (A string.) Read all characters until right after the specified character.

Reading Different Types of Data

You can use the as parameter to read text in your primary encoding (such as MacRoman) and several different Unicode encodings, including UTF-8 and UTF-16BE. You can also read files containing raw AppleScript data structures such as lists and records.

Opening and Closing File Access

Before writing to files, and sometimes before reading files, you have to open access to the file, which you can do with the open for access command. After you've opened the file and read or written to it, you should close it with the close access command.

The open for access command returns a temporary ID number that can be later used by the read, write, set eof, get eof, and close access commands to identify the file. The following script opens a file for access and then uses the resulting file ID to read the file and close access to it:

```
set file_ID to open for access alias "Macintosh HD:report export.txt"
set report_text to read file_ID
close access file_ID
```

Note that opening and closing access to a file does not change its "busy" status. These files can be opened by any other application even after AppleScript has opened them for access.

To write to a file, you have to open it with write permission. You do this as part of the open for access command:

```
set file_ID to open for access alias "Macintosh HD:report export.txt" ¬
    with write permission
```

Writing to Files

After you opened a file for access with write permission, you can use the write command to write any data to the file:

```
set file_ID to open for access alias "Macintosh HD:report export.txt" ¬
    with write permission
set eof file_ID to 0
write "Today's special: Pea soup" to file_ID
close access file_ID
```

When writing out a complete file, you should always use the set eof command to set the file's length to 0 before writing the new data to it. If you forget to do this and the new data is shorter than the old data, some of the old data will be left at the end of the new file.

Writing a Specified Number of Bytes

You can use the for and starting at parameters to specify how many bytes of data to write and where to start writing. The following script writes text from a variable starting at the tenth byte of the file for 20 more bytes. Any part of the text in the variable beyond the 20th byte will be omitted:

```
set file_ref to open for access alias "Macintosh HD:report export.txt" ¬
    with write permission
write the_long_text_variable for 20 starting at 10 to file_ref
close access file_ref
```

Writing Different Types of Data

You can write text data in several text encodings: your primary encoding (such as MacRoman) and two Unicode encodings (UTF-8 and UTF-16BE). You can also write native AppleScript values such as lists and records. You do that with the as parameter.

EOF

EOF describes the number of bytes in the file. For example, the EOF of a MacRoman text file that has only the word Apple in it will be 5.

You can get and set the EOF of a given file with the get eof and set eof commands. For example, before writing out a new file, you should set its length to 0 using:

```
set eof the_file to 0
```

Standard Additions also defines an eof constant that you can use as the write command's starting at parameter to make it write the new data at the end of the file. For example, the following script will append some new text to the end of an existing file:

```
set file_ID to open for access alias "Macintosh HD:report export.txt" ¬
    with write permission
write the_new_text to file_ID starting at eof
close access file_ID
```

Manipulating the File System

This chapter covers the different aspects of scripting the file system using the Finder and System Events applications and shows how to use the File Commands suite of the Standard Additions scripting addition.

Getting File Information

Whenever you need to get information about a file, folder, or disk, you can go to several places: the Finder, System Events, or the `info for` command.

The `info for` command is part of Standard Additions.

The power of the `info for` command is in the information it returns to you. The information about a file is returned in a record whose properties are shown in the following section.

From the Dictionary: info for

Here's the dictionary entry for the `info for` command; features that are new in OS X 10.4 are marked with an asterisk (*):

```
info for: Return information for a file or folder
    info for anything
        -- the alias or file reference to the file or folder
    [size boolean]
        -- Return the size of the file or folder? (default is true) *
    Result: file information
        -- a record containing the information for file or folder specified
```

The record returned from the `info for` command is also described in the Standard Additions dictionary:

```
Class file information: Reply record for the 'info for' command
Properties:
    name Unicode text  [r/o]  -- the name of the item
    displayed name Unicode text  [r/o]  -- the user-visible name of the item
    short name Unicode text [r/o]
        -- the short name (CFBundleName) of the item (if the item is
            an application) *
    name extension Unicode text  [r/o]
        -- the name extension of the item (such as "txt")
    bundle identifier Unicode text  [r/o]
        -- the item's bundle identifier (if the item is a package)
    type identifier Unicode text  [r/o] -- the item's type identifier *
    kind Unicode text  [r/o]  -- the kind of the item
    default application alias  [r/o]
```

```
                  -- the application that normally opens this kind of item
      creation date date  [r/o]  -- the date the item was created
      modification date date  [r/o]  -- the date the item was last modified
      file type string  [r/o]  -- the file type of the item
      file creator string  [r/o]  -- the creator type of the item
      short version string  [r/o]
          -- the item's short version string (from the Finder's 'Get Info'box)
      long version string  [r/o]
          -- the item's long version string (from the Finder's 'Get Info' box)
      size integer  [r/o]  -- the size of the item in bytes
      alias boolean  [r/o]  -- Is the item an alias file?
      folder boolean  [r/o]  -- Is the item a folder?
      package folder boolean  [r/o]
          -- Is the item a package (a folder treated as a file?)
      extension hidden boolean  [r/o]
          -- Is the item's name extension hidden from the user?
      visible boolean  [r/o]  -- Is the item visible?
      locked boolean  [r/o]  -- Is the item locked?
      busy status boolean  [r/o]  -- Is the item currently in use?
      icon position point  [r/o]
          -- the coordinates of the item's icon in its window or on the desktop
      folder window bounding rectangle  [r/o]
          -- the coordinates of the folder's window (if the item is a folder)
```

Using the info for Command

The nice feature of using the info for command is that because it's a scripting addition, you don't have to use it inside an application's tell block.

The following is a script that uses the info for command to calculate the number of days for which a chosen file has not been updated. The script will do that by subtracting the file's modification date from the current date and then calculating the whole number of days in the result.

```
set the_alias to (choose file)
set file_info to info for the_alias
set seconds_old to (current date) - (modification date of file_info)
set days_old to seconds_old div days
set file_name to name of file_info
display dialog "The file \"" & file_name & "\" hasn't been modified for " ¬
    & days_old & " days."
```

The following is a typical example of a file information record returned by the info for command on line 2 of this script (I've spaced it out a bit to make it easier to read than it would be in Script Editor):

```
{
    name:"report.rtf",
    creation date:date "Thursday, November 20, 2003 11:04:20 PM",
    modification date:date "Thursday, November 20, 2003 11:04:30 PM",
    icon position:{0, 0},
    size:6.961535E+6,
    folder:false,
    alias:false,
    package folder:false,
    visible:true,
    extension hidden:false,
    name extension:"rtf",
```

```
    displayed name:"report.rtf",
    default application:
        alias "Macintosh HD:Applications:Microsoft Office X:Microsoft Word",
    kind:"Microsoft Word RTF document",
    file type:"RTF ",
    file creator:"MSWD",
    type identifier:"public.rtf",
    locked:false,
    busy status:false,
    short version:"",
    long version:""
}
```

Other useful bits of information you can get from the file information record are the size of the specified file, the folder or disk in bytes, whether it's a folder, whether it's an alias file, and whether the file is locked.

ALL BUT THE SIZE

As you may know, it takes some time for the operating system to figure out the size of a folder, which can make the info for command take too long to work. For instance, the following script takes several seconds just because it has to calculate the size of the Applications folder:

```
info for (path to applications folder)
```

The remedy for this problem came in Tiger (OS X 10.4) with the addition of a new Boolean parameter, size, to the info for command. With the new size parameter, you can specify whether you want the size returned by using the info for command.

The following script, using the new parameter, returns the results instantaneously:

```
info for (path to applications folder) without size
```

The resulting record still includes a size property, but instead of a number, it now contains a missing value.

Getting the Paths to Standard Locations

Part of getting around in OS X is understanding the different domains and special folders that organize the different domain-related files. One way you can find these folders is by using System Events, which you'll look at later in the "Finder vs. System Events" section.

Another way you can locate them is by using the path to command, as defined in Standard Additions. For example, using the path to command, you can get the paths to the different font folders that sometimes seem to be randomly scattered around the system.

The path to command has two main parts: the folder you're looking for, which is indicated by a constant value such as desktop or home folder, and the domain in which you want to find the folder. You can specify a particular domain to search using the optional from parameter; otherwise, path to will use a suitable default. Standard Additions' dictionary lists all the folder and domain constants available. The following are a few examples:

```
path to fonts
--> alias "Macintosh HD:System:Library:Fonts:"

path to fonts from user domain
--> alias "Macintosh HD:Users:hanaan:Library:Fonts:"

path to launcher items folder from Classic domain
--> alias "Number Nine:System Folder:Launcher Items:"
```

The path to command has two other parameters. The as parameter allows you to ask for the result as a string instead of an alias:

```
path to startup disk as string
--> "Macintosh HD:"
```

The other parameter is folder creation. According to the dictionary, folder creation means that if the folder you're requesting a path for does not exist, the folder will be created. Also, the dictionary claims that the default is true. This works only for a few folders, though, and only in domains where you have sufficient permissions to make such changes.

Getting the Path for the Start-Up Disk and User Directory

Two of the most useful paths you can get are the paths to the start-up disk and the user's Home directory. Using built-in paths that represent these two containers can take you a long way to having a system-independent script.

The idea is to make your script as portable and flexible as possible. I know what you're thinking . . . this is just a script that'll run on your Mac, and it has a small chance of going anywhere else. That's not necessarily so. As you will discover, a small bit of code you write to perform a simple task can suddenly grow into a full-blown script and then become part of a larger scheme. It is at that point that you copy the script to some other Mac to test it, and wham! Nothing works since the other Mac's hard drive has a different name.

So, as much as you just want to get that pesky script quickly working, I urge you to take the time to replace the hard drive names using one of the few ways AppleScript has to refer to the start-up disk, no matter what its name is.

Let's say, for example, that your script refers to a folder called Client Jobs on the hard disk. You need a variable in your script that'll identify that folder. If you provide the full path as a literal string, your script line may look like this:

```
set the_jobs_folder_path to "Macintosh HD:Client Jobs:"
```

If you move the script to a Mac with a differently named hard drive, your script will break. Instead, use the command path to startup disk to get the first part of the path.

Declare a global variable called something like hd, and assign the name of the start-up disk to it up front. From that point, anytime you want to refer to the start-up disk, just use this variable:

```
global hd
set hd to path to startup disk as string
set client_jobs_folder_path to hd & "Client Jobs:"
```

Why did you get the path to the start-up disk as a string? This way, it's easier to concatenate it to names of other folders, to colons, and to other strings that make up path names. After the path name is complete, you can convert it to an alias if you need one, use it to create a Finder or System Events reference, and so on.

Using the path to me Command

One of the most useful commands you can use in your quest for script portability is path to me.

The variable me is usually used to refer to the current script object but is often used in the path to command to find out the script's location on disk. This doesn't work in every situation but is useful when it does.

A common use for path to me is to allow a script applet to find files and folders relative to its own position on disk. This comes in handy when your applet is part of some sort of folder structure. It's also one of the situations where path to me generally does what you want, which is good news.

The way I like to set it up is by having a folder I call the Main folder. Inside I have all the folders the system needs (even small systems). The folders may be resources, templates, in/out, and so on. One of my folders is always named System. In this folder I put the main applet that controls the whole system. Since the user will need to run this applet to start the system, I usually give the user an alias file in a more convenient place, just to keep their paws out of the system's folder structure. Figure 15-1 shows a sample of this folder structure.

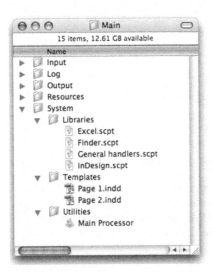

Figure 15-1. *A sample folder structure for an AppleScript system*

The script, however, needs to know where all the related files are. Since the position of these files within the Main folder is already known, all the script needs in order to work out their full paths is the path to the Main folder. To get that, I need to just get the container of the container of the script application's file. The applet's container is the folder System, and that folder's container is the Main folder. Here's the line in the script that assigns the Main folder's path to a variable:

```
tell application "Finder"
    set main_folder_path to container of (container of (path to me)) as string
end tell
```

The problem with using path to me is that, in fact, it became an official AppleScript feature only in Tiger (Mac OS X 10.4). On earlier versions of the Mac OS, it was actually interpreted as meaning path to current application. This meant in Panther and earlier, path to me would return the desired result only in script applets (where the application *is* the script) and in a few attachable applications that knew how to provide special support for it. Otherwise, it would return the path to the current application instead.

Beginning with Tiger, path to me is directly supported by AppleScript itself, so it should now produce the desired result in most—though still not all—applications.

One place that path to me still doesn't behave as I would like it to behave is in Apple's Script Editor. This may be sorted in a future version, but in Tiger and earlier it still returns the path to the Script Editor application itself. You can see that in Figure 15-2.

Figure 15-2. *The* path to me *command in Script Editor returns the path to the Script Editor application, not the saved script.*

To work around this, you'll need to hardwire the path to the applet file into your script during the development and testing stages. Once the script is finished, you should replace this fixed path with path to me to make it portable.

Other script editors do provide you with a bit more assistance here. In Satimage's Smile editor, path to me and path to current application always return the path to the saved script. Late Night Software's Script Debugger allows you to choose whether path to me returns the path to the application or to the script file. For my purposes, I usually want the path to the script file. For me, this feature alone was worth Script Debugger's price.

Finder vs. System Events

One of the AppleScript improvements that came with Mac OS X is the faceless background application known as System Events. System Events is a scriptable application that provides an alternative to some of the Finder's file system–scripting capabilities.

The idea behind the introduction of System Events was to allow scripters to manipulate the file system including files, folders, and so on, without having to use the Finder. On Mac OS 7, 8, and 9 you could always count on the Finder being available, which is not always the case with OS X. For example, some Mac users may prefer to disable the Finder and use a third-party file manager such as Cocoatech's Path Finder instead. This can be a problem for scripts that rely on the Finder for manipulating the file system; fortunately, the System Events application is always available, so you can use that instead.

While the System Events scripting responsibilities grow, the Finder still holds on to a few exclusive scripting features. For instance, System Events doesn't have access to Finder windows and icon positions, for obvious reasons.

You do have to refrain from assuming that the System Events scripting dictionary is merely a subset of the Finder's dictionary because there are actually many differences between their object models, some major and others minor, that can catch you by surprise. (The following section covers these differences in more detail.)

Although some file system–related functions are available through Standard Additions commands such as list folder and info for, these functions are informational only: they get information but can't really do anything. To perform file-related actions such as creating folders and deleting files, you have to use either the Finder or System Events.

Manipulating Files, Folders, and Disks

The first features that come to mind when scripting the file system are the different items you can control and the commands you can use on the items. Until OS X, AppleScript's ability to manipulate the file system was nothing to sink your teeth into, but at least it was all concentrated in one place: the Finder's dictionary. Now, to make matters more complex, you can also use System Events, which has a somewhat different object model.

The following sections will examine the object models of both the Finder and System Events.

The Finder's File System Object Model

The top of the food chain in the Finder's inheritance structure is a superclass called item. The item class describes the basic features found in every class of file system object you'll meet in Finder scripting: disk, folder, application file, document file, and so on.

Figure 15-3 illustrates how Finder's file system–related classes inherit properties, elements, and behaviors from one another. For example, if you follow the arrows on the diagram, you can see that the alias file class inherits many of its attributes from the file class, which in turn inherits many of its attributes from the item class.

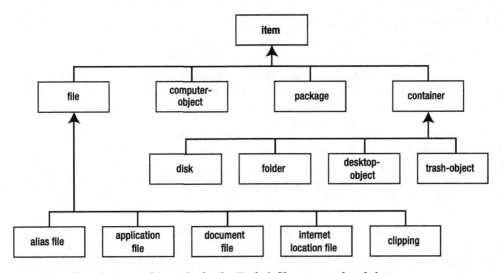

Figure 15-3. *The inheritance hierarchy for the Finder's file system–related classes*

For example, if you look at the Finder's dictionary, you can see that the item class defines a name property. From this, you can deduce that every disk object, every folder object, every document file object, and so on, also possesses a name property. This means you can ask any kind of file system object for its name, even when you don't know—or care—exactly what class of object it is. As long as you know it's some sort of item object, you know that asking it for its name will always work.

You can also use your knowledge of the Finder's inheritance hierarchy when creating references to file system objects. For instance, if you want to create a handler that takes a path string and uses the Finder to delete the corresponding file or folder, you can convert that string to a Finder object reference using item the_path_string:

```
on delete_item(the_path_string)
    tell application "Finder"
        delete (item the_path_string)
    end tell
end delete_item
```

You don't need to worry whether the path string points to a document file, a folder, a clipping, and so on, since you know these are all types of items. You can just say item the_path_string, and the Finder will produce a suitable reference, figuring out the finer details for you. Similarly, if you know that the delete command will work on any kind of item, you can be confident that the previous will work whether the item being deleted is a document file, an application file, or a folder.

The item class has four subclasses: container, file, package, and computer-object.

Containers

The container class defines the properties, elements, and behaviors that are common to all Finder items that can contain other items.

The container class has the following subclasses: disk, folder, desktop-object, and trash-object. The last two, trash-object and desktop-object, describe two special container objects that represent the current user's trash and desktop, respectively. These two objects are permanently found in the trash and desktop properties of the Finder's application object. The following are two examples of using trash and desktop:

```
tell application "Finder" to set trashed_items to every item of trash
tell application "Finder" to move every file of desktop to trash
```

Notice how the two preceding script lines (of which the second one you won't want to execute) use the words trash and desktop to refer to the two special Finder containers.

Referring to container elements is great when you want to execute any command on objects or get information about objects that you know are containers of some kind but are not sure exactly which—disks or folders. For example, the following script will back up every file of a given container, without caring whether that container object is a disk or a folder:

```
tell application "Finder"
    duplicate (every file of container the_path_string) ¬
        to (folder "backup" of home)
end tell
```

Notice the use of the word home in the preceding script. home happens to be a property of the Finder's application object and so is desktop, trash, and startup disk. What makes the trash and desktop properties different from the properties startup disk and home is that desktop and trash contain special, one-off objects representing those file system items, whereas the startup disk and home properties contain just ordinary references to disk and folder objects.

The disk and folder subclasses of container are similar, sharing many common characteristics and behaviors (in other words, all those they've inherited from the container class). You could almost think of a disk as a top-level folder, and for many scripting purposes they are the same, unless you want to use a command such as erase or eject. These commands work only with disks.

Files

The file class has five subclasses: alias file, application file, document file, internet location file, and clipping. Each subclass may add its own set of properties that no other class has. The application file class, for instance, defines a Boolean property called has scripting terminology. This property is true when the application is scriptable.

Although for the most part you will just use the class file in scripts, distinguishing between the different subclasses may be useful when getting lists of specific items from folders. For instance, you can create a script that goes through the hard drive and deletes all the nonworking alias files. The script will loop through all the alias files in each folder and try to fix them.

Heck, let's create that script right now!

I will show how to create a script that will loop through folders and delete all the alias files whose original items no longer exist. Later you can modify the script to ask the user to choose a new original item instead, but that is your homework.

Now, writing a script that can process the contents of a single folder is simple enough, but what if you also want it to process all of the folder's subfolders, each of those folder's subfolders, and so on? The answer to this problem is first to put all the code for processing a single folder into a subroutine. This subroutine will then call itself in order to process each one of the folder's subfolders too, and as the subroutine processes each of those folders, it'll call itself to process their subfolders too, and so on, and so on, until every single nested folder has been dealt with.

This ability of a subroutine to call itself (and call itself . . . and call itself . . .) is what's known as *recursion*, and it's terrific for dealing with deeply nested, or naturally recursive, structures such as the folders in a file system or the elements in an Extensible Markup Language (XML) document.

■**Note** Make sure you remember the difference between AppleScript's alias value class and the Finder's alias file class. alias file is a special "shortcut" file that opens another file or folder when you double-click it in the Finder, whereas alias is an AppleScript value that points to a file, folder, or disk in the file system. If you write alias where you actually mean alias file, or vice versa, the script won't work correctly.

Script 15-1 shows the script.

Script 15-1.

```
1. set the_folder to (choose folder)
2. clean_alias_files_in_folder(the_folder)

3. on clean_alias_files_in_folder(the_folder)
4.     tell application "Finder"
5.         --Check each of the alias files in this disk/folder
6.         set alias_files_list to alias files of the_folder
7.         repeat with the_alias_file_ref in alias_files_list
8.             if not (exists original item of the_alias_file_ref) then
9.                 delete the_alias_file_ref
10.            end if
11.        end repeat
12.        --Clean the alias files in each sub-folder
```

```
13.      set sub_folders_list to folders of the_folder
14.      repeat with the_sub_folder_ref in sub_folders_list
15.          my clean_alias_files_in_folder(the_sub_folder_ref)
16.      end repeat
17.   end tell
18. end clean_alias_files_in_folder
```

Line 1 of the script allows the user to choose a folder. This folder will be the top-level folder processed by the script. The script will then process all nested files in that folder.

In line 2 you call the main handler, clean_alias_files_in_folder. As you will see in a minute, what makes the script recursive is the fact that the handler calls itself.

The handler, which starts from line 3 through 18, treats only one folder. First, all the alias files are treated. That happens from line 5 through 11. You start by creating a list, listing only the alias files in the folder:

```
set alias_files_list to alias files of the_folder
```

Then, you loop through the list, check the original item property of each alias file, and delete the alias files whose original item doesn't exist.

From line 12 to 17 you do a similar thing: you list the subfolders that are in the current folder and loop through them. What you do with these subfolder references, however, is different. In line 15 you make the handler call itself, passing it one of these subfolder references. Now the handler goes off and processes the subfolder in the same way as before: first deleting any broken alias files, then processing each one of *its* subfolders, and so on. When no more subfolders are left to process, AppleScript knows to return to the spot it left off at and continue running through more folders.

Packages

Packages (also known as *bundles*) are special folders: they appear as single files in a Finder's window, but they're really disguised folders that contain other folders and files. In the System Events dictionary, they're referred to as *file packages*, not packages, but the object is the same. The most common form of package is the OS X application bundle, where the application binary and its various resource files (icons, audio files, help files, and so on) are all wrapped up in a bundle folder with the filename extension .app.

The Script Editor can also create packages. In fact, you can create two types of packages: script application (applet) bundles and script bundles. You'll learn more about that when I discuss saving scripts in Chapter 24.

You can read more about packages earlier in the "Getting File Information" section of this chapter.

The computer-object Class

The Mac OS X Finder likes to provide its users with a "worldview" of the entire file system—a special location named Computer where all local disks, mounted media, and other network-accessible computers are visible at once. You can easily view this location by choosing Computer from the Finder's Go menu. The Computer location is also represented in the Finder's scripting interface by a single object of class computer-object. You can find this object in the computer container property of the Finder's application object.

The computer-object class itself is a bit odd. The dictionary says that it inherits from the item class, so you can expect it to have all the properties defined by the item class. Most of these properties don't actually contain useful values, though, and can just be ignored. The one useful property you can extract from the computer container object is displayed name. The value of this property is the name of your computer, as defined in the Sharing panel in System Preferences.

The Finder's dictionary also claims that the `computer-object` class doesn't have any elements, which seems a bit odd. However, references to its `item`, `container`, and `disk` elements seem to work fine, so this is probably just an error in the dictionary:

```
tell application "Finder" to get every item of computer container
--> {item "Network" of computer container of application "Finder", ➥
startup disk of application "Finder", disk "Backup 5" of application "Finder"}
```

One other thing you can use it for is opening the Computer window from AppleScript:

```
tell application "Finder" to open computer container
```

System Event's File System Object Model

System Events' disk-folder-file suite describes a somewhat different object model than the Finder, although it serves the same purpose as the Finder's and mostly works in similar ways.

While the top dog in the System Events' inheritance hierarchy is `item`, the subclass of the `item` class that deals with file system items is the class `disk item`. I'll cover disk items now and other items in the following sections.

Figure 15-4 shows the part of the System Events inheritance hierarchy in which you're interested.

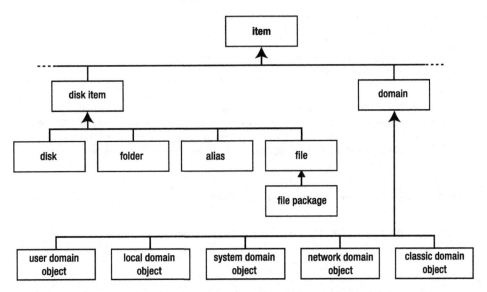

Figure 15-4. *The inheritance hierarchy for System Events' file system–related classes*

For now, let's concentrate on the classes that define individual disk, folder, and file objects. The top class, `disk item`, is also the most general one. Any object in the file system is a disk item of one sort or another: all folders are disk items, all files are disk items, and all disks are disk items.

The `disk item` class has four subclasses: `folder`, `alias`, `disk`, and `file`. Note how different they are from the Finder's object class hierarchy. For example, System Events doesn't distinguish between different kinds of files to the same degree as the Finder, so if you want to create a reference that identifies only application files, say, you'll find it harder to do in System Events. However different, the System Events' class hierarchy is pretty easy to understand. Let's look at the four subclasses in detail.

Files

Files include any disk item that can't contain other disk items. Unlike the Finder, System Events does not distinguish between application files, clippings, document files, and so on.

Here's a simple script that gets a reference to the first file in the user's Home folder, assuming there is one:

```
tell application "System Events"
    file 1 of home folder
end tell
```

As with Finder references, the System Events application also allows you to identify files by name, range, and so on, if you want, such as like this: file "Read Me.txt" of home folder.

The following example uses the file class's size property to filter files that are larger than 5MB (or 5 million bytes, to be exact):

```
tell application "System Events"
    set large_file_list to every file of the_folder ¬
    whose size > 5000000
end tell
```

The following, more complex example gets the names of the HTML files in a selected folder. The script does that by using the file class's type identifier property, which is available in Mac OS X 10.4 and later. You can find more information about type identifers in Chapter 12.

```
set the_path to (choose folder) as string

tell application "System Events"
    set file_names to name of every file of (disk item the_path) ¬
    whose type identifier is "public.html"
end tell
```

The file class has one subclass, which is file package. File packages are identical to what the Finder refers to as *packages*; they are special folders that look and behave like files in a Finder window but can secretly contain other items. One flavor of a file package is the application bundle. Cocoa applications and most Carbon-based applications are saved as application bundles, as shown in the following script:

```
tell application "System Events"
    every file package of folder "Applications" of startup disk
end tell
```

The preceding script lists all application bundles and any other bundles that may be in your Applications folder.

Folders

In scripting terms, folders are disk items that can have elements. These elements represent files and other folders that are contained by the folder.

For example, I can build up a reference to my Home folder by referring to each disk and folder element in turn:

```
tell application "System Events"
    folder "hanaan" of folder "Users" of disk "Macintosh HD"
end tell
```

Or I can create the same reference using a suitable path string:

```
tell application "System Events"
    folder "Macintosh HD:Users:hanaan:"
end tell
```

Like the Finder, System Event's application object also provides several useful properties that contain references to important locations. So, I can also get a reference to my Home folder using the following:

```
tell application "System Events"
    home folder
end tell
```

All three examples return a reference that looks like this:

```
folder "Macintosh HD:Users:hanaan:" of application "System Events"
```

Working with a folder object's elements is quite straightforward. For example, to get the name of every folder in the current user's Home folder, use this:

```
tell application "System Events"
    name of every folder of home folder
end tell
--> {".Trash", "Desktop", "Documents", "Library", "Movies", "Music", ➥
"Pictures", "Public", "Sites"}
```

To get a reference to the first visible file or folder in the Applications folder, use this:

```
tell application "System Events"
    disk item 1 of folder "Applications" of startup disk ¬
        whose visible is true
end tell
--> file package "Macintosh HD:Applications:Address Book.app:" ➥
of application "System Events"
```

Disks

In the Finder, the disk class is a subclass of the container class. In System Events disk is a direct subclass of the disk item class.

The following script lists the names of all available disks:

```
tell application "System Events"
    name of disks
end tell
--> {"Macintosh HD", "Number Nine", "Network"}
```

About System Events' alias Class

The alias class in System Events' dictionary is a bit of an oddity. It has no relation either to Apple-Script's alias value class or to Finder's alias file class; its actual purpose is to make it easier to write references in System Events.

Scriptable applications normally allow you to refer to their objects only using a full object reference such as text of document 1 or name of every track of playlist "Library". When dealing with the file system, however, it's common to refer to files, folders, and disks using AppleScript alias values.

Of course, you could convert your AppleScript alias value to a path string and use that to construct a new application reference in Finder or System Events. For example:

```
set the_alias to choose file
set the_path to the_alias as string
tell application "System Events" to set file_info to properties of file the_path
```

However, both the Finder and newer versions of System Events allow you to skip these extra conversion steps and just use the original AppleScript alias value directly in the reference:

```
set the_alias to choose file
tell application "Finder" to set file_info to properties of the_alias
tell application "System Events" to set file_info to properties of the_alias
```

So although seeing the nonstandard alias class definition in System Events' dictionary may be a bit confusing at first, don't worry about it. This is just System Events' way of making this trick work.

This extra flexibility makes dealing with AppleScript aliases a bit simpler and more convenient. Just remember to be careful if you need to ask for the value's class, since AppleScript alias values already have a class property of their own. This means a line like this:

```
tell application "System Events" to get class of the_alias
```

will return alias, not disk, folder, or file (or alias file, document file, and so on, in the Finder's case), as you probably wanted. So, you still need to use the longer method for that. But the rest of the time, it "just works."

Using Related System Events Classes

Up until now you have learned about those classes of objects in System Events that directly deal with the file system: file, folder, and disk. These are called *disk items*.

System Events' dictionary defines many other classes in addition to its disk item classes. Most of these other classes apply to unrelated tasks such as GUI scripting and XML processing, so I won't cover them in this chapter. Still, a few are of interest here: user, domain and login item. Let's take a closer look at them.

Using the user Class

No, not only you and your family members are privileged enough to be users on your OS X–equipped Mac. Try this script to see who else has an account on your Mac:

```
tell application "System Events"
    name of every user
end tell
```

If you're running Mac OS X 10.3, System Events will return the names of *all* users, including various special user accounts that belong to the operating system itself:

```
--> {"nobody", "root", "daemon", "unknown", "smmsp", "lp", "postfix", ¬
"www", "eppc", "mysql", "sshd", "qtss", "cyrus", "mailman", ¬
"appserver", "johanne", "olivia", "hanaan", "aylam"}
```

On OS X 10.4, however, only the names of regular users are returned, which is usually what you're interested in:

```
--> {"johanne", "olivia", "hanaan", "aylam"}
```

Now, let's see what properties each user has. I'll first check the properties of user hanaan:

```
tell application "System Events"
    properties of user "hanaan"
end tell
--> {full name:"Hanaan Rosenthal", name:"hanaan", ¬
home directory:"/Users/hanaan", ¬
picture path:"/Library/User Pictures/Animals/Dragonfly.tif", class:user}
```

Hmm . . . I have access to the users' picture path. Maybe I'll create an AppleScript Studio application that automatically changes users' pictures based on their mood. Or maybe not.

The following script looks for only the users whose Home directory is in the Users folder, which is useful if you're still running on OS X 10.3:

```
tell application "System Events"
    full name of every user whose home directory starts with "/Users"
end tell
```

Using the domain Class

Domain is yet another term Mac users have to get used to using. Domains are a Unix method of specifying regions in the start-up disk relating to different system functions.

The following script lists the name of each domain:

```
tell application "System Events"
    name of every domain
end tell
--> {"System", "Local", "Network", "User", "Classic"}
```

What other tasks are domains good for? For example, you know you can get the path to different system locations using the path to Standard Addition command. But what if you want to get the paths to all possible locations a scripting addition can be in or get the paths for all font folders in the system? To do that the easy way, you need System Events:

```
tell application "System Events"
    scripting additions folder of every domain
end tell
--> {folder "Macintosh HD:System:Library:ScriptingAdditions:" ➡
    of application "System Events", ➡
    folder "Macintosh HD:Library:ScriptingAdditions:" ➡
    of application "System Events", missing value, ➡
    folder "Macintosh HD:Users:hanaan:Library:ScriptingAdditions:" ➡
    of application "System Events", ➡
    folder "Number Nine:System Folder:Scripting Additions:" ➡
    of application "System Events"}
```

If you don't recognize the result, it is a list of references to all the Scripting Additions folders on your system. (The third item is missing value because there wasn't a Scripting Additions folder available for the network domain when I ran the script.)

The following example uses the different domains to collect a list of all the scripting additions installed on OS X:

```
set addition_names_list to {}
tell application "System Events"
    set os_x_domains to every domain whose name is not "Classic"
    repeat with domain_ref in os_x_domains
        set addition_names_list to addition_names_list & ¬
            (name of every file of scripting additions folder of domain_ref ¬
                whose name extension is "app" or name extension is "osax")
    end repeat
end tell
return addition_names_list
```

Using the login item Class

Remember the good ol' OS 9 times, when all you had to do was pop an alias of a file in the start-up disk's folder and it would launch when the system started?

Script 15-2 will prompt the user to pick an application and will create a login item for that app, which means the application will start by itself when that user logs in. (Remember, in Unix land you don't *start*, you *log in*. Also, OS X may log you in automatically each time it starts up, depending on your settings in System Preferences' Accounts pane.)

Script 15-2.

```
set the_app to choose application with prompt ¬
    "Choose application to startup automatically" as alias
set app_POSIX_path to POSIX path of the_app
tell application "System Events"
    make new login item at end with properties ¬
        {path:app_POSIX_path}
end tell
```

Now, after users have lots of fun with your script, they will have a surplus of unwanted login items. Script 15-3 will allow them to choose a login item from a list and delete it.

Script 15-3.

```
tell application "System Events"
    set login_item_names_list to name of every login item
    set the_selection to ¬
        choose from list login_item_names_list OK button name "Delete"
    if the_selection is not false then
        set selected_name to item 1 of the_selection
        delete login item selected_name
    end if
end tell
```

Your homework is to allow the user to delete multiple login items at a time and warn the user before deleting ("Are you sure?").

What Can You Do to Finder Items?

In the following sections, you will focus not on all the things you can do with the Finder application but rather all the things you can do with and to Finder items. Since the System Events commands are so similar to the Finder's commands, the following sections will concentrate on the Finder.

Using the open and close Commands

The open command can open any Finder item that you can open from the Finder. It acts as if you double-clicked the item. If you use the open command on a disk or folder, the disk/folder will open as a new Finder window. For example, this will open the current user's Home folder:

```
tell application "Finder" to open home
```

If you use it to open a file, the Finder will normally tell the file's default application to open it:

```
tell application "Finder"
    open file "index.html" of folder "Sites" of home
end tell
```

You can specify a different application with the open command's optional using parameter:

```
tell application "Finder"
    set textedit to file "TextEdit" of folder "Applications" of startup disk
    open file "index.html" of folder "Sites" of home using textedit
end tell
```

You can determine ahead of time which application will open a file by default. You do that by asking for the default application property found in the info for command's reply record.

This is one way to do it:

```
default application of (info for (choose file))
```

The close command works only on disks and folders, closing their windows if they're already open.

Using the duplicate Command

The Finder's duplicate command copies files and folders.

In its simplest form the duplicate command takes a single value as its direct parameter: a reference to one or more items to copy. For example:

```
tell application "Finder" to duplicate file "ReadMe.txt" of desktop
```

This has the same result as selecting Duplicate in the Finder's File menu: creating a copy of the file in the same folder as the original.

The duplicate command, along with other commands such as move and delete, can also accept an alias, or a list of aliases, as its direct parameter. This is handy when you already have a list of alias values obtained from somewhere else, because you don't need to convert them to Finder references before passing them to the command.

The other way you can use the duplicate command is to copy items from one folder to another. To do this, you have to specify a reference to the Finder items you want to duplicate and a reference to the container you want to duplicate them to:

```
tell application "Finder"
  duplicate every file of desktop to disk "Backup Disk"
end tell
```

The most useful feature, however, is being able to decide what to do if an item by that name already exists in the container you duplicate to. By default, the Finder will raise an error: "An item with the same name already exists in the destination." You can make it replace any existing items automatically by making the optional `replacing` parameter `true`:

```
duplicate file the_file_path to folder the_folder_path replacing true
```

One last thing . . . AppleScript allows you to write this:

```
tell application "Finder"
  copy the_items to folder "Documents" of home
end tell
```

as another way of saying this:

```
tell application "Finder"
  duplicate the_items to folder "Documents" of home
end tell
```

Be careful, though: using `copy items to container` in place of the normal `duplicate items to container` command works only if `container` is a literal Finder reference as shown previously. If it's a variable, AppleScript will get the referenced items and assign the result to the variable instead!

For example, this will duplicate the items to the user's `Documents` folder:

```
tell application "Finder"
  set destination_folder to folder "Documents" of home
  duplicate the_items to destination_folder
end tell
```

but this will assign the items to the variable `destination_folder` instead:

```
tell application "Finder"
  set destination_folder to folder "Documents" of home
  copy the_items to destination_folder
end tell
```

You can avoid any confusion by always using the `duplicate` command for duplicating application objects.

Using the delete Command

The `delete` command in the Finder's dictionary doesn't actually delete anything; it just moves the referenced Finder item to the trash. The following:

```
tell application "Finder" to delete file the_file_path
```

is identical to this:

```
tell application "Finder" to move file the_file_path to the trash
```

As with the `duplicate` command, the `delete` command can accept a reference identifying multiple items. For example, to delete all the labeled files on the desktop with help from the Finder's powerful `whose` clause, you can use this:

```
tell application "Finder"
  delete every file of desktop whose label index is not 0
end tell
```

You can also empty the trash by simply using the empty command:

```
tell application "Finder" to empty trash
```

or just this:

```
tell application "Finder" to empty
```

Using the move Command

Moving files works just like dragging files in the Finder: you have the file or folder you want to move and the folder or disk to which you're moving it. You can also specify whether you want to replace an existing item with the same name using the optional Boolean replacing parameter, as shown in Script 15-4.

Script 15-4. *(includes the following script)*

```
tell application "Finder" to move file the_file_path to container the_folder_path
```

or

```
tell application "Finder"
   try
      move file 1 of folder source_folder to folder dest_folder without replacing
   on error number error_number
      if error_number is -15267 then
         display dialog Can't replace the file, replace the scripter instead..."
      else
         display dialog "An error occurred: " & error_number
      end if
   end try
end tell
```

The preceding example asked the Finder not to replace the items if it encounters items with identical names in the destination container. (The default value for the replacing parameter is already false, but I've put it in anyway for emphasis.) This forces you to place the move command in a try block to capture the error. The preceding example also captured the error that the failed move generated and acted on it. If files already exist, the Finder will generate error number –15267.

Using the exists Command

The exists command is one of my favorites. It takes one parameter, a reference to the item whose existence is in question, and returns a Boolean: true if the item exists or false if it doesn't:

```
tell application "Finder"
   exists file "I am here!" of the desktop
end tell
```

By the way, a neat trick of AppleScript's is that it lets you put the exists keyword *after* the reference if you prefer, making the code read more like English:

```
tell application "Finder"
   file "I am here!" of the desktop exists
end tell
```

The fun thing about this ability to contemplate the existence of files is that because of the clean Boolean result, you can incorporate the command directly into statements that call for a Boolean value, such as if statements:

```
if exists the_file then delete the_file
```

Using the make Command

The make command allows you to create Finder items such as files, folders, and Finder windows, although most places where the make command is used, it is used to create folders.

The Finder's make command has one required parameter, new, which is the class of the object you want to create. The optional parameters are as follows:

- at, which is a reference to the folder or disk where a new file or folder should be created

- to, which is used when creating new alias files and Finder windows

- with properties, which allows you to supply initial values for many of the new object's properties instead of leaving the Finder to use its own default values

The following script creates a new folder on the desktop. The script will use the with properties parameter to name the folder My Files and assign a comment to it:

```
tell application "Finder"
    activate
    make new folder at desktop with properties ¬
        {name:"My Files", comment:"Place to put stuff"}
end tell
```

You can also use the make command to create blank text files and alias files. For example, to create an empty file on the desktop, you can do this:

```
tell application "Finder"
    make new document file at desktop with properties ¬
        {name:"My File", comment:"Place to put thoughts"}
end tell
```

When making an alias file, you specify the original item that it should point to using the to parameter:

```
tell application "Finder"
    set original_item to folder "Documents" of home
    make new alias file at desktop to original_item
end tell
```

The following script creates a new window in the Finder that displays the contents of the start-up disk. You can specify the disk or folder the window should show using the optional to parameter:

```
tell application "Finder"
    activate
    make new Finder window to startup disk
end tell
```

Using the sort Command

The Finder's sort command, available in Mac OS X 10.4 and later, sorts a list of Finder items by a particular property, such as name, creation date, size, and so on. The following example sorts a list of folders by name and by creation date:

```
tell application "Finder"
    set folder_list to folders of startup disk
    set folder_list_by_name to sort folder_list by name
    set folder_list_by_date to sort folder_list by creation date
end tell
```

One word of caution: although most Finder commands can understand a single reference that identifies multiple objects—for example, `every folder of home` or `every file of desktop whose label is 1`—the sort command can work only with a list of single-item references. For instance, the sort command in the following script will generate an error:

```
tell application "Finder" to ¬
  set folder_list to sort (folders of startup disk) by name
```

To solve this problem, you need to ask the Finder to resolve the multi-item reference `folders of startup disk` first, such as by inserting an explicit get command. You can then pass the resulting list of single-item references to the sort command, and it will run fine:

```
tell application "Finder" to ¬
  set folder_list to sort (get folders of startup disk) by name
```

Using the eject Command

The eject command takes a disk reference as the parameter and ejects that disk:

```
tell application "Finder" to eject disk "Removable 4000"
```

The following script will use the `ejectable` property of a disk object to eject only the disks that can be ejected:

```
tell application "Finder"
    eject (every disk whose ejectable is true)
end tell
```

Managing Files in Windows

A few commands control how files are displayed in a Finder window but don't really do anything to them. For instance, selecting a file or sorting the contents of a window doesn't change any files or folders, only how they appear in the window.

The select and reveal commands work similarly in the Finder. They both select a Finder item in the Finder window. If the disk or folder containing the item is closed, both commands will open it as a new window but do it slightly differently.

The select command will open the container to a window using the last viewing style (icon, outline, or browser). If the reveal command has to open a window to reveal the item, it will use the default browser viewing style:

```
tell application "Finder"
    select every folder of home
end tell
```

Revealing files and folders in Finder windows can come in handy. In the interface of any system or script dealing with files, it is a pleasant surprise for the user to have a button that reveals a related file or folder in the Finder—that is, of course, unless the intention of your script is to keep these users *out* of the file system . . . .

Getting the Contents of Folders

AppleScript gives you several ways to get a list containing the items in a particular folder. The two routes you can take are using the list folder command in Standard Additions or using the Finder. Each way has its advantages.

Using the list folder Command

list folder is a command defined in the Standard Additions dictionary. The list folder command returns a list containing the names of the files and folders in the container (either folder or disk) you specify:

```
list folder (path to startup disk)
--> {".DS_Store", ".hidden", ".hotfiles.btree", ".Trashes", ".vol", ¬
"Active accounts", "Applications", "automount", "bin", "client jobs",¬
"cores", "Desktop", "Desktop (Mac OS 9)", "Desktop DB", "Desktop DF",¬
"Desktop Folder", "Developer", "Games", "jobs", "Library", "mach",¬
"mach.sym", "mach_kernel", "Network", "obj", "Previous Systems",¬
"private", "sbin", "System", "TheFindByContentFolder",¬
 "TheVolumeSettingsFolder", "tmp", "Trash",¬
"User Guides and Information", "Users", "usr", "var", "Volumes"}
```

Oh no, what's all that stuff?! Do I really have all this junk right on my hard drive? Yes, I do. Luckily, most of these files are invisibles. In case I don't want to have them listed, I can omit the invisible files by making the invisibles parameter false:

```
list folder (path to startup disk) without invisibles
--Result:
{"Applications", "Developer", "Installer Log File"¬
, "Library", "mach", "mach.sym", "System", "Users"}
```

OK, this time I got less junk and a list I can actually use.

Using the Finder to Get the Content of Folders

Although list folder is great because you don't need any application to use it, the Finder offers a much more powerful solution. Using the whose clause, you can filter out just the set of files you want to work with.

Let's look at a few examples of using the Finder to filter files in different folders. The following script will list all files in a chosen folder that have not been modified in the last ten weeks and that have no label attached to them:

```
set the_folder to choose folder
tell application "Finder"
   get every file of the_folder whose ¬
      (modification date < ((current date) - (10 * weeks)) and label index = 0)
end tell
```

Notice how in the preceding script you can use a single command to look for files (not folders) that are of a certain age and label.

In Script 15-5, you will look for files that are larger than 10MB and are not applications. Unlike the last script, this script will use a recursive subroutine to search through all the subfolders as well, starting from the folder selected by the user.

Script 15-5.

```
1. set the_folder to choose folder
2. set mb_limit to 10
3. set byte_limit to mb_limit * 1024 * 1024
4. set list_of_large_files to get_large_files(the_folder, byte_limit)

5. on get_large_files(the_folder, minimum_size_in_bytes)
6.     tell application "Finder"
7.         --Find all the matching files in this folder
8.         set found_files_list to every file of the_folder ¬
              whose size ≥ minimum_size_in_bytes and class is not application file
9.         --Process each sub-folder in turn
10.        set sub_folders_list to every folder of the_folder
11.        repeat with sub_folder_ref in sub_folders_list
12.            set found_files_list to found_files_list & ¬
                  my get_large_files(sub_folder_ref, minimum_size_in_bytes)
13.        end repeat
14.    end tell
15.    return found_files_list
16. end get_large_files
```

The get_large_files handler appears on lines 5 through 16 of the script. The handler starts by asking the Finder for a list of references to all the applicable files in the current folder. That happens on line 8. After that, you get all the subfolders in the current folder so you can search through them as well. The loop on lines 11 to 13 takes each subfolder in this list and recursively calls the get_large_files handler to search through that folder—and any subfolders it has—and return a list of all the files it finds there.

What makes this script so fast and simple is the Finder's incredible ability to filter the right kind of files with the whose clause on line 8. If the Finder didn't have this built-in filtering support, you'd have to loop through each file in the folder to check them yourself, which would make the code more complex and run much more slowly as well.

Getting the Entire Contents

Another useful property defined by the container class in the Finder is the entire contents property. You can use the entire contents property to get a reference to every file and folder contained in a disk or folder and all of its nested folders as well.

Here is something *not* to try:

```
tell application "Finder"
    get entire contents of (path to library folder from system domain)
end tell
```

This would, at least in theory, give you a list of every file and folder in /System/Library, which contains way more than 100,000 items. In reality, you'll find that using entire contents to search through hundreds or thousands of folders like this takes far too long to be practical.

When dealing with a much smaller folder structure, however, the entire contents property can come in handy. For example, you can use it to quickly look for all the files with a particular name extension by combining it with the whose clause:

```
set the_folder to choose folder "Choose the folder to search:"
display dialog "Enter the file name extension to match:" default answer "mp3"
set desired_name_extension to text returned of result
tell application "Finder"
    get every file of entire contents of the_folder ¬
        whose name extension is desired_name_extension
end tell
```

Listing Disks

On a related topic, you can use the Standard Additions' list disks command to get a list of all your mounted disks. For example:

```
list disks --> {"Macintosh HD", "Network"}
```

Referring to Packages' Contents

Packages, also referred to as *bundles*, are a funny breed of file. In a Finder window, they look like files. However, to the system, they're not much more than a folder with more folders and files inside of it. The most common form that packages take is Cocoa applications, although many Carbon applications are also built as packages. The package format is also used by some kinds of files, such as TextEdit's .rtfd format and Script Editor's .scptd format. The folders and files inside the package make up the different components of the application or file.

Although the Finder's dictionary does define a package class, the Finder normally identifies package-based files as application files, document files, and so on. You can refer to a disk or folder's package elements, though, when you want to get a list of all the files that are really packages. For example:

```
tell application "Finder"
    get every package of folder "Applications" of startup disk
end tell
```

In the System Events dictionary, however, packages are represented by the file package class, which is a subclass of System Events' file class.

Dealing with the files and folders within packages becomes especially important when you work with your own AppleScript Studio applications. There you need to refer to the package from inside the Studio application itself, which you can do by using Studio's main bundle property and bundle class. Studio also provides several commands for loading common resources such as images, sounds, and so on, directly.

When dealing with packages from the outside, however, all you need to do is add a colon to the end of the package's path name and then add the rest of the path of the enclosed file or folder you want to work with.

You know that an application or other file is a package when you Ctrl-click it. If one of the menu items is Show Package Contents, as shown in Figure 15-5, then you know it's a package-based file you're dealing with, and you can open it and look around.

Figure 15-5. *The Show Package Contents menu item*

Figure 15-6 shows the package contents of the application Safari.

Figure 15-6. *The open package of the application Safari*

So, to refer to a file inside the package, you may have to do a couple of things. First, you will have to check whether the application has the .app filename extension. This extension has to be added to the path name.

After that, you have to add the colon, followed by the rest of the path. Packages always start with a single folder called Contents. Inside that there are usually additional folders; for example, Cocoa applications have a couple of folders called MacOS and Resources and sometimes others as well. Open them, and double-click some files. You will be surprised how much of your system you can mess up in a short period of time!

The following script gets an alias to a TIFF file in the Resources folder in the Safari package:

```
set safari_bundle to alias "Macintosh HD:Applications:Safari.app:"
set resource_path to (safari_bundle as string) & ¬
    "Contents:Resources:Autofill.tif"
set resource_file to resource_path as alias
--> alias "Macintosh HD:Applications:Safari.app:Contents:Resources:Autofill.tif"
```

If you're using Mac OS X 10.4 or later, you can also use Standard Additions' new path to resource command to locate files within a bundle by name:

```
set bundle_file to alias "Macintosh HD:Applications:Safari.app:"
set resource_file to path to resource "Autofill.tif" in bundle bundle_file
--> alias "Macintosh HD:Applications:Safari.app:Contents:Resources:Autofill.tif"
```

Mounting Volumes

You can mount volumes from servers, remote computers, or iDisks with the mount volume command. That command is defined in the File Commands suite of the Standard Additions.

You have two ways to specify the volume to mount. The first way is to supply the volume's name as the direct parameter to the mount volume command, followed by the name of the server as its on server parameter. For example:

```
mount volume "Macintosh HD" on server "OfficeMac.local"
```

The other way is to supply a URL string as the direct parameter and omit the on server parameter:

```
mount volume "afp://OfficeMac.local/Macintosh%20HD"
```

The URL string describes the server address and the protocol used to connect to the server such as Server Message Block (SMB) or Apple File Protocol (AFP).

■**Note** SMB and AFP are protocols for sharing files and printers across a network. SMB is normally used with Windows and AFP with Macs, although Mac OS X supports both. Your Mac's built-in Help file contains more information if you need it; just select Help ➤ Mac Help in the Finder and search for *connecting to servers*.

As well as the server name, you can provide several other pieces of information if you want: the name of the volume to mount, a username, and/or a password. You'll look at these shortly.

From the Dictionary: mount volume

Here's the mount volume command the way it appears in the dictionary:

```
mount volume: Mount the specified AppleShare volume
mount volume string
        -- the name or URL path (starting with 'afp://') of the volume to mount
        on server string -- the server on which the volume resides
        [in AppleTalk zone string]
            -- the AppleTalk zone in which the server resides
        [as user name string]
            -- the user name with which to log in to the server;
               omit for guest access
        [with password string]
            -- the password for the user name; omit for guest access
```

Using the mount volume Command

The basic command looks like this:

```
mount volume "afp://serverNameOrIPAddress"
```

Here are a couple of examples, one using a Bonjour name and the other using an IP address:

```
mount volume "afp://Jean-Grays-Macintosh.local"
mount volume "afp://192.168.200.2"
```

After running this command, the user will be shown a Connect to Server dialog box, allowing them either to connect as a guest user or to enter a username and password and connect as a registered user.

Note That same Connect to Server dialog box allows the user to add the server to the keychain. Adding the server login information to the keychain should not be taken lightly because it will make access to the server much easier from the computer the script ran on. However, if you don't want to have to enter the same login details each time the script is run, then storing this information in the keychain is still *far* more secure than hard-coding them in your script, which isn't secure at all (not even if the script is saved as run-only). Adding the login information to the keychain can cause other issues, as explained later in the "Mounting Volumes and the Keychain Feature" section.

If you want, you can supply the name of the specific volume to mount. This might be the name of a mounted disk or a particular user account:

```
mount volume "afp://Jean-Grays-Macintosh.local/Macintosh%20HD"
mount volume "afp://OfficeMac.local/jsmith"
```

If the URL doesn't include a volume name, Mac OS will list all the available volumes for the user to choose from.

You can also supply login information directly to the command in one of two ways. You can either include the username and/or password in the URL itself or use the command's as user name and with password parameters.

The following two script lines will work the same. The first includes the login information in the URL, and the second one uses parameters:

```
mount volume "afp://username:my_password@serverNameOrIpAddress"
```

```
mount volume "afp://serverNameOrIpAddress" ¬
    as user name "username" with password "my_password"
```

Or you can just supply the username by itself and leave the user to type the password into the Connect to Server dialog box.

You can also use other protocols instead of AFP, such as SMB. The protocol you use depends on the server setup.

For example, you can use the following subroutine as a general subroutine for mounting server volumes:

```
on mountVolume(userName, pswd, serverIP, volumeName)
    set serverString to ¬
        "afp://" & userName & ":" & pswd & "@" & ¬
        serverIP & "/" & volumeName
    mount volume serverString
end mountVolume
```

When using this mountVolume subroutine, it's useful to note that Standard Additions' mount volume command is pretty relaxed about URL encoding issues. For example, a volume name such as Macintosh HD should really be encoded as Macintosh%20HD, but in practice the unencoded version seems to work OK too. However, if any of your mountVolume parameters contain special URL characters such as forward slashes, you will need to encode these first, or it won't work as intended.

Mounting Volumes and the Keychain Feature

One of the issues that may cause problems when trying to access volumes with the mount volume command is the keychain. If the volume information is already entered into a keychain but the password has changed, you may get an error. It has been reported that this situation happens when the login information is embedded in the URL. Manually deleting the keychain entry from the keychain can solve this problem.

Faking Volumes with Disk Utility

One of the challenges you'll encounter when working on client scripts from your home office (another way to describe working from bed while watching football . . .) is tapping into the company's servers. Servers are often referred to in scripts but are guarded behind firewalls and are inaccessible from your home.

To get around this problem, I use a mirror of the server I create using a disk image. A mounted disk image will appear to AppleScript as if it were any other mounted server on the system. Since it would be unreasonable to replicate the entire folder structure of the server, you would want to copy only the parts that your script will use.

To replicate a server on your hard disk, you start by creating an empty disk image the size you need. Start the Disk Utility application in /Applications/Utilities. (OS X 10.2 users should use the Disk Copy application instead.) Then click the New Image icon in the toolbar, or choose New Blank Image from the Image menu. This will open a dialog box similar to the one shown in Figure 15-7.

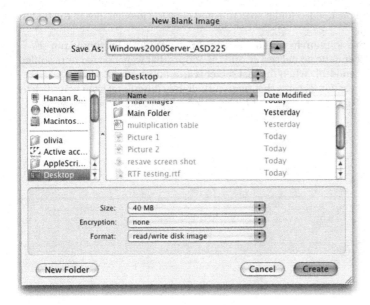

Figure 15-7. *The New Blank Image dialog box*

In the Save As field, type the name of the server you're replicating. From the dialog box choices at the bottom, choose a size that is going to be sufficient for the files you will be testing in your scripts. I usually use 100MB, but if you're working with large images, you'll need more. Just remember that the size of the disk image will be the size that you choose, so choosing 2GB will make the disk image huge. Also, choose read/write format.

After you click Create, the disk image will be created and also mounted on your system, as shown in Figure 15-8.

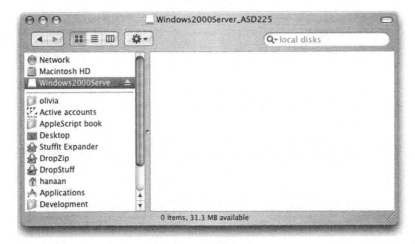

Figure 15-8. *The new mounted disk image*

In the mounted disk, create the needed folder structure and copy the needed files to the folders in the folder tree you've created.

Although you should test this solution in your own environment, AppleScript should not see the difference between that disk and the actual server, and the scripts that were created or modified using the fake disk should work smoothly when the real server is around.

You do have to watch, however, for features that may work slightly differently from your disk to the server, such as the sorting of files, the script's ability to delete files from the server, the availability of file labels, and so on.

CHAPTER 16

■ ■ ■

Working with the Clipboard

In this chapter, we will focus on scripting clipboard operations such as copying and pasting between applications and manipulating data residing in the clipboard. As you will see, you can get values in and out of the clipboard in a few ways, and the clipboard can move information that can't be handled as an AppleScript value.

Getting the Clipboard Data to AppleScript

The Standard Additions command the clipboard will return the contents of the clipboard. The class of the result of the the clipboard command depends on what sort of data was copied, however.

For example, if you copy some text from a TextEdit document, the clipboard will return a string of some sort:

```
the clipboard
--> "Some text from TextEdit."
```

If you get the class of this returned value, you'll see that it's Unicode text:

```
the clipboard
class of result
--> Unicode text
```

The the clipboard command also has an optional parameter, as. To understand how to use this parameter, you first need to look at how the Mac clipboard actually works.

Understanding How the Mac Clipboard Works

The Mac clipboard is a clever piece of software; it's simple to use but surprisingly sophisticated beneath the surface.

When a user copies some data from an application, the clipboard has no idea what kind of application the user is going to paste that data into next. To provide as much flexibility as possible when copying and pasting between applications, the clipboard doesn't just get the data in the native format used by that application; it gets it in as many different formats as the application can provide. This gives the clipboard a sort of "backup plan" when pasting the data into other applications. Less sophisticated formats may not contain as much of the original data as the native format, but they are likely to be understood by a greater number of applications—and something is better than nothing.

For example, when you copy text from a rich-text document in TextEdit, the Mac clipboard obtains this text in as many formats as it can, from the basic (string) to the richest (RTF).

It does this so that when you paste this text into another application, the receiving application can pick whichever format is best for it. For example, Microsoft Word can understand RTF data, so it will ask the clipboard for this because RTF contains not only character data but also lots of valuable style information that Word can put to good use. An application such as Terminal would take the UTF 8–encoded character data, since that's the richest format it can understand and use. An elderly, Carbon-based, plain-text editor that doesn't support Unicode text would make do with the basic string data.

Finding Out What's on the Clipboard

The `clipboard info` command returns some information about the contents of the clipboard, as shown in the following example:

```
set the clipboard to "Paste me!"
clipboard info
--> {{string, 9}}
```

The result shows that the clipboard contains a string of 9 bytes. Next, here's an example of the clipboard information after copying text from TextEdit:

```
clipboard info
--> {{Unicode text, 1142}, {scrap styles, 62}, {string, 571}, ➡
{uniform styles, 564}, {«class ut16», 1144}, {«class utf8», 575}, ➡
{«class RTF», 914}}
```

The result is a list containing all the formats TextEdit used to place the same data on the clipboard. It shows that the basic character information is available in any of four formats: `string` and three Unicode encodings (`Unicode text`, `«class ut16»`, and `«class utf8»`). Also, some separate style information is available (`scrap styles` and `uniform styles`) for applications that know how to combine this with one of the previous character-only formats. Finally, the data is available in RTF (`«class RTF»`), which combines both character and style information in a single format.

Getting Specific Types of Data from the Clipboard

Although the `the clipboard` command tries to return clipboard data in a format AppleScript can use, sometimes you want to retrieve data in one of the other available formats. You can specify which of the available formats you want by using the optional `as` parameter. For example, if RTF data is available, you might want to retrieve it so you can write it to a file:

```
set rtf_data to the clipboard as «class RTF»
set the_file to choose file name default name "untitled.rtf"
set file_ID to open for access the_file with write permission
write rtf_data to file_ID
close access file_ID
```

Setting the Clipboard Data

AppleScript and other applications allow you to set the content of the clipboard in a few ways.

Using the Cut, Copy, and Paste Commands in Applications

Some applications define `cut`, `copy`, and `paste` commands that perform the same operations as the standard Cut, Copy, and Paste menu options in their Edit menus. For example, the `copy` command (not to be confused with AppleScript's own copy...to... statement) will copy the application's current selection to the clipboard. The following example copies the selection in the front Photoshop document and pastes it:

```
tell application "Adobe Photoshop CS2"
    activate
    copy
    paste
end tell
```

Notice that the first command is activate. Clipboard-related operations require that the application you copy from or paste to is the frontmost application.

Other applications define their own version of the copy and paste commands. The following example copies the current selection in the front document in Word 2004 to the clipboard. The command in Word is copy object, and the direct parameter is selection:

```
tell application "Microsoft Word"
    copy object selection
end tell
```

Script 16-1 shows how to convert an RGB Adobe Illustrator document to a CMYK document. It does this by copying all the artwork from the current document (which is presumably RGB) and pasting it into a newly created CMYK document.

Script 16-1.

```
tell application "Illustrator CS"
    set selected of every page item of document 1 to true
    activate
    copy
    make new document with properties {color space:CMYK}
    paste
end tell
```

Note that in the preceding example, the script is responsible for two critical tasks: the first, on line 2, is selecting the items that need to be copied, and the second, on line 3, is activating the Illustrator application. The copy command works on the application only if it is the frontmost process.

Using the set clipboard Command

Use the set the clipboard to command to set the contents of the clipboard to a string or other value:

```
set the clipboard to "Paste me!"
```

The following script sets the clipboard to the short version of the date:

```
set the_date_string to short date string of (current date)
set the clipboard to the_date_string
```

Using GUI Scripting

You can usually copy selections from any application by using GUI scripting to manipulate the application's Edit menu directly. The example in the "Saving Clipboard Data to a PDF File" section shows how you can do this.

Saving Clipboard Data to a PDF File

Script 16-2 shows an ultracool script in regard to utilizing PDF data in the clipboard. It takes a selection you make with the marquee tool (Tools ➤ Select Tool) in a PDF document within the application Preview and saves it to a file you specify.

Note Since this script uses GUI scripting, to make it work you must go to the Universal Access tab in System Preferences and turn on Enable Access for Assistive Devices. Chapter 20 covers GUI scripting in detail.

Script 16-2.

```
1. --Use GUI Scripting to click on Edit -> Copy in Preview's menu bar
2. tell application "Preview" to activate
3. tell application "System Events"
4.    tell application process "Preview"
5.       click menu item "Copy" of menu "Edit" of ¬
             menu bar item "Edit" of menu bar 1
6.    end tell
7. end tell

8. --Get the PDF data from the clipboard
9. delay 1
10. activate
11. try
12.    set pdf_data to the clipboard as «class PDF»
13. on error number -1700 --the clipboard doesn't contain any PDF data
14.    display dialog "Make a marquee selection in a PDF document in Preview" & ¬
             " and try again." buttons {"OK"} default button 1 with icon stop
15.    return
16. end try

17. --Write the PDF data to file
18. set destination_file to choose file name default name "Selection.pdf"
19. set file_ID to open for access destination_file with write permission
10. set eof file_ID to 0
21. write pdf_data to file_ID as «class PDF »
22. close access file_ID
23. tell application "Finder"
24.    set file type of file destination_file to "PDF "
25. end tell

26. --Preview the new file
27. tell application "Preview" to open destination_file
```

The highlights of the script are as follows. Because Preview isn't yet scriptable, you have to use GUI scripting to trigger its Edit ➤ Copy menu item directly. Line 2 brings the Preview application to the front so that its GUI interface is active. Lines 3 to 8 use System Events' GUI scripting support to "click" Preview's Copy menu item. To keep this example simple, the script will assume that the user has remembered to open a file and make a marquee selection in it before running it. Preview's lack of proper scripting support would make this difficult to check automatically anyway.

Line 9 makes the script wait for a second before continuing. Without it, I found that the the `clipboard` command would sometimes raise an error, as if it didn't have time to catch up with the recent change to the clipboard. It's not an elegant or foolproof way to make the script behave (it's what experienced scripters would call a *kludge*), but it seems to do the trick here.

The `activate` command on line 10 returns the current application to the front before using the the `clipboard` command.

In line 12 you use the the `clipboard` command to get the raw PDF data («`class PDF`») from the clipboard. If the clipboard doesn't contain any PDF data—perhaps the user selected part of a JPEG file, not a PDF file like they're supposed to do—the command will raise an error, number –1700, instead. If that happens, the surrounding `try` block will catch this error, tell the user there's a problem, and stop the script from going any further.

Lines 18 to 25 create a new PDF file on disk. Line 18 asks the user to choose the name and location for the new PDF file, and lines 19 to 22 write the raw PDF data to this file using the commands in Standard Additions' File Read/Write suite. (These are discussed in detail in Chapter 14 if you need to refresh your memory.) Lines 23 to 25 use the Finder to set the new file's file type to `PDF`. This bit isn't absolutely essential—as long as the file's name includes a `.pdf` extension, then OS X will know it's a PDF file. However, if the user forgets to add a `.pdf` extension when choosing a new filename, the OS can still work out that it's a PDF file by looking at this code.

Finally, on line 26 you tell Preview to open the new file so the user can look at it. Even though Preview isn't scriptable, it can understand the basic `run`, `activate`, `open`, and `quit` commands that all Mac applications should understand.

TESTING TIP

When testing this script, you can insert the following temporary line after line 9 to check what types of data have just been put on the clipboard:

```
return clipboard info
```

The value in Script Editor's Result area will probably look something like this:

```
{{picture, 33546}, {TIFF picture, 29542}, {«class PDF », 59627}}
```

Notice how the clipboard contains PICT and TIFF versions of the copied data, as well as the obvious PDF version, so that other applications will have a range of formats from which to choose. For example, a bitmap graphics editor probably won't understand PDF data, but it can use TIFF or PICT data just fine. What you're interested in, though, is the PDF data, which is indicated by the «`class PDF`» entry. If you don't see «`class PDF`» in the list, it's probably because the front document in Preview isn't a PDF, so you'll need to open one that is. Once you're finished testing this part of the script, remember to delete or comment out this temporary line so that the rest of the script can execute.

Using Errors to Your Advantage

AppleScript has a few types of errors: bugs that prevent scripts from compiling; bugs that cause scripts to work incorrectly when run, either failing completely or not doing what you wanted; and errors triggered by external factors that you've deliberately designed your scripts to handle.

Since compile errors are easy to discover and usually easy enough to fix, this chapter will concentrate mainly on runtime errors.

Understanding Compile Errors

Compile errors are errors that prevent the script from compiling. The bad news is that they happen a lot when you start to script simply because the syntax is still foreign to you. Later, you still get them when your syntax is correct but some literal expression you used didn't work. The good news is that a compile error is a bit like losing your car keys down the drain. It's irritating, but at least it can't be made worse by someone driving away in your car . . . .

Let's look at a few common mistakes that will result in the code not compiling.

Encountering Simple Typos

The following script will not compile because of simple typing errors. There's no space between the to and the 10 in line 1; AppleScript expects the word to but instead it gets what it would consider to be a variable. On line 2, the command display dialog is misspelled.

```
repeat with i from 1 to10
   disply dialog i
end
```

Encountering Unbalanced Statements

One potentially irritating mistake you can make is not balancing your block statements, like in the following example:

```
repeat with i from 1 to 20
   if i > 10 then
      display dialog "Second half"
end repeat
```

Although the previous problem is easy to spot, block statements such as if, try, tell, and repeat can sometimes span across tens or maybe hundreds of lines in your script. Detecting where the missing end should be can be a challenge.

Encountering Unbalanced Parentheses and Unescaped Quotes

When forming complex expressions containing multiple sets of parentheses, you are bound to omit or include extra parentheses on either side of the expression. Another related, common mistake is using quotes in a string but not escaping them properly. Look at the following script:

```
if ((x < 0) or (x > 10) then display dialog "The "x" variable is out of range."
```

In this example, the expression ((x < 0) or (x > 10) is missing a closing parenthesis, and the string literal provided for the display dialog command contains unescaped quotes. Here's the fixed script:

```
if ((x < 0) or (x > 10)) then display dialog "The \"x\" variable is out of range."
```

Encountering Unrecognized Keywords

It is common to use keywords from applications outside the application tell block. The following line will not compile since the element names track and playlist aren't ones defined by AppleScript. They are defined by Apple iTunes, though, which is presumably what they're meant for.

```
get every track of playlist 1
```

To fix this problem, wrap the line in a tell application block, like this:

```
tell application "iTunes"
    get every track of playlist 1
end tell
```

FOLDER VS. TELL APPLICATION

A less obvious, noncompiling example is as follows:

```
folder "Applications"
```

If you compile the word folder by itself, you'll see it gets formatted as an application keyword. When you try to compile folder "Applications", though, you get an error. Why?

It compiles as an application keyword the first time because Standard Additions adds its own keyword definition for folder to AppleScript. However, AppleScript defines folder as a property name (see the file information record defined by the File Commands suite), not a class name, and an object specifier like folder "Applications" needs to start with a class name. But stick it inside a tell application Finder/System Events block, and it'll compile correctly, since both those apps define folder classes.

Encountering Reserved Word Mishaps

Using reserved words in ways that aren't allowed will cause the script not to compile. One common mistake is trying to use a class name as a variable name:

```
set list to {1, 2, 3, 4, 5}
```

Scripting additions may reserve words in addition to the ones reserved by AppleScript. To easily avoid collision with reserved words, stick to using camel case or underscore-separated multi-word variables.

Encountering Invalid Date and Alias Literals

Since the way date literals are compiled depends on the date format set on the Mac you're using, some dates may compile incorrectly or not compile at all. For instance, the date literal "3/14/2006" will compile as March 14th, 2006, using the default settings of a U.S. Mac system, but it won't compile on a European system.

More common yet, alias literals require that the file you point to actually exists. For instance, the following script won't compile if no folder named Letters exists on a mounted volume named Backup:

```
alias "Backup:Letters:"
```

Understanding How Runtime Errors Work in AppleScript

Runtime errors in AppleScript aren't all-out unanticipated mistakes that can't be recovered from. Rather, runtime errors are designed to let you know that the data provided for a certain statement to chew on doesn't fit and that AppleScript's next resort is to throw an error and terminate the script. Errors are the way out when the result of a statement isn't in the range of acceptable possibilities.

You have two categories of runtime errors to consider: those that should be anticipated (which are caused by external factors) and those that should be fixed. To understand the difference, you'll see a simple script that will look at a set of files in a folder and extract the first six characters of each file's name. Here's the first attempt:

```
tell application "Finder"
    set file_list to name of every file in (path to documents folder)
    repeat with the_file in file_list
        set the_code to text 1 thru 6 of name of the_file
    end repeat
end tell
```

Say you write the script, and it breaks the first time you run it. The problem is that although the script's syntax is correct, it has a bug that doesn't allow it to run past the fourth line. The bug is that the variable the_file in the repeat loop already has the filename in it, not a pointer to the file. This is a typical programmer's bug that's easy to fix in this case but can sometimes be more difficult to locate.

Once you fix the first problem, as shown here, the script seems to run well:

```
tell application "Finder"
    set file_name_list to name of every file in (path to documents folder)
    repeat with the_file_name in file_name_list
        set the_code to text 1 thru 6 of the_file_name
    end repeat
end tell
```

The script won't produce an error until you encounter a file whose name is shorter than six characters. This condition is a different kind of bug. Instead of being buggy code, it makes an incorrect assumption, namely, that all filenames will be six characters or longer. You can handle this problem rather easily with a simple conditional statement, as shown in lines 4–6 here:

```
tell application "Finder"
    set file_name_list to name of every file in (path to documents folder)
    if length of the_file_name ≥ 6 then
        repeat with the_file_name in file_name_list
            set the_code to text 1 thru 6 of the_file_name
        end repeat
    end if
end tell
```

So, are errors good or bad? Errors are actually good, much like pain is a good thing for our health for one reason, which is that we do our best to avoid it.

So, can you avoid errors altogether? Not really. But although you can't avoid them, you can anticipate them, trap them, analyze them, and sentence them to community service.

Understanding the Psychology of an Error

I've come up with four basic rules you should keep in mind with regard to errors when building scripts:

- As the scripter, you subconsciously avoid doing things that will generate errors, so you should have someone else test your script for you.

- As the scripter, you think you know best how your script will behave. Wrong! Give it to a novice user, and that user will likely provoke unexpected behavior and errors within the first three seconds.

- People don't read instructions. If you think to yourself, "I wrote an instruction in the dialog box telling the user to enter a date, so it's not my fault if they don't," you're wrong; it is your fault. The blame does not lie with what the user entered but with that you didn't anticipate all the different data that could be entered.

- Remember, Murphy's law applies to your scripts: any statement in your script that can generate an error because of user incompetence will generate an error. Furthermore, the error yet again is reflected on you, the AppleScript genius, not on the just-started-yesterday user.

By considering the psychology of both users and yourself, the developer, and by sticking to these four rules, you should be much better equipped to prepare for and fix errors.

Understanding the Anatomy of an Error

Every error that is thrown includes various bits of information that help you identify its cause. The two main values are the error text, which describes what went wrong, and the error number, which indicates what type of error it is and which can be used by the script in deciding what action it should take next.

The other pieces of information that may be available are the partial result and expected type. The *partial result* parameter applies only to commands that return results for multiple objects. In this case, the value is a list that can contain the objects that were handled correctly until one object caused an error. The *expected type* is the type of data the script would have liked to have gotten instead of the offending object.

To understand a bit better, start a script, and type the following:

```
1 + "abc"
```

When you run this script, you'll get the error message "Can't make 'abc' into type number." The error number is –1700, which indicates it's a coercion error. There's no partial result, but you do have an offender. The offending object is the string "abc", and the expected type is number. AppleScript tried to coerce "abc" into a number but couldn't.

Note You'll see how to find out what the error number is in the "Knowing What to Do in Case of an Error" section.

Understanding the two main properties of an error, the number and the message, is important both when you want to trap potential errors and when you conspire to take the offender's role and throw an error yourself! You'll learn more about this in the "Generating Errors" section.

Trapping Errors

How much effort you put into trapping errors really is up to you. You may be writing a script for your own use, or for a limited use, and don't want to turn it into a big production. In this case, you may want to test the script and explain to the user how to write down any error and let you know about it.

On the other hand, if you have to distribute the script among many users—or worse, to unknown users all over the place—you want to take every precaution that no potential error remains untrapped.

In the following sections, I will show how to trap errors.

Using the try Block

The one and only preferred way to trap errors in AppleScript is by using try statement blocks, which start with a line containing a single word, try, and end with a line containing two words, end try. Most try blocks also have an additional line in the middle that starts with on error, but you'll learn more about that in the "Knowing What to Do in Case of an Error" section.

The script that follows shows the basic try block:

```
try
    statement 1
    statement 2
    statement 3...
end try
```

If no errors occur in any of the lines containing statements 1, 2, and 3, then the try block is as much use as life insurance for a vampire. If one of the three statements does throw an error, then subsequent statements from there until the end try statement will be skipped. In fact, every time an error is thrown, AppleScript immediately stops executing the statement where the error occurred and looks to see whether this statement is enclosed by a try statement. In this case, it will find that try statement. If it doesn't find a try statement, then AppleScript has no choice but to air your dirty laundry and let the user know an error has occurred.

If AppleScript does find a try statement, AppleScript looks to see whether the try statement has an on error line. This example doesn't have an on error line, just an end try. This means AppleScript continues to execute the script from the line following the end try line, and you may never know that an error has occurred.

Using the Full try Statement

The following is the official definition of the try statement. Optional parameters appear in square brackets.

```
try
    --statement or statements that may throw an error.
on error [error_message] ¬
        [number error_number] ¬
        [from offending_object] ¬
        [to expected_type] ¬
        [partial result result_list]
    --the statement/s that will execute in case of an error...
end try
```

As you can see in this example, the try statement can be involved. It is usually much simpler, though. Out of all the different parameters, you'll usually need to deal with only the error message and the error number.

Knowing What to Do in Case of an Error

So far you have dealt with the try statement as a simple block with a start and an end. Now, however, you'll learn how to add the on error line in the heart of the try statement. From now on, your try statement block will have two compartments:

```
try
    --compartment 1
on error
    --compartment 2
end try
```

In compartment 1 you'll put all the statements you want to execute under normal operation. In compartment 2 you'll put all the statements you want to execute if anything goes wrong in compartment 1. Here's another way you can put it:

```
try
    light candles on cake
on error
    call fire department
end try
```

Do you usually invite firefighters to birthday parties? I know my wife wouldn't mind—she has a thing for firemen—but they always seem so busy. However, it is a good idea to have a plan to call the firefighters in case something goes wrong with the candles.

One of the most common uses of the on error clause is to trap error number –128, which is the "User canceled" error. The "User canceled" error can occur in various ways; for example, it is normally thrown by the display dialog command when the user clicks the Cancel button. Any other button is simply returned in the dialog reply record; only the Cancel button generates an error. Error –128, however, will not generate an ugly error message to the user. All that'll happen if the Cancel button is clicked is that the script will exit, or if it is saved as an application, the application will quit.

Note For more information about the display dialog command, see Chapter 12.

Script 17-1 shows a simple example of trapping the Cancel button error.

Script 17-1.

```
try
    display dialog "What's next?" buttons {"Cancel", "Go", "Run"}
on error
    display dialog "I'm out of here..." giving up after 5
end try
```

Now this is OK, but what you want to do in many cases is take action only if the error is a specific error. In this case, you want the dialog box displayed only for the "User canceled" error.

For that, you need to know the error number. Just for adventure's sake, let's pretend you don't know exactly what error is thrown or what the error number is. To figure it out, you need to create a little script, make sure that AppleScript throws an error at you, trap it, and analyze it. You do that with the error message and error number values that are returned by the error.

To get the error message, you can add a variable identifier immediately after on error. The error message will be assigned to this variable. Examine Script 17-2.

Script 17-2.

```
try
    display dialog "Do it?"
on error the_error_message
    display dialog "An error occurred. The message was:" & ¬
        return & the_error_message
end try
```

Figure 17-1 shows the message of the second dialog box. It shows that the value of the variable the_error_message you placed after the on error line was "User canceled."

Figure 17-1. *The error message trapped in the variable* the_error_message *is "User canceled."*

To trap the error number, you add the word number before the variable. For now, add the word number as shown in Script 17-3, run the script, and click the Cancel button. Figure 17-2 shows the dialog box displayed as a result of you clicking Cancel. Check out the error number the dialog box revealed. (I also changed the text of that second dialog box, but that shouldn't matter.)

Script 17-3.

```
try
    display dialog "Do it?"
on error number the_error_number
    display dialog "An error occurred. The number is:" & ¬
        return & the_error_number
end try
```

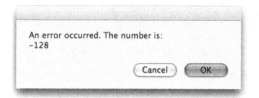

Figure 17-2. *The dialog box reveals the error number.*

Ah, the satisfaction of attaining hard-earned knowledge! Now, let's mix the error message with the error number; see Script 17-4.

Script 17-4.

```
try
    display dialog "Do it?"
on error the_error_message number the_error_number
    display dialog "An error occurred:" & return & the_error_message & ¬
        return & the_error_number
end try
```

If you return to the original 1 + "abc" example for a moment, you can use the same approach to capture the error message and number, plus all the other available error information:

```
try
    1 + "abc"
on error error_text number error_number ¬
    from offending_object partial result result_list to expected_type
    return {error_text, error_number, offending_object, result_list, expected_type}
end try
--> {"Can't make \"abc\" into type number.", -1700, "abc", {}, number}
```

Putting Error Numbers to Use

Now that you know how to figure out the error numbers, you can start using them. To start, modify the preceding script to display the second dialog box only if the error number is –128. To do that, you just have to replace the variable following the word number with the actual error number. Script 17-5 shows how the script will look.

Script 17-5.

```
try
    display dialog "Do it?"
on error number -128
    display dialog "You canceled the script. Bye!"
end try
```

The preceding script is OK, but it lets you act upon only one error. What if you anticipate two or more errors? For that you have two possible options: you have to either nest multiple try statement blocks one inside the other or put the error number into a variable and use an if-else if block to test for the different possible errors.

Testing for Multiple Errors

In many cases, the same statement may throw more than one type of error. To treat each error differently, you will need to use a simple conditional statement. You'll also need to identify the number of the errors you want to treat and leave one last open else clause to deal with any other error that may occur. This script will take two variables: one with a path pointing to a folder and one with a path pointing to a file. The script will attempt to duplicate the file in the folder.

Two things that can go wrong are that one path points to a nonexistent item, in which case the Finder will throw error number –10006, and that the file you're copying already exists in the destination folder, which is error number –15267.

Watch how the script acts differently based on the error, as shown in Script 17-6.

Script 17-6.

```
1. try
2.     tell application "Finder"
3.        duplicate file source_file_path to folder dest_folder_path
4.     end tell
5. on error error_message number error_number
6.     if error_number is -10006 then
7.        display dialog ¬
              "Either the file or folder you specify doesn't exist"
8.     else if error_number is -15267 then
9.        display dialog ¬
              "The folder already has a file with the same name"
10.    else
11.       display dialog "The following message has occurred:" & ¬
                 return & error_message
12.    end if
13.    display dialog "The script is going to stop now"
14.    return
15. end try
```

Nesting try Handlers

Another way to achieve a similar result is to use several nested try statements, as shown in Script 17-7.

Script 17-7.

```
1. try
2.     try
3.        try
4.           tell application "Finder"
5.              duplicate file source_file_path to folder dest_folder_path
6.           end tell
7.        on error number -10006
8.           display dialog ¬
                 "Either the file or folder you specify doesn't exist"
9.        end try
10.    on error number -15267
```

```
11.        display dialog ¬
                "The folder already has a file with the same name"
12.     end try
13. on error error_message
14.     display dialog "The following message has occurred:" & ¬
            return & error_message
15. end try
```

In the preceding example, the code whose error you want to trap is actually inside three nested try statements. Each one of the first two will trap only a specific error. If the error that occurred is not that error, the error will trickle down to the next try statement. At the end, the error will get to the outermost try block that you've designed to trap any error.

Being Careful Not to Trap Too Much

Error trapping is not a solution to errors! Well, it kind of is the solution, but only either for errors you anticipate or for freak, once-in-a-lifetime errors. During your testing and debugging stage, you should stay away from trapping errors. You want to see them as they come and treat them. Once you've managed to account for almost all situations, add some try statements just to be sure. See the "Using the Scriptwide try Statement" section later in this chapter.

You may also consider deactivating any error-trapping try statements. Simply comment out the try statement components. When all is done, uncomment the try statements to make them active again. You do that since during the testing stages you actually want to see the errors so that you can possibly find better solutions for them.

Dressing Up Errors

Sometimes you'll want AppleScript's own errors to be displayed but want to add some explanatory text of your own. The following script does just that—it traps an error and displays the error text along with some more script-specific text.

In this example, the script is looking for a related file needed for normal operation. If the file isn't found, the script displays a dialog box containing the actual AppleScript error following this text related to the script: "A problem occurred while getting the work manifest."

Here's the script:

```
property work_folder : "Macintosh HD:Users:Hanaan:Work:"

on run
   set manifest_file to work_folder & "manifest.txt"
   try
      set jobs_list to paragraphs of (read manifest_file)
   on error error_text
      --Stop the script immediately if the job manifest can't be found...
      display dialog "A problem occurred while getting the work manifest:" & ¬
         return & return & error_text buttons {"Quit"} with icon stop
      return
   end try
   --Otherwise start processing the new jobs...
   --rest of the code goes here
end run
```

Using the Scriptwide try Statement

One of the projects I'm working on is a bunch of scripts Sal Soghoian (AppleScript product manager) wrote for Showtime Networks. The scripts automate the creation of the Upcoming Shows menus for about ten of Showtime Networks' affiliate stations. Sal initially created the scripts as a public relations campaign for Showtime, and it really worked well. It also worked well for me to inherit the project, since besides billing for the time, I got to learn a lot from Sal's AppleScript mastery.

One of the neat features in these scripts was that, besides the localized error trapping that was implemented throughout the script, every script had one big try statement that covered it from head to toe.

The purpose of this try block's on error handler wasn't to notify the user that something wrong went down—AppleScript's built-in error dialog box would have done that. The purpose was to cause the script to display the error message in a nice dialog box instead of the typical error message AppleScript displays in case of unhandled errors, with the dreaded Edit button that, no matter what I tell them, users always seem to want to click. Figure 17-3 shows the AppleScript generic-style error message dialog box.

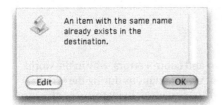

Figure 17-3. *AppleScript's generic error message dialog box with the dreaded Edit button*

Sal's scriptwide try statement worked well, but I needed a way for the user to know exactly where things went bad so I could troubleshoot faster. So, I came up with the following solution: I added a global variable called script_location and assigned a different number to it throughout the script. Every two or three lines of real code, I added something like this:

```
set script_location to 64
```

At the end, part of the job of that scriptwide on error handler was to report to me not only the nature of the error but the value of that script location variable, which allowed me to pinpoint the exact location of the error.

Although adding lines indicating the script location can be useful, what I usually do is remove most of them while the script has been in use for a while. As useful as they can be when an error happens, they do bloat the script quite a bit. Once a script proves that it runs smoothly in a working environment, you no longer need most of these script position indicators.

Logging Errors to a File

An even better error-hunting technique I use is to write the script's activity to a text file. Since doing this every second or third line of the script really will hamper performance, you will want the user to implement it only when there's a persistent error. Find a way for the user to flag the script that should log errors. You can also choose to log more of the script's activity, in which case the logical place in the script is between tasks the script performs. For instance, you can have the following comments logged in the proper places throughout your script: "Exporting Excel file <name> to tab-delimited file," "Now reading tab-delimited file into AppleScript," "Now inserting images into page template," and so on.

If you have an interface, then you can add a little check box called Log Activity. Otherwise, if your script has a dialog box that appears at the start, you may want to add a button to it called Settings. Clicking this button will display another dialog box that will allow users to turn logging on for the following execution of the script. This will turn a `log_error` global variable to `true`, which will then tell all the handlers in the script to log their activity.

The idea with logging activity is to create a text file on the desktop bearing the date and time and add some text to that file every few lines. The text should describe the location and include some of the actual values used in the script. This can provide clues for the error.

I tell my clients to e-mail me that resulting text file, which is handy for revealing the cause of the error.

Since you will be utilizing the error logging feature again and again, it is a perfect candidate for a handler with a couple of parameters such as the line number, the part of the script it's called from, and maybe the values of a few variables coerced into a string.

A handler call is much easier to embed multiple times in your script.

Generating Errors

Having spent the last portion of the chapter trying to contain and control errors, why in the world would you want to go around creating them yourself? Well, in some situations during the script's execution, you will realize that the best way to proceed is to throw an error. In many cases, this error will be handled by the same error trapping mechanism you set up to trap other possible errors.

To throw an error yourself, you use AppleScript's `error` statement. The most basic form of this statement is simply this:

```
error
```

Running this statement causes AppleScript to raise an unknown error with the generic message "An error has occurred" and with an error number of –2700. However, in most situations you'll want to supply a more meaningful error message and error number. Here's the full definition of the error statement:

```
error [error_message] ¬
    [number error_number] ¬
    [from offending_object] ¬
    [to expected_type] ¬
    [partial result result_list]
```

As you can see, the error statement has the same parameters as the `try` statement's `on error` line.

The error message and error number are the two parameters you'll usually use for throwing errors. For example:

```
error "E.T. could not phone home: wrong number" number 411
```

Figure 17-4 shows the error dialog box that this error, unhandled, will display.

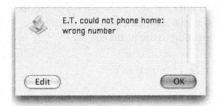

Figure 17-4. *The error message shown in an AppleScript application error dialog box*

Throwing your own errors is a good idea when part of your script hits a problem it can't deal with itself. Not only does this let other parts of the script know there's a problem, but it also gives them a chance to deal with it if they want by trapping and handling that error in a try block.

As an example, let's say you're writing a script where one part involves looking up a phone number based on a person's name. The names and phone numbers are stored in a list of lists like this:

```
set contact_table to {{"Joe", "5553712"}, {"Pam", "5550232"}, {"Sam", "5556795"}}
```

This list works as a simple lookup table: to get a phone number, you loop through each item in the main list, checking to see whether the name matches the one you want. When the loop finds a matching name, it returns the corresponding phone number. For example, if the name is Sam, then the value returned will be 5556795.

You'll encounter one other possibility, though: what if none of the entries in the table matches the desired name? Well, let's take a page out of AppleScript's book here. Just as saying get item 10 of {1, 2, 3, 4, 5} will cause AppleScript to raise a "Can't get item . . ." error, I'll have my table-searching subroutine generate a similar error when it can't find the entry that was requested. Here's the error statement I'll use:

```
error "The item was not found." number -1728
```

Since the type of error being reported is similar to an existing AppleScript error, I've used the same error code as AppleScript, –1728. But I could make up my own error code for it if I preferred, such as error number 6000, "Can't find an entry with the given key in a lookup table."

Here's the full table lookup subroutine:

```
on get_value_for_key(key_value_list, key_to_find)
    repeat with item_ref in key_value_list
        set {this_key, this_value} to item_ref
        if this_key = key_to_find then return this_value
    end repeat
    error "The item wasn't found." number -1728
end get_value_for_key
```

And here are some examples of its use:

```
get_value_for_key(contact_table, "Pam")
--result: "555-0232"

get_value_for_key(contact_table, "Frank")
--error: The item wasn't found.
```

Now when the get_value_for_key handler raises the error number –1728, the part of the script that called it can handle that error in any way it wants. For example, it might catch that particular error number and record the problem in a log file before continuing to the next task:

```
try
    set the_phone_number to get_value_for_key(contact_table, the_person)
on error number -1728
    add_to_log("Couldn't call " & the_person)
    set the_phone_number to missing value
end try
if the_phone_number is not missing value then
    --call the person at that number...
end if
```

Or, it might choose to ignore the error completely, letting the script stop straightaway, and display the standard AppleScript error dialog box. As the designer of the script, the choice is up to you.

Introducing Other Common Types of Errors

The following sections list all AppleScript-related error messages that don't belong to third-party scripting additions or scriptable applications. The errors are divided into operating system errors, Apple event errors, application scripting errors, and AppleScript errors.

Encountering Operating System Errors

An operating system error is an error that occurs when AppleScript or an application requests services from the Mac OS and something goes wrong (see Table 17-1). They are rare, and more important, you usually can't do anything about them in a script. A few, such as "File <name> wasn't found" and "Application isn't running," make sense for scripts to handle.

Table 17-1. *Operating System Errors*

Number	Description
–34	Disk <name> is full.
–35	Disk <name> wasn't found.
–37	Bad name for file.
–38	File <name> wasn't open.
–39	End of file error.
–42	Too many files open.
–43	File <name> wasn't found.
–44	Disk <name> is write protected.
–45	File <name> is locked.
–46	Disk <name> is locked.
–47	File <name> is busy.
–48	Duplicate filename.
–49	File <name> is already open.
–50	Parameter error.
–51	File reference number error.
–61	File not open with write permission.

Number	Description
–120	Folder <name> wasn't found.
–124	Disk <name> is disconnected.
–128	User canceled.
–192	A resource wasn't found.
–600	Application isn't running.
–609	Connection is invalid.
–905	Remote access is not allowed.
–906	<name> isn't running or program linking isn't enabled.
–915	Can't find remote machine.
–30720	Invalid date and time <date string>.

Encountering Apple Event Errors

An Apple event error is an error that is generated by a scriptable application or a scripting addition (see Table 17-2). Many of these errors, such as "No user interaction allowed," are of interest to users. Also of interest to users are errors that have to do with reference forms, as well as errors such as "No such object." In addition, AppleScript can generate some of the errors shown.

Table 17-2. *AppleScript Event Errors*

Number	Description
–1700	Can't make some data into the expected type.
–1701	Some parameter is missing for <commandName>.
–1702	Some data could not be read.
–1703	Some data was the wrong type.
–1704	Some parameter was invalid.
–1705	Operation involving a list item failed.
–1708	<reference> doesn't understand the <commandName> message.
–1712	Apple event timed out.
–1713	No user interaction allowed.
–1715	Some parameter wasn't understood.
–1717	The handler <identifier> is not defined.
–1719	Can't get <reference>. Invalid index.
–1720	Invalid range.
–1721	<expression> doesn't match the parameters <parameterNames> for <commandName>.
–1723	Can't get <expression>. Access not allowed.
–1727	Expected a reference.
–1728	Can't get <reference>.
–1730	Container specified was an empty list.

Continued

Table 17-2. *Continued*

Number	Description
–1731	Unknown object type.
–1750	Scripting component error.
–1751	Invalid script ID.
–1752	Script doesn't seem to belong to AppleScript.
–1753	Script error.
–1754	Invalid selector given.
–1755	Invalid access.
–1756	Source not available.

Encountering Application Scripting Errors

An application scripting error is an error returned by an application when handling standard Apple-
Script commands, which are commands that apply to all applications (see Table 17-3). Many of
these errors, such as "The specified object is a property, not an element," are of interest to users
and should be handled.

Table 17-3. *Application Scripting Errors*

Number	Description
–10000	Apple event handler failed.
–10001	A descriptor type mismatch occurred.
–10002	Invalid key form.
–10003	Can't set <object or data> to <object or data>. Access not allowed.
–10004	A privilege violation occurred.
–10005	The read operation wasn't allowed.
–10006	Can't set <object or data> to <object or data>.
–10007	The index of the event is too large to be valid.
–10008	The specified object is a property, not an element.
–10009	Can't supply the requested descriptor type for the data.
–10010	The Apple event handler can't handle objects of this class.
–10011	Couldn't handle this command because it wasn't part of the current transaction.
–10012	The transaction to which this command belonged isn't a valid transaction.
–10013	There is no user selection.
–10014	Handler only handles single objects.
–10015	Can't undo the previous Apple event or user action.

Encountering AppleScript Errors

An AppleScript error is an error that occurs when AppleScript processes script statements (see Table 17-4). Nearly all of these are of interest to users. For errors returned by an application, see the documentation for that application.

Table 17-4. *AppleScript Errors*

Number	Description
−2700	Unknown error.
−2701	Can't divide <number> by zero.
−2702	The result of a numeric operation was too large.
−2703	<reference> can't be launched because it is not an application.
−2704	<reference> isn't scriptable.
−2705	The application has a corrupted dictionary.
−2706	Stack overflow.
−2707	Internal table overflow.
−2708	Attempt to create a value larger than the allowable size.
−2709	Can't get the event dictionary.
−2720	Can't both consider and ignore <attribute>.
−2721	Can't perform operation on text longer than 32K bytes.
−2740	A <language element> can't go after this <language element>.
−2741	Expected <language element> but found <language element>.
−2750	The <name> parameter is specified more than once.
−2751	The <name> property is specified more than once.
−2752	The <name> handler is specified more than once.
−2753	The variable <name> is not defined.
−2754	Can't declare <name> as both a local and global variable.
−2755	Exit statement was not in a repeat loop.
−2760	Tell statements are nested too deeply.
−2761	<name> is illegal as a formal parameter.
−2762	<name> is not a parameter name for the event <event>.
−2763	No result was returned for some argument of this expression.

Power Wrap-Up

The following sections summarize the chapter in an intensive reference style. Use these sections to look up facts related to the chapter without the chatter.

Compile Errors

Compile errors are errors that occur while the script tries to compile. Compiling scripts is what happens before the script even runs. Typical compile errors are aliases that point to a nonexistent file, two variables in a row, not using a `tell` block when using application-specific terms, and so on.

Runtime Errors

Runtime errors are errors that happen only while the script runs. An error that is thrown while the script is running has a few components that either are used by the scripter to debug the problem during development or are used by the script itself to determine how it should precede in case the error is trapped. Untrapped errors will cause the script to stop, and usually AppleScript will display a dialog box containing the grim details of the error to the user.

The error components are the error text, error number, offending object, and expected type.

How to Trap Errors

You trap errors with the `try` block. Any runtime error that occurs in a statement inside a `try` block will not stop the script. The following is the basic `try` statement block:

```
try
    set x to 2 + "five"
end try
```

You can tell the script what to do in case there's an error anywhere within the `try` block by adding the `on error` line to the try statement, like this:

```
try
    set x to 2 + "five"
on error
    set x to 0
    display dialog "Couldn't get the value of x!"
end try
```

You can get the error components by placing variables after the `on error` line, like this:

```
try
    set x to 2 + "five"
on error error_text number error_number from offending_object to ¬
expected_type
    display dialog "There was an error, and here is what happened:" & ¬
        return & error_text
end try
```

How to Generate Errors

You can use the `error` command to throw errors at any point during the script, like this:

```
error "Something happened" number 999
```

Although I used only the error text and number components, you can use the other two as well. Be aware that Apple reserves negative error numbers.

■ ■ ■

Defining and Calling Subroutines

Although subroutines aren't the first thing you create when you learn AppleScript, they are the one facet of writing scripts that will have the most impact on your scripts, especially as they grow bigger and more ambitious. Subroutines are your tools for organizing scripts; they make your scripts efficient and give you a perfect way to store and reuse your code.

What Are Subroutines?

Subroutines allow you to create your own commands. A *command* is simply an isolated block of code that does something, defined by AppleScript, a scripting addition, or a scriptable application. This code is executed from somewhere else in the system and can be reused over and over again, wherever you need that functionality to occur. A command you use in AppleScript can trigger a few or many lines of code, depending on its complexity.

Your subroutines aren't much different; it's just that subroutines are commands written using AppleScript, which means you can easily write them and use them yourself. Rather than being part of the main body of the script, subroutines are organized away from it and are called, or *triggered*, from the main body of the script or from other subroutines.

■Note Subroutines are often referred to as *handlers* and sometimes as *functions* and *procedures*. All these, for this book's purposes, have the same meaning.

To better understand subroutines, I want you to imagine making a list of tasks before throwing a party in your house. The list may include baking a cake, washing dishes, buying chips, and sending invitations. Although this list is a great overview, it doesn't offer any details. If the list actually included all the details of baking a cake or looping through dishes in the sink and washing each one, the list would no longer be a snapshot that you could glance at to see what needed to be done. For items that do require directions, such as the exact steps for baking the cake, which you'll most likely need, you know where to go. So when the day of the party finally arrives, you pick your list and look for the directions. Each item on the list, instead of being the specific instructions for the task, calls your attention to the task, whose specific details you can look up somewhere else.

The same happens with a script that uses subroutines. The script in Figure 18-1 shows the party plan in the Script Editor the way you would organize it as a script with subroutines.

By looking at the script in Figure 18-1, you can easily differentiate between the master plan and the fine details.

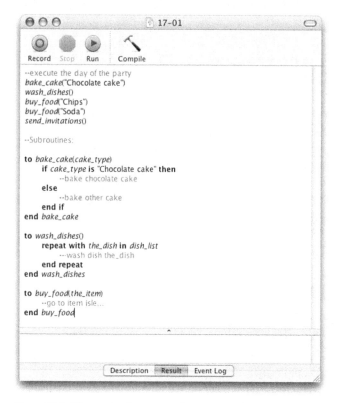

Figure 18-1. *The party plan as a script*

Later, as you gain experience, you can start spreading commonly used subroutines into different script files called *script libraries*. Doing so makes your scripts smaller and more manageable and allows you to package general-purpose subroutines for use by multiple scripts. These libraries may have subroutines that all perform related tasks. In the preceding example, you could have a "baker" script library. In this case, you would use this line to bake the cake: tell baker to bake_cake("chocolate cake").

Subroutines Have to Be Called in Order to Work

On their own, subroutines don't do anything other than occupy bytes in your script file. A subroutine is used only when it is called from an active part of your script. That active part may start at the run handler (see the section "Using the run handler" later in this chapter) and continue through any subroutine that is called. Subroutines may call each other as well, which means one subroutine can contain a call to another subroutine.

Imagine a job site without a foreman. You have a carpenter, electrician, landscaper plumber, and framer, but you don't have anyone to take charge and say, "OK, we start by digging a big hole . . . ." This foreman will assign tasks to the other workers. Each worker may then, based on their function, assign tasks to other people on the site. As soon as the workers have completed all the tasks the foreman had in the list, the job is considered done, and the workers can all go and have a drink (no matter what time of day it is . . .).

This job site with no foreman is the same as a script with a bunch of handlers but with no run handler (or other executing handler such as the open handler, but I'll cover more about that in Chapter 24).

The foreman may even come in, say "OK, start," and then leave. I've created scripts like that; here's how they look:

```
go()
on go()
  --perform all commands...
end go
```

In this case, the go subroutine call is the only line in the run handler, but it's enough to ignite the script and get it going.

Writing Your First Subroutine

Before I get into the specifics of subroutines, I'll show how to create one simple subroutine and call it. In this example, I will create a little subroutine that displays a dialog box. At this point, the dialog box will display some literal text, not different text every time, as it could.

Figure 18-2 shows the basic form of a subroutine.

Figure 18-2. *The basic form of a subroutine*

By looking at the script in Figure 18-2, you clearly can see the two components that make up any subroutine: the subroutine's definition and the call that triggers it. Although the positioning of the subroutine call in your script is pivotal, the subroutine definition can live almost anywhere in your script, or even in other scripts. The only place it can't appear is directly inside another subroutine definition. Subroutine calls can appear inside expressions or other commands, or all by themselves, just like any other command in AppleScript. They can even appear inside the subroutines they call—which is known as *recursion*. Anywhere in your script you need a subroutine executed, just stick in the appropriate call.

Using the run Handler

The run handler contains all the statements that will be executed when you run the script. A script can have only one run handler at most, but some scripts may have no run handler at all.

I've Never Seen No run Handler!

You may be wondering why you already wrote a bunch of scripts, but none of them has anything that looks like a run handler. This is because the run handler doesn't have to be explicitly defined. If a script doesn't contain an explicit run handler, then AppleScript assumes the script has an implicit run handler instead. An implicit run handler consists of all the statements found at the top level of the script, except for any property declarations, named script object definitions, and other handler/subroutine definitions.

The scripts in Figures 18-3 and 18-4 are identical; it's just that the one in Figure 18-4 explicitly defines the run handler, and in the script shown in Figure 18-3, the run handler is implied.

Figure 18-3. *The script has a* run *handler, but it is implied. The entire script shown is part of this* run *handler.*

Figure 18-4. *The* run *handler is explicitly written out.*

Now, try this:

```
display dialog "You can run..."
on run
    display dialog "But you can't compile"
end run
```

Why won't this script compile? The first display dialog command is inside the implied run handler, and the second display dialog command is in the explicit run handler. Two run handlers don't get along.

When Should You Make the run Handler Explicit?

Although in many situations leaving the run handler implicit (not actually wrapping the top-level statements with on run...end run) is OK, sometimes you'll want to explicitly identify the run handler.

The one time when you are required to specify the run handler explicitly is when you want to pass parameters to it, like in the following script:

```
on run {value1, value2, etc...}
    ...
end run
```

You would run the previous script with this call:

```
run script the_script with parameters {value1, value2, etc...}
```

For better readability, you could add the run handler when the script has some other unusual execution method. For instance, if the script is a droplet application, it will have another unique handler called the on open handler. This handler will be executed when a file is dropped on the script application. Although for the most part the user will utilize the script by dropping a file on it, you may want to have some code in the run handler that will execute if someone double-clicks the droplet application.

Script 18-1 defines both the run handler and the open handler in the same script. If you drop a file on the script application, it will show you the file's type, as defined in the open handler, and if you double-click the script application, you will get instructions, as defined in the run handler.

Script 18-1.

```
on open a_list_of_aliases
    set the_item to item 1 of a_list_of_aliases
    set the_item_type to file type of (info for the_item)
    display dialog "You dropped a file of type \"" & ¬
        the_item_type & "\"" buttons {"OK"} default button 1
end open

on run
    display dialog ¬
        "Drop something on me and I'll tell you what type it is!" ¬
        buttons {"OK"} default button 1 with icon note
end run
```

I will discuss the open handler in the Chapter 24, which covers droplets.

What Are Parameters?

Parameters, also referred to as *arguments*, are values passed to the subroutine by the subroutine call. Parameters let you explain to the subroutine how you want the different commands and statements executed.

When you stand at a coffee shop counter, asking for coffee is the statement you use. The parameters are the main details you provide about how you like your coffee: "I'd like a large coffee, black with one sugar." The "make coffee" subroutine has three parameters: size, whitener, and sweetener. Anywhere you get coffee in the country you can supply those parameters to the "make coffee" subroutine, and people will understand, even though the exact way they'll go about making it may be different.

The following is the "make coffee" subroutine the way AppleScript would have it:

```
to make_coffee(size, whitener, sweetener)
    put size cup on counter
    fill with coffee
    if whitener is not none then add whitener
    add sweetener number of sugar baggies
    stir
    return cup of coffee
end make_coffee
```

To execute this subroutine, you'd send it a make_coffee command containing the size, whitener, and sweetener values you want the subroutine to use in preparing your coffee. For example:

```
make_coffee(Large, none, 1)
```

You'll look at parameters in more detail shortly.

What's the Result?

In AppleScript, you may want your subroutines to return a value, or you may not. For example, a subroutine whose job is to close all open documents in InDesign may return no result. It will always just close any open documents, and that's that. You may want to test whether the operation was successful and return a true or false, or you may return the number of documents you closed. This is entirely up to you.

AppleScript will return a result from a subroutine when it reaches the return statement. If no return statement is provided, then the subroutine's result will be the result of the last statement the subroutine executed, even if you don't want to use it. The return statement starts with the word return and is optionally followed by a value, which becomes the subroutine's call result.

Let's look at a few examples—the following four subroutines will return the sum of the two parameters.

This is the first variation:

```
on add_up(a, b)
  return a + b
end add_up
```

This is the second variation:

```
on add_up(a, b)
  a + b
end add_up
```

This is the third variation:

```
on add_up(a, b)
  set the_sum to a + b
  return the_sum
  --any line beyond the return line will be ignored
end add_up
```

This is the fourth variation:

```
on add_up(a, b)
  set the_sum to a + b
end add_up
```

All four subroutines will return the same result. Notice that the second and fourth subroutines don't explicitly use the return statement, but AppleScript still returns the result of the last statement.

Returning a Result Midway

One reason to use a return statement in the middle of a subroutine is if you trapped an error. You can also use intermediate return statements as part of a conditional statement, as shown in Script 18-2.

Script 18-2.

```
on do_math(a, b, the_operator)
    if the_operator is "+" then
        return a + b
    else if the_operator is "-" then
        return a - b
    else if the_operator is "*" then
        return a * b
    end if
end do_math
```

Here's another example for returning a result before the end of the subroutine:

```
on find_position_in_list(the_list, the_value)
    repeat with i from 1 to count the_list
        if item i of the_list is the_value then
            --Once we find the item we want, we don't need to keep looking.
            --Executing a return statement here immediately stops the search
            --and returns its result
```

Collecting Results from Subroutines

So, you've just seen how generous subroutines are in returning results. What you need to do now is collect these results so you can put them to use later in the script. You can do that by assigning the result of the subroutine call to a variable. Here's an example of a subroutine that returns a result:

```
on calculate_cubic_feet(ft_tall, ft_wide, ft_long)
    return  ft_tall * ft_wide * ft_long
end calculate_cubic_feet
```

Now you'll call the subroutine, but you will make sure that the result it returns is assigned to a variable:

```
set this_room_volume to calculate_cubic_feet(8, 12, 10)
this_room_volume --> 960
```

Using Subroutines' Results in Expressions

Many application and scripting addition commands return a value as their result. AppleScript allows you to put commands inside expressions so the value returned by the command is used in the expression.

The same applies to user-defined commands: you can call a subroutine from inside an expression, and the result of that call will be used by the expression. For example, let's create a little subroutine that formats a U.S. phone number. Just for this example we will keep it simple. Script 18-3 shows the subroutine.

Script 18-3.

```
on format_phone(the_phone_number)
    return "(" & ¬
        (text 1 thru 3 of the_phone_number) & ") " & ¬
        (text 4 thru 6 of the_phone_number) & "-" & ¬
        (text 7 thru 10 of the_phone_number)
end format_phone
```

Now, let's create a statement that will use that subroutine, as shown in Script 18-4.

Script 18-4.

```
set the_message to ¬
    "You can reach my office at: " & format_phone("8005551234") & ¬
    " or on my cell at: " & format_phone("2125551234")
display dialog the_message
```

As you can see in Figure 18-5, the expression in the preceding statement incorporated two calls to the format_phone subroutine.

Figure 18-5. *The dialog box produced by the two scripts using the* format_phone *subroutine*

Can a Subroutine Return More Than One Result?

By the AppleScript rules, a subroutine may return only one value as a result. This would have been too restrictive, since many subroutines you create produce more than one result that you want to return to your script.

So, what can you do if a subroutine needs to return more than one value at the same time? All you do is collect the different values you want to return in a single list or record and return that list or record.

Script 18-5 will accept a full name as a string and return the first name and last name separately. To return both values to the calling statement, you will use a record.

Script 18-5.

```
on split_name(the_name)
    set first_name to first word of the_name
    set last_name to last word of the_name
    return {first_name:first_name, last_name:last_name}
end split_name
set name_record to split_name("Paul Revere")
-->{first_name:"Paul", last_name:"Revere"}
```

In the preceding example, you returned a record as a result. Personally, I like to use lists because they make it easier to map the values to individual variables—they are more flexible.

The advantage of a list in this case is that you can map the result directly to individual variables. Script 18-6 shows how you do that.

Script 18-6.

```
on split_name(the_name)
    set first_name to first word of the_name
    set last_name to last word of the_name
    return {first_name, last_name}
end split_name

set {first_name, last_name} to split_name("Paul Revere")
--> first_name = "Paul"
--> last_name = "Revere"
```

As you can see in this example, since the subroutine returned a list with two items and the list of variables you assigned the result to also has two items, each item from the returned list was assigned to its corresponding item in the subroutine's returned variable.

This is as close as it gets to returning multiple values.

Another fact that makes this example easy to follow is that the list names of the variables you used in the subroutine's return statement inside the subroutine are the same as the list names of the variables you assigned the subroutine's result to in the calling statement.

Specifying Subroutine Parameters

You can pass parameters to a subroutine in two ways: by position and by label. Specifying parameters by position is the simpler approach. Here the subroutine's name is followed by a pair of parentheses containing one or more parameters, for example do_something(parameter1, parameter2, ...). When using positional parameters, it is essential that both the command's parameters appear in the same order as the subroutine's; otherwise, the subroutine won't work correctly. Although commands with many positional parameters can be a bit hard to read, this style of parameter passing is easy to pick up and start using.

Labeled parameters are more complex but allow parameters to be passed to a subroutine in any order, and they make user-defined commands look more like application and scripting addition commands.

The advantage of using labeled parameters is that labels can clearly describe what each of the parameters stands for. For instance, imagine the following call to an imaginary subroutine:

```
Do_this_thing("1:00 PM", true, true, "AAA", 100293)
```

Just what do all these values stand for? Does the string "AAA" stand for roadside assistance or for the type of batteries the subroutine needs in order to work?

Now try this:

```
Do_this_thing from "1:00 PM" with do_it_right and ¬
clean_up_after given battery_type:"AAA", number_to_use:100293
```

Ah! Now you can look at the subroutine call and see exactly what the different parameters mean (given it makes sense to you . . .). I can't count how many times I've looked at subroutine calls I created in the past and had no clue what the different parameters did until I dug back into the subroutine definition.

Using Positional Parameters

You can start using positional parameter subroutines quickly, and they don't get any more complicated than what can be described in two paragraphs.

To understand positional parameter subroutines, imagine a cargo train where the cars aren't marked. The person loading the train knows in what order to organize the cars, and the person unloading is aware of the same order. If the first car is supposed to contain lumber and it contains straw instead, then your script will most likely end up trying to build a house of straw.

That's right: what's important in positional parameter subroutines is the order, or *position*, of the parameters.

Definition for Positional Parameter Subroutines

The following is the dictionary definition of the positional parameter subroutine (items shown in square brackets are optional):

```
to subroutine_name ( [ parameter_variable [, parameter_variable ]...] )
    --any local and/or global variable declarations
    --the statement/s to execute

end subroutine_name
```

If you omit the subroutine name after the end keyword, AppleScript will automatically add this for you when compiling the script. AppleScript also allows you to start the subroutine with on instead of to if you want—both mean the same thing.

The corresponding command will look like this:

```
subroutine_name ( [ parameter_value [, parameter_value ]...] )
```

Defining and Calling Positional Parameter Subroutines

You'll start this section by looking at another simple example of a positional parameter subroutine. The purpose of this subroutine will be to create a folder somewhere on the hard drive.

You'll start with the naked statements:

```
tell application "Finder"
    make new folder
end tell
```

Now, add a subroutine wrapper for it. For that you will need the subroutine identifier. The subroutine identifier will be used as the command name when you want to call the subroutine. Script 18-7 shows the basic subroutine definition.

Script 18-7.

```
on create_folder()
    tell application "Finder"
        make new folder
    end tell
end create_folder
```

The empty parentheses after the subroutine identifier create_folder are required. They are the currently empty home of any parameters the subroutine may use. To call this subroutine, you can use this line:

```
create_folder()
```

Note that this command has the same name as the subroutine, followed by the same set of empty parentheses. Create a new document in Script Editor, enter the subroutine and the command shown previously, and then run the script. As you can see, the command causes the subroutine to execute, creating a new folder on the desktop.

Adding Parameters

As it stands, the subroutine will create a folder named untitled folder on the desktop. This can't be what you want the script to do. What you want is to be able to specify a different location to the script and a different name for it as well.

As mentioned earlier, the important part of adding these parameters to the subroutine is deciding on their order. Here you will specify the location followed by name. Script 18-8 shows the new subroutine definition and call with the addition of these two parameters.

Script 18-8.

```
on create_folder(folder_location, folder_name)
    tell application "Finder"
        make new folder at folder_location ¬
            with properties {name:folder_name}
    end tell
end create_folder
```

Then, to call the subroutine from anywhere in this script, you can use this:

```
create_folder(path to documents folder, "My Stuff")
```

The result will be a folder named My Stuff placed in the user's Documents folder.

Using Labeled Parameters

Somebody please tell me, why? Positional parameters are so easy to use, they do everything you want, and they always work the same. So why complicate things by introducing labeled parameters? And if you don't figure them out, is anything wrong with you? Now, you may not want to tie yourself-esteem to your mastery of labeled parameters, because after all, if you never knew they existed, you could still script happily ever after. Nevertheless, they can be pretty cool.

Although positional parameters are recognized only based on their position, labeled parameter subroutines have a unique way to display parameters. For starters, labeled parameter subroutines do away with the parentheses. Instead, they use a combination of special keywords and user-defined labels to define the subroutine and have a command-like treatment of Boolean values for calling the subroutine.

To understand the structure of labeled parameter subroutines, I'll start with the basics and then move on to more complex features later.

The Definition and the Call

The main struggle with subroutines is making sure the subroutine definition (the part that actually does the work) properly uses the parameters the user wants to feed it. This feeding of parameters to the subroutine happens in the subroutine call: the part that tells the script to execute the subroutine.

Hence, your main effort here will be finding a way to pass values from the call to the definition.

Definition for Positional Parameter Subroutines

The following is the definition of the labeled parameter subroutine:

```
to subroutine_name [ of direct_parameter_variable ] ¬
    [ predefined_label parameter_variable ]... ¬
    [ given user_label: parameter_variable [, user_label: parameter_variable ]...]

    --any local and/or global variable declarations
    --the statement/s to execute

end subroutine_name
```

If you omit the subroutine name after the end keyword, AppleScript will automatically add this for you. You can also start the subroutine with on instead of to, and you can use in rather than of to indicate the direct parameter (both words have the same meaning).

And here's the definition for a positional parameter subroutine call:

```
subroutineName [ of direct_parameter_value ] ¬
    [ predefined_label parameter_value ]... ¬
    [ with user_label [, user_label ]...] ¬
    [ without user_label [, user_label ]...] ¬
    [ given user_label: parameter_value [, user_label: parameter_value ]...]
```

You can substitute the word of in the first line with the word with.

Starting with the Basics: Subroutine Parameter Labels

I'll start the labeled parameter subroutine discussion with the predefined subroutine parameter labels supplied by AppleScript. The subroutine parameter labels are 23 reserved words that you can use as labels to parameters. Let's look at these labels and at how you can use them.

The 23 labels are about, above, against, apart from, around, aside from, at, below, beneath, beside, between, by, for, from, instead of, into, on, onto, out of, over, since, thru (or through), and under.

You can use these labels in both the subroutine definition and the subroutine call in a coordinated way, which allows you to determine what values supplied by the subroutine call match up with certain variables in the subroutine definition.

All 23 labels function the same, but you should choose them based on how well they fit into the context of the subroutine. The people who thought them up must have wanted your script to read more like a poem . . . .

Say you have a subroutine that will return the highest number in a list of positive integers. The subroutine will require one parameter that is the list of integers. Out of the 23 labels, I chose the out of label to be most fitting for the subroutine parameter label assignment. Script 18-9 shows what my subroutine looks like.

Script 18-9.

```
to find_highest out of the_list
    set highest_for_now to item 1 of the_list as number
    repeat with the_item_ref in rest of the_list
        if the_item_ref as number > highest_for_now then
            set highest_for_now to the_item_ref as number
        end if
    end repeat
    return highest_for_now
end find_highest
```

To call the subroutine, I use the following line:

```
find_highest out of {1, 4, 12, 5}
```

Let's compare the calling line with the first line of the subroutine definition, but let's change the subroutine identifier and label.

Here's the definition:

```
to (name) parameter the_list
```

Here's the call:

```
(name) parameter {1, 4, 12, 5} -- The four-item list will be ➡
assigned to the variable the_list
```

As with positional parameter-based commands, the command's name identifies the subroutine that should be executed, and the parameter label specifies to which variable *inside* the subroutine the parameter value will be assigned. In the preceding example, you can clearly see that the value of the variable the_list in the subroutine will be {1, 4, 12, 5}.

Now let's try that with one more subroutine parameter. For this example, you'll add a top number. This time, the subroutine will just return a Boolean value: true if the top number is higher than the highest number in the list and false if the list contains a higher number than the top number we supply.

Script 18-10 shows the second subroutine definition.

Script 18-10.

```
to check_if_highest out of the_list above the_top
    repeat with the_item_ref in the_list
        if the_item_ref as number > the_top then return false
    end repeat
    return true
end check_if_highest
```

And here's the call:

```
check_if_highest out of {1, 4, 12, 5} above 16
```

Note that since the parameters are recognized by name and not by position, you could also use the following call:

```
check_if_highest above 16 out of {1, 4, 12, 5}
```

Making Up Your Own Labels

You've already seen how to make up custom names for your subroutines. Now you'll look at how to define custom names for a subroutine's parameters as well. All this means is that if you don't find any of the 23 labels reserved by AppleScript suitable for indicating what a parameter's job is, you can choose your own, more descriptive label instead.

There are three differences, however, between using your own labels and using the predefined subroutine label parameters: you have to precede the use of your own labeled parameters with the word given, your parameters must be separated by a comma, and you have to separate your labels from the variables (or values in the subroutine call) with a colon. A bit confusing, but together we can do it!

Let's start with a simple single-parameter subroutine. The subroutine will take a string and return the reverse of it (*word* ➤ *drow*).

You will need to invent three words for this subroutine: the subroutine identifier will be reverse_string, the parameter label will be a_string, and the identifier of the actual variable used in the subroutine will be string_to_reverse.

Script 18-11 shows how the subroutine definition will look.

Script 18-11.

```
to reverse_string given reversing_string:string_to_reverse
    set text item delimiters to ""
    return (reverse of (characters of string_to_reverse)) as string
end reverse_string
```

This really isn't as bad as it seems. You already know about the subroutine identifier and the parameter variable. All you did was add your own label to the parameter.

Here is the call for that subroutine:

```
reverse_string given a_string:"play time"
--> result: "emit yalp"
```

Now let's try it with two parameters. The following subroutine will calculate the area of a rectangle. The parameter labels will be width and height. Here you go:

```
to calculate_rectangle_area given width:w, height:h
    return w * h
end get_the_area
```

What's nice in this situation is calling the subroutine. The parameter labels make it easy to remember what the values stand for.

```
calculate_rectangle_area given width:12, height:5
```

Calling Subroutines with Boolean Parameters

Another unique feature of the labeled parameter subroutines is the ability to specify Boolean values, like you would in any other AppleScript command, using the with and without labels.

As an example, you will create a subroutine that trims tabs and spaces from strings. As for parameters, you will have four Boolean parameters and one direct parameter.

The direct parameter is the first parameter used in a subroutine definition. The label of the direct parameter is either in or of, and it always has to be the first parameter. The direct parameter will be the actual string you want to trim white text from. The four Boolean parameters will be from_front, from_back, trimming_spaces, and trimming_tabs. You can assume that for the subroutine to do anything, either one of the first pair of parameters and either one of the second pair of parameters must be set to true, but that's beside the point.

Now let's inspect the subroutine. Mainly pay attention to the first line in the definition and to the subroutine call. Script 18-12 shows the subroutine definition.

Script 18-12.

```
1. to trim_characters of the_text ¬
       given from_front:f, from_back:b, trimming_spaces:s, trimming_tabs:t
2.     --Assemble a list of characters to trim
3.     set characters_to_trim to {}
4.     if s then set end of characters_to_trim to space
5.     if t then set end of characters_to_trim to tab
6.     --Trim from the start of the text
7.     if f then
8.        repeat while character 1 of the_text is in characters_to_trim
9.           if length of the_text is 1 then
10.             return ""
11.          else
12.             set the_text to text 2 thru -1 of the_text
13.          end if
14.       end repeat
15.    end if
16.    --Trim from the end of the text
17.    if b then
18.       repeat while character -1 of the_text is in characters_to_trim
19.          if length of the_text is 1 then
20.             return ""
21.          else
22.             set the_text to text 1 thru -2 of the_text
23.          end if
24.       end repeat
25.    end if
26.    return the_text
27. end trim_characters
```

Notice that this is a normal labeled parameter definition. You have the labels marking the four labeled parameters, and you're ready to call the subroutine. In the subroutine call, you won't supply values to the parameters in the fashion you learned earlier, which would go something like this:

```
trim_characters of the_text given ¬
    from_front:true, from_back:true, trimming_spaces:true, trimming_tabs:false
```

Instead, you will treat the Boolean parameters like you would treat them in application and scripting addition commands—by using the with and without keywords:

```
trim_characters of the_text ¬
    with from_front, from_back, trimming_spaces and trimming_tabs
```

In the preceding call, all four Boolean parameters received a true value. In the call that follows, you will assign a false value to the trimming_tabs and from_front parameters:

```
trim_characters of the_text ¬
    with from_back and trimming_spaces without from_front and trimming_tabs
```

Whose Subroutine Is It Anyway?

First you learned about AppleScript commands and application commands. Then you saw that you can create your own commands, which is OK as long as you make up names for them such as do_this_thing_now.

Now, a problem often encountered by AppleScript novices is when they've just defined a subroutine in a script and it works fine when called from one part of their script but completely fails when called from another part, even though they've used the same command both times! What gives?

It all starts when you want to call your subroutine from inside an application tell block. Let's assume you created a subroutine for Valentine's Day called foreplay. If you call it from outside any tell block, all is well. But as soon as you try it from, say, inside the Finder's tell block, you get the following error: "Can't continue foreplay." Ouch! A second ago you were fine, but now you're trying it from the Finder, and you can't. That hurts. Here's the foreplay subroutine:

```
on foreplay()
    --Naughty stuff goes on here!
end foreplay

foreplay() --This works...

tell application "Finder"
    foreplay() --...but this causes an error: Can't continue foreplay.
end tell
```

Don't worry—all the script is experiencing here is a bit of uncertainty on top of some performance anxiety. See, when you called the foreplay subroutine from inside the tell block, AppleScript sent the foreplay command to the target object specified by that tell block—which in this case is the Finder, *not* your script. However, the only commands the Finder knows how to handle are the ones defined in its dictionary, and foreplay isn't one of them. At this point the Finder doesn't know what else to do with the command, so it sends a "Can't continue" error message back to AppleScript, which causes AppleScript to raise the "Can't continue foreplay" error you see.

Next time, try to specify whose foreplay you're trying to perform—in this case, your script's. To identify the current script, you refer to AppleScript's special built-in me variable. One way to do this is to use another tell block to change the current target object:

```
tell application "Finder"
    tell me
        foreplay()
    end tell
end tell
```

Another, more common way is to add the words of me after the command:

```
tell application "Finder"
    foreplay() of me
end tell
```

You can also write it like this:

```
tell application "Finder"
  my foreplay()
end tell
```

Preceding the subroutine call with the word my tells AppleScript to send the command to the script itself and not to the application that is the target of the tell statement you're in.

Overriding AppleScript Commands

You can redefine AppleScript and scripting addition commands. The code in your new definition will replace the code that usually runs when the command is called. For instance, let's try to meddle with the choose from list command defined in Standard Additions.

In your script, type the code shown in Script 18-13.

Script 18-13.

```
on choose from list theList
    display dialog "I'll choose for you" buttons {"OK"}
    return some item of theList
end choose from list
choose from list {1, 2, 3}
```

In the preceding script, you changed the functionality of the choose from list command. If it is called from anywhere in the script, instead of allowing the user to choose, the script will let the user know that it will choose an item from the list and then indeed proceeds to pick a random item from the list using the some item filtering statement.

In the same situation, you can possibly add to the command and then tell AppleScript to continue with the original command. Look at Script 18-14.

Script 18-14.

```
on choose from list theList
    display dialog "Should I choose for you?" buttons {"No", "Yes"}
    if button returned of result is "No" then
        continue choose from list theList
    else
        return some item of theList
    end if
end choose from list
choose from list {1, 2, 3}
```

In the preceding script, AppleScript first offers to make the decision for the user. If the user declines, then the script will tell AppleScript to *continue* to execute the command the way it was designed originally.

Introducing Recursion

Recursion is when a subroutine calls itself. Technically it means that the subroutine definition contains the subroutine call. The following example contains an example of a subroutine that will call itself an infinite number of times:

```
do_something()

on do_something()
    display dialog "Doing something now..."
    do_something()
end do_something
```

Recursion doesn't necessarily mean that the subroutine will call itself infinitely. In most cases, the subroutine calling itself will be subject to a condition.

One thing that recursion is used for is when processing files or folders nested in a folder hierarchy. In this case, the script starts by calling the handler and passing the top folder as a parameter. The handler gets the contents of the folder and processes each item; if the item is a folder, the subroutine then calls itself and passes that folder as the parameter's value.

Here's a cool example that creates a list of folders, each one indented based on its level in the folder hierarchy:

```
show_folder_hierarchy(choose folder, "")

on show_folder_hierarchy(the_folder, the_indent)
    --process this folder
    tell application "Finder"
        set the_result to the_indent & name of the_folder & return
    end tell
    --process each sub-folder in turn
    tell application "Finder"
        repeat with sub_folder_ref in (get every folder of the_folder)
            set the_result to the_result & ¬
                my show_folder_hierarchy(contents of sub_folder_ref, the_indent & tab)
        end repeat
    end tell
    return the_result
end show_folder_hierarchy
```

You can find more examples of recursive subroutines dealing with files and folders in Chapter 13.

Using Subroutines and Variables Together

In Chapter 8, we talked about variables being the memory of AppleScript. If you store a value in a variable, you can later use it anywhere in the script. Well, this is almost all true.

As a refresher, AppleScript has two main kinds of variables: global variables and local variables. The main difference between the two comes to light when you work with subroutines.

Declaring Variables

Although it is more organized and proper to do so, you are not required to declare local variables. Only global variables require proper declaration.

You declare variables anywhere in the script's run handler by typing the variable identifier following the word global:

```
global the_name
```

You can also declare multiple variables in the same statement, as follows:

```
global x, y, z
```

I think it is better to declare global variables one at a time, because this way you can add a comment for each variable in regard to its function.

Understanding the Scope of Local and Global Variables

In short, local variables are available only inside the subroutine they're used in, and local variables that were defined in the run handler (the main part of the script) have no meaning inside any other subroutine definition.

Global variables, on the other hand, are available throughout any part of your script. Let's look at an example—Script 18-15 shows a subroutine that calculates the area of a rectangle. It also uses a pair of local variables, the_width and the_height, which you will start by declaring only in the body of the script and not in the subroutine.

Script 18-15.

```
1. local the_width, the_height --not needed, but nice
2. set the_width to 3
3. set the_height to 5
4. set the_area to calculate_rectangle_area()

5. on calculate_rectangle_area ()
6. return the_width * the_height
7. end get_area
```

What happens when you run the script? You get the following error on line 6:

```
The variable the_width is not defined.
```

But how can that be when you had both variables defined in the script? Well, as soon as you started executing the subroutine, the local variables you declared and assigned values to at the top level of the script (in other words, in the implicit run handler) were no longer visible to you. So, what are your options? First let's look at global variables.

Let's run the same script with a slight modification; instead of declaring the variables the_width and the_height as local variables, declare them as global variables:

```
1. global the_width, the_height --Now it's needed, but is it nice?
```

Now that the variables are global, their reach—or in programming terms, their *scope*—spans the run handler and any other subroutine you defined.

Using Local Variables Nevertheless

To use the values from local variables in subroutines, all you have to do is pass them as parameters, like in Script 18-16.

Script 18-16.

```
local the_width, the_height --not needed, but nice
set the_width to 3
set the_height to 5
set the_area to get_area(the_width, the_height)

on get_area(the_width, the_height)
   return the_width * the_height
end get_area
```

They don't have to match the identifiers used in the subroutine itself, but they may. The subroutine definition may as well be like Script 18-17.

Script 18-17.

```
on get_area(x, y)
   return x * y
end get_area
```

Don't Yield to Global Temptation

It may be a wasted effort to try to explain that even though a couple of global variable declarations can spare you a lot of effort in passing parameters to subroutines, they can cause headaches later. Nevertheless, I'm going to try, so here we go.

First, so you don't say no one ever told you so, you should not use AppleScript global variables as a replacement to passing parameters in subroutines because you're too lazy to keep track of your parameters.

Global variables should be reserved for only the truly global values in your script. For instance, they should be reserved for the path to the main folder in the automation solution you're creating, the variable whose value is the loaded library script with many of the subroutines you use, and other such values that are used throughout the script—items whose usefulness covers many parts of the script, are used by many subroutines, and are global in nature.

Understanding the Scope of Properties

In the eye of a subroutine definition, script properties are identical to global variables. You can declare a property once, and that value will be attached to that variable throughout the script, including subroutine definitions.

Storing Individual Subroutines

The identifier you use when you specify a subroutine automatically turns into a variable whose value is the content of the subroutine.

As an example, you will use the split name subroutine created earlier. After the subroutine is defined, you can ask the script for the class of the variable split_name, as shown in Script 18-18.

Script 18-18.

```
on split_name(the_name)
    set first_name to first word of the_name
    set last_name to last word of the_name
    return {first_name:first_name, last_name:last_name}
end split_name
class of split_name
--> handler
```

OK, the variable has a handler value, so what can you do with that? Watch:

```
set script_file_path to (path to scripts folder) & "script.scpt" as string
store script split_name in file script_file_path
```

What will the two preceding lines do? They will create a compiled script file containing the split_name script. Figure 18-6 shows the resulting script file opened in the Script Editor application.

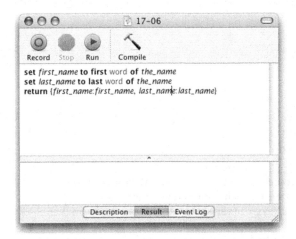

Figure 18-6. *A subroutine that was stored as a script is open in the Script Editor application. Notice that the* on wrapper *is gone.*

Moving Script Parts to Subroutines

One way that subroutines are created in your script is when a portion of your script "evolves" into a subroutine. It happens in the process of writing a script. You suddenly realize that the chunk of script you just created can be its own little thing, responsible for carrying out a single, well-defined task. You may be able to use it somewhere else in the script or in other scripts. Or maybe you just figured that it takes too much space in the body of the script, and you want to move it out of the way where it won't be so distracting.

What you need to do first is identify all the variables on which this part of the script depends. Some variables may be created inside the part you're trying to move, so you don't have to worry about them for the start. The rest will need their values to be passed into the subroutine, usually as parameters.

After you have some idea of which variables you will need to pass as parameters, you can move the entire part of the script to your subroutine area and wrap it in an on . . . end subroutine wrapper.

This would also be a good time to decide what values the subroutine call should return. If the portion of the script you're porting into a subroutine is a single value, you can return that value directly. However, if you need to return more than one value, you will need to wrap them up in a list (or record) before returning them.

In the following example, you will look at extracting part of a larger script into its own subroutine. The bit you're interested in is used to calculate the age in days of a given file, which is just the sort of nice, well-defined, logical task that can be easily made into a user-defined command.

Script 18-19 shows the script.

Script 18-19.

```
--some statement...
set the_file to choose file
--some other statement...
set file_properties to info for the_file
set file_creation_date to creation date of file_properties
set file_age_in_seconds to (current date) - file_creation_date
set days_old to file_age_in_seconds div days
--do something with days_old variable...
```

By looking at the script I can identify that the part I want to convert into a subroutine uses a few variables but requires only one variable to start, which is the variable the_file.

The subroutine will return the value of the days_old variable to the script, which can then assign it to a days_old variable of its own.

It's important to check whether the other variables used in that part of the script (such as file_age_in_seconds, file_creation_date, and so on) are used later in the script. If they are, you will need to have the subroutine return their values as well or reconsider which parts of the code should go in this subroutine and which should go elsewhere or stay where they are.

For example, if file_age_in_seconds is also used later, then it would probably be best to make a subroutine named get_file_age_in_seconds and leave the code that uses days_old to perform that final division itself. If file_creation_date is used elsewhere, then you should probably think about obtaining the file's creation date as a separate task and then passing it to a subroutine called calculate_age_in_days that takes a date value as its parameter.

Figuring out the best ways to divide code into separate subroutines can be hard at first, but you'll get better and better at it with practice. A good tip is to make a copy of your original script and experiment on that. That way, if you like what you come up with, you can keep it; if not, you can simply throw it away, and no harm has been done in trying.

Script 18-20 shows the new part of the script and the subroutine definition.

Script 18-20.

```
--some statement...
set the_file to choose file
--some other statement...
set days_old to get_file_age_in_days(the_file)
--do something with days_old variable...

on get_file_age_in_days(the_file)
  set file_properties to info for the_file
  set file_creation_date to creation date of file_properties
  set file_age_in_seconds to (current date) - file_creation_date
  set days_old to file_age_in_seconds div days
  return days_old
end get_file_age_in_days
```

Extending AppleScript Your Way

Although all of us AppleScript users use AppleScript for programming, we all use it slightly differently. These differences come to light when we see the applications we use and the type of tasks we automate. It is safe to say that many scripters have a specialty beyond scripting and that the Apple-Script scripting language is merely a tool we use to perfect whatever else we do. I write scripts, but my true specialty is publishing workflows. A system administrator may use AppleScript, but his true function is administering Macs.

After working with AppleScript for a while, you will realize that you use the same types of functions that relate to your area of expertise. Your next step then is to create your own language that makes scripting *your* tasks easier.

No, I'm not suggesting you learn C++, put on rags, and walk barefoot from city to city preaching the new code. All I want you to do is start doing a few little things to make you a better scripter.

Start collecting functions. Every collection starts small. My collection started with the subroutines I downloaded from the AppleScript website. I collected them into a file, renamed them to fit my subroutine naming style, and saved them in a script file. I slowly added little subroutines to that file and started loading that file to every script I created. Soon enough I realized that a large chunk of the volume of my scripts was code I called from my subroutine library. By now I have more than ten libraries, each with its own purpose, and most of the boring side of my coding is taken care of by dragging and dropping subroutine calls.

For your naming conventions, start with the large object such as the name of the application you're talking to, and go from there. Give your subroutines long, clear names. Shorthand is great at the time of writing, but a month down the road the subroutines look like someone else wrote them, died, and never left the instructions.

So you see? Once you have many of these subroutines collected in one or more files, also referred to as *script libraries*, your main scripts will mostly use commands you created earlier (your subroutines) instead of AppleScript or scriptable applications commands. You'll look at creating and using script libraries in much more detail in Chapter 19.

Working Smart with Subroutines

The following few sections contain tips for creating and using subroutines. Subroutines can be a boon for efficient script writing, and with the right organization, you will be able to spend more time on the function of the script and less time on messing with syntax.

Organizing Code with Subroutines

One of the brilliant factors subroutines add to your scripts is organization. They allow you to tell the story of your script in your language, rather than in a programming language.

You know those people who tell a story about something they did but feel compelled to go into every last detail, until you lose the whole story? Well, without subroutines, AppleScript can be like that too. As you read through a script and try to understand it, you don't want to be bothered with the 50 lines of script that made a certain function of the script work. What you want is to quickly get a general idea of the script's organization, what happens in what order, and the basic branching that makes up the script. That's true: out of 100 if-then statements and repeat loops in a given script, only a few actually play a part in the overall structure of the script and should be included in the main body (or, the run handler, as you saw earlier).

So, how do you organize a script with subroutines? You think logically as you write the script. You also periodically read the script back and pretend it's a story you're telling someone. If it sounds a bit heavy on the details, you may want to corral the code that has that extra detail you don't want to have in the main body of the script and turn it into a subroutine. This way, your script becomes more like an easy-to-understand story, and the details are buried in subroutines.

Reusing Code with Subroutines

Another big function of subroutines, if not the biggest one, is reusing code. The idea is that a subroutine is a closed nugget of code that, given the expected parameters, will perform reliably and return the expected result. This won't be the same result every time, but it will be a result within the expected range.

Once you have such a subroutine, even if it has been written for a specific purpose, you may find that you can reuse it elsewhere in the same script and in other scripts too. Another way to instantly know that a piece of a script will make a good subroutine is if you start copying chunks of script from one part of the script to another. If the same code, or similarly structured code, exists in more than one part of the script, you may want to consider turning it into a subroutine.

Thinking Ahead

When creating subroutines, it is good to consider not only the script you're working on right now but the wider scope of scripts you've created and are likely to create. Think about making your subroutines as general as possible without using any data specific to the subject matter your script is processing but rather to the process it is performing. For instance, if your script needs a subroutine that takes a list of files and returns a new list containing only the names of the Microsoft Word documents from the original list, try to make it more general: create a subroutine that takes a file list in one parameter and a file type in the other. The subroutine will return the names of the files from the list that are of the types in the second parameter. This subroutine focuses on the process of filtering files by type rather than on a script-specific need such as filtering Word documents.

Thinking Small

Make your subroutines as small as you can (while keeping them longer than their own calls). Small, generic subroutines are much easier to understand than big complicated ones that try to do lots of different things at once. They're also much easier to debug since you can often test them in isolation, and they're easier to reuse within the same script or even in other scripts.

What I personally use is a set of about 15 subroutine library files that have hundreds of subroutines dealing with different subjects. Some of the subroutines are long, but most have fewer than ten lines of script. This makes it so that most of my scripts consist of subroutine calls instead of commands. I name my subroutines deliberately and descriptively so that I can easily identify what the script is doing at any given time, such as `Excel subroutine library.scpt`, `Text manipulation subroutine library.scpt`, and so on.

Applications Aside

Another thing I like to avoid is littering my scripts with application `tell` blocks. I know, I know, a 200-line script that talks to seven applications is much cooler to look at, but once you've passed the "look, Ma" stage, you may want to consider chucking commands sent to applications into different subroutines and storing them all in the same library. I have a library of commands for each application, and every time I use a new command, object, or property in that application, I turn it into a subroutine and add it to the library.

Script Debugger makes placing library and subroutine calls easy with its clipping palette.

Power Wrap-Up

The following sections summarize the chapter in an intensive reference style. Use these sections to look up facts related to the chapter without the chatter.

Subroutines

Subroutines, also called *handlers*, are code capsules that can be used by the main script multiple times. A subroutine that is not called by the main body of the script, also called the run handler, will never be executed.

How to Use the Basic Subroutine

The basic subroutine starts with the definition line and ends with the end line. The definition line starts with either on or to; is followed by the subroutine identifier, which is a term you make up to name the subroutine; and finally ends with the list of subroutine parameters:

```
on do_something(parameter_1, parameter_2)
```

The last line of the subroutine starts with end followed by the subroutine identifier:

```
end do_something
```

The body of the subroutine includes any statements that appear between the definition and end lines:

```
on do_something(parameter_1, parameter_2, etc)
--do this
--do that
end do_something
```

Subroutines can have multiple parameters or no parameters at all, in which case the subroutine identifier is followed by empty parentheses:

```
on do_something()
--do this
end do_something
```

How to Get the Subroutine Result

A subroutine returns the result of the last statement to execute in the subroutine. To make subroutines more legible, the final statement uses the return command to return the final value. Not every subroutine returns a value, however.

```
on calculate_numbers (a, b)
  set the_result to a + b
  return the_result
end do_something
```

To return more than one result, collect the different results in a list, and return the list as the result.

How to Call Subroutines

To be executed, the subroutine has to be called from the main script, or from another subroutine, like this:

```
do_something(parameter_1_value, parameter_2_value, etc)
```

If the subroutine is called from inside an application `tell` block, you have to specify that the subroutine is not an application command but rather a script-defined command. You can do this in one of the following ways:

```
tell me to do_something()
my do_something()
do_something() of me
```

How to Use Positional Parameter Subroutines

The subroutine type shown previously is the positional parameter subroutine type. Each parameter is identified by its position within the other parameters. In this type of subroutine, the order of the parameters in the subroutine definition and the subroutine call must be identical.

How to Use Labeled Parameter Subroutines

Labeled parameter subroutines are a bit more complex to create and call. For more information regarding labeled parameter subroutines, read the corresponding section in this chapter.

How to Use Subroutines and Variable Scope

Any variable that is defined in one subroutine is valid only in that particular subroutine and not outside it. To use a value of a variable from the body of the script in a subroutine that is called from the body of the script, the value has to either be passed as a parameter or be defined as a global variable or a property.

■ ■ ■

Using Script Objects

Script objects are probably the most underutilized complex feature in the AppleScript language. This chapter explains the idea behind script objects and how to use them, and it discusses real-world techniques for putting script objects to use in your projects.

Note While reading this chapter, please be aware that you can use AppleScript to create some incredible scripts without ever using script objects. I personally didn't start using script objects until I had to when attempting a large-scale system. Script objects are good, but they are also an advanced feature with many hidden caveats that can drive you crazy.

Introducing Script Objects

So, you got through the basics and are now ready for the serious stuff. Understanding script objects after creating many scripts is like understanding the solar system after living on Earth. You have to imagine that each script you created so far is not an entire entity but rather an object that can be moved, reproduced, and made to accept your commands. Not only can the script accept commands, but so can any script objects the script contains, as you will soon see.

To understand what a script object is, try to understand what a script is in the first place. A *script* is a collection of commands in the form of subroutines (including the run handler) and/or data contained in properties. When you run the script, either from the scripting application, as a stand-alone applet, or in any other way, the run handler from that script executes, and any data stored in properties, if any, is used in that execution. Now imagine that a script object is just that: a collection of commands and data, but instead of being a stand-alone unit, it is loaded in one way or another to a different script. That script becomes the "parent" script and can run the loaded "child" script in its entirety or just call its subroutines to use and set the data stored in its subroutines.

Initially, it is a bit difficult to see what's so great about script objects; after all, you can do many, if not most, things without them. In fact, some scripters will never start using script objects but will still create some useful scripts. So, what's all the hoopla about script objects? Well, you have to be planning a project whose complexity calls for the use of script objects—script objects aren't useful at all in most situations. But when attempting a complicated AppleScript system, using script objects can make your system more modular and easier to handle.

Don't get me wrong—starting to use script objects isn't that complicated, and they quickly can become useful tools. Like many other things in life, though, it takes some time and practice to really master them.

You'd use script objects for two main reasons: for script libraries and for object-oriented programming.

Simple: Loading Script Libraries

Script libraries can help you maintain sanity when working on larger AppleScript projects in two ways: they reduce the size of your scripts, which makes the scripts more manageable, and they allow you to use the same subroutines in multiple scripts. In a way, script libraries are a bit like your local public library: instead of storing all the books you want to read in your house, you can go there once a week and check out any book the library has. You have full access to thousands of books, but the library maintains the space it takes to store these books. On top of that, other people can use the same library to check out the same books. In AppleScript, a library holds subroutines that any script can check out and use at any time.

The most common use for script objects is in assembling powerful collections of useful subroutines that can be quickly and easily reused from script to script. This method of using script objects is not only easy to use but highly recommended. All you do is load a script to another script with the load script command.

Although this method doesn't use the more advanced abilities script objects have to offer, it has an instant organizational benefit: you can now take all those handlers you keep copying and pasting between your scripts and give them a final resting place in one or more script files. You can load these files, also referred to as script *libraries*, into your different scripts. You can then call the subroutines in the loaded script and execute them without them crowding your actual script. In effect, you will be writing your own scripting addition–like extensions to AppleScript, except you can write these extensions yourself using simple AppleScript instead of a much harder, low-level language such as C (ah—cool!).

Advanced: Defining Your Own Custom Objects

A second, more advanced use for AppleScript's script objects is in defining custom objects for use in your scripts (what programmers refer to as *object-oriented programming* [OOP]).

Just as subroutines allow you to define your own custom commands, script objects allow you to define your own custom objects. For example, AppleScript lacks a built-in command for sorting lists, but you can easily define a sort_list subroutine yourself to provide this functionality.

Similarly, although AppleScript already defines several basic value classes for you to use in scripts—integer, string, list, record, date, and so on—you may sometimes find yourself wishing it provided other types as well. For example, what if you need an object that can store values according to string-based keys, rather than by numerical index (lists) or property label (records)? Although AppleScript might not provide such an object, you can build your own by using existing structures such as lists to hold the raw key and value data, defining subroutines that can add and retrieve this data, and then wrapping the whole lot in a script object. Then, any time you need an object that stores values by string-based keys, you can just ask AppleScript to make you another one of these custom script objects. Sure, you could keep the data and the subroutines separate, but your code will be a lot more organized and convenient to use if you group related things—and good organization and ease of use become increasingly important as your scripts grow larger and more complex.

For example, imagine using AppleScript to program a checkers game. The main script can contain a list where each item is a script responsible for a single piece. Each such game-piece script can contain subroutines that move the piece and deal with different situations, as well as properties that keep track of the piece's position and state. The main script will then just tell the piece to move, either left or right, and the piece will be able to do the rest.

Here's a skeleton of the checkers script object:

```
script checkers_piece
    property piece_position : {3, 5}
    property is_queen : false
```

```
on move_piece(move_direction)
    -- what to do if the piece should move...
end move_piece

on terminate_piece()
    -- what to do if the piece should die...
end terminate_piece

on promote_piece()
    -- The piece reached the end of the board...
end promote_piece

end script
```

Creating and Using Scripts

Perhaps one of the most used and useful forms of script objects is the form that doesn't specifically use the "object-oriented" aspect of script objects. Instead, the benefit of loading scripts from files allows you to organize your scripts and increase code reusability.

Loading scripts from files is simple: you need a path to a compiled script file, and you need a variable identifier to which you want the script assigned.

Understanding Script-Loading Basics

To avoid confusion, let's walk through all the steps. Start by creating a new script. In it, type the lines of code in Script 19-1.

Script 19-1.

```
display dialog "You can run but you cannot hide"

on do_something_else(the_thing)
    display dialog "I'm now "& the_thing
end do_something_else
```

What you have done is created a script with an implicit run handler that consists of a single display dialog statement and an additional subroutine, do_something_else, that takes one parameter and consists of one display dialog statement.

Next, save your script on your desktop, and name it my scriptlibrary.scpt. Then close the file you just created. Now start a new script file, and type the following:

```
set script_path to ((path to desktop as string) & "my scriptlibrary.scpt")
set my_script_variablelibrary to load script file script_path
tell my_script_variable to run
```

What you should pay attention to here is the load script command and the run command. The load script command, which is defined in Standard Additions, loads a script from disk. And you can then assign it as the resulting script object to the my_script_variablelibrary variable.

In the following statement, you send a run command to the script object assigned to the my_script_variable, telling it to execute its run handler. The run command expects to find a script object assigned to the my_script_variable variable, and it executes this script object's run handler.

Now remember that the script you saved has more to it than just a `run` handler. It also has a subroutine you defined called `do_something_else`. To call this subroutine, you can call it either in the script object's `tell` block:

```
tell my_script_variablelibrary
    do_something_else("cooking lunch")
end tell
```

or in this form:

```
my_script_variable's do_something_else("cooking lunch")
```

Either way, the result is that your main script has loaded a script file as a script object into a variable, and now you can call subroutines from that script object by using the variable to which it is assigned.

Forming Script Libraries

The most common reason people use the `load script` command is to organize subroutines in script libraries. Unlike the scripts you've written in previous chapters, script libraries aren't intended to be run directly. In other words, you'll have compiled scripts that don't contain a `run` handler at all. Instead, those script files contain collections of useful subroutines that you can use in any other script.

If you don't yet have a script library you're using, then start one right now. Working with script libraries is easy and addictive, although it does require an ounce of discipline. It forces you to evaluate every chunk of code you write. From now on, start writing scripts as small chunks that perform one little task after the other. Instead of creating one long script that interacts with many applications and consists of hundreds of script lines, break it into units.

Each nugget of code should have a small function and a name, such as `finder_delete_file` or `create_word_document`. The smaller the subroutines you put in your library, the more they will fit into your scripts, and the more modular your scripts will be.

To start your own library, create a new script in Script Editor and add to it some subroutines. You'll find some useful list-related subroutines in a script called `list subroutines.scpt` in this chapter's folder in the code download. Copy the subroutines from there, and paste them to your script. In the following sections, you will save and use this library.

Where Should You Save Your Library?

Another important aspect of a library is where you save it. Of course, if you're writing scripts for yourself, the location of your library doesn't make too much difference. But sooner or later you will need to make your scripts available to other people on other Macs. At that point, you must ensure your script can always find the subroutine library and that you don't go crazy with installation.

The best solution is to find a folder you can later access using the `path to` command, preferably somewhere in the current user's `Library` or `Scripts` folder. Use the `Application Support` folder to store libraries that are used by specific script applications, and use the `ScriptingAdditions` folders for general-purpose libraries. Placing your library in one of these folders allows your scripts to find them no matter which OS X computer they run on.

As an exercise, save the script you created earlier containing list subroutines. Call it `list_commands_library.scpt`, and save it in the `/Library/ScriptingAdditions/` folder on your hard disk.

Loading the Library

Now that you have a library, let's see how you can use it in a script. For example, let's say you named your script command_library.scpt and put it in the Applications Support folder in the user's Home folder. You will load the list library you just created to a new script.

To load that library, start your new script, and add the following two lines:

```
set library_path to ¬
   (path to application supportscripting additions from user local➥
      domain as string) & "list_command_library.scpt"
set my list_commands_library _lib to load script file library_path
```

Since every Mac OS X has an Applications Support folder (and if it doesn't exist, the command will create it), you are safe. After that, all you have to do is type my_lib before the command name to properly call it. To use the loaded library, add these lines to your script:

```
set the_list to {3, 7 ,1 ,9 ,2 , 0}
set sorted_list to list_commands_library's sort_list(the_list)
--> {0, 1, 2, 3, 7, 9}
```

You still have to make sure the computer the script is running on has your library in that folder. For computers running Panther, you can take advantage of script application packages. Just save your script as a package, place your library file in the resources folder in that package, and use the path to me command to access that resources folder. For a complete description, see Chapter 21, which explains how to install scripting additions.

Creating and Running Script Objects

Script objects can be a rather complex matter to grasp, so this section starts from the beginning and moves along slowly. I will also try to stick to more doing and less talking.

I will start with script objects by showing how to create the script code first. Start a new script file, and type the following lines:

```
set x to "Hello"
display dialog x
```

Now run the script. The outcome is, as expected, a dialog box.

Next, let's turn this code into a script object. Wrap the two lines with the script wrapper, like this:

```
script
   set x to "Hello"
   display dialog x
end script
```

Now run the script. Nothing happens, but look at the result of your script: it's a script! Try adding the following line after the end script line and then running it again:

```
display dialog (class of result as string)
```

The dialog box displays "script" on your screen.

Now, replace the last line with the last line of Script 19-2.

Script 19-2.

```
script
    set x to "Hello"
    display dialog x
end script
run result
```

Aha! You got the script to run, but it's a bit awkward. Do you really have to ambush the script until it's done "passing through" just to capture it? Not really. What you did previously was simply create the script object, but you didn't leave yourself a comfortable way to use that script.

What you will do next is give the script a name. Naming the script object will create a neat situation: the script object's name will become a variable that has the script object assigned to it. Now here is the punch line: because the named script object is defined at the top level of the main script, it's assigned to the variable while the script compiles! This is cool because you can start referring to the script object (by name) right from the beginning of the script—it has already initialized itself. Here's how you name a script (I'm using the name simon):

```
script simon
    set x to "Hello"
    display dialog x
end script
```

Now, you don't have to wait for the script to run as if it were a statement. Instead, you can give it commands from the beginning and push the actual code of the script to the end, as you do in Script 19-3.

Script 19-3.

```
tell simon to run
script simon
    set x to "Hello"
    display dialog x
end script
```

Proliferating Your Script Object

So far, you've met script simon. Although script simon is nice and has great intentions, it acts a bit too much like a simple subroutine. What is the difference between telling simon to run and calling any subroutine with the same code? Not much.

What you will do next, however, takes a script object. You will now give simon a couple of siblings: jack and judy. The way you do that is by copying simon to the variables judy and jack.

To make matters more interesting, you will also declare a property inside the script simon, and instead of a run handler, you will place the display dialog statement in a subroutine called say_something. To start, refer to the new simon script, shown in Script 19-4.

Script 19-4.

```
script simon
    property x : "Hello"
    on say_something()
        display dialog x
    end say_something
end script
```

Now simon is a script with a purpose: it has a property and a subroutine like any useful script should. Let's see what you can do with it.

Start by copying simon to jack and to judy. Then, set the x property of jack and judy to two different values. After that, tell both judy and jack to call the say_something subroutine and see what happens.

Script 19-5 shows the complete script.

Script 19-5.

```
copy simon to jack
copy simon to judy

set x of judy to "Hi, I'm Judy"
set x of jack to "Hello, I'm Jack"

tell jack to say_something()
tell judy to say_something()

script simon
    property x : "Hello"
    on say_something()
       display dialog x
    end say_something
end script
```

In the first two lines, you copy simon to judy and jack. How can you do that right at the start? Remember, simon was a script object before the main script even started to run; in fact, simon was a script object since the main script was compiled!

The following two lines set the x property of judy and jack. Remember, two copies of the script simon are now live as two separate scripts, each with its own x property that you can set to anything you want. And since judy and jack are objects, you can set their properties at will.

Lines 5 and 6 of the script actually call the say_something subroutine of judy and jack. As you can see for yourself when you run the script, each of them has something different to say.

Note Although you use copy here to replicate the script, it's hardly a great way to do it in the real world. The reason is that using copy to replicate a script performs what is called a *deep copy*. This copies the script object along with any script object that is loaded into that script object, and so on. This situation can overload the script and crash it.

Using Subroutines to Create Script Object Instances

So far you've counted on the script objects being there, but you didn't really have control over when and where they became available. It was nice to have the script objects already in a variable upon recompiling the main script, but that can be a bit of a drag as well. What you'll see now is how to make the main script manufacture new script objects on demand. You do that by placing the script objects in a subroutine. This way, only when you call that subroutine is a script object created.

Also, the script doesn't need to have a name. If you give the script a name by placing an identifier after the word `script` in the opening line, this name will have no meaning outside the subroutine scope. Instead, when you call the subroutine containing the script, you must assign the result that the subroutine returns to the variable to which you want the script object to be assigned.

Script 19-6 shows you how to create a subroutine that can create the same person you looked at earlier. The script's single subroutine, `make_new_person`, will create a script object containing its own property and subroutine. The script is structured in such a way that when each instance of the script object is created, the initial greeting for that person is set. Later, when you call that script's `say_something()` subroutine, the script will display the value stored in the `greeting` property, which you supplied when you created the script's instance.

Script 19-6.

```
set judy to make_new_person("Hi, I'm Judy")
set jack to make_new_person("Hello, I'm Jack")

tell jack to say_something()
tell judy to say_something()

to make_new_person(their_greeting)
    script
        property greeting : their_greeting
        on say_something()
            display dialog greeting
        end say_something
    end script
end make_new_person
```

Introducing Libraries and Variable Scope

Although global variables are visible throughout the hierarchy of nested scripts, properties are good only in the script in which they are defined. If you create a main script that has a `page_template` property and then load a script library into that script, the loaded script will not have access to the main script's `page_template` property (or anything else in the main script, for that matter).

The only connection these two scripts have to each other is from the loading script to the loaded script. This means the loading script can set and get properties and call subroutines in the loaded script, but the loaded script has no way to speak to the script that loaded it. This means if there's a property in the loaded script that has to be set based on a variable value in the loading script, only the loading script can make that assignment, not the loaded script.

Let's say you have a script application you run, which you will call Main Script. This Main Script application has to process different files and use different templates and folders. This applet and all the files and folders it uses are located in a folder structure, the topmost folder of which is named `main system folder`. To make life easier, you have a property in the applet called `main_folder_path`, and when you run the applet, it starts by figuring out the main folder's path and assigning it to the `main_folder_path` property.

To make things a little clearer, Figure 19-1 shows the system's folder structure.

Figure 19-1. *The multiscript system folder structure*

Figure 19-2 shows the two scripts used by the system: the main application script called Main Script and the library script it will load called Library.scpt.

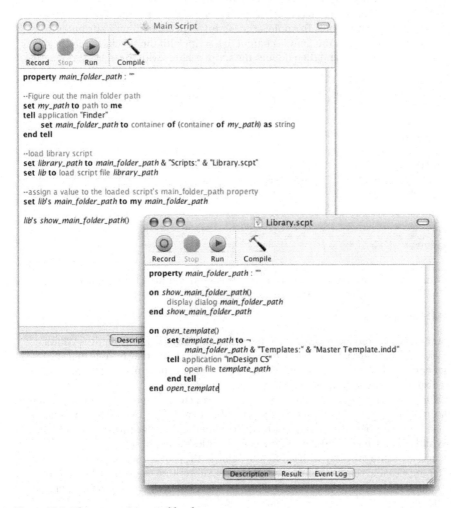

Figure 19-2. *The two scripts used by the system*

The main script starts by figuring out the path for the main folder's path. This is then used to find the path to the script library and load it to the property lib. After an instance of the Library.scpt script is loaded to the lib property, Main Script assigns the loaded script's main_folder_path property. To check that the loaded script now has a value for the main_folder_path property, Main Script can call a test subroutine, show_main_folder_path, in the loaded script.

Introducing Inheritance: When Scripts Start to Have Children

So far I have discussed how to create instances of script objects and how to call subroutines and set properties in them. Now, it's time to take it one step further. Script object inheritance has more to do with inheriting traits than inheriting fortune. To better understand inheritance, imagine a book called *Mac OS X Unleashed* (so geeky . . . I get to pick any book, and here I go). You can read it because it has content. Now, imagine a second book: *Mac OS X Unleashed II*. However, the content of the second book, instead of being original, looks like the contents of the first book, only it includes any changes or additions introduced in the second book.

In the case of the books, the first book is the parent. The second book is the child, which has inherited everything from the first book. In AppleScript, script objects can inherit attributes from other script objects in a similar way. You define a parent to a script with the special parent property. Script 19-7 defines the script wilma and then defines the script pebbles with the wilma script acting as the parent.

Script 19-7.

```
script wilma
    property hair_color : "red"
    property the_name : "Wilma"
    on say_your_name()
        display dialog "My name is " & the_name
    end say_your_name
end script

script pebbles
    property parent : wilma
end script
```

What you can do after defining the two script objects is send commands to the pebbles script as if it were the wilma script. Insert this line at the end of the script:

```
tell pebbles to say_your_name()
```

Now I know pebbles is pretty tiny, but there's no excuse for answering, "My name is Wilma" when she was asked for her name. If you figure out why she did that, you may be able to fix it. Pebbles said her name was Wilma because the script pebbles inherits not only the say_your_name subroutine but also the the_name property and its value.

One nice feature of script object inheritance is that you can choose which attributes (properties and subroutines) you want the child script object to inherit and which ones you don't. In this case, the say_your_name subroutine fulfills its purpose well, but the the_name property should be restated in the child script, which should do wonders for Pebbles's sense of self.

To do this, add the same property with a different value in the pebbles script. Also, add the words of me after the variable the_name in the say_your_name subroutine (see line 5). When the say_your_name command is sent to the pebbles script, you need it to use the the_name property that is defined in the pebbles script, even though the handler itself is located in the wilma script. If the subroutine in wilma asked for the_name by itself, then AppleScript would just return the value of the the_name property in the same object (wilma). Your code should now look like Script 19-8.

By asking for the_name of me (or my the_name), you tell AppleScript to start looking for a property named the_name in the script object that originally received the say_your_name command, which in this case is pebbles. Since pebbles now has her own the_name property, AppleScript gets the value of that; if she didn't, AppleScript would continue looking for a the_name property in her parent (wilma), and so on, until it found one (or ran out of parents to look in).

Script 19-8.

```
script wilma
    property hair_color : "red"
    property the_name : "Wilma"
    on say_your_name()
        display dialog "My name is " & the_name of me
    end say_your_name
end script

script pebbles
    property parent : wilma
    property the_name : "Pebbles"
end script

tell pebbles to say_your_name()
```

Now Pebbles will answer correctly, because although the subroutine is inherited from her mom, her name is different. To see the subroutine work from the parent script as well, try to change the last line of the previous script to this:

```
tell wilma to say_your_name()
```

In the preceding example, you saw that the pebbles script can redefine a property it inherited from the wilma script. The child script can also redefine a subroutine that exists in the parent script. When the appropriate command is sent to the child script, the new, redefined subroutine will be called, as expected. Script 19-9 defines a say_your_name subroutine in both the parent and child scripts.

Script 19-9.

```
1. script wilma
2.     property hair_color : "red"
3.     property the_name : "Wilma"
4.     on say_your_name()
5.         display dialog "My name is " & the_name of me
6.     end say_your_name
7. end script

8. script pebbles
9.     property parent : wilma
10.     property the_name : "Pebbles"
11.     on say_your_name()
12.         display dialog "Yabadabado!"
13.     end say_your_name
14. end script

15. tell pebbles to say_your_name()
```

Oh, come on now, Pebbles, that's not your name! At this point, Wilma can't take it any longer. She needs to help Pebbles say what she wants to say. To help that happen, you can use the continue keyword in pebbles's version of the say_your_name handler. The continue keyword followed by a subroutine call tells the parent script to execute its own version of the called subroutine. To do that, add the continue keyword followed by the say_your_name command inside the subroutine defini-tion in the child script:

```
on say_your_name()
    display dialog "Yabadabado!"
    continue say_your_name()
end say_your_name
```

Now things seem to work OK. The dialog boxes you get are "Yabadabado" for Pebbles followed by "My name is Pebbles."

Got No Life: Using Inheritance in a Shoot 'Em Up Game

One example I will talk about (but won't go into too much detail on) is an alien "shoot 'em up" game that uses script objects to control every aspect of the game. In this script, among the many defined script objects, a few define the alien spaceships. One script object defines all the basic characteris-tics common to each type of alien ship, although it isn't used directly in the game. To add variety, I created three other child scripts. Each one has a parent property, which defines this "base" object as its parent. The child scripts redefine some of the parent's subroutines and properties to also create variety. For instance, the red alien will be sometimes cloaked and sometimes visible, and also the pointValue property is different from one alien script to the other to make sure you get different scores for shooting different kinds of aliens.

Script 19-10 shows a small portion of the script that deals with the inheritance.

Script 19-10. *(excerpt)*

```
to makeAlienBaseObject()
    script
        property currentSpot : 1
        --Child objects will define their own pointValue, r1 and r2 properties

        on advanceAlien(columns)
            if alive then
                --...
            end if
        end advanceAlien

        on explode(alienPositionInList)
            -- Explode alien...
        end explode

        on firstRow()
            return my r1
        end firstRow

        on secondRow()
            return my r2
        end secondRow
    end script
end makeAlienBaseObject
```

```
to makeGreenAlien()
    script
        property parent : makeAlienBaseObject()
        property pointValue : 100
        property r1 : "0 0"
        property r2 : "000"
    end script
end makeGreenAlien

to makeRedAlien()
    script
        property parent : makeAlienBaseObject()
        property pointValue : 200
        property r1 : " W "
        property r2 : "W W"
        (* Unlike green aliens, which are always visible,
            red aliens have a 50% chance of being cloaked. *)
        property cloaked : some item of {true, false}

        on firstRow()
            if cloaked then
                return " • "
            else
                return continue firstRow()
            end if
        end firstRow

        on secondRow()
            if cloaked then
                return "    "
            else
                return continue firstRow()
            end if
        end secondRow
    end script
end makeRedAlien
```

You can find the complete Script 19-10, the alien-game script, on the Apress website (www.apress.com). To play, change the TextEdit preferences to create text documents by default.

You can see another example of inheritance on line 27. The redAlien script decides whether to use its own version of the secondRow subroutine or whether to continue to the parent's version of that same subroutine.

Case Study: Stock Tracker Example

In this section, you will explore a script that uses script objects to track stocks. The movement is, as can be expected, random—so if AAPL gets lower than MSFT, just restart the script . . . .

Before getting into the specifics of the script, shown in Script 19-11, let's take a moment to understand its structure. The core of the script is a list (stock_script_list) in which each item is a script object representing one stock. The script object has a few properties and two subroutines: start_stock and update_stock. When the start_stock subroutine is called, the stock is initialized. For that reason, you will call this subroutine only once at the start. The second subroutine, update_stock, changes the value of the stock and refreshes its view in the Finder window.

The part of the script that deals with the script objects consists of three distinct parts. First the list of script objects is created (lines 16 through 19). This is rather simple: the script loops once for each item in the symbol list, and each repetition, an instance of the script stock is tacked onto the scripts list.

The instances of the script object are created using the stock_instance subroutine. Since this subroutine returns an instance of the script object, you can add that object directly to the list (line 18).

Now for the second part. After you have gathered a list of instances of the same script object, you can start working with them. To start, call the start_stock subroutine in each instance.

The make_new_stock subroutine holds the key to the future success of the stock. It assigns random values to the variables that will determine whether the stock's general direction will be up or down. One of the parameters of that initialization subroutine holds the name of the stock.

To call the make_new_stock subroutine in each instance, the script loops through the script object instances list (lines 19 through 21).

Notice that in the repeat loop you address each item of stock_script_list one at a time. That's right: since every item of this list is an instance of a script object, you can tell it to execute a command defined in the script object definition.

The third and final part of the script (lines 23 through 28) has two nested repeat loops. The outer one is an endless loop with no way out. That's right: if you don't stop the script, the stocks will go up and down forever. The inner loop is similar to the last repeat loop. It loops in the list of script object instances and calls the update_stock subroutine for each script object instance in the list.

Script 19-11.

```
1. property stock_symbols : ¬
      {"IBM", "AAPL", "MSFT", "AOL", "ARC", "AHT", "GLFD", "OXBC"}
2. global stocks_folder

3. --Prepare stocks display
4. tell application "Finder"
5.    if not (exists folder "Stocks" of desktop) then
6.       make new folder at desktop with properties {name:"Stocks"}
7.    end if
8.    set stocks_folder to folder "Stocks" of desktop
9.    make new Finder window to stocks_folder
10.    tell result
11.       set toolbar visible to false
12.       set bounds to {30, 70, 830, 770}
13.       set current view to icon view
14.       set arrangement of its icon view options to not arranged
15.    end tell
16. end tell

17. --Create stock scripts list
18. set stock_scripts_list to {}
19. repeat with i from 1 to count stock_symbols
20.    set end of stock_scripts_list to make_new_stock(item i of stock_symbols, i)
21. end repeat
```

```
22. --Update each item in the list
23. repeat
24.     repeat with stock_ref in stock_scripts_list
25.         tell stock_ref to update_stock()
26.     end repeat
27.     delay 0.5
28. end repeat

29. --Subroutine for creating new stock objects
30. on make_new_stock(the_stock_symbol, the_stock_number)
31.     script stock
32.         property stock_symbol : the_stock_symbol
33.         property stock_number : the_stock_number
34.         property stock_value : 400

35.         to initialize()
36.             --prepare display
37.             tell application "Finder"
38.                 activate
39.                 if not (exists folder stock_symbol of stocks_folder) then
40.                     make new folder at stocks_folder with properties ¬
                            {name:stock_symbol}
41.                 end if
42.                 tell folder stock_symbol of stocks_folder
43.                     set position to {stock_number * 80, 770 - stock_value}
44.                     set label index to 0
45.                 end tell
46.             end tell
47.         end initialize

48.         to update_stock()
49.             --update stock value
50.             set the_change to random number from -15 to 15
51.             set stock_value to stock_value + the_change
52.             --update display
53.             tell application "Finder"
54.                 tell folder stock_symbol of stocks_folder
55.                     set position to {stock_number * 80, 770 - stock_value}
56.                     if the_change < 0 then
57.                         set label index to 2 --red = the stock value went down
58.                     else
59.                         set label index to 6 --green = the stock value went up
60.                     end if
61.                 end tell
62.                 update stocks_folder
63.             end tell
64.         end update_stock
65.     end script
66.     tell stock to initialize()
67.     return stock
68. end make_new_stock
```

Case Study: AutoGraph

AutoGraph is an automated publishing system I created for clients in the financial field. Besides making some neat use of Extensible Markup Language (XML), Scalable Vector Graphics (SVG), and Adobe InDesign tagged text, this system is made expandable by means of script objects.

The system uses script objects in two ways—one is for the basic purpose of organizing functions away from the main scripts. In fact, it uses 11 such libraries, each one containing functions for a specific purpose. These script files (which I call *engines*) can be loaded independently to other scripts and provide functionality in the form of subroutines, each covering a slightly different area. One engine covers InDesign commands, one covers Adobe Illustrator commands, one interacts with SQL, one creates SVG contents, and so on.

The second way the system uses script objects is for processing the actual graph-bearing pages. Each script file has the code to create a unique type of graph: one creates a pie chart, one creates a bar graph, and so on. The challenge in creating this system was that I knew even after the system started being used that I would have to add more of these graph scripts, for about 40 more types of graphs, but I didn't want to have to change the main script or have to update it every time with a call to a new script.

The solution was to make all the scripts share the same main subroutine. Each one of those graph-processing scripts has a subroutine called process with the same parameters. The main script starts by loading instances of all the scripts into a list of script objects. It also creates a sister list that contains a code name for each graph type in the same order in which they are stored in the script object list.

As the main processor runs, it is fed data for each one of the graphs. From that data it figures out the graph's code name and uses it to get the offset in the script object list of the script object that can produce that graph type. Now, the main script has the data for the graph, and it knows where in the script object list it can find the script that can process that graph. All that happens next is that the main script calls the process subroutine for the correct script object and waits for it to finish running (see Figure 19-3).

The advantage of this setup is that as long as I create the new graph-processing scripts using the same method, one main process subroutine with the same parameters, I can add them to the system without having to change the main script.

In addition, all the graph-processing scripts load these same "engine" library scripts for their own functionality.

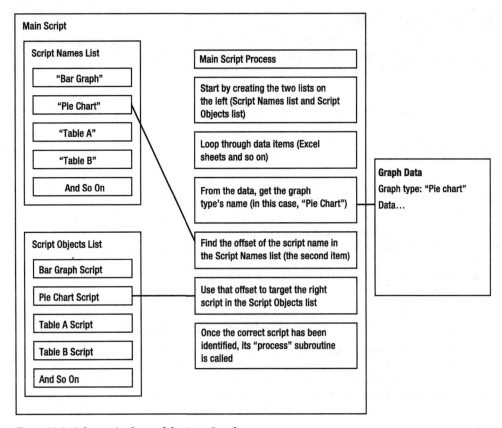

Figure 19-3. *Schematic chart of the AutoGraph system*

Power Wrap-Up

The following sections summarize the chapter in an intensive reference style. Use these sections to look up facts related to the chapter without the chatter.

What Are Script Objects?

Script objects are special objects containing a script. This script can then run independently from the main script and keep its own properties and subroutines. Script objects can be scripts you load from another file or script objects you declare inside the main script. A script object that exists in the same script document as your main script has to be wrapped in a script block, like this:

```
script simon
    property identifier : initial value
    on run
        --statements
    end run
    on do_something()
        --statements
    end do_something
end script
```

The preceding script has a run handler and a subroutine. It doesn't need both. This script is also named (simon). You are required to name scripts in this way only if they are not initialized with a subroutine.

In the case of the preceding script object, the script object is instantiated when the script is compiled.

How to Create Script Instances with a Subroutine

You can place your script object in a subroutine. In this case, the script object will not be instantiated when the main script is compiled. The script object will become available only when the subroutine in which it lives is called. Script 19-12 shows an example of a script object instantiated by a subroutine and later called to run.

Script 19-12.

```
set my_script_object to load_script()
tell my_script_object to run

on load_script()
    script
        display dialog "I'm running!"
    end script
end load_script
```

How to Declare Script Objects

When named script objects appear in your compiled script, they become instantiated as soon as the script compiles. In this case you do not need to instantiate the script, and you can refer to it by name, as shown here:

```
tell simon to run
script simon
    display dialog "I'm running!"
end script
```

How to Replicate Scripts

Once you have a script object in a variable, you can make copies of it with the copy command:

```
set script_1 to load_script()
copy scipt_1 to script_2
```

If you use the set command instead of copy, you will end up with two variables referencing the same script object, instead of two copies.

How to Use Script Objects and Inheritance

A script object can contain the property parent. The value of the parent property is usually another script. The script whose parent property is set immediately inherits all the properties and subroutines from the parent script (named as the value of the parent property). In some rare instances, an application is the parent; for instance, when embedding AppleScript scripts in a FileMaker Pro script, you can omit the tell application "FileMaker Pro" block, since the implied application is FileMaker Pro.

The child script can redefine properties set in the parent script and also rewrite subroutines specified in the parent script. Such redefined subroutines can include the command continue followed by the name of the subroutine. This will cause the same subroutine to execute as it is defined in the parent. You can read much more about this earlier in the chapter.

How to Load Scripts

You can load script into variables in other scripts by using the load script command. The script you load has to be saved as a compiled script. The loading script must assign the loaded script to a variable. This variable will then be used to give the script commands. Here's an example:

```
set my_script to ¬
   load script file "Macintosh HD:Scripts:subroutine library.scpt"
tell my_script to do_something()
```

In the preceding example, the subroutine do_something() is defined in the loaded script.

How to Use the run script Command

The run script command takes a script in the form of a string and tries to run it as AppleScript. See the following example:

```
run script "on run (x)
display dialog x
end " with parameters {"Hello World"}
```

In this example, the run script command runs a three-line script and passes it the string "Hello World" as a parameter.

The Wild World of AppleScript

■ ■ ■

Using AppleScript Amenities in Mac OS X

Following the great success companies had automating tasks with AppleScript in pre–OS X times, Apple has taken the time to make AppleScript even better, faster, and easier to integrate into applications. As soon as the OS X diagrams started circulating in 1999, it became clear that the days when AppleScript was a mere extension, riding on top of the code and begging for some processor cycles, were coming to an end. By Mac OS X, we were in.

The tight integration of AppleScript into OS X brought about some great stuff. For instance, applications created using Cocoa, Apple's new programming environment, are much easier to make scriptable. Also, user interface element scripting (graphical user interface [GUI] scripting) became an integrated part of the operating system, giving scripters access to almost all user interface (UI) elements in any application—not to mention the integration of AppleScript into OS X developer tools in the form of AppleScript Studio. Other things didn't come as easily. For Finder recordability, we had to wait for several years until it finally emerged unannounced with OS X 10.3 (Panther). Folder actions (re)appeared in Jaguar (OS X 10.2), although they didn't become reliable until Panther.

Another feature I'll discuss in this chapter is the systemwide Script menu. This menu is versatile and easy to use, and it provides a great way to launch scripts from any application.

In this chapter, you will look at some of the AppleScript amenities included with OS X 10.3 and later.

Using the AppleScript Utility

New to Tiger, the AppleScript Utility is a wee application that provides an easy way to adjust several AppleScript-related settings. Instead of having to sift through various System Preferences panels, this is one-stop shopping. You can find the AppleScript Utility application in the /Applications/ AppleScript/ folder.

Figure 20-1 shows the main screen of the AppleScript Utility application.

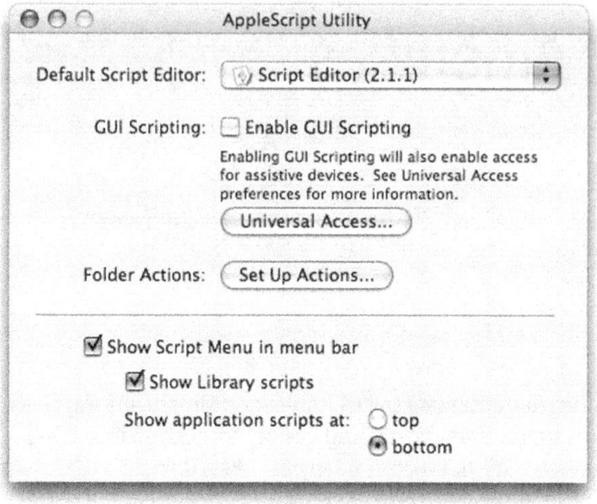

Figure 20-1. *The AppleScript Utility application*

A nice feature enabled by the AppleScript Utility application is the ability to set the default AppleScript editor. Until now, Apple's Script Editor was the default editor, and to change that you had to use the Get Info window, but now you can pick from several editors in the pop-up menu. You can pick from Script Editor and any third-party editors you've installed yourself: Script Debugger, Smile, and so on.

These are the other features you can set in the AppleScript Utility application:

- You can enable and disable GUI scripting.

- You can launch the Folder Actions Setup utility.

- You can set Script menu options.

Using the Systemwide Script Menu

Yet another optional OS X user interface item is the systemwide Script menu. OS X does not come with the menu installed because the stylish black-and-white icons at the top right of the menu bar were meant strictly for hardware controls such as monitor control, volume control, AirPort, and so on. The Script menu, however, blends in quite nicely, and installing it is easy. To see the Script menu, simply launch the AppleScript Utility (found in /Applications/AppleScript/), and check Show Script Menu in Menu Bar. Figure 20-2 shows the open Script menu.

Figure 20-2. *The open Script menu*

Preinstalled Scripts

As you can tell from looking at the menu shown in Figure 20-1 (or by gazing at your own Script menu), it already has quite a few scripts. It contains two sets of scripts separated by a divider line, with scripts above the divider and scripts below the divider. The scripts above the divider are those installed in the local domain's Scripts folder inside /Library/, and those below the divider are those installed in the user domain's Scripts folder inside ~/Library/. The divider may not have anything below it yet since the current user's Scripts folder is initially empty (see the "Other Menu Items" section).

Scripts reside in different folders on your system. The preinstalled scripts are in Startup disk/Library/Scripts/. The user scripts shown in the menu are in /User Folder/Library/Scripts/. The submenus shown in the Script menu are subfolders of the Startup disk/Library/Scripts/ folder.

Other Menu Items

The Script menu contains two additional items on top of the scripts and script folders. The first item, Open Scripts Folder, simply opens the system's Scripts folder in the Finder. This gives you quick access to adding or removing scripts. The second item launches the AppleScript Utility application.

Application-Specific Scripts

Another cool feature of the Script menu is that it can show a set of scripts only when specific applications are active. See the grayed-out Finder Scripts item shown in Figure 20-2. The script names that follow reside in a special folder and will be visible only when the Finder is the active application. In fact, you can have a different set of scripts for any application.

To add exclusive scripts for an application, activate that application (the Finder, for example), and then from the Script menu, choose Open Scripts Folder ➤ Open Finder Scripts Folder. Any scripts you place in that folder will appear only when the Finder is active.

If a folder for that application doesn't exist, it will be created as you make your selection.

Running and Launching Scripts from the Script Menu

To run a script from the Script menu, simply select it from the menu. To launch a script using the default AppleScript editor, select a script from the menu while clicking the Option button. You can set the default AppleScript editor by using the AppleScript Utility application.

Getting Your Hands on Apple's Sample Scripts

One feature that makes working with AppleScript great is the AppleScript community. You would think that competition in this small field would cause an unattractive "every man for himself" atmosphere, but not here! In the AppleScript community, people are sometimes so eager to help you that they will share with you anything from chunks of code to entire scripts that will help you with your quest.

Besides handouts here and there, the AppleScript website contains many sample scripts, mostly written in the deliberate teacherly style of Sal Saghoian, AppleScript's product manager.

The first batch of scripts you have access to are the scripts in the Scripts folder I just spoke of in the section "Preinstalled Scripts." Following that, you will find more resources for free scripts. Although many of these scripts may not be exactly what you need, they make a great starting point, and you are encouraged to open them and copy portions to your own scripts. You can look in two main places on Apple's website for sample scripts; one is the applications page on the AppleScript web page at www.apple.com/applescript/apps/. From there, go to the application of interest, and look for sample scripts.

The following page also contains links to a great collection of utility subroutines: www.apple.com/applescript/guidebook/sbrt/.

Using Folder Actions

Folder actions allow you to create hot folders on your Mac that trigger a script whenever the folder is modified. You create a folder action by attaching a script to a folder. Such a script may contain special event handlers that activate when the folder window opens, closes, or moves or when items are either added to or removed from the folder.

Folder actions are great for any hot-folder setup you need to create. Imagine any workflow in which files need to be processed automatically but a person has to trigger the automation by telling the script which file or files to process. Although you could have created the same workflow using a script application saved as a droplet (that is, containing an open handler), folder actions give you a wider variety of action-triggering events and allow users to trigger scripts by dropping files into a folder, which may be more workflow-like than dragging and dropping files on an application droplet.

Folder actions became a feature in OS 10 starting with OS X 10.2 but became reliable only in OS X 10.3 (Panther).

Starting Out with Folder Actions

For folder actions to work, you have to meet a couple of conditions. First, you must have folder actions activated on the Mac that the actions should run on. Second, you must attach a script with at least one folder action event handler to a folder.

You have three ways to start folder actions. You can run a script that will start them, use the Folder Actions Setup utility, or use the contextual menu.

To turn folder actions on or off using a script, look no further than /Library/Scripts/Folder Actions. In that folder, you will find, among others, two files named Enable Folder Actions.scpt and Disable Folder Actions.scpt. You can run these scripts either from a script editor or from the Script menu.

The scripts are simple. This one enables folder actions:

```
tell application "System Events" to set folder actions enabled to true
```

And this one disables folder actions:

```
tell application "System Events" to set folder actions enabled to false
```

The Folder Actions Setup utility application also allows you to enable and disable folder actions, as shown in Figure 20-3.

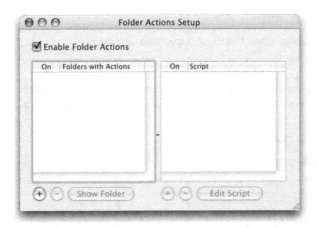

Figure 20-3. *The Folder Actions Setup utility*

To turn folder actions on with the Finder's contextual menu, Ctrl-click anywhere on the desktop, and choose Enable Folder Actions from the pop-up menu. Unless you have some other utility installed, the folder action menu items should be at the end of the menu.

You can also show the Folder Actions Setup utility by choosing Configure Folder Actions from the Finder's contextual menu.

Setting Up Your First Folder Action

After you enable folder actions, you may want to get started by creating a folder action script, attaching it to a folder, and testing it.

Let's start by creating a simple script that will randomly change the labels of the items you drop in the folder. You will use the Folder Actions Setup utility to administer the operation.

Step 1: Create Your Script

Start a new script with Script Editor. Your first lines will be the event handler that is triggered when a file is added.

Type into the script window the script lines shown in Figure 20-4.

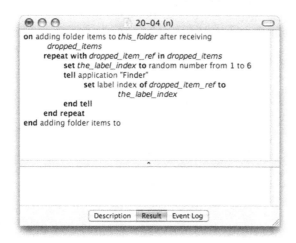

Figure 20-4. *The event handler that gets activated when files are dropped into the folder*

Let's try to analyze the script shown in Figure 20-4. The script's one handler is the adding folder items handler. This handler will be called automatically when any files or folders are added to the folder that this script is attached to as a folder action—that is, after you turn the script into a folder action and attach it to a folder.

Note A script can contain more than one folder action handler.

Step 2: Save Your Script

For your script to become folder action material, you need to save (or move) it to the Folder Action Scripts folder. There is an existing Folder Action Scripts folder at /Library/Scripts, or you can create one at ~/Library/Scripts if you want a folder action script to be available to the current user only.

Step 3: Create Your Hot Folder

Create a folder on the desktop, and call it My Hot Folder. This will be the folder that will be the target of the folder action events.

Step 4: Activate the Folder Actions

If it's not already running, start the Folder Actions Setup utility. It should be in the AppleScript folder in your Applications folder.

Once the utility is started, select the Enable Folder Actions check box, also shown in Figure 20-3.

Step 5: Attach the Folder Action to Your Folder

You can add a folder item to a folder in a few ways. You can use a script or the Finder's contextual menu. Here, you will use the Folder Action Setup utility.

To attach the folder action script you created, you start by adding the folder to the folder list, and then you attach the script to it. In the Folder Action Setup utility application, click the + button under the folder list on the left. This will open the Choose Folder dialog box. Choose the hot folder you created on the desktop, and click OK. The folder will appear in the folder list.

Next, click the folder in the folder list to see the list of scripts currently in the Folder Actions Scripts folder. Choose your script, and click OK.

Setting Up Folder Actions Events

Although the obvious thing to do with folder actions is to perform some action when items are added to the folder, folder actions provide you with four other events that can trigger handlers in your scripts. The five events in total are adding a folder item, closing the folder window, moving the folder window, opening the folder, and removing a folder item.

Here are the definitions of the events:

```
adding folder items to: Called after new items have been added to a folder
    adding folder items to  alias  -- Folder receiving the new items
        after receiving  a list of alias  -- a list of the items the folder received

closing folder window for: Called after a folder window has been closed
    closing folder window for  alias  -- the folder that was closed

moving folder window for: Called after a folder window has been moved or resized
    moving folder window for  alias  -- the folder whose window was moved or resized
        from  bounding rectangle  -- the previous coordinates of folder window
                                    (you can get the new coordinates from the Finder)

opening folder: Called after a folder has been opened into a window
    opening folder  alias  -- the folder that was opened

removing folder items from: Called after items have been removed from a folder
    removing folder items from  alias  -- the folder losing the items
        after losing  a list of alias  -- a list of the items the folder lost. For
                                    permanently deleted items, only the names
                                    (in strings) are provided.
```

More About the Folder Actions Setup Utility

Notice that you can check and uncheck folders in the left list to enable or disable all their attached actions.

To view the folder action scripts attached to a particular folder, you must first select that folder in the folder list. Also, each folder can have more than one folder action script attached to it, and you can enable and disable the scripts individually with the check boxes in the list on the right.

Where Are Folder Action Scripts Stored?

Folder action scripts reside in the Folder Action Scripts folder in the Scripts folder of either the current user's Library folder or the Library folder in the startup disk. Out of the box, the Folder Actions Scripts folder already exists in the local domain, and it contains several samples of folder action scripts you can open and play with or attach to folders.

Using the Contextual Menus with Folder Actions

After some struggle, the folder action feature finally made it to the Finder's contextual menu in OS X 10.3. By default, the bottom of the menu has the options Enable Folder Actions and Configure Folder Actions.

Once you enable folder actions, a third option, Attach a Folder Action, becomes visible, allowing you to attach actions to folders from the Finder.

When you Ctrl-click a folder with one or more folder action scripts already attached to it, you get yet more options for editing and removing those scripts (as shown in Figure 20-5).

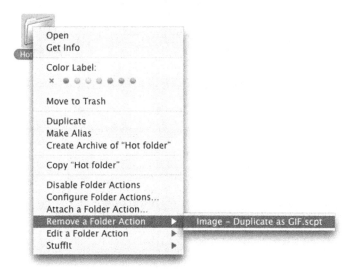

Figure 20-5. *The contextual menu after Ctrl-clicking a folder with a folder action attached to it*

Using Scripts to Manage Folder Actions

You may be in a situation where you need to be able to set up multiple Macs with some folder action functionality. If you want to use scripts to automate the process of creating folder actions, you should check out the scripts that come with the Mac in the /Library/Scripts/Folder Actions folder. In this folder you will find scripts for enabling and disabling folder actions as well as attaching to and removing folder actions from folders. All scripts, of course, are open, and you're encouraged to copy parts of them into your own scripts.

One of the features used in the folder action–related scripts is Standard Additions' path to command:

```
path to Folder Action scripts
--> alias "Macintosh HD:Users:hanaan:Library:Scripts:Folder Action Scripts:"
```

Scripting the User Interface

When applications have good AppleScript support, a working object model, and a solid dictionary, scripting the graphical user interface (or GUI as I will refer to it here) is simply not needed. GUI scripting is used to plug holes in the scriptability of your system, including applications, utilities, and any other thing you'd want to automate.

Although GUI scripting is a relative newcomer to the AppleScript scene, it works really well within its limitations and in a way is satisfying, mainly because it allows you to automate almost any feature that can be invoked from the user interface. It can also be a bit frustrating, however, since the script sometimes works faster than the user interface and therefore trips over itself. You can easily remedy this situation, however, with a small delay in the script.

Despite any issues it may have, GUI scripting is a welcome addition, and in many cases it is the only option you have to bridge the scriptability gaps in the applications you use in your process.

GUI scripting also lets you get and set attributes of a UI element that are not defined in the System Events dictionary, and it lets you perform actions that aren't defined in that dictionary by using technical terms defined by Apple and by third-party applications to support Apple's Accessibility technology—such as get value of attribute "AXPosition" of window 1 or perform action "AXRaise" of window 1. For example, the Finder responds to several new technical terms of this nature, and GUI scripting can use this technique to get at them. You can use tools such as Apple's UI Element Inspector and PreFab's UI Browser to learn what these technical terms are.

Enabling UI Scripting

By default, running scripts that use UI commands won't work. To enable UI scripting on any Mac, the Mac has to be running Mac OS X 10.3 Panther or newer and has to have a little-known check box selected in a System Preferences panel.

To enable GUI scripting, launch the AppleScript Utility application (/Applications/AppleScript/), and check Enable GUI Scripting. Alternatively, you can launch System Preferences, and in the Universal Access panel, select the Enable Access for Assistive Devices check box at the bottom of the window. You can leave it turned on all the time without ill effects.

Using the GUI Scripting Dictionary

The GUI scripting commands and objects are defined in the System Events dictionary under the Processes suite. The Processes suite defines five commands and many classes. The five commands are click, perform, key code, keystroke, and select. The list of classes in the Processes suite is a bit longer. It contains 45 classes, almost all of them being subclasses of the class named UI element. On top of that, each UI element has many elements and properties of its own. You can set the values of many of the properties using AppleScript's set command, and you can evaluate them using the get command.

Although some logic applies to the hierarchy of the elements—such as a window element can contain a button element, a button cannot contain a window, and a menu bar contains menus that contain menu items—the dictionary doesn't hint at any of that. In the eyes of the System Events dictionary, all elements are equal under the UI element superclass, of course.

So, figuring out which element in the UI of a given application contains which other elements is difficult—unless, of course, you have the right tool.

Only after you discover the cryptic nature of UI elements can you understand that without a tool such as Prefab's UI Browser (created by Bill Cheeseman and available at www.prefab.com/uibrowser/), you wouldn't get very far. A less powerful but free utility called UI Element Inspector is available from Apple (www.apple.com/applescript/uiscripting/).

Some Object Structure

Even though the dictionary isn't much help when it comes to the UI object model, I can try to shed some light on the situation. In GUI scripting, two main types of objects contain all others: windows and the menu bar. Windows, then, can contain all elements that belong in a window such as text fields, buttons, and pop-up buttons. Menu bars can contain menus, and menus contain menu items, and so on.

It is also important to note that any object (such as a table) that appears to have a scroll bar really doesn't. In reality, the scroll bar is part of a scroll view in which the object resides. This means in some cases to get to the UI element you want to change, you will have to dig through the scroll element. See the "Using UI Browser to Locate Elements" section later in this chapter.

Basic UI Scripting Example

Let's look at a few examples of putting UI scripting to use. The first attempt will be discovering the basic structure of an application's UI. Launch Preview, and open one file (you can take a screenshot and open it). Now, run the following script:

```
tell application "Preview" to activate

tell application "System Events"
    return every UI element of process "Preview"
end tell
-- {window "6536f2002.tif" of application process "Preview" ¬
    of application "System Events",¬
 menu bar 1 of application process "Preview" of application "System Events"}
```

Notice that the only command you sent to the Preview application was the activate command. When scripting an application's UI, you usually activate these applications first and then send the rest of the commands to the process element of the System Events application. In this case, the element is process "Preview". Also notice that the result of the script has two elements: a window and a menu bar. The menu bar is the main element you use to identify and select menu items. The rest of the UI elements usually are part of some window.

In the next example, you will flip the front image open in Preview. To do that you will use the click command to click a specific menu item:

```
tell application "Preview" to activate

tell application "System Events"
    tell process "Preview"
        click menu item "Flip Vertical" of menu "Tools" of menu bar 1
    end tell
end tell
```

What Can You Do with GUI Scripting?

Having only five commands makes it seem like your options are limited; however, what you can do in this case has more to do with which object you perform the command on than with the command itself. On top of that, every UI element has many properties that can be set with AppleScript's set command. This by itself will account for a lot of what you can do with GUI scripting.

Before you see how to dig out the object you want from a pile of UI elements, you'll look at four out of the five commands (you'll skip select for now).

click

The click command makes the UI element behave as if you clicked it with the mouse. This applies to buttons, text fields, menu items, and so on.

If you were going to the desert and could take just a single UI command with you, click would be it. Most UI tasks you will perform will boil down to clicking some UI element. It is finding that element that will pose the challenge.

In the following script, the click command selects a UI element of the dock process:

```
tell application "System Events"
    tell process "Dock" to click UI element "iTunes" of list 1
end tell
```

perform

The perform command is a bit different from click but can sometimes have the same effect.

The perform command will perform the action associated with a particular UI element. You use perform instead of click when the UI element whose action you want to execute is not one you can click, such as a text field. Clicking a text field will place the insertion point in it but will not perform any action that is built into it. Another example is that a window element may perform the raise action, which brings it to the front of other windows in the application.

keystroke

The keystroke command allows you to simulate the action of a user pressing keys on the keyboard. All you have to do is follow the keystroke command with a string you want System Events to enter via your keyboard.

This command is handy in two situations: one is when you want to type text, and the other is when you want to execute a keyboard shortcut with the Cmd key (or other key).

You can use modifier keys with your keystrokes in two ways. You can use the keystroke command's optional using parameter to specify one or more modifier keys just for the next keystroke, like this:

```
keystroke "n" using command down
```

To use multiple modifiers, put them in a list, like this:

```
keystroke "n" using {command down, shift down}
```

key code

The key code command is a bit like keystroke, but instead of typing based on a character, it uses the hardware-based integer key code of a particular key.

This method has the advantage of giving you access to keys that aren't characters, such as the Delete key, the arrow keys, and the function keys on the top row of your keyboard.

Like the keystroke command, the key code command provides an optional using parameter for specifying one or more modifier keys to "hold down" at the same time.

For what it's worth, though, key codes 123 through 126 are the arrow keys (in this order: left, right, down, and up), and code 51 is Delete. Utilities such as Prefab's UI Browser can show you the key code of any key you press.

Script 20-1 will start a new document in TextEdit and type the word *Apple*. Then it will go back one character and select the one before last by using the left arrow with the Shift key.

Script 20-1.

```
tell application "TextEdit"
    activate
end tell
tell application "System Events"
    keystroke "n" using command down
    keystroke "Apple"
    key code 123
    key code 123
end tell
```

In a few pages you will look at using the get and set commands to get and set the values of UI elements.

Using UI Browser to Locate Elements

Working with AppleScript's GUI scripting means working with Mac OS X user interface elements, and the only sane way to do that, especially when dealing with complex windows containing lots of nested elements, is by using Prefab's UI Browser (www.prefab.com).

The reason why you need UI Browser is because when the Mac GUI was created, it wasn't created with you scripting it in mind. It is a bit messy, and finding your way around means wasting a lot of time. For instance, if you want to know what's in the first column of the first row of Apple's Mail, you have to use the following syntax:

```
tell application "System Events"
    tell process "Mail"
        value of text field 1 of row 1 of table 1 ¬
        of scroll area 1 of splitter group 1 of group 1 of window 1
    end tell
end tell
```

So if you don't yet own UI Browser, go to www.prefab.com, and download a demo. You can manipulate menu items of simpler window elements rather easily without UI Browser.

Exploring the UI Browser Interface

Using UI Browser is simple. You start by picking the application whose interface you want to script from the Target pop-up menu. This pop-up menu shows all open applications and also allows you to choose an application. Figure 20-6 shows UI Browser with the Target menu exposed. Once you choose an application, the main browser view shows you the main set of UI elements. These usually are the menu bar and the main open windows.

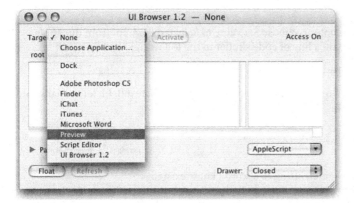

Figure 20-6. *UI Browser with the Target menu exposed*

In the first UI exercise, you will create a search script for Preview. You will first look at a simple script that enters a search string in the search field. Then, you will develop it further to catalog the search results it will pick right from the interface.

Using UI Browser

Start by opening a text PDF file with Preview. Try looking through the developer documentation for one. Also, make sure the bookmarks drawer is open. Next, choose Preview from UI Browser's Target menu. If you already have, you may want to refresh your screen. I also expanded the Path to Element disclosure triangle to show the path to the currently selected element.

Next, click the standard window element representing your PDF document in the second browser column, and continue clicking the objects listed in the subsequent browser columns. If you check the helpful Highlight check box, UI Browser will highlight the interface element with a yellow rectangle.

After you select the window, click drawer 1 and then search text field 1. This is the search text field. You will use the keystroke command to type something in that field, but you first need to create an AppleScript tell block that identifies the text field.

In UI scripting you don't tell applications what to do. Instead, everything you do happens under the System Events application. You tell different process objects of System Events what to do. Script 20-2 shows a typical tell block to start off a UI scripting script.

Script 20-2.

```
activate application "Preview.app"
tell application "System Events"
    tell process "Preview"
        -- GUI Scripting statements:

    end tell
end tell
```

In UI Browser, choose Tell Block Wrapper (short) from the AppleScript menu. Then, copy and paste the result in a new script window in Script Editor.

Targeting the UI Element

After you clicked the last text field element, choose Set Value of Selected Element from the Apple-Script pop-up menu. This will give you a line of code similar to the following:

```
set value of text field 1 of drawer 1 of window "file name.pdf" to "<string>"
```

Copy this line into your script, but since you will work more with this text field, let's separate it and give it its own `tell` block, like this:

```
tell window "file name.pdf"
  set value of text field 1 of drawer 1 to "iPod"
end tell
```

Notice that I also switched the search string to a word I knew existed.

Now, you need to click the Search button. In the UI, the Search button resides inside the text field and therefore will appear in UI Browser in the browser column to the right of the text field, as shown in Figure 20-7.

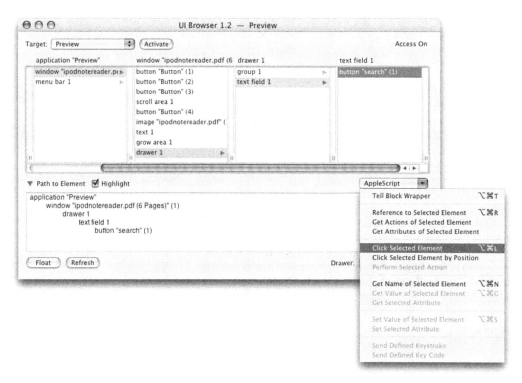

Figure 20-7. *UI Browser's main browser with the Search button element selected*

Script 20-3 shows the script so far, after you pasted the new `click` line into it and worked out the window's `tell` block.

Script 20-3.

```
activate application "Preview.app"
tell application "System Events"
    tell process "Preview"
        tell text field 1 of drawer 1 of window 1
            set value to "iPod"
            click button "search"
        end tell
    end tell
end tell
```

This script is supposed to find the occurrence of the word *iPod* in the front Preview document.

Getting Fancy with Table Data

As in many other applications, Preview uses GUI tables to display data in rows and columns. The table you're interested in is the one containing the search results, which appears in the same drawer as the search field when one or more matches are found. Note that if there are no matches, you will end up with some unexpected tables.

After digging a bit with UI Browser, you discover that the table object is as follows:

```
table 1 of scroll area 1 of group 1 of drawer 1 of window 1
```

and that it has rows, and every row has two text fields.

For example, if you just want a list of pages the matching text appears in, you can use the following line:

```
value of text field 1 of every row of table 1 ¬
    of scroll area 1 of group 1 of drawer 1 of window 1
```

The following is the entire script:

```
activate application "Preview"
tell application "System Events"
    tell process "Preview"
        value of text field 1 of every row of table 1 ¬
            of scroll area 1 of group 1 of drawer 1 of window 1
    end tell
end tell
--> {"1", "1", "1", "3", "5"}
```

Dictionary UI Scripting Example

The following simple script will use the text the user typed into a dialog box and search for that term in the Dictionary application. In addition to looking up the result in Dictionary, the script will set the term_definition variable to the definition's text.

```
display dialog "Enter a term to lookup:" default answer ""
set term_to_lookup to text returned of result

activate application "Dictionary"
tell application "System Events"
    tell process "Dictionary"
        tell window 1
            keystroke term_to_lookup
            keystroke return
```

```
            tell scroll area 1 of scroll area 1 of group 1
                set term_definition value of UI element 1
            end tell
        end tell
    end tell
end tell
```

Using the Services Menu

One of the nice features that OS X introduced is the Services menu. The Services menu is actually a submenu of the Application menu of almost all OS X applications. It allows software vendors to make some of the useful features found in their applications available from within any other application. You can see the Services submenu in Figure 20-8.

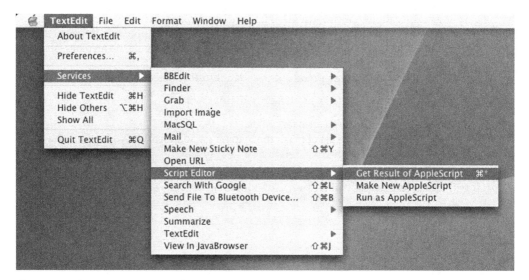

Figure 20-8. *The Services menu with the Script Editor options shown*

Some great services are Mail's Send Selection service, Search with Google service, and (one of my favorites) Script Editor's three available services. The services that get installed with Apple's Script Editor are Get Result of AppleScript, Make New AppleScript, and Run As AppleScript. These services mean you can highlight any text from an application that supports services and try to perform the action you chose.

To try it, open TextEdit, type **12 * 7**, highlight it, and choose Services ➤ Script Editor ➤ Get Result of AppleScript. This will replace the selected text with the result.

If you choose Make New Script, the text you highlighted becomes a new Script Editor script.

Digital Hub Actions

You can set digital hub actions in the CDs & DVDs panel of System Preferences, as shown in Figure 20-9. The idea is that you can specify a script (or other action) that will be executed when you insert different kinds of CDs and DVDs into the Mac. This feature can be invaluable to people in the imaging, video, and graphics fields who have to deal with CD or DVD media on a regular basis. For instance, you can set a script to open a picture CD, process all the pictures, and so on.

You can find example scripts at www.apple.com/applescript/digitalhub/.

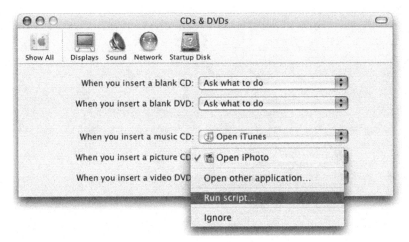

Figure 20-9. *The CDs & DVDs panel of System Preferences*

CHAPTER 21

■ ■ ■

Extending AppleScript with Scripting Additions

Scripting additions, also referred to as OSAX (or osax), are special files that add commands to AppleScript. Using existing scripting additions is easy, although writing new ones takes a bit more programming experience than possessed by the average AppleScripter because they have to be written in a lower-level language such as C.

Since authoring scripting additions is beyond the scope of this book, the chapter will discuss existing scripting additions from Apple and third-party developers.

Note The acronym OSAX comes from the creator type and now, in Mac OS X, the filename extension of a scripting addition, which is `.osax`. OSAX stands for Open Scripting Architecture eXtension.

These are the three main reasons to use scripting additions:

- They may make your scripts run faster since C code generally runs faster than AppleScript.

- They may make your development cycle shorter since using the commands in scripting additions saves you the time it would take to program the same functionality.

- They may allow you to perform tasks that vanilla AppleScript simply can't do since a lot of the functionality provided by the Mac operating system—file system access, graphical user interfaces (GUIs), audio features, and so on—are accessible only through lower-level languages such as C.

Although a few widely used scripting additions exist, most scripting additions are created by people who simply need certain functionality and know how to create it. Therefore, many scripting additions are available as free downloads. You can find most, if not all, of them at www.macscripter.net and www.osaxen.com.

Scripting Additions and the AppleScript Language

When scripting scriptable applications, any command that is defined in the application's dictionary can be compiled correctly and executed only from inside that application's `tell` block:

```
open file "Macintosh HD:Jobs:1234.indd"

tell application "InDesign CS"
   open file "Macintosh HD:Jobs:1234.indd"
end tell
```

In the preceding script, since the first open command is outside the application tell block, it will not run as intended since AppleScript itself doesn't know how to handle an open command.

The commands defined in scripting additions, on the other hand, are made directly available to your scripts from within AppleScript itself, so you do not need to enclose them in a tell block in order to use them. For example, you can script for a long time and not know that certain commands you use are not part of AppleScript, but rather defined in the Standard Additions dictionary.

The fact that scripting additions lack a tell block forces developers to use the same command name universe with other scripting addition developers and with AppleScript itself. This means any variable you use anywhere in your script can potentially be a word reserved by a scripting addition. Although scripting addition developers are generally careful to use unique word combinations for their classes and commands, you may also want to stick to camel case or underscore word separation when naming variables, which should keep name collision to a minimum.

Scripting Additions and Mac OS X

Although scripting additions are supported by the AppleScript shipped with Mac OS X, not many developers upgraded their additions. This phenomenon can be explained based on several factors.

One of these factors is the introduction of Unix shell scripting in Mac OS X in general and shell scripting integration with AppleScript using the do shell script command. Much of the functionality that scripters used to rely on additions for is now available freely with different shell commands, which can be invoked right from AppleScript. Shell commands are fast, relatively easy to master, and are prolific in the variety of commands they offer.

Another contributing factor to the slow coming of new additions was that AppleScript was slow under OS 9, making scripting additions important. Using a scripting addition command instead of writing a vanilla AppleScript handler that will perform the same task could speed up execution by seconds or even minutes. Nowadays, however, AppleScript (and the Mac it runs on) is so fast that speed is not really an issue.

Installing Scripting Additions

Scripting additions simply need to reside in a ScriptingAdditions folder in one of your Mac's three domains in order to work. More specifically, these folders are as follows:

- The system domain, which is for Apple's scripting additions only: /System/Library/ScriptingAdditions/

- The local domain, which makes scripting additions available to all users: /Library/ScriptingAdditions/

- And finally, the user domain, which is where you can place scripting additions that will be available to you only: /User/Library/ScriptingAdditions/

Note that you may have to create the ScriptingAdditions folders in the local and user domains. The name of the folder has no space between the two words.

The icon of scripting additions is an unmistakable Lego cube, shown in Figure 21-1.

Figure 21-1. *The scripting addition icon*

Standard Additions

The Standard Additions scripting addition comes preinstalled with AppleScript and contains a variety of useful, basic commands. Not that you would ever need to get your hands in there, but you can find the Standard Additions scripting addition in the system domain's ScriptingAdditions folder: /System/Library/ScriptingAdditions/StandardAdditions.osax/.

You can see the definitions of the commands and records used in Standard Additions by selecting File ➤ Open Dictionary in Script Editor and choosing Standard Additions from the list, as shown in Figure 21-2.

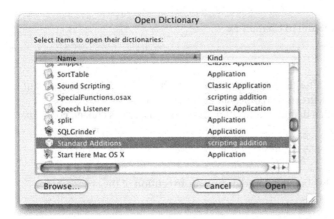

Figure 21-2. *Choose Standard Additions from the application list in the Open Dictionary dialog box.*

In the following sections, I will describe the Standard Additions commands but will not provide a detailed explanation because the book is structured around usability, not around the programming language structure. Therefore, you can find the full explanation of each Standard Additions command in the respective chapter of the book.

Standard Additions commands are divided into nine suites based on functionality: User Interaction, File Commands, String Commands, Clipboard Commands, File Read/Write, Scripting Commands, Miscellaneous Commands, Folder Actions, and Internet. Note that the Folder Actions and Internet suites are special cases and will be discussed in their respective sections later in this chapter.

The following sections summarize the Standard Additions commands, organized by suite, along with examples of their use.

User Interaction

I explain most of the user interaction commands in detail in Chapter 12, which discusses user interaction.

beep

This sounds a beep or a number of beeps using the system alert sound. For example:

```
beep 3
```

choose application

This displays the Choose Application dialog box, which looks similar to Script Editor's Open Dictionary dialog box shown in Figure 21-2. This returns either an AppleScript application value or an alias value identifying the application file. Here are two examples:

```
choose application
--> application "Address Book"
```

And, here's an example for getting the result as an alias:

```
choose application as alias
--> alias "Macintosh HD:Applications:Adobe InDesign CS:InDesign CS.app:"
```

You'll learn more about this command in Chapter 12.

choose color

This displays the Choose Color panel. After the user chooses a color, the command returns a list of three integers specifying the 16-bit red, green, and blue values for that color.

The following script will start with a default white color and return the user's chosen color (in this case red):

```
choose color default color {65535, 65535, 65535}
--> {65535, 0, 0}
```

Figure 21-3 shows the Colors dialog box displayed during the execution of the choose color command.

Figure 21-3. *The Colors dialog box shown during the execution of the* choose color *command*

choose file

This displays the Open dialog box and allows the user to choose a file. The script can restrict the user to choosing files that are of specific file types. The result is either an alias or a list of aliases. Figure 21-4 shows the Choose a File dialog box displayed by the following script line:

```
set the_alias to choose file without invisibles
-->alias "Macintosh HD:test.xml"
```

Figure 21-4. *The Choose a File dialog box*

choose filename

This displays the Save dialog box. This command allows you to choose a location and specify a filename. It works for choosing a file that you want your script to create. Figure 21-5 shows the Choose File Name dialog box displayed by the following script line:

```
set the_file to choose file name
-->file "Macintosh HD:Users:hanaan:Desktop:job report.txt"
```

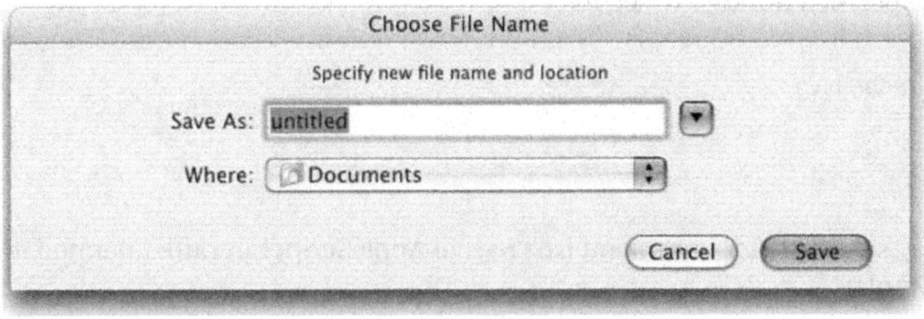

Figure 21-5. *The Choose File Name dialog box*

choose folder

This command is like choose file, but it allows only the user to choose a folder.

choose from list

This displays a simple dialog box containing items from a list. The user can then choose no items or one or more items, depending on the parameters given. The following is a script line that shows the dialog box in Figure 21-6:

```
set chosen_name to choose from list {"Al", "Bill", "Sara"}
-->{"Al"}
```

Please make your selection:

```
Al
Bill
Sara
```

Cancel   OK

Figure 21-6. *The* choose from list *dialog box*

choose remote application

This command, introduced in Mac OS X 10.4, allows you to choose a remote application running on another Mac on your network. This is useful for remote Apple events, covered in Chapter 31.

```
choose remote application
--> application "Mail" of machine "eppc://10.0.1.3/?uid=504&pid=4351"
```

choose URL

The choose URL command allows the user to choose a uniform resource locator (URL) from Apple's URL browser. Here's an example allowing you to specify a server:

```
choose URL showing File servers
--> "afp://production-mac-3.local"
```

You'll learn more about this in Chapter 12.

delay

This delays the script by the specified number of seconds:

```
delay 3 -- delay 3 seconds.
delay 1.5 -- delay 1-1/2 seconds.
```

display dialog

Who knew that the good ol' display dialog command isn't part of AppleScript but rather defined in Standard Additions? For example:

```
display dialog "Hello World!"
```

You'll learn more about this and all other user interaction commands in Chapter 12.

display alert

This is a new command in OS X 10.4, similar to the `display dialog` command, but it always displays an icon and has only one default OK button. For example:

```
display alert "Houston, we have a problem"
```

You'll learn more about this in Chapter 12.

The dialog reply record

This is a record containing the result of the `display dialog` command. It may contain information about the buttons returned from a dialog box, about the text the user typed in, or about whether the dialog box gave up.

say

This speaks any text you provide using one of Apple's built-in speech voices. Note that the voice names are case sensitive. Here's an example:

```
say "Hello" using "Victoria"
```

File Commands

I explain all the file-related scripting additions in detail in Chapter 13, which is dedicated to working with files.

info for

The `info for` command is useful for getting information about files, folders, and disks in your file system.

The command will return the `file information` record containing the file's name, name extension, type, creator, size, creation and modification dates, and more.

The file information record

The `file information` record returned by the `info for` command contains lots of values describing the specified file, folder, or disk. For example:

```
info for alias "Macintosh HD:Users:hanaan:Desktop:results.doc"
--> {
  name:"results-all-1.doc",
  creation date:date "Tuesday, March 9, 2004 2:06:41 PM",
  modification date:date "Tuesday, March 9, 2004 2:06:41 PM",
  icon position:{0, 0},
  size:2.71134E+5,
  folder:false,
  alias:false,
  ...
```

long list disks

This returns a list of the currently mounted disks.

list folder

This lists the names of all items in a folder. The list may or may not contain the names of invisible files and folders depending on the parameters used. For example:

```
set names_list to list folder alias "Macintosh HD:Applications:" without invisibles
--> {"Address Book.app", "AppleScript", "Automator.app", "Calculator.app", ...}
```

mount volume

Mac administrators everywhere love this command! It allows you to mount a volume with or without a username and password. If you don't provide login information, you will be prompted to enter it every time. For example:

```
mount volume "afp://user_name:pass_word@server_name/volume_name"
```

path to

The path to command is useful for getting an alias or path string to one of many special folders on your Mac. Not only can you get the path to that specific folder, but when possible, the command will also create one if it doesn't exist.

When you use the path to command, you can also specify the folder's domain; for instance, when you want the path to the Fonts folder, you have to decide whether it's the Fonts folder in the current user's Library folder, the startup disk's Library folder, or the Mac OS X system. Here's how it works:

```
path to fonts folder from user domain
--> alias "Macintosh HD:Users:hanaan:Library:Fonts:"

path to fonts folder from local domain
--> alias "Macintosh HD:Library:Fonts:"

path to fonts folder from system domain
--> alias "Macintosh HD:System:Library:Fonts:"
```

The following are the other paths to command parameter values:

application support	applications folder	desktop	desktop pictures folder
documents folder	favorites folder	folder action scripts	fonts
frontmost application	help	home folder	internet plugins
keychain folder	library folder	modem scripts	movies folder
music folder	pictures folder	preferences	printer descriptions
public folder	scripting additions	scripts folder	shared documents
shared libraries	sites folder	startup disk	startup items
system folder	system preferences	temporary items	trash
users folder	utilities folder	voices	apple menu
control panels	control strip modules	extensions	launcher items folder
printer drivers	printmonitor	shutdown folder	speakable items
stationery			

The path to command is useful since it allows you to specify folder locations on the Mac system without having to use specific information such as the name of the hard disk or the name of the user. For instance, look at the following command:

```
path to documents folder
--> Macintosh HD:Users:hanaan:Documents:
```

The result shown previously contains both the username and the name of the hard disk, but the path to command figured it out on its own.

The path to command also takes other parameters. You can use it in the following ways:

```
path to me -- returns path to the running script or applet
path to current application
path to frontmost application
```

path to resource

Resources are files found in the Resources folder inside an application bundle. The main use of this command, new to Mac OS X 10.4, is to get a handle on a resource you added to the script applet. You may have included templates or other files needed by the application.

Try the following: create a script, and insert this:

```
set script_path to (path to resource "main.scpt" in directory "Scripts")
set icon_path to (path to resource "applet.icns")
tell application "Script Editor" to open script_path
tell application "Preview" to open icon_path
```

Now, save the script as a bundle application, and run it. In the first two lines, the script will get a reference to the file of the main script and to the icon file using the path to resource command. The last two lines open the main applet script using Script Editor and the icon using Preview.

String Commands

I describe most of the text-related commands in detail in Chapter 3, which is dedicated to working with text.

ASCII character

This returns the character associated with the ASCII code you provided. For example:

```
ASCII character 38
--> "&"
```

ASCII number

This is the opposite of ASCII character; the ASCII number command takes a single character as an argument and returns the ASCII number associated with that character.

The following line of script will return the ASCII number of the tab character:

```
ASCII number tab
--> 9
```

localized string

New in Mac OS X 10.4, `localized string` will get you a string in the current language that corresponds to the string given in the direct parameter. This command is intended to help you make your script display alerts and use strings in the local language. For that to work, however, you have to do the legwork and create all the localized files with the strings you will want to use in the different languages. By default, the localized string will look in the bundle of the current application, but you can also specify another bundle and get a localized string from that application.

offset

The `offset` command takes two strings as parameters. It returns the position of the first string in the second string or 0 if the first string isn't found:

```
offset of "far" in "how far is it"
--> 5
```

The string `"far"` starts at the fifth character of the string `"how far is it"`.

summarize

This returns a summary of a long string, using a specified number of sentences. It can also summarize a text file. For example:

```
summarize file "MacHD:My Life Story.txt" in 1
```

Clipboard Commands

I describe the clipboard-related commands in Chapter 14 in detail, which is dedicated to working with the clipboard.

set the clipboard to

This sets the content of the clipboard to an AppleScript value. Here are a couple examples:

```
set the clipboard to "Some text"

set the clipboard to (read file "Macintosh HD:Picture 1.pdf" as «class PDF »)
```

the clipboard

This returns the contents of the clipboard. Here are a couple examples:

```
the clipboard
--> "Some text"

the clipboard
--> «data PDF 255044462D312E320D25E2E3CFD30D0A312030206F626A0D3C3C200D2F54...»
```

Read more about scripting the clipboard in Chapter 16.

clipboard info

This returns a list describing the types of data that are being held on the clipboard and the size in bytes of each.

The following example shows that the clipboard contains information for a styled string, 6 bytes of character data, and 22 bytes of corresponding style data:

```
clipboard info
--> {{scrap styles, 22}, {string, 6}}
```

File Reading/Writing

I describe all the file-related commands in detail in Chapter 13, which is dedicated to working with files.

open for access

This opens a file for access to read it or to write to it. This command returns an ID number identifying the open file. You can then use that ID number in the five other commands in the File Read/Write suite to identify that file.

You can open for access files that do not exist yet, which will in turn create the file for you:

```
open for access file "Macintosh HD:test.xml"
--> 1568
```

You can use the ID number returned by open for access only for as long as the file remains open. As soon as the file is closed, it is no longer valid and should not be used again. (You can close files by using the close access command or by quitting the application that's running the script.)

If you want to write to a file, you need to open it for access with write permission:

```
open for access file "Macintosh HD:my text.txt" with write permission
```

close access

After you opened a file for access, you should close it again once you're finished with it:

```
close access file "Macintosh HD:my text.txt"
```

Or, if you have the ID number returned by the open for access command, you could also use it as a parameter:

```
set file_ID to open for access file "Macintosh HD:test.xml"
set the_text to read file_ID
close access file_ID
```

read

The read command reads the content of any file to a variable. Some optional parameters can read the file to a list or read only a part of the file. You can read more about this command in Chapter 14.

```
read file "Macintosh HD:my text.txt"
--> "Some text..."
```

write

This writes any data to a file. To use this command, you must open the file for access with write permission first. The following script writes the contents of the clipboard to a file:

```
Set the_path to "Macintosh HD:my text file.txt"
set file_ID to open for access file the_path with write permission
set eof file_ID to 0
write ("Hello World!") to file_ID
close access file_ID
```

Note that the third line sets the "end of file" to 0. This in effect erases any data in the file. Not doing so may leave some of the old text if you write to an existing file that has more text than you are writing at the moment. Read more about the write command in Chapter 14.

get eof

EOF is the acronym for *end of file*. The get eof command returns the number of bytes in the specified file:

```
get eof file "Macintosh HD:test.xml"
--> 524
```

Read more about the get eof command in Chapter 14.

set eof

This sets the size of a file in bytes. This command can wipe out the contents of a file by setting the EOF to zero:

```
set eof file "Macintosh HD:test.xml" to 0
```

Read more about the set eof command in Chapter 14.

Scripting Commands

I describe some of the script-related commands in detail in Chapter 18, which is dedicated to working with script objects.

load script

This reads a compiled AppleScript file and returns a script object.

store script

This writes a script object to disk as a compiled AppleScript file.

run script

This executes a string, source code file, or compiled script file. The default language used is AppleScript, or you can use other Open Scripting Architecture (OSA) languages if you have them installed. For example:

```
run script "5+5"
--> 10
```

scripting components

This returns the names of the scripting components installed on your Mac:

```
scripting components
--> {"JavaScript", "AppleScript Debugger", "AppleScript"}
```

Miscellaneous Commands

I describe some of the miscellaneous commands in detail in other chapters.

current date

This returns a date value containing the current date and time:

```
set now to current date
--> date "Wednesday, March 10, 2004 7:25:27 AM"
```

Read more about this command in Chapter 5.

set volume

This sets the volume for the alert input and output. To set the volume, use one of these parameters with a volume value from 0 to 100. Here are the parameters:

```
alert volume
input volume
output volume
```

The following example sets the alert volume to 50 percent:

```
set volume alert volume 50
```

You can also mute the sound output altogether with the output muted parameter, like this:

```
set volume with output muted
```

Or, to turn sound back on, use this:

```
set volume without output muted
```

system attribute

Experienced programmers use the system attribute command to look up low-level hardware and software information. Although the new system info command introduced in Tiger provides a much easier way to look up common system information, system attribute is still useful if your script needs to run on Panther or earlier.

You can get two types of information using the system attribute command: Gestalt values and shell environment variables.

Looking Up Gestalt Values

Gestalt values are a low-level legacy technology inherited from Mac OS 9 and earlier, so you'll find them rather cryptic to use.

Although most Gestalt values aren't of any interest to AppleScripters (and many are obsolete in OS X anyway), you may find a few useful, such as those for getting the system number, the processor speed, or the amount of random access memory (RAM) installed. You can find a full list of available Gestalts in the Gestalt Manager documentation on Apple's website:

```
http://developer.apple.com/documentation/Carbon/Reference/Gestalt_Manager
```

To obtain a Gestalt value, you pass a string containing its four-letter code as the command's direct parameter. If the code is recognized, the result will be a 32-bit number containing the requested system information. Depending on how that information is represented, you may have to do some additional processing to make sense of it.

For example, to get the version of Mac OS X that is running on your computer, use this command:

```
system attribute "sysv"
```

The resulting value will be a decimal number such as 4166. That number translates into the hexadecimal value 1046, which indicates the current system version is 10.4.6. Here's a handy subroutine to calculate this for you:

```
get_system_version()
--> {10, 4, 6}

on get_system_version()
    set n to system attribute "sysv"
    set major_version_number to (n div 4096 * 10) + (n div 256 mod 16)
    set minor_version_number to n div 16 mod 16
    set patch_number to n mod 16
    return {major_version_number, minor_version_number, patch_number}
end get_system_version
```

Looking Up Shell Environment Variables

Although OS X inherits Gestalt values from its classic Mac OS side, shell environment variables come from its Unix side. To obtain a list of available shell environment variable names, just run the `system attribute` command without any parameters:

```
system attribute
--> {"PATH", "SECURITYSESSIONID", "HOME", "SHELL", "USER", ...}
```

You can then use any of these strings as the direct parameter to the command to look up the corresponding value:

```
system attribute "USER"
--> "hanaan"

system attribute "SHELL"
--> "/bin/bash"
```

system info

Introduced in OS X 10.4, this useful command simply returns a record containing system information. When I run it on my Mac, I get this result:

```
{AppleScript version:"1.10.6", AppleScript Studio version:"1.4", ➥
system version:"10.4.6", short user name:"hanaan", ➥
long user name:"Hanaan Rosenthal", user ID:501, ➥
user locale:"en_US", home directory:alias "Macintosh HD:Users:hanaan:", ➥
boot volume:"Macintosh HD", computer name:"Hanaan Rosenthal's PowerBook G4 17\"", ➥
host name:"hanaan-rosenthals-powerbook-g4-17.local", IPv4 address:"10.0.1.2", ➥
 primary Ethernet address:"00:0b:85:dc:16:20", CPU type:"PowerPC 7450", ➥
CPU speed:1333, physical memory:1024}
```

time to GMT

This returns the number of seconds the current location is from Greenwich mean time:

```
time to GMT
--> -18000

(time to GMT) / hours
--> -5.0
```

Read more about this command in Chapter 5.

random number

This returns a random number. You can specify a range or get the default result, which is a random number from 0 to 1:

```
random number
--> 0.918785996622

random number from 1 to 100
--> 39
```

Read more about this command in Chapter 4.

round

This rounds a given real value to a whole number:

```
round 5.2 rounding up
--> 6

round 5.2 rounding as taught in school
--> 5
```

Read more about this command in Chapter 4.

do shell script

This performs a Unix shell script. One of the new commands with the most explosive use, the do shell script command gives you unparalleled access to commands available in the Unix operating system under the Mac OS X hood.

For instance, the shell script command wc returns the number of lines, words, and bytes (characters) in a text file. Here's how you can use this functionality from AppleScript:

```
do shell script "wc /Users/hanaan/some_file.txt"
--> "     66     158     1448 /Users/hanaan/some_file.txt"
```

It is your responsibility to parse the resulting text, however:

```
set {line_count, word_count, character_count} to words 1 thru 3 of result
--> {"66", "158", "1448"}
```

Ah, that is better . . . . Still think that do shell script is just for geeks? Well, you may be right, but now you may also want to become one . . . .

Read more about this command in Chapter 30.

class: POSIX file

You can use the POSIX file keyword to convert a Unix-style path string into an AppleScript file reference value:

```
set posix_file_path to "/Applications/TextEdit.app"
set the_file to POSIX file posix_file_path
--> file "Macintosh HD:Applications:TextEdit.app"

"/Applications/TextEdit.app" as POSIX file
--> file "Macintosh HD:Applications:TextEdit.app"
```

I'm not sure why POSIX file should be defined in Standard Additions' dictionary instead of AppleScript's, but it works OK, so don't worry about it.

See Chapter 13 for more information about POSIX file.

Folder Actions

Unlike the other suites you've looked at so far, the Folder Actions suite in Standard Additions' dictionary doesn't define normal commands that you call from your script. Instead, it supplies AppleScript with the terminology you'll need to write folder action event handlers in your scripts.

Chapter 19 has more information about writing and using folder actions.

opening folder

This is the event handler in your folder action script that is executed when the folder is opened in a window.

closing folder window for

This is the event handler in your folder action script that is executed when the folder window is closed.

moving folder window for

This is the event handler in your folder action script that is executed when the folder window is moved.

adding folder items to

This is the event handler in your folder action script that is executed when an item or items are added to the folder.

removing folder items from

This is the event handler in your folder action script that is executed when an item or items are removed from the folder.

Internet Suite

The Internet suite contains several Internet-related items.

open location

This opens a URL with the default application for that type of URL. For example, a URL using Hypertext Transfer Protocol (HTTP) will open in your default web browser. For example:

```
open location "http://www.apple.com"
```

Internet-Related Records and Coercions

The "classes" section of Standard Additions' Internet suite defines a few record structures related to Internet scripting.

Standard Additions installs a special coercion into AppleScript that allows you to break down URL strings and extract various information from them. The URL and Internet address entries define the structure and property names of the records returned by this coercion. For example:

```
set my_url to "http://www.apple.com" as URL
--> {class:URL, scheme:http URL, path:"http://www.apple.com", ¬
   host:{class:Internet address, DNS form:"www.apple.com", port:80}}
```

The other two record definitions, Web page and FTP item, provide AppleScript with some basic Internet-related terminology that third-party applications can use if they want, although I'm not aware of any that do. These records don't do anything by themselves, however, so you can just ignore them.

Read more about folder actions in Chapter 20.

Third-Party Scripting Additions

Until now you have looked at the scripting additions that are put out by Apple and are yours for free. In the following sections, you will look at some third-party scripting additions. Although many third-party scripting additions are on the market, only a handful of them ever got upgraded to work with OS X. Nevertheless, the ones that did make the transition are worth exploring.

Where to Find Third-Party Scripting Additions

The one-stop place to shop (or more likely, browse) for scripting additions is MacScripter.net (www.macscripter.net or www.osaxen.com). The folks at MacScripter.net are mostly volunteers who put a good bit of effort into a well-organized and fresh AppleScript website. Among other features, they boast the most complete and up-to-date searchable collection of scripting additions.

The following are some of the scripting additions worth investigating. You can get information and download any of these from www.osaxen.com. The list is followed with more details regarding a few of these scripting additions.

- 24U Appearance X
- ACME Script Widgets
- Jon's Commands X
- List & Record Tools
- Property List Tools
- Satimage
- ScriptDB
- SQLiteAddOns
- XMail
- XMLLib

ACME Script Widgets

ACME Script Widgets by ACME Technologies (www.acmetech.com) has been around for more than ten years and is one of the most successful commercial scripting additions available.

ACME Script Widgets is known for its string and list manipulation commands.

The following is a brief description of some of the commands included with ACME Script Widgets.

Acme replace

Acme replace makes string replacement a snap. Although it is not that difficult to create your own text-replacement handler using AppleScript, this command can do it for you faster and with some additional features. Here's a simple example of the Acme replace command:

```
Acme replace "Boston" in "Go to Boston by train" substitution text "New York"
--> "Go to New York by train"
```

Using different parameters you can choose whether to replace all occurrences and whether the search is case sensitive.

change case

If you need to change the case of text in your scripts on a regular basis, this command just might be worth the price of admission. The change case command allows you to change the case of text in a string to uppercase, lowercase, title case, or sentence case or to toggle the current case of each letter. For example:

```
change case of "THAT DAMN CAPS-LOCK KEY DID IT AGAIN." to lower
--> "that damn caps-lock key did it again."
```

Satimage

Satimage is a French company that is responsible for the development of Smile, the free AppleScript script editor. Another tool Satimage developed and keeps on improving is a great set of text and math commands bundled in the Satimage scripting addition.

My favorite two commands in the Satimage collection are the find text and format commands.

find text

What separates find text in Satimage from anything you could easily do in AppleScript alone is the use of regular expressions. Sure, you can create a handler that replaces one word with another, but regular expressions take text replacement to a whole other level.

Here's a simple example:

```
find text "l+" in "Hello World!" with regexp and all occurrences
--> {{matchPos:2, matchLen:2, matchResult:"ll"}, ➥
    {matchPos:9, matchLen:1, matchResult:"l"}}
```

This command searches the string "Hello World!" for a sequence of one or more l characters. (The + symbol is a special character in regular expressions meaning "find one or more of the preceding pattern.") The all occurrences parameter at the end tells find text to find all matches for the l+ pattern.

Another simple pattern you could try is [[:alnum:]]+. This will find a sequence of one or more alphanumeric characters in the string, in this case Hello and World. (The brackets mean "match any character inside the brackets," and [:alnum:] is shorthand for the characters a–z, A–Z, and 0–9.)

You could use more complicated patterns to find web addresses, reformat U.S. phone numbers, or extract certain rows from a tab-delimited table of data. If you regularly work with text, regular expressions are a must-have for your toolbox.

You can read more about it in Chapter 28.

format

The format command can also save you a lot of frustration in formatting numbers. You can use it to format numbers and return them as strings with the right number of decimal places, commas, parentheses, and so on.

```
format 1234.5678 into "#,###.00"
"1,234.57"
```

ScriptDB

ScriptDB is a scripting addition written from scratch for OS X. It is put out by Custom Flow Solutions (www.customflowsolutions.com), which is a company operated by yours truly.

ScriptDB's main goal was to give scripters a set of built-in database commands and tools. The scripting addition doesn't use a database file to maintain the data but rather keeps the whole database in memory.

The purpose of such a database is to assist you in manipulating data in a table-like structure during script execution.

As scripters, we constantly make lists, some of them synchronized with each other to form sorts of tables, and then we loop through to get the data we need from them. ScriptDB allows you to take these lists, or data from text files or FileMaker Pro .xml files, and manage them like a database.

See Chapter 26 for more about ScriptDB.

Missing Additions and Garbled Scripts

Anytime you're counting on a third-party addition, you should also count on the day you (or someone else) will open the script on a Mac that doesn't have those scripting additions installed.

If the script is supplied in compiled form (that is, as a .scpt file), then when you open it in Script Editor the osax commands will appear in their raw forms. If the script is in source code form, then the osax commands won't compile unless written in raw form. Either way, you'll get an error when the script tries to execute that command.

For example, if you open a compiled script that uses the Acme replace command but don't have the ACME Script Widgets addition installed on your Mac, then a line like this:

```
Acme replace old_string in the_string substitution text new_string
```

will appear instead as this:

```
«event WaynRPLC» old_string given «class in  »:the_string, «class with»:new_string
```

and the script will raise an error saying that the value of the old_string variable doesn't understand the «event WaynRPLC» message.

Fortunately, the problem isn't permanent: as soon as the required scripting addition is installed, the script will run normally, and Script Editor will compile and decompile it normally using the familiar English-like terminology from the addition's dictionary.

If it's important to you not to get an error in these cases, you can make your script check to see whether the scripting addition is installed before trying to use it. You can do that by looking for it in the various ScriptingAdditions folders on that system. The subroutine in Script 21-1 uses System Events to obtain a reference to the scripting additions folder in each domain and then checks to see whether a file with the given name exists in that folder.

Script 21-1.

```
is_scripting_addition_installed("Satimage.osax")
--> true

on is_scripting_addition_installed(file_name)
    tell application "System Events"
        repeat with sa_folder_ref in (get scripting additions folder of every domain)
            if (contents of sa_folder_ref is not missing value) and ¬
                (exists (file file_name of sa_folder_ref)) then return true
        end repeat
    end tell
    return false
end is_scripting_addition_installed
```

Scripting Additions and Script Portability

Just as we like to travel light, so do our scripts. They just don't like to have too many strings attached. If you use scripting additions in your script, installing your script correctly on other Macs isn't quite as simple as copying the script itself across. You also need to make sure all the required scripting additions are installed on those Macs; otherwise users could get an unexpected error when they try to use the script. So if you want to make a script foolproof, you'll need to supply all the scripting additions it needs along with it *and* arrange for those additions to be automatically installed when not already present.

Although you could use the PackageMaker utility included in Developer Tools to package everything into a .pkg file, it's often nicer to supply users with a single .scpt application file that they can install simply by copying it straight to their hard disk. With script bundles, you can save your script as a bundle that can contain other files such as scripting additions. Although a bundle-based applet can't use an embedded scripting addition directly, it can check to see whether the user has that scripting addition already installed and, if not, copy the embedded into one of the standard ScriptingAdditions folders.

Let's pretend you need to create a script application that uses the ScriptDB scripting addition. Start a new script, and type this:

```
display dialog "test"
```

Now, save the script as an application bundle, as shown in Figure 21-7.

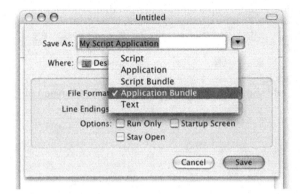

Figure 21-7. *Saving a script as a bundle*

After the script is saved, go to the Finder, and locate it. Ctrl-click it, and choose Show Package Contents, as shown in Figure 21-8.

Figure 21-8. *Choose Show Package Contents from the contextual menu.*

Figure 21-9 shows the contents of the package.

Figure 21-9. *The contents of the package*

The file `main.scpt` in the `Scripts` folder is your compiled script.

Let's get back to scripting additions. You can actually copy the scripting addition (given your license allows you to) to the `Resources` folder of your application bundle, and it will be distributed with your script application.

What you need now is a script that will check whether the scripting addition is already installed and, if not, install it.

First, test the `path to me` command. Open the script application in Script Editor, and change the script to this:

```
set my_path to path to me as string
display dialog my_path
```

Now save the application, and double-click it.

The dialog box shown in Figure 21-10 should show you that the path to the application actually looks like a path to a folder.

Figure 21-10. *The dialog box showing the path to the application*

You could get the path to your internal scripting addition like this:

```
set my_path to path to me as string
set my_scripting_addition to my_path & "Contents:Resources:name of sa.osax"
```

But wait, you may not even need to use your internal scripting addition. First you have to check whether there's already one installed. To do that, use the subroutine shown in the "Missing Additions and Garbled Scripts" section. This subroutine checks whether a given scripting addition is already installed.

Now, you need to put it all together: you should check whether the scripting addition exists and, if it doesn't, install it in the user's domain. For example, I use a scripting addition named `initials.osax`. Here's the complete script, omitting the definition of the subroutine shown previously:

```
set sa_name  to "initials.osax"
if not is_scripting_addition_installed(sa_name) then
    set my_path to path to me as string
    set my_sa_path to (path to me as string) & "Contents:Resources:" & sa_name
    tell application "finder"
        duplicate file my_sa_path to (path to scripting additions from users domain)
    end tell
    display alert ➡
        "A scripting addition was installed. Quit and relaunch this application."
end if
```

Faceless Scriptable Applications

Another method of adding functionality to AppleScript is by using faceless background applications. These invisible applications play a similar role to scripting additions, providing additional commands for AppleScripts to use. The main difference is that scripting additions are chunks of code that are loaded into existing programs; faceless scriptable applications are applications with their own scripting dictionary.

In the following sections, you will explore three such faceless applications. All three are not only free but come preinstalled with every Mac, so you don't run a risk that someone won't have them installed.

URL Access Scripting

Although this little application has only two scriptable commands, it can be quite useful. It allows you to use AppleScript to upload and download files to and from the Internet.

ColorSync Scripting

If you use ColorSync on a regular basis, you may want to take a good look at this little utility, which provides commands for adding, removing, and examining the ColorSync profiles attached to image files and converting images from one color space to another.

In the /Library/Scripts/ColorSync folder, you will find 18 scripts that use ColorSync scripting. I urge you to open them and figure out how they work (it is a bit beyond the scope of the book).

Image Events

Image Events is another scriptable utility that has only a handful of commands and classes but can be invaluable when you don't want to use a full-blown application such as Adobe Photoshop or Lemke Software's GraphicConverter (www.lemkesoft.de/en/graphcon.htm) to perform basic operations such as rotating, flipping, and resizing.

Another task that Image Events is ideal for is getting information about image files. You can open an image file and then use the properties defined by the image class to get that image's bit depth, resolution, size, color space, file type, and more. This can prove invaluable in publishing workflows.

Script 21-2 changes the comment of a chosen file into a description of the image containing the resolution, file type, bit depth, and so on.

Script 21-2.

```
1. set image_file to choose file with prompt "Please select an image file:" ¬
     of type "public.image"

2. try
3.    tell application "Image Events"
4.       set my_image to open image_file
5.       tell my_image
6.          set {the_width, the_height} to dimensions
```

```
7.          set file_type to file type
8.          set color_space to color space
9.          set bit_depth to bit depth
10.          set res to resolution
11.          close
12.       end tell
13.    end tell
14. on error error_text
15.    display dialog "The file you picked couldn't be analyzed for some reason." ¬
          buttons {"OK"} default button 1 with icon stop
16.    return
17. end try

18. set image_information to "Image information:
       File type: " & file_type & "
       Width: " & the_width & ", height: " & the_height & "
       Resolution: " & res & "
       Color space: " & color_space & "
       Bit depth: " & bit_depth
19. tell application "Finder"
20.    set comment of image_file to image_information
21. end tell
```

Note that the value used with the of type parameter in line 1 will work in only Mac OS 10.4 or newer.

The main parts to notice in the preceding script is that the open command returns a reference to an image element representing the newly opened file. You then get information about that image file by referring to the image object's properties. If an error occurs—for example, because the chosen file wasn't of a type Image Events understands—the surrounding try block informs the user there's a problem and stops the script.

■ ■ ■

Understanding the Fundamentals of Automating Applications

One point I have made again and again throughout the book is that the AppleScript language is pretty small on its own. It has merely five commands and a handful of objects and properties. What gives life and substance to AppleScript is the scriptability of various applications and scripting additions.

As you become an experienced scripter, you will learn specific commands and objects that relate to the individual applications that you need to script. Also, you will learn the common structure that applications share, which will help you tackle new scriptable applications.

In this chapter, you will look at how to attack a new application you want to start scripting. You will start with dictionary basics and object model structures such as classes, properties, and elements. From there you'll see how to refer to objects and how to use the powerful whose clause.

Understanding Scripting Dictionary Basics

Every scriptable application has a scripting dictionary that defines all the application's commands and classes available for use with AppleScript. To view an application's dictionary, go to the Script Editor application, and choose File ➤ Open Dictionary. Then, choose the application whose dictionary you want to open, and click Open.

You can also drop the application's icon on the icon of the Script Editor application.

Note These two methods also work with Late Night Software's Script Debugger.

The nicest way, however, to keep track of your scriptable applications and their dictionaries is to use the new Library palette in Script Editor 2 (or later). The Library palette, shown in Figure 22-1, lists scriptable applications whose dictionaries you like to view often.

Figure 22-1. *The Library palette*

You can add applications to the Library palette by clicking the + button, and you can open an application's dictionary by clicking the third button from the left (the icon that looks like books on a shelf). A similar feature has existed for a while in Late Night Software's Script Debugger. Figure 22-2 shows the dictionary for FileMaker Pro.

Although a scripting dictionary is an invaluable source of information, you still need additional documentation in order to script a given application. This is because although the dictionary lists all the application's related commands and classes (object types), it doesn't explain the connection between them. For instance, although the Apple iTunes dictionary will reveal the make command and the track class, iTunes doesn't allow you to combine the two to create a new track object. Thus, a command such as the following, although it looks as though it ought to work correctly, will just generate an error when you run it:

```
tell application "iTunes"
    make new file track at playlist 1 with properties ➡
    {location:alias "Macintosh HD:some.mp3"}
end tell
--iTunes got an error: Can't make class file track.
```

You can create new track objects in other ways, however. For example, using the following code, you can create them automatically:

```
add alias "Macintosh HD:some.mp3" to playlist 1
--> file track id 247 of library playlist id 142 of source id 38 of ➡
application "iTunes"
```

When extra documentation isn't provided, you'll need to study example scripts, ask other scripters, or even resort to plain ol' trial-and-error experimentation to figure out the right combinations.

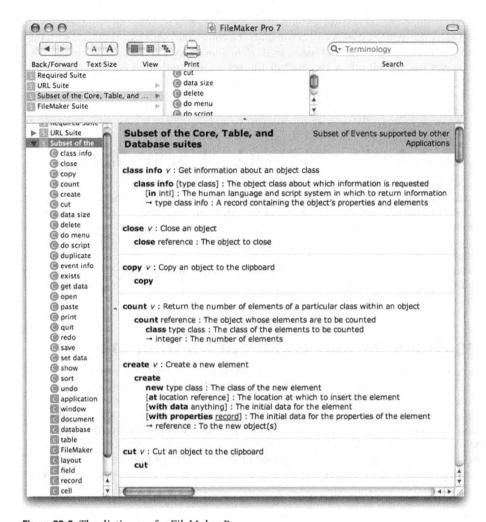

Figure 22-2. *The dictionary for FileMaker Pro*

Nevertheless, whenever you get any new application, the first step to take is to drop it on the Script Editor (or Script Debugger) icon to see whether it is scriptable. Figure 22-3 shows the disappointing dialog box you get when the application is not scriptable.

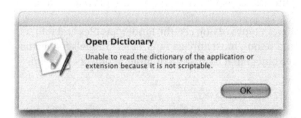

Figure 22-3. *The dialog box you get when you try to open the dictionary of a nonscriptable application*

The Script Editor dictionary viewer window distinguishes between classes and commands with small icons before the name of the class or command. The command names are preceded with the letter *c* in a small blue triangle, and the classes, listed right after the commands, are preceded with a *c* in a violet square (see the left side of Figure 22-2). Classes are descriptions of the objects you work with, and commands are what you use to manipulate those objects.

In the following sections, you'll explore commands and classes and the way they appear in the application dictionary.

Look, Look Again, and Then Look Some More

Although companies that put out scriptable applications try to make the commands and property names as descriptive as possible, sometimes the names can be a bit misleading. Some properties or commands, despite having funny names, can be exactly what you need to fill a gap in your script. Before searching the Web or posting messages on Apple's AppleScript Users list in search of an answer, explore the dictionary. Any property or command that appears to not have any obvious purpose might be the one you need.

Try to teach yourself a new property or command every week by reading the dictionary, looking up information on the Net, and reading the scripting reference for that application. Doing this will keep you moving forward.

Things (Objects) and Things to Do (Commands)

An application's scriptability consists of two realms: objects and commands. *Commands* are instructions you tell the application to do, and *objects* are the things that will change in the application after you give certain commands.

For instance, Apple's TextEdit application includes a command named open. The open command is designed to open one or more text documents in the TextEdit application. When run successfully, one or more new objects of class document are created in the TextEdit application. Each document object possesses all the properties defined by the document class, and as you are aware, you can have any number of such objects. You'll look at objects, classes, and properties in the next section.

Understanding the Object Model

A well-thought-out object model in an application is what separates applications with good AppleScript support from those with not-so-good AppleScript support. Even though most applications have some sort of internal object model where all the application's data is held, it takes a good amount of effort on the behalf of the development team to translate this object model into an AppleScript object model.

Although different applications have different types of objects (the Finder has files and folders, Adobe InDesign has pages and text frames, and so on), most applications' object models follow the same overall structure: a top-level application object that contains a number of objects, some of which contain other objects . . . and so on.

To understand this structure, imagine a large office building. The building is divided into floors, each floor is divided into offices, and an office may have desks and people in it. Every object has a specific address that anyone in the building can use to find it. For instance, the receptionist's desk is the third office on the second floor. The office also has a name, Reception, so another way you could identify it would be by saying "the office named 'Reception' on the second floor." Figure 22-4 can help you visualize it.

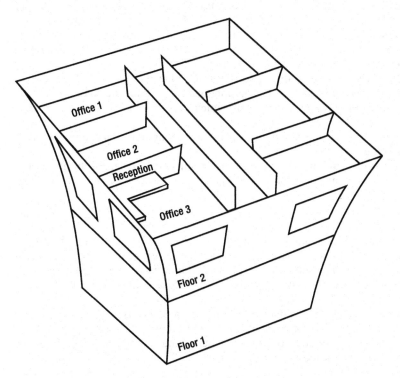

Figure 22-4. *The office building described as an object model*

The following mocked-up dictionary shows the dictionary-style listing of the classes illustrated in Figure 22-4:

```
class building
  Elements
    floor -- by index

class floor
 Elements
    office -- by index, name

class office
    Properties
    name : string -- the office name
  Elements
    desk -- by index
    person - by index, name
[etc...]
```

Notice that you were able to identify the desired office using two methods: by its position and by its name. Locating objects in order to script them is the first order of the day.

Scriptable applications use a similar method of addressing their objects: the Finder has disks that can contain files and folders. Folders can have files or more folders. In InDesign, you have a document that contains pages. The pages may contain, among other things, text frames that can contain words and characters. In FileMaker Pro, you have a database that can have tables with fields and records. Addressing the objects in these applications is also similar to the building example: in the Finder you can refer to the file report.txt in the third folder of the disk Server; in InDesign you can refer to the fifth text frame on page 2 of the document Annual Report.indd, and in FileMaker Pro you can talk to cell Last Name of record 5 of table Contact of database 1. All are different types of objects, but the way each object model works is pretty much the same.

On top of addressing, each object in an application has three other sides to it. An object consists of the DNA of a specific class; an object can have properties that describe the object such as size, name, and so on; and an object can have elements. Elements are the objects that the object in question contains.

In scripting dictionaries, classes (object definitions) are listed separately from commands, and they are also structured a bit differently.

Every class shows a little description followed by the list of other classes that may be elements (see the "Elements" section later in this chapter). The list of elements is followed by a list of properties.

Classes

A *class* is what defines how an object should behave. Every object is the product of a class. In nature, we are all objects derived from the "human" class. When we are born, we get human traits such as an upright posture and a disposition toward talking too much. When you create an object, say, a document in InDesign, this document is an instance of the document class, and it takes all its characteristics from that class.

Classes can also have subclasses. The Finder, for instance, has a superclass called item. This item class has subclasses such as files, folders, and disks. Each of these subclasses inherits all the traits of the item class and then adds some of its own. For instance, the file subclass has a file type property, but the folder subclass doesn't.

Properties

Properties are the object's traits. If your car was an object in the application of your life, its properties would include the car's color, manufacturing year, make, model, plate number, and so on. Unlike elements in an object, every object may have only one value for a given property, even though that one value can be a list or a record containing many values. Your car can't have more than one plate number or multiple model names (this is a Toyota Camry . . . and a Celica).

An InDesign image object's properties may include the rotation angle, resolutions, and bounds, and a file in the Finder may have properties such as the size, creation date, and icon position.

The more properties listed in the dictionary under the different classes, the better the scripting support is. Every listed property stands for another feature you can script in this application. In InDesign CS, for example, the application class and the document class have more than 100 properties; FileMaker Pro lists about 13. Granted, these are different applications, but when InDesign was designed, Adobe deliberately attempted to make it the most scriptable application it could be, which makes it a favorite among scripters.

The following is a list of properties of the playlist class as specified in the iTunes dictionary. The first three properties are defined by the item class that the playlist class inherits from; the rest are added by the playlist class itself.

```
container  reference  [r/o]  -- the container of the item
name  Unicode text  -- the name of the item
persistent ID  double integer  [r/o]  -- the id of the item. This id does not
                                       -- change over time.
duration  integer  [r/o]  -- the total length of all songs (in seconds)
index  integer  [r/o]  -- the index of the playlist in internal application order
name  Unicode text  -- the name of the playlist
parent  playlist  [r/o]  -- folder which contains this playlist (if any)
shuffle  boolean  -- play the songs in this playlist in random order?
size  double integer  [r/o]  -- the total size of all songs (in bytes)
song repeat  off/one/all  -- playback repeat mode
special kind  none/folder/Party Shuffle/Podcasts/Purchased Music/Videos  [r/o]
     -- special playlist
```

Notice that each property in the list represents a true attribute of an iTunes playlist. Also notice that the name of each property is followed by the expected value type. That value type specification is helpful but is not always a complete disclosure of all data types or values expected. Sometimes figuring out the property value takes some investigation.

The best way to figure out the value of a particular property is to investigate an existing object. Whether it's a folder in the Finder, an image document in Adobe Photoshop, or a track in iTunes, write a reference to the object and ask it for the value of that property—or even of all its properties at once. Many classes include a properties property, and getting this will return a record containing most or all of the properties of a given object. Examining the properties property of an object can prove to be an endless source of education. You can compare the result with the dictionary to learn even more about the scriptability of a particular object. For example:

```
tell application "Finder" to get properties of disk 1
--> {class:disk, name:"d1", index:2, displayed name:"d1", name extension:"", ...}
```

The best way to explore an object's properties (and elements, for that matter) is by using the Explorer window in Late Night Software's Script Debugger, as shown in Figure 22-5. The difference between the Explorer window and the dictionary is that while the dictionary shows classes, which are object definitions, the Explorer window shows actual objects that currently exist in the application along with their properties, property values, and elements. This window is one feature that makes Script Debugger worth the price.

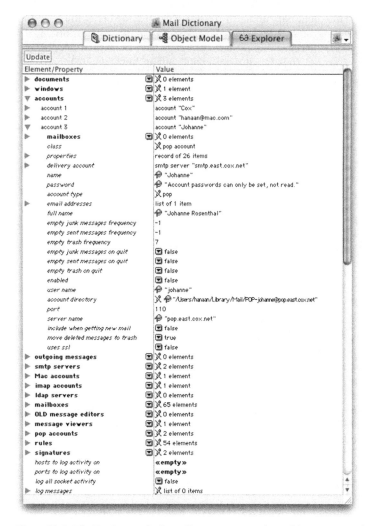

Figure 22-5. *The Explorer window allows you to explore objects, properties, and object elements in an expandable outline view.*

Working with Properties

When it comes to manipulating application objects' properties, two commands do most of the talking: set and get.

The get command allows you to get properties' values. Most times you don't even have to write the get keyword yourself: AppleScript will automatically send a get command for you when one is needed. Whenever you want to use the value of any object property in your script, such as the width of a Photoshop image or the modification date of a file in the Finder, you have to use the get command. Similarly, when you want to change a property's value, such as the name of a file, you use the set command.

Using an application's get and set commands can be a bit confusing at first, since AppleScript also defines its own get and set commands that look the same but work differently. Refer to Script 22-1.

Script 22-1. *(includes the following two scripts)*

```
tell application "Finder"
    set the_size to physical size of file the_pdf_file_path
end tell
```

By looking at the preceding statement, at first glance it appears as if I used the Finder's set command. In fact, I used the Finder's get command to get the value of the physical size property of the file and AppleScript's set command to assign that value to an AppleScript variable. I could have written the statement in the following way, which would have exposed the usage of the different commands:

```
tell application "Finder"
    --Use the Finder's get command:
    get the physical size of file the_pdf_file_path
end tell
--Use AppleScript's set command:
set the_size to the result
```

Working with Special Property Values

Although the values of many properties adhere to AppleScript's own data types such as text, number, list, and so on, many properties don't. Instead of using AppleScript's built-in data classes, these properties use constants defined in the application dictionary. Take, for instance, InDesign's local display setting property used by different page items. The property has four possible values. By looking in the InDesign dictionary, you can tell that the possible values are high quality, typical, optimized, and default. These aren't strings but rather keywords that are part of InDesign's scripting terminology.

Another related type of property is one containing a reference to an application object. For instance, the Finder application defines a home property, whose value is a reference to the home folder, which is a specific object in the Finder. Another example is the general preferences property of InDesign's dictionary. The value of this property is the general preference object.

You Can Get It, But Not Set It

Object properties in scriptable applications are divided into two categories: read-only and editable. As you may imagine, the object model of an application doesn't always let you change every property of every object. For instance, the creation date property of a file object in the Finder can't be changed; after all, a file can be created only once in its life, and the date and time it was created on doesn't change. Some other properties can't be changed simply because the developers decided they shouldn't be.

Read-only properties are marked as [r/o] in the dictionary, but if you really need to be able to change a read-only property, try to change it anyway; although rare, it is possible that the dictionary information is not fully accurate.

Assigning Property Values to New Objects

An understanding of a class's properties can come in handy when creating an object of that class. When you use the make command to create a new application object, the application will normally assign default values to all the new object's properties. However, you'll often want to supply your own values for at least some of these properties, and to do this you can use the make command's with properties parameter. This method isn't always allowed but is much faster than the alternative of changing properties once the object has been created.

The most common example of creating an object with properties is probably creating a folder in the Finder (see Script 22-2).

Script 22-2. *(includes the following two scripts)*

```
tell application "Finder"
   make new folder at desktop with properties ¬
      {name:"my files2", label index:1}
end tell
```

Notice that although I set two legal properties on the folder while creating it, the Finder chose to use the name property but completely ignore the label index property because of an annoying little bug in the Finder on Panther and Tiger. This may be fixed in a future release, of course, but for now you just have to work around it—fortunately this is easy to do.

To add the label to the folder after the fact, you can use the rule of thumb that when you create an object with the make command (in most applications), the result of that operation will be a reference to that object. Knowing that, you can complete the operation by setting the label index to the resulting value of the Finder's make command:

```
tell application "Finder"
   set myFolder to make new folder at desktop with properties ¬
      {name:"my files"}
   --myFolder is:
   --folder "my files" of folder "Desktop" of folder "hanaan" ¬
   --   of folder "Users" of startup disk
   set label index of myFolder to 1
end tell
```

Hey, You! Referencing Objects

Even the best-placed command with perfectly positioned parameters isn't useful if you can't direct it at the right object. Targeting objects can be tricky at times, but you can do a few things to make it better. For starters, you have to understand your application's object model. An application with a solid object model makes it easier to identify objects.

You can talk to elements directly in six ways: by index, by name, by ID, by relative position (before page 3), by range (pages 3 thru 6), and by test (every line whose weight is 0).

Starting with the Parents

Every object is an element of another object—other than the application object itself, of course. Armed with this fact, you can go around asking different objects to identify their element objects. This can go a long way to finding the object you want to use. Whether it is asking for every item of a folder in the Finder or every text frame in an InDesign page, the result will be a list in which each item is an object.

After you get the list, you can either loop through it in order to target each object or, better yet, command them all to dance at the same time directly, as shown here:

```
tell application "Finder"
  -- looping through every element (slower):
  repeat with the_folder in (every folder of startup disk whose name contains "old")
    delete the_folder
  end repeat

  -- commanding multiple objects directly (faster):
  delete (every folder of startup disk whose name contains "old")
end tell
```

Whenever you can avoid looping (and you can't always), do so—your script will work faster as a result. Script 22-3 shows a few scripts that target multiple objects and manipulate them with a single command.

Script 22-3. *(includes the following two scripts)*

```
-- Example 1:
tell application "Finder"
  duplicate every item of source_folder to destination_folder with replacing
end tell

-- Example 2:
tell application "InDesign CS"
  tell page 1 of active document
    set stroke weight of every graphic line to 4
  end tell
end tell

-- Example 3:
tell application "TextEdit"
  get first paragraph of text of every document
end tell
```

You can specify different classes of elements to be more or less selective in the types of objects identified by a reference. For instance, in the Finder, referring to items of a specific folder encompasses all items including folders, files, applications, and so on. You can narrow it down to files, which will not include any containers such as folders, or narrow it even further by referring to specific file types such as application files or document files:

```
tell application "Finder"
  get every item of the_folder --most general
  get every file of the_folder --more specific
  get every document file of the_folder  --most specific
end tell
```

The dictionary shows you which class is on top by listing a special property called *inheritance*. This property shows the superclass to which the class you're looking at belongs. An object inheritance appears after the class's name in square brackets, like this: folder n [inh. container > item]. By looking at this text you can tell that the folder class inherits its properties from the container class, which in turn inherits its properties from the item class.

Figure 22-6 shows the Finder's dictionary with two classes highlighted: file and folder. You can see that the file class inherits all its properties from the item class and the folder class inherits its properties from the container class, which in turn also belongs to the item class.

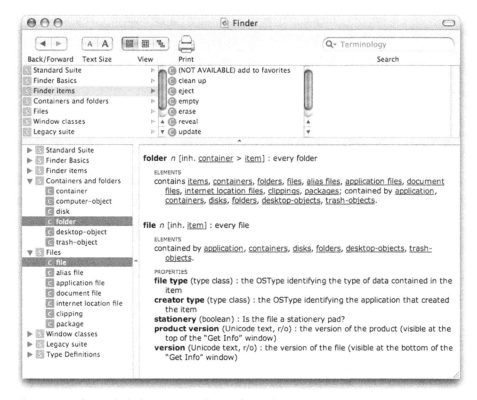

Figure 22-6. *The Finder's dictionary with two classes highlighted:* file *and* folder

Specifying a Range of Elements

A common form of referencing a set of object is by range. To reference elements by range, you must know the reference to the first and last elements in the range, and you have to know that every element between (and including) these outer elements will be affected. For instance, the following script will close all but the front TextEdit documents:

```
tell application "TextEdit"
  close (documents 2 thru -1) saving no
end tell
```

Or, the following will reference a range of records in a FileMaker Pro database:

```
tell application "FileMaker Pro"
  records 12 thru 16 of database 1
end tell
```

Knowing "Whose" Hot and Who's Not . . .

This kind of wholesale object manipulation is fast and powerful, but wait, there's more! You can push it even further by isolating the objects you want to work with even more using the powerful by-test reference form, also known as the whose clause.

The whose clause allows you to construct multi-object references that identify only those objects whose property and/or element values meet certain conditions. For instance, what if you want to change the line weight of the lines like you did previously but only for the lines that are thinner than half a point? Script 22-4 shows how you can do that.

Script 22-4. *(includes the following two scripts)*

```
tell application "InDesign CS"
    tell page 1 of active document
        tell (every graphic line whose stroke weight ≤ 0.5)
            set stroke weight to 0.5
        end tell
    end tell
end tell
```

You can also combine properties, as you can see in the following script, which deletes specific files from a folder:

```
tell application "Finder"
    tell every file of the desktop
        delete (every file whose size < 1000 and name extension is not "pdf")
    end tell
end tell
```

Activating Applications

When scripting different applications, you have to decide whether the applications should be in the foreground or background when the script runs. The basic rule is that applications perform better in the background, not in the foreground, and you should bring your script to the foreground for maximum performance. Applications perform better in the background because there's less screen redraw activity, which can slow things down quite a bit. Since the script itself has no display tasks or user interface, it does better in the front.

You need to consider a few issues here, starting with screen redraw. Although it's really cool to see an application jumping around while processing documents at the speed of light, it does run slower this way. If speed is a critical issue, which it isn't always, then you will be served well by timing your script in the foreground and background and comparing the results.

Some commands, such as copy and paste, require that the application be in the foreground, so you don't really have a choice there, but you can perform the operation and then send it back again.

What I usually do is create a should_activate property. Then, instead of just using the activate command, I do this:

```
tell application "Some Application"
    if should_activate then activate
end tell
```

This way, when I know some VP will be checking out the system, I turn this property on, and all hell breaks loose on the screen. The system may run a few paces behind the usual speed, but no one cares at this point.

Debugging Scripts

Debugging your scripts is not something you do as the final step of script writing. You should do your debugging while you're writing the script, every step of the way. As your mom always told you, it is better to clean as you go.

Although there are many tricks to debugging, there's no better overall way than to do it with Script Debugger from Late Night Software (www.latenightsw.com). I know, it does cost about $190 U.S., but if you spend a good chunk of your time writing scripts, it will pay for itself. It is currently the only AppleScript editor written for Mac OS X that gives you step-by-step debugging.

Script Debugger, as the name suggests, has useful tools for debugging scripts. The main debugging feature, and the one Script Debugger is most known for, is the ability to run through the script step-by-step and set breakpoints where the script pauses. I'll return to some Script Debugger debugging techniques later in the chapter. In the meantime, you'll learn about some other ways you can get the bugs out of your scripts with any script editor.

Don't Try to Understand the Problem, Just Solve It!

Fixing scripts does not always require you to know *precisely* what exact external forces caused them to break, but it does require you to know *where* they broke and what part of the script isn't working anymore. If necessary, you can often find a way around the problem without ever fixing it.

My clients always crack up when they ask me what the problem was and my reply is "I don't know, but I did make the script work again."

Of course, understanding the source of the problem can be extremely beneficial, but it may be far beyond your reach—for instance, say the client is switching servers, and suddenly the script can't delete files. You can't change the server's behavior, but you can provide a workaround. Also, if a specific application acts buggy when you script one of its features, you don't have to get to the bottom of it and spend a week on the phone with the developers of this application. File a bug with the developer, and then find a suitable workaround for your script.

Don't Confuse User Errors with Bugs

Not too many scripts don't rely on any user action whatsoever, and as long as the user's action is required, some user at some point will cause your script to break. With complex scripts, it can be difficult to figure out whether the script broke or some file the script is expecting or other required element is not in place.

Although it may be tempting to get right into your script and find a workaround, you should stop to think. If the script has been operating successfully for some time, it is most likely still working OK, and the user is probably the cause.

For example, if the script unexpectedly errors because the user has recently moved certain files or folders that the script relies on, you may want to modify the code that raised the error so the next time this specific error-causing condition occurs, it will trap the error and deal with it sensibly. This might be something simple like improving your error reporting so the user is notified gently with a dialog box explaining what the problem is and how to rectify it. Or you might design the error handling code so it rectifies the problem automatically, creating replacement folders or using some default files instead.

As you become more experienced in designing and writing scripts, you'll learn to anticipate most ways that a user could accidentally mess up the smooth running of your script and add the code to handle these errors right from the start. That way, your scripts will always behave intelligently and gracefully regardless of what your users manage to throw at them.

Values Are a Window to Your Script Statements

When you write a script statement, there's a chance that somewhere in that statement there's a bug. The bug can be in one of two levels: it's either a syntax error that will prevent the script from compiling or a runtime error. The first error type is in a way nicer, since AppleScript lets you know right away where the issue is. Runtime problems are a different issue altogether. The script's syntax is OK, but somewhere along the line, the code was unable to run. Or else it appears to have run OK but has actually produced the wrong result. Imagine telling AppleScript to delete a file that doesn't exist or trying to get the value of the fifth item in a four-item list. Or perhaps it overwrote a file's existing content when it was supposed to add the new data to the end of the file instead. The script's grammar is correct, but the actual instructions it's giving to AppleScript aren't quite what you'd intended.

Assuming that all the required application objects exist and the problem is somewhere in your script logic, one way you can spot the problem is by examining the values that contributed to the problematic statement.

To do that, you will look at a few ways of observing values while the script is running.

Using the return Statement

The first value-exposing debugging method you'll use is the return statement. Using the return statement allows you to return any value currently set in the script. The downside is that it will also stop the script right then and there. Using return within subroutines doesn't work the same, since it will simply return the value from the subroutine to the part of the script that called it. In that case, you'll need to add further return statements to return the value all the way. However, using return is nice because it will return the value in a pure AppleScript format for you to examine.

To use the return statement for debugging, create a new line somewhere in the middle of your script, before the place where the error happens but after the place where the value in question has been created. Let's assume you have the script in Script 23-1 that is supposed to remove some text from the name of files. Since all the files in the folder are named by another script, you can count on them having the same length.

Script 23-1.

```
set file_name_list to list folder the_jobs_folder
repeat with the_file_name in file_name_list
    set new_name to text 1 thru 12 of the_file_name
    tell application "Finder"
        set name of file the_file_name of the_jobs_folder to new_name
    end tell
end repeat
```

When you run the script, if the folder path stored in the_jobs_folder contains invisible files, you get an error on line 3 that looks something like this: "Can't get text 1 thru 12 of '.DS_Store.'" You realize that there's some issue with the file list the script is using, so you add a line of script returning the value of file_name_list after it has been created:

```
set file_name_list to list folder the_jobs_folder
return file_name_list -- TEST
repeat with the_file_name in file_name_list
    set new_name to text 1 thru 12 of the_file_name
    ...
```

Tip Note that the comment at the end of the line in the previous script is TEST. Adding a reminder that a specific line was intended for temporary testing or debugging purposes is a good way to avoid leaving it there by mistake.

By looking at the list in the Result area of Apple's Script Editor window (shown in Figure 23-1), you can clearly see that the list includes the OS X–generated .DS_Store invisible file.

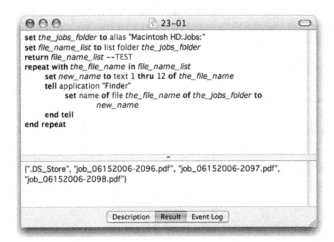

Figure 23-1. *The* return *statement stops the script and returns the value of the* file_name_list *variable, which is displayed in the Result area.*

You can then trace the problem to the statement that assigned the file list value to the file_name_list variable. The solution is to make the invisibles parameter of the list folder command false:

```
set file_name_list to list folder the_jobs_folder without invisibles
```

One pitfall with using this form of debugging is that you may forget to remove the temporary return statement from your script once you're finished with it. This is not likely, but if it happens, your script will stop in the middle, and this time it *will* be your fault. Adding a TEST comment to such debugging lines, as you did here, can help avoid that.

Dialog Boxes to the Rescue

One of the basic forms of debugging is using the display dialog command. All you do is display a dialog box showing the value in question.

The display dialog command is best for debugging string values or values that can be coerced into strings such as numbers, Booleans, and dates. To display application references values, you will need to add more sophisticated code that displays the index of the application element or uses another way to show you, with a string, which application reference is in question.

For the most part, you can just insert a line of code that looks like this:

```
display dialog variable_in_question
```

with the identifier of the real variable you want to test, of course.

The main advantage dialog boxes have over the return command you looked at before is that after you click the OK button, the script continues. This allows you to check multiple items in the same debug session. Also, the dialog box gives you as much time as you need to make notes or do some good ol' thinking before you're ready to continue.

Using the dialog box debugging technique is great for checking the values of variables that change in a repeat loop. While the loop is crunching statements with slightly varying values in every repetition, a dialog box on every loop can reveal a lot about what's going on in there.

If you like the idea of debugging with dialog boxes, you may want to facilitate it a bit. The first thing you will need is a debug property. This property will be set to true when you're debugging and false when you're not. It is mainly a fail-safe mechanism to make sure you didn't leave any dialog box surprises for the script's end users.

The subroutine itself should have a short name, such as msg (short for *message* and a bit like the msgbox Visual Basic command).

The contents of the subroutine can be simple:

```
on msg(the_value)
    if debug then display dialog the_value
end msg
```

If you want to get a little fancier, Script 23-2 shows a beefed-up subroutine that uses dialog boxes for debugging all sorts of values.

Script 23-2.

```
1. property debug : true
2. msg({1, 2, 3, 4})

3. on msg(the_value)
4.     if debug then
5.         set the_class to class of the_value
6.         set the_class_string to the_class as string
7.         if the_class is in {integer, real} then
8.             display dialog the_class_string & return & the_value
9.         else if the_class is string then
10.            display dialog the_class_string & return & "\"" & ¬
                   the_value & "\""
11.        else if the_class is date then
12.            set the_string_value to the_value as string
13.            display dialog the_class_string & return & ¬
                   "date \"" & the_value & "\""
14.        else if the_class is list then
```

```
15.         set text item delimiters to ", "
16.         set the_string_value to the_value as string
17.         set text item delimiters to ""
18.         display dialog "List of " & (count the_value) & ¬
                " items" & return & "{" & the_string_value & "}"
19.       else
20.         try
21.           set the_string_value to the_value as string
22.           display dialog the_class_string & return & ¬
                  the_string_value
23.         on error error_text
24.           display dialog "Debug error:" & return & ¬
                  the_class_string & return & error_text
25.         end try
26.       end if
27.     end if
28. end msg
```

The preceding subroutine will give you a slightly more descriptive dialog box based on the class of the value you're testing. Figure 23-2 shows the dialog box that will be displayed if a list is passed to the subroutine.

List of 4 items
{1, 2, 3, 4}

Cancel   OK

Figure 23-2. *The debugging subroutine handles a list that was passed to it for display.*

Error Messages Tell a Story

A mix between the return value and the dialog box methods is the error method. Simply throw the value as an error. Say you want to see the value of the variable my_file_list in the middle of the script's execution; simply type the following:

```
error my_file_list
```

AppleScript will display the value of the variable my_file_list in an error message.

This method is useful when you want to test your script when it is running as an application. In such cases, the return value method simply won't work.

Using the Event Log

The event log is the one debugging feature actually built into AppleScript. Debugging with the log includes using the Event Log area in Script Editor (or Script Debugger). Let's start with the Event Log area itself. When the event log is open in the script-editing application, AppleScript logs each application and scripting addition command that is sent by your script, along with its result. Figure 23-3 shows a simple script and the results that the event log has captured.

Figure 23-3. *A simple script and the results that the event log has captured*

Logging Anything with the log Command

You can force anything to be added to the event log by using the log command. The log command, followed by a value, will add the given value to the log, wrapped in comment brackets: (*value*). The value is wrapped in a comment because anything that appears in the event log is actually legally compiled AppleScript code.

Figure 23-4 shows how you can force the result of $x * 12$ to appear in the log.

Figure 23-4. *By using the* log *command, you can force the result of* X * 12 *to appear in the log.*

Using the start log and stop log Commands

If you're using Script Debugger, you have two more commands at your disposal: start log and stop log. These two commands will start and stop logging to the Apple Event Log area. For these commands to work, the Apple Event Log area must be open.

When you want to log only specific statements or parts of your script, you can add a line saying start log before the part you want to log and a stop log line after that part. Since the log starts automatically when the Event Log area is open, you may want to start your script with the stop log command.

To use these commands inside an application tell block, make sure to write the full command and reference: tell me to start log or tell me to stop log.

Showing Log History

Apple's Script Editor 2 actually creates a history for the event log. You can check out the event log history by choosing Window ➤ Event Log History.

Figure 23-5 shows the Event Log History dialog box. The left column allows you to select the script whose log you want to see, and the right side displays the actual log.

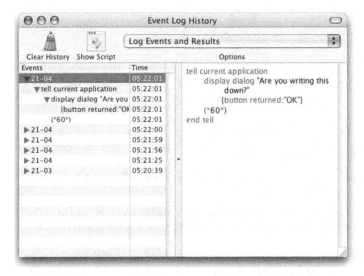

Figure 23-5. *The Event Log History dialog box in Script Editor 2*

Debugging with Script Debugger

As mentioned, Script Debugger is the best debugging tool for AppleScript. If you own Script Debugger, then check the following sections out for a few debugging how-tos; if you don't own it, read on and consider getting it.

To debug with Script Debugger, you can switch to a special mode called AppleScript Debugger X. This mode is similar to AppleScript in any respect having to do with running the scripts, but you have to switch back to normal AppleScript mode before deploying your script in any way.

To switch to debugging mode in Script Debugger, choose Script ➤ Enable Debugging.

Using the Script Debugger Script Window

The most notable part of the Script Debugger script window is the Properties panel, shown at the top right of the window in Figure 23-6. This panel shows all the script's properties, global variables, top-level variables, declared local variables, and their values.

Figure 23-6. *Script Debugger's script window with the Properties panel open at the top right*

Beside the value, you can see what type of string the value is by the little icon to the left of the value. Unicode text has a square with the text *UTF XVI* next to it, and style text has a red *A* and a blue *a* icon.

This properties and variables list is great when you want a glimpse of the script's current state. The result of the last line to execute is displayed in the Result area at the top of the Results drawer.

Using the Script Debugger's Debugging Mode

Next, you will convert the example script to AppleScript debugger language. You do that by choosing Script ➤ Enable Debugging. When the script is in Debugger mode, the Properties panel turns into the Debugging panel.

The most notable addition to the main scripting window is a row of diamonds to the left of the script. Each diamond represents a potential breakpoint next to a line of code. Clicking that diamond turns it red, which indicates that the script should stop at this line the next time it runs. The script's "playback head," shown as a blue arrow, stops at the line with the breakpoint before this line is executed.

Figure 23-7 shows Script Debugger's script window in AppleScript Debugger mode.

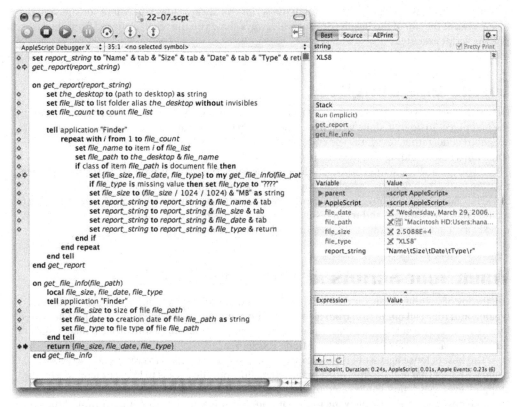

Figure 23-7. *Script Debugger's script window in AppleScript Debugger mode*

The left side of the Debugging panel is now a list of handler calls. When the playback head is stopped inside a subroutine, then that subroutine is selected in the list, and all of its variables appear in the property area to the right.

By default, undeclared local variables do not appear in the list. If you want to examine the values of local variables, you have to declare them as local variables at the top of the subroutine definition. After doing so, these declared local variables and their values will appear in the yellow-shaded area in the Properties panel.

Stepping Through Scripts

When in AppleScript Debugger mode, Script Debugger allows you to perform four additional script navigation commands besides the usual run and stop. The commands are pause, step into, step over, and step out.

The pause command (Cmd+Shift+. [period]) is good when you want to pause a long-running script just to see where you are. Otherwise, you can't use this command to pause at an exact point.

Stepping is really where things heat up. The step into (Cmd+I) and step over (Cmd+Y) commands allow you to execute one line of script at a time. The difference is that step into will go into subroutine calls and step through every line there, while step over will skip the subroutine call and move right to the next line.

The step out command is handy if you happened to have stepped into a subroutine but you want to get out of it.

In any case, the blue arrow at the left of the script will always show you where you are, and the Result area at the top of the Results drawer will always show you the result returned from the last line the script executed.

Divide and Conquer

One of the best ways to avoid bugs is to make sure you don't introduce them into your scripts in the first place. To do that, don't write new code directly into your already overcomplicated bowl of spaghetti code; rather, test your new code on the side first—just as you would crack an egg into a small bowl before adding it to the mix, just in case it is rotten.

If you create little script chunks on the side and integrate them into the main script only once they are tested, you will have much less need to go around fixing bugs in your script.

This also goes for debugging. If there's a problem in the script, try to isolate it, copy the code to a different script window, and try to resolve it there. Besides having less code to deal with, you can quickly try a few scenarios without messing with that mammoth script.

When Your Scripts Are Used by Clients

Oh, the joy of writing scripts for cash. The problem is that those scripts never seem to forget their creator, and they call out to him from all around the globe. Yes, once you create a script that is used by someone, they will hunt you down whenever anything goes wrong. I still have clients I wrote scripts for years ago calling me with questions about them.

The best defense against being swamped with fixing old scripts is to create good scripts to begin with (not that good scripts don't break—they do—but the trick is to know exactly where they stopped, even years after you created them).

The best way I know to allow me to troubleshoot scripts remotely (other than Timbuktu, of course) is to give the script the ability to create a log that records its activity. This log can be enabled somehow by the client and, when enabled, will create a file where it adds lines of text each time certain things happen in the script.

This may sound like overkill, but truly, once you create the log subroutine, you can use it in any script you create.

The most important part of constructing the log subroutine is to not make the mistake of creating a string variable, adding log text to it, and writing it to a file at the end. What will happen is that the script will stop in the middle because of the bug, the string variable with all that good log information will be erased from memory, and you will still be clueless.

Instead, use `write log_test to the_file at eof`. This will ensure that each line you want to log will be added to the end of the text file right away.

CHAPTER 24

■ ■ ■

Saving and Running Scripts

Although any script you write using AppleScript still looks the same and generally utilizes the same system resources to run, the Mac makes that AppleScript functionality available to you in a few ways. The most common forms used to save and run scripts are script applets, script droplets, and compiled scripts. This chapter will cover the different ways you can put scripts to work.

You can find most of the options for saving scripts in the Save dialog box of whichever script editor you're using. Figure 24-1 shows the Apple Script Editor Save dialog box.

Figure 24-1. *Apple Script Editor's Save dialog box*

Table 24-1 shows the file formats available for saving AppleScript files.

Table 24-1. *AppleScript File Formats*

Type	Description	Options	Features	Name Extension	Icon
Application applet	A normal application applet that runs when you double-click it.	Run only, stay open, start-up screen	Simple applet.	`.app`	run me
Droplet application applet	An application applet containing an on open handler.	Run only, stay open, start-up screen	Allows your script to process files dropped on it.	`.app`	drop me a file

Continued

Table 24-1. *Continued*

Type	Description	Options	Features	Name Extension	Icon
Application applet bundle	An application applet saved as a Cocoa bundle.	Run only, stay open, start-up screen	Can also be saved as a droplet by including the on open handler. The bundle can hold any files such as templates, and so on.	.app	Bundle
Compiled script	The native AppleScript file format. Can be executed from within the script editor or loaded into other scripts.	Run only	Can also be run from the Mac OS X Script menu or other "script runner" utilities.	.scpt	Basic.scpt
Compiled script bundle	The same as a compiled script but uses Cocoa's three-bundle format.	Run only	The script bundle can hold any files such as templates, and so on.	.scptd	basic bundle.scptd
Text file	An ASCII plain-text file that contains the noncompiled version of the script.	Line encoding	Opens without requiring referenced application applets to be open.	.applescript	plain text.applescript

Using Compiled Scripts

A compiled script file is AppleScript's default file format. What is the difference between a compiled script and plain text? When you compile the script, a few things happen. The first thing you may notice is that the script text gets formatted based on the AppleScript formatting settings you specified in the Script Editor's preferences.

In addition, you may have noticed that if AppleScript didn't recognize any of the applications you used in the script, it asks you to locate them, and then it launches them in order to compare the keywords you used in this application's tell block with the ones defined in the application's dictionary. In the compiled script, AppleScript actually includes several kinds of information identifying each application used—its filename, its creator type, and an alias to its last known location—any of which can be used to find that application again later. This allows it to recognize that application even if it is renamed, moved, or even upgraded. That's right—if you created a script a year ago with Adobe Illustrator 10 and you're opening it now, AppleScript may recognize Illustrator CS as the target.

AppleScript also converts the syntax from AppleScript's hallmark English-like syntax into what appears to be cryptic text that is actually tokens that can be understood only by the AppleScript interpreter. A compiled script file containing the simple script display dialog "Hello" looks like the following when viewed raw in Bare Bones Software's BBEdit:

```
FasdUAS 1.101.10
˘˘˘˘
l˘
¸
I˘˘˘ ¸˘˘.sysodlogaskrTEXT
m\\ Hello˘¸˘
¸
.aevtoappnullÄê****   ˘˘˘˘˘
```

```
ˇˆˇˇ.aevtoappnullÄê****
kˇ₁ˇ₁ˇˇˇ
\ˇÙˇÙ.sysodlogaskrTEXTˇˆ\‡jascr
ˆfifi≠
```

From a system standpoint, forcing you to compile a script before saving it can prevent many runtime issues such as syntax errors, missing applications, and so on. It also brings the script one step closer to the machine language understood by the AppleScript interpreter.

Having said all that, the reverse is also true: Script Editor acts as a decompiler. Whenever you open a script with Script Editor, it has to decompile the script, locate all the referenced aliases and applications, and apply the AppleScript formatting.

Another function of compiled scripts not saved as applications but rather as scripts is that they can be loaded into other scripts and can act as subroutine libraries. As discussed in Chapter 20, loading scripts into other scripts is fairly easy and can help you reuse your code in an efficient way.

Using Script Applets

What's easier to use than a script applet? You write AppleScript code, test it, and save it as an applet. All the user has to do is double-click it. When the script is done executing all the code in the run handler, it quits.

A script applet handles two events when run: run and quit.

When you launch a simple applet, the run handler immediately executes. Since you may have not included an explicit run handler, any code that is not a part of any other handler is by default part of the run handler. Once the run handler returns, the program automatically executes the quit handler, if one exists, and then quits.

Script Editor also allows you to save applets in a stay-open form if you want. This means that instead of quitting automatically as soon as the run handler is finished, they will remain open until explicitly quit. This allows them to handle additional events such as user-defined subroutine calls and idle events. You'll learn more about stay-open applets later in the "Using Stay-Open Applets" section.

Using Droplets

Droplets are script applets with a twist: they can process files that are dropped on them. Using droplets allows you to create script applets that apply certain processes to dropped files.

To turn an applet into a droplet applet, simply include the open handler somewhere in it. The one parameter of the open handler is a variable that will contain a list of aliases to all the files and folders dropped on the droplet. This means the open handler doesn't actually do anything; it doesn't move the dropped items to any particular place, unless, that is, you write the script to do that. All that happens is that your script gets a wake-up call with a reference to a bunch of files: "Hey, wake up! Here are the files you will be processing . . . ."

Figure 24-2 shows a small (and rather crude) example of the open handler. The script tells you how many files and how many folders were dropped on it. The only purpose of it is to show the basic operation of the open handler and the function of its parameter.

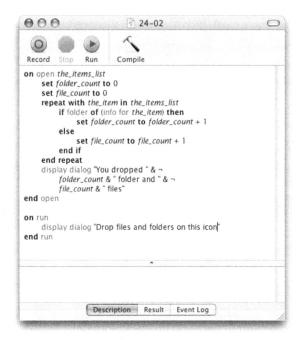

Figure 24-2. *The basic droplet applet script*

Notice a couple of things about the script in Figure 24-2. I named the variable the_items_list, and it can have any identifier name you want (as long as it adheres to variable naming rules, of course).

In the script, I use the value of this variable as I would use any other list. This time, I'm looping through the items in the list.

Also notice that there's a run handler. Although it's not required, it is nice to have something happen when some unsuspecting user tries to double-click the droplet. Remember, the droplet is just an applet and will execute the run handler if double-clicked.

You can find some more templates and examples of droplets on the AppleScript web page. Go to www.apple.com/applescript/resources/, click Essential Subroutines, and then click Finder Droplets.

Using Stay-Open Applets

So far you have looked at normal applets and at droplet applets that perform a single run or open event and quit when done. Script Editor also allows you to save them in stay-open form so they don't quit automatically as soon as they finish handling that first event. Instead, they become idle and wait around until you explicitly quit them, allowing them to handle additional events in the meantime.

Some big advantages a stay-open applet has over a big repeat loop with a delay are that during the execution of a delay command, the applet isn't responsive, it can't execute any other commands, and the only way to quit it is by pressing Cmd+. (period) or by force quitting.

Although a normal script applet or droplet can use only the run/open and quit handlers, the stay-open applet can have two more: reopen and idle. It can also have any number of user-defined handlers, or subroutines, that can be called from other scripts.

Let's look at a brief description of all these event handlers before getting into some more details regarding the idle handler and its function. The following handlers aren't ones that your script applet's script would normally call of its own accord. (The only exception might be the quit handler, which will be executed anytime another handler sends the applet a quit command.) Instead, they respond automatically to natural events in the life of a script applet. The code inside the event handlers will execute when the specific event occurs.

run

The run event handler is called once when a stay-open applet is launched by double-clicking it in the Finder or by sending it a run command from another script. It won't be called again automatically while the script is running (although other scripts can call it as often as they like). You can use this handler to initialize values, give instructions, or do anything else the applet has to do once. After the run handler has completed, the idle handler (if one exists) will be called. If your stay-open applet is also a droplet, then any initialization has to happen in a separate handler; otherwise, the same initialization code will repeat in the run handler and in the on open handler. The following is a script that shows the basic code responsible for initialization in a stay-open droplet:

```
property is_initialized : false

to initialize()
    if is_initialized then return
    set is_initialized to true
    -- do initialization here
end initialize

on run
    initialize()
end run

on open dropped_items
    initialize()
    -- process dropped items here
end open

on quit
    continue quit
    set is_initialized to false
end quit
```

open

If a stay-open droplet is launched by dragging files or folders onto it or by sending it an open command from another script, its open handler will be executed instead of its run handler. After the open handler has finished handling this initial event, the idle handler (if one exists) will be called. Additional files and folders can be dropped onto an already-running droplet; this will cause its open handler to execute again, allowing the new items to be processed.

reopen

The reopen event handler will be called when an already-running script applet is relaunched by clicking its Dock icon or by double-clicking it in the Finder again.

quit

The quit event handler is called when the user chooses Quit from the File menu of the script applet's menu and when the scripter calls the quit handler either from the same script or from another script (done by using the quit command).

If you include a quit event handler in your applet, you are in effect intercepting the normal quit command that tells the applet to stop running. That means the applet will not automatically quit; instead, it will do what you ask it to do.

You can use the continue quit statement to let the applet's script stop the main event loop and quit.

The following quit event handler asks the user whether they're sure they want to quit, and it quits only if the answer is yes:

```
on quit
    display dialog "Are you sure you want to quit?" buttons {"No", "Yes"}
    if button returned of result is "Yes" then
        continue quit
    end if
end quit
```

In the preceding example, if the user tries to quit the applet but then clicks the No button, the applet will remain open.

idle

The idle event handler is really where most of the action happens. As you saw earlier, the run handler executes once at the start, the quit event handler executes once at the end, and the reopen handler is really a "just-in-case" handler.

The idle event, however, happens all the time. Does that mean the idle event acts like a huge repeat loop? Well, sort of. The idle event handler works a bit like a repeat loop with a built-in delay. You can tell it to cool off for a given period of time before it starts again. You do that with the idle event's version of the return command.

At the point where you want the idle handler to be done executing code for a while, use the return statement, followed by the number of seconds you want to wait until the next time the idle event handler is called.

For instance, the following script, if saved as a stay-open applet, will remind you to take a break every 15 minutes:

```
on idle
    activate
    display dialog "Time to stretch!" giving up after 30
    return (15 * minutes)
end idle
```

In the preceding script, the idle event handler will be executed for the first time as soon as the script has finished executing its run handler. The idle handler will bring the applet to the front and display the "Time to stretch!" dialog box. On returning, it will instruct the script applet to invoke the idle event handler again when 15 minutes (15 × 60 seconds) have passed.

Calling Handlers from Other Scripts

Another cool thing about stay-open scripts is that you can call their handlers from an outside script while they are running. Let's say the stay-open script applet shown in Figure 24-3 is running. Another script can call its tell_time subroutine like it would call a command defined in any other applet:

```
tell application "My Clock"
    activate
    tell_time()
end tell
```

Figure 24-3. *The script of the* My Clock *script applet*

Using the Quit Command in a Script

One thing you will find yourself trying to do once in a while is quitting the script applet from inside the script based on a certain condition. For instance, there may be a dialog box asking the user whether they want the applet to continue running or quit. In this case it is common to try to use the quit command to force the applet to quit. Although using the quit command will cause the applet to quit eventually when it is done handling the current event, you will be better served raising an error –128 (the "User canceled" error) to force the applet to quit immediately.

Bundling Up

Starting with Panther and now in Tiger, you can now save both compiled scripts and script applets as bundles. Bundles are the format used for all Cocoa applications and many Carbon applications, as well as various file formats such as TextEdit's .rtfd documents. Bundles are really disguised folders that appear in the Finder as if they were regular files and behave like them too when you double-click them. You can open a bundle like a folder, however, should you need to view or change its actual contents.

To open it like a folder, Ctrl-click the bundle with the mouse, and choose Show Package Contents from the contextual menu. With Tiger and newer, you can also view the contents of a script or applet bundle by opening it in Script Editor and clicking the Bundle Contents icon in the document window's toolbar.

Once you see the bundle's content, you can browse the script or application's folder structure.

Bundles can come in handy when your script needs to use external files such as templates, icons, sounds, scripting additions, or some text files containing data the script needs. After saving the script, place these files inside the Resources folder inside the bundle, and use the command path to me to get the path to the bundle:

```
set template_path to (path to me as string) & "Contents:Resources:Template.indd"
```

With Tiger and newer, you can also use the path to resource command to locate bundle resources directly by filename:

```
set template_path to path to resource "Template.indd"
```

The functionality and usefulness of the path to me statement has been made better in Tiger. You can find the full details in Chapter 8.

Locking Scripts with Run Only

Unless you are saving your script as text, you can choose the Run Only save option to lock the contents of your script. Doing so will strip your script from the data, which would allow the script to be read by a script editor later.

This feature may have severe consequences: if the locked script is the only version of your script, you will never gain access to it, other than for the purpose of running it. It is highly advised to save a copy of your scripts as text for backup, or you'll risk losing them.

Note Locking your only copy of a script is almost as disastrous as trashing it! If you lock your source code often by saving scripts as run only, you have to be extra careful, or you will lose your code.

I personally never lock any of my scripts. As a consultant, I want my clients to open my scripts and look at them. All they can say is, "Wow, we better not touch that stuff!" For me, locking a script would be like Apple locking the containers of its computers so you couldn't open them.

Sometimes, however, saving scripts as run only is a good idea. The obvious reason is protecting your scripting secrets, especially if your scripts are distributed to a mass audience. Another reason is to prevent the users of the scripts from messing them up intentionally or unintentionally.

Customizing the Start-up Screen

When saving a script applet, you can check the Startup Screen check box, found in the Save dialog box. The next time the applet runs, the text you typed in the Description panel of your Script Editor script window will display in a rather crude welcome window.

Figure 24-4 shows the script's Description panel, which will be displayed when the script applet is launched if the Startup Screen check box is checked when the applet is saved.

Figure 24-4. *You can add formatted text to the Description panel in the Script Editor script window. This text will be displayed when the script applet starts.*

Implementing Healthy Scriptwriting Practices

Once the euphoria of running your first script settles (hold on—it has been eight years, and I'm still not over it . . .), you can turn yourself from a mere scripter into a lean, mean, scripting machine. This chapter is dedicated to teaching you a few good practices that can help you turn scripting into more of a business, from a product-management viewpoint. When you script, someone benefits from your scripts financially. I get there by applying the simple "time is money" rule. Remember that even with the immense time savings a single script can offer, you can still improve your scriptwriting in several ways.

In this chapter, I will cover using good general script-writing practices, implementing naming conventions, being cautious with global variables and literals, using comments, enhancing performance, using subroutine libraries, getting user feedback, and delivering code to external sites.

There Are No Bad Scripts, Just Bad Scripters

Well, not really—catchy title, though! What makes scripts "bad" is when scripters think of the code they are writing as black boxes that will be closed at the end of the day and never looked at again. In fact, writing the script and making it do what it was supposed to in the first place is only the beginning. It's the next steps, such as debugging, maintaining, and updating, where the quality of the script can make your job a joy or drive you to insanity.

The following sections will touch on several aspects of healthy scriptwriting: maintainability, foolproofness, performance, and cross-project reusability.

Maintainability

Your script is meant to serve a purpose and use external influences, such as user input, data files, templates, or databases to perform its functions. These external influences are most certain to change during the scriptwriting process or after the script has been put in use. It is when you need to either fix bugs or update your script to meet the changing environment that your own demons will come back to haunt you.

You should consider a few tips when attempting to make your script easier to maintain:

- Limit the use of global variables and script properties. These staples are really easy and tempting to use but will make the script difficult to untangle.

- Comment, comment, comment. Looking at your script again after a period of time can make it seem more like some ancient scriptures. Well-placed, clear comments that explain what different parts of the script do can mean a ten-point difference on your blood-pressure test.

- Another way to make scripts more legible is by properly naming variables and handlers. Well-named variables can make debugging and updating the script much easier. For instance, which of these would be easy to understand: using `set n to (x + y) * z`, using `set amountDue to (totalPrice + shipping) * taxRate`, or simply calling a handler called `calculateTotalPrice()`?

I'll cover these topics in more detail throughout the chapter.

Foolproofness

So, you think that in the months of testing your script you managed to foresee any possible issue a user can encounter, is that right? Well, go live with it, give it to a user, and wait five minutes.

Never underestimate a user's ability to find ways to crash your script. While deemed an idiot by the phrase *idiot proofing*, this user teaches you an important lesson on just how many ways they can make a script stop on its track, even after a long testing period. Part of the problem is that you, as the developer, will naturally tend to avoid doing things that'll make your script choke. Always let someone else use the script, preferably someone who's a novice, or at least the most novice among the people who will end up using the script. Novices have a way of doing things that can trigger the weirdest problems.

When writing a script that will depend on user activity, expect this "idiot proofing" to take up a good chunk of time. Try to foolproof a four-line script that has some user interaction, and you'll soon end up with a 20-to-30-line script that doesn't do much more than the original did but does it more reliably.

Performance

Although not as much of an issue as in pre–OS X scripting, making your scripts run as fast as they can makes a difference. See more about this in the "Enhancing Performance" section later in this chapter.

Cross-Project Reusability

As explained in the "Using Subroutine Libraries" section later, writing handlers in a way that will make them useful in other scripts can help you develop your future projects faster. Take, for instance, a script that relies on Microsoft Excel as the data source. You decide to create a handler that will get the data from the workbook by quoting specific ranges where the data resides. Now imagine turning that handler into a more general-purpose handler that gets data from a given range in a given Excel file. The handler can open the Excel file, extract the data from a list of ranges, and close the file at the end. This handler would be rather easy to use in future projects that also require similar interaction with Excel.

Implementing Naming Conventions

One more sign of becoming a grown-up scripter is understanding the importance of naming conventions. Usually that understanding hits you when you open a large production script you (or someone else) wrote a few months ago to make some changes—fix some problems, add new features, and so on. Unless you're blessed with superhuman memory, you'll naturally have forgotten all the details of how it works over time, so you'll need to learn how it works all over again. Unfortunately, if the author of the code didn't bother to pick good, descriptive, consistent names for any of the dozens (or even hundreds) of variables in your script when it was written, understanding it is going to be a tough challenge . . . and all because a little more care in choosing good variable names wasn't taken.

Before I go into detail and lay out a comprehensive naming convention system, I'll cover some simple tips.

First and foremost, you have to follow AppleScript's rules for naming variables and subroutines (also called *identifiers*). Chapter 8 and Chapter 18 define them in detail. These include not starting an identifier with a digit and not inserting any spaces or other special characters. One special character that is allowed and used quite a bit is the underscore (_).

Two common conventions exist for writing identifiers consisting of multiple words: one is the intercap method, where the words are not separated but each word starts with a capital letter:

```
totalPageCount
TotalPageCount
```

The other is the underscore method, where the words in the identifier are separated by underscores:

```
total_page_count
```

In this chapter, I will assume you know the basic naming rules defined by AppleScript and that what I refer to here as "wrong" may actually be a legal variable or subroutine name—it's just not a *good* one.

Looking at a Comprehensive Naming Convention System

For any type of conventions relating to AppleScript, I always return to one source of information: Mark Munro. Mark is the founder and president of Write Track Media (www.writetrackmedia.com) and has created some incredible automation systems for the Associated Press, Sony Music, and others. Mark is obsessed with the process of script writing and has dissected and categorized every aspect of his scripting process.

Among other things, Mark has come up with the following description of his naming conventions for subroutines and variables.

Naming Subroutines

The following sections discuss Write Track Media's standards for naming subroutines.

Basic Formula

The basic formula for subroutine naming is as follows:

```
«Group»«Entity»«Action»
«Group»«Entity»«Action»«Attribute»
```

Group is typically the application or functional group the subroutine deals with. If the subroutine deals with a single application and contains code that is as generic as possible, it should get the application name (finder, filemaker). If instead it deals with a single type of process that may involve several applications, it should get the function name. For routines that are not typically open-ended enough to be harvested, Mark tends to make the group be the client name or code to help distinguish these routines as being exclusive to the client's project. The primary group serving as the first part of the name helps to keep you thinking in a structured way, encouraging you to keep a subroutine focused on one primary task or function. It also aids in sorting the subroutines when viewing them in a list.

The `Entity` (or noun) is the item upon which the action will be taken. This can be something straightforward such as a folder or a file in the Finder or a record or a database in FileMaker Pro, or it can be something more complex such as a department (`accounting`). Although many people tend to want to put the action in the second place and the entity in the third place (`delete folder` rather than `folder delete`), I advise against that. Why? Sorting a list by entity first and action second makes it far easier to locate the subroutine you want.

The `Action` is the type of processing that will be undertaken on the `Entity`.

The `Attribute` is an optional naming position that is reserved for identifying the attribute of the `Entity` that will be modified in a manner described by the `Action`. For example, you might say `finderFolderSetName()` to denote which of the folder's properties will be changed. The attribute can also be an item that is further down the hierarchical chain. For example, you might say `finderFolderCreateFile()` to indicate you are going to create a file within the folder. The file is not really an attribute of the folder exactly . . . but you can use this position in the naming formula this way.

Here are some simple examples:

```
filemakerFieldGetData()
filemakerFieldSetData()
filemakerRecordDelete()
finderFolderDelete()
finderFolderOpen()
finderItemCopy()
finderItemDelete()
finderItemMove()
```

Here are some more complex examples:

```
calendarDatesCreate()
clientDataParse()
```

Complex Formulas

Sometimes the preceding basic formula is not sufficient to convey all the information necessary about the activity within a subroutine. Therefore, some additional rules can guide the exceptions. This is especially true with complex applications such as desktop publishing. With Finder or File-Maker Pro routines, you are typically changing one attribute of a primary item. For example, you might change the name of a file or its file type. In FileMaker Pro, you might change the contents of a cell.

In QuarkXPress, however, you may need to change the leading of some paragraph in the contents of a text box. When more levels of hierarchy in the `Entity` and `Attribute` are required, you can simply add another level:

«Group»«Entity»«Action»«Attribute»«SubAttribute»

An example of this is `quarkTextSetParagraphTabs()`.

Another example of a complex exception is one that contains a combination of items. This is somewhat rare but can be accommodated by simply adding a conjunction as follows— `finderFolderSetNameAndLabel()`.

Remember, the idea is to not limit your description . . . just to make it as formulaic as possible. If you need to be more specific, add words to the end of the basic formula—while trying to keep the basic formula intact. A crazy example is `quarkDocumentReplaceWordsStartingWithTECWithTECSoft()`.

Case-Sensitivity

Always make the Group (the first part) lowercase. All other parts of the name are title case. Avoid using an underscore to separate naming sections because it removes the possibility of double-clicking the name to select it.

Here are some properly named subroutines:

```
finderAppActivate()
finderFolderCreate()
finderFolderDelete()
```

Here are some improperly named subroutines (though legal by AppleScript):

```
FinderAppActivate()
finder_folder_delete()
FINDERFOLDERCREATE()
```

Stay Consistent

If one subroutine creates a new record in FileMaker Pro and another creates a text file in the Finder, it can be helpful to use the same action term such as Create or Make. However, when you start mixing terms (especially words with the same meaning), it can become a little confusing.

Single Words

Each part of the formula should be a single word. This is especially important with automated harvesting, when you want to pull out the application name, and with sorting.

Note Automated harvesting in this case means having a script examine the content of another script and extract the names of all the handlers.

Spell It Out

Avoid "hyperabbreviation." This is a remnant from the days when memory was limited and every byte of space was like gold. People would write docChgClr() instead of documentChangeColor or, worse, setTOD instead of SetTimeOfDay. Abbreviations like this will always come back to haunt you, since you are likely to forget the initial meaning of the abbreviation. As a rule, try to spell everything out except for common, long words. If confronted with a long word, try using a different word before resorting to a cryptic abbreviation.

Avoid "Cute" Expressions

I always try to avoid "cute" expressions. Instead, I try to keep things professional. cdPlayThatFunkyMusic() might show your personality, but isn't cdPlayTrack more accurate, serious, and helpful to others as well as to yourself in the future? I once saw a script with a subroutine called MakeHTMLWhoopie(). Eh?

This is the conclusion:

```
Turn this --> into this
setMyGroovyDesktopColorBlue() --> finderDesktopSetColor()
MakeFileMakerRecordsSorted() --> filemakerRecordsSort()
crunchSomeFunkyNumbers() --> numberCalculatePercentage()
```

Naming Variables

The following sections discuss Write Track Media's standards for naming variables.

Variable Naming Formula

Variables should always be named in an efficient manner without compromising a clear description of what the variable contains. If a variable is too long, you should reword it in such a way that it doesn't lose the general meaning. If it is too short and will not be easily understood, you should expand it a little. Most important, all variables should have a descriptive prefix that helps quickly identify the contents they hold or the type of window object whose name they contain. Some variable names require a *superprefix* to help establish their relationship to the script and their placement and usage within it. The basic formula for naming a subroutine is as follows:

```
«Optional Super Prefix»«Prefix»«Description»«Etc»
```

As with subroutine naming, lowercase the first prefix, use title case for the rest, don't include "cute" words, be descriptive without being too verbose, and so on. The Description can be as many words as you need to describe the contents of the subroutine and can follow any pattern you choose. There are no current standards for how this part of the name should be configured besides using general brevity and clarity.

Variable Naming Prefixes

Prefixes allow you to easily distinguish the use and purpose of the variable. You can tell the variable's purpose simply by glancing at it.

Primary Variable Prefixes

Primary variable prefixes denote the basic type of data contained within a variable. You will find that once you start using these, you will be instantly hooked. Variables become more quickly recognized, and you can deal with your code more efficiently. Here are a few examples:

bln: Identifies variables that contain Boolean (true or false) values.

data: Identifies variables that contain some unknown data type. This is useful when receiving a value from a subroutine that could be a text string, a list, or a number depending on the operations performed. Typically this implies you should check for the presence of certain values such as Error where you might be expecting a list.

list: Identifies variables that contain any list values. Although you can use this to identify lists containing sublists, you should not use it to denote records.

name: Identifies variables that contain a name of an item.

num: Primary prefix that identifies variables containing numeric values. If a number is converted to a string, this prefix should not be used. Rather, you should use text—such as textNumServerItems or textServerItemCount.

path: Identifies variables that contain a path to an item. Typically, for readability, this should take the form of pathTo«Item» (pathToTemplate or pathToProjectFolder).

rec: Identifies variables that contain records.

script: Identifies variables that contain a loaded AppleScript or script object.

text: Identifies variables that contain any kind of text values including numbers that have been converted into text. path, name should be used in place of text to allow for more specific identification of certain types of text.

Secondary Variable Prefixes

Secondary variable prefixes are a little more specific than primary variable prefixes. At the moment they all deal with a more specific type of path or the path to a disk or mounted server volume. These are optional and can be interchanged with their primary counterparts. Some examples follow:

disk: A secondary type of text prefix for paths that can identify variables containing text values indicating the path to a disk. It should include the full path, such as Server Name:, not just the name of the disk. This is slightly more specific than the path prefix, but you can use either.

file: A secondary type of text prefix for paths that identify variables containing text values indicating the path to a file. This is slightly more specific than the path prefix, but you can use either.

folder: A secondary type of text prefix for paths that can identify variables containing text values indicating the path to a folder. This is slightly more specific than the path prefix, but you can use either.

vol: A secondary type of text prefix for paths that can identify variables containing text values indicating the path to a server volume. It should include the full path, such as Volume Name:, not just the name of the disk. This is slightly more specific than the path prefix, but you can use either.

Variable Superprefixes

A *superprefix* is a prefix that goes in front of a primary or secondary prefix to help identify additional information about the status of the variable. The remainder of the variable name should be formatted as if the superprefix were not present.

c: Used for the current item in any repeat statement. For example, if a variable contains the current item in a list, it might be named cNameFile, cNumToProcess, or cPathToStatusFile.

g: Used for all globals (except standard wtm template globals, which may not follow this standard).

p: Used for all properties.

db«DatabaseName»: May be used when a variable contains something relating to a database. The database superprefix has a slightly different rule in terms of the formatting of the rest of the variable. Rather than use a primary or secondary prefix after the superprefix, you should use the name of the database first. Then, following that, you should use the type of data and then the descriptor of that data. The formula is db«DatabaseName»«DataType»«Descriptor»—for example, dbContactsFieldFirstName or dbProjectsScriptBuildCatalog. Currently, this superprefix is optional because it is aberrant from the normal standards. At some time in the future, this prefix may be modified to conform to the primary and secondary prefix requirements.

Development Variable Prefixes

The following are the development variable prefixes:

dev: Used to denote a variable containing data that is used only when in development mode and should not be accessed or used in any way for the final release of a solution or product.

Note Although the conventions detailed in the previous section are obviously useful, I have included them to give you an idea of how far you can take this if you want. You don't *have* to go this far with your practice of good naming conventions—for most scripters it should be enough to adhere to a few commonsense rules such as being consistent, avoiding abbreviations, and generally giving your variable naming more thought. If you can read a variable name outside the context of the script and right away understand the meaning of the value it stores, then you're in good shape.

Use Global Variables Cautiously

Using global variables and properties in your scripts gives you power you should not abuse. In small scripts it may not be an issue, but as your scripts grow, using properties and global variables will cause your scripts to become entangled and unmanageable.

Overusing global variables disrupts the flow of values in the script. It can become difficult to figure out at what point a value of a variable changed and what caused the change. The result of having too many unjustified global variables is that it can become difficult to debug small parts of the script and, in turn, be difficult to debug anything in the script.

In addition, you'll try to move a subroutine to another script and realize you can't because it uses a global variable or property you first have to isolate. Think about script properties as properties of the script, not as a convenient method of passing values (or not having to) between subroutines. Even if a few of the subroutines in your script use the same variable, it still does not make it a candidate for a property or global variable. It may be a property of those few subroutines, and if it is, you should get them all into a separate script file and load them as a script object using the load script command. Once these subroutines are isolated and have their own secret society, they can have their own properties inside that script object.

It's also important to realize that in some cases, the values of global variables and properties are saved when the script quits and then read again when the script launches again. If you store large lists or large script objects in global variables or properties, they can slow down the loading and quitting time of your script, bloat its size, or prevent the script from saving altogether if the values stored in these variables are too complex.

Commenting Scripts

You don't just comment scripts in case some other scripter opens them a few years from now. You comment your script so that when you open it a few months from now you won't have to rack your brain trying to figure out what that absolutely brilliant code that doesn't seem to work anymore actually meant.

For me, discipline and organization came with a great deal of pain and took a long time to be ingrained in my scripting; however, I can say I have been sloppy and I have been disciplined, and disciplined is better. I feel much better not wasting time dealing with my own scripts that I can no longer understand, descriptive variable names that don't make that much sense a month later, or rationale behind a certain subroutine.

Comments can seem to be dumb, like so:

```
--This subroutine cleans blank data cells from the data for the page.
```

or like so:

```
--This subroutine was created to prevent files from being created if
--the job is old
```

But man, you can seem much dumber to yourself when you can't understand your own code, which happens quite often.

Another important type of comment is one that dates itself. Every time I return to an old script and make an adjustment, I comment out a copy of the old code and add a visible comment such as this:

```
--•••-- Changed by Hanaan on 4/12/2006. Reason: include date in
-- report file name.
```

This leaves a trail of evidence for what was part of the original script and what other statements were added later.

Another important use of comments is in documenting handlers. If you consider that writing handlers is adding your own commands to the mix—commands that potentially require specific parameters, perform an action, and/or return a result—documenting these items is more than preferred. For example:

```
-- This handler gets data from an Excel file.
-- The handler will open the given file, get the data from
-- the given sheet and close the file.
-- The result is a list of  Excel data taken from the worksheet
-- Parameters:
-- filePath (alias): the path to the Excel file
-- sheetName (string): The name of the worksheet to get the data from.
-- closeFile (boolean): true will close file after getting the data.
```

In addition, when updating the script, you should make sure to update any related notes to make sure they're still correct.

Literal Expressions Can Bring You Down (Dramatization)

Even if you're certain a specific value in your script will never change, you should still not embed it directly into the operations or statements in which it is used. This will make your scripts much less debugging friendly. Instead, just before the operation the value is used in, assign it to a descriptive variable name.

For instance, instead of writing this:

```
set daysWorked to hoursWorked / 8
```

write the following:

```
set workHoursInWorkday  to 8
set daysWorked to hoursWorked / workHoursInWorkday
```

The second version is longer but is easier to read, and if the value has to change, you can find it and update it much easier.

Enhancing Performance

John Thorsen of TECSoft, the original AppleScript training company (www.tecsoft.com), claims that the value AppleScript automation adds to any workflow is so drastic that the actual speed in which the script runs doesn't really matter. After all, does it really matter whether the process that used to take 3 hours now takes 20 seconds or 30 seconds?

Although this is true, some scripts do need to perform as fast as possible, since after a while, people start comparing how fast they are in relation to other scripts, not how fast the manual process was. People forget quickly . . . .

For instance, a script that processes jobs in a queue can process that many more jobs an hour if it runs faster.

The following sections highlight some issues you should consider when trying to speed up your scripts.

OS X, Baby!

If you're still limping along with OS 9, you are running scripts slower than you could. I know that there are many other considerations for upgrading the operating system, but if you're looking for reasons to upgrade, then you should know that, because of the tighter integration of AppleScript in the OS, your scripts are likely to run faster on OS X.

Writing More Efficient Code

A few simple design techniques can help speed up your code.

Adding Items to Lists

When you have a list and you want to add an item to it at the end, you can do it in two ways.

This is one way:

```
set the_list to the_list & the_item
```

This is the other way:

```
set end of the_list to the_item
```

Since adding items to a list usually happens multiple times inside a repeat loop, it is important to realize the implication of the method you choose. In the first way, adding items will take a bit more time since AppleScript needs to create a completely new list each time. The second method, where you tack on items to the end of the existing list, allows you to add items to a long list much more quickly, so you should favor this method.

Concatenating Huge Strings

Generally, when you assemble a string from smaller strings, you use the & operator to concatenate two strings at a time to form a longer string. In a repeat loop, it looks something like this:

```
set the_string to ""
repeat until done
    ...
    set the_string to the_string & new_text
    ...
end repeat
```

This works well; however, if the final string you're generating is rather large, you may want to add all the strings to a long list and then coerce the final list into a string, like this:

```
set temp_list to {}
repeat until done
    ...
    set end of temp_list to new_text
```

```
    ...
end repeat
set text item delimiters to ""
set the_string to temp_list as string
```

Note that in the previous script, text item delimiters is set to an empty string. If each item in the list represents a separate line or paragraph in the text and the individual strings don't yet have a return character appended to the end, then you can set the text item delimiters value to return instead of a blank string, which will add a return character between the string items when the list is coerced into a string.

Exiting Looping After a Result Is Gotten

Although some repeat loops are meant to go through every item in a list or object in an application, the function of some repeat loops is to find a specific item or object and move on after it is found. If this is the case, use the exit repeat statement to exit the loop right after you found the information desired. In Script 25-1, the repeat loop looks for a match in the list and returns the index in the list of the matching item.

Script 25-1.

```
repeat with i from 1 to (count the_list)
    set the_item to item i of the_list
    if the_item is equal to the_other_item then
        set item_index to i
        exit repeat --mission accomplished!
    end if
end repeat
```

Reducing Application Interaction

Interacting with applications slows AppleScript down. Although you can't eliminate this interaction altogether, you can try to limit it in various ways.

Retrieving Application Values in Batches

One way to do that is by getting as much data from the application as you can in one visit and then working your way through that data in AppleScript. For example, when working with Excel, get the value of an entire range of cells, then loop through them, and process that data in AppleScript, instead of going to Excel for the value of each individual cell.

This is not so good:

```
tell application "Excel"
    set firstValue to value of cell "A1"
    -- process firstValue
    set secondValue to value of cell "A2"
    -- process secondValue
    -- etc...
end tell
```

This is better:

```
tell application "Excel"
    set firstValue to value of cell "A1"
    set secondValue to value of cell "A2"
```

```
end tell
-- process firstValue
-- process secondValue
-- etc...
```

Using Single Commands to Manipulate Multiple Objects

Oftentimes in application scripting you want to apply the same commands to many application objects. One of the coolest abilities you'll find in many scriptable applications is that they'll allow you to apply a single command to multiple objects.

To do this, you create a single multi-object reference that identifies all the objects you want the command to operate on. This is much more efficient than getting a list of references to the individual objects, looping over the list, and applying the same command to each object in turn.

You can use three sorts of multi-object reference: those that identify all the elements of an object, those that identify a range of elements, and those that identify all the elements that match certain conditions (otherwise known as the whose clause). Some application commands are better than others at dealing with these sorts of complex references, but it's always worth a go, especially when you know you have a lot of objects to process. It helps to make your code shorter and simpler too.

For example, to get the name and modification date of every file in a folder, you could write the following:

```
set file_names_list to {}
set last_modified_list to {}
tell application "Finder"
    set files_list to every file of some_folder
    repeat with file_ref in files_list
        set end of file_names_list to name of file_ref
        set end of last_modified_list to modification date of file_ref
    end tell
end tell
```

However, it's much simpler to write the following code—it will perform the same task much more quickly since it uses only two get commands in total, instead of two get commands per file plus an additional get to retrieve the list of file references at the start:

```
tell application "Finder"
    set file_names_list to name of every file of some_folder
    set last_modified_list to modification date of every file of some_folder
end tell
```

Here's another example, this time using TextEdit's close command and a range reference to close all but the front document in TextEdit:

```
tell application "TextEdit" to close (documents 2 thru -1)
```

Using the whose Clause Instead of Looping to Filter Application Objects

Chapter 22 discusses using the whose clause when filtering objects in applications. Using the whose clause instead of looping through objects and testing each one yourself in AppleScript can add a real-time boost to the script execution, especially when dealing with application commands that can accept these multi-object references directly.

Imagine using Script 25-2 instead of the following:

```
tell application "Finder"
    set files_list to every file
    repeat with the_file_ref in files_list
        if name of the_file_ref starts with "job" then
            set label index of the_file_ref to 2
            move the_file_ref to folder "jobs"
        end if
    end repeat
end tell
```

Script 25-2.

```
tell application "Finder"
    tell every file whose name starts with "job"
        set label index to 2
        move to folder "jobs"
    end tell
end tell
```

Not only have you saved yourself from testing each filename in AppleScript, you've also reduced the entire operation to one set command and one move command in total. This is much more efficient than using separate set and move commands to process each job file, plus all the extra get commands needed to get the initial list of file references and then obtain the name of each one in turn.

Using Subroutine Libraries

To greatly reduce development time, you can collect subroutines in library files and then load these libraries into your other scripts. Libraries aren't special files, so you will not find a "Library" file format in the Save dialog box. A library is simply a compiled script that usually has no run handler, only subroutine definitions. You then use Standard Additions' load script command to load the file with the subroutine definitions into other scripts, which gives you access to all their subroutines.

Creating Many Little Chunks

How you organize your scripts' code can help you make it more reusable and more efficient. One of the best ways to organize scripts is by means of subroutines.

The more of your scripts that are made of many subroutine calls instead of long, drawn-out conditional statements, repeat loops, and tell blocks, the better. Subroutines allow you to group related statements and then execute them all with a simple command. Once you've written and tested them, these self-contained units of code are easy to use and, in many cases, reuse. As long as you know what these subroutines will do and how to call them, you can ignore all the finer technical details of how they work internally while using them. As far as the rest of your code is concerned, they "just work." Using the same subroutines in multiple scripts can save you a lot of time, not only by reducing the amount of new code you need to write but also by reducing the amount of code you have to keep track of in your head at any one time.

When you write any script, you should always be asking yourself whether you can use the actual functionality you're scripting, as small or large as it may be, somewhere else in any future scripts. If yes, give it a name, and declare a subroutine—it's a bit more work but will pay for itself many times over.

Creating and Managing Your Own Script Libraries

Once you get over the initial mental barrier of using script libraries, you will want to facilitate their use. The most important decision you need to make is where those library files should live. The two main options here are whether each script should be using its own set of libraries and you duplicate all your library files for each "project" or whether you find one place on the Mac where all script libraries are shared by all scripts.

Even though it is more efficient to have a global set of script libraries, since that way you have only one unique set of files to worry about, it may be easier to start out by having each "project" use its own set. This decision also has a lot to do with the scope of your projects. In my line of work, I create a few large systems for large clients, so for me it makes sense to have a separate `libraries` folder for each system. However, if you work for the one company that will be using your scripts, it may be smarter to store all your subroutine libraries in the `Scripts` folder, the `ScriptingAdditions` folder, or anywhere else that can be accessed with the `path to` command.

Loading Libraries Up Front and Keeping in Properties

Repeatedly loading a library each time you want to call one of its subroutines can be a bit time-consuming. It's usually best to have your script load all the libraries it needs into properties at the top of the script. That way, your script needs to load each library only once, and they can all be accessed from anywhere in your script. You can load all your libraries either when the script is compiled or each time it is run. Chapter 19 discusses how to load and use libraries in more detail.

Keeping on Top of Things: Code Buried in Script Objects Can Be Time-Consuming

Once you have multiple scripts calling subroutines that are buried in other script files and these subroutine calls are embedded in lengthy `repeat` loops, you may want to watch out that you don't lose track of your subroutine calls. It is fairly easy to forget a seemingly benign subroutine call inside a loop, which then loops itself a few times and in the process causes the script to complete thousands of unnecessary operations.

If the script appears to be taking a long time to run, try to audit different parts of it to see whether some handler buried somewhere still performs an unnecessary function that takes forever. Script Debugger built-in script timers can come in handy.

Getting Feedback

Most people who will run your scripts are used to performing small commands and getting instant feedback from the Mac. Running a script that takes more than ten seconds without knowing whether it is still working can be frustrating. Your scripts must keep even the most anxious user informed.

Keeping the Users Informed

With scripts that take longer than one minute to run, which is rarer now that both AppleScript and the Macs it runs on are so much faster, your users may get agitated if the only feedback they get from your script is the occasional spinning cursor and a "done" dialog box message at the end.

The best thing to do is create a little face-only application in Studio, as explained in Chapter 12, to be used by your script for the sole purpose of telling the user to which general process the script is going. Time your processes in a way that the message updates every one to two seconds.

This way, instead of the users thinking, "This is taking so long," they are finally made aware of the sheer volume of things the script is doing for them.

Script 25-3 shows a simple way to display a status report dialog box inside an application. The `ignoring application responses` block prevents your script being held up while the message is displayed.

Script 25-3.

```
tell application "System Events"
   activate
   ignoring application responses
      display dialog "Moving files to server..." buttons {"OK"} giving up after 3
   end ignoring
end tell
```

Note This scenario may be problematic if Script Editor has not yet loaded the Standard Additions OSAXen before the `ignoring application responses` clause starts. To resolve this issue, force the Standard Additions OSAXen to be loaded by executing a benign command prior to the `ignoring application responses` clause, like this: `round 0`.

Timing Scripts

You may want to make a habit of timing portions of your scripts. This can come in handy when finding and fixing performance bottlenecks.

Timing scripts is easy. At the point in your script where the "stopwatch" should start, add the following line:

```
set start_timer to current date
```

Then, at the end of the timed process, use this line:

```
set run_time to (current date) - start_timer
```

It always makes a good impression to display the number of seconds a script took to run, especially if the process has recently been done manually.

If you need to measure script times in fraction of seconds, a scripting addition such as GetMilliSec and Jon's Commands X will provide a suitable solution.

Delivering Scripts to Other Sites

Things can change dramatically once your children leave home. Managing scripts in other locations can be a drag, especially when they break for any reason and your only source of information is a person with a distinct inability to form meaningful sentences.

In this case, a program such as Timbuktu, Apple Remote Access, or the free Chicken of the VNC can be a real lifesaver; you can log in remotely and see the problem for yourself. They are easy to find using Google.

When this is not possible, you will want to make solid arrangements regarding the support of your off-site scripts. The following are a few tips.

Managing Script Preferences That the User Can Change

While writing scripts for other people to use, you have to always keep in mind that some of the values you defined in your script will be subject to change. Font names, type sizes, folder paths, usernames—the list goes on.

You have a few ways to manage these script user preferences. Picking the format that works for you has to do with the frequency of the changes and the savvy of the users.

For not-so-savvy users who need to change settings more frequently, you can use a dialog box start-up screen. Every time the script starts, a dialog box appears letting the user know what is about to happen. The dialog box sneaks in a button called Settings that, when clicked, takes the user through a set of dialog boxes with text input or buttons that account for the different settings they can change. These settings are then stored in properties for the next time the script runs. This is useful also for the first time the script runs when the user may have to initialize a few values.

The option for savvier users with scripts that may need to change every few months is to simply place the well-named properties at the top of the script and teach those users how to open the script and change these properties.

Updating and Upgrading Your Solutions

One aspect of deploying script solutions in other locations or multiple systems that can become a nightmare is version control. Keeping track of script versions to track updates and system disparity can be challenging, and many things can go wrong.

One thing you have to do when version control becomes an issue is to sit down and work out a simple system for dealing with it. A good start would be a property at the top of the script with a version number and another one with the last date of modification. Another simple idea is to add release notes in the description area, as shown in Figure 25-1.

Figure 25-1. *A simple script containing properties for the latest release date and version number, as well as release notes in the description area*

Should You Lock Your Code?

You can lock your AppleScript code by saving your scripts as run only. They can still run and be loaded into other scripts, but they can never be opened.

You would lock scripts for one of two reasons: the first is to protect clients from themselves. If they can't open the scripts, they can't mess things up and give you the work you dread most. The other reason for locking your scripts is to protect your code from unauthorized access. Otherwise, nothing is preventing any scripter at the installed location from opening your scripts and copying your subroutines into their own scripts.

Nevertheless, I always leave my scripts unlocked. Yes, I do have clients who like to poke around in them, but I just explain the possible consequences, and they usually do it on a separate machine designated as a test environment. Another benefit it can give me is that I can use a person as a remote-controlled AppleScripter to help me fix scripts on-site when they break. Besides, I'm an open source guy. Sharing code is what makes the AppleScript community so great, and I want to be a part of that. If someone can open my scripts and actually learn something, more power to them. Of course, there's that whole competition thing, but really, what are the chances that a script I wrote will be used against me if it falls into the wrong hands? In my eyes this is an unlikely situation.

You may also use a combination by locking your general cache of subroutines and leaving the main scripts unlocked for easy access.

Adding a Debug Mode to Your Scripts

One trick that can help you debug scripts from afar is making up your own debug mode. You have two reasons for running a script: to get things done with it (which is the reason why you wrote it in the first place) or to debug and fix it. You may want the script to go through several steps while debugging that you wouldn't want it to go through while doing live work.

You can facilitate this debug mode with a Boolean property called something like debug. Any part of the script that should run only while debugging can be conditional on the debug property being set to true, like so:

```
if debug then log myVariable
```

or like so:

```
if debug then
    set log_text to "Now running subroutine 'main_process'"
    log_to_file(log_text)
end if
```

The debug property can be either set manually inside the script or set externally. Earlier I discussed a Settings button in a greeting dialog box for your script. Asking whether the user wants to turn on debugging can be one of the settings indicated there.

Creating Detailed Text Logs

One of the debugging operations I like to use in my scripts is the creation of a detailed runtime log. Every few operations I write a little blurb to a file describing the current position of the script. I later have the clients e-mail me that log file, which I use to quickly determine where the script had an error.

Power Wrap-Up

Getting to be an experienced scripter is a funny thing: the more I work with AppleScript, the slower and more deliberate I become at writing the scripts, but because of that, the systems I create are more solid and thought-out. I used to rush into things by writing scripts, but now I jot down diagrams and flow charts before I even get to the script editor.

Furthermore, I can appreciate the time I spend on writing better scripts when I have to refer to some of my older work. It spreads out on a sort of an evolutionary timeline, with older scripts looking a bit childish and "bad habits" slowly disappearing from them the more current they are.

The take-away from this chapter is that it's OK to take your time and plan things as soon as you feel ready to do so. Channel your new-project excitement not through writing new code but through figuring out the best way to lay out that code and what things did or did not work for you in the past. Soon enough, this by itself will become the exciting part of the project.

CHAPTER 26

■ ■ ■

Scripting Apple Apps

In OS X's first year or two of existence, things were a bit hectic. Apple was in the midst of its largest operating system rollout ever, and it was scrambling to get applications out to hungry users. We AppleScripters were just happy that AppleScript was going strong in OS X and improvements were made on a monthly basis. What we didn't like so much was that none of the shiny new applications called iApps were scriptable. Now, a few years later, things have changed for the better: not only are Apple iTunes, iPhoto, iCal, Mail, and Address Book all scriptable, but scripters can access the databases used by OS X to manage contacts, music, and mail.

The subject of this chapter, as you can imagine, could fill its own little book. Therefore, my intention is not to cover every aspect of scripting Apple's applications but rather to give you a solid start in scripting the six most important ones: iTunes (and the iPod), iChat, Mail, Address Book, iCal, and Automator.

Scripting iTunes + iPod

Starting with version 3, iTunes became a scriptable application with a solid dictionary and a fine object model describing tracks and various playlist types. Scripts for scripting iTunes fall into two categories: maintenance scripts and usability scripts. Maintenance scripts are great for features such as cleaning up your library and managing your tracks and playlists. With the ability to have thousands of tracks—some from CDs, some from the music store, and some, well, from less respectable places—AppleScript can be a saving grace when you want to organize the iTunes part of your life.

The other type of scripts can help you enjoy music more easily and efficiently on a day-to-day basis. You can easily create little AppleScript Studio utilities that perform tasks that would require several steps in the iTunes interface.

Note You can find iTunes sample scripts on Apple's AppleScript web page at `www.apple.com/applescript/itunes/`. You will find a collection of about 30 scripts you can use, open, and learn from.

Understanding iTunes Scriptable Objects

iTunes has a well-designed object model, a quality that can make scripting easier. When examining the iTunes dictionary, you will see that there are more objects than commands, which is also an attribute of a well-crafted scripting environment. To complement how you think about music organization in general, iTunes has two main types of object: playlists and tracks. Most other object types are variations of these two. In fact, it has five types of playlists and five types of tracks.

Before accessing these known goodies, you will have to go through an object of class source. The source object you will work with most is the library source. On English-speaking systems, this source object is named Library, although the name may differ for other languages. In the library source, you will find your playlists and, in there, your tracks.

Other sources may be useful as well. If an iPod is connected to your Mac, for example, the iPod becomes its own source with playlists and tracks. Some other source types are audio CD, MP3 CD, and shared library.

In turn, each source object can contain various playlist elements. For example, the library source contains a special playlist of class library playlist. This library playlist is also called Library (or its equivalent in other languages) and contains every file, uniform resource locator (URL), and shared track that iTunes is aware of. The library source can also contain any number of user-defined playlists, each one containing whatever file, URL, and shared tracks you put in it. So, in order to work with a particular track (or tracks), you have to refer to a specific playlist in a specific source.

Figure 26-1 illustrates this part of the iTunes containment hierarchy, showing how different kinds of tracks are contained by different kinds of playlists, which in turn are contained by the source elements of the application.

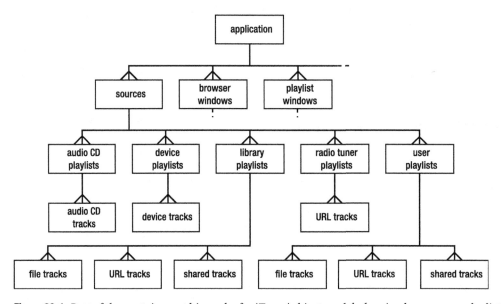

Figure 26-1. *Part of the containment hierarchy for iTunes' object model, showing how source, playlist, and track elements are contained by one another*

The following example plays a random song from the library:

```
tell application "iTunes"
    play some track of playlist "Library" of source "Library"
end tell
```

The library source has many playlists, which include your user playlists, but it has only one playlist of the subclass library playlist. This means the following script has the same effect:

```
tell application "iTunes"
    play some track of library playlist 1 of source "Library"
end tell
```

Working with Tracks and Playlists

Creating new playlists in iTunes is simple: just use the make command, optionally passing the new playlist's name via its with properties parameter:

```
tell application "iTunes"
   make new user playlist with properties {name:"My First Playlist"}
end tell
```

You don't need to specify a location since iTunes will automatically add the new playlist object to your main Library source object.

You can find out the names of all your playlists using this:

```
tell application "iTunes"
   name of every user playlist of source "Library"
end tell
```

Creating new track objects is a little different. To add existing tracks to a user playlist, use the duplicate command to copy the desired track objects from one playlist (usually the main library playlist) to the other. To import new audio files into iTunes, use the add command. iTunes will automatically create the corresponding track objects for you in the main library playlist. If you want, you can use the add command's optional to parameter to add them to a user-defined playlist at the same time.

Script 26-1 allows the user to enter a keyword. It then creates a new playlist based on that word and duplicates to that new playlist every track object whose name contains that keyword. As an example, I used the word *Yellow*. See Figure 26-2 for the resulting playlist.

Script 26-1.

```
display dialog "Enter a key word" default answer ""
set track_criteria to text returned of result
tell application "iTunes"
   set my_playlist to make new playlist ¬
      with properties {name:Songs with " & track_criteria}
   tell playlist "Library" of source "Library"
      duplicate (every track whose name contains track_criteria) to my_playlist
   end tell
end tell
```

Figure 26-2. *The playlist created by Script 26-1*

Scripting the Equalizer

iTunes allows you to control the equalizer using AppleScript. The equalizer contains properties for each one of the ten bands and for the preamp, which is the leftmost slider in the equalizer. Although it could be nicer if every band in the equalizer was an element of the equalizer, it makes sense to have them as properties since the equalizer has a fixed number of bands and all you can do is get and set their values.

Script 26-2 will be music to your ears, especially if you value alternative forms of music. It will, until stopped, change the bands of the manual equalizer preset to random numbers from –12 to 12.

Script 26-2.

```
tell application "iTunes"
    play
    set current EQ preset to EQ preset "Manual"
    repeat
       tell EQ preset "Manual"
          set preamp to random number from -12 to 12
          set band 1 to random number from -12 to 12
          set band 2 to random number from -12 to 12
          set band 3 to random number from -12 to 12
          set band 4 to random number from -12 to 12
          set band 5 to random number from -12 to 12
          set band 6 to random number from -12 to 12
          set band 7 to random number from -12 to 12
          set band 8 to random number from -12 to 12
          set band 9 to random number from -12 to 12
          set band 10 to random number from -12 to 12
       end tell
    end repeat
end tell
```

Scripting the iPod

No, the iPod is not scriptable. Apple does provide some iPod-related scripts from its website, but most of these simply help manage the iPod notes, and so on.

iTunes' iPod-specific command is the update command, which updates the track contents of a connected iPod.

iTunes also has an eject command that can eject an iPod. You can specify the iPod to eject by referring to the source object pointing to the iPod. If you know the iPod's name, you can simply refer to it that way:

```
tell application "iTunes"
    eject (some source whose kind is iPod)
end tell
```

Or, just eject all connected iPods:

```
tell application "iTunes"
    eject (every source whose kind is iPod)
end tell
```

As discussed previously, when an iPod is connected to your computer, iTunes regards it as another source.

Scripting Mail

Scripting Mail can be fun, although earlier versions could also be a bit frustrating because of certain functions, such as accessing attachments, being buggy or unavailable. Mail 2, which is included with OS X 10.4, has addressed many of the original problems.

The structure of Mail's object model is simple: you have accounts, mailboxes, and messages. Each account has mailboxes, and mailboxes can contain both messages and other mailboxes. Figure 26-3 shows how it all fits together.

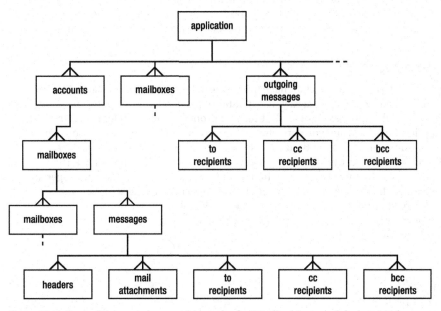

Figure 26-3. *Part of the containment hierarchy for Mail's object model, showing how account, mailbox, and message objects can be contained by one another*

This script lists the mailboxes of the first account:

```
tell application "Mail"
    return name of every mailbox of account 1
end tell
--> {"INBOX", "Drafts", "Sent Messages", "Deleted Messages", "Junk"}
```

Mailboxes can also be elements of the application itself without having to belong to a specific account. Mailbox objects can contain other mailboxes too. You can directly access any mailbox in Mail that is created "on your Mac," as shown in Script 26-3.

Script 26-3.

```
tell application "Mail"
    tell mailbox "lists"
        tell mailbox "applescript-users list"
            count messages
        end tell
    end tell
end tell
```

Six standard top-level mailboxes are also accessible via properties of Mail's `application` object: `drafts mailbox`, `inbox`, `junk mailbox`, `outbox`, `sent mailbox`, and `trash mailbox`.

Mailbox objects are fairly simple with only a few properties, all of which are read-only except for the `name` property. Each mailbox object also has two types of elements, messages and mailboxes, that you can manipulate from AppleScript to work with the messages and/or submailboxes that are inside that mailbox.

The `account` class is much more extensive with three subclasses, `Mac account`, `pop account`, and `imap account`, that represent the different types of e-mail accounts that Mail supports. Each account object contains plenty of properties for manipulating the account's settings. (These are the same settings you see in the Accounts panel of Mail's preferences.) In addition, each account object has mailbox elements representing all the mailboxes that belong to that particular account.

Referring to a Message

To get information from a message, you first have to provide a reference to it. You can locate messages in Mail's object model in several ways: you can obtain a list of references to the currently selected messages from the application object's `selection` property, you can refer to one or more messages in a top-level mailbox, and you can refer to one or more messages in a mailbox that belongs to a specific account. Which method you use depends on what you want to do, of course.

Let's say I'm about to cancel one of my e-mail accounts with my service provider. I will want to notify every person who previously sent mail to that address. Assuming all those messages are still in the original Inbox for that account, Script 26-4 shows how I can get a list of their senders' addresses. I start by referring to my soon-to-be-canceled `Flybynight.net` account and then to the mailbox named `INBOX` within that account. Finally, I ask Mail to get the sender of every message in that mailbox, as shown in Script 26-4.

Script 26-4.

```
tell application "Mail"
    tell account "Flybynight.net"
        tell mailbox "INBOX"
            set address_list to sender of every message
        end tell
    end tell
end tell--> {"Jo Brown <jo@foo.com>", "Alan Green <a.green@bar.org>", ...}
```

If the message is in a local mailbox you created, you can start by referring to a `mailbox` element of the top-level `application` object. For example, on my Mac I've created a top-level mailbox called `lists` that contains submailboxes for each of the mailing lists to which I subscribe. If I want to count all the messages in the submailbox named `applescript-users list`, I refer to it as shown in Script 26-5.

Script 26-5.

```
tell application "Mail"
    tell mailbox "lists"
        tell mailbox "applescript-users list"
            count messages
        end tell
    end tell
end tell
--> 12374
```

One other way to refer to messages is via the six standard mailbox properties in Mail's application object: inbox, outbox, drafts mailbox, and so on. These are equivalent to the standard large mailbox icons that appear on the left side of a viewer window in Mail and are used in much the same way. For example, the mailbox object in the inbox property acts as a convenient shortcut that allows you to refer all the messages in all your accounts' INBOX mailboxes at once. So, a command like this:

```
tell application "Mail"
    get every message of inbox
end tell
```

would return a long list like this:

```
{
    message id 21 of mailbox "INBOX" of account "Work" of application "Mail",
    message id 52 of mailbox "INBOX" of account "Work" of application "Mail",
    ...
    message id 38 of mailbox "INBOX" of account "Personal" of application "Mail",
    ...
    message id 97 of mailbox "INBOX" of account "Temp" of application "Mail"
}
```

Creating a Message

Creating a message is pretty straightforward: just use Mail's make command to create a new object of class outgoing message, and assign suitable values to its properties and elements. See Mail's dictionary to figure out the different properties and elements this object can have. Script 26-6 shows an example of a script that creates a new e-mail message.

Script 26-6.

```
set the_subject to "Hello there"
set the_body to return & "Please read the attached file"
set the_file to choose file
tell application "Mail"
    set new_message to make new outgoing message ¬
        with properties {subject:the_subject, content:the_body, visible:true}
    tell new_message
        --add recipients
        make new to recipient at end with properties ¬
            {name:"George", address:"george@cox.net"}
        make new cc recipient at end with properties ¬
            {name:"Georgia", address:"georgia@cox.net"}
        --add attachment
        make new attachment at end of first paragraph of content ¬
            with properties {file name:the_file}
    end tell
end tell
```

The preceding message has two recipients. Mail's dictionary defines three kinds of recipients you can use when adding new recipients to a message: to recipient, cc recipient, and bcc recipient. All three are subclasses of the recipient class, which defines the name and address properties used to store the person's details.

Tip When creating new recipients, make sure you specify either to recipient, cc recipient, or bcc recipient in the make command. If you use recipient by accident, you'll get an error because Mail can't make objects of that class.

Notice that when you create the attachment, you insert it at the end of the first paragraph of the message's content. This is because attachment objects are actually elements of Mail's text class, not its message class as you might expect. This approach seems a bit odd at first, but it does make sense if you think about how Mail works: when you view an e-mail message on the screen, notice how attachments appear within the message's body.

This means whenever you want to attach a file to a message, you must tell the make command to insert the new attachment object somewhere within the content property's text object. In this example, I've started the content text with a blank paragraph for neatness and added the attachment there; you could insert the attachment at the end or somewhere in the middle of the content text if you prefer.

You can top it off by sending your message with the send command, like this:

```
Tell app "iTunes" to send new_message
```

Gathering Information from Message Headers

For some, message headers are the inexplicable gibberish text that appears at the top of any e-mail message you get. For others, it is a treasure of information, tracing the e-mail message path from its origin, through each mail server, all the way to its destination. Apple made a nice effort to break each header into its own element, giving you fairly clean access to the information.

One thing you can extract from headers, if you care to, is the Internet Protocol (IP) addresses of the different servers the message traveled through. To do that, you first have to get a list of all the headers and then parse out the IP address from the content of each header. Script 26-7 shows how it can be done.

Script 26-7.

```
tell application "Mail"
    set the_message_selection to selection
    set the_message to item 1 of the_message_selection
    set header_list to content of every header of the_message ¬
        whose name is "received"
end tell
set text item delimiters to return
set header_text to header_list as string
set address_list to find text "[0-9]{1,3}\\.[0-9]{1,3}\\.[0-9]{1,3}\\.[0-9]{1,3}" ¬
    in header_text with regexp, string result and all occurrences
set address_text to address_list as string
set text item delimiters to ""
display dialog ¬
    "This message visited the following IP addresses:" & return & address_text
```

A couple of notes about Script 26-7: first, it utilizes the Satimage osax's find text command (www.satimage.fr/software/en/downloads_osaxen.html), and second, the code for extracting the IP address is meant for demonstration purposes and isn't 100% accurate.

Using String Utilities

For your convenience, Mail's dictionary includes two string-related commands that can be helpful when you need to extract information about a message's sender. These are extract name from and extract address from. These commands will accept a string containing the sender's name and their email address in angle brackets (<>). Here's an example of how they work:

```
tell application "Mail"
    set the_sender to sender of message 1 of inbox
    --variable the_sender contains string like "Mickey T. Mouse <mickey@disney.com>"
    set sender_name to extract name from the_sender
    set sender_address to extract address from the_sender
end tell
return {sender_name, sender_address}
--> {"Mickey T. Mouse", "mickey@disney.com"}
```

Scripting Address Book

One of the hidden jewels scripters get with OS X is the ability to script Address Book. The reason why it is so nice is that you get access to the operating system's contact database. Other Apple applications such as Mail use this database, which is open to any developer who wants to use it.

What makes Address Book scripting so nice is the well-structured object model, which reflects the database structure itself. The object model in Address Book is designed for flexibility. It does not limit you to a specific number of addresses or phone numbers per person. Instead of numbers and addresses being properties of the person, they are elements. As you are aware, an object can have only one of each property, but you can add as many elements as the application allows.

The most important class in Address Book is person. A person object has various properties containing their first name, last name, title, birth date, and so on. A person object may also contain any number of address elements and various kinds of contact information elements.

Contact information elements are phone numbers, e-mails, related names, and other type of contacts that can be described in a label-value pair. For instance, a person's work phone number would typically appear in Address Book's main window as follows:

work 401-555-1212

This would be represented by an object of class phone, which is a specific subclass of the general contact info class, and would have the label work and the value 401-555-1212. To get every work phone number of the currently selected person in Address Book, you would use the following:

```
tell application "Address Book"
    set the_person to item 1 of (get selection)
    value of every phone of the_person whose label is "work"
end tell
--> {"401-555-1212", "401-555-5237"}
```

Addresses are similar but contain more specific properties such as city, state, and so on. This structure allows Address Book to contain entries without any phone number but with three e-mail addresses and to contain others with no e-mails but several phone and fax numbers—or any mix in between.

Figure 26-4 shows part of the containment hierarchy for Address Book's object model.

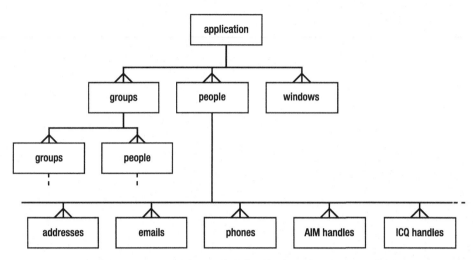

Figure 26-4. *Part of the containment hierarchy of Address Book's object model (some contact information elements not shown because of page space constraints)*

As you can see from Figure 26-4, you can refer to person objects as elements of the top-level application object; every person in the Address Book is accessible this way. You can also refer to person elements within specific groups such as every person of group "Friends". To add and remove people to and from a particular group, use the add and remove commands. For example, the following script creates a group named Birthday People and adds every person with a known birthday to it:

```
tell application "Address Book"
    if not (group "Birthday People" exists) then
        make new group with properties {name:"Birthday People"}
    end if
    add (every person whose birth date is not missing value) ¬
        to group "Birthday People"
end tell
```

In Script 26-8, I created a little utility that allows you to quickly look up contact information by a person's first or last name. The script taps the contact database structure and shows only the available phone numbers and e-mail addresses.

The script starts by letting the user pick a character from the alphabet. Then it gets the full name of all people in the Address Book database whose first or last name starts with the chosen character.

Once the user picks a name, the script will show the e-mail and phone numbers of the chosen contact and will create an e-mail message for that person if the user wants.

Script 26-8.

```
1. --Ask user to select a letter from A to Z
2. set character_list to characters of "ABCDEFGHIJKLMNOPQRSTUVWXYZ"
3. set the_selection to choose from list character_list
4. if the_selection is false then return --User canceled
5. set chosen_character to item 1 of the_selection

6. --Get the names of people whose first/last names start with that letter
7. tell application "Address Book"
```

```
8.    set name_list to name of every person ¬
          whose first name starts with chosen_character ¬
          or last name starts with chosen_character
9.  end tell
10. if name_list is {} then
11.    display dialog "No matching people were found." buttons {"OK"}
12.    return
13. end if

14. --Ask user to select a person's name
15. set the_selection to choose from list name_list
16. if the_selection is false then return --User canceled
17. set chosen_name to item 1 of the_selection

18. --Get all the email and phone contact info for the chosen person
19. tell application "Address Book"
20.    set chosen_person to first person whose name is chosen_name
21.    tell chosen_person
22.       set email_label_list to label of every email
23.       set email_value_list to value of every email
24.       set phone_label_list to label of every phone
25.       set phone_value_list to value of every phone
26.    end tell
27. end tell
28. if email_label_list is {} and phone_label_list is {} then
29.    display dialog ¬
          "The person you selected has no email or phone details." buttons {"OK"}
30.    return
31. end if

32. --Assemble a string containing the contact information
33. set the_message to "Contact information for " & chosen_name & ":" & return
34. repeat with i from 1 to (count email_label_list)
35.    set the_label to item i of email_label_list
36.    set the_value to item i of email_value_list
37.    set the_message to the_message & ¬
          the_label & " email: " & the_value & return
38. end repeat
39. repeat with i from 1 to (count phone_label_list)
40.    set the_label to item i of phone_label_list
41.    set the_value to item i of phone_value_list
42.    set the_message to the_message & ¬
          the_label & " number: " & the_value & return
43. end repeat

44. --Display the contact information, with the option of creating a new email
45. if email_label_list is {} then
46.    display dialog the_message buttons {"Thanks"} default button 1
47. else
48.    display dialog the_message buttons {"e-mail", "Thanks"}
49.    if button returned of result is "e-mail" then
50.       tell application "Mail"
51.          activate
52.          set new_message to make new outgoing message ¬
                with properties {visible:true}
53.          tell new_message to make new to recipient with properties ¬
                {name:chosen_name, address:item 1 of email_value_list}
```

```
54.        end tell
55.     end if
56. end if
```

After the user picks a letter from the alphabet, the script needs to create a list of full names whose first or last name starts with that letter. This takes place in lines 7 through 9.

In the Address Book dictionary, the person class defines several name-related properties: name, first name, middle name, last name, title, suffix, nickname, maiden name, and then phonetic first name, phonetic middle name, and phonetic last name. That makes eleven name options—better safe than sorry, I guess. Actually, you can control only ten name-related properties. The property name is a read-only property that is comprised of the person's title; first, middle, and last names; and suffix details.

Once you collect the list of names, the user gets to pick the one they want. That happens in line 15.

In line 20 you get the reference to the person based on the full name the user picks from the list. Note that if there are two identical names, the script will arbitrarily pick the first one. Just make sure you fix that little issue before you package this script and sell it as shareware.

Once you assign the person to a variable, you can collect the phone numbers and e-mails assigned to that person. As you saw earlier, phone numbers and e-mails are represented as elements of a person object.

Since you need both the label and the value of the e-mails and phone numbers, you collect both. This takes place in lines 22 through 25. First you create a pair of lists containing all the person's e-mail details: one list contains all the labels (home, work, and so on), and the other list contains all the values (that is, the e-mail addresses). Then you create another pair of lists containing the person's phone details.

Each label string in the first list corresponds to the value string at the same position in the second address. For example:

```
phone_label_list --> {"home", "work", "work"}
phone_value_list --> {"401-555-7999", "401-555-1212", "401-555-5237"}
```

Why do it this way? You could have built up a single list of label-value pairs using the following method:

```
tell application "Address Book"
    set phone_info_list to {}
    repeat with phone_ref in (get every phone of chosen_person)
        set end of phone_info_list to {label, value} of phone_ref
    end repeat
end tell
phone_info_list
--> {{"home", "401-555-7999"}, {"work", "401-555-1212"}, {"work", "401-555-5237"}}
```

However, it's often simpler just to write this:

```
tell application "Address Book"
    tell chosen_person
        set phone_label_list to label of every email
        set phone_value_list to value of every email
    end tell
end tell
```

This gives you two separate lists, but as long as you remember how the labels in one list relate to the values in the other list, this isn't a problem when using that data.

Note The second approach also has performance advantages when retrieving data from large numbers of objects. See Chapter 25 for more information.

Between lines 33 and 43 you construct a string using the values from these lists. This string is stored in the variable the_message and will be used to display the collected information to the user at the end.

Finally, the contact information appears to the user in a dialog box. If the script has detected one or more e-mail addresses, it will display a dialog box that has an Email button. If the user clicks that button, the script will create a new e-mail message in Mail with the selected person's e-mail address.

Scripting iCal

The next iApp I will cover is iCal, which has a small but well-crafted scripting dictionary. In iCal you have calendars that can have todos and events.

A *todo* (that's "to-do" without the hyphen) represents a task that you need to do sometime, such as write an article or arrange a vacation. A todo object is fairly simple with a summary and description of the task to do, an optional due date for the task to be done, and a few other useful properties such as the date the task was finally completed (if it has been yet). If you're using OS X 10.4 or later, iCal 2.0 also allows todo objects to have alarm elements, used to trigger various reminders for tasks that haven't been completed yet.

An event represents a particular occurrence at a specific time (or times) and place, such as a 90-minute meeting with several colleagues that you need to attend every Monday morning at 9:30 AM for three weeks or such as the much-anticipated summer vacation you'll be taking from July 15 to July 30. Not surprisingly, event objects are a bit more complex than todo objects, with properties for the start date, end date, and location of the event and whether the event repeats at regular intervals and with elements for specifying who'll be attending the event and triggering various alarms.

Calendars in the iCal dictionary correspond to the different named calendars you can specify in iCal. Each calendar has todo elements and event elements. In iCal's window, you can identify which events belong to which calendars by their color.

Note Although iCal can have multiple calendars, they all appear in the same calendar window.

Figure 26-5 shows the containment hierarchy for iCal 2.0's object model. As you can see, it's straightforward. iCal 1.5 has the same hierarchy, except that its todo objects don't have any elements.

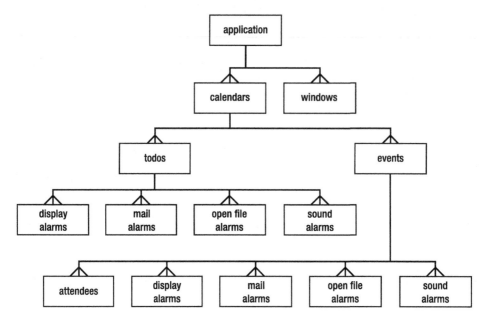

Figure 26-5. *The containment hierarchy for iCal's object model*

Creating Calendars

The calendar class is the core element of any iCal application. Any event you want to manipulate or create has to belong to a calendar.

To create a calendar named Sports in iCal on OS X 10.4 and newer, run the following script:

```
tell application "iCal"
    make new calendar with properties {name:"Sports"}
end tell
--> calendar 9 of application "iCal"
```

Earlier versions of iCal had a slightly different dictionary where the calendar class had a title property instead of the current name property. This was changed in OS X 10.4 to make it easier to refer to calendars by name; for example, you can now say calendar "Sports" instead of first calendar whose title is "Sports" to identify the Sports calendar. If your script needs to run on Panther, you should use the title property instead:

```
tell application "iCal"
    make new calendar with properties {title:"Sports"}
end tell
```

Tiger's iCal still supports these old-style scripts for backward compatibility, although the now obsolete title property is no longer shown in its dictionary.

Note The earliest versions of iCal also required you to supply a value for the make command's at parameter: end of calendar. Newer versions are smart enough to work this out for themselves.

Creating Events

As you can imagine, one of the most useful classes in iCal is the event class. Events are what make the calendar useful in the first place: dinner party Tuesday at 6 PM, sales meeting Friday from 3 to 4:30 PM, and so on.

The event class has a few obvious properties such as start date and end date, both of which accept AppleScript's date value. You can also set the summary text you want displayed in the iCal window. Script 26-9 shows a simple script that creates a new event and assigns it a few basic properties.

Script 26-9.

```
tell application "iCal"
    tell calendar 1
        set new_event to make new event at end of events
    end tell
    tell new_event
        set start date to date "Monday, May 1, 2006 4:00:00 PM"
        set end date to date "Monday, May 1, 2006 4:30:00 PM"
        set summary to "Feed ferret"
        set location to "Providence"
        set allday event to false
        set status to confirmed
        set recurrence to "FREQ=DAILY;INTERVAL=2;UNTIL=20060531"
    end tell
end tell
```

Note You could have assigned the properties to the iCal event all at once using the properties parameter in the make command, like so: make new event with properties {start date:date "Wednesday, May 3, 2006 04:00:00", end date....

Let's look at the seven properties of the new event object set in this example. The first two properties are start date and end date. These are probably the most important properties that define the date and time boundaries of the event.

The summary and location properties are two strings that provide information about the event.

The event's status property can be none, confirmed, tentative, or cancelled, and the allday event property's value is a Boolean that determines whether the event appears as a variable-sized block that runs between the start and end times given by your date values or as an all-day block that automatically runs from midnight to midnight.

The recurrence property is where Apple engineers could have definitely spent more time. Right now, as of iCal version 2.0.3, the recurrence property is an ugly string that includes information about the recurrence frequency, intervals, and duration of the event. Here is an example of the string again:

FREQ=DAILY;INTERVAL=2;UNTIL=20060531

The string has three properties in it, which appear next to their possible values.

Frequency

Represented with FREQ, this can be followed by the value DAILY, WEEKLY, MONTHLY, or YEARLY.

Interval

If the frequency is set to DAILY, for instance, INTERVAL specifies how many days between event occurrences. In the preceding example, the interval is 2, which means the feed ferret event will recur every two days.

Duration

The duration either can be the word UNTIL followed by a YYYYMMDD-style date string or can be the word COUNT followed by the number of occurrences that will happen before the event repetition expires. In the earlier example, I used the following UNTIL value: 20060531. This means the event will stop recurring at midnight on May 31, 2006.

An UNTIL duration of –1 indicates that the event never expires.

Event Elements

An object of the event class can have elements of its own. An event can have attendees and four types of alarms: open file alarms, sound alarms, display alarms, and mail alarms. I will not get into these in detail right now, but the script in the next section should shed some light on their use and creation.

Creating a New Event Based on Mail

Script 26-10 shows how to parse an e-mail sent by Microsoft Exchange Server when a new meeting is scheduled. I took the text from the e-mail message and converted it into a new event in iCal.

The script is broken down into three parts: getting the information from Mail, extracting the dates and other information from the message, and finally creating the new event.

Note Line 38, which adds the attendees to the event, doesn't work in Panther or older because of bugs in iCal 1.5 scriptability. If you're still using iCal 1.5, you'll need to omit that line and add the attendees by hand. The good news is that this bug is fixed in iCal 2.0, which comes with OS X 10.4.

Script 26-10.

```
1. --Get message information from Mail
2. tell application "Mail"
3.    set selection_list to selection
4.    set my_message to item 1 of selection_list
5.    tell my_message
6.       set attendee_count to count every recipient
7.       set attendee_name_list to name of every recipient
8.       set attendee_address_list to address of every recipient
9.       set message_subject to subject
10.       set message_text to content
11.    end tell
12. end tell
```

```
13. --Parse message text for the start date, end date and location
14. set message_paragraph_list to paragraphs of message_text
15. repeat with the_paragraph in message_paragraph_list
16.    if the_paragraph starts with "When:" then
17.       set date_string to text (word 2) thru (word 5) of paragraph_ref
18.       set time_start_string to text (word 6) thru (word 8) of paragraph_ref
19.       set time_end_string to text (word 9) thru (word 11) of paragraph_ref

20.       set start_date to date (date_string & space & time_start_string)
21.       set end_date to date (date_string & space & time_end_string)
22.    else if the_paragraph starts with "When:" then
23.       set where_string to text 8 thru -1 of the_paragraph
24.    else if the_paragraph starts with "*~" then
25.       exit repeat
26.    end if
27. end repeat

28. --Create event in iCal
29. tell application "iCal"
30.    set my_cal to calendar 1
31.    set new_event to make new event at end of my_cal with properties ¬
              {summary:message_subject, start date:start_date, end date:end_date}
32.    tell new_event
33.       make new mail alarm at end of mail alarms ¬
              with properties {trigger interval:-30}
34.       --make attendees
35.       repeat with i from 1 to attendee_count
36.          set attendee_name to item i of attendee_name_list
37.          set attendee_address to item i of attendee_address_list
38.          make new attendee at end of attendees with properties ¬
                  {display name:attendee_name, email:attendee_address}
39.       end repeat
40.    end tell
41. end tell
```

In the first portion of the script, between lines 1 and 12, you extract information directly from the mail message. Figure 26-6 shows the original mail message you get.

From: Julie@att.com
Subject: **Project management meeting**
Date: April 27, 2004 2:50:46 PM EDT
To: jane@att.com, drake@att.com, bob@att.com
Cc: joe@att.com

When: Thursday, April 29, 2004 10:00 AM-11:00 AM (GMT-05:00) Eastern Time
(US & Canada).
Where: Meeting room 12, 6th floor

~~*~*~*~*~*~*~*~

Weekly meeting to assess progress.

Figure 26-6. *The original mail message you need to parse*

The information extracted is the message subject you will use as the summary of the event, the list of recipients that will be used to add attendees to the event, and the body of the message from which the start and end date for the event will be extracted.

When testing this script in full, you'll need to make up a dummy message in Mail with similar content to that in Figure 26-2 and send it to yourself. Once you receive it, select it in Mail, and run the script as normal. If you're testing only the second and third parts of the script, you could comment out the first part of the script and add some temporary code to supply the test data directly:

```
set attendee_count to 4
set attendee_name_list to ¬
   {missing value, missing value, missing value, missing value}
set attendee_address_list to ¬
   {"jane@att.com", "drake@att.com", "bob@att.com", "joe@att.com"}
set message_subject to "Project management meeting"
set message_text to "When: Monday, May 29, 2006 10:00 AM-11:00 AM (GMT-05:00) ➡
Eastern Time (US & Canada).
Where: Meeting room 12, 6th floor


*~*~*~*~*~*~*~*~*~*


Weekly meeting to assess progress."
```

Once you've finished testing, remember to delete or comment out the test code, and then reenable the original code for getting the data from Mail.

In the second part, lines 13 through 27, you parse out the information you need from the mail message. You can do that in many ways, but the result has to be pretty much the same. You need to end up with three pieces of information for the iCal event: start time, end time, and location.

The way I tackled it in the script is by breaking the message into paragraphs and then examining each paragraph using a repeat loop. If the paragraph starts with When:, then I know it has the date information; if it starts with Where:, then it has the location. More specifically, I parse out the date information from the When: paragraph in two steps.

The full line (broken onto two lines) is as follows:

```
When: Thursday, April 29, 2004 10:00 AM-11:00 AM
         (GMT-05:00) Eastern Time (US & Canada)
```

but I needed this:

```
Thursday, April 29, 2004 10:00 AM-11:00 AM
```

So, I start by getting all the text from the second to the fifth word (line 17), which also omits the end time, which I don't need.

The final part of the script creates the event (lines 28 through 41). You create the actual event object in line 31, assigning custom values to the summary and assigning start and end date properties during the creation process. You then assign the result of the make command to the variable new_event.

In lines 32–40 you add the elements to the event. You start by adding a single e-mail alarm element, and then you loop through the list of attendee e-mail and name lists to add them as attendees to the event.

Using iCal to Schedule Scripts

Another neat feature of iCal is that you can schedule compiled AppleScript files to run. To do that, create a new event in iCal, and set the date and time you want the script to execute on. Then add an open file alarm, and specify the script file you want to execute.

Scripting iChat

iChat is a small application, so it's not surprising it has only three classes and three commands defined in it. Besides the application class, iChat has an account class and a service class.

Different account elements in the iChat application correspond to different people you chat with. Accounts can be referenced either from the service they belong to or from the application directly.

iChat has only a handful of properties, as you may imagine, and you can't change most of them. In fact, the only two significant properties belong to the application class, and they are status and status message. All properties of the account and service classes are read-only.

One of the properties scripters like to have fun with is the status message property. This is the message that appears both at the top of your iChat window and as your status on your buddies' iChat windows.

The property is simple; you can simply set it to any string:

```
tell application "iChat" to set status message to "Honey, I'm Home"
```

Script 26-11 acts as an iChat status message agent. It is saved as a stay-open application and uses the on idle handler.

The script will check to see the current track name and playlist name in iTunes and alternate them every five seconds as the status message. This way your buddies can know you're available and know what song you happen to be listening to at the moment.

Script 26-11.

```
1. property flag : true
2. property original_message : ""

3. on run
4.     tell application "iChat"
5.         set original_message to status message
6.     end tell
7. end run

8. on idle
9.     try
10.        tell application "iTunes"
11.            set this_track to name of current track
12.            set this_playlist to name of current playlist
13.        end tell
14.        set status_message to "Available and listening to "
15.        if flag then
16.            set status_message to status_message & ¬
                   "track: " & this_track
17.        else
18.            set status_message to status_message & "playlist:" & ¬
                   this_playlist
19.        end if
20.    on error
21.        set status_message to "Available and listening to nothin'"
22.    end try
23.    tell application "iChat"
24.        set status message to status_message
25.    end tell
```

```
26.     set flag to not flag
27.     return 5
28. end idle

29. on quit
30.     tell application "iChat"
31.         set status message to original_message
32.     end tell
33.     continue quit
34. end quit
```

The script uses two properties: original_status and flag. The flag property changes from true to false to indicate to the script whether the next status should be the name of the playlist or the track.

The original_status property is set in the on run handler, which executes once when the script application is launched. It holds the original status message. This original message is reinstated in the on quit handler, which is called when the script application quits.

A minimal amount of error handling has been added, in case iTunes has no current track or playlist information available.

Also notice that if you want your script application to be able to quit normally, you must execute the statement continue quit at some point in the quit handler. Otherwise, the quit operation will never be completed, and the only way to stop the script application then will be to force it to quit.

Scripting Automator

Automator is a cool new application that comes bundled with Mac OS X 10.4 Tiger. It allows you to automate various tasks on your Mac by arranging premade Automator actions into workflows.

Automator interfaces with AppleScript in three ways:

Actions created with AppleScript: Many of the actions that ship with Automator and ones created by third-party developers are created using AppleScript as the main programming language. These actions are created with Xcode, which is part of Apple's Developer Tools (included with your OS X installer disks or available as a free download from http://developer.apple.com).

The Run AppleScript action: One action in Automator is the Run AppleScript action, which allows you to run any script, most likely performing an operation on the input, which was returned from the previous action, and possibly returning a result to be used as input in the next action.

ScriptingAutomator: Like many other Mac applications, the Automator application is scriptable. Although most of Automator's dictionary is used to define the classes, commands, and events needed to write AppleScript-based actions, it also defines a number of classes and commands you can use to edit and run workflows from AppleScript.

Figure 26-7 shows the Automator workflow window.

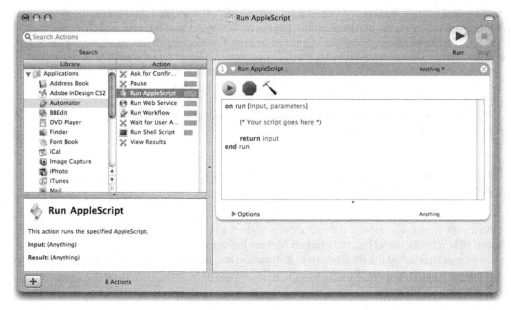

Figure 26-7. *The main Automator workflow window with the Run AppleScript action*

In this chapter, you'll be dealing with the two later points.

Using the Run AppleScript Action

To add the Run AppleScript action to your workflow, you have to first create a new workflow window if none exists; you do that by choosing File ➤ New in Automator.

The Run AppleScript action is under the Automator category, so click the Automator icon in the Library column on the left of the window. Now, drag the Run AppleScript action to your workflow on the right of the window. Your workflow window should look similar to the window in Figure 26-7.

As you can tell, the Run AppleScript action is not blank but rather has some code in it:

```
on run {input, parameters}
  (* Your script goes here *)
  return input
end run
```

In short, any code you place inside the run handler will execute when the action you're editing is executed. In this case, it will happen as soon as the entire workflow is executed, since this is the first action in the workflow.

input

By examining the short script in the Run AppleScript action's body, you probably see two things that may need explanation: the two parameters passed to the run handler, input and parameters, and the return input statement at the end. As you can imagine, the script in its current form doesn't do much. It does, however, do something. The input that is passed as a parameter in the run handler is the result of the previous action. The last line of the run handler, return input, faithfully passes that input to the next action in the workflow. This means that although the action doesn't do anything spectacular, it also doesn't ruin the flow.

What is the input, however? Which data class is it, and what sort of values can you expect? That completely depends on the previous action, whichever it may be, and the type of data it produces. For the most part, however, that data is arranged in a list. For instance, a Finder action may return a list of file references or aliases, and a Mail action may return a list of references to Mail messages.

To see the input, you will use the Run AppleScript action's Result area. This area is right below the script in the Run AppleScript action's pane but is initially hidden; you make it visible by dragging the dot at the center-bottom area of the script area.

To examine an action's result, drag the Get Selected Finder Items action from the Finder category and drop it above the Run AppleScript action.

Tip It is easy to locate an action if you enter the action's name or part of it in the Search Actions search field at the top-left corner of the Automator window.

Once the workflow contains the two actions, go to the Finder, and select a few files on your desktop (if you're like me, at least 20 random files are lurking there in disarray).

After you've selected the files, return to Automator, and run the workflow. You'll see the result in the Result area at the bottom of the Run AppleScript action, as shown in Figure 26-8.

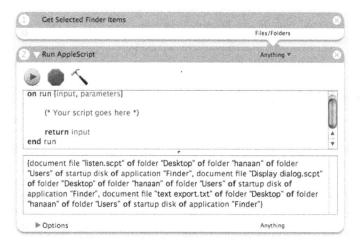

Figure 26-8. *The workflow containing the two actions and the Run AppleScript's action result*

What you see is a list of Finder file references. The script can process this list of files.

Note The easiest way to view the result of an Automator action is by using the View Result action.

Parameters

OK, so the input can be almost anything, such as a list of files or anything else the previous action spits out. What are the parameters, though? To find out, change the return line in the script from return input to return parameters. Now run the workflow. The Result area should contain something like this:

```
{|temporary items path|: ➡
"/Users/hanaan/Library/Caches/TemporaryItems/com.apple.Automator.9UZVzc", ➡
|ignoresInput|:false, |action|:item id 2, |source|:"on run {input, parameters}

..(* Your script goes here *)

   return parameters
end run"}
```

The parameters are some Automator built-in environment variables, which you will probably not use. One parameter variable you may be looking at is the |ignoresInput| variable. This variable tells you whether the user chose to have the action ignore any result returned from the previous action, which, in other words, is the user asking the script to ignore the input variable.

Let's Get Some Code Down

I will now show how to create a script that filters files larger than a certain size, specified by the user. Since the Run AppleScript action can take advantage only of AppleScript user interface features, I will show how to use the display dialog command to get the user input.

The backbone of the script is a repeat loop that will loop through the files in the input variable (remember, the input variable is going to have a list of files returned from the previous action), checking the size of each one. If the file size is greater than the size specified by the user, then the file reference will be added to a new list. This new list will be returned at the end of the script.

Script 26-12 shows the rather simple script you will enter for the Run AppleScript action.

Script 26-12.

```
on run {input, parameters}
   if class of input = list then
     set file_list to input
   else
     error "Input must be a list of aliases"
   end if
display dialog "Enter minimum file size in KB" default answer "20"
   set min_size_in_kb to text returned of result as number
   set filtered_file_list to {}
   repeat with the_file_ref in file_list
     set the_alias to the_file_ref as alias
     if (size of (info for the_alias)) > (min_size_in_kb * 1024) then
       set end of filtered_file_list to the_alias
     end if
   end repeat
   return filtered_file_list
end run
```

One possible problem the script may have is if the user enters text that is not numerical. You can add some try statement to check for that. Another thing you may want to verify is that the result returned from the last action is a list of aliases.

Note the first line of code in the run handler: set file_list to input. This line isn't really needed; you could just use the original input identifier, but I chose a more descriptive one. You could also mess with Automator's default variable naming and name the input variable file_list instead: on run {file_list, parameters}.

Also notice this line: set the_alias to the_file_ref as alias. Remember that the original list has Finder-style file references. Since you'll be using Standard Additions' info for command to get each file's size, you need to coerce each Finder reference into a value the info for command will understand, in this case an AppleScript alias value.

The following line uses the info for command to get a record containing the file's details and then gets the size of the file from the record's size property. The script then compares the size of the file with the minimum size entered by the user. Since the info for command returns the file size in bytes, I multiply the value of the min_size_in_kb variable by 1,024 to convert it to a size in bytes as well.

The final line of the script's run handler may be the most important: return filtered_file_list. This line ensures that the following action in the workflow gets the new file list as its input.

Finishing the Workflow

What this workflow will do is apply a red label to the files that are larger than the value specified by the user. To do that, add the Label Finder Items action to the end of the workflow. Check the red label in the action's interface.

After doing that, run the workflow. It will apply a red label to the files larger than the size specified by the user (you in this case).

Scripting the Automator Application

The Automator application is scriptable, as would be expected, and several classes and commands are useful for automating the automation program. The classes of objects you will be using are workflow and Automator action. As you would imagine, Automator action objects are elements of workflow objects. There are a few other classes, but they are less important than these two.

Three commands are defined in the Automator Suite of Automator's dictionary: add and remove add and remove Automator action elements from and to a workflow object. The execute command can execute a workflow.

Let's look at a simple script using Automator. Script 26-13 will ask the user to pick an iTunes Automator action, add that action to the workflow, save the workflow, and execute it.

Script 26-13.

```
tell application "Automator"
  activate
  set action_list to name of Automator actions whose target application = {"iTunes"}
  set action_name to (choose from list action_list) as string
  if action_name is false then return -- in case user cancels
  set my_workflow to make workflow with properties {name:action_name & "Workflow"}
  add Automator action action_name to my_workflow
  save my_workflow in (path to desktop as string) & action_name & "Workflow"
end tell
```

Other than the save and make commands, all the commands used in this script are from the Automator suite.

Note that the script creates the workflow object, assigning the string containing the action's name and the word Workflow to its name property, and assigns the resulting reference, workflow "My Random Workflow" of application "Automator", to the variable my_workflow. If the name of the workflow changes later, the reference stored in that variable would no longer refer to that workflow, since it uses the workflow's name, not its unique ID, to identify it.

I would assume if you create a system that utilizes Automator workflows, you would want to use the execute command to run these workflows. Otherwise, I found the Automator scripting useful when I was writing my Automator book. I used AppleScript to add one action at a time to a workflow and take screenshots of each action's interface.

CHAPTER 27

■■■

Scripting Data and Databases

Take a piece of paper and make a simple shopping list: one column for the items you need and one column for the number of items you want. Did you just create a database? I think you did: you can sort it and find items in it; you can cross-reference items in the store's price list, which makes it a relational database; and you can add it to a longer list of all the shopping you've ever done. OK, so it's not that fast or efficient, but it has data organized in fields and records.

Three factors make a database what it is: the data structure, which basically consists of the fields and field definitions; the data itself; and the functionality, such as sorting, searching, and exporting.

AppleScript has no built-in database tools, but you can get a bit done with lists and records. For instance, you can collect data in a list of records, as shown here:

```
set people_table to {¬
    {first_name:"Jo", last_name:"Brown", age:31}, ¬
    {first_name:"Sam", last_name:"Green", age:24}, ¬
    {first_name:"Adam", last_name:"Smith", age:29}, ¬
    }
```

Later you can loop through the records in this list, getting and setting the values of their properties as needed. However, although this approach works for basic operations on small amounts of data, more advanced tasks such as sorting or searching the data will be slow and complicated to do using AppleScript alone.

In this chapter, you will look at four ways AppleScript can connect to or be used as a database.

You will start with scripting FileMaker Pro 8, then move on to connecting to SQL databases using MacSQL, then look at a scripting addition that acts as a built-in database engine for AppleScript, and finally investigate the new Database Events application that is included in Mac OS X 10.4 and newer.

Note Please note that the FileMaker Pro and MacSQL sections assume prior experience with the respective application and with basic database concepts and terminology.

Automating FileMaker Pro with AppleScript

FileMaker Pro is one of the oldest and most loved applications used on the Mac. It started out through Claris, an Apple subsidiary, and is now created and sold by FileMaker Inc. (www.filemaker.com). FileMaker Pro is known for its ease of use, robust scripting, and layout tools, which give developers the ability to develop database-driven applications quickly.

One thing you should know about FileMaker Pro's AppleScript support is that it's designed for manipulating the data in existing databases, not constructing new ones. You still have to do tasks such as creating new databases and editing their layouts using FileMaker Pro's graphical interface. As a result, you'll find that many properties and elements are noneditable. For example, you can't use AppleScript to create and delete database or layout elements, and you can change only one important property, cellValue, using the set command.

Although this might sound like a significant limitation, it really isn't. The beauty of scripting FileMaker Pro isn't in how you can construct the database but rather in how you can use an already established database to help you with script execution. Given an existing database, you can use AppleScript to get and set the values of records' cells, create and delete records, and perform advanced operations such as finding and sorting records. As a scripter, I like that I can use File-Maker Pro to put together a back-end database for my script with minimal effort. I can give the users a nice user interface, set up reports, control security in a jiffy, and best of all, have full access to the underlying data.

Although the following sections describe the important aspects of FileMaker Pro scripting, they are by no means a comprehensive guide. FileMaker Pro does come with a database that explains the different classes and commands available to scripters.

Versions

FileMaker Pro was never known for comprehensive AppleScript support; however, it gave scripters consistent support through the years. Even now with the introduction of the all-new FileMaker Pro 8, the scripting dictionary remains virtually unchanged.

One thing that did change with FileMaker Pro 8 is the introduction of the table class. In earlier versions of FileMaker Pro, each file represented a single database table. Now, a single file can contain multiple tables, with each of these tables being represented as an element of the database object for that file.

Having multiple versions of FileMaker Pro on the same Mac, all with the same name, may be a problem. To ensure that your script editor points to the right version of FileMaker Pro, you can change the name of the application to FileMaker Pro 7 or change the name of the old one. Alternatively, you can refer to the copy you want using its full path. For example:

```
tell application "Macintosh HD:Applications:FileMaker Pro 8:FileMaker Pro"
    --some commands here...
end tell
```

The FileMaker Pro Object Model and the Commands You Can Use

The FileMaker Pro object model is reasonably simple. Before you dive in, here's a quick overview of the main object classes to help you get started:

- Database/document objects represent open FileMaker Pro files. Databases consist of tables and layouts.

- Tables, which consist of rows and columns (records and fields) of cells, store your data.

- Windows allow you to organize and view your data. Windows use layouts to control exactly how and where that data is presented.

In the following text, I'll discuss all of these in much more detail.

Databases and Documents

The main elements of the top-level application object are database, document, and window. There's also menu, but I will not cover it here.

In FileMaker Pro 7 and newer, the application object's database and document elements represent pretty much the same thing: an open FileMaker Pro database file. In fact, although FileMaker Pro's dictionary shows slightly different definitions for the database and document classes, you'll find they're more or less interchangeable in practice.

You can refer to database/document objects either by index (which depends on the current window order) or by name (which is the same as its filename, except that the name extension bit is optional). For example:

```
tell application "FileMaker Pro"
    database 1
end tell
--> database "Inventory.fp7" of application "FileMaker Pro"

tell application "FileMaker Pro"
    database "Inventory"
end tell
--> database "Inventory.fp7" of application "FileMaker Pro"
```

A modern FileMaker Pro database file contains one or more tables, which hold your data, and defines one or more layouts for viewing that data in various ways. Not surprisingly, FileMaker Pro's dictionary defines table and layout classes to represent database tables and layouts too. Using table objects is good when you want direct access to all the data in that table, and using layouts is useful when you want to work with a found set of records. You'll look at using tables and layouts in later sections.

Windows

Windows display some or all of a database's data. Although you can generally ignore window objects in other applications when scripting them, in FileMaker Pro scripting you need to refer to window objects and their layout elements whenever you want to work with found sets.

Window objects appear both as elements of the top-level application object and as elements of each document/database object. The latter is particularly useful when you already have a reference to a particular database and want a reference to the window (or windows) that belongs to it. For example:

```
tell application "FileMaker Pro"
    tell database "Inventory"
        window 1
    end tell
end tell
--> window "Inventory" of database "Inventory.fp7" of application "FileMaker Pro"
```

Each database can have one or more windows open at the same time, and each window can show its own found set of records. For example, one window might show all the records in your database, although another shows only the records that match a recent find request. You can refer to windows either by index (which depends on their onscreen order) or by name. If a database has multiple windows open, make sure you refer to the window that contains the found set you want.

Each window uses a layout from the database to display the records in its found set, and you can switch between layouts whenever you like to display that data in different ways. To get and set values in a found set, you need to use a layout that includes fields that show those values. Later in the "Layouts" section I'll discuss how to go to different layouts in a window, how to use them to manipulate the found set, and how to get and set values.

Tables

Tables are where your actual data is stored. Simple databases will have just a single table, but more sophisticated relational designs can contain multiple tables whose records are related to one another in various ways.

For example, a sales database might have one table containing its product details, a second table containing its customer details, and a third table for keeping track of which customers buy which products. FileMaker Pro will use the predefined relationships between the database's tables and unique IDs stored in the key fields of each table to determine which records are related to one another (hence the phrase *relational database*).

FileMaker Pro allows AppleScripts to have direct access to a database's table objects. This is useful when you want full access to all the fields in that table and to the data in every cell of every record.

Script 27-1 shows a typical script for getting values from a table.

Script 27-1.

```
tell application "FileMaker Pro"
    tell document "Inventory"
        tell table "equipment"
            tell record 1
                set the_date to cell "date purchased"
                set the_cost to cell "value"
            end tell
        end tell
    end tell
end tell
```

Note that this script asks for the first record in the table. In a table, records always appear in the order they were added, so the first record is the oldest and the last record is the newest. You cannot change the order of records in a table; you can only add and delete them. New records are automatically added at the end, of course.

Layouts

Layouts present particular views of a database's data to its users, both human and AppleScript. You can use layouts to find only those records that match certain criteria (the found set) and to sort records in a particular order. A layout may show some or all of the fields from a single table or from several related tables if portal views are used.

For example, the sales database mentioned earlier might provide one layout for viewing the company's product details (name, model number, description, and price) and another layout for viewing its customer details (contact name, mailing address, and account number). In addition, since this is a relational database, the customer layout could include a portal view showing which of the company's products a customer has purchased.

Working with layouts in AppleScript is a lot like working with them by hand. To use a layout, you first have to refer to a window in which it's displayed. FileMaker Pro's document objects helpfully include window elements, which makes it easy to locate the window (or windows) currently displaying the data for a particular database.

Script 27-2 shows a typical script for getting values from a layout.

Script 27-2.

```
tell application "FileMaker Pro"
    tell document "Inventory"
        tell window 1
            go to layout "equipment"
            tell current record
                set the_date to cell "date purchased"
                set the_cost to cell "value"
            end tell
        end tell
    end tell
end tell
```

As you can see, this script has some similarities to the previous one but also some differences. Notice that instead of referring to table "equipment" of document "Inventory", you now start by referring to window 1 of document "Inventory". Next you use the go to command to tell the window which layout you want it to display. In this case, you go to a layout named equipment, which is set up to display various data from the equipment table. Once the desired layout is visible, you can identify the record you're interested in and get the values from its cells.

Since windows and layouts are used for controlling how data is displayed, they have some extra abilities that tables don't; for example, you can ask FileMaker Pro for the currently selected record by referring to the window's current record property. If you wanted the first record currently shown in that layout, you could get that by referring to record 1 of layout "equipment" of window 1. Of course, which record that is will depend on which records are in the window's found set and the order in which they are sorted.

One other difference when working with layouts rather than tables is that you can refer only to fields that are actually present on the layout itself. For example, if a table includes a "product code" field but the layout you're using doesn't display this field, you won't be able to get the product code from that particular layout—you'll need to use a different layout or access the table directly instead. On the other hand, a single layout can have portal views that allow you to access data held in multiple tables, whereas a table object allows you to access the data only in that particular table.

Incidentally, if you're designing a FileMaker Pro database yourself, you might sometimes find it useful to set up some layouts especially for your AppleScripts to use, in addition to the layouts you provide for human users. That way, your scripts can get access to additional fields that human users don't need to see, but you can still enjoy the extra benefits that working with layouts rather than tables provides (found sets, sorting, and so on).

Scripting Older Versions of FileMaker Pro

If you're still using FileMaker Pro 6 or older, you'll find its object model is a bit different. The most obvious difference is that there's no table class in its dictionary since each database file can hold only a single table anyway. To get access to all the records in a database file, you need to start by referring to a database object. For example:

```
tell application "FileMaker Pro 6"
    tell database "Employees"
        count every record
    end tell
end tell
--> 47 --the total number of records in this database
```

To refer only to the records in the current found set, you have to start with a document object instead. For example:

```
tell application "FileMaker Pro 6"
   tell document "Employees"
      count every record
   end tell
end tell
--> 13 --the total number of records in the current found set
```

In FileMaker Pro 6 and older, AppleScript could refer to a special layout element, layout 0, to access all the fields in a table. Although this still works in FileMaker Pro 7 and later, it allows access only to the first table in the database, so you're better off referring directly to the database's table elements instead.

You should also notice in the previous examples that you refer directly to the database and document objects' record elements, even though the database and document class definitions in File-Maker Pro's dictionary don't actually show database and document objects as having field, record, or cell elements. FileMaker Pro provides several "hidden" shortcuts like this that aren't listed in its dictionary, although you will find them mentioned in its Apple Events Reference database if you look carefully.

Again, although you can still find these hidden shortcuts in the current version of FileMaker Pro, they don't support newer features such as multiple tables, so when using FileMaker Pro 7 and newer, it's best if you always refer explicitly to the table, window, and layout objects you want to use.

Records, Fields, and Cells

In FileMaker Pro you can get and set the data of an individual cell or of an entire record or field at once.

Although the cell class has a cellValue property, just referring to the cell object returns its value, as shown in Script 27-3.

Script 27-3. *(includes the following two scripts)*

```
tell application "FileMaker Pro"
   tell document "Inventory"
      tell record 3 of table "equipment"
         get cellValue of cell "value"
      end tell
   end tell
end tell
--> "495.0"
```

As you can see, getting the value of the cell's cellValue property returns a string, but FileMaker Pro also allows you to retrieve the same value just by using this:

```
tell application "FileMaker Pro"
   tell document "Inventory"
      tell record 3 of table "equipment"
         get cell "value"
      end tell
   end tell
end tell
--> "495.0"
```

Getting either the cell or the cellValue of the cell always returns a string, no matter from where the field type the data comes.

Script 27-4 sets the value of a cell in certain records of a table.

Script 27-4.

```
tell application "FileMaker Pro"
   tell database "Inventory"
      tell table "equipment"
         tell (every record whose cell "type" is "222")
            set cell "model" to "AB-222"
         end tell
      end tell
   end tell
end tell
```

The preceding script represents more than merely a way to set data. As you can see, you can also use a whose clause to specify *which* records you want a command to act on. Think of the whose clause as AppleScript's own answer to FileMaker Pro's Find Mode, although you can use AppleScript to control that too if you want; you'll look at doing this later in this chapter.

You can also set or get data of an entire field or record at once. For example, the following script gets all the values from the quantity field of the database's equipment table:

```
tell application "FileMaker Pro"
   tell database "Inventory"
      get field "quantity" of table "equipment"
   end tell
end tell
--> {"120", "135", "76", "3", "47", ...}
```

Here's another example that gets all the cell values from a record:

```
tell application "FileMaker Pro"
   get record 5 of table 1 of database "test scores"
end tell
--> {"Jan", "Smith", "95"}
```

You can even retrieve all the data in the table at once by writing this:

```
get table 1 of database "test scores"
```

or by writing this:

```
get every field of table 1 of database "test scores"
```

depending on whether you want the cell values grouped by record or by field. Both commands will return a list of lists.

When you work with table and layout objects, you have to be aware of the order FileMaker Pro uses when it sets and returns data.

As explained earlier, the field order in a table is the field creation order, and the record order is the record creation order. You can't change that order, even by sorting the records. However, when you get data from the layout instead of the table, the records will be returned from the found set in the current sort order.

This means that although the table object is more flexible and has greater access to the data, it may be beneficial sometimes to use the layout object to get or set the same data, since you can specify the sort order and found set you want before you change or get the data, and this way have more control over what you do.

Script 27-5 first uses FileMaker Pro's show command with a whose reference to tell FileMaker Pro to show the records you want in the current window. It then sorts the displayed records based on the contents of the value field before retrieving the data from this field.

Script 27-5.

```
tell application "FileMaker Pro"
    tell table "equipment"
        show (every record whose cell "type" is "222")
    end tell
    tell layout "equipment" of window 1
        sort by field "value"
        set value_list to field "value"
    end tell
end tell
value_list --> {"150", "185", "200"}
```

In the preceding script, you use FileMaker Pro's show command as a simpler alternative to its find command. The actual find command in FileMaker Pro's AppleScript dictionary will perform a find using the most recent find settings. Although you can use AppleScript to create and execute new find requests from scratch, for most tasks it's easier just to use the show command with a whose reference.

Notice that for the show command you turn to the table object, not the layout object. Remember, the layout object knows only about the currently found set, so it will show the records that fit the criteria you set, if they are already in the found set. Even if you use the following line, FileMaker Pro may not show all the records in the table:

```
show every record of layout "equipment"
```

To show all the records in the table, you will need to do the following:

```
show every record of table "equipment"
```

To sort records, on the other hand, you have to use the layout object since the table object doesn't handle the sort command.

Just as you get data from the database a whole field at a time, you can also insert data a whole field at a time.

Script 27-6 sets the cell serial number of every record in the found set to values from a list. The values will be applied to the records in the order they happened to be sorted in at the time.

Script 27-6.

```
set serial_list to {"AB-222", "AB-223", "AB-224", "AB-225", "AB-226"}
tell application "FileMaker Pro"
    tell layout "equipment"
        set field "serial number" to serial_list
    end tell
end tell
```

If the inner tell block had been directed at the table object instead of the layout object, then the data in the field would apply to the records in the table, starting from the first one in the creation order, going up until the last record or the last item in the list (whichever comes first), completely ignoring the found set and the sort order.

Finding Data Quickly with the whose Clause

You probably have used the Find Mode menu option in FileMaker Pro many times. When writing scripts for FileMaker Pro, however, you may want to avoid using either the dictionary's find command or any reference to a FileMaker Pro script that performs a find command—not necessarily because they don't work, but rather because there's a better way to refer to the set of records you want to use. That way is AppleScript's powerful filtering whose clause.

For most operations such as get data and set data, you don't even need to actually find the data and display the found set but rather isolate the records you want to work with inside your script. The whose clause is great for that.

As you've seen, you can use a single whose clause to retrieve complex sets of data. Script 27-7 shows an example.

Script 27-7.

```
tell application "FileMaker Pro"
   tell database "campaign"
      tell table "donors"
         tell every record whose ¬
            (cell "State" = "RI") and ¬
            (cell "Income" > 100000)
            set address_list to cell "address"
            set phone_list to cell "tel01"
            set name_list to cell "full name"
         end tell
      end tell
   end tell
end tell
```

The preceding script allows you to get data quickly from a specific set of records without changing any interfaces, running any scripts, or invoking any FileMaker Pro find commands.

Using the whose Clause to Retrieve Relational Data

Using the whose clause search techniques you saw previously, you can perform complex relational searches with minimal effort and without having to set up or refer to any FileMaker Pro relationships.

The idea is to first find the key field and then use the value in that key field to find related records. For example, let's say you have a contacts database. In that contacts database you have two tables: people and numbers. The numbers table contains all the fax and phone numbers for all the contacts, and every number is linked to the contacts with the person id field. Each number record has four cells then: number id, person id, number label, and number value.

Now let's imagine you have a person named John L. Smith from Boulder, Colorado, and you need to get all the numbers related to his record. All you have to do is find the value of the person id field in the people table and then find all the records in the numbers table that have that same number in that table's person id field. Script 27-8 shows how the script goes.

Script 27-8.

```
tell application "FileMaker Pro"
    tell table "people" of database 1
        tell every record whose ¬
            (cell "first name" = "John") and ¬
            (cell "middle name" starts with "L") and ¬
            (cell "last name" = "Smith") and ¬
            (cell "city" = "Boulder") and ¬
            (cell "state" = "CO")
            set person_id to cell "person id"
        end tell
    end tell
    tell table "number" of database 1
        tell every record whose ¬
            (cell "person id" = person_id)
            set person_number_list to cell "number value"
        end tell
    end tell
end tell
```

Using the find Command

Using the whose clause for filtering records is great in many cases, but FileMaker Pro still may have search criteria that perform filtering functions not available in AppleScript, such as searches for duplicates and searches that need to perform complex tests on cells' values. In these situations you'll want to use FileMaker Pro's find command instead.

For example, Script 27-9 will find all the Wednesday morning meetings that will be attended by employee John Smith. A whose clause is no good here because there's no way to make it match only records whose dates fall on a Wednesday, so you have to use find.

Script 27-9.

```
tell application "FileMaker Pro"
    tell database "Company Calendar"
        show every record of table "Meetings"
        tell window 1
            tell layout "Meeting Details"
                go to it
                if requests exists then delete requests
                set my_request to create request
                tell my_request
                    set cell "Date" to "=Wednesday"
                    set cell "Start Time" to "8 AM...12 PM"
                    set cell "Attendees::First Name" to "==John"
                    set cell "Attendees::Last Name" to "==Smith"
                end tell
            end tell
            find
        end tell
    end tell
end tell
```

Figure 27-1 shows a typical result after this script is run.

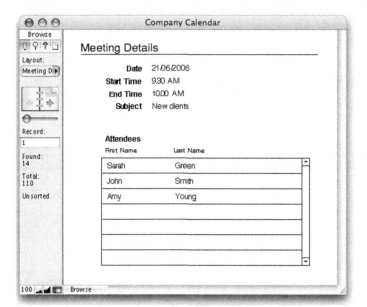

Figure 27-1. *The result of running the* find *script. As you can see from the sidebar, FileMaker Pro has found 14 out of 110 records matching the request.*

You start by identifying the window you want to work with, window 1 of database "Company Calendar". Next you tell this window to go to the Meeting Details layout, which lets you view the information you want. You then tell this layout to delete any previous find requests; otherwise, these would interfere with your new search.

Now you can construct the new search request. First you use the create ("make") command to add a new request element to the layout. You then add the search values to this request. To match a particular day in the date field named Date, you use a string containing an equals (=) sign followed by the name of the day. To match a range of times in the Start Time field, you write the starting time followed by three dots and then the finishing time. The Meeting Details layout uses a portal view of the database's Attendees table to show the first and last names of the employees who will be attending each meeting, so you refer to those cells as Attendees::First Name and Attendees::Last Name. To exactly match the text in those fields, you add two equals signs to the start of your strings. You can find full instructions on how to use FileMaker Pro's special find symbols in its built-in Help.

Once you've finished setting up the request, you tell the window (not the layout) to perform the find command. Any records that don't match all the criteria in the search request will be eliminated from the found set, leaving just the ones you want.

Running AppleScripts from Inside FileMaker Pro

FileMaker Pro allows you to run AppleScripts that are embedded in FileMaker Pro scripts. To do that, you use the Perform AppleScript script step in a FileMaker Pro script.

Figure 27-2 shows the dialog box in FileMaker Pro that allows you to specify the AppleScript script you want to run.

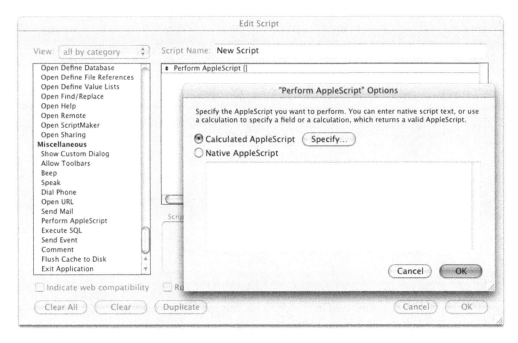

Figure 27-2. *The Perform AppleScript script step in a FileMaker Pro script*

This script step is used to execute AppleScript code in the middle of a FileMaker Pro script. As you can see in Figure 27-2, you have two ways to perform AppleScripts from FileMaker Pro scripts. You can either specify a calculation, whose text result is a valid AppleScript script, or dictate the actual script text.

If you choose to enter the native AppleScript code, FileMaker Pro will attempt to compile your script and check your syntax when you click the OK button. You will be able to exit the dialog box only if the script you entered compiles or if you cancel. Note that unlike other AppleScript editors, FileMaker Pro does not reformat your source code or colorize its keywords after it has been compiled. For instance, if you typed `tell app "Finder"` instead of `tell application "Finder"`, that is the way your source code will remain. Don't worry, though; as long as you can click the OK button, you'll know it has been compiled correctly.

In the case of calculated fields, FileMaker Pro compiles the script right before execution, since the script can change any time leading up to that point.

You can use the Native AppleScript option when you want the database to execute the same script every time. The Calculated AppleScript option is great when you need the database to choose from a selection of prewritten scripts or generate the script's code on the fly; for example, you might want it to run a different script depending on what day of the week it is.

I prefer to put all my scripts into calculation fields—even the ones that could be typed into. That way, whenever I need to make manual changes to a script, I need to edit only a field in the database, rather than having to dig up the original FileMaker Pro script step each time.

See the next section for a few tips regarding using calculation fields with Perform AppleScript script steps.

Working Smart with FileMaker Pro

You can make scripting FileMaker Pro easier and cleaner in a few ways. Here are a few of them.

Default Application

When running AppleScript scripts from a FileMaker Pro script step, FileMaker Pro is considered to be the default application. This means if you choose, you don't have to use the `tell application "FileMaker Pro"` line.

I recommend you do, though, in order to make your scripts also usable outside the context of a FileMaker Pro script. This also lets you write your script in your usual AppleScript editor and then just copy and paste the finished code into FileMaker Pro once you're happy with it. (Writing Apple-Scripts in Script Editor or Script Debugger is a lot nicer than doing it in FileMaker Pro!)

Get the Data and Run

Although AppleScript interaction with applications such as FileMaker Pro is necessary to get the work done, you want to limit this interaction to the minimum. This can speed up your script and make it more efficient.

The way I like to interact with FileMaker Pro is by first getting all the data I need from it using as few commands as possible and then using that data in my script.

For example, it is better to let AppleScript access the data using the `table` object and make heavy use of the `whose` clause in order to filter the record set you want to use, rather than using an AppleScript `repeat` loop through each record one at a time to find the ones you want. See Chapter 25 for additional tips on writing efficient scripts.

Work from Behind

AppleScript scripts that interact with FileMaker Pro work much faster when FileMaker Pro is in the background and the script is in the foreground. This is somewhat true for many applications but makes a big performance difference in FileMaker Pro.

The best way to put FileMaker Pro in the background is to send the script the `activate` command, like this:

```
tell me to activate
```

Use a Dedicated AppleScript Scripts Table

One structural piece I include with some solutions is a separate FileMaker Pro table I call `AppleScript`. In that table, each record contains the text for a different AppleScript script used by the entire database. This gives me easy access to the scripts from a central location, rather than having them buried in lots of different FileMaker Pro script steps.

Avoiding Terminology Conflicts in Embedded AppleScripts

Because FileMaker Pro acts as the default application when you run AppleScript scripts from inside FileMaker Pro, some scripting addition commands normally won't compile because of conflicts with existing keywords in FileMaker Pro's dictionary. For example, FileMaker Pro's dictionary defines `read` and `write` constants for describing the access privileges for tables, records, and so on. This means Standard Additions' `read` and `write` commands don't compile unless you place them in another application's `tell` block, such as the Finder.

Scripting Runtime Labs' MacSQL

In many cases your AppleScript scripts have to connect to different enterprise SQL databases. These databases span Microsoft SQL Server, MySQL, Oracle, FrontBase, OpenBase, Sybase, and others.

When your AppleScript solution calls for integration with a SQL database, one product stands out: Runtime Labs' MacSQL (www.rtlabs.com).

MacSQL is a simple program that gives you GUI access to many flavors of SQL databases, including the few I mentioned previously. In addition to helping you create queries and view the schema of the SQL database, MacSQL is "AppleScriptable" to a point that you can perform any SQL command with AppleScript code. You will, of course, need the proper SQL statements that will get the job done, but these are usually easy to get. The best thing to do, if you are not familiar with SQL syntax, is to find a good reference book that details the syntax of the specific SQL flavor you're using and ask someone from IT to help you get a handle on the SQL statements you need.

Note MacSQL's dictionary has undergone a number of changes since version 2, including significant alterations to the way the do query command works. This means many scripts written for older versions won't work correctly on version 3, and vice versa. This chapter covers version 3 of MacSQL, which is the current release at the time of writing, so if you're using version 2, you will need to modify the following scripts to work correctly there. See MacSQL's dictionary, documentation, and example scripts for additional information.

Getting Connected

The biggest challenge you will face when scripting a SQL database with MacSQL is the initial stage of getting access to your database. Once you're over that part, it's usually smooth sailing.

To get connected, you will need database access settings such as the host, database name, and user login information. Start by choosing File ➤ New. In the New Connection dialog box, shown in Figure 27-3, choose the database type you will be using. Once you do that, MacSQL will display the fields you need to fill in order to establish a connection with your database. Write down the settings you will require, and ask someone from IT for the values to enter.

Figure 27-3. *MacSQL's New Connection dialog box*

After some back and forth action with IT, you should be able to establish a connection with the database. This connection will represent itself in the form of a MacSQL document. Save this document to the hard drive, and keep a note somewhere with the settings the administrator gave you.

The document you saved is your new best friend. Every time your script needs to connect to that database, all you have to do is open that document. Then, you will direct any SQL statement to MacSQL's front document object, which has all the settings.

Speed

I always knew that SQL databases were generally fast, but what surprised me was just how fast I could execute SQL commands with AppleScript in the middle. It would execute tens of operations per second, which may sound slow in SQL terms but is usually fast enough for AppleScript projects that don't need to access the database that often.

Simple select Command

Interacting with SQL databases using MacSQL is a bit more complicated than just using the do query command. Script 27-10 gets data from two fields from the entire contact_table table. Let's look at the script and then analyze it line by line.

Script 27-10.

```
set query_text to "SELECT first_name, last_name FROM contact_table"
tell application "MacSQL3"
    tell front document
        set the_result_set to ¬
            do query query_text results as none with prefetching results
    end tell
    set the_data to values of every row of the_result_set
    delete the_result_set
end tell
return the_data
--> {{"Liz", "Brown"}, {"Jason", "Green"}, ...}
```

The first line of the script is simply the string that makes up the SQL command. Usually, you will be concatenating strings in AppleScript to get to the final SQL statement you want.

Next, you will talk to the front document. Remember, this is the document you saved in the "Getting Connected" section. This script assumes that this document is already open and frontmost in MacSQL.

In the following line, you do the query. You supply the do query command with a direct string parameter that contains the raw SQL command. The SQL statement you use has been put in the variable query_text in the first line of the script.

When the do query command's results as parameter is none and the command is successful, the result is a reference to a result set. A result set is a MacSQL object that can contain rows and columns (more on that later). In this script you assign the reference returned by the do query command to the variable the_result_set. The following line then extracts the values from every row of the result set and assigns the result to the variable the_data.

Now, the value of the variable the_data contains a list of lists, and it contains all the data you fetched from the SQL table.

The last line before the end tell line deletes the result set. This is essential housecleaning. If you don't delete the result set once you've finished with it, MacSQL will jam after a number of queries.

More on Result Sets

Because of the way MacSQL communicates with database applications, result set objects behave a bit differently from other application objects. Depending on the type of database (such as Microsoft SQL Server) and how you use the do query command, the rows of the result set may be "indeterminate"—that is, MacSQL doesn't know how many rows there are or what they contain until you actually ask for each one.

This means a command such as get every row of the_result_set won't work as intended when a result set has indeterminate rows. Instead, you have to loop an unlimited number of times, getting the next row of the result set until an error occurs. You can then trap that error, using it to break out of the repeat loop.

Another option is to use the do query command's prefetching results parameter, as shown in the previous script. If prefetching results is true (the default is false), MacSQL will obtain the data for all the rows from the database in advance. However, the MacSQL documentation warns that this could cause problems if there is a large amount of data, so sometimes you may want to use the looping approach instead.

Script 27-11 is one of the sample scripts that come with MacSQL, which forces you to loop through the rows and then through the items in each row for the purpose of generating a tab-delimited string.

Script 27-11.

```
set theQuery to "select * from foo"
set rs to ""
tell application "MacSQL3"
    tell front document
        set rs to do query theQuery results as none
    end tell
    set d to ""
    set rowNum to 1
    try
        repeat
            set theRow to row rowNum of rs
            set ro to tab delimited values of theRow
            set rowNum to rowNum + 1
            set d to d & ro & (ASCII character 10) --add row and newline
        end repeat
    on error err
    end try
    delete rs
    d
end tell
```

Although this is a good example of the row and result set objects, know that each row object has not only the values property whose value is a list but also the tab delimited values property, which contains the string version of the data in the row.

___

▪Note When working with Microsoft SQL Server, it is important to always retrieve all the rows for a result set; otherwise, it won't behave correctly. If you use prefetching results, this will be done for you; otherwise, you *must* loop through every single row in the result set yourself until no more are found.

___

Clean Up or Go Overboard

As discussed previously, deleting each result set once you're finished with it is essential. Each result set object uses a separate connection to the database, and database applications put a maximum limit on the number of connections you can have open at the same time (the exact number depends on the database setup). So, if you don't clean up after yourself, you will eventually get the error "Connection pool limit reached."

In the next section, note in the subroutine in Script 27-12 that the script attempts to delete the result set if there has been any error in the script. If the error occurred after the result set has been established but before it has been deleted, then you will eventually get that "Connection pool limit reached" error.

MacSQL Subroutines

The following are two subroutines I created for my own use. They use a document pointing at a Microsoft SQL Server database. The first one returns data that the SQL statement gets from the database, and the other one sets data, so it doesn't need to return anything. The following are the subroutines, each with a sample subroutine call.

Script 27-12 gets data from MacSQL.

Script 27-12.

```
set query_text to "SELECT first_name, last_name FROM contact_table"
set the_result to sql_query_select(query_text)

on sql_query_select(query_text)
    try
        tell application "MacSQL3"
            tell front document
                set rs to do query query_text ¬
                    results as none with prefetching results
            end tell
            set the_data to values of every row of rs
            delete rs
        end tell
        return the_data
    on error err_msg number err_num
        --display dialog err_msg & return & query_text
        try
            delete rs
        end try
        error err_msg number err_num
    end try
end sql_query_select
```

And Script 27-13 sets data.

Script 27-13.

```
set query_text to ¬
    "INSERT INTO contact_table (first_name, last_name) VALUES ('Dan', 'Smith')"
set the_result to sql_query_insert(query_text)

on sql_query_insert(query_text)
    try
        tell application "MacSQL3"
            tell front document
                set rs to do query query_text results as none
                delete rs
            end tell       end tell

    on error err_msg number err_num
        try
            delete rs
        end try
        --display dialog err_msg & return & query_text
        error err_msg number err_num
    end try
end sql_query_insert
```

Using ScriptDB

ScriptDB (www.applescriptdb.com) is a new scripting addition that gives you powerful database capabilities within AppleScript. It is created by Custom Flow Solutions, which I own, and it is sold as a commercial product; it is also possible to download a demo of it from www.applescriptdb.com.

Although you can export and import a ScriptDB database to a file, the purpose of it is really to be used in memory. The ScriptDB object is part of your script, and any operation you perform on it returns another ScriptDB object as the result.

You would use ScriptDB to manage any data in your script that needs to be stored and manipulated in a more comprehensive manner than a simple list or record can provide by itself. Among other things, it replaces all those clunky routines you have for sorting lists and finding items in lists, although this is only the tip of what ScriptDB can do.

All commands in the ScriptDB suite start with the letters DB. This makes some commands read a bit funny but ensures that the commands don't collide with other scripting addition or Apple-Script commands.

ScriptDB is also fully Unicode compliant, so databases can contain text from different languages without any special setup.

In this section, you will look at some of the capabilities of ScriptDB and see why it should be a staple in anyone's tool chest.

Classes and Commands

ScriptDB has custom records that represent a database, a field, a record, and other smaller related objects. The ScriptDB object is the main record object used by the scripting addition. Its main properties are DBName, DBFields, and DBData.

The DBFields property is a list made of field definitions. You specify those definitions when you create the database.

Creating a Database

You can create a ScriptDB database in two ways: you can either create it from scratch or load an existing file. The file can be a tab-delimited text file or an XML file exported from either ScriptDB or FileMaker Pro. ScriptDB can also export data to these formats.

The script that follows creates a simple database called contacts with three fields: first name, age, and date of birth:

```
set field_list to ¬
    {{"first name", string}, {"married", boolean}, {"age", integer}}
set my_db to DB create with properties ¬
    {DBName:"contacts", DBFields:field_list}
```

This is the resulting database object:

```
{class:ScriptDB, DBName:"contacts", ➡
    DBFields:{ ➡
        {DBFieldName:"first name", DBFieldClass:string}, ➡
        {DBFieldName:"married", DBFieldClass:boolean}, ➡
        {DBFieldName:"age", DBFieldClass:integer} ➡
    }, ➡
    DBData:{} ➡
}
```

Although the resulting data structure is a bit complex, it is easy to extract data from it when you need to do so. In the result, each field is no longer a simple list but rather a record. This, however, shouldn't concern you at this point.

Database Management and Variables

Almost every operation you perform with ScriptDB returns a modified ScriptDB object. This means, for example, that after you use the DB add record command, the command will return a fresh copy of the database object you gave it with a new record added.

Note Using a scripting addition command to add a new record might seem overly complex when AppleScript already allows you to append items to lists directly. You should always use ScriptDB's commands to perform these sorts of operations, however, because ScriptDB will ensure your new data is valid before it's added to the database or complain if it isn't. If you bypass these commands and attempt to change the data structures directly, you won't get this automatic checking, and any mistakes you make will damage the integrity of your data.

As with other AppleScript statements, if you keep assigning the result to the same variable, you will write over the last version of the database.

In the preceding example, you assign the resulting database to the variable my_db. From now on, whenever you want to perform any operation on that database, you will need to use the my_db variable.

Adding Data to Your Database and Deleting It

You can add one record at a time, one field at a time, or multiple records at once.

To add a single record, you use the DB add record command. The following statement adds a single record to the database:

```
set my_db to DB add record {"James", true, 28} to db my_db
```

The DBData property of the ScriptDB object will now be as follows:

```
DBData:{{"James", true, 28}}
```

You can also add multiple records with the DB add records command. You use the DB add records command the same way, only you supply a list of lists, with each sublist representing a database record, like the one shown here:

```
{{"James", true, 28},{"Joan", false, 24},{"Mario", false, 15}}
```

Let's assume you added these three records to the database. To delete a record, you can use the DB delete records command. The DB delete records command can be simple but also powerful. In the following statement, you delete the second record from the database:

```
set my_db to DB delete records from db my_db number 2
```

To delete multiple records by their number, simply supply a list of records.

But what if you want to delete records based on their data? For instance, what if you want to delete all the records of people younger than 18? Here's how you'd do that:

```
set my_db to DB delete records from db my_db where {"field(age)", "<", 18}
```

Finding Data

ScriptDB allows you to find data subsets that can be returned as a list of lists, as a new ScriptDB object, or as row numbers, representing the rows in which the matching data exists.

You do that with the DB get data command, which has some unique parameters for maximum flexibility.

Narrow the Field

The first way to restrict your search is by specifying the records and/or fields from which you want the data. This may be all you need to do.

For instance, if you want just the second record, you can write this:

```
DB get data from db my_db in records 2
```

For record ranges, use a string with dashes to specify a range and comma to separate ranges:

```
DB get data from db my_db in records "20-30, 45-55"
```

This can be useful since you can use AppleScript to create the range string on the fly.

Use the fields parameter to restrict the returned result to specific fields:

```
DB get data from db my_db fields "age"
--> {28, 24, 15}
```

Or specify multiple fields by name or position:

```
DB get data from db my_db fields {1, "married"}
--> {{"James", true}, {"Joan", false}, {"Mario", false}}
```

You can also mix the in records and fields parameters, like this:

```
DB get data from db my_db in records "1,2" fields {1, "married"}
--> {{"James", true}, {"Joan", false}}
```

Search by Criteria

The most powerful search option is the use of the where parameter, which is a list describing the test or tests to perform. (Think of it as the ScriptDB scripting addition's equivalent to an application's whose clause.) This list may seem a bit awkward at first, but it does give you some great flexibility for finding data in your ScriptDB database object.

The list consists of fields names, math and comparison operators, values, and Boolean operators such as OR and AND. You must write field names and operators as strings. The following are a few examples of searches:

```
DB get data from db my_db where {"field(age)", "<", 55}
```

And also the following:

```
DB get data from db my_db ¬
    where {{"field(married)", "=", false}, "AND", {"field(age)", ">", 18}}
```

Now, match that with the previous parameters, in records and fields, and you can pinpoint any data in your lists. For instance, to get the name of the only single person older than 21 in the database, use the following search:

```
DB get data from db my_db ¬
    fields "first name" ¬
    where {{"field(married)", "=", false}, "AND", {"field(age)", ">", 18}}
--> {"Joan"}
```

Search Result Formats

When you perform a search, you can ask for the data as a list of lists, a list of row numbers, or as a ScriptDB object. To specify the result, you use the as parameter. The as parameter can have the following values, which correspond to the items mentioned previously: database, data only, or row numbers.

When you ask for the result as data only, which is also the default, you have the choice of transposing the data. For example, if the result would have been this:

```
{{"James", true}, {"Joan", false}, {"Mario", false}}
```

then asking for it transposed would return this:

```
{{"James", "Joan", "Mario"}, {true, false, false}}
```

Sorting Data

The DB sort db command sorts the records in your database object. You can sort by any number of fields and refer to them by name or number. Here is an example of a database sorted by the first name field:

```
set my_sorted_db to DB sort db my_db by "first name"
```

To sort by descending order, you can put a minus sign before the field name or number. If you specify fields by name, then the minus sign has to be inside the quotes, like this:

```
set my_sorted_db to DB sort db my_db by "-first name"
```

You can also supply a list of fields to sort by:

```
set my_sorted_db to DB sort db my_db by {2, "-first name", -3}
```

The preceding example will sort first by the second field, then by the field first name in descending order, and then by the third field in descending order.

Adding and Deleting Fields

When you write scripts, you keep a lot of the script data in lists. Each database record is represented as an AppleScript list, with each item in the list representing a specific field in that record.

This is why it is useful to be able to add fields to and delete them from a ScriptDB object.

Let's say you created the database with three records that look like this:

```
{{"James", true, 28}, {"Joan", false, 24}, {"Mario", false, 15}}
```

The data here is really three fields: first name, married, and age. To add a gender field, you can use this command:

```
set my_db to DB add field {"gender", string} to db my_db with data {"M", "F", "M"}
```

The new ScriptDB object now contains the following record data:

```
{{"James", true, 28, "M"}, {"Joan", false, 24, "F"}, ➡
{"Mario", false, 15, "M"}}
```

If you want, you can get the data transposed, like this:

```
DB get data from db my_db with transposed
--> {{"James", "Joan", "Mario"}, {true, false, false}, ➡
{28, 24, 15}, {"M", "F", "M"}}
```

You can also specify a default value via the optional using default parameter, in case the list is not long enough or you provide no data at all.

To delete a field, use the DB remove field command, like this:

```
DB remove field "married" from db my_db
```

Working with Files

ScriptDB allows you to save and load database files. You can use either XML or a tab-delimited format. The DB save and DB load commands allow you to specify the format and delimiters for the text file. The neat feature is that ScriptDB uses a FileMaker Pro–compliant XML format, so you can load XML files exported by FileMaker Pro and have all the field formats preserved. You can also export the data from ScriptDB in XML and then import that XML file right into a FileMaker Pro database or just open it with FileMaker Pro.

Database Events

One of the new features added to the Mac OS with the arrival of Tiger is Database Events scripting. Database Events is a small faceless application based on the SQLite database that is a part of the operating system. Although Database Events uses SQL as the back end, it really doesn't allow you to script SQLite but rather use SQLite for the limited functionality provided by the Database Events suite.

Database Events scripting allows you to create databases that are stored in files. The database name and folder path you specify while creating them determine the file path where the data is stored. Each record in the database is created individually and can contain any number of field elements, each of which has its own name and value properties.

Database Events Classes and Commands

You can find the Database Events application in /System/Library/CoreServices/. Here are the database-related classes from its dictionary:

```
Class database:
  A collection of records, residing at a location in the file system
Plural form: databases
Elements:
  record by name, by numeric index, before/after another element,
  as a range of elements, satisfying a test, by ID
Superclasses: item
Properties:
  class type class [r/o]
    -- (inherited from the "item" class) The class of the object.
  properties record
    -- (inherited from the "item" class) All of the object's properties.
  location alias [r/o] -- the folder that contains the database
  name Unicode text [r/o] -- the name of the database

Class record: A collection of fields, residing in a database
Plural form: records
Elements:
  field by name, by numeric index, before/after another element,
  as a range of elements, satisfying a test
Superclasses: item
Properties:
  class type class [r/o]
    -- (inherited from the "item" class) The class of the object.
  properties record
    -- (inherited from the "item" class) All of the object's properties.
  id integer [r/o] -- the unique id of the record
  name Unicode text [r/o]
    -- the name of the record, equivalent to the value of the field named "name"

Class field: A named piece of data, residing in a record
Plural form: fields
Superclasses: item
Properties:
  class type class [r/o]
    -- (inherited from the "item" class) The class of the object.
  properties record
    -- (inherited from the "item" class) All of the object's properties.
  name Unicode text [r/o] -- the name of the field
  value anything -- the value of the field
```

As you can see from the dictionary, there are three main classes, besides the application class, of course. These classes are database, record, and field. Unlike FileMaker Pro, there is no table class or cell class. Also, Database Events doesn't require that neighboring records all have the same structure. Each record can have completely different fields, with different names and data types.

To see how Database Events scripting works, let's create two scripts: one will be create the database and populate it with records, fields, and data; the second script will read the data.

Script 27-14 will create a database named cars and will have two records; each record will hold information about one car in three fields, say, make, model, and year. When the script is run, a file named cars.dbev will be created automatically on your desktop if it doesn't already exist; otherwise, the existing file will be used.

Script 27-14.

```
set theFolder to path to desktop
tell application "Database Events"
  set theDB to make new database with properties {name:"cars", location:theFolder}
  tell theDB
    set theRecord to make new record with properties {name:"Toyota"}
    make new record with properties {name:"Mercedes"}
  end tell
  tell theRecord
    make new field with properties {name:"Make", value:"Toyota"}
    make new field with properties {name:"Model", value:"Camry"}
    make new field with properties {name:"Year", value:1993}
  end tell
  tell record "Mercedes" of theDB
    make new field with properties {name:"Make", value:"Mercedes-Benz"}
    make new field with properties {name:"Model", value:"300TD"}
    make new field with properties {name:"Year", value:1997}
  end tell
  save theDB
end tell
```

Let's take a look at a few points in this script. First, note the use of variables for referencing database elements and the database object itself. The script starts by creating a new database and assigning it to the theDB variable. Later in the script, you refer to the database using this variable.

Also, references to the records you create in the database are assigned to variables as they are created. The first record the script adds fields to is assigned to, and later referenced, using the variable theRecord. The second record isn't assigned a variable. Instead, it's referenced using its name in the script line tell record "Mercedes" of theDB.

The last command in the script is the save command: save theDB. This line saves the changes to the cars.dbev database file on your desktop.

The following script will get data from a single field from the database:

```
tell application "Database Events"
  tell database "~/Desktop/cars.dbev"
    set carModel to value of field "Model" of record "Mercedes"
  end tell
end tell
carModel --> "300TD"
```

Notice how you identify the database using a POSIX path to the existing database file. The ~ character is shorthand for the path to the current user's home folder, which Database Events understands.

After you established a link with the database, you can go down the object hierarchy: database ➤ record ➤ field.

Although Database Events doesn't provide any way to execute SQL commands, it supports the usual range of AppleScript reference forms, allowing you to perform basic database-style operations. For example, to get the make of every car, use this:

```
tell application "Database Events"
    tell database "~/Desktop/cars.dbev"
        set carMakes to value of field "Make" of every record
    end tell
end tell
carMakes --> {"Toyota", "Mercedes-Benz"}
```

Remember, though, that Database Events doesn't require every record in a database to contain the same fields, so this script will work only if all records contain a field named Make.

Similarly, to delete all the records for cars made before 1995, use this:

```
tell application "Database Events"
    tell database "~/Desktop/cars.dbev"
        delete every record whose value of field "Year" < 1995
    end tell
end tell
```

To extract all the values from the database as a list of lists (assuming that every record contains identically named fields in the same order), use this:

```
tell application "Database Events"
    tell database "~/Desktop/cars.dbev"
        set field_names to name of every field of first record
        -- field_names contains {"name", "Make", "Model", "Year"}
        set record_values to value of every field of every record
    end tell
end tell
record_values --> {{"Toyota", "Toyota", "Camry", 1993}, ➡
{"Mercedes", "Mercedes-Benz", "300TD", 1997}}
```

CHAPTER 28

■ ■ ■

Using Smile: The AppleScript Integrated Production Environment

Emmanuel Lévy from Satimage-software contributed this chapter. Satimage, located in Paris, is the creator of Smile.

Smile is an integrated development environment (IDE) for writing and executing scripts and much more. You can download Smile from www.satimage.fr/software.

Introducing Smile

In the following sections, I'll introduce you to Smile and its main features.

Introducing Smile's Integrated Engine Architecture

Smile can perform many tasks for you, and although the interface of Smile looks simple—the menus are not especially long, and the dialog boxes do not have loads of buttons and pop-up lists—Smile is not a huge download. How does that work? Well, most of Smile's features, including some of the more powerful ones, do not have an interface but are available in the software, waiting for you to call them in a script.

Smile's interface was designed to help you edit and test your scripts efficiently. For instance, if you are writing a script to process text files, Smile lets you test it in a text window first. And when you make a PDF or an image, you view the document in a window as you are building it.

Smile's architecture enables it to offer a particularly wide range of well-implemented technologies. Indeed, when you work with Smile, you work simultaneously with the following:

- An editor (and runner) of scripted Aqua interfaces, including palettes that you can associate with any application.

- A text editor supporting both styled ASCII text and Unicode, including an extended Extensible Markup Language (XML) validator. Specifically, *styled text* refers to styled MacRoman ASCII, and *Unicode* refers to UTF-8 and UTF-16. That said, Smile can convert between the various high ASCII encodings such as ISO-8859-1, the "PC encoding."

- A text search-and-replace tool for ASCII text and Unicode.

- A regular expression engine for ASCII text and Unicode.

- An XML engine.

- A graphic generation engine capable of producing high-quality vector PDFs, JPEGs, and movies.

- A scientific environment with fast computational libraries for numbers and for arrays of numbers.

- A data visualization environment with the finest features: ready-to-publish vector PDF production, default settings of professional quality, 1D, 2D, and 3D plots; 3D objects library; 3D triangular mesh generation; easy animations; easy customization of figures using the graphic generation engine; Unicode support; and more.

- An industrial interface able to handle RS232 serial communication and some digital input/output (I/O) universal serial bus (USB) devices.

Since you control everything by script, you can use any of these technologies in any automated process.

Introducing Smile's Terminal

To operate the various features available in Smile, you communicate with your machine through the AppleScript language. To that effect, Smile includes a unique command-line interpreter for AppleScript. Smile's command-line interpreter, called AppleScript Terminal, is basically a modified version of the Terminal window.

Smile does include a script editor for AppleScript, but Smile's AppleScript Terminal is more than that—it's a fully interactive command-line environment. In fact, even if you don't use any of Smile's special features, you will still find it helpful to use Smile's AppleScript Terminal as the environment in which to control your machine: the Finder, the shell commands, the OSAX, and your preferred applications.

Why Should You Use Smile?

Smile is the perfect complement to AppleScript because it makes the most of some of AppleScript's features:

- AppleScript supports persistent contexts. Smile embeds you in a context that augments as you work. You can see the benefits right away and also in the long term. In other words, once you program a routine, it is straightforward to include it in the context as a library. Smile's context is itself a script, and you can dynamically load new handlers into that context easily.

- In AppleScript, you can compile and execute in one operation a single line or a block of lines. In the standard Script Editor, you must run all lines every time, but Smile is way more versatile—in Smile's AppleScript Terminal, you can run any part of a script independently, and that execution will happen in a persistent context.

- In AppleScript, scripts are scriptable. Any script, running or not, is an object (it owns handlers and properties) that can be scripted. A script can send commands to another script and change its properties. Furthermore, whether it's running or not, a script retains its current state. All of Smile's objects (including the application itself) are scriptable objects; each one has its own script, which can provide it with specific properties and behaviors.

- An AppleScript program supports handling quantities belonging to any class, including classes that did not even exist at the time the program was written. For instance, it will seem natural to the AppleScript user that the same commands that used to work with ASCII now work transparently with Unicode text.

Downloading Smile

Smile is available in two distributions: the standard edition (free) and the full edition. The full edition includes all the features of the standard edition plus some additional features (SmileLab and Smile Server as of Smile 3.1.9) that require paid registration licenses. I recommend you download the full edition, since the full edition is required for some of the examples in this chapter. However, if you download the full edition and do not pay to register, the SmileLab features will run in demo mode, which is enough for testing all the examples in this chapter.

To install Smile, visit Smile's home page at `www.satimage-software.com/en/index.html`, where you can download an installer. Usually, when the download is complete, an image disk will automatically mount in a new Finder window. If no image disk mounts, double-click the .dmg file you downloaded. The image disk contains one file, the installer package. Double-click that file, which will launch Smile's installer. To install Smile, just follow the instructions in the installer.

■**Note** I've gathered the script samples in this chapter into one text file, which you can download from `www.apress.com` or from `www.satimage-software.com/downloads/hr_book_samples_v2.html`. If the file does not expand by itself once downloaded, double-click its icon. It will then expand into a (Smile) text document named `hr_book_samples`.

Using Smile

The following sections will get you a bit more familiar with Smile and some of its components.

Using the AppleScript Command-Line Environment

Launch Smile by double-clicking the saucer icon in `/Applications/Smile/`. If this is the first time you are launching a copy of the full edition of Smile, a splash screen offers several options that introduce Smile's features. You can practice a moment using the splash screen and then proceed.

Smile's primary tool is its unique AppleScript Terminal. This text window is an interpreter for AppleScript; pressing the Return key executes the current line or the selected lines. To run a single line, you do not need to select the line. When no text is selected, the Return key runs the line where the insertion point is located, and then the insertion point moves to the beginning of the next line, making it natural to run a script line by line (see Figure 28-1).

Try it—open `hr_book_samples`, found in the code download for this book, and click somewhere in the first uncommented line:

tell application "Finder" to set x to name of startup disk

When the cursor is blinking somewhere in the line, press Return. Now the cursor is blinking at the beginning of the following line:

display dialog "The startup disk's name is " & x

Press the Return key again. As you can see, Smile remembers the value of x, which you would not expect if you were working in another script editor.

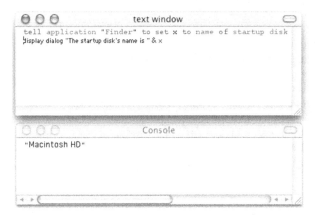

Figure 28-1. *A line is compiled and executed by pressing Return, and the result is then displayed in the console.*

■ **Note** The preceding example was possible because Smile maintains a persistent AppleScript context. When you run one line or a block of lines in the AppleScript Terminal, that is, in a text window, the variables and handlers remain defined until you quit. They are available at a global level, that is, to any script running from any text window. You'll get familiar with this as you work more with Smile.

Now type in these two lines:

```
set pdf_url to "http://www.satimage-software.com/downloads/mc0306.pdf"
set pdf_file to ((path to desktop) as text) & "mc0306.pdf"
```

Click anywhere in the first line to put the insertion point in that line. Press the Return key twice. Now pdf_url and pdf_file are defined. Unless you assign them different values later, their contents will be preserved.

If your computer is connected to the Internet, you can now execute the following line. Choose to copy it first in a new text window; you can check that all text windows share the same context.

```
do shell script "curl " & pdf_url & " -L -o " & (get POSIX path of pdf_file)
```

This will download a PDF file that you will use in the "A Tutorial: Making a Tool to Add Text to an Existing PDF Document" section later in this chapter. As long as the command executes, the script is suspended; the insertion point will blink again once the download is complete. As you see, the latest line uses the variables that were defined in a previous run. In the PDF application you'll build in this chapter, you will use the pdf_file variable again.

Such variables compiled on the fly in text windows live in Smile's persistent context.

Using Smile's Custom Dialog Boxes

Smile consists of an editor—and creator of graphical interfaces—known as Smile's *custom dialog boxes*. Later in the chapter, I'll show you how to create a graphical interface, but I suggest you experiment now with custom dialog boxes. In the following two sections, I'll show you how to create a simple application interface to display a date. It should take you less than one minute.

Creating the Interface

To create the user interface, do the following:

1. Select File ➤ New Dialog. This opens a new dialog box and also the Controls palette (which is a Smile dialog box).

2. Click the New button in the Controls palette, and drag it to the empty dialog box.

3. Close the Controls palette.

4. Double-click New button, and enter **Date & time** for its name.

Programming the Functionality

The interface of the first dialog box is final; let's program it now:

1. Select Dialogs ➤ Edit Dialog Script. This opens a new colored window, which will contain the dialog box's script.

■**Note** Alternatively, click anywhere in the dialog box (don't click a button, though) with the Cmd and Opt keys pressed, like with HyperCard.

---

2. By default the dialog box's script contains two empty handlers: prepare and click in. Remove the prepare handler. In the click in handler, insert the following line:

   ```
   dd(current date)
   ```

3. Verify that your handler now looks like this:

   ```
   on click in theDialog item number i
   dd(current date)
   end click in
   ```

4. Next, select File ➤ Save to save the script, and then select File ➤ Close to close the script's window.

5. Select Edit ➤ Edit Mode to toggle your dialog box from edit mode to normal mode. You should also now save the dialog box to disk, so select File ➤ Save. Then provide a name.

6. You can now test your first dialog box by clicking the button. Doing this will send the click in event to the dialog box, which will execute your script line. Figure 28-2 shows the dialog box and script.

Note that your script uses dd, a term not included in native AppleScript. Smile's built-in libraries include a number of handy terms documented in the Help menu. To get information about a specific term such as dd, select the term, and then select Edit ➤ Find Definition (or press Cmd+Shift+F). Find Definition is also available in the contextual menu.

Figure 28-2. *The simplest working dialog box ever: one button, one line of script*

Using Regular Expressions

Smile offers an AppleScript implementation of regular expressions, which supports both ASCII text (MacRoman) and Unicode. Regular expressions (known as grep in the Unix systems) are the basic tools for most text-matching tasks, such as extracting a given substring or finding all the e-mail addresses contained in a file; therefore, they are useful in a wide range of situations.

The Find dialog box understands regular expressions and is the best place to test a regular expression on text windows before using it in a script. The same Find dialog box works both in text windows and in Unicode dialog boxes.

Next, try the Find dialog box:

1. Select Edit ➤ Find. This opens the Find dialog box.

2. Enter **[0-9]+** as the Find string.

3. Enable the Regular Expression check box.

4. Click Find.

This will find the next sequence of several (+) digits ([0-9]) in the front window.

The script to perform the same task implies using the find text command. Make sure the dialog box just behind hr_book_samples is a text window, and execute the following line:

```
find text "[0-9]+" in window 2 with regexp, string result and all occurrences
```

Note that you can replace window 2 with a reference to a file.

Figure 28-3 shows an example of a regular expression script statement that looks for Devanagari letters.

Figure 28-3. *In Smile, the regular expressions understand Unicode.*

If you are curious to experiment further with regular expressions, you will want to have the list of the regular expressions' metacharacters handy. You will find one in the pop-up list in the Find dialog box, on the right of the Regular Expression check box.

Satimage's website provides exhaustive documentation on regular expressions. You can find it at www.satimage-software.com/en/reg_exp.html.

Using the Graphic Engine

Smile includes an AppleScript PDF graphic library. This is the facet of Smile that you will explore most in the "A Tutorial: Making a Tool to Add Text to an Existing PDF Document" section. Here, you'll get a small taste of it first.

In the hr_book_samples window, select the block shown in Script 28-1, and press the Return key.

Script 28-1.

```
set c to {250, 250}
set r to 100
set i to first character of (system attribute "USER")
BeginFigure(0)
SetPenColor({1 / 8, 1 / 4, 1 / 2})
SetFillColor({1 / 4, 1 / 2, 1, 1 / 2})
CirclePath(c, r)
DrawPath("fill-stroke") -- or: 3
TextMoveTo(c)
SetTextSize(1.5 * r)
SetTextFont("Courier")
SetFillGray(1)
DrawString("[h]" & i)
DrawPath("fill") -- or: 0
EndFigure()
```

Running this script will create the image shown in Figure 28-4. Alternatively, you can produce JPEGs, BMPs, PNGs (often an optimal solution for synthetic graphics), and so on, as well as Apple QuickTime movies.

Figure 28-4. *By default, saving a drawing in Smile makes a PDF document.*

Here you are using Smile's graphic library: BeginFigure(0) prepares a default graphic window for drawing. SetPenColor and SetFillColor let you specify a color, either as RGB or as RGB-alpha (alpha being the opacity).

In a PDF document, you define shapes (*paths*), and then you draw them—usually in "stroke" mode or in "fill" mode. However, you have other options. Here CirclePath defines a circular path, with the center and radius as specified in pixels (1 pixel equals 1/72 inch), and then DrawPath draws it, using the current graphical settings such as the pen color and fill color.

Finally, EndFigure is what terminates the PDF record and displays the final graphic in the default graphic window.

Again, if you are curious about a particular term, select the term, and then press Cmd+Shift+F (or select Edit ➤ Find Definition). To open the documentation for the graphic engine, use the Help menu, and follow the links.

Working with XML

XML is a cross-platform data format. For more information about XML, the best place to go is www.w3.org.

Smile offers an AppleScript implementation of the XML Document Object Model (DOM) to browse and edit XML documents by script, which supports several useful XML technologies such as XPath (to perform sophisticated searches in XML documents) and Extensible Style Language Transformations (XSLT, to transform your XML documents into other structures, HTML [Hypertext Markup Language], or entirely different markup languages) and which supports several kinds of validations (syntactic validation, DTD conformance, Schema, and RelaxNG validation). Smile's XML Suite works with references to the nodes rather than with data: for this reason, the XML Suite is able to work with very large XML files.

In Unicode windows, you can edit XML files such as XHTML files written as Unicode, or *plist* files. Smile's Unicode windows check an XML document's syntax. To check the syntax of an XML document in a Unicode window, press the Return key. If Smile detects an XML error, it will select the line where the error occurred, and it will display the error message. Pressing Cmd+Return checks the validity of the XML with respect to its DTD. Checking an XML document frequently while you are editing it may save you time.

Using SmileLab

Smile includes graphical objects for numerical data visualization and additional libraries that go together to form SmileLab. The graphical objects can make curves, plots, color maps, 3D surfaces, and so on, to represent numerical data and to change them into PDF vector graphics.

Smile also has a set of mathematical functions that allows you to program, in AppleScript, C-fast computations on numbers and on arrays.

Next, you will learn how to generate some data and then plot it.

Note Script 28-2 requires the full version of Smile. Demo mode is enough, though.

Enter Script 28-2, or find it in the code download, in the hr_book_samples file.

Script 28-2.

```
-- create data
set n to 1000
set x to createarray n
set y to runningsum (randomarray n range {-1, 1})
set y to multlist y with sqrt (3)

-- display data as a curve
set c to QuickCurve(x, y, 0)
set v to c's container -- the curve belongs to a plot ...
set w to v's container -- ... which belongs to a window

-- display equations as curves
set c1 to QuickCurve(x, "sqrt(x)", v)
set c2 to QuickCurve(x, "-sqrt(x)", v)

-- customize appearance
set name of v to "A random walk of " & n & " steps"
set legend kind of v to 3
set legend abscissa of v to n / 2
set legend text size of v to 14
set legend fill color of v to {1, 1, 1, 1}
set label text size of v to 14
set xlabel of v to "n"
set name of c to "\\Sigma_{i=1.." & n & "}\\ Rnd_i"
set name of c1 to "n^{1/2}"
set name of c2 to "-n^{1/2}"
draw w
```

Run the whole script (or run it block by block if you'd like—you can run a block by pressing the Return key once the lines are selected). Figure 28-5 shows the results.

Block 1 creates the data. Smile introduces a datatype equivalent to an AppleScript list of numbers such as {1.0, pi, 300}, the array of real. Computations on arrays of real are fast, and arrays of real have virtually no size limit (AppleScript native lists are not adapted for extensive calculations).

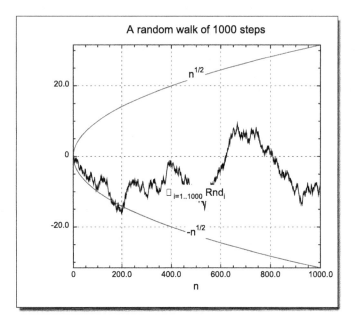

Figure 28-5. *In many situations the default settings are perfectly adapted, which makes scripts shorter.*

createarray is one way of making a new array of reals. By default, createarray n creates an array of the n-first integers. The dictionary shows that createarray accepts optional parameters. To view the entry for createarray in the dictionary where it belongs (namely, the dictionary of the Satimage OSAX), select createarray, and then press Cmd+Shift+F (or select Edit ➤ Find definition or use the contextual menu.)

As its name suggests, randomarray returns an array of random numbers in the given range, [-1 .. 1].

y contains * as its item of rank k, the sum of the previous k random numbers. This is called a *random walk* (on the line); after k steps, the random walker's position may be any value between -k and k.

Block 2 will display the random walk as a curve: position vs. time. QuickCurve belongs to QuickPlotLib, a library included with SmileLab: pressing Cmd+Shift+F on QuickCurve will open the documentation for the command.

As you see, the curve you made lives in a plot view, which in turn requires a graphic window to exist.

Which class of objects may contain which other class of objects is part of the information that the dictionary supplies: select Smile ➤ Smile dictionary, and then use the Index menu in the dictionary's toolbar to view the entry for curve. Be aware that the entry for a given class shows which classes of objects it can contain (its elements), not which class of object can contain itself (its container).

Note If you prefer to use dictionaries with hypertext links, use the online versions, available at www.satimage.fr/software/en/dicts.html.

Scientists know that a random walk (with n steps chosen randomly in [-1 .. 1]) will essentially scale like √n. Let's confirm the fact and plot the two curves -√n and +√n: this is what the two lines in block 3 do. You can run the script several times to observe different draws. Also, you can increase n.

Finally, the fourth block controls the visual appearance of the graph; you can adjust each visual feature of an object by setting the corresponding property to the desired value. The Graphic Settings dialog box has a script button to generate such scripts automatically. The list of the properties of an object in a given class is provided in the dictionary, in the entry for that class. To view the entry for a given class, you do the same as when viewing the entry for a given command: select the class's name, such as plot view, and then press Cmd+Shift+F.

Smile is one of the few software packages that implements AppleScript's properties property feature, intended for setting several (and getting all) properties in one instruction.

Here's an example:

```
set properties of v to ¬
    {name:"A random walk of " & n & " steps", ¬
    legend kind:3, legend abscissa:n / 2, legend text size:14, ¬
    legend fill color:{1, 1, 1, 1}, label text size:14, xlabel:"n"}
```

You can use this as a shortcut for the following:

```
set name of v to "A random walk of " & n & " steps"
set legend kind of v to 3
set legend abscissa of v to n / 2
set legend text size of v to 14
set legend fill color of v to {1, 1, 1, 1}
set label text size of v to 14
set xlabel of v to "n"
```

A Tutorial: Making a Tool to Add Text to an Existing PDF Document

You'll now learn how to make a program in Smile to add some text to a PDF document. Usually, you'd do this with Adobe Acrobat. However, Acrobat is not free, so it's great to be able to write a program to update PDFs for free! So that you can test your program on a real PDF document as you develop it, you have been given clearance by the state of California to use one of its forms from the Department of Health Services. However, you can use any PDF document for this tutorial.

Preparing the PDF

If you ran the sample scripts earlier in the chapter, the PDF file should already be downloaded to your desktop, and its path will be stored in the pdf_file variable.

Otherwise (or if you have quit Smile since), execute the following lines to download the PDF file to your desktop (remember that you need to be connected to the Internet):

```
set pdf_url to ¬
    "http://www.satimage-software.com/downloads/mc0306.pdf"
set pdf_file to ((path to desktop) as text) & "mc0306.pdf"
do shell script "curl " & pdf_url & " -L -o " & (get POSIX path of pdf_file)
```

If you want to use another file, store its path (as a string) in the `pdf_file` variable. It's useful to know that dropping a file on a text window inserts its path in the window.

Now open the PDF file in Smile (see Figure 28-6). If you double-click the file's icon, Finder will choose to open it in Acrobat Reader or in Preview; let's explicitly tell Smile to open it. Execute the following line:

```
set w to open pdf_file
```

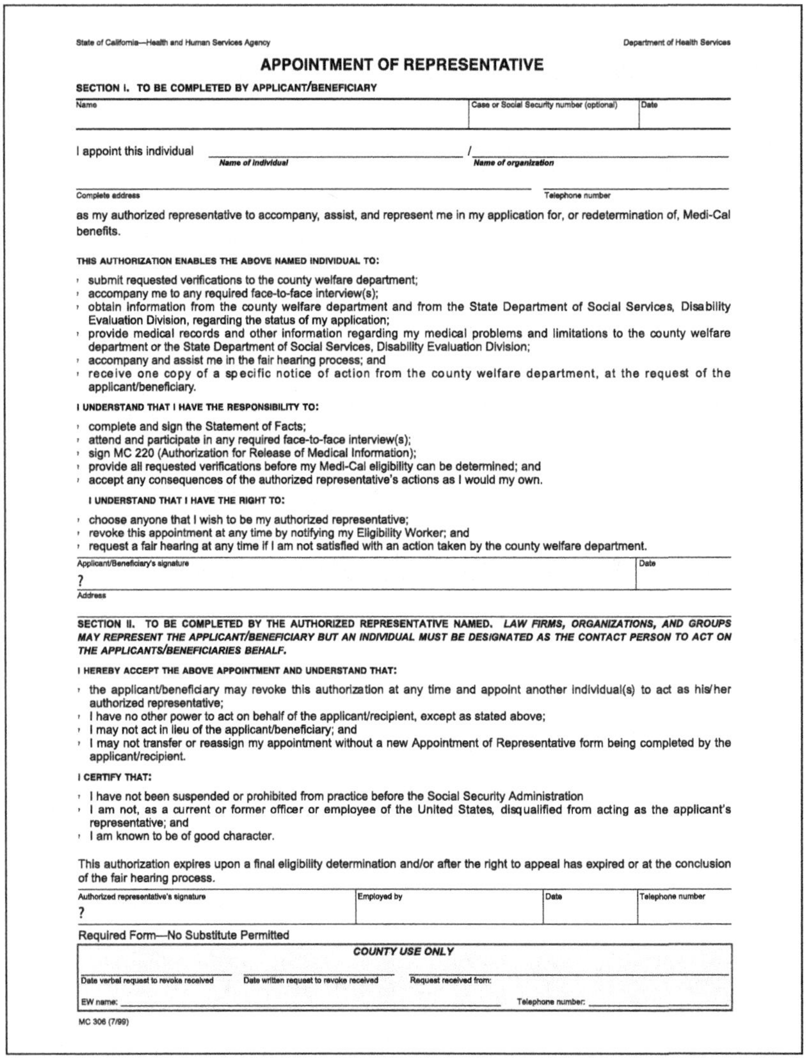

State of California—Health and Human Services Agency   Department of Health Services

APPOINTMENT OF REPRESENTATIVE

SECTION I. TO BE COMPLETED BY APPLICANT/BENEFICIARY

Name | Case or Social Security number (optional) | Date

I appoint this individual ______ / ______
Name of individual   Name of organization

Complete address   Telephone number

as my authorized representative to accompany, assist, and represent me in my application for, or redetermination of, Medi-Cal benefits.

THIS AUTHORIZATION ENABLES THE ABOVE NAMED INDIVIDUAL TO:

- submit requested verifications to the county welfare department;
- accompany me to any required face-to-face interview(s);
- obtain information from the county welfare department and from the State Department of Social Services, Disability Evaluation Division, regarding the status of my application;
- provide medical records and other information regarding my medical problems and limitations to the county welfare department or the State Department of Social Services, Disability Evaluation Division;
- accompany and assist me in the fair hearing process; and
- receive one copy of a specific notice of action from the county welfare department, at the request of the applicant/beneficiary.

I UNDERSTAND THAT I HAVE THE RESPONSIBILITY TO:

- complete and sign the Statement of Facts;
- attend and participate in any required face-to-face interview(s);
- sign MC 220 (Authorization for Release of Medical Information);
- provide all requested verifications before my Medi-Cal eligibility can be determined; and
- accept any consequences of the authorized representative's actions as I would my own.

I UNDERSTAND THAT I HAVE THE RIGHT TO:

- choose anyone that I wish to be my authorized representative;
- revoke this appointment at any time by notifying my Eligibility Worker; and
- request a fair hearing at any time if I am not satisfied with an action taken by the county welfare department.

Applicant/Beneficiary's signature | Date
?
Address

SECTION II. TO BE COMPLETED BY THE AUTHORIZED REPRESENTATIVE NAMED. *LAW FIRMS, ORGANIZATIONS, AND GROUPS MAY REPRESENT THE APPLICANT/BENEFICIARY BUT AN INDIVIDUAL MUST BE DESIGNATED AS THE CONTACT PERSON TO ACT ON THE APPLICANTS/BENEFICIARIES BEHALF.*

I HEREBY ACCEPT THE ABOVE APPOINTMENT AND UNDERSTAND THAT:

- the applicant/beneficiary may revoke this authorization at any time and appoint another individual(s) to act as his/her authorized representative;
- I have no other power to act on behalf of the applicant/recipient, except as stated above;
- I may not act in lieu of the applicant/beneficiary; and
- I may not transfer or reassign my appointment without a new Appointment of Representative form being completed by the applicant/recipient.

I CERTIFY THAT:

- I have not been suspended or prohibited from practice before the Social Security Administration
- I am not, as a current or former officer or employee of the United States, disqualified from acting as the applicant's representative; and
- I am known to be of good character.

This authorization expires upon a final eligibility determination and/or after the right to appeal has expired or at the conclusion of the fair hearing process.

Authorized representative's signature | Employed by | Date | Telephone number
?

Required Form—No Substitute Permitted

COUNTY USE ONLY

Date verbal request to revoke received | Date written request to revoke received | Request received from:

EW name: ______ Telephone number: ______

MC 306 (7/99)

Figure 28-6. *Smile opens PDF files in graphic windows, where you can make custom graphics.*

As you can see in Figure 28-6, the result returned (the value of `w`) is a graphic window.

Let's get some information about that object class. Select graphic window, and press Cmd+ Shift+F; this displays the entry for the graphic window class. For this project, you'll focus only on two properties: back pdf and front pdf; those are where the graphic window stores PDF data. Here is an excerpt of Smile's dictionary describing the class graphic window:

```
Class graphic window : (inherits from window) a window where
you can draw pictures of various kinds by script, and that you can
save as a PDF file or as a tiff file.
Plural form:
   graphic windows
Properties:
   frame a list of small real -- {x origin, y origin, width, height} [...]
[...]
   back pdf string -- The PDF data for the background of the window.
 Can be set to a file, to some Graphic Kernel output or to raw PDF
 data as string.
   front pdf string -- The PDF data drawn after the background and the
   graphic views of the window. Can be set to a file, to some Graphic
   Kernel output or to raw PDF data as string.
```

Making a PDF drawing consists of filling the back pdf and/or the front pdf fields of a new graphic window with PDF data (a string, actually). Here is an excerpt of the PDF data in the file you just opened:

```
%PDF-1.3
%fÂÚÂÎßÛ −fΔ
2 0 obj
<< /Length 1 0 R /Filter /FlateDecode >>
stream
xú+T_T(_c}Σ\C_ó|dæ_ú_
endstream
[...]
xú•Ωk"-Σm&˙Ω≈:ÛIûrñöwrÊì,ÀâO˘_KI*)WMŸ€íÂ_...ÌH_Â◊_>Ï^k_Ïáç~ÀÂ*K[__1ç
[...]
```

As you can see, PDF is not as intuitive as AppleScript. Thus, you will not make PDF data directly; rather, Smile's graphic library will. You will use natural commands such as MoveTo, LineTo, and DrawString, and Smile's graphic library will turn them into regular PDF data.

When you program the graphic library, you will find the documentation useful, which is available in four forms:

- The hypertext documentation for all commands is available via the Help menu.

- A PDF document is included in the download "Smile—Scripted graphics" (and includes guide and reference).

- A chapter in the online documentation is available from Smile's home page (and includes guide and reference).

- A drawing palette, available from the Window menu, displays each graphical command as a button. To display the description for a given command in the (resizeable) Message floating window, place the mouse over the button. To insert a command in the frontmost window, click the button.

Note To enjoy the tutorial, you do not have to use the documentation. I merely mention it for further reading.

To have Smile generate the PDF and provide it to the back pdf property of a given graphic window, w, your script proceeds in three steps. First, you initiate the PDF with BeginFigure(w), and second, you include the graphic commands specific to your graphic. Finally, you close the PDF with EndFigure(). This is the instruction that will notify Smile to compile the graphic commands into PDF data and to load the PDF data into the back pdf field of w so the window will display your graphic.

When you open the PDF file mc0306.pdf, Smile loads the PDF into back pdf. You do not want to replace the original graphic; rather, you want to superimpose a new graphic. Here you have to use the foreground layer—the front pdf field of the window. The instructions are the same as for drawing in the background layer, except you must call BeginFrontFigure() and EndFrontFigure() instead of BeginFigure() and EndFigure(). Let's try it by drawing a line from one corner to the other, over the opened PDF. Here you'll use basic graphic commands: MoveTo and LineTo. Both want a point as their argument, the list {x, y} of two numbers (MoveTo moves the pen without drawing; LineTo defines a line starting from the current pen location). The scale is 1 pixel (1 pixel = 1/72 inch ≈ 0.35 mm). x/y coordinates increase rightward/upward.

```
BeginFrontFigure(w)
MoveTo({0, 0})
LineTo({600, 840})
Endfrontfigure()
draw w
```

As usual, select the text, and press Return . . . ouch! Nothing happens.

This is because the program does not draw! All it does is define a shape (a *path*)—here, the diagonal line. After having defined a path, you then have to draw it in a separate operation, which is why you use DrawPath. The parameter of DrawPath will specify whether to draw the stroke of the path, will specify whether to fill the path (which makes little sense for this line, of course), and will propose more options such as using the path, not to draw but as a mask. The most often used values are DrawPath("fill-stroke"), which draws the stroke and fills the path; DrawPath("fill"); and DrawPath("stroke").

Usually, before firing a DrawPath command, you specify the pen and fill settings you want it to use. Here you'll use the default settings: by default the pen and the fill colors are black, and the pen size is 1 pixel:

```
BeginFrontFigure(w)
MoveTo({0, 0})
LineTo({600, 840})
DrawPath("stroke") -- or: 2
EndFrontFigure()
draw w
```

Select the text, and then press Return—you'll notice that a slash has been drawn on the page, as shown in Figure 28-7.

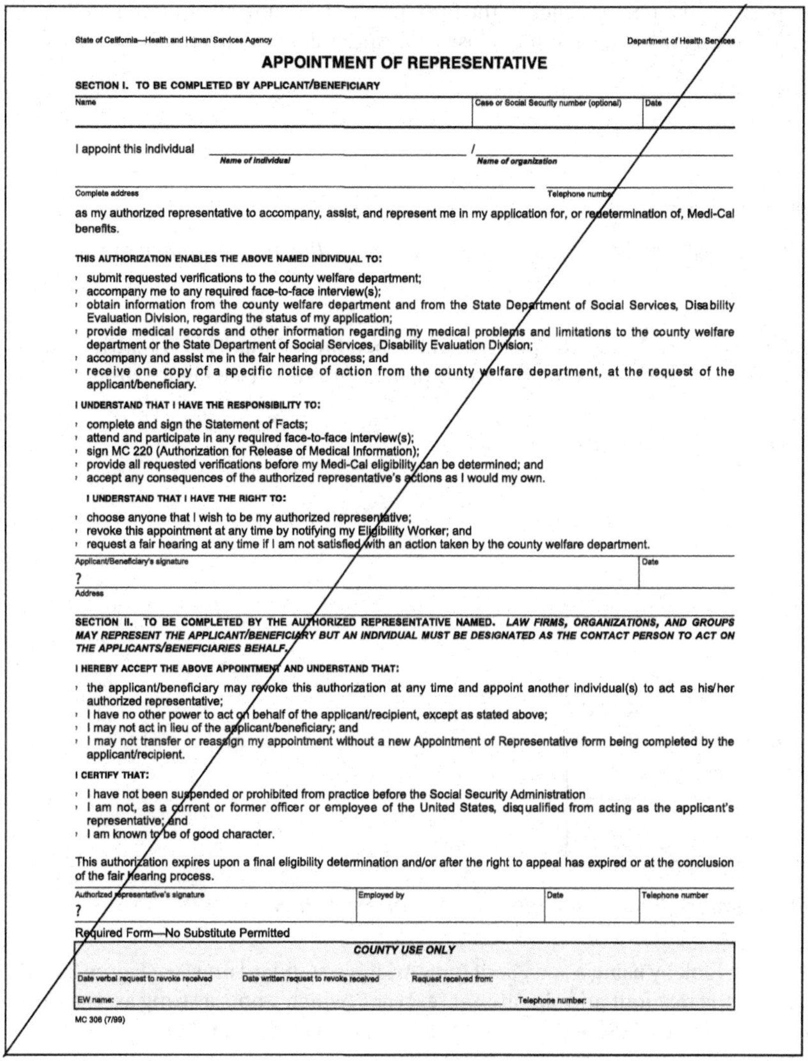
State of California—Health and Human Services Agency

Department of Health Services

APPOINTMENT OF REPRESENTATIVE

SECTION I. TO BE COMPLETED BY APPLICANT/BENEFICIARY

Name	Case or Social Security number (optional)	Date

I appoint this individual ______ (Name of individual) / ______ (Name of organization)

Complete address ______ Telephone number ______

as my authorized representative to accompany, assist, and represent me in my application for, or redetermination of, Medi-Cal benefits.

THIS AUTHORIZATION ENABLES THE ABOVE NAMED INDIVIDUAL TO:

- submit requested verifications to the county welfare department;
- accompany me to any required face-to-face interview(s);
- obtain information from the county welfare department and from the State Department of Social Services, Disability Evaluation Division, regarding the status of my application;
- provide medical records and other information regarding my medical problems and limitations to the county welfare department or the State Department of Social Services, Disability Evaluation Division;
- accompany and assist me in the fair hearing process; and
- receive one copy of a specific notice of action from the county welfare department, at the request of the applicant/beneficiary.

I UNDERSTAND THAT I HAVE THE RESPONSIBILITY TO:

- complete and sign the Statement of Facts;
- attend and participate in any required face-to-face interview(s);
- sign MC 220 (Authorization for Release of Medical Information);
- provide all requested verifications before my Medi-Cal eligibility can be determined; and
- accept any consequences of the authorized representative's actions as I would my own.

I UNDERSTAND THAT I HAVE THE RIGHT TO:

- choose anyone that I wish to be my authorized representative;
- revoke this appointment at any time by notifying my Eligibility Worker; and
- request a fair hearing at any time if I am not satisfied with an action taken by the county welfare department.

Applicant/Beneficiary's signature	Date
?	

Address

SECTION II. TO BE COMPLETED BY THE AUTHORIZED REPRESENTATIVE NAMED. *LAW FIRMS, ORGANIZATIONS, AND GROUPS MAY REPRESENT THE APPLICANT/BENEFICIARY BUT AN INDIVIDUAL MUST BE DESIGNATED AS THE CONTACT PERSON TO ACT ON THE APPLICANTS/BENEFICIARIES BEHALF.*

I HEREBY ACCEPT THE ABOVE APPOINTMENT AND UNDERSTAND THAT:

- the applicant/beneficiary may revoke this authorization at any time and appoint another individual(s) to act as his/her authorized representative;
- I have no other power to act on behalf of the applicant/recipient, except as stated above;
- I may not act in lieu of the applicant/beneficiary; and
- I may not transfer or reassign my appointment without a new Appointment of Representative form being completed by the applicant/recipient.

I CERTIFY THAT:

- I have not been suspended or prohibited from practice before the Social Security Administration
- I am not, as a current or former officer or employee of the United States, disqualified from acting as the applicant's representative; and
- I am known to be of good character.

This authorization expires upon a final eligibility determination and/or after the right to appeal has expired or at the conclusion of the fair hearing process.

Authorized representative's signature	Employed by	Date	Telephone number
?			

Required Form—No Substitute Permitted

COUNTY USE ONLY

Date verbal request to revoke received ______ Date written request to revoke received ______ Request received from: ______

EW name: ______ Telephone number: ______

MC 306 (7/99)

Figure 28-7. *With five script lines, you have programmed your first graphic.*

By default, Smile did not refresh the window. It is designed that way so you can avoid useless or disgraceful updates. To request that the window refresh explicitly, use the following:

```
draw w
```

Now you'll go further with the text-drawing experiments.

First you have to position the text. So, click in the form under the Name prompt; the toolbar of the window displays the values for x and y—values close to 55 and 702, respectively (see Figure 28-8).

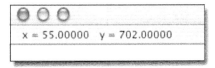

Figure 28-8. *The graphic window's toolbar displays information regarding the location of the mouse pointer.*

A command analogous to MoveTo sets the position of the pen for writing. This is TextMoveTo. The following script uses the simplest command for writing text, DrawText (see Figure 28-9):

```
BeginFrontFigure(w)
TextMoveTo({55, 702})
DrawText("John Smith")
EndFrontFigure()
draw w
```

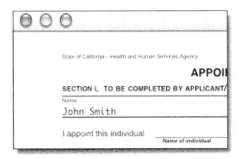

Figure 28-9. *By default the graphic library's text-drawing routines start in Monaco 10.*

You'll now improve the look by using a sans-serif font. Arial is a standard one (see Figure 28-10). The commands for setting the text font and size are SetTextFont (which wants a string as its argument, the name of a font) and SetTextSize (which accepts any positive real number). The script is now the following; run it:

```
BeginFrontFigure(w)
SetTextFont("Arial")
SetTextSize(12)
TextMoveTo({55, 702})
DrawText("John Smith")
EndFrontFigure()
draw w
```

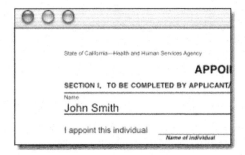

Figure 28-10. *Now the string is in the right place with the right font and size.*

You still have one task to perform. You want to be able to address several strings, so you have to put each string in independent objects in picture view, each containing one string.

First, you can empty the front layer to reinitialize the PDF.

```
BeginFrontFigure(w)
EndFrontFigure()
draw w
```

Then, you make a new picture view and fill it with the string. A *picture view* is a rectangular object living in a graphic window, which has the front pdf and back pdf properties, like a graphic window. Its frame property specifies its position inside its container window and its size.

```
set {the_width, the_height, dy} to {100, 50,-3}
set v to make new picture view at w with properties {frame:{55, 702 + ➥
  dy, the_width, the_height}}
BeginFrontFigure(v)
SetTextFont("Arial")
SetTextSize(12)
TextMoveTo({0, 0-dy})
DrawText("John Smithson")
DrawPath("stroke")
EndFrontFigure()
draw w
```

You have finished the program! You now have a (small) script capable of writing any text in any location of a PDF, using any font. You can even enhance it. For example, you could adjust the frame of the picture view by calling the measuretext command to compute what the rectangle's sizes must be exactly to display a given string using a given font.

Here is the entire script listing:

```
-- replace with actual document's path
set pdf_file to ((path to desktop) as text) & "mc0306.pdf"
set w to open pdf_file
-- run the following block as many times as needed,
-- adapting the parameters to suit
set text_font to "Arial"
set text_size to 12
set s to "John Smithson"
set {dx, dy, the_width, the_height} to measuretext s font {text font: text_font,➥
  text size: text_size }
set v to make new picture view at w with properties {frame:{55, 702 + dy,➥
  the_width, the_height}}
```

```
BeginFrontFigure(v)
SetTextFont(text_font)
SetTextSize(text_size)
TextMoveTo({0, 0-dy})
DrawText(s)
DrawPath("stroke")
EndFrontFigure()
draw w
```

Keeping productivity gains as large as possible sometimes means making the minimal effort required to have the work done. Here you are not implementing any error checking, any user notifications, or any of the other bells and whistles you would expect for an application that you would distribute. You have just externalized the variables and added a few comments to make the program reusable later.

Rolling Up the Scripts into a Graphical Interface

In this section, you will add a user interface to the script you created earlier. Once you have made a task doable in Smile, you may want to make it available for nonscripters to use. This interface will allow users to select the PDF they want to edit and specify the text they want to add to it.

Smile makes creating a graphical interface easy using *custom dialog boxes*. When you save a custom dialog box, you get a document that will open in Smile when double-clicked: each graphical interface can be seen as a separate application able to run in Smile's environment.

For your first experience of a custom dialog box, you'll keep it simple: you'll have the user enter each quantity as a string, in text fields. So far you identified the following inputs: the string, the font, the text size, and the location, which consists of two numbers, so you need five text entry fields (*editable text boxes*) and five *static text boxes* to let the user know what to type there.

In your tests, you obtained a reference to the graphic window (w) because you opened the PDF file yourself. In a real situation, the user opens a PDF file, and then they may use the custom dialog box to edit the PDF. So that the user is able to target any open PDF file (any graphic window), you'll add a sixth text field in which the user will type the name of the window to target. Obviously, you could design a user-friendly way of targeting the desired window, but for the purposes of this example, let's restrict the tutorial to a simple tool.

The user will trigger the actions with buttons. You won't update the window's display each time the user changes any quantity in the text fields, but rather you'll have the user decide when to show the result: a first button will display the new string with the current settings. You also want to validate the current drawing before editing a new string; you need a second button for that.

To have the dialog box open with one click, you will install it in the User Scripts menu (the menu with a parchment icon). To install a new item in the User Scripts menu, you copy it into a specific location in the user's domain, namely, /User/<login>/Library/Application support/ Smile/User scripts/.

This makes you ready to create your Smile tool. In the first step, you'll build the interface—the dialog box the user will see. Then you'll provide the scripts that will bring the dialog box to life.

Building the Interface

The first action is to make a new dialog box. Select File ➤ New Dialog. This opens a new dialog box and also the Controls palette from which you will copy the desired controls (see Figure 28-11). Note that the Controls palette is merely a dialog box. It is part of Smile's philosophy to define a limited number of window classes so that you can script Smile more easily. The Controls palette is where you find one copy of each of the controls you can install in your dialog box.

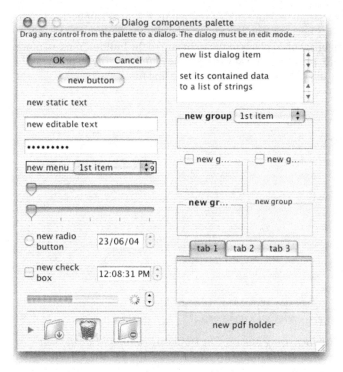

Figure 28-11. *The Controls palette is in edit mode; you copy a control into your dialog box by dragging and dropping.*

As you can check by selecting the Edit menu, both windows are in edit mode, which is the mode where you can make structural changes to the dialog box. This is because you used File ➤ New Dialog. When you open an existing dialog box by the usual means, it opens in running mode, the normal use mode. Selecting Edit ➤ Edit mode lets you toggle the dialog box into edit mode and immediately make any change.

You can also check that, since the dialog boxes are in edit mode, the menu bar displays a Dialog menu with several commands to help with editing a dialog box.

Now you'll populate the empty, new dialog box. Enlarge the new dialog box. Click the new static text control in the Controls palette, hold down the mouse button, and drag the control to the new dialog box, close to the upper-left corner. You have installed your first control.

Sooner or later you'll have to save the dialog box to disk, so let's do that now. Select File ➤ Save, and save the dialog box by entering **Add text to a PDF file** as its name in /User/<login>/Library/ Application support/Smile/User scripts/.

This changes the dialog box's name into the file's name. Check that the User Scripts menu now offers one new item, with the name you supplied.

Proceeding as you did for new static text, install a new editable text control in the dialog box. Place it to the right of new static text. It is better that the two controls do not overlap: drag the new editable text control sufficiently to the right, and/or resize the new static text control to a shorter size: select it with the mouse, and then move its frame's bottom-right corner.

Instead of dropping more items, you'll duplicate the two existing items (see Figure 28-12). Select them both, in the creation order (new static text, then new editable text), using the Shift key. Or, deselect any item by clicking in an empty spot in the dialog box, and then select Edit ➤ Select

All. Now press Cmd+D, or select User Scripts ➤ More Smile Commands ➤ Edit ➤ Duplicate. (Duplicate is better than copying and pasting, because Duplicate leaves the clipboard untouched.) The duplicated items are created with an offset of 20 pixels to the right and to the bottom. You can move them with the arrows on the keyboard; press the Shift key to have the items move by 20 pixels, and use the left and the bottom arrows to align the new controls with the first ones.

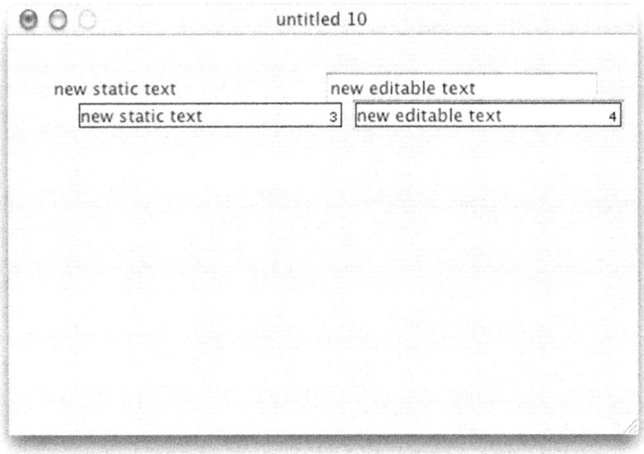

Figure 28-12. *New items are created with increasing indexes. The* Duplicate *command creates new copies at an offset of (20, 20) with respect to the original.*

Repeat this step four times (to end up with six copies of each).

Still using drag and drop from the Controls palette, create (for instance, both at the same height, under the array of text fields) two new buttons. Now you can resize the dialog box so as to enclose the controls only.

When you write the script for the dialog box, you'll refer to the controls by their indexes. A control's *index* is the number that its frame displays in the bottom-right corner when selected. Check that the indexes are in the natural order, that is, from left to right and then from top to bottom. The rightmost button in the bottom should assume the index 14. If you have more items, use Edit ➤ Clear to suppress the extra controls. If the order is not what it should be, proceed as follows. Unselect any item by clicking an empty spot. Then press the Shift key, and click each item once in the desired order so as to finally select them all. Now, select Edit ➤ Cut and then Edit ➤ Paste; the controls will be pasted in the same order as you selected them.

The script will handle the contents of the editable text boxes, but you have to name the other eight controls. For the editable text boxes, I suggest `string to display:`, `text font:`, `text size:`, `x (pixels):`, `y (pixels):`, and `current target:`; for the buttons I suggest `refresh` and `validate` (see Figure 28-13). For each of the eight controls to be renamed successively, double-click each to open its Control dialog box, set its name to the desired string, and then close the Control dialog box.

You will not need another new control for the moment, so close the Controls palette.

The interface of the dialog box is now operational—if not fully finalized from a cosmetic point of view. I won't demonstrate cosmetic-oriented features here. It may be enough to say that in addition to moving and resizing, you can, using the Dialog ➤ Align Items menu item, copy the sizes from a control to another and align and/or distribute the controls vertically or horizontally. More sophisticated, user-contributed editing tools are available for free at Satimage's website.

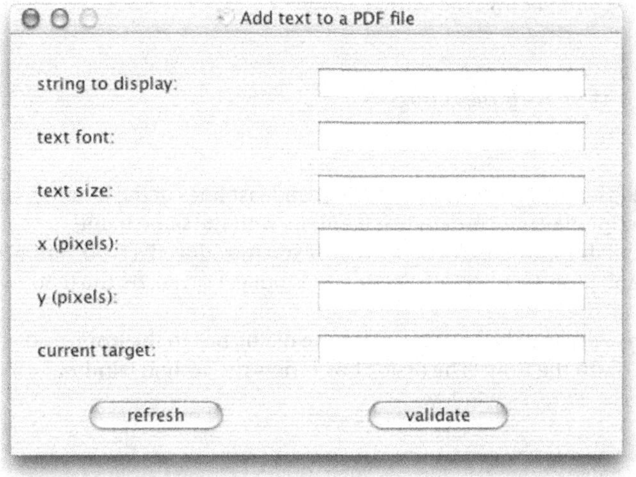

Figure 28-13. *When a dialog box is in edit mode, the bottom-right corner shows a grow box, which resizes the dialog box. Here no grow box is visible.*

Programming the Dialog Box

Last but not least, you have to program the dialog box by providing it with scripts. All the lines you wrote for the first tests are still available, so your task will have much to do with copying and pasting.

In Smile, when the user acts on a control (for instance, typing a character in an editable text box or clicking a button), Smile notifies the script of the control's container—the dialog box; the control itself is not notified. More precisely, the script of the dialog box will receive the following event:

```
click in d item number n
```

where d is a reference to the dialog box (the owner of the script) and n is the index of the control that the user's action addresses. Thus, you won't write as many click in handlers as you have active controls—you need only one.

The other handler you need to write is prepare. When a custom dialog box opens, Smile sends the following event to its script just before making it visible:

```
prepare d
```

where d is a reference to the dialog box. Any initialization should be performed in the prepare handler. Most often, the job of the prepare handler is to prepare the appearance of the dialog box and to assign initial values to the global variables that the script of the dialog box may use. However, at this step you won't use global variables (properties); the prepare handler will mainly reset the entry text fields.

Let's write the prepare handler. With the dialog box still in edit mode, select Dialog ➤ Edit Dialog Script: this will open the script of the dialog box. (Alternatively, press Cmd+Opt-click in an empty spot of the dialog box.) The name of the new (colored) window is the same as the dialog box's name, with .Script appended. It may be helpful to note here that the script of the dialog box is different from, say, the script of an applet, in that it will never "run"; the script will receive events that it will handle in the handlers you'll write, but under normal conditions it will never receive a run event.

Type or copy the following `prepare` handler into the script window:

```
on prepare theDialog
    repeat with i from 2 to 12 by 2
        set contained data of dialog item i of theDialog to ""
    end repeat
end prepare
```

(By default, the script of the dialog box already includes the first and last lines of the handler, so you have only three lines to type. A script may not contain two handlers with the same name.)

Now let's save the script into the dialog box. Select File ➤ Save. If you introduced a typo, Smile throws an alert to notify you of a compilation error, and the script does not get saved; fix the typo, and try again.

In Smile, you test as you develop—let's test the handler. Bring the dialog box to the front, and then bring the hr_book_samples window to the front. The dialog box is now the second window. Execute the following line in the hr_book_samples window:

```
set d to window 2
```

This returns to d an absolute reference to the dialog box, which will remain valid even when the dialog box is no longer the second window and until it gets deleted. Now to test the handler, execute the following:

```
tell d to prepare it
```

This should clear the editable text fields.

If it does not, the first thing to do—if you are sure the script was saved—is to install an error output. Indeed, in the spirit of a behavior ready for automatic applications, Smile keeps silent the errors triggered in a `prepare` handler, unless the scripter explicitly handles them. You'll now see how you would install an error handler. Specifically, you'll introduce a typo into the script that follows and see how the error code you will insert handles the error.

To experiment with the error handler, bring the dialog box's script window to the front, and replace its content with the following lines:

```
on prepare theDialog
    try
        repeat with i from 2 to 12 by 2
            set contained data of dialog item i of theDlog to ""
        end repeat
    on error s
        FatalAlert(s)
    end try
end prepare
```

Do not forget to save the script with File ➤ Save to make the change effective. Now, as you have done already, put the cursor in the following line, and press Return:

```
tell d to prepare it
```

AppleScript attempts to run the `prepare` handler. But in the `set contained data...` line, it will choke on a variable that was not defined before: `theDlog` (the variable passed as the argument to `prepare` is `theDialog`, not `theDlog`). This is a typical runtime error. AppleScript thus jumps to the first line after the `on error` clause. There you see `FatalAlert`; `FatalAlert` is nothing but a shortcut that Smile defines for convenience, which is really one option of `display dialog` (with a stop icon and one OK button), and is adapted for displaying error messages.

Now correct the typo (replace `theDlog` with `theDialog`), and save the script.

You are finished with the prepare dialog box; now let's program the click in handler. It is good practice not to directly handle the event in the click in handler but instead to write routines that click in will call.

Reviewing the sequence of test scripts, you see that you can reuse the picture view to enable text modifications. You just have to store its reference to address it later or to reinitialize it when validating. It will be a good idea, as a visual confirmation, to blank the string to display once the current front graphic is merged in the background graphic.

Bring the script of the dialog box back in view if needed, and type (or copy) the three new handlers shown in Script 28-3. Remove the built-in sample click in handler, but keep the prepare handler you entered previously.

Script 28-3.

```
property v:0
on prepare theDialog
      set v to 0
      repeat with i from 2 to 12 by 2
          set contained data of dialog item i of theDialog to ""
      end repeat
end prepare
on RefreshDisplay(d)
   tell d
      set s to contained data of dialog item 2
      set text_font to contained data of dialog item 4
      set text_size to contained data of dialog item 6
      set x to contained data of dialog item 8
      set y to contained data of dialog item 10
      set w_name to contained data of dialog item 12
   end tell
   set w to graphic window w_name
   set {dx, dy, the_width, the_height} to measuretext s font {text font: Â
     text_font, text size: text_size }
   try
      set frame of v to {x, y + dy, the_width, the_height}
   on error
      set v to make new picture view at w with properties {frame:{x, y + dy, Â
        the_width, the_height}}
   end
   BeginFrontFigure(v)
   SetTextFont(text_font)
   SetTextSize(text_size)
   TextMoveTo({0, -dy})
   DrawText(s)
   DrawPath("stroke")
   EndFrontFigure()
   draw w
end RefreshDisplay

on MergeCurrent(d)
   set v to 0
   set contained data of dialog item 2 of d to ""
end MergeCurrent
```

```
on click in d item number n
   if n = 13 then
      RefreshDisplay(d)
   else if n = 14 then
      MergeCurrent(d)
   end if
end click in
```

Now your dialog box should look like Figure 28-14 (with possibly an additional try...on error...end try structure in the prepare handler).

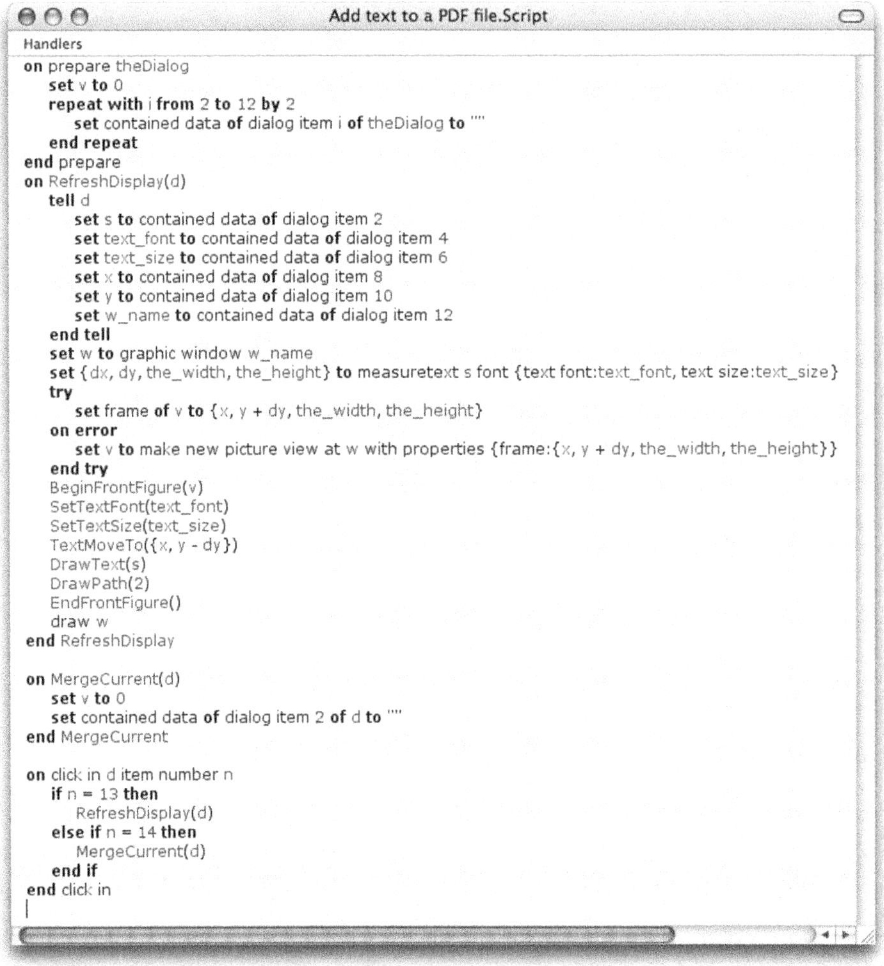

Figure 28-14. *The whole dialog box works with one short script only. Yet, the dialog box does not handle any errors, and its features are basic.*

Save the script, and select File ➤ Close to close its window. Bring the dialog box to the front, and save it as well. This will save to disk the changes you made to the dialog box, including the script you just wrote.

You are now ready to test and use the new Smile tool. If it is still open, close the PDF file, discarding the changes. If it is still open, close the dialog box, too.

Now, open the PDF file in Smile like a user would do normally. In other words, drop its icon on the Smile icon, use File ➤ Open in Smile, or use a script as shown here:

```
open pdf_file
```

Open the dialog box. If you followed the instructions verbatim, your new dialog box should be available as an item in the User Scripts menu. Otherwise, just double-click the icon of the dialog box in the Finder.

Now you can use your new tool. Let's add a first string to the document; say you want to set the name information to Bart Simpson. To fill in the x/y (pixels) information, click the graphic window at the location where "Bart Simpson" should print. The toolbar displays the values for x and y—something like 55 and 702. Now you can fill the text fields in the dialog box, such as Bart Simpson, Lucida Grande, 13, 55, 702, or mc0306.pdf. At this point, you'll need to fill all the fields; you have not installed any error handling or any system of default values.

To view the result, click Refresh. If nothing happens, probably a field is not filled in or is incorrectly filled in—for instance, a letter in a numeric field.

If some setting does not suit you, change it, and click Refresh again until you are satisfied with the result. Then, to validate that first string, click Validate. This resets the string to display to the empty string, suggesting you can now work on a second string. Proceed for the second string like you just did for the first string. If the second string is on the same horizontal as the first one, keep the same value for y (pixels).

Handling User Clicks

Obviously, reading the window's toolbar and copying its content manually into the dialog box is not productive. You should have the graphic window send the location of the click to the dialog box.

When the user clicks in an active graphic window, Smile sends `pick in` to the graphic window's script. You should install a handler for `pick in` in the graphic window's script. Let's open the script of the graphic window. As for the dialog box, you must first change the graphic window to edit mode. With the graphic window being the active window, select Edit ➤ Edit mode (or press Cmd+Y), and then Cmd+Opt-click the graphic window. This will open its script; by default, the script is empty.

Type the following lines:

```
on pick in w at {point:{x, y}, step:i}
    set d to dialog "Add text to a PDF file"
    set contained data of item 8 of d to x
    set contained data of item 10 of d to y
end pick in
```

(This is assuming you named the dialog box "Add text to a PDF file." Otherwise, change the string in the script accordingly.) Note that `pick in` passes a step argument. The value of `step` is 1 when the user presses the button ("mouse down"), 2 when the user is moving the mouse while the button is down ("drag"), and 3 when the user releases the button ("mouse up"). For more sophisticated handling—for instance, if you wanted to implement the ability to constrain the drag with the Shift key—you would use the value of `step`.

Also, if you look carefully at the script, you'll observe that you set the `contained data` property of an editable text field not to a string but to a number. This is something special to Smile. Text fields can be filled with numbers, and you can customize the way they will display numbers by setting their format property (editable in the contextual menu in edit mode).

On the other hand, reading the `contained data` property of an editable text field always returns a string unless you coerce the string to a number by specifying `as real`.

Select File ➤ Save and then File ➤ Close to close the script's window, and then select Edit ➤ Edit Mode (or press Cmd+Y) to change the PDF's graphic window to running mode.

Now click and drag the mouse; the dialog box should display the mouse's location in the x/y (pixels) field.

Note that you can now hide the toolbar, because it does not display the coordinates any longer when you drag the mouse. This is because you did not supply a `continue pick in [...]` line in the handler, so the handler overrides the standard behavior.

If you want nonprogrammers to use your tool, you should have the script installed "automagically." You'll make a third button that will implement the `pick in` script in the target graphic window. For this, change the dialog box to edit mode (Edit ➤ Edit Mode), click the Validate button to select it, move it a little to the left with the left arrow key, duplicate it (User Scripts ➤ More Smile Commands ~TRA Edit ➤ Duplicate), and align it (arrow keys with or without the Shift key pressed). Double-click the new button, and name it auto click.

Now let's program the new button. Cmd+option-click the dialog box to open its script (or select Dialog ➤ Edit Dialog Script). Add the handler in Script 28-4 to the script (in addition to `RefreshDisplay`, `MergeCurrent`, and `click in`) at any location in the script (not inside another handler, though).

Script 28-4.

```
on InstallScript(d)
    set w_name to contained data of item 12 of d
    set w to graphic window w_name
    set script of w to "on pick in w at {point:{x, y}, step:i}
    set d to dialog \"" & name of d & "\"
    set contained data of item 8 of d to x
    set contained data of item 10 of d to y
end pick in"
postit ("Loaded")
    smilepause 5
    postit ("")
end InstallScript
```

In this handler you use a sophisticated feature, scripted scripting. In Smile you can dynamically provide a script to an object; you can set the `script` property of an object to a string—provided the string is an AppleScript source that can be compiled. Smile lets you manipulate—by script—scripts as well as the individual handlers and properties of a script.

You have chosen to display feedback when the action is done: the floating Message window will display "Loaded" for 5 seconds (`postit ("")` closes the Message window).

The handler uses a unique command of Smile's: `smilepause`. Inserting `smilepause` in a script pauses the script (for the time specified, which can be 0) while letting the application be fully responsive. You can use `smilepause` for a wide variety of occasions. Here you use it to have the message go away after five seconds yet let the user work normally as soon as the action is done.

Of course, you must have the new handler called when the user clicks the Auto Click button. This is the job of the `click in` handler, where you should install (before `end if`) the two following lines:

```
else if n = 15 then
    InstallScript(d)
```

You can check your script against the code download. The order of the routines is arbitrary. If there is no error, save and close the script. Once the dialog box is the front window, save it as well.

Now you can click the new button and finish filling in the form if you want, and then you can save it too. Finally, you can view the file by double-clicking its icon. Depending on your settings, this will open the file in Preview or in Adobe Reader (or Acrobat Reader), and you can see the strings you have added. You can use a high magnification to check that you have vector graphics.

Exercises

Obviously, you have made a working tool yet a minimal one. What you should do now depends mostly on who will be using the tool and how often they will use it.

Here are some standard improvements you may want to implement later. For the sake of brevity, we leave them as exercises for you to do on your own.

- Have the dialog box systematically work on the first graphic window (even if the window is not the second window) while also displaying its name as a visual feedback. Or, install a load window 2 button.

- Install a menu for the text font. For the text size, install the small arrows control.

- The pick in script should support the Shift key to pin one coordinate.

- The user should be allowed to type a numeric expression such as 55+200 as x or y.

- Install a live check box for live update.

- The user should be allowed to switch between picture views so that all the text remains editable until the user saves it as PDF.

- Graphic windows support widgets that you can use like scriptable handles to an object. Rewrite Adobe Illustrator using the widgets.

CHAPTER 29

■■■

Automating Unix Applications

One of the biggest boosts for Mac users, and scripters in particular, is the new operating system under the hood of OS X. I am, of course, referring to Unix. *Shell scripts* are Unix command-line-style scripts. Shell scripting consists of a few flavors, hundreds of commands, and endless possibilities. One of the most exciting additions to AppleScript comes in the form of a single command: do shell script.

The world of Unix offers scripters an endless source of free scriptable applications. Many free Unix applications are available, each performing little commands and actions. You can utilize most of these applications in your AppleScript solution by means of the do shell script command.

Why and When Are Shell Scripts Used in AppleScript?

Although working with the Unix command line is different from working in AppleScript, in many situations the two can complement one another nicely. Many tasks where AppleScript is known to be weak, such as advanced text processing, raw performance, and access to lower-level operating system features, are long-time strengths of the Unix world. Decades of Unix development have produced a wide range of powerful, fast, and reliable command-line applications, many of which are freely available over the Internet or already installed on Mac OS X ready for you to use. At the same time, AppleScript provides terrific support for controlling scriptable GUI applications on Mac OS X—something that's crucial to many Mac users and an area where its Unix side is still playing catch-up.

By combining the two, you get the best of both worlds. Your AppleScripts can call into Unix scripts to help out with heavy-duty data-crunching tasks, and the Unix scripts can call into Apple-Script when they want to work with Apple iTunes or Apple iCal. Although the integration isn't completely seamless and you still need to watch out for a few issues, it is still a highly valuable addition to an AppleScripter's toolbox, alongside traditional AppleScript solutions such as script-able applications, scripting additions, and script libraries.

Even in situations where AppleScript is already strong, such as manipulating the file system, sometimes you may prefer to use Unix commands instead, perhaps because they perform a task in a slightly different way or provide extra options that aren't available elsewhere. For example, when working with the file system, Unix commands won't produce a Finder progress dialog box when deleting or copying files. Also, a shell script can process a large number of files much more rapidly than an AppleScript script can. If you have a folder with more than 1,000 files and you need to extract a few files from it or if you need to search for a file in a directory tree, Unix commands can do that much faster than Finder commands.

Sometimes it's not that the Finder lacks a command; it's just that the shell script equivalent is a bit more convenient. For instance, if you need to duplicate a file to a different folder and rename it, with the Finder you first need to use the `duplicate` command to copy it and then use the `set` command to change the name of the new file. However, this can cause problems if the target location already contains a file with either the old name or the new name. Using shell scripts, you can copy a file to another file that will duplicate it and rename it in one shot.

Understanding Unix Scripting Concepts

In the following sections, you will learn about some basic concepts of Unix scripting, which will stand you in good stead when starting to work with the command line on your Mac.

The Unix Command Line and Mac Desktop Compared

The Unix command line is like a giant toolbox, packed full of really useful tools for performing a huge range of tasks. Each tool in this toolbox is designed to do a single job and do it well. This is a bit different from the way that graphical user interface (GUI) applications such as the Finder, TextEdit, and Mail work, because each of these is designed to perform a range of related tasks. For example, you can use the Finder to eject a disk, copy a file or folder, list the contents of a folder, mount an iDisk, and so on. In the Unix world, you would perform each of these actions using a *separate* application: the Unix application for copying items is called `cp`, the one for listing the contents of folders is `ls`, and so on.

Another difference is that many Unix applications are designed to launch, perform a single task, and quit as soon as that task is done. By comparison, a GUI application such as Mail takes much longer to start up and then stays open so you can perform any number of e-mail–related tasks until you quit it. Some Unix applications do provide similar interactive options: for example, you can use the `top` application to get a one-off list of running processes, or you can have it display a constantly updating list of process information. (Incidentally, AppleScript can interact only with those Unix applications running in noninteractive mode.)

A third difference between the Unix world and the Mac desktop is that Unix applications are designed to connect to one another easily so that the output from one can be fed directly into the next. Some Mac applications are designed to interact with one another to a limited degree; for example, Safari allows you to Ctrl-click an image in a web page and add it directly to your Apple iPhoto library. For anything more serious, however, you have to resort to AppleScript—and hope the applications you're using provide the commands you'll need. By comparison, Unix applications are designed from the ground up so that users can seamlessly plug them together with little or no effort.

Even if you've never used Unix before, you may still find all this sounds a bit familiar if you've used Apple's Automator application at all. An Automator *action* is equivalent to a Unix application and performs a single, specific task; the Automator application fills a similar role to the Unix command line in that it allows you to link multiple actions together and run them as a single unit. Of course, some differences exist: Automator has a friendly, easy-to-use GUI interface while the Unix command line has many advanced (and cryptic!) power-user features. Overall, though, you can probably guess where Apple got the original idea for Automator from!

You should be able to see the similarities between what AppleScript lets you do (connect GUI applications to create powerful workflows) and what the Unix command line lets you do (connect Unix applications to create powerful workflows), even if the ways they go about it are a bit different.

How the Unix Command Line Works

You need to understand a number of key concepts before starting to work with the Unix command line. The following sections summarize these concepts in order to give you a feel for the subject if you're new to Unix scripting; for a much more detailed discussion, you should refer to books and tutorials that are dedicated to the topic.

The Shell

When you open a new Terminal window or call `do shell script`, you'll first meet a Unix command line, or *shell*. A Unix shell application is basically a scripting language, a command-line interface (for working interactively), and a script interpreter all rolled into one.

When a shell application is running interactively, you can enter commands and other code at the command line. As soon as you hit Return, the line of code you've just entered will be read and executed. For example, if you open a new Terminal window, type in `ls`, and then hit Return, the shell will read that line of text, figure out that `ls` is the name of a command, look for a Unix application with the same name, and run it for you. In Figure 29-1, you can see the `ls` command being executed in the Terminal.

Figure 29-1. *The* `ls` *command executed in the Terminal application with the result below it*

Note Another approach is to write a shell script in a text editor, save it as a text file, and then tell a shell application to read and execute that file. Since this chapter is about using the Unix command line from AppleScript, I won't discuss this approach here. However, you will learn how to create a Unix shell script as an AppleScript string and then use Standard Additions' `do shell script` command to execute that script.

Mac OS X includes a number of Unix shell applications as standard. These have names such as `sh`, `tcsh`, `zsh`, and `bash`, and each one offers users a slightly different set of features for working on the Unix command line. You don't need to worry too much about the differences as long as your shell scripts are simple, since they all deal with basic tasks such as issuing commands in the same way. More advanced shell scripting features such as setting variables and using `repeat` loops do vary from shell to shell, however, so you'll need to read the manual for the particular shell you're working in if you want to use the advanced features.

Note Terminal uses your default shell, which on Tiger is `bash` (unless you've changed it). The `do shell script` command always uses `sh`.

Commands

I discussed earlier how Unix uses lots of small, single-purpose applications to perform tasks. To run Unix applications from the Unix shell, you use *commands*. A command is just the name (or the path) of the application to run, followed by any options and arguments you want passed to the application.

You'll find that Unix commands are not unlike AppleScript commands, which consist of the name of a command handler you want to execute followed by the parameters you want to pass to the handler. Here is a typical Unix command:

```
ls -l /Applications/
```

The command's name is ls, which is the name of the Unix application for listing a folder's contents. The -l bit is an *option*, and the /Applications/ part is an *argument*. Notice that each option and argument in a command is separated by a space. In general, arguments are values for the application to process, and options control exactly how that processing is performed. In the previous example, /Applications/ is the path to the folder whose content you want to list, and the -l option is a simple on/off flag that tells ls to provide a detailed description of each item rather than just its name (the default).

Many Unix applications provide an additional way to pass in data known as *standard input* (often abbreviated to stdin). Although arguments are useful for passing in small pieces of data such as file and folder paths, you can pass any amount of data via standard input. This data is usually (though not always) plain text, and many Unix programs process this input on a line-by-line basis, where each line is separated by a linefeed (ASCII 10) character.

Most Unix applications also return a result, which is often also plain text. Not surprisingly, this is known as *standard out* (or stdout). For example, the ls application returns a list of file and folder names/descriptions as text, with each item separated by a newline.

Finally, when a Unix application encounters a problem it's unable to cope with, it will generate an error. These error codes are given as numbers. In addition, a description of the problem is often given; this appears as *standard error* (stderr). Standard error works a bit like standard out, except that it's used for error messages, not normal results. Standard error is also used for warning messages describing nonfatal problems that the application was able to deal with by itself but still wants the user to see.

Pipes

By default, a Unix application takes its input from the Unix shell that started it, and its output is displayed by that same shell. You can see this for yourself by typing ls -l /Applications/ in a Terminal window and hitting Return.

One of Unix's key features is that it enables you to link multiple applications together to create powerful data-processing workflows, or *pipelines*. It does this by allowing you to redirect the standard output of one Unix application to the standard input of another. These connections are called *pipes*, and on the command line they are written as a single vertical bar, |.

For example, let's say you want to list the name of every item in your home folder whose name contains the letter *D*. To get the name of each item, you'll use the ls command, which outputs the item names as linefeed-delimited text. To extract only the lines containing the letter *D*, you'll use a second command, grep, which is used to match lines that contain a particular pattern of text. grep takes the text to search as its standard input and the pattern to look for as its argument. To join the two commands, you put a pipe character between them:

```
ls | grep D
```

When you run this script, the result is—you guessed it—a list of names containing the letter *D* as newline-delimited text.

> ■**Note** You may notice that when you run the previous example, only names containing uppercase *D*s are matched. If you want to make grep ignore case, add the -i option between the grep command's name and its argument, as shown here: ls | grep -i D.

Other Redirections

Usually the first command in a pipeline takes its standard input from the shell that started it, and the last command's standard output and standard error are displayed by the same shell. Sometimes it's useful to use a different source for standard in or different destinations for standard out and/or standard error.

For example, let's say you want to use grep to match lines in a plain-text file. To do this, you need to tell the shell to read the standard in data for the grep command from your text file. (grep can also read files directly, but don't worry about that here.)

To redirect standard input, you use the < symbol followed by the path of the file to read from:

```
grep some-pattern < /path/to/input/file
```

Similarly, to specify a different destination for standard out, use the > symbol followed by the file to write to:

```
ls -l /Applications/ > /path/to/output/file
```

You can use other redirection symbols for redirecting standard error, appending standard out to an existing file, and so on, but I won't cover them here.

Getting Help

For users used to the comforts of the Mac desktop, learning to use the Unix command line and the many powerful tools it offers can be a bit intimidating at first. Fortunately, plenty of assistance is available.

Built-in Help

Unix comes with extensive built-in documentation that you can easily access from the command line. Almost every Unix application comes with a detailed manual that describes what it does and how to use it. To view a manual, you use the man tool. For example, to view the manual for ls, type the following:

```
man ls
```

You can use the cursor keys to scroll through longer manuals. When you're done, just type q to exit man.

Some Unix applications also provide built-in help. For example, the popular curl tool (used to upload and download files via File Transfer Protocol [FTP] and Hypertext Transfer Protocol [HTTP]) will provide a short description of each option you can use, which is handy when you don't want to search through its full manual just to look up something. To view curl's built-in help, just type curl followed by the -h option:

```
curl -h
```

Another handy tool is apropos. This searches through a list of brief descriptions for every installed Unix application and displays those that contain a given search word or phrase. For example, try typing this:

```
apropos text
```

This will return dozens of matching manuals, not only for Unix tools but also for things such as low-level system calls that are of interest only to C programmers, Perl, and Tcl libraries, and so on. Fortunately, apropos puts a number in parentheses after the manual name that tells you what section it came from. The most useful section is section 1, which contains general commands. Section 8, which contains system administrator tools, might also be of occasional interest.

For example, to do a quick and dirty filter for section 1 manuals, you could use this:

```
apropos text | grep '(1)'
```

The man tool also provides some powerful manual search tools if apropos doesn't find what you're after; see its manual for details.

Other Sources of Help

Unix is a popular operating system that has been around for many years now, so plenty of good books and tutorials about Unix scripting are available; you'll also be able to find online newsgroups and other sources of information and assistance. A quick online search for the phrase *Unix tutorial* will produce tons of links for you to rummage through and find one you like!

Things to Watch Out For

Although the Unix command line is sophisticated in some respects, it can be quite primitive in others. I'll quickly cover some common issues that you may encounter, particularly when using the Unix command line from AppleScript.

Data in Unix Is "Dumb"

Although AppleScript provides a variety of well-defined value classes for representing different kinds of data (integers, reals, strings, dates, lists, records, and so on), to the Unix command line all data is just a dumb series of bytes, and it's up to individual applications to interpret that data in a particular way.

Many Unix applications treat data as plain ASCII text, and when they want to represent a "list" of "strings," they use a single block of ASCII text where each "list item" is a single line followed by a linefeed (ASCII 10) character. For example, if you're passing data to a command that expects linefeed-delimited text as its standard input, make sure that's what you're giving it.

An easy mistake is to use return characters (ASCII 13) to separate your lines because that's what's often used in AppleScripts and many older Mac applications. As you know, AppleScript provides a built-in return constant but not a linefeed constant, so if you want to be sure of getting a linefeed character, then you'll have to use the ASCII character command. For example:

```
set AppleScript's text item delimiters to (ASCII character 10)
set input_string to the_list as string
```

Unix Doesn't Know About Different Character Sets

Another difference is that few Unix applications work with text understand character sets such as MacRoman and Unicode: the only character set they know about is ASCII. Perhaps some day it will finally catch up, but for now it's just something command-line users have to accept.

To compensate for Unix's ignorance of modern (and not-so-modern) text encodings, a common technique is to represent non-ASCII text as UTF-8 encoded Unicode. This provides a reasonable degree of compatibility since the first 128 characters in UTF-8 also happen to the same 128 characters that make up the ASCII character set. Most Unix tools that deal with ASCII text will understand these 128 characters as usual while paying no special interest to any others. For example, the `ls` command actually returns file and folder names in UTF-8 format, so if a filename or folder name contains non-ASCII characters, then these characters will be preserved, although they may not display properly in a Terminal window.

Fortunately, you don't have to worry too much about text encodings when using the `do shell script` command, since it will convert AppleScript strings to UTF-8 data and back again for you. However, you do need to watch out when using Standard Additions' `read` and `write` commands to read and write text files that are used by shell scripts. See Chapter 14 for more information about how to read and write UTF-8 encoded text files in AppleScript.

Unix Understands POSIX File Paths Only

Although AppleScript prefers to use colon-delimited HFS paths to identify files and folders (for example, `Macintosh HD:Applications:TextEdit.app`), the Unix shell always uses slash-delimited POSIX paths (for example, `/Applications/TextEdit.app`).

Watch Where You Use Spaces and Other Special Characters!

Because Unix shells already use spaces to separate command options and arguments from one another, you have to be careful not to add any extra spaces where you shouldn't when constructing shell scripts. You also need to watch out for other special characters used by Unix shells (this includes most punctuation characters).

For example, the following command will list the items in the `Applications` folder:

```
ls /Applications/
```

However, the following command, which is supposed to list the contents of the folder named `FileMaker Pro 8`, won't work as expected:

```
ls /Applications/FileMaker Pro 8/
```

Instead of treating `/Applications/FileMaker Pro 8/` as a single argument, the Unix shell actually sees three arguments: `/Applications/FileMaker`, `Pro`, and `8/`. At best, this sort of mistake results in the shell script immediately halting with an error message. At worst, the script may perform a different action than the one you intended. This could be bad news if your script is performing a potentially dangerous task such as writing or erasing files: you could easily end up deleting a completely different part of your file system instead!

Fortunately, Unix shells allow you to escape or quote spaces and other special characters, and you should take great care always to do so whenever appropriate. I'll discuss this further in the "Quoting Arguments" section.

Unix Assumes You Know What You're Doing

Unlike the Mac OS desktop, Unix was designed by programmers for programmers. It places few restrictions on what you can do and rarely provides "Are you sure?" warnings before performing potentially dangerous operations such as replacing or deleting files. A simple mistake such as forgetting to escape spaces in a file path when using the `rm` command to delete files and folders could easily lead to disaster. See the "Quoting Arguments" section for some examples of how dangerous mistypes can be in Unix.

Some Useful Unix Commands

The following is a list of some particularly useful Unix applications that are included with Mac OS X. Since this book is about AppleScript, not Unix, I won't be covering most of them here, but you might like to check them out sometime. I've included a brief description of what each one does to help you get started.

- `cd`: Changes the working directory (that is, the default folder used by other commands)
- `ls`: Lists the items in a folder
- `mv`, `cp`: Moves and copies files and folders
- `rm`: Deletes files and folders
- `find`: Searches for files and folders
- `chown`, `chmod`: Changes the owner and access permissions for files and folders
- `date`: Gets the current date as a custom-formatted string
- `curl`: Uploads and downloads files using HTTP, FTP, and so on
- `grep`: Extracts lines that match a regular expression pattern
- `awk`: Extracts pieces of data from lines
- `textutil`: Converts text files from one format to another (`.txt`, `.rtf`, `.html`, `.doc`, `.webarchive`, and so on)
- `zip`, `unzip`: Packs and unpacks ZIP archive files
- `perl`, `python`, `ruby`, `tcl`: Allows you to use powerful general-purpose scripting languages

Running Shell Scripts from AppleScript

You can run shell scripts from AppleScript in two ways: scripting the Terminal application and using Standard Additions' `do shell script` command.

Scripting the Terminal Application

Apple's Terminal application provides a basic scripting interface. Dictionary defines just two classes, `application` and `window`. Window objects include properties for manipulating various window settings. The main command is `do script`, which tells it to run a Unix shell script or command.

From the Dictionary

Here's the definition of the `do script` command:

```
do script: Run a Unix shell script or command
    do script  string  -- data to be passed to the Terminal application as the
                            command line
        [in  reference]  -- the window in which to execute the command
```

This takes a shell script string as a direct parameter and executes it either in a new window or in an existing one depending on whether you supply an `in` parameter; see the syntax in the "Example" section.

Note that `do script` doesn't wait for the shell script to complete; it just starts it and returns immediately. It doesn't return a result, and it doesn't raise an error if the shell script fails.

Example

This will open a new Terminal window and use the ls Unix command to list the contents of a folder (or *directory* in Unix jargon):

```
tell application "Terminal"
   do script "ls /Applications/AppleScript/"
end tell
```

Alternatively, if you want to run the script in an existing window, use the in parameter to supply a reference to the window you want to use:

```
tell application "Terminal"
   do script "ls /Applications/AppleScript/" in window 1
end tell
```

Like many other shell script commands, the ls command may take no arguments, in which case it uses the current working directory. In this example, a single argument passed to the ls command is a POSIX path pointing to the AppleScript folder in the Applications folder (/Applications/AppleScript/). The slash at the start of the path name indicates that the path is an absolute path and not a relative path. (You'll learn more about working directories and relative vs. absolute paths in the "Absolute Paths, Relative Paths, and the Working Directory" section.) The result is a string listing the names of the files and folders in the folder.

Limitations

The following are the limitations of scripting the Terminal application:

- You can't pass data directly in or out (you need to read to/write from separate files for that).
- The do script command won't wait for the script to complete before returning.
- The do script command won't raise an error if the shell script fails (again, you need to make the shell script writes any error information to a separate file and then check that; this requires extra work and is often clumsy to do).

Using the do shell script Command

The do shell script command is simple: it takes a string as its direct parameter and executes it as if you had typed it in the Terminal application and pressed Return (though it has a few differences, which I'll discuss along the way).

Note Apple provides a very good FAQ on using do shell script at http://developer.apple.com/technotes/tn2002/tn2065.html.

From the Dictionary

The do shell script command is defined in the Miscellaneous Commands suite of Standard Additions:

```
do shell script: Execute a shell script or command using the 'sh' shell
   do shell script  string  -- the command or shell script to execute.
                            Examples are 'ls' or '/bin/ps -auxwww'
     [as  type class]  -- the desired type of result; default is Unicode text
                          (UTF-8)
```

```
      [administrator privileges  boolean]  -- execute the command as the
                                                 administrator
      [user name  string]  -- use this administrator account to avoid a password
                             dialog (If this parameter is specified, the
                             "password" parameter must also be specified.)
      [password  string]  -- use this administrator password to avoid a password
                            dialog
      [altering line endings  boolean]  -- change all line endings to Mac-style
                                           and trim a trailing one (default true)
   [Result:  string]  -- the command output
```

Setting the do shell script Command Parameters

The following sections discuss some of the do shell script command's parameters.

The administrator privileges Parameter

The administrator privileges parameter allows you to enter the Mac administrator's username and password in the operating system's Authenticate dialog box. This authentication will hold for as long as the script is open. Every time it's opened, it will require authentication the first time it runs. If it's a script applet, it will require authentication every time it runs. This may be annoying, but it ensures that someone can't use AppleScript to bypass the Unix tight permissions scheme.

The user name and password Parameters

You can use user name and password together as an alternative to the administrator privileges parameter, although you can supply any username and password, not necessarily an administrative one. Using these has the generally bad security implication of hard-coding potentially sensitive login information right into your script. Try not to get fired over this! Here's an example:

```
do shell script "cd /secure/server/directory/" user name "admin" password "URaQT"
```

The altering ending Parameter

This Boolean parameter allows you to alter the line endings of the do shell script command's result from the original Unix line endings to the Mac's line endings. By default, the line endings will be altered and become Mac line endings. You would want to specifically not alter the line endings if you plan on feeding the result of one statement as the parameter of the next do shell script command.

Direct Parameter and Result Unicode Caveats

Although the dictionary still lists the results from a shell script as being of type string, it is actually of type Unicode text. In reality, the do shell script command converts the direct parameter you hand it, which is the shell script you want to execute, from a string or Unicode text to UTF-8 and then converts the UTF-8 encoded result back to Unicode text type before returning it to you. In general, this is of no consequence to you. But in case you need to use the read and write commands for reading and writing text files used by the do shell script command, you will need to consider these issues. Chapter 14 discusses reading and writing UTF-8 files.

> **Note** The UTF-8 format may contain the first 128 characters that are the same as in ASCII, which makes them compatible with an ASCII-oriented shell. It may also contain any other Unicode character represented as a sequence of 2–6 bytes. You can learn more about this in Chapter 14.

Example

Here's an example of using the do shell script command to return a result in a usable datatype:

```
do shell script "ls /Applications/AppleScript/"
```

Unlike Terminal's do script command, do shell script can return a result. Figure 29-2 shows the value returned when the previous script is run.

Figure 29-2. *Running the* ls *Unix command from AppleScript using the* do shell script *command*

The result is a Unicode text string containing the names of the items in the folder. Each name appears on a separate line in the string, separated by a linefeed (ASCII 10) character. Many Unix commands will represent a list of values in this way. You can easily split the returned multiline string into a list of strings if you want:

```
every paragraph of (do shell script "ls /Applications/AppleScript/")
--> {"AppleScript Utility.app", "Example Scripts", ➥
  "Folder Actions Setup.app", "Script Editor.app"}
```

Limitations

The following are some known limitations to using the do shell script command.

No User Interaction

In many cases, the shell scripts you want to run require user interaction. Because the do shell script command doesn't allow for that, you have to direct shell scripts to the Terminal application instead by using its scripting capabilities.

Speed

Although shell scripts often execute quickly, do shell script has to start a new shell each time it's called, which can add overhead time. This can start to add up if you're calling do shell script frequently.

Supplying Data to Standard Input

Unfortunately, the do shell script command doesn't provide any way to supply data directly to standard input. I'll cover a couple of ways to work around this limitation in the "More Examples of Using Quoted Form" section.

Running AppleScript from Shell Scripts

Reversing the tables on the do shell script command is the osacompile shell command. This command allows you to run AppleScript scripts from the command line.

The osacompile command can run scripts in two ways: it can run the actual code you supply as a string, or it can run a script stored in a file, either as text or as a compiled script.

For example, to execute a script right from the command line, use -e, followed by the script in quoted string form. The following shell script will tell iTunes to start playing:

```
osascript -e 'tell app "iTunes" to play'
```

You can supply multiple lines of script by including more -e options, each one followed by a line of code. The following shell script will run a four-line AppleScript that will activate the Finder and display an alert showing the name of disk 1:

```
osascript -e 'tell app "Finder"' -e 'activate' -e ➥
   'display alert (get name of disk 1)' -e 'end tell'
```

Note how the script lines are quoted with single quotes.

To run a script stored in a file, you specify the file path right after the command. For this example, I created a text file with the text return (get current date as string) and then saved it in my user directory with the name my script.applescript.

The following shell script will run it and as a result return the current date to the command line:

```
osascript 'my script.applescript'
```

You can also pass parameters to the script's run handler. What you have to do is include a parameter variable at the end of the on run line. The value of this variable will be a list containing the arguments passed from the command line.

Here's the simplest way to pass parameters: create a new document in Script Editor, and type the following:

```
on run folderNames
   tell application "Finder"
      repeat with thisFolderName in  folderNames
         make new folder at desktop with properties {name:thisFolderName}
      end repeat
   end tell
end run
```

Save this script as a text file in your home folder, and name it make folder.applescript.

Now, enter the following text into the Terminal:

```
osascript 'make folder.applescript' 'My Cool Folder'
```

osascript will compile script in the text file and call its run handler, passing it the list {"My Cool Folder"} as its parameter. The script in turn will loop through each item in this list, creating a new folder on the desktop and using the string as the name of the folder. To pass multiple parameters, separate each argument in the osacompile command with a space.

Other AppleScript-related commands, which I won't be covering here, are osalang, which lists all the open scripting architecture (OSA) languages you have installed, and osacompile, which compiles text and saves it as a compiled script. Use man to find out more about these commands.

You can also read more about running scripts from the command line using the cron application in Chapter 30.

Assembling Shell Script Strings

The following sections discuss ways to assemble AppleScript strings that can be used as shell scripts.

Unix File Paths

While AppleScript uses colon-delimited HFS paths to describe the locations of files and folders on a hard disk, Unix requires slash-delimited POSIX paths. This means any time you want to pass a path from AppleScript to a shell script or back, you have to convert from one format to the other.

Chapter 13 discusses how to convert between HFS- and POSIX-style paths, but here's a quick refresher. When going from ActionScript to a shell script, use an alias/file object's POSIX path property to get the equivalent POSIX path string. (This also works on strings.)

```
set posix_path_string to POSIX path of  alias➥
"Macintosh HD:Applications:AppleScript:" --> "/Applications/AppleScript/"
```

When going from a shell script to ActionScript, use a POSIX file specifier to convert a POSIX path string back into a file object:

```
set the_file_object to POSIX file posix_path_string
--> file "d1:Applications:AppleScript:"
```

Because of some long-time bugs, all these conversions will work correctly only when the named hard drive is mounted; otherwise, you'll get a malformed path as a result. For example, the following:

```
POSIX path of "Unmounted HD:Folder:"
```

returns the following:

```
"/Unmounted HD/Folder/"
```

but it should be the following:

```
"/Volumes/Unmounted HD/Folder/"
```

In addition, the following:

```
POSIX file (get "/Volumes/Unmounted HD/Folder/")
```

returns the following:

```
file "Macintosh HD:Volumes:Unmounted HD:Folder:"
```

but it should be the following:

```
file "Unmounted HD:Folder:"
```

Quoting Arguments

Forgetting to quote arguments is a common mistake and also potentially serious because, unlike the Mac's GUI interface, the Unix command line is extremely unforgiving of user mistakes (it assumes you already know what you're doing). For example, it's all too easy to accidentally ask it to delete your entire home folder, and before you know it, you'll be restoring your entire account from backups (uh . . . you do always keep up-to-date backups, don't you?); there are few "Are you sure?" confirmations and no Undo. Although the most common result of a missing or misplaced quote is that the script halts with an error or produces an incorrect result, it really is possible to do some serious damage if you're not careful.

For example, even forgetting some quotes can have serious implications if you are playing with commands such as rm, which will just delete what you ask it to and not think twice about it. Imagine if you wanted to use the POSIX path /Users/hanaan/Documents Backup in an rm command and didn't quote it:

```
set the_path to "/Users/hanaan/Documents Backup"
do shell script "rm -rf " & the_path --DO NOT RUN THIS CODE!
```

This would erase your Documents folder and the item named Backup in the current working directory, not your Documents Backup folder!

Assuming you're not quite that careless, you'll remember to quote it, but here's where unsuspecting folk run into another pitfall. If you try to add the quotes yourself, such as in the following:

```
do shell script "rm -rf '" & the_path & "'"
```

then you avoid the previous, more obvious bug, but you still leave yourself open to another. Specifically, what happens if the string you're quoting contains a single quote character? The shell will see that character and assume it's the closing quote and treat what follows as regular code. Here's a relatively benign example that causes an error when run:

```
set the_text to "Use a pipe '|' symbol"
do shell script "echo '" & the_text & "'"
--Error: sh: line 1:  symbol: command not found
```

What the shell sees is the line like this (with extra spaces added to make it more obvious):

```
echo 'Use a pipe' | symbol
```

It executes the echo command and then tries to pipe its output to a command named symbol. In this case, the script errors because a symbol command isn't available, but imagine what damage it could do if some destructive command *was* triggered, either accidentally or possibly even deliberately. (For example, malicious Internet hackers often use carefully crafted strings to trick carelessly written programs that have these flaws into executing code that hijacks the whole machine.)

Therefore, before using an AppleScript string as a literal string in a shell script, *always* make sure it's correctly quoted and escaped first. Asking a string for the value of its quoted form property will do this for you easily and effectively. Quoting POSIX path strings is an obvious example, but you should do it for *any* string whose contents should be treated as data, not code. For example:

```
set shell_script to "rm -rf " & quoted form of the_posix_path

set shell_script to ¬
    "echo " & quoted form of input_text & ¬
    " | grep " & quoted form of match_pattern
```

Absolute Paths, Relative Paths, and the Working Directory

When executing file-related shell script commands either in AppleScript or in the Terminal, you need to pass the path of the target file or directory as arguments to the Unix command. You can specify file paths in Unix commands in two ways: either as an absolute path or as a relative path.

Passing an absolute path means you disregard your current location and assume that the starting point (which is also the top directory, in this case) is either the startup disk or the current user's home directory. Relative paths start from the current working directory.

When specifying an absolute path starting from the startup disk level, you start the path with a slash. To indicate the startup disk only, you pass a slash by itself. The following shell script will list the content of the startup disk:

```
do shell script "ls /"
```

In a way, when executing the do shell script command from AppleScript, it is easier to use absolute paths starting from the startup disk since this is the path that is returned by the POSIX path property of alias file references. In the following script, you first get the path to the user's Documents folder using AppleScript's path to command, and then you get the POSIX path property of the result and use it with the ls command in a shell script:

```
set mac_path to path to documents folder from user domain
--> alias "Macintosh HD:Users:hanaan:Documents:"
set unix_path to POSIX path of mac_path
--> "/Users/hanaan/Documents/"
do shell script ("ls " & unix_path)
```

If you want to start from the current user's home directory, you have to precede the slash with a tilde: ~/. The following script will have the same result as the previous one, listing the contents of the Documents folder in the home directory:

```
 do shell script ("ls ~/Documents")
```

To do this, however, you will need to build the path yourself without much help from Apple-Script's various POSIX path amenities.

You can also refer to disks other than the startup disk. To do that, you need to precede the name of the disk with the word Volumes. The script that follows lists the contents of the hard disk External2000:

```
do shell script ("ls /Volumes/External2000")
```

When writing shell scripts in the Terminal application, where they belong, the most common way to pass path arguments is as relative paths. Relative paths use an implied working directory for all your file-related commands. You can add on to that working directory or change the working directory and work from there.

Imagine giving someone directions to the kitchen in your house. You may tell that person to go to the front door or a room and start from there (absolute paths), or you may ask that person where they are standing at the moment and give directions from that point. After all, they might be one doorway away, so why send them all the way to the front door to start?

You can change the working directory with the cd command, after which you can see the path to the working directory in the Terminal as the prefix to the commands. Figure 29-3 shows the Terminal after the working directory was changed with the cd command.

The first line (after the welcome line) shows the cd command change the working directory to the AppleScript folder in the Applications folder on the startup disk. The next line starts with that directory as part of the command prompt.

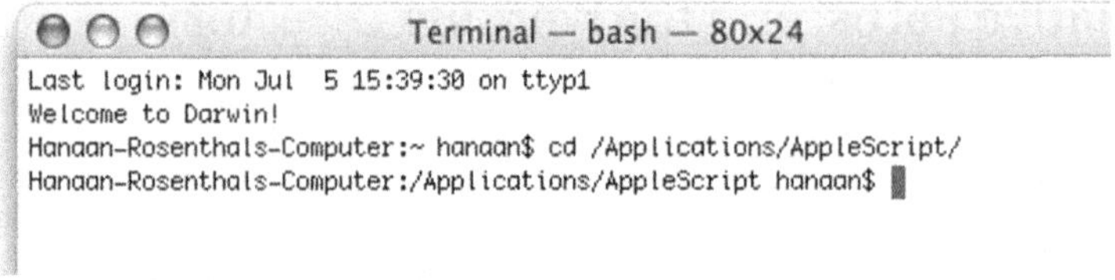

Figure 29-3. *The Terminal window shown after the* cd *command. Watch how the command prompt changes.*

To describe the enclosing directory when using relative paths, you can use `../`. The following script lists the directory that encloses the current working directory:

```
do shell script to "ls ../"
```

The problem with using the working directory in AppleScript's do shell script is that, unlike the Terminal, AppleScript forgets the working directory between executions of the do shell script command. You could execute multiple commands by separating them with a semicolon. The following script will change the working directory with the cd command and list the working directory with the ls command:

```
do shell script "cd ~/Documents; ls"
```

The fact that AppleScript doesn't retain the working directory between do shell script calls does make working directories less helpful, though, and for most tasks absolute paths are the method of choice.

More Examples of Using Quoted Form

Earlier, you saw how to use quoted form to help you when writing shell scripts. This section goes a bit further into this subject, showing you some more practical examples of what you can do with it. Here's a simple example to show how to list the contents of a folder:

```
do shell script "ls " & quoted form of POSIX path of the_folder
```

The ls command is always a good one to experiment with because it's nondestructive and won't cause any damage if accidentally misused. You can take this further with a more potentially dangerous example involving your old friend rm:

```
do shell script "rm -rf " & quoted form of POSIX path of the_file_or_folder
```

Passing Data to Standard Input

Although the do shell script command doesn't provide any way to feed data directly to standard input, you can supply standard input yourself in a couple of ways, each with its own advantages and disadvantages.

Using echo

The simplest way to get data into a Unix application's standard input is to include it in the shell script. To do this, you use the echo application, which takes your input data as an argument (correctly quoted, of course!) and passes it directly to standard out. You can then use a pipe to redirect this output to the standard input of a second command.

To demonstrate, here's how you could use grep to find all lines in a linefeed-delimited string containing the specified pattern (also correctly quoted):

```
do shell script ¬
    "echo " & quoted form of input_text & ¬
    " | grep " & quoted form of pattern_to_match
```

For example, to find all the strings in a list that contain at least one digit (0–9), do this:

```
set the_list to {"hello", "bob42", "three", "0.197"}
set AppleScript's text item delimiters to (ASCII character 10)
set input_text to the_list as string
set pattern_to_match to "[[:digit:]]"

do shell script ¬
    "echo " & quoted form of input_text & ¬
    " | grep " & quoted form of pattern_to_match
every paragraph of result
--> {"bob42", "0.197"}
```

This echo-based approach has a couple of disadvantages, however. The first is that the Unix shell sets a maximum length for scripts (on Tiger this is roughly 128KB), so if you try to pass too big a string, you'll get an error. The second is that if your string contains any ASCII 0 characters, you'll get an error because Unix often interprets ASCII 0 to mean "end of string" and will stop reading your shell script before it gets to the actual end.

For some tasks these limitations won't be an issue, but when they are, you'll need to use the next approach.

Using Temporary Files

Another way to get data from AppleScript to a Unix application's standard input is to write it to a temporary file and then redirect the shell script's standard input to read from that file. Although this approach takes a bit more work, it doesn't have the limitations of the echo-based approach you just saw.

This approach has three steps. The first step is to create a suitable file path for writing the temporary file to. The second step is to write the temporary file using Standard Additions commands. The last step is to tell your shell script to read its standard input from this file.

If you want, you can add some code that uses the rm command to erase the temporary file once it's no longer needed. This step isn't strictly necessary if you write the file to one of Mac OS X's temporary folders, however, because the Mac OS X will eventually clean up any leftovers in those locations for you. To keep the following example simple, I've left out this cleanup stage, but you can add it if you want.

Creating the File Path

To create your temporary file path, use a couple of Standard Addition commands: path to and random number. The path to command gets the path to the temporary items folder where you'll write the file. The random number command generates a random filename that (you hope!) won't overlap with any existing temporary files. To be certain of this, once you've generated a random filename, you can use the list folder command to get the names of all the current temporary items and check that the new name isn't in that list. If it is, you just try a different random name until you come up with one that is original. In practice, the chances of another temporary item having the same name are pretty low, but since you're sharing the temporary folder with other applications, it's best to be sure.

Script 29-1 shows the finished subroutine.

Script 29-1.

```
on make_temp_posix_path()
    set temp_folder to path to temporary items
    set new_name to "dss" & (random number from 100000 to 999999)
    set existing_temp_names to list folder temp_folder
    repeat while new_name is in existing_temp_names
        set new_name to "dss" & (random number from 100000 to 999999)
    end repeat
    return (POSIX path of temp_folder) & new_name
end make_temp_posix_path
```

Notice how this subroutine returns a POSIX-style file path. You'll need to convert this to a file object before passing it to the file-writing subroutine, but you can use it in the shell script as is. I've also prefixed the filename with dss (short for do shell script) just so the files are easy to identify if I need to look in the temporary items folder while debugging scripts that use this approach.

Writing the Temporary File

This step is easy. You'll write the file's content as UTF-8 encoded Unicode text («class utf8»), because that gives you a good level of compatibility with the ASCII-oriented Unix shell while also preserving any non-ASCII characters. The subroutine shown in Script 29-2 is a just modified version of one of the file-writing subroutines shown in Chapter 14.

Script 29-2.

```
on write_text_to_utf8_file(the_file, the_text)
    set file_ref to open for access the_file with write permission
    set eof file_ref to 0
    write the_text to file_ref as «class utf8»
    close access file_ref
end write_text_to_utf8_file
```

Redirecting the Shell Script

To make the shell script read its standard input from a temporary file, you use the < symbol followed by the path to the temporary file:

```
grep 'pattern to match' < '/path/to/input text'
```

The do shell script equivalent of this is as follows:

```
do shell script ¬
    "grep " & quoted form of pattern_to_match & ¬
    " < " & quoted form of temp_path
```

The following example uses grep to find all the items in a list that contain at least one digit (remember to include the two handlers from the previous sections):

```
set the_list to {"hello", "bob42", "three", "0.197"}
set AppleScript's text item delimiters to (ASCII character 10)
set input_text to the_list as string
set pattern_to_match to "[[:digit:]]"

set temp_path to make_temp_posix_path()
write_text_to_utf8_file(POSIX file temp_path, input_text)
```

```
do shell script ¬
    "grep " & quoted form of pattern_to_match & ¬
    " < " & quoted form of temp_path
every paragraph of result
--> {"bob42", "0.197"}
```

Changing Permissions

One of the biggest headaches Unix integration brought to the Mac platform is permissions. I know, it's all for the best, but it is still a pain. Although you can use the Finder's Get Info dialog box or third-party GUI applications such as BatChmod (http://macchampion.com/arbysoft/) to do this, sometimes you may want to use the powerful chmod Unix command to do this.

Since this is not a Unix book and many Unix books are available, I will not go into it too deeply; however, I do want to cover the basics of using chmod and how to integrate it with AppleScript. chmod, which is short for change mode, changes the permission modes of a file or folder. Besides the file you want to change, it takes a mode argument, which is a single code that describes the new permissions settings for the file.

Note Mac OS X 10.4 adds support for access control lists (ACLs), a newer and more flexible way to control file permissions. Traditional Unix permissions are still in common use, though, and should be sufficient for most users.

---

chmod also takes several options, allowing you to customize the way it works. An important option is -R, which determines whether folders are processed recursively, and the same options you applied to the folder apply to all the files and folders in it.

The mode argument is a bit more complicated because it allows the same information to be specified in different ways. For this exercise, you'll specify the mode in its absolute form, which is easy to calculate in AppleScript. Imagine a three-digit number in which the first digit represents the owner, the second digit represents the group, and the third represents anyone else. Now, say the number 4 stands for "allow to read," number 2 stands for "allow to write," and 1 is for "allow to execute." Let's put a simple one together: the mode 444 means allow the owner to read, the group to read, and anyone else to read.

What if, however, you want to let the owner read and write? Well, read is 4 and write is 2, so read and write is 6. The mode number in that case would be 644. Table 29-1 offers a quick reference.

Table 29-1. *Mode Numbers for Different User Permissions Settings*

Permission Level	Mode Number
Read	4
Write	2
Execute	1
Read/write	6
Read/execute	5
Write/execute	3
Read/write/execute	7

Looking at Table 29-1, you can tell why a popular choice is 777, which allows anyone to do anything. Also, 775 is useful, because it prevents anyone other than the group and owner from writing to the file.

To learn more about chmod, use the man page: type man chmod in the Terminal application. (I won't be discussing ACLs here, so you can ignore the ACL Manipulation Options section for now.)

Script 29-3 is a droplet that loops through nine dialog boxes that represent the nine options: owner read, owner write, owner execute, and the same for group and others. After collecting the information from the user, the script assembles a string that will be run as a shell script. The script is followed by a brief explanation.

Script 29-3.

```
1. on open the_item_list
2.     set shell_script to "chmod"

3.     --Ask the user what mode to use
4.     set this_mode to 0
5.     repeat with the_entity_ref in ¬
            {{"owner", 100}, {"group members", 10}, {"others", 1}}
6.         set {entity_name, entity_val} to the_entity_ref
7.         repeat with the_action_ref in ¬
                {{"read", 4}, {"write to", 2}, {"execute", 1}}
8.             set {action_name, action_val} to the_action_ref
9.             display dialog ¬
                    "Allow " & entity_name & " to " & action_name & "?" ¬
                    buttons {"No", "Yes"} default button "Yes"
10.            if button returned of result is "Yes" then
11.                set this_mode to this_mode + (entity_val * action_val)
12.            end if
13.        end repeat
14.    end repeat

15.    --Ask if folders should be processed recursively
16.    display dialog ¬
            "When processing folders, change all enclosed items as well?" ¬
            buttons {"No", "Yes"} default button "Yes"
17.    if button returned of result is "Yes" then
18.        set shell_script to shell_script & space & "-R"
19.    end if

20.    --Add the mode argument to the command string
21.    set shell_script to shell_script & space & this_mode

22.    --Add the file path arguments to the command string
23.    repeat with this_item_ref in the_item_list
24.        set shell_script to shell_script & space & ¬
                quoted form of POSIX path of this_item_ref
25.    end repeat

26.    --Run the shell script
27.    display dialog "Make these changes as an administrator?" ¬
            buttons {"No", "Yes"}
28.    set run_as_admin to button returned of result is "Yes"
```

```
29.    try
30.        do shell script shell_script administrator privileges run_as_admin
31.    on error err_msg
32.        display dialog "The following error(s) occurred:" & return & err_msg ¬
               buttons {"OK"}
33.    end try
34. end open
```

The preceding script consists of a few parts.

Lines 4 to 14 find out what permissions the user wants to use. The outer loop cycles through each entity (owner, group, and everyone else), and the inner loop goes through the permission options for that entity (read, write, execute). Each time, a dialog box asks the user to choose whether to allow or disallow a particular permission. It starts with the owner's read permission, then the owner's write permission, and so on. If the user clicks Yes, the script adds the appropriate number to the value in the this_mode variable.

Lines 16 to 19 ask the user whether items inside folders should be changed as well. If the user clicks Yes, the -R option is added to the chmod command.

Once the command's options have been added, the next step is to add its arguments. Line 21 adds the mode argument that was constructed earlier. Lines 23 to 25 loop through the list of dropped items, getting the POSIX path of each, quoting it (don't forget this bit!), and adding it to the command.

Lines 27 and 28 let the user decide whether they want to make the changes as an administrator or as a regular user. Line 30 executes the shell script. If the user decides to perform it as an administrator, the do shell script command will ask for an administrator name and password to be entered before running the shell script. Users who don't have administrator access can still change the permissions on files they already own. Any errors that occur will be trapped by the surrounding try block and reported to the user.

Note You can find out the current permissions for a file or folder in the Finder by choosing File ➤ Get Info and looking at the Ownership & Permissions tab or by using AppleScript (open the Finder's dictionary in Script Editor, and look for the three privileges properties defined in the item class). The ls Unix command also provides an l option for displaying detailed information about a file or a folder's contents, as in ls -l /Applications/.

Analyzing PDFs

In addition to the Unix applications that come as standard on Mac OS X, many free Unix applications are available, and you can figure out how to script many of them with the do shell script command.

As a small example, I will show how to script a Unix application called pdffonts, which is part of the open-source Xpdf package by Glyph & Cog (www.glyphandcog.com). You can download Xpdf from its website at www.foolabs.com/xpdf/. (There should be a Mac OS X binary installer on the downloads page.)

pdffonts takes the path of a PDF file and returns detailed information about the fonts in that PDF file—whether the font is embedded, the font type, and so on. The following is sample output from pdffonts:

Name	Type	Emb	Sub	Uni	Object ID	
TZJIIJ+Palatino-Roman	CID Type 0C	yes	yes	yes	17	0
RJPWGN+Palatino-Bold	CID Type 0C	yes	yes	yes	23	0
QBFQSP+Palatino-Italic	CID Type 0C	yes	yes	yes	9	0

The meaning of the different columns is as follows:

Name: The font name, including the subset prefix, which is the text before the +.

Type: The font type. (Type 1, Type 3, TrueType, CID Type 0, and so on.)

Emb: Whether the font is embedded in the PDF.

Sub: Whether the font is a subset.

Uni: Whether the PDF contains an explicit "to Unicode" map. For details, see www.glyphandcog.com.

Object ID: The font dictionary object ID, which includes the number and generation.

It is up to you to extract the information you want from this.

Script 29-4 creates a droplet that accepts a PDF file and tells you how many fonts it uses and how many of them are embedded.

Script 29-4.

```
1. on open {pdf_file}
2.     set shell_script to "/usr/local/bin/pdffonts " & ¬
           quoted form of POSIX path of pdf_file
3.     try
4.         set shell_result to do shell script shell_script
5.     on error error_message
6.         display dialog "Error:" & return & error_message
7.         return
8.     end try
9.     --first 2 lines are table headings, so we ignore those
10.    if (count paragraphs of shell_result) > 2 then
11.        set font_info_list to paragraphs 3 thru -1 of shell_result
12.        set embedded_font_count to 0
13.        repeat with font_info_ref in font_info_list
14.            --the embedded column is fifth from the right
15.            set is_embedded to word -5 of font_info_ref
16.            if is_embedded is "yes" then
17.                set embedded_font_count to embedded_font_count + 1
18.            end if
19.        end repeat
20.        display dialog "This PDF contains " & ¬
               (count font_info_list) & " fonts, out of which " & ¬
               embedded_font_count & " are embedded."
21.    else
22.        display dialog "No fonts were found."
23.    end if
24. end open
```

In line 2 of the script you get the POSIX path to the dropped PDF, quote it, and construct the shell command.

Lines 3 to 8 are responsible for running the shell command and reporting any errors that might occur (for example, whether the file dropped is not a PDF).

Line 10 checks to see whether there were any fonts found in the PDF. The first two lines of the result string are table headings, so you ignore those. If it contains more than two lines, you can start extracting the data from the remaining lines; otherwise, you just let the user know that no fonts were found.

In line 11 you create a list that includes all the paragraphs of the result, starting from the third paragraph (paragraphs 1 and 2 are the title and underscore).

Once you have the list, you loop through each font information line and pick out the information you need. Although the finished solution looks simple enough, coming up with one that will work reliably isn't always as easy, so let's look at how this one was arrived at and some of the potential traps discovered along the way.

As is common for command-line tools, table-style data isn't presented as simple tab-delimited text but arranged as vertical columns designed for viewing in a monospace font on a command-line display. This sort of format is rather trickier to parse reliably because the number of spaces between each item in a table row will vary as the application tries to arrange everything into vertical columns.

If you're lucky, the columns will all be fixed widths that never, ever change, in which case you can extract the bits you want using references like this:

```
text start_position thru end_position of the_line
```

Unfortunately, this is not always the case. For example, if a left column contains a long value, then all the remaining columns may be pushed to the right to fit it in. These sorts of issues often aren't obvious at first glance, so be careful; otherwise, you could introduce all sorts of subtle, hidden bugs into your code. Faulty code that happens to produce correct results most of the time but occasionally slips in an incorrect answer can easily often go unnoticed for a long time if it doesn't cause an actual error.

In this case, testing pdffonts with a PDF file whose font names are known to be longer than 37 characters (the width of the first column) quickly shows that this approach won't be an option here.

Another common way to break down these sorts of tables is to use another Unix application, awk. awk is a basic pattern-matching language for identifying and extracting sections of data from a single line. It's ideal for dealing with command-line table data where spaces appear between items but never appear inside them because it treats any number of adjoining spaces as a single divider. For example, to extract the third column from such a table, you would pipe the table data from the previous command into an awk command like this:

```
some_command | awk '{print $3}'
```

Alas, this won't help you either because the values in the second column of the table may often contain spaces (for example, Type 1), so a value that appears as item 3 on one line could be item 4 or 5 on the next.

Still, it feels like you're getting closer to a solution, doesn't it? Looking at the columns on the right, notice that they're all a lot more regular; therefore, I reckon you'll be OK if you count columns from the right instead of from the left. Using awk would be trickier here because it normally counts from left to right. However, the values in the right columns are all either numbers or words, so you should be able to get the one you want using a word -5 of... reference in AppleScript. Problem (you hope) solved!

Once you've extracted the desired yes/no value from the line's Embedded column, you can see whether it's a yes and increment the value of embedded_font_count if it is. This happens on lines 16 to 18.

Finally, on line 20, the finished message is assembled and displayed.

Calling Other Languages

Mac OS X ships with several popular general-purpose scripting languages installed as standard: Perl, Python, Ruby, and Tcl. Because this is a book about AppleScript, I don't want to spend lots of time teaching you how to use those languages as well, but scripters who already know a little about using these languages (or are willing to learn) can easily call them from AppleScript via the do shell script command.

You'll now look at a couple of quick examples using Python (www.python.org), a popular general-purpose scripting language with a clean syntax and plenty of useful libraries included as standard.

Encoding URLs in Python

The following script uses Python's urllib module to convert an AppleScript string for use in URLs:

```
on encode_URL(txt)
    set python_script to ¬
        "import sys, urllib; print urllib.quote(sys.argv[1])"
    set python_script to "python -c " & ¬
        quoted form of python_script & " " & ¬
        quoted form of txt
    return do shell script python_script
end encode_URL

encode_URL("photos ƒ")
--> "photos%20%C6%92"
```

In a URL, only numbers, characters *a* to *z* and *A* to *Z*, and a few symbols (such as - and _) are left intouched. Everything else should be converted to the UTF-8 equivalent and then formatted as hex numbers with a % symbol in front of each one. As you'll recall, do shell script already converts text to UTF-8 when passing it to the Unix shell, and UTF-8 is just what the quote function in Python's urllib module wants, so you can pass it to that without any extra conversions. Similarly, the quote function returns ASCII text, so you don't need any extra conversion there either.

In the Python script, the import statement imports the libraries you need. The sys.argv[1] bit gets the text to convert; this is supplied as an extra argument to the python shell command, which passes it to the script. The quote function converts this to the desired format, and the result is printed to standard out.

In the previous example, the command executed by the Unix shell will look like this:

```
python -c 'import sys, urllib; print urllib.quote(sys.argv[1])' 'photos ƒ'
```

The -c option is followed by the script you want Python to execute. This is followed by the argument you want it to pass directly to the script for processing.

Remember that although the actual string-to-URL conversion is fast, calling this subroutine repeatedly will be relatively slow because of the time it takes to start a new Unix shell followed by a new python interpreter. If you want to convert lots of strings at once, you could speed things up by concatenating them into a return-delimited string, passing that to the encode_url subroutine in a single call and then splitting the result into a list (remember that returns will be converted to %13, so you'll need to use text item delimiters, not "every paragraph of . . .," to split it back up).

Changing Case in Python

The following script is quite similar to the previous one, except this time you're using Python to convert a string to uppercase. Here's the subroutine, followed by an example of its use:

```
on uppercase_text(txt)
    set python_script to ¬
        "import sys; print unicode(sys.argv[1], 'utf8').upper().encode('utf8')"
    return do shell script "python -c " & ¬
        quoted form of python_script & " " & ¬
        quoted form of txt
end uppercase_text

uppercase_text("Mon résumé est excellent!")
--> "MON RÉSUMÉ EST EXCELLENT!"
```

Since you'll want any non-ASCII characters to be converted correctly, you'll use Python's Unicode support. You do this by asking Python to convert the UTF-8 data it receives into a unicode object (equivalent to AppleScript's Unicode text, only more powerful), change the case of that, and then convert the result into UTF-8 data. As you can see from the example result, non-ASCII characters, in this case the two é characters, are correctly converted.

You can easily adapt this code to take advantage of other basic text manipulation features built into every unicode object in Python. For example, to change the text to lowercase, sentence case, or title case instead, replace the upper() call with lower(), capitalize(), or title(). If the input text is large, you'll want to pass it via stdin instead of argv, in which case you'd need to use the temp file–based technique described earlier in the chapter and change the Python script to this:

```
"import sys; print unicode(sys.stdin.read(), 'utf8').upper().encode('utf8')"
```

CHAPTER 30

■ ■ ■

Scheduling Scripts

So far I have covered the scripts themselves: how to write them, save them, and run them. But what if you want a script to run automatically at any time of the day or night?

In this chapter, I cover a few options for scheduling scripts to automatically run at any time on your Mac.

Using iDo Script Scheduler

Perhaps the most well-known option for automating the launch of scripts is iDo Script Scheduler by Sophisticated Circuits. You can buy it or download a demo from Sophisticated Circuits' website at www.sophisticated.com.

iDo Script Scheduler allows you to select a script file and specify when it should run. Your choices are Once Only, Repeating, Days of Week, Day of Month, Hot Key, and System Idle. The Days of Week and Day of Month choices are variations of the Repeating option. They allow you to specify in what intervals your scripts will run.

The System Idle option lets you set a number of minutes that the system can be idle before your script executes. Hot Key is also a neat alternative for attaching key combinations to script execution.

You can have iDo Script Scheduler run scripts from many languages, including Perl, the Unix shell, Python, and others. You have to identify these scripts with special filename extensions. It's a reliable and easy-to-use utility, and most of its windows and dialog boxes are self-explanatory. The main window, shown in Figure 30-1, lists the scheduled events and allows you to add, delete, or edit an event.

Figure 30-1. *The scheduled events in iDo Script Scheduler's main window*

Clicking the New or Edit button opens a simple Event window, which allows you to set the trigger for the script and specify the script file. The Event window also lets you specify parameters for the script, but for that, your script must be saved as a compiled script with a run handler containing parameters, like this:

```
on run {parameter1, parameter2, ...}
--script
end run
```

Some similar utilities you could use are Script Timer (find it at www.appsandmore.com) and MacAT (check out www.macsos.com.au/macat/).

Using iCal to Schedule Scripts

Another neat way of scheduling script execution is by using Apple iCal. To do that, create a new event in iCal, and set the start date and time to the date and time on which you want the script to execute. After you have the event, choose the Open file alarm, and choose the script file you want to run. This can be either a compiled script or a script application. Set the alarm to execute 0 minutes before the event.

The example in Figure 30-2 will run the Backup user folders.scpt script every night at 12:20 AM.

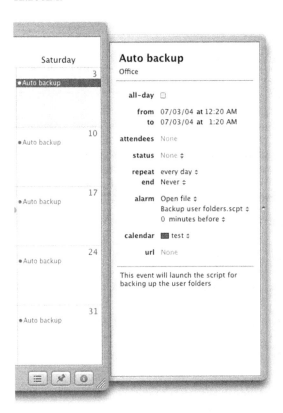

Figure 30-2. *The event shown will run the* Backup user folders.scpt *script every night at 12:20 AM*

Managing Stuck Scripts

In Chapter 23 you looked at many ways to avoid having your script error out. As much as you try, however, you can never eliminate the possibility that your script will crash.

The consequences of your script hanging or crashing may be small; someone will eventually find it and restart it. In other cases, however, it may control an automated system that processes critical jobs that people are waiting for and has to be up 24/7. In these cases, a crashed script has to be attended to immediately.

I encountered this situation in a recent project. The project was a system that produces financial documents in a fully automated fashion. Users drop source files into hot folders, and the finished Portable Document Format (PDF) file is e-mailed to them within minutes. Not only that, but the company's offices in Australia, Japan, and the United Kingdom use the system, so it was critical to have it start itself if needed.

The solution for this problem was Kick-off, a hardware-software combination made by Sophisticated Circuits, the company that makes iDo Script Scheduler. Kick-off is part of a family of products that allow you to control the computer power from scripts, among other ways.

Kick-off connects between the power strip and your Mac's power cord and also connects to the Universal Serial Bus (USB) port. You can configure it to restart your Mac in the event that a particular script hangs.

The way it works is by using an application called PowerKey Daemon. PowerKey Daemon is a scriptable utility that has a built-in timer. To use it, you include the command `tickleAppTimer` with the number of seconds the timer should be set to, like this:

```
tell application "PowerKey Daemon" to tickleAppTimer 300
```

After the PowerKey Daemon gets the "tickle," it starts the timer. If the timer expires, meaning the number of seconds you set in the timer pass before you tickle the timer again with `tickleAppTimer`, Kick-off starts the restart sequence. First, Kick-off tries to restart your Mac the nice way a specified number of times. If it can't restart, the hardware part takes over, and the power to your Mac is stopped and then started again.

All you have to do is make sure you have a start-up script in the start-up items that restarts your system.

To make sure Kick-off doesn't restart your Mac after the script quits normally, add this `quit` handler:

```
on quit
    tell application "PowerKey Daemon"
        tickleAppTimer 0 -- clear the timer before exiting.
    end tell
    continue quit -- let the script quit normally.
end quit
```

Using Unix cron

The Unix `cron` utility allows you to schedule Unix commands to run at various times and intervals. As well as running Unix commands and shell scripts, you can make `cron` execute AppleScripts via the `osascript` shell command. I discuss the `osascript` command in more detail in Chapter 29.

Each user, plus the operating system itself, has their own crontab file that lists the tasks for `cron` to perform. If you aren't intimidated by Unix, you can use the `crontab` shell command to edit crontab files at the command line. Alternatively, the freeware application CronniX provides a convenient graphical interface for editing crontab files. You can download CronniX and read more about it at www.abstracture.de/projects-en/cronnix/. Another crontab editor you could use is piTime from piDog Software (www.pidog.com/piTime/). Figure 30-3 shows CronniX's main window displaying a list of tasks in a typical crontab file.

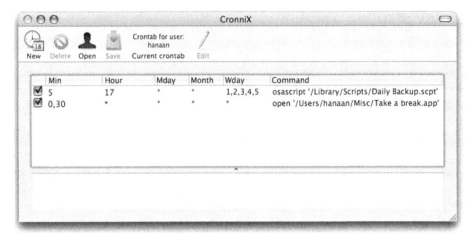

Figure 30-3. *Using CronniX to view and edit a user's crontab file*

■**Note** The first task in the list uses osascript to execute a compiled AppleScript, Daily Backup.scpt, at 5:05 PM every Monday to Friday. The second task uses the open shell command to launch a script application every half hour.

■■■

Controlling Remote Applications

Did you know you can use AppleScript to control applications across the network or across the world? This chapter discusses scripting remote Macs and remote applications.

Scripting Remote Macs over IP

One of AppleScript's features is the ability to run a script on one Mac that controls applications on another Mac. You do this with remote Apple events over Internet Protocol (IP). Beside a couple of extra lines you have to wrap your code with, the scripts themselves are the same as if they were made to run locally.

Enabling Remote Apple Events

Before you can even start scripting remote Macs, the Mac you want to script has to be able to accept them. By default, Macs are set to not allow access by remote Apple events. This issue is crucial to security: imagine the risk if anyone who knew your IP address could control your Mac from afar. Well, they would also need your username and password, but in a multi-Mac environment those may not be the most difficult things to get.

To activate remote Apple events on any OS X Mac, check the Remote Apple Events check box in the Services tab of the Sharing pane of System Preferences, as shown in Figure 31-1.

While you're in the Sharing pane, check out the user's Bonjour name. (Bonjour was previously known as Rendezvous in OS X 10.3 and earlier.) It is noted under the computer name with the .local name ending. This name will come in handy later.

Note Attention network administrators: OS X uses port 3031 for remote Apple events.

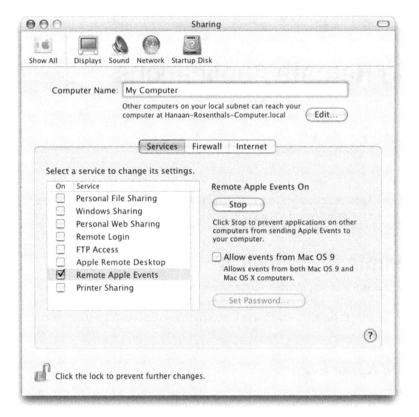

Figure 31-1. *The System Preferences Sharing pane, where you turn on remote Apple events*

Talking to Machines

When you write scripts that run locally, the scripts run on the default machine, which is your Mac—therefore specifying the machine is unnecessary. When scripting other Macs over IP, however, you need to specify the Mac (or *machine* as it is referred to in the script) to which you want to send events.

You can specify the remote machine either by using its IP address or, if it is on your local network, by using its Bonjour name. You can find the Bonjour name in the Sharing pane of its System Preferences, as noted earlier. You can get the IP address from the Network pane of its System Preferences.

Once you figure out the IP address or Bonjour name of the target machine, you can compose the tell block. Let's say you want the Finder of the target Mac to create a folder. For argument's sake, you are talking to a Mac whose IP address is 101.2.3.4. You'll need to tell the application Finder of the machine in this way:

```
tell application "Finder" of machine "eppc://101.2.3.4/"
    make new folder...
end tell
```

The beginning of the machine uniform resource locator (URL) string is always eppc:// followed by either the IP address or the Bonjour name.

The basic `tell` block for a Mac on the same local network is as follows:

```
tell application "Finder" of machine "eppc://bonjour-name.local"
    ...
end tell
```

Note Application names are case sensitive when used in a remote machine `tell` block.

Authentication

And you thought for a second that OS X security would let you by without identifying yourself! Not a chance. In fact, even if the target Mac allows incoming remote Apple events over IP, you will still need to have a username and password of a user on that Mac with administrator privileges.

You can embed the username and password for that Mac in your machine name string, like this:

```
machine "eppc://username:password@101.2.3.4/"
```

or in the case of using the Bonjour name, like this:

```
machine "eppc://username:password@bonjour-name.local"
```

If you don't use the name and password, when you run a script for the first time, you will have to enter the login information in a dialog box and ask to keep it in the keychain. Although the first method of embedding login information in the machine name is a bit easier, using the keychain is more secure, since the login information isn't hard-coded in a script somewhere.

Note It is tempting to hard-code usernames and passwords directly into scripts, but this has serious security implications. Before you know it, you install your script on some user's Mac, and suddenly your password is everywhere. Instead, try to use the keychain whenever possible.

Process ID and User ID

Along with the machine's name, you can add either a process ID (`pid`) or a user ID (`uid`).

The process ID is given to a specific process on that machine when the process (application) launches. This makes it less useful since you can't rely on it being constant. You can tell a process ID by looking at the first column in the Activity Monitor application on the remote Mac. Also, the result of the `choose remote application` command includes the `pid` of the selected remote application. Here's an example of specifying the `pid`:

```
tell application "Finder" of ¬
    machine "eppc://Hanaan-Rosenthals-Computer.local/?pid=131"
    get home
end tell
--> folder "hanaan" of folder "Users" of startup disk of application "Finder" ➡
of machine "eppc://Hanaan-Rosenthals-Computer.local/?pid=131"
```

Another way of specifying the exact process you want to target is the user ID (uid). Including the uid in the tell block allows you to target an application running on a specific user's account. This is useful when more than one user is logged into the Mac at a time.

You can determine the name of the user of a certain uid in a couple of ways. You can use the terminal on the remote Mac by typing id followed by the username:

```
hanaan$ id hanaan
uid=501(hanaan) gid=501(hanaan) groups=501(hanaan),➥
  81(appserveradm), 79(appserverusr), 80(admin)
```

Or, if you use the choose remote application command, the uid will be specified in the result:

```
application "Finder" of machine "eppc://10.0.1.4/?uid=502&pid=3896".
```

From here, you can figure out the username associated with that uid by asking the Finder of that Mac for the name of home, like this:

```
using terms from application "Finder"
    name of home of application "Finder"➥
      of machine "eppc://10.0.1.4/?uid=502"
end using terms from
-- "Olivia"
```

The using terms from Block

Although you can connect and talk to applications on remote Macs, you may not want to have a live connection to them while you're writing and compiling the script. For that purpose, you can enclose any code that is aimed at a remote application with the using terms from block. This tells AppleScript to compile the code intended to be executed by a remote application, using terms from the same application locally. This makes the tell block look like Script 31-1.

Script 31-1.

```
tell application "Finder" of machine (get "eppc://101.2.3.4/")
    using terms from application "Finder"
        --code aimed at the remote Finder
    end using terms from
end tell
```

The reason why the machine name is in parentheses is to allow the script to compile even if the remote machine isn't available on the network for some reason. Using the code (get machine_name) prevents AppleScript from looking for the machine during compilation. The script will compile using the terms taken from the application mentioned in using terms from, and the real machine will be evaluated and found only when the script runs.

Another thing you can do is allow the user to specify which application they're controlling using the choose remote application command, like this:

```
 set the_application to ¬
  choose remote application with prompt "Choose the remote InDesign to use:"
tell the_application
  using terms from application "Adobe InDesign CS2_J"
    --code aimed at the remote InDesign
  end using terms from
end tell
```

Launching Applications

Another caveat of scripting remote applications is that if the application isn't running when you target it with a script, your commands won't go through, even if you use the launch command.

What you have to do is use the Finder on the remote machine to first launch the application file and only then target it with commands. You use the Finder since it is almost certain to be running. For example:

```
tell application "Finder" of machine "eppc://johns-mac.local/"
    open file "Macintosh HD:Applications:TextEdit.app"
end tell
```

Using Aliases

The alias file–reference form is useful on the local Mac since it keeps track of files even as they move or change names. In scripting remote applications, however, using the alias reference form can cause AppleScript to get confused. Instead, store file paths in variables as strings or use POSIX file values.

Controlling XML-RPC and SOAP

AppleScript has taken a bold step to integrate the Extensible Markup Language–Remote Procedure Call (XML-RPC) and SOAP technologies into its core language. XML-RPC and SOAP are data formats for *web services*, packets of functionality that allow applications to communicate with one another over a network, usually the Web. Unlike remote Apple events, which is a Mac-only technology, web services use standard web technologies such as Hypertext Markup Language (HTTP) and Extensible Markup Language (XML) to communicate, allowing any operating system or programming language to use them.

With AppleScript, you don't need to know or write any XML or create your own HTTP requests, since AppleScript handles all the communication with the remote application for you. What you do have to know are the service's URL, method (command) name, what parameters the method takes (if any), and what values it returns. For SOAP calls, you also need to provide some standard configuration values. Each web service provider should provide all this information as part of its documentation, so using web services in AppleScript is mostly a matter of finding out what values to use and adding them to your script in the right way.

A few websites, such as XMethods (www.xmethods.com), list many such services along with information about how to use them. Converting that information into a fruitful AppleScript call is a different story, but you should get the hang of it with a bit of practice.

You can use AppleScript to make a call to a SOAP service or an XML-RPC service. Both call types are done using syntax similar to that for targeting any other application.

XML-RPC

The syntax for XML-RPC service calls looks like this:

```
tell application "http://url-to-xml-rpc-service"
    call xmlrpc {method name: the_method, parameters: parameter_list}
end tell
```

SOAP

SOAP is a more advanced successor to XML-RPC. The syntax for making a call to a SOAP service looks like Script 31-2.

Script 31-2.

```
tell application "http://url-to-soap-service"
    call soap {¬
        method name: the_method, ¬
        SOAPAction: the_action, ¬
        method namespace uri: the_namespace, ¬
        parameters: parameters_record}
end tell
```

Although the `call soap` syntax looks a bit complex, using it is mostly just a matter of looking up the documentation for the service you want to use and filling in all the values from that.

If the service requires parameters, you can supply them using the `parameters` property in the call record shown previously; otherwise, you can just omit it. Unlike XML-RPC, which uses positional parameters, SOAP calls use labeled parameters. In AppleScript, these parameters are supplied as properties in a record, where each property's name is an AppleScript identifier. For example:

```
set parameters_record to {|name|:the_name, |size|:the_size, cost:the_cost}
```

Note Remember, when writing an identifier name in AppleScript, you can avoid conflicts with existing Apple-Script keywords or preserve a particular case by wrapping it in a pair of vertical bars. For example, `name` is a reserved keyword, but `|name|` is an ordinary identifier.

SOAP Examples

So, you went to the XMethods website and found a service you want to test. Figuring out how to use it takes a little extra work. AppleScript's SOAP support is fairly basic, so you'll have to supply the configuration details yourself. You should find this information in the documentation for the SOAP service you want to use.

For example, on the XMethods site, go to the service's main page, and click the Analyze WSDL or View RPC Profile link. This will give you the application URL; the values to use in the main record's `method name`, `SOAPAction`, and `method namespace url` properties; and the names and types of the parameters to use, if any.

If the parameters or return values are complex, you'll probably need to look for additional documentation on the SOAP service provider's own website to find out exactly how to use them.

The following is an example of a service that uses no parameters but returns a record as a result. I first list the service specifics exactly as they appear on the XMethods website and then the way the same information should be turned into an AppleScript script.

The service, called `getRandomBushism`, simply returns a record with two properties: `bushism` and `context`.

On the website, the service's specifications are listed as follows:

- Method name: getRandomBushism
- Endpoint URL: http://greg.froh.ca/fun/random_bushism/soap/index.php
- SOAPAction: urn:RandomBushism#bushism#getRandomBushism
- Method namespace uniform resource indicator (URI): urn:RandomBushism
- Input parameters: N/A
- Output parameters: N/A
- Return: RandomBushism

The AppleScript code for calling that service looks like Script 31-3.

Script 31-3.

```
tell application "http://greg.froh.ca/fun/random_bushism/soap/index.php"
    set the_result to call soap {¬
        method name: "getRandomBushism", ¬
        SOAPAction: "urn:RandomBushism#bushism#getRandomBushism", ¬
        method namespace uri: "urn:RandomBushism"}
end tell
display dialog  "Bush: " & bushism of the_result
display dialog context of the_result
```

Here's another example that converts regular text into "Swedish chef" dialect, as fans of the Muppets will recognize. First, you look up the technical specification on the XMethods site:

- Method name: Bork
- Endpoint URL: http://a3.x-ws.de/cgi-bin/bork/bork.wsdl
- SOAPAction: #Bork
- Method namespace URI: SoapInterop
- Input parameters: Chef (string)
- Output parameters: Bork (string)

As you can see, the Bork SOAP call takes a single parameter, Chef, whose value is a string and returns another string as the result. Here's how the AppleScript code looks once you add this information to it:

```
tell application "http://a3.x-ws.de/cgi-bin/bork/bork.wsdl"
    call soap {¬
        method name:"Bork", ¬
        SOAPAction:"#Bork", ¬
        method namespace uri:"SoapInterop", ¬
        parameters:{Chef:"Swedish meatballs!"}}
end tell
--> "Svedeesh meetbells! Bork Bork Bork!"
```

Summary

Even though AppleScript supports XML-RPC and SOAP calls natively, a usability gap makes it difficult for any scripter to look up a SOAP or XML-RPC application on the Web and quickly put it to use with AppleScript. Regardless, the promise of such web services should keep you interested; they are slowly turning into a valuable, and mostly free, resource for the scripting community. You can use these web services to get weather information and stock quotes, verify e-mail addresses and credit card numbers, get ample data on places in the United States based on their ZIP codes, find television listings in Iceland, and obtain a list of famous people whose birthday is on a given date. This list is endless, and it keeps on growing all the time.

Quite a few websites list useful web services that you can call from AppleScript, as well as XML-RPC and SOAP specifications, such as XMethods (www.xmethods.com) and UserLand's XML-RPC's website (www.xmlrpc.com).

Another place to find information and help is from Apple's AppleScript website (www.apple.com/applescript/resources/). From there, look for the XML-RPC and SOAP references.

CHAPTER 32

■ ■ ■

Entering the Business of Automation

If you use AppleScript for more than the occasional script you write for yourself, then you are saving someone time and increasing their productivity. All that goodness translates into money that someone is either saving or making. An AppleScript return-on-investment study published a few years ago by GISTICS suggests that media producers saved more than $100 million during 1998 using AppleScript automation techniques. (For more information about this study, see the "Taking the Next Step" section).

As the scripter, you can do certain things to get in on the action. You can either push your position as a scripter within your organization or become an independent automation consultant and write scripts for living, as I have been doing for almost ten years. In any case, you need to understand what makes AppleScript automation unique and how you can use it to dramatically improve the workflows of companies that use Macs for their business.

This chapter discusses some of the business aspects of AppleScript and gives advice to those who want to capitalize on this incredible technology.

Starting to Make an Impact

As in any other business, when you're just starting, you have to stand out in the crowd in order to be noticed. Luckily for you, you are not trying to direct a major Hollywood film or sell your paintings to a museum. What you're trying to do is write scripts for your organization, slowly get recognized, and then slowly get paid. What may make this possible is part of what makes AppleScript so great: you can make a substantial impact without too much work.

Before jumping to asking for a budget or writing up a six-figure proposal for a project, you have to remember a simple rule: what you can do for others always comes before the reward you get back (or at least the monetary reward).

Rolling Up Your Sleeves

To make it as a scripter, you can't sit around waiting for someone to promote you to that position; it has to be all you. If there's little automation going on in the company you work for, then it is a typical company. You have to be the one who looks around for scripting opportunities; when you find them, don't ask whether you should try to automate them, just do it. In your spare time, during lunch, or on your work hours—no matter what it takes, find a problem or task that can be helped with scripting and work on solving it. Wait as long as you can before revealing your work; the more complete it is when you show it, the better off you will be.

Now that you have something to show, make sure you have a clean demo arranged in order to show off your script. Collect some basic numbers such as "This used to take three hours, but now it can be done in six minutes," or something to that effect.

Before long, you will find that little automation issues come to you: "Could you script this?" "Could you automate that?"

Taking the Next Step

If you have what it takes to script and you decide you want to take a more serious crack at it, start by looking around your own company but this time with a bit more ammunition. To start, you have to be fully aware of the value and impact that scripting and automating can have on your department and company. A good starting point is a return-on-investment study published by GISTICS. To get the full study, go to Google, and type **AppleScript ROI GISTICS**; you will encounter numerous websites that have posted the full study. Among other facts, the study claims companies saw their investment in AppleScript returned 2.4–4.3 times during the first year of adaptation; usually, the expectation is to return the investment once within a few years. This information can help you convince your company, or other companies, to give you a nudge upward on the pay scale.

Joining Apple's Consultants Network

The Apple Consultants Network is a network of certified consultants maintained by Apple Computer. The consultants are "skilled in the setup, use, and maintenance of Apple products and solutions," and prospective clients can search for consultants by geographic location and area of expertise. The Apple Consultants Network's website is at http://consultants.apple.com.

To become a consultant, you need to pass a few tests and pay the membership fee. Membership doesn't make sense for everyone, but if you're looking to become an independent consultant, you should look into it.

Figuring Out the Value of Automation

It is quite difficult to figure out the monetary value of a scripting project, since it can stretch across many areas in a company and have impact that is far greater than the time saved by having Apple-Script do the work instead of a person.

In fact, the time-saved estimation is where you have to be the most cautious. Let's assume you ran some tests and some numbers and you figured out that the catalog takes 20 hours to produce in the current manual workflow, but you can create scripts that will produce it in 1 hour. Let's also assume, for argument's sake, that you are right. Will that mean the company can lay off 95% of the employees working on the catalog as soon as the script is working? No. The company won't be able (and shouldn't want to) lay off anyone for a while.

By manual workflow, I don't refer to X-Acto knives and tape, rather to the workflow that uses Macs but is not (yet) automated.

The reality is that even with the type of drastic results you can get with AppleScript, change is always slow. This is good in a way, since you can now avoid those nightmares about having your co-workers lose their jobs because of you. In reality, if you save your company or department 10% of the workforce after a year, which can happen through attrition and promotion instead of layoffs, you have done a great job of increasing team efficiency/productivity. It is important, however, to have realistic expectations as far as the immediate impact your scripting work will have on your department.

The Broad Impact

Let's get back to the catalog you are working to automate. If you can shorten the production time from 20 hours to 1 hour, you can imagine that the production lead time, which is the amount of time you have to start the work before the catalog has to be ready, will shorten by, say, 50%. Even though production sees a direct improvement of 95%, the lead time has to take into account much more than just the raw production. An improvement of 50%, however, is huge. It means all the information in the catalog can be much more up-to-date, which is essential in some markets. The fact that a script will now be inputting the prices instead of a person means errors will be reduced drastically, which means much less work for proofreaders and graphic designers. An automated process also means you in effect taught the Mac how to do all the boring repetitive work and all those designers who spent days and nights correcting copy and retyping prices can now concentrate on design instead.

The Art of Prototyping

Back to selling your work. You will come to realize that with AppleScript development, the 80-20 rule applies: you can finish 80% of the project in 20% of the time. This by itself doesn't mean much, since you will have to spend the rest of the 80% of the time on the small things (believe me, it is unavoidable). Where you do take advantage of it is that you can create a working prototype of the project in a short amount of time.

The key is to have a meeting with a prospective client, be it in your company or as a consulting job somewhere else. In that meeting, try to gain an understanding of the terms they use and of their workflow. Pay special attention to the raw materials, the documents, and the final output (raw materials being the data they use to produce whatever it is they produce, the material being their templates, and so on, and the output being the finished job). Try to take as much of it with you, with permission, of course; sign a confidentiality agreement if you have to do so. Then, make a meeting with them a couple of weeks later.

At this point, you should get busy: make sure you have a good prototyping tool such as AppleScript Studio, FileMaker Pro, or Late Night Software's FaceSpan to use for a basic interface. Now, create some basic scripts that take their material and turn them into parts of the final product. I like to have a dialog box come up at the end that says, "The process is complete and took 23 seconds" or something to that effect. It is impressive for people at a company to see their product or part of it created automatically and so fast.

Is It Possible?

A question you will get again and again is whether one thing or another is possible to automate. In reality, anything is possible, as long as the client is willing to pay for it. As far as your experience goes, unless they're asking for things that are way beyond your ability, you should assume you can figure out how to get anything done, even if you haven't done it yet.

Charging for Automation

Automation is valuable, and unless you're in the process of starting out and trying to get any experience, you should charge good money for it. Along with charging money comes the question of how much to charge.

To figure out how much to charge, you have to look at two variables: one is the value of your services to the client, and the other is the value of your time. The ultimate situation is where the difference between the two is the greatest—for instance, say you figure out that the job will save the company approximately $200,000 over two years, and it will realistically take you 50 hours to create. Now, even if you figure your time is worth $250 per hour, you come out at $12,500. The ratio is huge. You can easily ask for $20,000 to $30,000 and know that even at less than that you will do fine.

Another way to charge is for time. You can charge either hourly or by the day. Hourly, you can expect $120–$225 per hour, depending on with the company. Although this may appear to be less than what you get if you charge by the project, you are covered if you exceed your estimates. Charging by the day is also possible. Try not to place yourself at less than $1,000 per day, or $500–$700 or so if you're new at this.

Always keep in mind that the value of your work will be far greater than anything you will ever dream to ask, so don't be afraid to ask for what you want.

Scope Creep

You may or may not have heard the term *scope creep* (also called *feature creep*), but the problem is very real, and as a sole developer, you have to protect yourself from it. Scope creep is bound to happen sometimes during development: clients periodically realize that the system or script you're creating can do just a wee bit more than initially thought. They approach you with the idea and see whether they can squeeze it in.

Usually, these requests are small enough that you don't feel like you can say no to them. A half hour here or an hour there really isn't much, especially for a project of a particular size. In reality, the larger the project, the more you have to avoid this creep. Anything you agree to will mean more benefit to the client, more work for you, more features for you to later support, and not any more reward. The only reward is that this client now knows they can get more out of you for less money.

Here's how I deal with scope creep: I start by defining what the system will do and make the description as tight as I can, not leaving open-ended items such as "may connect to SQL database" or "could have intranet interface." Then, I encourage the client to come up with more features they want to add, but instead of agreeing to them, I write them down. My point to the client is this: you have to keep your eye on the target. After you're done, or at some point during the development, you can look at all the proposed additions and adjust the price accordingly. This way, you add features in a more organized way, instead of just creeping in, and mainly you get paid more for adding them.

Another reason to avoid bloating the project is that as much fun as it is to be useful to your client, anything you agree to do, you own. By own, I mean owning the problem; if that feature ends up being a problem in any way, you are stuck with having to solve it. It doesn't matter that you were nice enough to suggest it; you can't take it back without taking a hit.

Supporting Your Solutions

Another facet of creating scripts for clients is that those scripts depend on the client's environment remaining static. Many things can go wrong, and 99% of them have nothing to do with you. For that reason, you have to be ready to support your scripts, and the client has to be willing to pay for this support.

The way I calculate the cost of support is by adding up the cost of the entire system, taking 20% of that amount, and spreading it over 12 months. If the client is more than 60–90 minutes away, I charge extra for being on-site. Using this formula, if you had a $24,000 project, the annual support agreement will be $4,800, which will be $400 a month.

This should cover everything you have to do to make sure their system works. Having that on your head also helps you create a system that is as maintenance free as possible.

Also insist that the client have one point person for contacting you in order to avoid having several people contacting you with the same problem.

Index

Symbols

~/ home directory
    specifying file paths in Unix commands, 703
~ character, Database Events, 658
< redirection symbol, Unix, 693
> redirection symbol, Unix, 693
& (concatenation) operator
    see concatenation operator

A

a reference to operator, 242–244, 256
absolute paths
    POSIX paths, 384
    Unix commands, 703
accents
    ignoring diacriticals clause, 54
access
    close access command, 545
    open for access command, 545
access errors
    AppleScript event errors, 465
    application scripting errors, 466
    operating system errors, 465
account class, iChat, 629
account class, Mail, 615, 616
Acme replace command, 552, 554
ACME Script Widgets, 552
Acrobat
    adding text to existing PDF, 671
acronyms, use of, 326
Action, for building subroutine names, 596
activate command, 195
    applications, 194
    clipboard data, 447
    running FileMaker Pro in background, 647
    saving clipboard data to PDF file, 449
    using custom dialog box in script, 346
Activity Monitor application
    determining process ID on remote Mac, 721
add command
    Address Book, 620
    Automator, 634
    creating tracks in iTunes, 613
adding folder items event, 522, 523, 550
addition operator, 104, 238
Address Book
    add command, 620
    contact info class, 619
    object models, 619
    name-related properties, 622
    person class/object, 619
    phone class, 619
    remove command, 620
    scripting, 619–623

addressing objects, 564
add_to_log handler, 404
administrator privileges parameter
    do shell script command, 698
AFP (Apple File Protocol), 440
ages
    calculating time differences, 126–127
alarm clock
    creating an alarm clock script, 140–142
alert box
    see also display alert command
    adding text to, 304
    designated default button, 305
    informational/warning/critical constants, 305
alias class, System Events, 427–428
alias data type
    folder kitchen timer example, 109
    writing random number script, 18
alias file class, Finder, 421
    alias value class compared, 423
    original item property, 424
alias files, creating, 434
alias literals
    compile errors, 453
alias values
    alias file-tracking example, 381
    alias value class, 380–382
    converting aliases to/from other values, 382
    converting Finder references to, 391
    converting HFS path to, 382
    obtaining POSIX path string, 382
aliases
    deleting out-of-date alias files, 423
    description, 410
    direct parameters, 178
    duplicate command, Finder, 431
    file references compared, 382
    file-related choose commands, 310
    Finder references, 391
    how aliases work, 380
    path to command, 542
    pre–OS X, 383
    scripting remote Macs over IP, 723
    valid paths for, 326
alien spaceships game
    script object inheritance, 506
Alignment panel
    FaceSpan for OS X, 375
allday property
    event class, iCal, 625
altering ending parameter
    do shell script command, 698

Printed in the United States
By Bookmasters